# THE ROUTLEDGE COMPANION TO DIGITAL HUMANITIES AND ART HISTORY

*The Routledge Companion to Digital Humanities and Art History* offers a broad survey of cutting-edge intersections between digital technologies and the study of art history, museum practices, and cultural heritage.

The volume focuses not only on new computational tools that have been developed for the study of artworks and their histories but also debates the disciplinary opportunities and challenges that have emerged in response to the use of digital resources and methodologies. Chapters cover a wide range of technical and conceptual themes that define the current state of the field and outline strategies for future development. This book offers a timely perspective on transdisciplinary developments that are reshaping art historical research, conservation, and teaching.

This book will be of interest to scholars in art history, historical theory, method and historiography, and research methods in education.

**Kathryn Brown** is a lecturer in art history and visual culture at Loughborough University, UK.

# THE ROUTLEDGE COMPANION TO DIGITAL HUMANITIES AND ART HISTORY

*Edited by Kathryn Brown*

Routledge
Taylor & Francis Group
LONDON AND NEW YORK

First published 2020 by Routledge

2 Park Square, Milton Park, Abingdon, Oxon OX14 4RN
605 Third Avenue, New York, NY 10017

*Routledge is an imprint of the Taylor & Francis Group, an informa business*

First issued in paperback 2022



*Library of Congress Cataloging-in-Publication Data*
Names: Brown, Kathryn (Kathryn J.), editor.
Title: The Routledge companion to digital humanities and art history / edited by Kathryn Brown.
Description: New York : Routledge, 2020. | Series: [Routledge art history and visual studies companions] | Includes bibliographical references and index.
Identifiers: LCCN 2019056562 (print) | LCCN 2019056563 (ebook) | ISBN 9781138585584 (hardback) | ISBN 9780429505188 (ebook)
Subjects: LCSH: Digital humanities. | Art—Historiography—Data processing.
Classification: LCC AZ105 .R68 2020 (print) | LCC AZ105 (ebook) | DDC 001.30285—dc23
LC record available at https://lccn.loc.gov/2019056562
LC ebook record available at https://lccn.loc.gov/2019056563

ISBN: 978-1-138-58558-4 (hbk)
ISBN: 978-1-03-233639-8 (pbk)
DOI: 10.4324/9780429505188

Typeset in Bembo
by Apex CoVantage, LLC

# CONTENTS

# FIGURES

# TABLE

# CONTRIBUTORS

**Walid Ahmad** is an applied mathematician who obtained his Bachelor's degree, cum laude, in applied mathematics with a minor in mechanical engineering from Columbia University. He went on to complete a Master's degree in mathematical modeling and scientific computing at the University of Oxford where he wrote his dissertation on the study of temporal networks in continuous time. His most recent research and professional work has focused on developing machine learning systems for industry.

**Alessio Assonitis** received his doctoral degree in Renaissance art history from Columbia University in 2003. He has published extensively on the Italian Renaissance and has been at the Medici Archive Project since 2004, becoming director in 2009. He has served as principal investigator for digital projects supported by the Andrew W. Mellon Foundation, including BIA (2010–2012, 2013–2014) and MIA (2015–2017, 2017–2019).

**Christina Bartosch** studied art history in Paris (Paris IV—Sorbonne University) and in London (UCL). She researched the history of Austria's exhibitions at the Venice Biennale, resulting in the publication of *Austria at the Venice Biennale 1895–2013*, edited by Jasper Sharp (Nürnberg 2013) and the "Biennale Archive Austria" (http://biennalearchiv.at/). From 2013 to 2017, she was a board member of the Austrian Art Historians' Association (VöKK) and the editor of the association's journal. She participated in writing the proposal for the research project "Exhibitions of Modern European Painting 1905–1915" with Raphael Rosenberg and Tanja Jenni and was principally responsible for the preliminary research on Wassily Kandinsky's exhibitions. Bartosch wrote her doctoral dissertation about the exhibitions of works by abstract artists from 1908 to 1915 (University of Vienna).

**Christl Baur** is Co-producer at Ars Electronica. She has an interdisciplinary background in art history, cultural management, and natural science. Her research encompasses video art, new media technologies, computer art, biotechnology, and interactive art, and she works at the nexus of art and science. In recent years, she has developed, co-produced, and delivered large-scale exhibitions and performances, research residencies and publication projects, most recently in cooperation with universities and scientific associations including Google Arts & Culture,

Microsoft, Hyundai, and the Chinese University of Art Beijing. She works closely with artists whose practice is situated at the interface of art, science, and technology.

**Koenraad Brosens** is a professor and chair of art history at the University of Leuven (KU Leuven). He has published widely on Flemish and French tapestry and European markets for tapestry. Brosens is PI of *Project Cornelia* (https://projectcornelia.be). This is a slow digital art history project developed in close collaboration with the University's Computer Science Department. It aims to gain better understanding of how the digital can or should be used by art historians addressing traditional and new questions that are fueled by complex and "biggish" archival data. Brosens was visiting professor at the University of Pennsylvania (2007), the *Peter Paul Rubens Chair* at the University of California Berkeley (2013), and J. Paul Getty Museum Scholar (2019). Finally, he tries to be a good husband and father while thoroughly enjoying scuba diving and all things Dylan.

**Kathryn Brown** is a lecturer in art history and visual culture at Loughborough University in the United Kingdom. Her publications span computer art, artists' books, nineteenth- and twentieth-century French art, and the art market. Her books include *Women Readers in French Painting 1870–1890* (Routledge, 2012), *Matisse's Poets: Critical Performance in the Artist's Book* (Bloomsbury Academic, 2017), *Matisse: A Critical Life* (forthcoming, Reaktion) and (as editor and contributor) *The Art Book Tradition in Twentieth-Century Europe* (Ashgate, 2013), *Interactive Contemporary Art: Participation in Practice* (IB Tauris, 2014), and *Perspectives on Degas* (Routledge, 2016). Brown has been a visiting fellow at Tulane University and the Australian National University. Her research has been supported by numerous awards, including most recently from the Terra Foundation for American Art. Brown is the series editor of *Contextualizing Art Markets* for Bloomsbury Academic.

**Daniel Burckhardt** is a research assistant at the Institute for the History of the German Jews in Hamburg and the German Historical Institute Washington DC. He received a diploma in mathematics from ETH Zurich and a Master's in the history of science of technology from TU Berlin. He has held positions in various digital history projects such as H-Soz-Kult, Pictorial Atlas: Art in the GDR and Clarin-D and was the technical developer of the DoME exhibitions database.

**Bruno Cardoso** is a postdoctoral researcher at KU Leuven. His research interests are focused on the field of Human-Computer Interaction (HCI)—more specifically, on the topics of emotion, usability, context-awareness in mobile devices, and domain-specific languages. Bruno was awarded a BSc and MSc in computer engineering at the University of Évora (Portugal), then spent some years as a consultant and freelance developer before embarking on a PhD with a focus on HCI at the Nova University of Lisbon (Portugal). After obtaining his PhD, Bruno started work as a postdoctoral researcher at KU Leuven (Belgium), first in the Computer Science Department and now in the Faculty of Arts.

**Erik Champion** is currently Professor and UNESCO Chair of Cultural Visualization and Heritage at Curtin University, and visualization theme leader at Curtin Institute for Computation. Prior to joining Curtin University, he was Project Leader of DIGHUMLAB in Denmark, working with EU research infrastructures and projects, and was "Research and Public Engagement" co-leader for http://dariah.eu/. His recent books are *Organic Design in Twentieth-Century Nordic Architecture* (Routledge, 2019), *Critical Gaming: Interactive History and Virtual Heritage* for

Routledge's Digital Research in the Arts and Humanities Series (2015), and *Playing with the Past* (Springer, 2011). He was Editor of *The Phenomenology of Real and Virtual Places* (Routledge, 2018), *Game Mods: Design, Theory and Criticism* (ETC Press, 2012) and Co-editor of *Cultural Heritage Infrastructures in Digital Humanities* (Routledge, 2017).

**T.L. Cowan** is an assistant professor of media studies (digital media cultures) in the Department of Arts, Culture and Media and the Faculty of Information at the University of Toronto. T.L.'s research/creation focuses on cultural and intellectual economies, networks and methods of trans- feminist and queer digital media and performance practices. Recent essays are published in *American Quarterly*, *Women & Performance*, and *First Monday*. She is currently completing a monograph, *Transmedial Drag and Other Cross-Platform Cabaret Methods*. T.L. is also a cabaret artist and curator, and is co-director of two digital research/creation projects, The Digital Research Ethics Collaboratory (DREC) and The Cabaret Commons.

**Jodi Cranston** is a professor in the Department of History of Art and Architecture at Boston University. She is the author of *The Poetics of Portraiture in the Italian Renaissance, The Muddied Mirror: Materiality and Figuration in Titian's Later Paintings* (Penn State University Press, 2010), and *Green Worlds of Renaissance Venice* (Penn State University Press, 2019), and editor of, and contributor to, *Venetian Painting Matters, 1450–1750*. She received a Kress Foundation digital grant to develop *Mapping Paintings*, a mapping platform for users to visualize the provenance of any painting, drawing, or print. This project builds on her first digital project, *Mapping Titian*.

**Rosário Salema de Carvalho** is a researcher at ARTIS, the Art History Institute of the School of Arts and Humanities of the University of Lisbon. She coordinates the research group Az—*Azulejo* Research Network and supervises projects concerning the study, inventory, and cataloguing of tile decorations, namely the group's anchor project, *Az Infinitum—Azulejo Referencing and Indexation System*. She holds a PhD in history/art history (2012) from the University of Lisbon and a Master's degree in art, heritage and restoration (2007) from the same university, with both theses focused on eighteenth-century tile decorations. She has conducted research in the field of Portuguese *azulejo* decorations, and has published several books and articles in national and international journals. Her current research interests include Baroque tile frames and related decorative systems, the cataloguing of tile patterns, and the development of inventory and cataloguing tools in the context of digital art history.

**Javier de la Rosa** is a postdoctoral fellow at UNED Digital Humanities Innovation Lab. He holds a PhD in Hispanic studies with a specialization in digital humanities from the University of Western Ontario, and a Master's in artificial intelligence from the University of Seville. Javier previously worked as a research engineer at the Stanford University Center for Interdisciplinary Digital Research and as the technical lead at the University of Western Ontario CulturePlex Lab for Cultural Complexity. His interests range from natural language processing applied to historical texts to the analysis of networks of fine arts artifacts and the visual culture of the past.

**Stefania De Vincentis** is a PhD candidate and research fellow at the Department of Humanities of the University of Ferrara. Her research is on digital humanities for art history and on museum studies, with a focus on ICT tools for the dissemination of art history and the enhancement of cultural heritage. She cooperates with TekneHub laboratory, developing communication activities and facilitating the involvement of cultural institutions in research projects. Her background in research and production of contemporary art during her MA degree in visual arts at IUAV–Architecture Institute of Venice University and her postgraduate degree in management of cultural heritage (MuSeC) at the University of Ferrara has led her to work with international centers for art history such as the Ermitage Italia Foundation.

**Marei Döhring** is a uni:docs fellow at the University of Vienna and is writing her PhD thesis on early twentieth-century picture frames. Her primary research centers on the emergence of colored frames that increasingly replaced gilt frames in European avant-garde exhibitions at the turn of the century. During her studies she worked as a researcher for a renowned frame workshop, where she gained practical knowledge on frames and further built her expertise in that field. She received her degrees in art history at the Ruprecht-Karls-University in Heidelberg and at the University of Vienna. From 2017 to 2018 she was a member of the FWF-funded research project "Exhibitions of Modern European Painting 1905–1915." In her subsequent position as university assistant (prae doc) she continued to support the team with database development and research while also teaching and supervising undergraduate students.

**Anna Dot** is an artist and researcher with a degree in fine arts from the University of Barcelona. She holds a PhD in Translation and Visual Studies from the Translation, Interpretation and Applied Languages Department of the University of Vic (Spain), where she is also member of the Research Group on Gender Studies: Translation, History, Literature and Communication (GETLIHC). She collaborates with the Associació Arxiu Muntadas, Centre d'Estudis i Recerca (ARXIU/AM) and participates in the collaborative international project *Beyond Text* (funded by Erasmus +) that brings arts-based practice research into education.

**Johanna Drucker** is the Breslauer Professor of Bibliographical Studies in the Department of Information Studies at UCLA. She is internationally known for her work in artists' books, the history of graphic design, typography, experimental poetry, fine art, and digital humanities. Recent titles include *Graphesis: Visual Forms of Knowledge Production* (Harvard University Press, 2014), *The General Theory of Social Relativity* (The Elephants, 2018), *Downdrift: An Eco-fiction* (Three Rooms Press, 2018), and *Visualization: Modeling Interpretation* (MIT Press, 2020). In 2014 she was elected to the American Academy of Arts and Sciences and awarded an honorary doctorate of fine arts by the Maryland Institute College of Art in 2017. In 2019 she was in residence as the inaugural Distinguished Material Cultures Fellow at Yale University. Her 1988 work, *Bookscape*, was featured in the "Artists and their Books" exhibit at the Getty Research Institute in summer 2018

**Amanda Du Preez** is a professor in the School of the Arts at the University of Pretoria, where she teaches visual culture studies and digital culture. She obtained a DPhil in English from the University of South Africa on the topic of cyberfeminism and embodiment in 2003. She has co-edited *South African Visual Culture* (2005), edited *Taking a Hard Look: Gender and Visual Culture* (2009), and authored *Gendered Bodies and New Technologies: Rethinking Embodiment in a Cyber-era* (2009). In 2018 she edited *Voices From the South: Digital Arts and Humanities*. She served as assistant editor of two journals, *Image & Text* and *De Arte*. Currently, she serves on the Advisory Board of the international journal *Persona Studies*. She is also a member of the Governing Board of the International Association for Visual Culture and serves as the Digital Humanities Association of Southern Africa's (DHASA) representative on the Conference Coordinating Committee (2019) for the Alliance of Digital Humanities Organizations (ADHO).

**Pamela Fletcher** is a professor of art history at Bowdoin College. Her research and teaching center on Victorian and Edwardian painting, with a focus on questions of narrative, sentiment, and sensation in the context of nineteenth-century exhibition culture. Recipient of fellowships from the Center for Advanced Study in the Visual Arts, the Getty Research Library, and the Paul Mellon Centre for British Art, she is the author of *Narrating Modernity: The British Problem Picture 1895–1914* (Ashgate, 2003) and the co-editor (with Anne Helmreich) of *The Rise of the Modern Art Market in London 1850–1939* (Manchester University Press, 2011). Together with David Israel, she created *The London Gallery Project* (2007, revised 2012), an interactive digital map of London's nineteenth-century art market.

**Anna Foka** is Scientific Leader of the Digital Humanities Initiative at the Department for Archives, Libraries, Museums and Cultural Heritage (ALM) Uppsala University, and Associate Professor in Information Technology and the Humanities at Humlab, Umeå University in Sweden. Her research interests are a blend of digital technology with historical and artistic disciplines. Anna has a background in classics, ancient history, and archaeology (MA 2006, PhD 2009, University of Liverpool) as well as media and performance studies (NCU Athens, Greece). She has published on classical studies, ancient history and archaeology, gender and humor, classical reception in film and TV, game studies, cultural heritage studies, augmented and virtual reality for museums, digital art history, digital visualizations, and digital geography.

**Susan Elizabeth Gagliardi** is Associate Professor of Art History at Emory University in Atlanta, Georgia. She is the author of *Senufo Unbound: Dynamics of Art and Identity in West Africa* (The Cleveland Museum of Art and 5 Continents Editions, 2014). Research for the book led her to develop *Mapping Senufo*—an in-progress, collaborative, digital publication project she now co-directs with Constantine Petridis of the Art Institute of Chicago—and to participate in the August 2014 Kress Summer Institute on Digital Mapping and Art History at Middlebury College. During the spring of 2016, she launched MAP IT | Little Dots, Big Ideas, a series of lectures and workshops at Emory focused on digital mapping and the humanities.

**Anne Collins Goodyear** co-directs the Bowdoin College Museum of Art. Specializing in the relationship of American art to science and technology and the construction of identity in modern and contemporary art, Goodyear co-edited *This Is a Portrait if I Say So: Identity in American Art, 1912 to Today* (Yale University Press, 2016), with Kathleen Campagnolo and Jonathan F. Walz; *AKA Marcel Duchamp: Meditations on the Identities of an Artist* (Smithsonian Institution Scholarly Press, 2014), with James W. McManus; and *Artefacts: Studies in the History of Science and Technology Volume 9: Analyzing Art and Aesthetics*, with Margaret Weitekamp (Smithsonian Institution Scholarly Press, 2013). She is president of the Digital Art History Society, and serves as a member of the Advisory Committee for Virtual Asian American Art Museum, the editorial board of *American Art*, and the National Committee for the History of Art. She is president emerita of CAA.

**Anne Helmreich** is Associate Director, Digital Initiatives, Getty Research Institute. Her most recent monograph is *Nature's Truth: Photography, Painting, and Science in Victorian Britain* (Penn State University Press, 2016). Her current research focuses on the history of the art market and the productive intersection of the digital humanities and art history. She co-edited *The Rise of the Modern Art Market in London, 1850–1939* (Manchester University Press, 2011) with Pamela Fletcher, and co-authored with Pamela Fletcher, "Local/Global: Mapping Nineteenth-Century London's Art Market," (*Nineteenth-Century Art Worldwide*) which won the ARIAH 2015 prize for best online essay. Her scholarship has been supported by grants and fellowships from the Getty Research Institute, the National Endowment for the Humanities, the Clark Library, the

Harry Ransom Center, the Huntington, the Yale Center for British Art, and the Paul Mellon Centre for British Art.

**Leonardo Impett** works at the intersection of art history and machine vision, in the intellectual tradition of distant reading; in 2020 he defended his PhD on the topic at EPFL. His research focuses on the operationalization of theories of visual form, using computational approaches to explore historiographic, as well as historical, questions. He previously read engineering, with a thesis on machine learning for musical acoustics, at Cambridge where he was later a visiting scholar at the Rainbow research lab and is currently visiting Methods Fellow in Digital Humanities. He has held visiting fellowships at Microsoft Research and Villa I Tatti, and is currently based at the Bibliotheca Hertziana in Rome. Alongside his research in computational visual studies, he frequently collaborates with sound and media artists, including projects shown at the Royal Opera House (2014), Maggio Musicale (2016), Transmedile (2019), Liverpool Biennale, and the Whitney Museum (2020).

**Ben Jackson** is a research fellow in digital humanities at the University of Sussex. His research interests (apart from digital humanities) include heritage informatics, digital media, and virtual prototyping, large-scale collaborative simulation and distance learning systems. Jackson is currently focused on building a macroscope to explore information. His early career focused on technology in entertainment systems. He holds a BSc in multimedia and digital systems and a DPhil in engineering and design both from the University of Sussex.

**Paul B. Jaskot** is a professor of art history at Duke University and the Director of the Wired! Lab for Digital Art History & Visual Culture. His work focuses on the relationship between architecture and politics in modern Germany, with a specific emphasis on the National Socialist period. He is the author, editor, and co-author of multiple articles and books on this topic, including, most recently, *The Nazi Perpetrator: Postwar German Art and the Politics of the Right* (2012) as author and *New Approaches to an Integrated History of the Holocaust: Social History, Representation, Theory* (2018) as co-editor. Jaskot is a founding member of the Holocaust Geography Collaborative, an international collective of scholars working on how digital mapping and other computational methods can advance questions concerning the genocide of the European Jews. In 2014 Jaskot co-directed the Kress-sponsored Summer Institute on Digital Mapping and Art History.

**Amy Jeffs** holds a PhD from the University of Cambridge concerning illustrated manuscripts of history and legend from England, 1240–1340 (especially British Library, Egerton MS 3028). The project has led to her to explore questions of genre, the history of education, and the political application of historical legend. During the first part of her PhD, Amy co-convened the Digital Pilgrim project, which applied digitization, 3D modeling, and GIS mapping to collections of pilgrim souvenirs and secular badges, working partially in the British Museum. The project explored the potential for digital technologies to facilitate art-historical engagement with large collections of miniature artworks, especially those with archaeological provenance.

**Lauren Jimerson** is an art historian whose research examines late nineteenth- and early twentieth-century art in France and the United States, with a focus on gender studies, women artists, and the intersections of art and literature. She holds a PhD from Rutgers University, a Master's degree from the Courtauld Institute, and a Bachelor's degree from Cornell University. Her research has benefited from grants including a Fulbright fellowship to France, a Mellon Dissertation Fellowship, and a doctoral exchange program at the École normale supérieure in

Paris. Her writings have appeared in scholarly publications, including *Woman's Art Journal*. She is currently a lecturer at the Paris Institute for Critical Thinking and is writing a book on women artists in early twentieth-century France and their representations of the nude.

**Béatrice Joyeux-Prunel** was an associate professor in modern and contemporary art history at the École normale supérieure in Paris from 2007 to 2019. She is currently full professor in digital humanities at the University of Geneva. She works on the global history of the avant-gardes, the visual culture of petroleum, and the digital turn in the humanities. She founded and has managed the Artl@s project (www.artlas.ens.fr) since 2009. In 2016 she founded Postdigital (www.postdigital.ens.fr), a research project on digital cultures and imagination. Among her recent publications, the volume she edited with Thomas DaCosta Kaufmann and Catherine Dossin (ed.), *Circulations in the Global History of Art* (Routledge, 2015) was republished in 2017. Joyeux-Prunel is the author of *Les Avant-gardes artistiques. Une histoire transnationale* (Gallimard, 2016/2017) and *Naissance de l'art contemporain 1945–1970. Une histoire mondiale* (Editions du CNRS, 2020).

**Baris Kandemir** earned a PhD in information sciences and technology in 2019 from The Pennsylvania State University and is finalizing his dissertation from The Pennsylvania State University. He received a Bachelor's degree in electrical and electronics engineering from Boğaziçi University, Turkey. His research interests include computational aesthetics and emotions, gender differences and personalization, and automated visual composition analysis. He is currently with DeepMap, Inc.

**Harald Klinke** teaches digital art history at the LMU Munich, Germany. He studied art history, media theory, painting, philosophy, and information systems in Karlsruhe, Berlin, Norwich (UK) and Göttingen, and received his PhD at the Karlsruhe University of Arts and Design and an MSc from the University of Göttingen. From 2008 to 2009, he worked as a lecturer of visual studies (Bildwissenschaft) at the Art History Department at the University of Göttingen. From 2009 to 2010, he conducted research, supported by a grant from the Deutsche Forschungsgemeinschaft, as a visiting scholar at Columbia University, New York. He is editor of the *International Journal for Digital Art History*.

**Alison Langmead** holds a joint faculty appointment at the University of Pittsburgh between the Dietrich School of Arts and Sciences and the School of Computing and Information. She is the Director of the Visual Media Workshop (VMW), a humanities lab located in the Department of the History of Art and Architecture that focuses on the investigation of material and visual culture in an environment that encourages technological experimentation. Alison is also the principal contact for the DHRX: Digital Humanities Research at Pitt initiative, which represents a transdisciplinary network of scholars who use digital methods to study the ways in which humans interact with their environments, whether social or cultural, natural or human-created.

**Allison Leigh** is an assistant professor of art history and the SLEMCO/LEQSF Regents Endowed Professor in Art & Architecture at the University of Louisiana at Lafayette. She is a specialist in European and Russian art of the eighteenth and nineteenth centuries and her first book, *Picturing Russia's Men: Masculinity and Modernity in 19th-Century Painting*, is forthcoming from Bloomsbury Press in 2020. Her primary research interests include the development of new art-historical methodologies, masculinity studies, the history and historiography of modernism, and the philosophy of art and aesthetics in the modern era. A recipient of numerous grants and fellowships, she formerly taught as a postdoctoral fellow in the Faculty of Humanities and Social Sciences at the Cooper Union for the Advancement of Science and Art in New York City.

**Inês Leitão** is a researcher at ARTIS, the Art History Institute of the School of Arts and Humanities of the University of Lisbon, where she is part of the research group Az—*Azulejo* Research Network. She holds a Master's degree in art, heritage, and restoration theory from the same university (2016), with a dissertation on contemporary *azulejos* and public art, and was awarded a doctoral fellowship by the Foundation for Science and Technology (FCT) to study contemporary *azulejos* applied in public spaces (1950–2020). She is the author of book chapters and scientific articles, and has participated in various research projects, namely *Az Infinitum—Azulejo Referencing and Indexation System* and *Off-Off Lisbon: Alternative Urban Narratives*. Her current research interests include contemporary *azulejos*, art theory, and public space.

**Jia Li** is a professor of statistics at The Pennsylvania State University and an amateur painter. She holds an MS degree in electrical engineering, an MS degree in statistics, and a PhD in electrical engineering, all from Stanford University. Her research interests include statistical modeling and learning, data mining, computational biology, image processing, image annotation and retrieval, and composition analysis of paintings and photos. She currently serves as the Editor-in-Chief for *Statistical Analysis and Data Mining: The ASA Data Science Journal*.

**Matthew D. Lincoln** is the research software engineer at Carnegie Mellon University Libraries, where he focuses on computational and data-driven approaches to the study of history and culture, and on making library and archives collections tractable for data-driven research. His current book project with Getty Publications, co-authored with Dr. Sandra van Ginhoven, uses data-driven modeling, network analysis, and textual analysis to mine the Getty Provenance Index Databases for insights into the history of collecting and the art market. He earned his PhD in art history at the University of Maryland, College Park, and has held positions at the Getty Research Institute and the National Gallery of Art. He is an editorial board member of *The Programming Historian*.

**Anne Luther** is a researcher with a focus on digital scholarship, cultural heritage data, and data visualization. She is currently the Principal Investigator for research projects in the Departments of Modern Art History at TU Berlin (VW Foundation), Fordham University (NEH), and MARKK (Siemens Foundation). As Research Manager at the Center for Data Arts at The New School, she specialized in the analysis of museum data, leading data sprints, software development and publications between 2015 and 2018. She received her PhD from Central Saint Martins College of Art and Design, London.

**Elspeth Mitchell** is an art historian and cultural theorist. She completed her PhD in 2013 at the University of Leeds with a thesis titled *Feminine Becomings: Theories of the Girl and the Moving Image*. She was associate editor for the journal *parallax* and has published in journals including *Australian Feminist Studies Journal* and *Girlhood Studies Journal*. In 2016, Elspeth co-founded *Feminist Readings Networks/Réseau Lectures Féministes* with colleagues at the University of Leeds, University of Helsinki, University of South Africa, and University of Paris 8, supported by a gender and education network funding grant.

**Nirmalie Mulloli** studied BA Combined Honours in the History of Art & Anthropology at Durham University. She completed her Master's in the History of Art & Visual Culture at the University of Oxford in 2016. She was the Database Development Manager of the *Exhibitions of Modern European Painting 1905–1915* (DoME) research project. In this capacity, she was responsible for planning and managing the ongoing database construction, including retrieval of archived data from Europe and North America, hiring and managing the project team to conduct technical back-end work, and also managing the construction of a user-friendly front-end interface. She is the co-ordinator of The International Art Market Studies Association (TIAMSA) and is part of the Portfolio/Showroom management team at the University of Applied Arts Vienna. Her research interests focus on the impact of alternative exhibitions spaces at the beginning of the twentieth century.

**David Newbury** is the Enterprise Software Architect at the J. Paul Getty Trust, where he works with museum professionals, researchers, scientists, and technologists to find common solutions to technical and scholarly problems. He has also worked on other collaborative museum technology projects such as Art Tracks, a provenance project at the Carnegie Museum of Art, and the American Art Collaborative, working with 14 museums on standardizing models and software around linked data. He has previously worked with Carnegie Mellon, the University of British Columbia, the University of Illinois, and PBS.

**Nuria Rodríguez-Ortega** is a full professor of digital art history at the University Málaga and the director of the iArtHis_Lab research group. She is also president of the Sociedad Internacional de Humanidades Digitales Hispánicas (HDH). Rodríguez-Ortega has vast experience leading international digital projects on digital art history, including exploring new tools and methods for art-historical research and publication, in collaboration with the Getty Research Institute, and the Exhibitium Project, devoted to enhancing studies on art history exhibitions from data science and cultural complex network perspectives. She is also engaged with the design of new curricula to promote the digital training of students and the scholarly community and has led several seminars on this topic, such as the Digital Art History Summer School (DAHSS), a joint initiative of the University of Málaga, UC Berkeley, and LMU Munich.

**Raphael Rosenberg** obtained a master's degree in art history, archaeology, and Egyptology at the University of Munich and a PhD in art history at the University of Basel. He was Assistant Professor at the University of Freiburg i.B. and the Collège de France in Paris, held the chair for Early Modern and Contemporary Art History at the University of Heidelberg, and is currently professor at the Department of Art History of the University of Vienna. He is a member of the Heidelberg Academy of Sciences and Humanities and of the Academia Europaea. His research focuses on the sculpture of the Italian Renaissance, on the history of art history, and the history of amimeticism (abstraction) in art before and after 1900. He is the founder of the Lab for Cognitive Research in Art History (CReA) and a specialist of eye tracking research.

**Pablo Santa Olalla** was a research trainee in the Department of Art History at the University of Barcelona, where he taught the subject "Artistic Languages." He has a BA degree in fine arts and an MA degree in advanced studies in art history, both from the University of Barcelona. Pablo is currently working on a PhD thesis about relational networks between conceptualist art practices in Latin America and Spain and is part of the research group Art Globalization Interculturality (AGI) and the research project Decentralized Modernities: Art, Politics and Counterculture in the Transatlantic Axis During the Cold War (MoDe(s)). He has collaborated with the Associació Arxiu Muntadas, Centre d'Estudis i Recerca (ARXIU/AM) for more than three years and co-ordinates the training seminar *On Mediation* on curatorial theory and practices.

**Sanja Sekelj** is a research assistant at the Institute of Art History in Zagreb, Croatia, and a PhD candidate at the postgraduate program in humanities at the University of Zadar. She is working on a PhD dissertation titled *Digital Art History and Artists' Networks in Croatian Art of the 1990s and 2000s*. She holds MAs in French language and literature and art history from the Faculty of Humanities and Social Sciences, University of Zagreb. She is currently researching artists' networks, art associations, and art groups of the 1990s and early 2000s, with an emphasis on new media networks and the strategic networking of cultural workers in the independent cultural scene. She was a member of the scientific research project ARTNET (2014–2018). She is a member of the curatorial team of the Gallery Miroslav Kraljević and executive editor of the scientific journal *Život umjetnosti*. She recently co-edited a thematic issue of *Život umjetnosti* on the topic of digital art history with Ljiljana Kolešnik and Sanja Horvatinčić.

**Lisa M. Snyder** is the director of Campus Research Initiatives and acting director of the Research Technology Group within the Office of Information Technology at the University of California, Los Angeles (UCLA). She has a Master of Architectural History from the University of Virginia and a PhD in architecture from UCLA. Her primary research is on pedagogical applications for interactive computer models of historic urban environments. Lisa developed the reconstruction model of the Herodian Temple Mount installed in 2001 at the Davidson Center in Jerusalem, and expanded the project in 2007 with a reconstruction of the early Islamic structures on the site during the eighth century. With funding from the National Endowment for the Humanities, she leads the team developing VSim, a software interface that enables publication and dissemination of academically generated 3D models. Lisa's primary obsession is her reconstruction model of the 1893 World's Columbian Exposition.

**Emma Stanford** is the Digital Curator at the Bodleian Library, University of Oxford. She manages the Bodleian's digitized collections and specializes in digitization planning, migrating legacy collections, and user training and engagement. She holds a BA from Middlebury College and an MSc from City, University of London.

**Juan-Luis Suárez** is the Director of the CulturePlex Lab at Western University, Canada, an interdisciplinary lab focused on digital innovation and cultural networks. He is the author of several books on humanism and the Baroque, and is the co-author of more than 80 articles on cultural analytics, digital humanities, and networks, among other themes. He holds a PhD in philosophy from Salamanca, a PhD in Hispanic literature from McGill, and an MBA from IE Business School.

**Fred Truyen** is a professor at the Faculty of Arts, KU Leuven. He publishes on digitization, photography, and e-learning. He is in charge of the mediaLab CS Digital. His research interests are mostly related to digitization of cultural heritage, web technology, and e-learning. He is involved in projects on open educational resources and open learning (currently E-SLP), and on digitization of cultural heritage: IDEM, RICH, 3PI, Digital Husserl (Hercules funding), Europeana Photography and Europeana Space (EC CIP), Europeana DSI (aggregator for photography), and Migration in the Arts and Sciences and Kaleidoscope (EC CEF Generic services). He has extensive experience in data modeling for image databases in the cultural-historical field, and contributes on this aspect to the Cornelia project. Truyen is President of Photoconsortium, the aggregator of Photography for Europeana, and part of the Europeana Member's Council and member of DARIAH-BE.

**Katherine R. Tsiang** is Associate Director of the Center for the Art of East Asia in the Department of Art History, University of Chicago. Her research has concentrated on the art and visual culture of medieval China as known from tombs and temples, focusing on intersections of religious beliefs and art production and the significance of imagery. She has also directed research projects on Chinese Buddhist cave temples that have been seriously damaged in recent history, employing digital imaging of the caves and their sculptural art now held in collections outside China. She has curated exhibitions showing the results of these projects that include the virtual reconstruction of Buddhist cave shrines.

**Luca Nicolò Vascon** studied mechanical engineering and industrial design. A pioneer of digital panoramic photography since the late 1990s, he has contributed to the development and popularization of the technology (hardware and software) related to interactive imaging. At first working in the IUAV University of Venice multimedia lab and then as co-founder and CEO of the visual services company "Officine Panottiche," he has participated in major cultural and educational projects in Italy and abroad involving immersive imaging, arts, heritage, and new technologies. Since 2019, Vascon has been an annual conference speaker at the International VR Professionals Association (IVRPA) and a member of the board of directors of the World Wide Panorama dissemination project.

**James Z. Wang** is a professor of information sciences and technology at The Pennsylvania State University. He received a Bachelor's degree in mathematics and computer science summa cum laude from the University of Minnesota, and an MS degree in mathematics, an MS degree in computer science, and a PhD in medical information sciences, all from Stanford University. His research interests include computational aesthetics and emotions, automatic image tagging, image retrieval, biomedical informatics, and computerized analysis of paintings.

**Robert Wellington** is a senior lecturer and Australian Research Council, Discovery Early Career Research Award fellow at the Centre for Art History and Art Theory, Australian National University. His project, *Travelling Objects: Art and Cultural Diplomacy*, investigates the prints and commemorative medals presented as diplomatic gifts from the court of Louis XIV. Wellington has a strong interest in digital art history, convening several conference panels and public symposiums on the topic. He leads a project team creating a digital critical edition of the eighteenth-century songbook, *Choix de Chansons*. His monograph, *Antiquarianism and the Visual Histories of Louis XIV: Artifacts for a Future Past*, was published by Ashgate in 2015.

**Martin White** is a reader in computer science in the Creative Technology Group, Department of Informatics at the University of Sussex. He has an HNC in electronic engineering from Bournemouth University, a BSc in computer systems engineering and a PhD in computer science (3D computer graphics) both from the University of Sussex. White's early career focused on hardware and software algorithms for computer graphics. His current research interests largely focus on cultural informatics (digital heritage), the Internet of Things, and blockchain technologies—particularly the application of blockchain and smart contracts to cultural, digital, and shared economy applications.

**Rafaela Xavier** is a researcher at ARTIS, the Art History Institute of the School of Arts and Humanities of the University of Lisbon, where she is part of the research group Az—*Azulejo* Research Network. She holds a degree in art history from the same university (2017) and is currently working on a Master's dissertation on the cataloguing of Mudejar *azulejos* in the National Palace of Sintra. The work is part of the projects *Cataloguing Portuguese Tile Patterns* and *Az Infinitum—Azulejo Referencing and Indexation System*. Her current research interests include *azulejos* and art theory.

# INTRODUCTION

*Kathryn Brown*

In 2015, Lev Manovich argued that "To 'see' contemporary culture requires use of computers and data science." Importantly, however, he added that while "seeing enabled by data science may be radical in terms of its scale—how much you can see in one 'glance,' so to speak—it continues the humanities' traditional methodology."[1] The latter approach involves, at the very least, the comparison and detailed analysis of cultural artifacts, periods, authors, genres, themes, and techniques. Manovich's comments capture an idea that runs throughout the present volume, namely, that research techniques drawn from the digital humanities and from art history are related to each other and can be deployed in mutually illuminating ways. They both entail acts of seeing and are equally dependent on the quality of research question that motivates the relevant analysis. To that extent, human vision and computer vision are not so far apart. While some scholars have worried that the rise of computational analytical techniques, reliance on big data, and use of quantitative research methods entail the "subordination" of art history to computer technologies, the following chapters show how the latest initiatives in digital humanities research relate to and develop key themes that are central to histories and theories of art.[2] Equally, if computational methods offer the possibility of examining and visualizing data in new ways, art history's ability to interrogate the very act of looking brings an important perspective to this exercise and to our understanding of the role of the researcher within it.

The present volume offers a broad survey of intersections between digital humanities and the study of art history. Authors focus not only on new technological tools that have been developed for the study of artworks and their histories but also debate the disciplinary opportunities and challenges that have developed in response to the emergence and use of those tools. Chapters cover a wide range of technical and conceptual themes that define the current state of the field and outline strategies for future development. Contributors debate the extent to which the use of computational methods can reshape conceptions of the art-historical canon and open new branches of research. Equally, however, they explore some of the gaps that have emerged within this branch of study and consider various conceptual biases to which it has fallen prey. The points at which "computer-assisted" and "traditional" methods of analysis come apart are as important for disciplinary self-reflection as is the study of their congruence. As scholars continue to debate the advantages and limitations of integrating computational methods into humanities disciplines, this volume offers a timely perspective on transdisciplinary developments that are reshaping art-historical research, conservation, and teaching.

"Digital art history" has emerged and gathered impetus over the past two decades and is now a familiar part of the research landscape. This has led to debate about whether the field is a sub-branch of art history, a revolution of the discipline, or just a distraction from art history's core concerns and subject matter. In 2013 Johanna Drucker drew what has become a classic distinction between "digitized art history" ("one built on the use of online resources") and "digital art history" ("the use of analytic techniques enabled by computational technology"). The latter, she argues, is "the proper domain of *digital* art history" on the grounds that it can "reveal features of art historical artifacts in novel ways," "extend traditional methods of observation and analysis," and yield "different points of inquiry."[3]

Although the term "digital art history" has become familiar, the decision has been made to title the present volume *Digital Humanities and Art History*. This has not been done with the aim of suggesting the existence of yet another discrete genre within this field. Nor does it seek to challenge the notion of "digital art history." Rather it signals an intention to probe what the term "digital humanities" means in the context of art-historical research and to examine how scholars have taken up and adapted techniques from the digital humanities for the purpose of generating new analytical tools for the study of visual art. Understanding the connection between the digital humanities and art history is key to conceptualizing "digital art history." As Jorge Sebastián Lozano has noted, "the technical possibilities of computing have not progressed at the same pace for each field," and art history has, in many cases, taken up concepts and approaches familiar from literary studies.[4] Questions concerning what art historians have found useful from other disciplines and how their needs and approaches differ from other branches of humanities scholarship are discussed throughout this book.

Chapters problematize the use and impact of digital techniques, identify gaps in the management and analysis of data, and debate the ethics of various initiatives that have emerged from the digital humanities. This includes problematizing reliance on biased archival or canonical material, examining the persistence of unequal access to resources needed to undertake digital humanities projects, and revealing legacies of gender and racial prejudice in technological research and development.[5] Studying the emergence of new epistemological models in the digital humanities helps to stimulate questions about the ambitions of art history itself, including critical reflection on the assumptions that underpinned the emergence of this field of study.

It is also important to point out that the present volume extends beyond narrow conceptions of "art history." Chapters showcase ways in which the use of computer technologies can stimulate new approaches to a broad set of topics ranging from the analysis of artifacts and expressive styles from contrasting geographies and time periods to themes relating to provenance, the art market, social history, heritage, museum studies, and art historiography. For reasons of space, it has not been possible to cover the full range of innovative projects that are currently being undertaken by scholars in this fast-paced field, but the breadth of examples is representative of recent developments and provides an overview of major methodological approaches and techniques. An attempt has also been made to include a range of different voices and perspectives in the volume. In consequence, contributions have been made by researchers in various branches of art history and visual culture, computer science, digital media studies and informatics, mathematics, engineering, design, software development, heritage, information services, pedagogy, museology, curating, and fine art.

The book is divided into five parts: (I) Histories and Critical Debates; (II) Archives, Networks, and Maps; (III) Museums: Real, Virtual, and Augmented; (IV) Computational Techniques for Analyzing Artworks; and (V) Digital Resources, Publication, and Education. Part I surveys a range of important debates that have shaped the intersection of art history with digital methods of analysis. These include the ways in which art historians manage and analyze data, visualize information, and reflect on their own positions as researchers. Authors are sensitive not only to the ways in which technology is transforming the discipline of art history but also to productive ways in which such innovations connect to existing methodologies and approaches.

Part II explores some of the cornerstones of digital humanities research—archives, networks, and maps—and considers a range of practical and ethical issues that arise in the production and use of such digital tools.[6] Understanding how to manage quantitative and qualitative data and thinking through the implications of different mapping techniques are central to re-evaluating and, in some cases, rewriting familiar art-historical narratives. Chapters in this part of the book examine how the use of technology can bring to public attention works that have been omitted from museum collections, present hitherto underrepresented histories, and stimulate the study of new connections between artists, dealers, and the circulation of art objects. Rather than focusing solely on the answers that digital technologies can provide, chapters debate the new range of questions that such technologies can stimulate. This includes, for example, consideration of the ethical issues that arise when digitizing and making public materials that have been created by, and experienced in, small groups and communities.

Part III turns to ways in which new technologies are impacting on museum experience and curatorial strategies. As museums develop their content through techniques of augmented or virtual reality and encourage visitors to navigate collections with the help of mobile devices, the experience of art has undergone radical change. Chapters show that museums can no longer be understood as single "sites" but rather as visual, discursive, and virtual environments supported by a range of digital platforms. In particular, the intersection between digital resources and gaming offers a new kind of art experience that has the potential to engage a broader public. While digitization and online materials have the advantage of broadening access to collections, they necessarily have repercussions for the status of the art object. Against this background, authors debate potential shortcomings of computer technologies for understanding and analyzing issues of complex cultural heritage. Chapters reflect critically on the creation and use of digital surrogates and the limitations of experiencing artifacts in virtual or augmented reality. While new technologies have ushered in important mechanisms for the preservation of endangered or lost artifacts, it is also necessary to inquire into the aesthetic, cultural, and ontological consequences of replacing unique objects with digital replicas.[7] Many parts of the discussion are, therefore, embedded in wider critical debates that motivate the dynamic field of digital heritage and museum studies.

Part IV contains practical guidance for readers interested in using or developing computer techniques for analyzing artworks. While each part of the book combines "state of the field" chapters with discussion of specific projects and, in many cases, examples of the code used to create the relevant program, chapters in this section are specifically concerned with the use and implementation of computational tools, including the mapping of surface structures, 3D and other types of modeling, the use of metadata, image processing, and computer vision. Here—and throughout the volume—theoretical discussion is combined with practical advice and the inclusion of open-source material. Where case studies are used, contributors explain the broader significance of the relevant example, discuss the lessons learned from it, and illustrate ways in which it can impact on, or stimulate the creation of, new projects. Chapters contain, therefore, methodological guidance ranging from how to use and maximize the potential of particular technologies to the identification of pitfalls when implementing such approaches.

It is noteworthy that nearly a third of the chapters in this volume (particularly those focused on the production of new computational methods and databases) are co-authored, and that many other contributions build on and extend work undertaken by research groups. Located at the intersection of the humanities and the sciences, the use of digital methodologies in art history has the potential to reshape the social nature of research and to introduce or strengthen collaborative working models and knowledge exchange. By including "how-to" guides, models, and samples of open-source software, it is hoped that this book will stimulate wider conversations, encourage teamwork across disciplines, and help to produce scholars who are capable of taking up and extending the latest analytical and technological methods of investigation.

Over the past decade, computational technologies have transformed not only research in art history but also pedagogical approaches to the discipline. As technology has become an integral part of daily life, so too it shapes students' expectations about the delivery of course content, use of analytical tools, and participation in systems of communication within scholarly environments. Building on important work in this area, I considered it important to include a section that examines ways in which museum professionals and university scholars are disseminating their research, integrating technology into educational programs, and transforming students' learning experiences.[8] Aspects of this discussion relate to the use of social media, the publication of open access materials, and the creation of methods of connectivity capable of stimulating innovative analytical approaches to new and established fields of study.

By giving rise to mapping and analytical tools that are capable of bringing underrepresented artistic networks and career trajectories to light or by visualizing material at a level inaccessible to human sight, computational methodologies promise to disrupt familiar histories and methods of analysis. Indeed, "disruption" is often a term that is used in a positive sense in discussions about the promise of interaction between digital and traditional humanities.[9] Yet digital methods are, themselves, subject to disruption and are rarely—if ever—completely "clean" or orderly. As many contributors to the present volume note, the development and use of computational tools have been shaped by the untidiness of history and the vagaries of human character: They are subject to accident, glitches, noise, and mismatches between software and hardware. Machinery itself is vulnerable to environmental hazard. As Paul Dourish and Genevieve Bell argued in 2011, "the practice of any technology in the world is never quite as simple, straightforward, or idealized as it is imagined to be. [. . .] Mess is always nearby."[10] For Dourish and Bell, "mess" relates not only to the relationship between technology and daily life but also to the contestation of "technological realities."[11] Against this background, the digitally informed methodologies discussed in this volume are—like histories of art—rooted in, and subject to, the unpredictability of human life. The ambition of this book is to examine patterns of mutual support and disruption that emerge as we navigate the productive messiness that underpins the intersection of digital humanities and art history.

## Notes

1. Lev Manovich, "Data Science and Digital Art History," *DAH-Journal* no. 1 (2015), 14–35 (33).
2. On the "subordination" of art history to digital methods, see Claire Bishop, "Against Digital Art History," Humanities Futures, Franklin Humanities Institute, accessed November 28, 2019, https://humanitiesfutures.org/papers/digital-art-history/: "subordinating art history [. . .] to computational analysis" is a method that "perpetuates uncritical assumptions about the intrinsic value of statistics." For a discussion of art history driven by the exponential growth in amounts of data (including images and visualization), see Maximilian Schich, "Figuring Out Art History," *DAH-Journal* no. 2 (2016), accessed November 29, 2019, https://doi.org/10.11588/dah.2016.2.24761.
3. Johanna Drucker, "Is There a Digital Art History," *Visual Resources: An International Journal of Documentation* 29, no. 1–2 (2013): 5–13 (7 and 8), doi:10.1080/01973762.2013.761106.
4. Jorge Sebastián Lozano, "Digital Art History at the Crossroads," in *Critical Approaches to Digital Art History*, eds. Angela Dressen and Lia Markey, *kunsttexte.de* 4 (2017): 1–14 (2). On the adoption of techniques from literary studies, consider, for example, the impact of Franco Moretti's, *Distant Reading* (London: Verso, 2015). See also Pamela Fletcher's discussion of this and other issues affecting the

emergence of digital art history in "Reflections on Digital Art History," *caa.reviews*, June 18, 2015, www.caareviews.org/reviews/2726#.XbbCtJP7SV4.

5. See, for example, Roopika Risam, "Decolonizing the Digital Humanities in Theory and Practice," 2018. English Faculty Publications, Salem State University, 7, accessed November 28, 2019, https://digitalcommons.salemstate.edu/english_facpub/7.
6. In 2011, Elijah Meeks identified the "pillars" of digital humanities as text analysis, spatial analysis, and network analysis, then adding the potential of a fourth—image analysis. "More Networks in the Humanities or Did Books Have DNA?" *Digital Humanities Specialist* (blog), Stanford University, December 6, 2011, https://dhs.stanford.edu/visualization/more-networks/. See also Pamela Fletcher's discussion of this point in "Reflections on Digital Art History"; Miriam Kienle, "Between Nodes and Edges: Possibilities and Limits of Network Analysis in Art History," *Artl@s Bulletin* 6, no. 3 (2017): 4–22.
7. For a recent discussion of this, see Carolyn Korsmeyer, *Things: In Touch With the Past* (Oxford: Oxford University Press, 2019), 150–59.
8. For previous work in this area, see *Digital Art History: A Subject in Transition*, eds. Anna Bentkowska-Kafel, Trish Cashen, and Hazel Gardiner (Bristol and Portland, OR: Intellect, 2005); Kelly Donahue-Wallace, Laetitia La Follette, and Andrea Pappas, *Teaching Art History With New Technologies: Reflections and Case Studies* (Newcastle: Cambridge Scholars Publishing, 2008). For more recent work, see Roger C. Schonfeld and Matthew P. Long, *Supporting the Changing Research Practices of Art Historians* (Ithaka S + R, 2014), https://doi.org/10.18665/sr.22833; Diane M. Zorich, "Transitioning to a Digital World: Art History, Its Research Centers, and Digital Scholarship," A Report to the Samuel H. Kress Foundation and the Roy Rosenzweig Center for History and New Media, George Mason University (May 2012), www.kressfoundation.org/uploadedFiles/Sponsored_Research/Research/Zorich_TransitioningDigitalWorld.pdf; Stephen Bury, Ralph Baylow, Samantha Deutch, Sumita Duncan, Julie Ludwig, Ellen Prokop, and Louisa Wood Ruby, *Art History in Digital Dimensions*, Digital Art History Lab, Frick Art Reference Library, Symposium Funded by the Getty Foundation and the Samuel H. Kress Foundation (February 2017), accessed November 28, 2019, http://dah-dimensions.org/report/.
9. See, for example, Janneke Adema and Gary Hall, "Posthumanities: The Dark Side of 'The Dark Side of the Digital,'" *The Journal of Electronic Publishing* 19, no. 2 (Fall 2016), http://dx.doi.org/10.3998/3336451.0019.201.
10. Paul Dourish and Genevieve Bell, *Divining a Digital Future: Mess and Mythology in Ubiquitous Computing* (Cambridge, MA: MIT Press, 2011), 4–5.
11. Ibid., 4.

## Bibliography


Bentkowska-Kafel, Anna, Trish Cashen, and Hazel Gardiner, eds. *Digital Art History: A Subject in Transition*. Bristol and Portland, OR: Intellect, 2005.

Bishop, Claire. "Against Digital Art History." Humanities Futures, Franklin Humanities Institute. Accessed November 28, 2019. https://humanitiesfutures.org/papers/digital-art-history/

Bury, Stephen, Ralph Baylow, Samantha Deutch, Sumita Duncan, Julie Ludwig, Ellen Prokop and Louisa Wood Ruby. *Art History in Digital Dimensions*, Digital Art History Lab, Frick Art Reference Library, Symposium funded by the Getty Foundation and the Samuel H. Kress Foundation, February 2017. http://dah-dimensions.org/report/

Donahue-Wallace, Kelly, Laetitia La Follette, and Andrea Pappas. *Teaching Art History with New Technologies: Reflections and Case Studies*. Newcastle: Cambridge Scholars Publishing, 2008.

Drucker, Johanna. "Is There a Digital Art History." *Visual Resources: An International Journal of Documentation* 29, no. 1–2 (2013): 5–13.

Fletcher, Pamela. "Reflections on Digital Art History." *caa.reviews*, June 18, 2015. www.caareviews.org/reviews/2726#.XbbCtJP7SV4

Kienle, Miriam. "Between Nodes and Edges: Possibilities and Limits of Network Analysis in Art History." *Artl@s Bulletin* 6, no. 3 (2017): 4–22.

Korsmeyer, Carolyn. *Things: In Touch with the Past*. Oxford: Oxford University Press, 2019.

Lozano, Jorge Sebastián. "Digital Art History at the Crossroads." *Critical Approaches to Digital Art History*, edited by Angela Dressen and Lia Markey, *kunsttexte.de* 4 (2017): 1–14.

Manovich, Lev. "Data Science and Digital Art History." *DAH-Journal* no. 1 (2015): 14–35.

Meeks, Elijah. "More Networks in the Humanities or Did Books have DNA?" *Digital Humanities Specialist* (blog), Stanford University, December 6, 2011. https://dhs.stanford.edu/visualization/more-networks/.
Moretti, Franco. *Distant Reading*. London:Verso, 2015.
Risam, Roopika. "Decolonizing the Digital Humanities in Theory and Practice" (2018). *English Faculty Publications*, vol. 7. Salem State University. https://digitalcommons.salemstate.edu/english_facpub/7.
Schich, Maximilian. "Figuring Out Art History." *DAH-journal*, no. 2 (2016). https://doi.org/10.11588/dah.2016.2.24761
Schonfeld, Roger C., and Matthew P. Long. *Supporting the Changing Research Practices of Art Historians* (Ithaka S + R, 2014). https://doi.org/10.18665/sr.22833.
Zorich, Diane M. "Transitioning to a Digital World: Art History, Its Research Centers, and Digital Scholarship." A Report to the Samuel H. Kress Foundation and the Roy Rosenzweig Center for History and New Media, George Mason University, May 2012. www.kressfoundation.org/uploadedFiles/Sponsored_Research/Research/Zorich_TransitioningDigitalWorld.pdf

# PART I

# Histories and Critical Debates

# 1

# DIGITAL METHODS AND THE HISTORIOGRAPHY OF ART

*Paul B. Jaskot*

Art history is almost by definition a field that rests on "big data."Traditional methods of training as well as interpretation—such as iconographic analysis—have required scholars to accumulate vast amounts of knowledge about visual tropes, for example. We are long familiar with thinking typologically as well as encyclopedically about forms, functions, and artists. In a word, art history has been digital art history seemingly without knowing it for some time. Yet still, digital methodologies clearly bring new challenges to the field. This chapter introduces the reader to the relationship between digital methods and art historiography. It will locate debates in the digital humanities within the debates of art history itself, to see how the one field illuminates the areas of study in the other. It will raise such questions as what is the relationship between digital methods and canonical art historiographic subjects of study? How are digital methods a critical new intervention in the theory and practice of art history? Which art-historical methodological approaches are best suited to digital epistemologies? And what is different (if anything) between digital art history and its predecessors? By focusing on these issues, I will argue for a need to concern ourselves with a more critical digital art-historical practice that is integrated with (and interrogates) long-standing art-historical subjects and interests.

But why this look backwards to historiography when the very notion of the digital seems to speak solely to the brave new world of the future? As Hubertus Kohle has recently argued, the digital humanities promises radical new results, modes of analysis, and publication. At the same time, it may very well not change the interest in fundamental human questions in the process, questions that, after all, are profound and at the core of the human experience.[1] If this is so, it is worthwhile to lay out those human questions and concerns at the same time that we outline the strengths and weaknesses of computational methods. In what follows, I will try to do just that. On the one hand, this chapter is concerned with the "big interests" of art history, as they can be seen in important historiographical developments over the past century. On the other, it is equally invested in the "big approaches" of computational methods that cross many different digital applications. It is only by exploring the conjuncture and divergence of these two diverse streams of thought that we can understand where that critical potential may lie.

****

While art history famously claims to be one of the most interdisciplinary of disciplines, it has certain borders and specific areas of interest that define its methodologies and subjects. Some of these are obvious: Think, for instance, of Erwin Panofsky's iconographic approach to particular complex images from early modern Europe such as Albrecht Dürer's oeuvre.[2] It is unlikely that anyone but an art historian would delve so deeply into the history of the form and subject matter to analyze its significance and meaning. On the other hand, other art-historical questions seem to be less clearly a matter solely of a single discipline, such as whether a set of stylistic patterns may be part of a specific cultural geography that can be defined as "German" art.[3] Aside from particular methodological debates in the field and trends in subjects of study, there are nevertheless some larger patterns in art-historical interests that have crossed almost all periods and times.

First, art historians are interested in typologies. Classification of groups and types is foundational to art history, as it is to many disciplines. Notably, the question of a group style and specific artistic genres were seen as crucial points as the field initially developed its subject of study in the late nineteenth and early twentieth centuries. Heinrich Wölfflin's interest in identifiable chronological and culturally specific styles is the most obvious place to start. For Wölfflin, looking at vast numbers of examples of early modern European art required the analytical ability to characterize them effectively through categories like "Renaissance" and "Baroque" or "Italian" versus "German."[4] While Wölfflin's samples were by today's standards small and often relied on easily accessible museums near where he taught (such as the Alte Pinakothek in Munich), his range of visual knowledge was nevertheless impressive for the period and complemented by relatively new modes of presentation such as side by side photographic comparisons. He was joined in this attempt to characterize art by others such as Alois Riegl, who, in a quite different approach, developed a distinctive analysis of Dutch portraiture. He, too, thought that artworks could be described in more collective terms through gesture and composition in order to analyze the dynamic relationship between artwork and audience, for example.[5]

Such early art-historical typologies have since been roundly criticized as too hermetic, emphasizing a narrow canon that pretends to be universal in its claim as a stable notion of "art history," among other points of critique.[6] While important, these criticisms often glide over the point that the very subject of art history needed to be defined in this early period, however faulty that initial work proved to be. Since then, though, typological thinking has also been used effectively and critically to relate artworks to social systems by, for example, Richard Krautheimer, in his studies of the formal and ideological influence of early Christian church plans on later European building.[7] In digital humanities, scholars have emphasized the importance of developing typologies to establish entirely new areas of knowledge, especially from marginalized groups, as a form of what Kim Gallon calls the "technology of recovery."[8] The power of typological thinking is, of course, its ability to characterize a field by organizing its subject; that method can be as dangerous in forming an unyielding canon as it can be critical in blasting open a set range of problems by introducing entirely new categories of evidence. In this regard, typological thinking is as much a part of the foundations of a field as it is of its latest (digital) critique.

Second, art historians are also interested in visual form, not only in individual works but at scale. Early attempts by Roger Fry, for example, to define a Post-Impressionist style can be put in this category as well as the centuries-long practice of connoisseurship in the study and analysis of Chinese art.[9] In either case, close looking and characterization of form is coupled with the categorization of visual patterns. What constitutes "style" in a visual sense was countered by other art historians who began to think of style in more social terms, as in the work of Meyer Schapiro in his fundamental essay "Style."[10] Formal critique at the scale of a definition of "style" can often be as theoretical as it is based on visual evidence, as in the case of Rosalind Krauss's argument for sculpture in the "expanded field."[11] As with close reading in literature, formalist art historians in the post-1968 world have faced criticism that visual analysis for its own sake is ahistorical and ultimately subjective. More recently in the digital era, we can speak of Franco Moretti's concept of distant reading as a critique of the limitations of analysis that fetishizes the close exploration of form, among other criteria.[12] Such recent debates indicate that the question of the scale of evidence at the basis of the analysis is an important point of consensus or disagreement when one considers the validity of an argument driven by visual evidence.

Third, art historians are interested in subject matter. Since Panofsky, the study of the significance of iconography has weighed heavily on art historians who focus on painting, sculpture, print, and photography, among other media. Panofsky's influential theory and method of iconographic analysis emphasized understanding the subject matter chosen within the history of that subject matter's depiction.[13] The result of this method means that the art historian must have as thorough a knowledge of other depictions of the same subject as she does of the object under investigation. As with other foundational approaches, the limitations of iconography have been well noted by subsequent generations, even while the importance of understanding the broader patterns in the content and context of subject matter choices have extended into important works in diverse areas such as the study of Chinese painting, feminist art history, and the ideological critique of art.[14] For all of these approaches, art historians concern themselves with locating the significant meaning of a work of art by placing it in dialogue with dozens if not hundreds of others.

And finally, art historians are interested in the social world in which art functions. From the initial biographical approach of Giorgio Vasari in the sixteenth century to the emphasis on social class and art in the works of Frederick Antal or Arnold Hauser, the place of an artwork in time has been an important criterion for many art historians across a diverse theoretical spectrum. In these cases, emphasis on the social requires an art historian to research vast areas of human history and experience covering ever more terrain at both the micro level of the work and the artist and at the macro level of the social system. While systemic questions have been especially of interest to Marxist art historians like Schapiro and Hauser,[15] specific social research extended in the post–World War II era to the broader field of art history through institutional studies of the global spread of national art academies, interest in artists beyond the white male canon, and a more diverse geography of art.[16] Art historians have also been critical of this work, particularly on the question of the role of mediation between the meaning of a work and its social context, as in the famous critique of Hauser by Ernst Gombrich.[17] These criticisms, though, have not dampened the continued interest of a wide array of art historians across the discipline in seeing the most crucial question in art history as how artworks and artists interact with social environments and systems. Such an interest has also been taken up in digital analysis as well.

This excursus on (mostly) old white men of art history helps us to see key patterns and trends in the discipline that are well known and established. I have intentionally emphasized the two eras of the first decades of the twentieth century and the post–World War II moment in order to draw out the point that these subject areas carry over in art history beyond specific methodological trajectories or periods. Not surprisingly, scholars today of diverse theoretical positions continue to be concerned with these areas. Of course, these are not the only fields of art-historical interest, but they are ones that cut through more than a century of historiography; in addition, they are also interests that depend methodologically on what constitutes "big data" in art history. These issues intersect with evidence—visual, social, or otherwise—at scale, unlike much of the theoretically driven art history that focuses on questions of representation. In this sense, they are the ones that can be most closely associated with the work of the digital humanities, and they are the trends that can engage most productively with digital methods.

As with the historiography, not all digital methods are equally well suited to art-historical questions and current debates. The relationship between the two intellectual fields is strategic and selective, not transparent. There are, though, at least three dominant areas in which the two clearly and productively intersect

First, digital methods favor large scalable questions that require big data. While there are few art-historical data sets that constitute "big data" in the typical digital humanities sense, the issue of evidence at scale and how to analyze it is obviously important to all four areas of art-historical inquiry just described.[18] In particular, the potential for mobilizing computational strategies to analyze thousands or even millions of images addresses historiographic concerns at the foundation of the field as well as its most recent interests. Being able to extend our data sets infinitely certainly brings us back to the issue of characterization and typology. It also shows potential, as Lev Manovich has shown, in analyzing form in new ways.[19] The sheer number of sources and images available in the last decade because of digitization in and of itself offers a real challenge to our analyses that is quickly becoming the norm.[20] The rapid expansion of art-historical evidence, while daunting in terms of our current methodological strategies and the overall *lack* of integration of computational methods across the discipline, also holds great promise for critical scholarship. For example, the ability to use new computational methods to analyze large bodies of visual evidence from cultures without extensive print traditions or, complementarily, the ability to highlight through sheer number the contributions of art-historical actors of marginalized class, ethnicity, or gender status allow for new challenges to an all-too market-driven choice of subject matter standard in the field.[21]

Second, digital methods deal with networks. Few issues have been as important to many of the categories of art-historical interest than the relationship between artists, artworks, and artistic movements. Such an interest has only increased with the growth of art-historical scholarship over the last century. This comes not only from scholars invested in formal issues or the social embeddedness of art, but also those who question such visually or historically driven research in favor of more theoretically inclined work influenced by epistemologies of representation. In the latter category, the question of affiliations, relationships, conceptual or personal connections, or the status of one body of work among many all still hinge on some concept of a network.[22] Of course, digital methods favor the former much more than the latter, and they have already shown rich potential in analyzing market systems or social relationships.[23] The complexity of the historical evidence as well as the ability to structure that evidence for computational analysis greatly favor these kinds of questions. In this regard, again, it is a matter of which parts of art-historical debate are most suited to developing computational approaches in the humanities.

Finally, digital methods allow for a more complex spatial analysis. The fundamental importance of spatial analysis to art history—from, for example, the physical object in space to the spread of vast artistic networks over diverse geographies—makes this aspect of the discipline in many ways the most productive point of intersection with digital methods.[24] Spatial computational methods can both examine large-scale spatial data but also have a morphological power to visualize this data analytically, such as in the early digital example of "Mapping Gothic France."[25] As indicated in the sources cited previously, these new digital methods extend questions that have been addressed in other ways in the historiography, especially questions of typological patterns over space and time or the movement of objects and artists through different cultural and social geographies. The deep art-historical interest in spatial questions (especially typological, formal, and social) intersects with the equally rich explosion of computational modes of spatial analysis. Rapid developments in Geographic Information Systems (GIS), 3D modeling, photogrammetry, and other digital approaches to space make this a particularly important area for the intersection of art-historical concerns and computational methods now and into the future.[26]

In laying out broad areas of interest in the art historiography as well as intellectual fields in digital analysis, we have seen how there are important overlaps especially in regards to art-historical evidence at scale. In stepping back from the mutual areas of interest, however, there are two opposing and equally problematic ways of thinking about the rapid rise in digital methods in relation to art-historiographical interests: on the one hand, the tyranny of the object; on the other, the dominance of the system. For example, a "big data" project might include all the possible data that could be gathered about a single work of art. Such a project could require hundreds of hours, large teams, and of course vast amounts of financial support.[27] As a result, this approach has the potential to limit our ability economically and institutionally to expand our inquiry into other areas of art-historical concern that may or may not be as relevant to a particular object. It could, therefore, favor iconography at the expense of the social. In contrast, "big data" also could favor a broad, systemic approach to millions of art-historical data points.[28] This result could easily limit an understanding of the particularity of an artist or artwork and reduce individual histories to pure abstraction.

And yet, more productively, if we focus on the database as the actual element that mediates between the computational method and the art-historical subject, we can also conceive of a more critical potential of such an intersection of interests, especially when large art-historical data sets come into play. The database used to structure this evidence can be conceived more dialectically than the impossible opposition of tyranny and domination just discussed. A database ontologically maintains the individual status of the evidence—artwork, artist, iconography, or any other category one wishes—within an environment that is structured for digital analysis. Such a method thus allows for both an individual and systemic approach to art-historical questions. In this sense, the database has the great potential to open up another debate in a difficult but important art-historical question: How do we connect the (singular) work of art to its social (systemic) significance? The database helps us think about that mediation in entirely novel ways even while it allows for the visualization of the relationship between the individual element and the "big data" of a system as absolutely the center of its concern. This takes us into some of the most critical questions of art history, especially those raised by the social history of art. The social history of art is an historiographic area that in particular has much to gain from a developing art-historical interest in computational methods.

★★★★

As the last point makes clear, I am arguing that digital methods intersect with the field of art history in particular ways. As with any approach, it is better suited to answering some questions more than others, taking on some subjects at the expense of others, and promoting particular intellectual areas of the discipline. The important issue is thus which art-historical question is of greatest concern to the scholar. The digital response to some questions may be deeply positivist and reactionary, as many of our critics assume. At the same time, it can respond to others by, for example, opening up completely new areas of the field for critical analysis that have been overlooked by market-driven canons.

We may thus be at a very new beginning, or rather returning to a new foundational moment.[29] In some sense, we need to go back to such fundamental work by scholars such as Wölfflin to rethink what the very core substance of our field is, and constituting that through new methods and approaches. This will of necessity be partial and require the collaborative work of many art historians. It will result in incomplete analyses, promissory notes that await ever larger data sets and more appropriate computational methods. And yet, if we want change in the field to contribute to a broad social function of scholarship—which is after all the goal of a critical digital humanities—we have the potential through these means radically to reorient historiographic debates, make visible what has been rendered invisible, and address art-historical questions of true significance to an analysis of individuals and systems. Still, dialectically speaking it must be noted that such a power can also be used to ossify the most canonical and narrow of subjects and interests with a massive concentration of social, institutional, and financial resources. As with any intellectual and political debate, it is up to us to explore what computational methods are capable of and for which art-historical and social interests. By doing so, we may identify their critical potential to disrupt the discipline's all-too-frequent subservience to a dominant culture.

## Acknowledgment

My thanks to Kathryn Brown and Robert Buerglener for their critical comments on this chapter.

## Notes

1. Hubertus Kohle, "Die Geisteswissenschaften und das Digitale: Ein Quantensprung oder *business as usual?*" in *#DigiCampus: Digitale Forschung und Lehre in den Geisteswissenschaften*, ed. Harald Klinke (Munich: Open Publishing LMU, 2018), 17.
2. Erwin Panofsky, *The Life and Art of Albrecht Dürer* (Princeton: Princeton University Press, 1955). In an elegant recent play off Panofsky's method and a novel new analysis, see also Mitchell B. Merback, *Perfection's Therapy: An Essay on Albrecht Dürer's Melancolia I* (Brooklyn: Zone Books, 2017).
3. Thomas DaCosta Kaufmann, *Toward a Geography of Art* (Chicago: University of Chicago Press, 2004).
4. Developed most famously in Heinrich Wölfflin, *Principles of Art History: The Problem of the Development of Style in Early Modern Art (Hundredth Anniversary Edition)*, trans. Jonathan Blower (Los Angeles: Getty Publications, 2015). For a thorough and critical recent evaluation of Wölfflin and his influence in the broader art-historical context, see Evonne Levy, *Baroque and the Political Language of Formalism (1845–1945): Bruckhardt, Wölfflin, Gurlitt, Brinckmann, Sedlmayr* (Basel: Schwabe Verlag, 2015).
5. Alois Riegl, *The Group Portraiture of Holland*, trans. Evelyn Kain (Los Angeles: Getty Publications, 1999). See also Wolfgang Kemp's excellent introduction to this translation.
6. The epistemological limits of typologies have been most effectively criticized by Michel Foucault as in *The Order of Things: An Archaeology of the Human Sciences* (New York: Vintage Books, 1970); see, especially, the chapter on classification. Poststructuralist art historians have pointed to this and other work to condemn typological methods that inevitably result in canon formations, which exclude specific discursive and representational strategies and interpretations. See broadly on this point, Michael Ann Holly, *Past Looking: Historical Imagination and the Rhetoric of the Image* (Ithaca, NY: Cornell University Press, 1996).
7. Richard Krautheimer, "The Carolingian Revival of Early Christian Architecture," *Art Bulletin* 24 (1942): 1–38.
8. Kim Gallon, "Making a Case for the Black Digital Humanities," in *Debates in the Digital Humanities 2016*, eds. Matthew K. Gold and Lauren F. Klein (Minneapolis: University of Minnesota Press, 2016), 42–49.
9. For an extended exemplar of Fry's work, see Roger Fry, *Cézanne: A Study of His Development* (London: L. & V. Woolf, 1927). For China, see, among many examples, Ankeney Weitz, *Zhou Mi's Record of Clouds and Mist Passing Before One's Eyes: An Annotated Translation* (Leiden: Brill, 2002).
10. Meyer Schapiro, "Style," in *Anthropology Today*, ed. Alfred L. Kroeber (Chicago: University of Chicago Press, 1953), 287–312.
11. Rosalind Krauss, "Sculpture in the Expanded Field," *October* 8 (Spring 1979): 30–44.
12. Franco Moretti, *Distant Reading* (London: Verso, 2013). For a highly productive recent critique of Moretti, see Carolyn Lesjak, "All or Nothing: Reading Franco Moretti Reading. A Review of *Distant Reading* and *The Bourgeois: Between History and Literature* by Franco Moretti," *Historical Materialism* 24, no. 3 (2016): 185–205.

13. The classic first text in English is Erwin Panofsky, "Jan van Eyck's Arnolfini Portrait," *The Burlington Magazine* 64, no. 372 (March 1934): 117–19, 122–27.
14. While in very different keys from Panofsky, innovative scholars in these areas include James Cahill, *Hills Beyond a River: Chinese Painting of the Yüan Dynasty, 1279–1368* (New York: Weatherhill, 1976); Carol Duncan, "Virility and Domination in Early Twentieth-Century Vanguard Painting," in *Feminism and Art History: Questioning the Litany*, ed. Norma Broude and Mary D. Garrard (London: Harper & Row, 1982), 292–313; Patricia Leighton, *Re-Ordering the Universe: Picasso and Anarchism, 1897–1914* (Princeton: Princeton University Press, 1989).
15. See an overview in Andrew Hemingway, "Marxism and Art," in *Oxford Bibliographies* (Oxford: Oxford University Press, 2014), accessed July 12, 2018, doi:10.1093/obo/9780199920105-0023.
16. Interesting examples of these trends include Jean Charlot, *Mexican Art and the Academy of San Carlos, 1785–1915* (Austin: University of Texas Press, 1962); Anne Sutherland-Harris and Linda Nochlin, *Women Artists 1550–1950* (New York: Alfred Knopf, 1976); George Kubler, *Mexican Architecture of the Sixteenth Century* (New Haven: Yale University Press, 1948).
17. An interesting recent review of this debate can be found in Jim Berryman, "Gombrich's Critique of Hauser's *Social History of Art*," *History of European Ideas* 43, no. 5 (2017): 494–506.
18. Drucker discusses this potential for changing the nature of iconographic analysis, for example, in her seminal article Johanna Drucker, "Is There a 'Digital' Art History?," *Visual Resources* 29, no. 1–2 (March–June 2013): 5–13.
19. Most recently in Mehrdad Yazdani, Jay Chow, and Lev Monovich, "Quantifying the Development of User-Generated Art During 2001–2010," *PLoS One* (August 8, 2017), accessed July 15, 2018, https://doi.org/10.1371/journal.pone.0175350.
20. To this point, see Harald Klinke, "Vorwort: Die digitale Transformation in den Geisteswissenschaften," in *#DigiCampus: Digitale Forschung und Lehre in den Geisteswissenschaften* (Munich: Open Publishing LMU, 2018), esp. 3–4.
21. Paul B. Jaskot, "Digital Art History as the Social History of Art: Towards the Disciplinary Relevance of Digital Methods," *Visual Resources* 35, no. 1–2 (March–June 2019): 21–33.
22. Compare how groups and affiliations have been treated in, for example, Thomas Crow, *Painters and Public Life in Eighteenth-Century Paris* (New Haven: Yale University Press, 1987); Amelia Jones, *Body Art/Performing the Subject* (Minneapolis: University of Minnesota Press, 1998).
23. See, for example, Matthew Lincoln and Abram Fox, "The Temporal Dimensions of the London Art Auction, 1780–1835," *British Art Studies* 4 (November 28, 2016), accessed July 15, 2018, http://britishartstudies.ac.uk/issues/issue-index/issue-4/london-art-auction-1870-1835. For social relationships, see the example of women's artist collaboratives analyzed in Joanna Gardner-Huggett, "Extrapolating Influence: The Challenges of Mapping the History of ARC and Artemesia Galleries, Chicago (1980–1985)," *Historical Geography* 45 (2017): 37–65.
24. I have made this argument previously in Paul B. Jaskot, "Commentary: Art-Historical Questions, Geographic Concepts, and Digital Methods," *Historical Geography* 45 (2017): 92–99.
25. Stephen Murray, Andrew Tallon, and Rory O'Neill, "Mapping Gothic France" (2010), accessed July 12, 2018, http://mappinggothic.org/.
26. For an overview, see Ian N. Gregory and Paul S. Ell, *Historical GIS: Technologies, Methodologies, and Scholarship* (Cambridge: Cambridge University Press, 2009). See also the foundational work of Anne Kelly Knowles in this area, including Anne Kelly Knowles, ed., *Past Time, Past Place: GIS for History* (Redlands, CA: ESRI Press, 2002).
27. See, for example, the impressive Ghent Altarpiece project, "Closer to Van Eyck" (2011), Accessed July 12, 2018, http://closertovaneyck.kikirpa.be/.
28. Maximilian Schich, Chaoming Song, Yong-Yeol Ahn, Alexander Mirsky, Mauro Martino, Albert-László Barabási, and Dirk Helbing, "A Network Framework of Cultural History," *Science* 345 (2014): 558–62.
29. Benjamin Zweig has argued that we need to see the long history of digital's relation to art history well before the internet. I agree with this important point, although I do think, as my chapter implies, that we also need to emphasize the last decade as a new moment in the re-evaluation of what constitutes digital art history. Benjamin Zweig, "Forgotten Genealogies: Brief Reflections on the History of Digital Art History," *International Journal for Digital Art History* 1 (2015): 38–49.

## Bibliography


Berryman, Jim. "Gombrich's Critique of Hauser's *Social History of Art*." *History of European Ideas* 43, no. 5 (2017): 494–506.

Cahill, James. *Hills Beyond a River: Chinese Painting of the Yüan Dynasty, 1279–1368*. New York: Weatherhill, 1976.

Charlot, Jean. *Mexican Art and the Academy of San Carlos, 1785–1915*. Austin: University of Texas Press, 1962.

Crow, Thomas. *Painters and Public Life in Eighteenth-Century Paris*. New Haven: Yale University Press, 1985.

Drucker, Johanna. "Is There a 'Digital' Art History?" *Visual Resources* 29, no. 1–2 (March–June 2013): 5–13.

Duncan, Carol. "Virility and Domination in Early Twentieth-Century Vanguard Painting." In *Feminism and Art History: Questioning the Litany*, edited by Norma Broude and Mary D. Garrard, 292–313. London: Harper & Row, 1982.

Foucault, Michel. *The Order of Things: An Archaeology of the Human Sciences*. New York: Vintage Books, 1970.

Fry, Roger. *Cézanne: A Study of his Development*. London: L. & V. Woolf, 1927.

Gallon, Kim. "Making a Case for the Black Digital Humanities." In *Debates in the Digital Humanities 2016*, edited by Matthew K. Gold and Lauren F. Klein, 42–49. Minneapolis: University of Minnesota Press, 2016.

Gardner-Huggett, Joanna. "Extrapolating Influence: The Challenges of Mapping the History of ARC and Artemesia Galleries, Chicago (1980–1985)." *Historical Geography* 45 (2017): 37–65.

Gregory, Ian N., and Paul S. Ell. *Historical GIS: Technologies, Methodologies, and Scholarship*. Cambridge: Cambridge University Press, 2009.

Hemingway, Andrew. "Marxism and Art." In *Oxford Bibliographies*. Oxford: Oxford University Press, 2014. Accessed July 12, 2018. doi:10.1093/obo/9780199920105-0023.

Holly, Michael Anne. *Past Looking: Historical Imagination and the Rhetoric of the Image*. Ithaca, NY: Cornell University Press, 1996.

Jaskot, Paul B. "Commentary: Art-Historical Questions, Geographic Concepts, and Digital Methods." *Historical Geography* 45 (2017): 92–99.

———. "Digital Art History as the Social History of Art: Towards the Disciplinary Relevance of Digital Methods." *Visual Resources* 35, no. 1–2 (March–June 2019): 21–33.

Jones, Amelia. *Body Art/Performing the Subject*. Minneapolis: University of Minnesota Press, 1998.

Kaufmann, Thomas DaCosta. *Toward a Geography of Art*. Chicago: University of Chicago Press, 2004.

Klinke, Harald, ed. *#DigiCampus: Digitale Forschung und Lehre in den Geisteswissenschaften*. Munich: Open Publishing LMU, 2018.

Knowles, Anne Kelly, ed. *Past Time, Past Place: GIS for History*. Redlands, CA: ESRI Press, 2002.

Krauss, Rosalind. "Sculpture in the Expanded Field." *October* 8 (Spring 1979): 30–44.

Krautheimer, Richard. "The Carolingian Revival of Early Christian Architecture." *Art Bulletin* 24 (1942): 1–38.

Kubler, George. *Mexican Architecture of the Sixteenth Century*. New Haven: Yale University Press, 1948.

Leighton, Patricia. *Re-Ordering the Universe: Picasso and Anarchism, 1897–1914*. Princeton: Princeton University Press, 1989.

Lesjak, Carolyn. "All or Nothing: Reading Franco Moretti Reading. A Review of *Distant Reading* and *The Bourgeois: Between History and Literature* by Franco Moretti." *Historical Materialism* 24, no. 3 (2016): 185–205.

Levy, Evonne. *Baroque and the Political Language of Formalism (1845–1945): Bruckhardt, Wölfflin, Gurlitt, Brinckmann, Sedlmayr*. Basel: Schwabe Verlag, 2015.

Lincoln, Matthew, and Abram Fox. "The Temporal Dimensions of the London Art Auction, 1780–1835." *British Art Studies* 4 (November 28, 2016). Accessed July 15, 2018. http://britishartstudies.ac.uk/issues/issue-index/issue-4/london-art-auction-1870-1835.

Merback, Mitchell B. *Perfection's Therapy: An Essay on Albrecht Dürer's Melancolia I*. Brooklyn: Zone Books, 2017.

Moretti, Franco. *Distant Reading*. London: Verso, 2013.

Panofsky, Erwin. "Jan van Eyck's Arnolfini Portrait." *The Burlington Magazine* 64, no. 372 (March 1934): 117–19, 122–27.

———. *The Life and Art of Albrecht Dürer*. Princeton: Princeton University Press, 1955.

Riegl, Alois. *The Group Portraiture of Holland*. Translated by Evelyn Kain. Los Angeles: Getty Publications, 1999.

Schapiro, Meyer. "Style." In *Anthropology Today*, edited by Alfred L. Kroeber, 287–312. Chicago: University of Chicago Press, 1953.

Schich, Maximilian, C. Song, Y.-Y. Ahn, A. Mirsky, M. Martino, A.-L. Barabási, and D. Helbing. "A Network Framework of Cultural History." *Science* 345 (2014): 558–62.

Sutherland-Harris, Anne, and Linda Nochlin. *Women Artists 1550–1950*. New York: Alfred Knopf, 1976.

Weitz, Ankeney. *Zhou Mi's Record of Clouds and Mist Passing before One's Eyes: An Annotated Translation*. Leiden: Brill, 2002.

Wölfflin, Heinrich. *Principles of Art History: The Problem of the Development of Style in Early Modern Art (Hundredth Anniversary Edition)*. Translated by Jonathan Blower. Los Angeles: Getty Publications, 2015.

Yazdani, Mehrdad, Jay Chow, and Lev Monovich. "Quantifying the Development of User-Generated Art During 2001–2010." *PLoS One* (August 8, 2017). Accessed July 15, 2018. https://doi.org/10.1371/journal.pone.0175350.

Zweig, Benjamin. "Forgotten Genealogies: Brief Reflections on the History of Digital Art History." *International Journal for Digital Art History* 1 (2015): 38–49.

# 2

# BLIND SPOT

## Information Visualization and Art History

*Johanna Drucker*

Visual images participate in the production and transmission of knowledge in many disciplines. In the sciences, they serve particular roles in generating and representing research.[1] In the arts, they express cultural scenes, preoccupations, and values. In communications, they argue and persuade. Graphic recording of direct observation goes back into prehistory. The configuration of the heavens and the physical features of mega-fauna, for instance, provoked some of the earliest recorded graphic expressions. The extension of human sight by technological means, first by telescope and microscope, then radar, sonar, and magnetic resonance imaging, has been augmented more recently by computational processing into visualizations. The images of subatomic traces in cloud chambers, or use of electron microscopy, or photon lithography at the nanoscale intensify the prosthetic effects of techno-vision. Many of these processes work beyond the scale of human perception. Others create images that have no relationship to a visual object. Among these are the many visualizations of data that populate the graphic world with charts and graphs and diagrams.

Critical attention to the role of images in knowledge production has a substantial history in science and technology studies.[2] Even a short list of outstanding scholarship by authors Peter Galison, Lorraine Daston, Bruno Latour, Karen Knorr-Cetina, Alina Paine, David Freedberg, and others concerned with the connection of visuality and knowledge shows the intellectual vibrancy and seriousness of this critical engagement.[3] In addition to attention to specific practices and topics (such as Claudia Swan's work on botanical illustration), newer work (such as Lev Manovich's or my own) addresses the ways imaging technologies have expanded the cultural role of analogue and digital visualization.[4] Critical reflection on the intimate connection of seeing and knowing reflects philosophical engagement with epistemology: the premises on which justified claims for true belief can be assessed and argued. Questions of resemblance, difference, describing, and mimesis are central to the investigation of the links between cognition, perception, and conventions of graphical presentation in scientific images, but so are concerns rooted in hermeneutic, rather than empirical, frameworks.[5] Visual epistemology is not only a matter of accuracy of iconic resemblance, legibility of symbols, or authority of indexical connection. The rhetorical structure of argument is equally important to the creation and communication of knowledge. The interpretative dimensions of knowledge are integral to its authority and constitution. Attitudes about what constitutes an image of a specimen or map of the movement of planets are as ideologically charged and hermeneutically rich as those concerned with, for instance, portraiture in any culture or period. *How* something is depicted always reveals at least as much as *what* is shown.

In general, less scholarly attention has been paid to diagrammatic and schematic graphical forms of expression, than to pictorial ones. But charts, graphs, and data visualizations are increasingly subject to historical and critical study.[6] The use and awareness of large data have expanded exponentially, and information visualizations have become ubiquitous, easily produced on common platforms. These graphic and schematic forms have their own histories, only some of which overlap with that of iconography. The imprint of the domains within which they originate still functions as part of the structuring principles on which they produce meaning.[7] Trees imply consanguinity to establish legitimate pedigree. Grids structure content types as discrete, defined categories for accounting purposes. Circular and radial forms imply wholeness of the original phenomena in business applications. Bar charts and scatter plots distance quantitative information from sources in human experience for the purpose of demographic and bureaucratic analysis and management. And x-axes are almost always used to plot change over time in alignment with Western conventions of reading sequence from left to right.[8] In each instance, the semantics of structure operate almost invisibly, so familiar and encoded are the instructions for reading.

Graphic designers, scholars working in digital humanities, and also those in the history of science, have taken to tracking circles, bar charts, pies, and trees to supply them with origin myths and to recover lost or abandoned projects.[9] In his 1958 work, *Logic Machines and Diagrams*, Martin Gardner linked graphical forms, conceptual organization and workings, and conditions of invention.[10] For example, he showed what the medieval Kabbalist Ramon Lull's volvelles made possible and how they differed from modern combinatorics processes. The mechanics of signification and the intellectual roots of graphical practices became apparent through Gardner's analysis. In a more curatorial approach, Edward Tufte's compendia provide a rich array of examples and a good descriptive vocabulary for specimens of what he terms "the visual display of quantitative information."[11] How-to books offer manuals of techniques and guidelines, such as *Show me the Numbers* (2004) by Stephen Few or *Statistical Graphics* (1983) by Calvin Schmid.[12] Coffee-table collections like Manuel Lima's *Visual Complexity* (2011) and Anthony Grafton and Daniel Rosenberg's *Cartographies of Time* (2010) present myriad examples culled from a rich historical inventory.[13] Also, art associated with dataflow and visual complexity finds its way into galleries and museums. But little of this work is underwritten with critical investigation of historical conditions or intellectual traditions. Almost none asks how graphical knowledge is related to ideology or how the epistemological assumptions structuring the images are expressed.

Work in art history is curiously sparse in these studies and debates. Why? James Elkins's *The Domain of Images* (1998) was a pioneering application of art-historical principles to the analysis of scientific images.[14] John Bender and Michael Marrinan's *The Culture of Diagram* (2010) offers another exception to the general rule, as does S.K. Heninger Jr.'s *The Cosmographical Glass* (1977).[15] Bender and Marrinan situated the concept of the "diagram" within eighteenth-century intellectual activities as a basic organizing principle of knowledge, using the French *Encyclopédie* as their main focus. Heninger's study placed Renaissance diagrams in the history of mathematics, showing the connections and tensions between classical geometry, Pythagorean theory, and emerging humanist constructs.

In another exception, *Prints and Visual Communication* (1953), William Ivins made a case for the way changes in print technology in the Renaissance increased specificity in the depiction of plant species.[16] His careful attention to the syntax of engraving practices—and their graphic qualities—linked observational and inscriptional aspects of visualization. He showed how refinement of line, tone, and approaches to rendering and the manipulation of metal plates and the needles, roulettes, and burins that inscribed them, changed the communicative capacity of botanical reproductions. Ivins did not isolate scientific images from those of other graphic works, and his inclusive discussion emphasized a tension between mechanical methods and aesthetic principles. He argued that techniques of increased precision could advance the certainty on which medical knowledge depended. He also argued that the replication of information and its circulation in printed multiples made it effective in stabilizing knowledge through shared references. But even supplementing these titles with lists of other published articles, or occasional conference proceedings, shows how limited the bibliography on diagrammatic forms remains by contrast to that on art in natural history, let alone, art history more broadly.

The question of "why" art history has not engaged more with information visualizations is largely rhetorical of course. More interesting is what the art-historical insight into these works might offer. The parallel question—what art history has to gain by this engagement—will also weave through this discussion. Perhaps the answer is that the field's engagement with visual epistemology changes from a soft "social" knowledge—of cultural trends, social relations, political events, and so on—to a far more ambitious place in the analysis of epistemology itself. What are knowledge claims and how do images make them? With these preliminaries in place, we can turn to the specific challenges of information visualizations.

Charts and graphs are conceptual objects, not representational ones. They have no referent in the visual world and bear no morphological resemblance to specimens or phenomena observed. They are rooted in practices of statistical mathematics put to the purpose of demographic, political, commercial, or other analyses. They are also images whose aesthetic features participate in visual communication as surely as other prints and visual works. Oddly, they lose their stature as *images* by virtue of their *work* in the (apparent) service of knowledge production. The implication is that their forms are determined by their purpose and thus not worthy of consideration on visual grounds. We don't look *at* them, but *through* them for their information. But if this line is drawn between epistemological images and art-historical ones on the grounds that the former serve empirical science and the latter are expressions of cultural conditions, we create a false binary. Art-historical methods could engage these graphical works differently—not as expressions of data (assessed as good, bad, inadequate, or indifferent in their degree of success) but as visual works whose properties are part of larger conditions of conception, execution, and ideological effect.

In the late eighteenth century, William Playfair created some still justly renowned graphical expressions of political statistics. His work often serves as a starting point for the history of modern information visualization.[17] Playfair, as various scholars have pointed out, did not invent his graphical forms wholesale.[18] Coordinate systems, for instance, had been developed by Descartes more than a century earlier.[19] As a focus, Playfair's work has the advantage of being familiar to many and much-studied. The work is highly aesthetic—it makes optimal use of the late eighteenth-century graphic arts to create rhetorically persuasive arguments whose import is as much bound to formal values as to intellectual ones. In other words, skill of presentation, as much as accuracy of information, makes Playfair's work appealing and enduring. These qualities also give it the potency to address ways visual epistemology *works* in hermeneutic terms. The Playfair plates are assertions of justified true belief. They make statements about how knowledge is produced and of what it consists. They are not the unmediated presentation of information, let alone simple correlations between graphics and phenomena in the world.

Playfair's first major publication was the 1786 *Commercial and Political Atlas and Statistical Breviary*. The term "Atlas" in his title asserts an association with cartographic methods. An atlas is a compendium of graphical expressions of interpretations of physical, geographical phenomena, and is fundamentally hermeneutic from the outset. Graphical projections of space are constructed projections, not unmediated representations of territory. They are distortions made through mathematical calculation, not observation.

The graphical features of the plates in the 1786 edition of the *Atlas* are professionally engraved and hand-colored. In addition to the line, column, and area features, they contain texts engraved in a recognizable business hand of the period as well as others that imitate printed type. The depicted medallion on which the explanatory title is inscribed attaches itself like a plaque to a building front, official in its public declaration. This hybrid approach to text was common to engraved book title pages in the period, and the style, size, scale for reading, and other graphic features situate these images among several realms. First, they are clearly designed to circulate in book format (as opposed to broadsides or popular ballads or newssheets). Many well-known painters in the period also made works designed to be produced and presented in book publications, such as John Martin and J.M.W. Turner, to name just two. The medium of engraving thus provided common ground for fine art and informational graphics. They are technologically indistinguishable. The muted earth-tone color palette used to tint Playfair's images is very close to that used in coloring Turner's landscapes of sea, sky, land, and clouds. Playfair is credited with being the first person to conceive of color-coding a chart, though tinting pictorial prints was a widespread practice.[20] But these images also belong to a larger system of visual print artifacts within commercial and legal frameworks. The handwriting on the plates is the same as that which would have appeared on written documents passed across a desk for accounting transactions, or bills of sale, lading, or other official and commercial purposes.[21] The graphical codes of the business hand (masculine, round, and clear, was distinguished from the more delicate italic models used by women) immediately place these images in a commercial context.[22]

When Playfair's work is read diachronically, solely within a lineage of information graphics, rather than synchronically, in relation to a broad array of graphic images, the approach isolates him from the graphical languages through which his work would have been read by his contemporaries. In that diachronic reading, he is a pioneer inventor in a linear narrative of progress. But read in his own context of media, the notion that Playfair's graphics are "informational" while Turner's or Martin's are "imaginative" starts to break down. A binary between imagined illustrations for fictional works and medical ones might hold, but images that accompanied travel narratives or naturalists' accounts of rambles and views are harder to sort into clearly opposed categories of imagined versus reported sights. Playfair's images are not, of course, "naturalistic" and have no prior visual object on which they can be based. They belong to the graphical realm of quantitative tables, nautical charts, and account ledgers which they clearly resemble through shared features.

Beginning with Playfair's work, information graphics are often assessed on whether they are adequate or inadequate to the task of communicating data.[23] That approach already assumes that the value of the image is determined by its ability to communicate a pre-existing referent. The "information" of the image is understood as equivalent to the values contained in the mathematical table of which it is an expression. Transparency and accuracy are equated as if data have an ideal form and the purpose of the graph is to express it.[24] The graphic is assumed to be legible solely as an efficient and accurate expression of data. Aesthetic properties are perceived as mere elements of period style—attractively generating nostalgia—not as structuring principles and assumptions about knowledge production.

This approach ignores the provocative features that come into play in an *aesthetic reading* of graphical objects. The statement is deliberate. The point is not simply, merely, to shift visualizations into the category of aesthetic objects, the goal is to show how, as aesthetic objects, they provoke a reading in accordance with the terms of critical hermeneutics. What *kind* of knowledge do these information visualizations express and how, in so doing, do they extend the boundaries of art history by their inclusion? This question opens the way to read Playfair and any of the wide range of information visualizations produced into the present through the same problematic conditions as those through which we read other works of art. The work is a hermeneutic object, fraught with interpretative qualities and dimensions of contingent and co-dependent relations of form to interpretation within cultural codes of production and reception. How is an information visualization to be understood as an epistemic object if it is *not* assessed in terms of the accuracy of alignment between referent and expression? In an aesthetic reading, attention to "accuracy" is replaced with attention to ways of knowing, and assumptions about how that process is inscribed in graphical modes of expression. In other words, reading information visualizations as arguments structured graphically is a radically different approach from reading them as representations. Graphics *make* knowledge, they do not simply represent it. An information visualization is *not a picture*. The common statement that information visualizations are "metrics expressed as graphics" misses the point that they are also reifications of misinformation—that is, that they make declarative statements that hide the complex life cycle of decisions on which their production depends.[25] Data do not exist in raw form.[26]

With this critical frame in mind, we can turn again to the plates of the *Atlas*. Playfair did not deal in probabilities, but in presumed actualities. His images are depictions of that which he takes to be "what is," that is, a seemingly unproblematic representation of quantitative information, such as the relation of one value to another across time, whether that is wages, prices, imports, or exports. Playfair's methods have their conceptual foundation in a burgeoning managerial culture, in a shift toward larger scale bureaucratic control of information and its consequences. They represent a way of "knowing" economic patterns and values over a period of time. The notion of extracting "data"—quantitative values of specific phenomena in the cultural world—from the complex of transactions among multiple domains and then presenting it in compact form as a means of making such information both legible and tractable arose within a rapidly changing economic environment. The very act of extraction and representation in a graphic form is an ideologically inflected epistemological act. It suggests that knowledge can be constituted through these processes of parameterization and reduction—and asserts that the graphic presentation is itself a legible and uncomplicated instrument of knowledge dissemination. The graphic convention presupposes that after the transformation of complex phenomena into metrical values, the graphic is simply a report, an account in visual form.

The canonical images from Playfair's *Atlas* make use of continuous line chart conventions that had been in (albeit infrequent) use for centuries.[27] Playfair was articulate about the extent to which the "graphical method appeals to the eye" and provided a "way of simplifying the tedious and complex."[28] The same statements are used in the present to describe (and justify) the presentation of quantitative information in graphical form. The host of issues hidden by the term "simplify"—such as the obfuscation of intellectual models of data production, rhetoric of graphical means, and glossing of statistical techniques—were no more apparent to Playfair's audience than they are to anyone reading a chart produced from the library of displays in a standard spread sheet application.

With the work of John Graunt and William Petty, Playfair's built on the cultural transformations of early modern statehood.[29] Graunt's *Natural and Political Observations Made upon the Bills of Mortality* (1662) and Petty's *Treatise of Taxes and Contributions* (1662) were foundational for the development of the field known as "political arithmetic."[30] Ian Hacking's work on the emergence of ideas of probability details the development of ideas of chance and inference within scientific and economic theory starting even earlier, in the fifteenth century.[31] The term "statistics" derives from *stasticum collegium* (Council of State) and thus associates the concept directly with bureaucratic techniques of government management.[32] Insofar as Playfair made any pioneering contribution, it was in the "use of graphs to represent empirical historical data" rather than "abstract mathematical functions."[33] His goal was to communicate, not to calculate new findings. The climbing rates of numeracy, though slower than those of literacy, play a part in the publication of these plates as the knowledgeable audience for them increased.[34]

The print context for Playfair's work, including the use of copperplate engraving and scientific treatises, tracks back to the fifteenth century, but the notion of vetted professional knowledge production coincided with the establishment of Royal Academies in the seventeenth century. Though Playfair was far from being an academician, he worked at least briefly with James Watt, who was a Fellow of the Royal Society.[35] The professional context is important in positioning Playfair's graphics, since popular prints (satiric, topical, political) circulated widely on their own, while illustrations, engraved title pages, and technical drawings in manuals for medical, engineering, mathematical, and other fields appeared in serial and bound publications like the *Atlas*.[36] His originality was synthetic rather than expressive.[37] Though Playfair's work spawned a host of imitators, the popularity in information graphics was not a steady upward climb, as charted by Friendly.[38]

Playfair's graphical work always depends on tables of individual data points. Methods of "curve fitting and interpolation," introduced a few decades earlier by Johann Lambert, are employed to create smooth lines of change plotting variables against each other (generally using the x-axis to chart time).[39] Playfair's much reproduced 1821 chart "Showing at One View the Price of the Quarter of Wheat and Wage of Labor by the Week" (Figure 2.1) for a 250-year span makes use of a number of different scales and methods of grouping time periods (by century, by monarch, by decades). The wheat price values are determined by the average in five-year divisions, while the information that shapes the curve of the line depicting wages is taken on a weekly basis. This discrepancy is amplified by the graphic, where the wheat prices are shown in bars that stair step up and down the graph, and the wages are shown as a single continuous line. Aside from the basic violation of graphic grammar—making a continuous line from discrete data points—the graphic displays some interesting features. The stair-step pattern of the bars makes for a skyline effect, and the fade-out below the hard-edged rectangular forms at the top creates a sense of fading mist, as if the wheat city floated on a sea of smoke and fog. This floating sensation disconnects the skyline from the wages, which have an aspirational upward curve, but one that never approaches the value of the wheat. The area below the curve has a solid tone and the use of color in tinted versions turns the upward sloping line purple-pink and the area below it aquamarine. This lightness contrasts with the ominous stacks of the dark, jagged edge of the skyline above, which hovers with threatening mechanical force in contrast to the organic harmony of the line. Mood and atmosphere are palpable. Data presentation is not neutral.

As already mentioned, tinting of engravings was common. Color in medical and botanical illustrations in this period had become saturated, even lurid in some instances. Lorraine Daston, in a study of "epistemic images" mostly from the eighteenth century, argues that the use of color was increasingly disparaged in scientific works where they intersected with the classification of species.[40] Carl von Linneaus was particularly disturbed by the extent to which the depiction of individual specimens in color was misused to proliferate species identifications.[41] According to Daston, Linneaus urged illustrators to keep to the basic structural features of "Number, Shape, Position, and Proportion."[42] Color was to be confined to the decorative depiction of flora, in those images and prints designed for delight and amusement rather than for scientific purposes. Color even came to be associated with a "hermeneutics of deception."[43] The down-played tones in Playfair's prints speak more authoritatively than vivid color would.

The enunciative force of Playfair's graphics is reinforced by the forward-facing orientation of the plate and print. The images declare themselves to be mere statements of fact, in part because

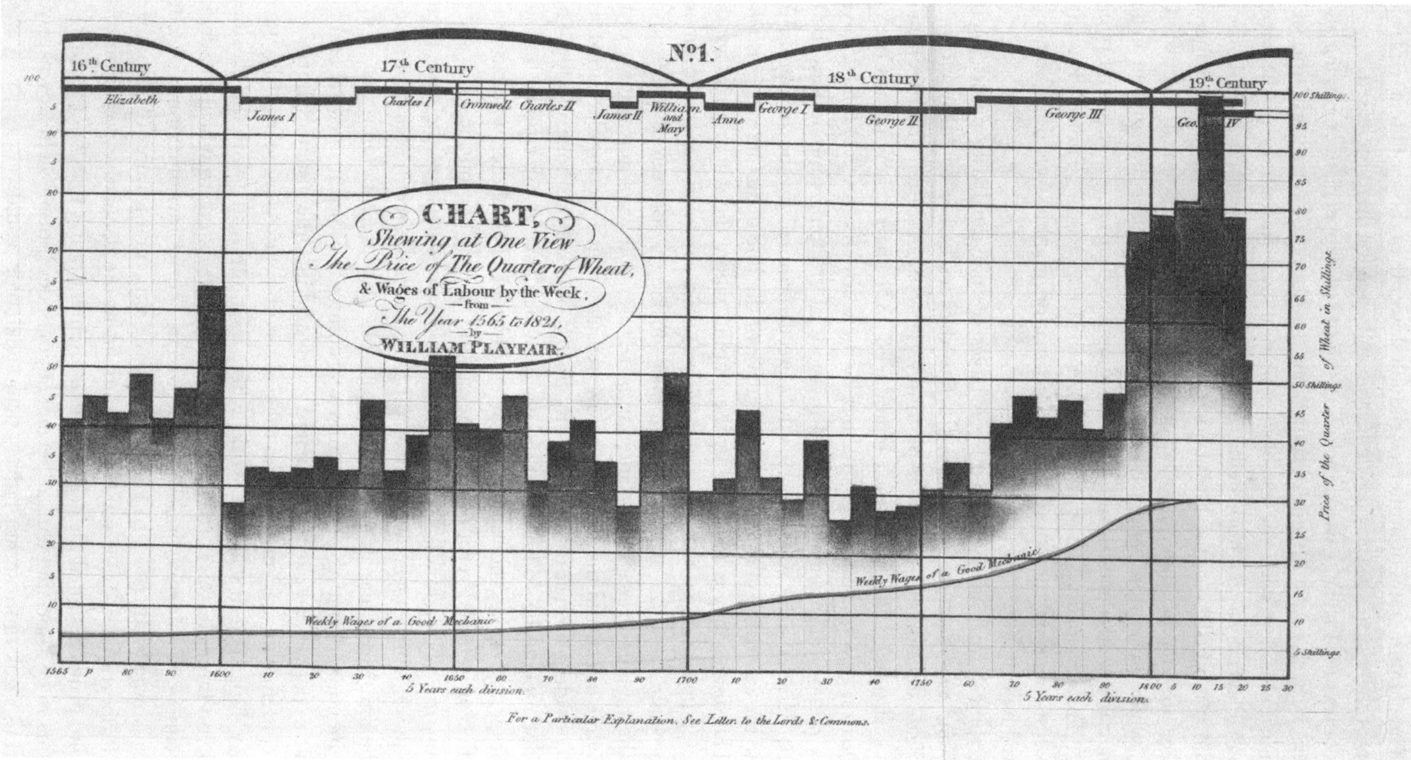


*Figure 2.1* William Playfair, 1821. *Letter on our agricultural distresses, their causes and remedies; accompanied with tables and copperplate charts shewing and comparing the prices of wheat, bread, and labour from 1565 to 1821.*

they differentiate themselves entirely from those created within the perspectival conventions of pictorial prints. Because they refuse the conventions used for scenes, vignettes, stories, and tales, Playfair's images function very differently in their truth claims from those of illustrational or pictorial works. They are meant to be read as plain statements of facts. Their layout, like those of technical drawings in isomorphic projection or of botanical and biological specimens in cross sections correlated across views (back, front, sliced), makes clear that Playfair's plates are fully rational in their conception and production. Their assertion of truth claims is not based on the legibility of figures, believability of circumstance, or correlation to the expectations of a reader/viewer looking into the proscenium of a pictorial frame, but on the treatment of surface with regular metrics and standardized values. The graphic is without spatial depth. The very flatness proclaims its honesty—declares its incapacity to lie. The work speaks directly, and its viewer is addressed in such a way that no position can be identified. We are not in a point-of-view system but merely offered an account, a balance sheet, as if its claims were self-evident.

We could extend this argument with an infinite number of other examples. But one useful addition is W.E.B. DuBois's set of sixty graphics created in 1900 for a presentation at the Pan-African Conference in London.[44] As Josh Jones has argued, these charts, with their hand-drawn lettering and graphics, are vivid cultural artifacts. The iconographic force of the works is striking. To show the growth of the percentage of the "Negro" [sic] population of the United States between 1800 and 1890, DuBois (and his team at Atlanta University) devised an image of a small-scale United States in black silhouette sitting inside the red (in the original) outline border of the continental States (Figure 2.2). The scale of the images increases, and though the percentages appear to drop (from one-fifth to one-eighth), the size of the black figure within the body of the country grows.[45] The multiple graphics show different aspects of Black experience—the "Routes of the American Slave Trade from Africa to South America/Brazil and to Georgia," or "The percentage of Negro Business Men in the United States," and other graphic presentations of information. They are rhetorically striking. The geometric language of the "Business Men" looks like a modern painting, decades in advance of the work of Piet Mondrian or Kasimir Malevich, engaging the language of abstraction for potent social ends. Likewise, the spiral forms that contrast the "Value of Household and Kitchen Furniture Owed by Georgia Negroes" in another one of the many images anticipates the vivid tones of pop and minimalist paintings from the 1960s. These inventions are clear statements, interventions in a bureaucratic system that typically muffled information in conventional presentations of dull gray tones. DuBois's team invented a striking graphical language as an act of disruption to communicative norms. Its interventions enact an avant-garde shock effect to "make strange" the normalized facts of racism and give them potency. How should we look at these images except through the lens of art history?

Compare these hand-lettered and hand-painted images with those published in 1914 by Williard Brinton in another classic work, *Graphic Methods for Presenting Facts*.[46] Brinton's book, published by the Industrial Management Library, was a textbook to guide government graphics offices. It is filled with graphics produced by technical instruments such as ruling pens and straightedges. Later editions added red to the original monochrome palette of halftone patterns and shading techniques. The handmade quality of DuBois's graphics evidences a passionate rhetoric in sharp contrast to the dispassionate style of those in Brinton's pages. DuBois's graphics speak volumes about the need to produce arguments in graphic form as a force for social change. The graphic features make the case for the Atlanta University research group.[47] Each image feels like a statement arrived at through considerable effort, consideration, and careful reflection, not simply a mechanical translation. Brinton's bureaucratic graphics express an administered culture in muffled tones.

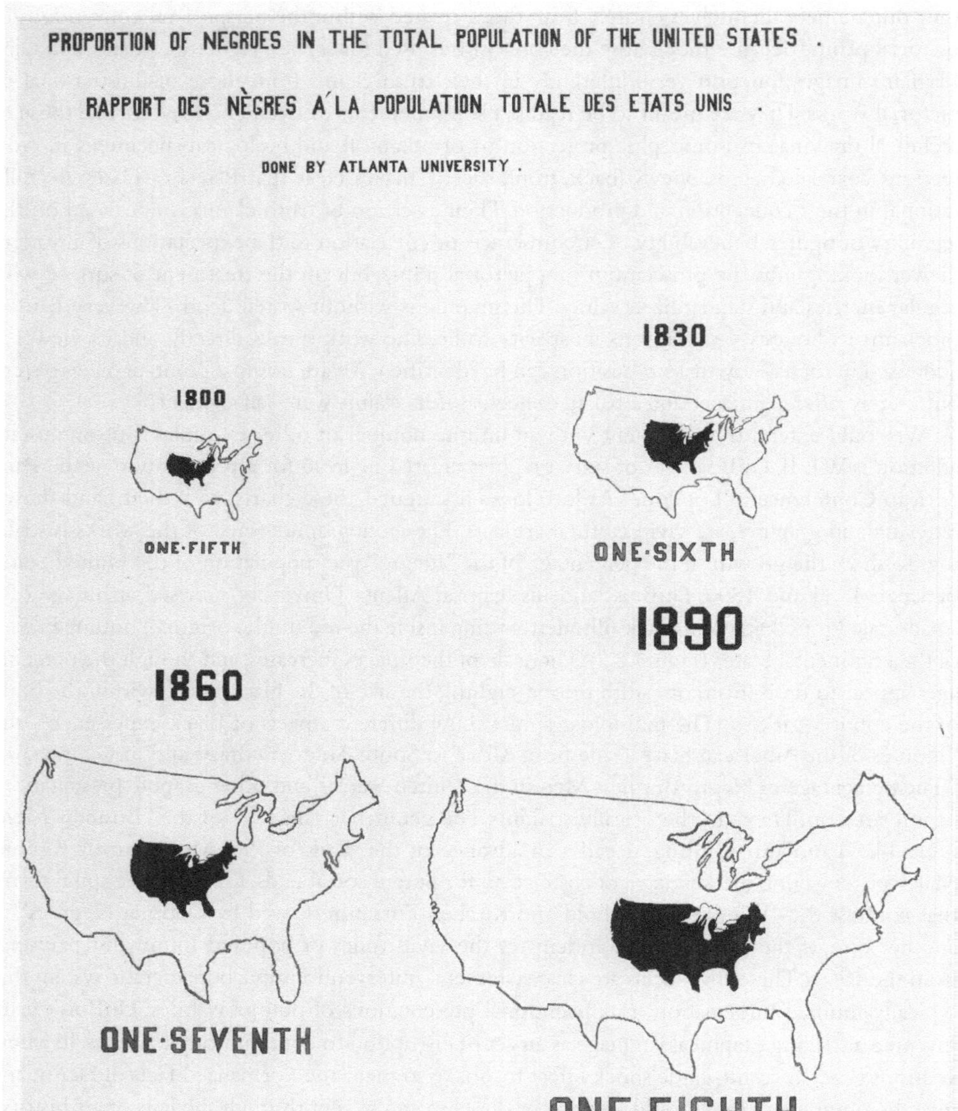


*Figure 2.2* W.E.B. DuBois and Thomas Calloway, graphics for the Exposition Universelle, Paris, 1900. *Source*: Library of Congress, LC-11931, no. 42.

Treating Playfair's works, or those of DuBois, or Brinton, or any of the many practitioners, anonymous or named, as images whose ingenuity at presenting information in graphical form, or whose qualities of presentation, are to be gauged simply in terms of accuracy of data imaging, keeps them in a category apart from art-historical ones. These are not empirical images. They are graphic presentations of hermeneutic processes, interpretative statements formulated within social conditions. They participate in cultural history as images.

The current vogue for data visualizations positions them in gallery and museum settings, recognizing them as aesthetic objects. Meanwhile, the disparaging of many graphics in the visualization world as "chart junk," to use the term coined by Edward Tufte to dismiss works that use figurative, metaphoric, referential imagery, asserts old class biases in high/low binarisms. The iconography of charts provides rich material for interpretation as we see in DuBois's images of the nation and Playfair's stair-stepped skylines. Visual studies and art history have never quite reconciled their differences, and that breach (in part) leaves the work of analysis and study of graphical forms of expression of information in a limbo. When examined by practitioners of science and technology studies, they are assessed within shifting paradigms of scientific accuracy. But the graphical modes of expression on which they perform are created from and circulate within visual culture and its codes.

The blind spot of art history, its considerable disregard for epistemological images as images, contributes to the disbalanced cultural authority of data visualizations. They are taken as statements of information rather than expressions of belief and ideology. Neither Playfair's nor DuBois's works should be judged on the grounds of their truthfulness, accuracy, or degree of empirical rigor. Instead, they should be assessed in terms of the ideological beliefs they embody and legitimate. The idea that knowledge—rather than information—can be expressed in graphical forms and formats should include the recognition that the production of that "information" is a process, often concealed in the final statement the graphic presents. A knowledge framework attends to the assumptions and conditions of production, not just the outcome. The notion that information floats free of the context in which it is modeled, turned into data through a process of selective extraction, and then given graphical expression in accordance with conventions that create apparent values that can be manipulated through scale, changes in axes, units, and other features are all aspects of these works that have to be addressed. The complex cultural workings of knowledge processes are concealed behind a surface of information that appears to be self-evident. The issue is not *how factual such graphics are*, but *how they presume to be factual*. How do we see the epistemological claim as an ideological one? We are familiar with the critiques of realism, its conventions and codes, with its styles and techniques. But we have less experience with assessing graphical empiricism and its epistemological claims. We consume such images every day. The lessons of examining past images is just a start. Daily graphical presentations also deserve to be examined through the critical frameworks of art history. Epistemological images and the tenets of visual epistemology deserve richer critical engagement through the study of these images *as images*. The art-historical capacity to formulate arguments about images as graphic expressions of knowledge production will increase as well.

## Notes

1. Peter Galison, *Image and Logic* (Chicago: University of Chicago Press, 1997) makes clear that images are not just a record of knowledge production but are part of the process of creating knowledge.
2. Wilfred Blunt and William T. Stearn, *The Art of Botanical Illustration: An Illustrated History* (London: Collins, 1950) would be one example of the synthetic work that sits between the magnificently illustrated volumes of natural objects and the work of studying this field of graphical production in its historical dimensions. Michael E. Lynch and Steve Woolgar, *Representation in Scientific Practice* (Cambridge, MA: MIT Press, 1990); Harry Robin, *Scientific Images From Cave to Computer* (New York: Abrams, 1992) are more recent overview works, but the bibliography on historical reflection on the work of artists drawing the natural world or creating scientific records is enormous.
3. Galison, *Image and Logic*; Tim Lenoir, *Inscribing Science: Scientific Texts and the Materiality of Communication* (Stanford, CA: Stanford University Press, 1998); Lorraine Daston and Katherine Park, *Wonders and the Order of Nature 1150–1750* (New York: Zone Books, 2001); Bruno Latour, "Visualization and Cognition: Drawing Things Together," in *Knowledge and Society Studies in the Sociology of Culture Past and*

*Present*, ed. H. Kuklick, vol. 6, 1–40 (Greenwich, CT: Jai Press, 1979); Karin Knorr-Cetina, *Epistemic Cultures* (Cambridge, MA: Harvard University Press, 1999); Alina Payne, ed., *Vision and Its Instruments* (College Station, PA: Penn State University Press, 2014); David Freedberg, *Eye of the Lynx* (Chicago: University of Chicago Press, 2002).

4. Claudia Swan, "Illustrated Natural History," in *Prints and the Pursuit of Knowledge*, ed. Susan Dackerman (Cambridge, MA: Harvard University Press, 2011); Lev Manovich, *InfoAesthetics* (London: Bloomsbury Press, 2015); Johanna Drucker, *Graphesis: Visual Forms of Knowledge Production* (Cambridge, MA: Harvard University Press, 2014).
5. Freedberg, *Eye of the Lynx* is an in-depth study of changes in knowledge paradigms in the seventeenth century and the shift from resemblance to difference.
6. Michael Friendly, *Milestones in the History of Thematic Cartography, Statistical Graphics, and Data Visualization*, is a good place to start: www.datavis.ca/milestones/; also the bibliography in Drucker, *Graphesis*.
7. Stephen Few, "What Ordinary People Need Most From Information Visualization Today," *Perceptual Edge: Visual Business Intelligence Newsletter* (2008), accessed August 9, 2018, www.perceptualedge.com/articles/visual_business_intelligence/what_people_need_from_infovis.pdf; Lev Manovich, "What Is Visualization?" *Visual Studies* 26, no. 1 (2011): 36–49.
8. Drucker, *Graphesis*; Stephen Few, *Show Me the Numbers* (Burlingame, CA: Analytics Press, 2012); Calvin Schmid, *Statistical Graphics* (New York: Wiley Interscience, 1983).
9. Manual Lima, *The Book of Trees* (New York: Princeton Architectural Press, 2014); *The Book of Circles* (New York: Princeton Architectural Press, 2016). See Lauren Klein, *Data by Design 1786–1900*, http://lklein.com/data-by-design/ and her work on Elizabeth Palmer Peabody and Emma Willard, accessed August 9, 2018, http://lklein.com/data-by-design/.
10. Martin Gardner, *Logic Machines and Diagrams* (New York: McGraw-Hill, 1958).
11. Edward Tufte, *The Visual Display of Quantitative Information* (Cheshire, CT: Graphics Press, 1983).
12. Few, *Show Me the Numbers*; Schmid, *Statistical Graphics*.
13. Manuel Lima, *Visual Complexity* (New York: Princeton Architectural Press, 2011); Anthony Grafton and Daniel Rosenberg's, *Cartographies of Time* (New York: Princeton Architectural Press, 2010).
14. James Elkins, *The Domain of Images* (Ithaca, NY: Cornell University Press, 1999); Caroline A. Jones and Peter Galison, *Picturing Science Producing Art* (New York: Routledge, 1998).
15. John Bender and Michael Marrinan, *The Culture of Diagram* (Stanford: Stanford University Press, 2010); S.K. Heninger Jr., *The Cosmographical Glass: Renaissance Diagrams of the Universe* (San Marino, CA: Huntington Library, 1977).
16. William Ivins, *Prints and Visual Communication* (Cambridge, MA: Harvard University Press, 1953).
17. Friendly, *Milestones in the History of Thematic Cartography*.
18. Patricia Costigan-Eaves and Michael Macdonald-Ross, "William Playfair (1759–1823)," *Statistical Science* 5, no. 3 (1990): 318–26.
19. Costigan-Eaves and Macdonald-Ross, "William Playfair (1759–1823)"; Jonathan Sachs, "1786/1801: William Playfair, Statistical Graphics, and the Meaning of an Event," in *BRANCH: Britain, Representation, and Nineteenth-Century History*, ed. Dino Franco Felluga, Extension of *Romanticism and Victorianism on the Net*, accessed August 9, 2018, www.branchcollective.org/?ps_articles=jonathan-sachs-17861801-william-playfair-statistical-graphics-and-the-meaning-of-an-event; Ian Spence and Howard Wainer, "Who Was Playfair?" *Visual Revelations*, accessed August 9, 2018, www.psych.utoronto.ca/users/spence/Spence_Wainer_1997b.pdf; On Descartes, see www.encyclopedia.com/education/news-wires-white-papers-and-books/descartes-and-his-coordinate-system, accessed August 6, 2018.
20. Cara Giaimo, accessed August 9, 2018, www.atlasobscura.com/articles/the-scottish-scoundrel-who-changed-how-we-see-data.
21. Howard Wainer and Ian Spence, eds., *The Commercial and Political Atlas and Statistical Breviary* (Cambridge, UK: Cambridge University Press, 2005) (based on the 1801, 3rd edition). Jeremy Norman, "William Playfair Founds Statistical Graphics [. . .]," History of Information, accessed July 6, 2018, www.historyofinformation.com/expanded.php?id=2929.

Thomas Boylston, correspondence with Thomas Jefferson on "Maritime Insurance Premiums." https://en.wikipedia.org/wiki/Commercial_Revolution#/media/File:Insurance_Contact_2.jpg; Roger Wohner, *Accounting Basics: History of Accounting*, accessed August 9, 2018, www.investopedia.com/university/accounting/accounting1.asp.

On account books, see www.rareamericana.com/18th-19th-century-manuscript-account-books/, accessed August 9, 2018. Hugh Grant, "Bookkeeping in the Eighteenth Century: The Grand Journal

and Grand Ledger of the Hudson's Bay Company*," Archivaria #43, accessed August 9, 2018. https://archivaria.ca/index.php/archivaria/article/viewFile/12179/13191.
22. Stacey Sloboda, "Between the Mind and the Hand: Gender, Art and Skill in Eighteenth-Century Copybooks," *Women's Writing* 21, no. 3 (2014): 337–56, accessed August 9, 2018, doi:10.1080/09699082.2014.922298.
23. Costigan-Eaves and Macdonald-Ross, "William Playfair (1759–1823)."
24. This is Tufte's argument, Tufte, *Visual Display of Quantitative Information,* throughout.
25. Schmid, *Statistical Graphics*; Few, *Show Me the Numbers*, and manuals for Tableau, and other platforms all contain a version of this formulation.
26. Lisa Gitelman, ed., *Raw Data Is an Oxymoron* (Cambridge, MA: MIT Press, 2013).
27. Costigan-Eaves and Macdonald-Ross, "William Playfair (1759–1823)." For a history of conventions, see Michael Friendly, *A Brief History of Data Visualization*, 4, accessed August 9, 2018, www.datavis.ca/papers/hbook.pdf
28. Cited in Costigan-Eaves and Macdonald-Ross, "William Playfair (1759–1823)."
29. Accessed August 9, 2018, www.britannica.com/biography/John-Graunt.
30. Accessed August 9, 2018, www.britannica.com/science/probability#ref849464.
31. Ian Hacking, *The Emergence of Probability* (Cambridge: Cambridge University Press, 1975)
32. Accessed August 9, 2018, https://en.wikipedia.org/wiki/History_of_statistics.
33. Jonathan Sachs, accessed August 9, 2018, www.branchcollective.org/?ps_articles=jonathan-sachs-17861801-william-playfair-statistical-graphics-and-the-meaning-of-an-event.
34. Sean Takats, "Domestic Expertise: Literacy and Numeracy in the Eighteenth-Century Kitchen," *Journal of the Western Society for French History* 32 (2004), accessed August 9, 2018, https://quod.lib.umich.edu/w/wsfh/0642292.0032.004?view=text;rgn=main.
35. Information on Playfair's connection to Watt comes from Costigan-Eaves and Macdonald-Ross, "William Playfair (1759–1823)," 325.
36. Sachs, Accessed August 9, 2018, www.branchcollective.org/?ps_articles=jonathan-sachs-17861801-william-playfair-statistical-graphics-and-the-meaning-of-an-event. Jonathan Sachs notes, "Playfair's charts emerge at a particular historical moment" that includes periodical writing but also as the idea of "centuries as time designations," became common, according to Lynn Hunt (cited by Sachs). Time as a sequence, and its explanatory power, were ideas entering public debate. Adam Smith, whose work influenced that of Playfair (who actually edited "the controversial eleventh edition of *The Wealth of Nations*"), as Sachs goes on to note, was an advocate of analysis that shifted from small to larger scales of time, phenomena, and patterns of data.
37. Giaimo, Accessed August 9, 2018, www.atlasobscura.com/articles/the-scottish-scoundrel-who-changed-how-we-see-data.
38. Friendly, *A Brief History.*
39. Ibid., 9.
40. Daston, L. "Epistemic Images," in *Vision and Its Instruments, Art, Science, and Technology in Early Modern Europe,* ed. A. Payne (University Park, PA: The Pennsylvania State University Press, 2015), 13–35.
41. Ibid.
42. Ibid.
43. The phrase is Bender and Marrinan's, *The Culture of Diagram*, though they were not applying it to Playfair (55).
44. Accessed August 9, 2018, www.openculture.com/2016/09/w-e-b-du-bois-creates-revolutionary-artistic-data-visualizations-showing-the-economic-plight-of-african-americans-1900.html.
45. It is unclear how to interpret the discrepancy of graphic size and percentage values in numbers.
46. Willard Cope Brinton, *Graphical Methods for Presenting Facts* (New York: The Engineering Magazine Company, 1914).
47. In 1988, Atlanta University merged with Clark College to form the current Clark Atlanta University.

## Bibliography

Bender, John, and Michael Marrinan. *The Culture of Diagram*. Stanford: Stanford University Press, 2010.
Blunt, Wilfred, and William T. Stearn. *The Art of Botanical Illustration: An Illustrated History*. London: Collins, 1950.

Boylston, Thomas correspondence with Thomas Jefferson on "Maritime Insurance Premiums." Accessed August 9, 2018. https://en.wikipedia.org/wiki/Commercial_Revolution#/media/File:Insurance_Contact_2.jpg.

Brinton, Willard Cope. *Graphical Methods for Presenting Facts*. New York: The Engineering Magazine Company, 1914.

Costigan-Eaves, Patricia, and Michael Macdonald-Ross. "William Playfair (1759–1823)." *Statistical Science* 5, no. 3(1990), 318–26.

Daston, Lorraine. "Epistemic Images." In *Vision and Its Instruments: Art, Science, and Technology in Early modern Europe*, edited by A. Payne, 13–35. University Park, PA: The Pennsylvania State University Press, 2015.

Daston, Lorraine, and Katherine Park. *Wonders and the Order of Nature 1150–1750*. New York: Zone Books, 2001.

Drucker, Johanna. *Graphesis: Visual Forms of Knowledge Production*. Cambridge, MA: Harvard University Press, 2014.

Elkins, James. *The Domain of Images*. Ithaca, NY: Cornell University Press, 1999.

Few, Stephen. *Show Me the Numbers*. Burlingame, CA: Analytics Press, 2012.

Freedberg, David. *Eye of the Lynx*. Chicago: University of Chicago Press, 2002.

Friendly, Michael. *A Brief History of Data Visualization*, vol. 4. www.datavis.ca/papers/hbook.pdf

———. *Milestones in the History of Thematic Cartography, Statistical Graphics, and Data Visualization*. www.datavis.ca/milestones/

Galison, Peter. *Image and Logic*. Chicago: Chicago University Press, 1997.

Gardner, Martin. *Logic Machines and Diagrams*. New York: McGraw-Hill, 1958.

Giaimo, Cara. Accessed August 9, 2018. www.atlasobscura.com/articles/the-scottish-scoundrel-who-changed-how-we-see-data.

Gitelman, Lisa, ed. *Raw Data is an Oxymoron*. Cambridge, MA: MIT Press, 2013.

Grafton, Anthony, and Daniel Rosenberg. *Cartographies of Time*. New York: Princeton Architectural Press, 2010.

Grant, Hugh. "Bookkeeping in the Eighteenth Century: The Grand Journal and Grand Ledger of the Hudson's Bay Company*." *Archivaria* #43. Accessed August 9, 2018. https://archivaria.ca/index.php/archivaria/article/viewFile/12179/13191.

Hacking, Ian. *The Emergence of Probability*. Cambridge: Cambridge University Press, 1975.

Heninger Jr., S. K. *The Cosmographical Glass: Renaissance Diagrams of the Universe*. San Marino, CA: Huntington Library, 1977.

Ivins, William. *Prints and Visual Communication*. Cambridge, MA: Harvard University Press, 1953.

Jones, Caroline A., and Peter Galison. *Picturing Science Producing Art*. New York: Routledge, 1998.

Klein, Lauren. *Data by Design 1786–1900*. Accessed August 8, 2018. http://lklein.com/data-by-design/.

Knorr-Cetina, Karin. *Epistemic Cultures*. Cambridge, MA: Harvard University Press, 1999.

Latour, Bruno. "Visualization and Cognition: Drawing Things Together." In *Knowledge and Society Studies in the Sociology of Culture Past and Present*, edited by H. Kuklick, vol. 6, 1–40. Greenwich, CT: Jai Press, 1979.

Lenoir, Tim. *Inscribing Science: Scientific Texts and the Materiality of Communication*. Stanford: Stanford University Press, 1998.

Lima, Manuel. *Visual Complexity*. New York: Princeton Architectural Press, 2011.

———. *The Book of Trees*. New York: Princeton Architectural Press, 2014.

———. *The Book of Circles*. New York: Princeton Architectural Press, 2016.

Lynch, Michael E., and Steve Woolgar. *Representation in Scientific Practice*. Cambridge, MA: MIT Press, 1990.

Manovich, Lev. *InfoAesthetics*. London: Bloomsbury Press, 2015.

Norman, Jeremy. "William Playfair Founds Statistical Graphics [. . .]." *History of Information*. Accessed July 6, 2018. www.historyofinformation.com/expanded.php?id=2929.

Payne, Alina, ed. *Vision and Its Instruments*. College Station: Penn State University Press, 2014.

Robin, Harry. *Scientific Images from Cave to Computer*. New York: Abrams, 1992.

Sachs, Jonathan. "1786/1801: William Playfair, Statistical Graphics, and the Meaning of an Event." In *BRANCH: Britain, Representation, and Nineteenth-Century History*, edited by Dino Franco Felluga. Extension of Romanticism and Victorianism on the Net. Web. Accessed August 9, 2018. www.branchcollective.org/?ps_articles=jonathan-sachs-17861801-william-playfair-statistical-graphics-and-the-meaning-of-an-event.

Schmid, Calvin. *Statistical Graphics*. New York: Wiley Interscience, 1983.

Sloboda, Stacey. "Between the Mind and the Hand: Gender, Art and Skill in Eighteenth-Century Copybook." *Women's Writing* 21, no. 3 (2014), 337–56. doi:10.1080/09699082.2014.922298.

Spence, Ian, and Howard Wainer. "Who Was Playfair?" *Visual Revelations*. Accessed August 9, 2018. www.psych.utoronto.ca/users/spence/Spence_Wainer_1997b.pdf
Swan, Claudia. "Illustrated Natural History." In *Prints and the Pursuit of Knowledge*, edited by Susan Dackerman. Cambridge, MA: Harvard University Press, 2011.
Takats, Sean. "Domestic Expertise: Literacy and Numeracy in the Eighteenth-Century Kitchen." *Journal of the Western Society for French History* 32 (2004).
Tufte, Edward. *The Visual Display of Quantitative Information*. Cheshire, CT: Graphics Press, 1983.
Wainer, Howard, and Ian Spence, eds. *Playfair's Commercial and Political Atlas and Statistical Breviary*. Cambridge, UK: Cambridge University Press, 2005.
Wohler, Roger. *Accounting Basics: History of Accounting*. Accessed August 9, 2018. www.investopedia.com/university/accounting/accounting1.asp.

# 3

# THE DIGITAL TRANSFORMATION OF ART HISTORY

*Harald Klinke*

The academic discipline of art history is currently in a state of transition owing to the increasing integration of digital methods.[1] Just like the digital humanities in general, art history makes use of databases, data analysis, and visualizations in order to support existing approaches to the history of art as well as to probe new opportunities for the field. Whereas Diane Zorich concluded in her 2012 report for the Kress Foundation that there was ambivalence in the art history community on whether digital methods would change the way research is conducted,[2] much has advanced since then. To name just a few milestones: In 2014 the *International Journal for Digital Art History* was founded in Munich and published its first volume in the following year. In 2016 the *Art History in Digital Dimensions* symposium at the University of Maryland developed a White Paper recommending future steps that were presented at the subsequent College Art Association conference.[3] At the beginning of 2019 the U.S.-based *Digital Art History Society* and the *European Digital Art History Network* announced their existence.

While ambivalence remains in the larger community of art history, it is increasingly swept aside by the growing awareness that digital art history is a growing field that cannot be ignored.[4] Digital art history has grown from its infancy by building its own infrastructure. The digital art history community organizes itself via social media, publications, summer schools, hackathons, and conferences. A growing number of projects and doctoral theses chart the possibilities of digital applications in art history. With recognition of the field's growing importance, it becomes apparent that digital art history might become more than just an additional method. Rather, it has the potential to transform art history in general. It makes sense, therefore, to look back on what art history is, has been, and what we might want it to be in the future.

## A Brief Media History of Art History

The object of art history is the history of art. That means, broadly, that scholars describe the development of human artistic production over time in its societal context and interdependencies with political history, social history, the history of media, etc. As a historical science it focuses on cultural objects as sources of information about the past rather than relying merely on text-based media. As such, visual analytics stand at the core of art-historical methodology.

In order to define art history as a science, Heinrich Wölfflin established a description of images not by their content but by their formal appearance.[5] "Style" became the central term in order to tackle the main challenge of dating and attribution. Erwin Panofsky, on the other hand, developed a kind of visual epistemology in order to rediscover the meaning of artworks on several levels in order to embed the object in its cultural-historical context.[6] "Meaning" seemed to be the goal of that endeavor.

Those methods were developed largely with originals (i.e. individual physical objects) in front of the researcher. But with developments in the visual media capable of representing artworks, art history was increasingly carried out on the basis of reproductions. That opened up many new methodological opportunities. Wölfflin was able to present art history to a larger audience by using slides and established the comparison of two images projected next to each other as a standard method.[7] Aby Warburg brought more objects into spatial proximity and included works in different media.[8] He interlinked many images independently of their artistic value (including stamps and postcards). In order to open the field to a global science of the image, André Malraux even highlighted the possibility of comparing works of art only by means of their form in a large-scale vision of global art through images.[9] Not least, the introduction of slide libraries changed the method and focus of art history and widened the possibilities of access to the works of art created in human history. This, in turn, changed our idea of the object.

## Introducing Digital Technology

It should not come as a surprise that the changing technology of our time has a profound impact on the process of "doing art history." New technology, namely digital technology, has the potential to challenge long held beliefs about art production and its genealogy and to put old questions in new contexts. Art history is often considered to be conservative, maybe because it is a retrospective endeavor. Yet the truth is that art history has consistently evolved and will continue to develop. That we currently cannot estimate the results of digital change should not keep us from taking the advantage of the opportunities that may open up for us. We have to walk the path to understand where it leads. And we need to expect to stumble in order to understand where the pitfalls are. We should also be aware that it is likely that by walking the path, our objectives will change.

The basis of art history is data. The term "data" in Latin means "the given." It is the basis of any science to start with the given—with what is. Art history starts with the individual object. By describing it, we gather data about what we see. By finding words for what we see, we bring to our conscious mind the contents of the partially unconscious process of seeing, recognizing, and understanding. By writing it down, we make it accessible for our and others' later use. Our data is visual data that we process in comparison with other images that are present as originals or reproductions or that are located in our mental archive. We describe, compare, and contextualize. We then write in order to communicate the findings to a scholarly community that might verify or falsify statements and build upon generated knowledge. This is how art historians have charted the history of art in depth and detail.

The basis of digital art history is digital data. In order to eliminate the interference of noise in transmissions, Claude Shannon proposed in 1948 to send discrete signals that have one of only two values, a high and a low state.[10] Those digital signals can be computed using calculation rules of binary numbers developed by Gottfried Wilhelm Leibniz in 1697.[11] The term "binary" means "on the basis of two." In contrast to the decimal system, the binary numeral system has only two possible digits, usually "0" and "1." Information encoded in digital data has the advantage that it can be processed on a machine with speed and precision. In art history we have created digital data in image databases for a long time, but we have just started to probe how that data can serve as a basis for knowledge. That is the difference between what has been called "digitized" and "digital" art history: using it for more than a substitute for the slide library and, instead, making it fruitful for data analysis in the service of art-historical epistemology.[12] Progress in the latter is the real potential for the field and opens up a number of methodological opportunities.

## A Closer Look: Distant Viewing

One such opportunity is "distant viewing." The term is often used to describe a method for art history to attain a new relationship to visual data. However, the term "distant viewing" is often used without a concise definition. There is not yet a discussion of its history and meaning.

It seems obvious that the term is derived from Franco Moretti's term "distant reading." In contrast to reading individual books (close reading), Moretti's literary method, originally termed "serial reading,"[13] allows looking at the canon of (in his case) world literature as a whole and discovering lesser known works, recurring patterns, and long term developments that are indistinguishable in close reading. In 2000 he wrote: "Distant reading: where distance, let me repeat it, is a condition of knowledge: it allows you to focus on units that are much smaller or much larger than the text: devices, themes, tropes—or genres and systems."[14]

Empirical literary studies had existed for a long time (e.g. word count done manually)[15] before the term "distant reading" came into being. And distant reading had been discussed before computational methods came about. When Moretti coined the term, he signified a way to de-isolate the single object and embed it into the context of a *longue durée*. Ted Underwood points out the existence of that trend since the 1960s and concludes: "Distant reading has evolved into a name for a more specific approach to literary history, but the approach described significantly predates this particular name for it."[16] However, computational automation and more advanced statistical methods brought the method to a new level.

Equally, there has also been a form of distant viewing before the use of the term in its newer context and before the use of computers. Moreover, the term existed earlier with a different meaning.[17] In 1897/98, Alois Riegl distinguished in his manuscript *Historische Grammatik der bildenden Künste* between three distances the observer can take to an artwork ("Nahsicht," "Normalsicht," and "Fernsicht") and discusses their respective epistemic advantages.[18] Benjamin Zweig recently pointed out that the translation for "Fernsicht" in the English edition is "distant viewing."[19] In 2017, Moretti cited the literary critic Northrop Frye and the German poet Johann Wolfgang von Goethe with suggestions similar to those of Riegl: that being close to the canvas allows us to see brushstrokes and if we step back we recognize the organizing design of the picture. And if one arrives in a new town, a person might want to find a higher ground from which to see the city as a whole. Moretti states that close and distant examination are equally valuable approaches: "it all depends on what you are interested in."[20] Distance creates an epistemic viewpoint that differs from close proximity. One sees differently by embedding individual objects in a broader context. And that is probably nothing else than what Malraux had in mind as a globally wide scope of comparison: Distant viewing before the term "distant viewing" and before the use of computers.

Earlier uses of the term can be found on Wikipedia: it relates to "television" since the first idea of what later became TV was described as "distant electric vision" in 1908 by Alan Archibald Campbell-Swinton, who suggested the use of a cathode ray tube for that matter.[21] Today, the term is also used to applications of visual computing in order to analyze visual culture such as in the *Distant Viewing Lab* at the University of Richmond that devotes one project particularly to cultural analysis within TV studies, i.e. moving images.[22]

The shift from "distant *reading*" to "distant *viewing*"—the step from literature to art—was perhaps too obvious to mention. It appeared in the context of art history on February 5, 2014, in a blog entry published by K. Bender in which he juxtaposed quality and quantity in art history:

> There is endless discussion in art history about the quality of artworks and how to recognise a masterwork. [. . .] Unfortunately many monographs focus only on works considered as the greatest masterpieces of art. Art history is shallow if lesser artists and their works are forgotten. This also implies that quantity in the arts cannot be dismissed: it is part of the historical complexity of art production.[23]

Referring to Moretti, he writes in a later post:

> Obviously, "distant viewing" in art history [. . .] should be a method for a much broader objective: the different branches of visual arts (sculpture, painting, etc.), their styles (renaissance, mannerism, baroque, rococo, neo-classicism, etc.) or the many themes in painting—history, portraiture, landscape, marine, genre, still life, etc.—could be analysed quantitatively, provided of course that the appropriate databases are available.[24]

He subsequently published those thoughts on a broader scope in the first issue of the *International Journal for Digital Art History* in June 2015.[25]

Accordingly, distant viewing is the presentation of connections between multitudes of images (Big Image Data) in meaningful spatial proximity to each other in order to gain an overview of a corpus that would not be possible without digital means.[26] It allows the interactive exploration of that visualization, by browsing swiftly through the images and to find something relevant (e.g. similar objects). The idea behind it is that the computer can process more images than a human can see (and remember in the mental archive) in a lifetime. The *quantity* is expected to be limitless. And that makes the difference.

Sheer quantity requires processing in order to make it usable for the human sensory system. How much such processing can augment connoisseurship is not yet proven. What becomes clear, however, is that now and then, in addition to quantitative analysis, we have to return to a qualitative analysis (i.e. going to a library or gallery). From distant viewing—the overall view of all works—we might want to come back to close viewing, the single inspection of particular works. It cannot be stressed enough that digital methods are no substitute for classical approaches. They are, however, an extension of those approaches. Digital art history works best in a constant exchange with conventional methods.

There are two ways of doing art history: going into depth (and becoming an ever greater expert in an increasingly narrow field) or emphasizing breadth (losing detail and gaining an overview of patterns over longer time periods). Neither is exclusive. What digital art history allows is a macro-analysis, a computerized breadth that would be otherwise impossible.[27] The "great unread" of books that have not reached the attention of research, as Margaret Cohen lamented already in 1999,[28] turns into the "great unseen" of art. Digital art history now brings them within the purview of scholarly attention.

However, simply applying what information science has to offer is not enough. Art history itself needs to tighten its methods at this point. We need to chart both the possibilities and limits of distant and close viewing. In terms of distant viewing we are not at the point of an established method for our field, but at the beginning of a rocky path. The challenges we face are on multiple levels:

1. It is not yet clear how a meta-image (an image made of a multitude of images) helps to answer particular research questions on the grounds that its "relevance" is not given, but

depends on the user's interests. For example, someone interested in portraits in general would like to see other portraits in a certain time period. While someone with an interest in paintings in a certain geographic region would like to see more examples from that context.

2. This means that similarity between objects can be defined in many ways. Some of these can be derived from the images via feature extraction, others by making use of metadata. For others, additional data and sources (such as textual) need to be accessed or collected.[29]
3. From this it follows that the data we have today are mostly collection data (e.g. from museums) that are not necessarily suitable for the breadth of research questions art history wants to pose. The data might not be (1) sufficient, (2) relevant, and/or (3) valid. With the data we have, we can hardly make universal statements about general art history, but only about our respective basis of data. Thus, talking about the results, we need to be linguistically exact, i.e. we can only talk about the data we have and draw conclusions about the history of the collection, for example.
4. Visualizations of meaningful similarity measures are not necessarily two- or three-dimensional spaces, but we need to develop new ways of showing meaningful connections between images. That encompasses developing a grammar of visualization for our field. For example, we always have several options to visualize data (bar or pie chart etc.) and many parameters (e.g. the axis limits). Those options can be used to focus on what is essential for the statement we want to make, but it can also serve to manipulate, create false evidence, and hide premises.
5. Finally, visualizations should not be thought of as static, but as interactive. In the end, visualizations could turn into a graphical user interface of a general research platform for art history via which we access visual data and are supported in gaining knowledge from a large image corpus. What such a platform might look like is far from obvious today.

In order to make good on the promises of distant viewing, we have to ensure its prerequisites: data infrastructure and research infrastructure. We do not yet have the necessary data in abundance. Nor do we have a research platform for digital art history. Such a system will allow an overview of a corpus, find relevant objects, and incorporate objects that are not typically part of the narrative.

## Transitioning to a New Art History

In order to develop such a system and to be acquainted with digital technology, a new generation of students has to be taught digital practices. Part of the syllabus of art history should be (and will be) the use of such systems for research on a user level. As such a system does not yet exist, students need training in data analysis, data visualization, and other techniques. As this slowly becomes natural, it may emerge that digital art history is not just an extension of art history, but can spark the transition to a new art history.

First, teaching is changing. Art history is usually taught in lectures and seminars. The goal of such formats is the transfer of knowledge and the organization of discourse. Working with software and data, however, is only in part knowledge or theory. Rather, it is a time-consuming trial and error by playing around with data in order to understand systems, structures, and content. Thus, digital art history requires new formats and new frameworks in which students are allowed to embark on a journey of experience and creativity, reconsidering research questions and approaches. Workshops and collaborative project work seem to be more suitable for this type of learning.

Second, the role of the teacher is changing. In this new environment, the teacher is no longer the encyclopedic mind. Nobody can know the functionalities of every package in the programming language Python. Nor is that necessary, since manuals and tutorials can be found on the web in abundance. The teacher's role is, instead, to organize a process from an art-historical research question, making use of software tools, data acquisition, and processing. The teacher can give an introduction to core principles, processes, hardware and software, allow and suggest group work and peer-teaching.

Third, the role of the department of art history is changing. Once, the library and the slide library were the center of every department of art history. They were the meeting points for scholars and students. Slides were produced for the slide library and returned to it after use. It grew and became a visual repository for consultation. With the process of digitalization, image databases were established, but in practice, digital reproductions for teaching and research are sought with search machines on the web or are individually scanned from books. Thus, they no longer enter a central repository, but rest on private hard discs. In the absence of a consistent and shared infrastructure, departments lose a central task and relevance as a place of access to knowledge. This is even more so with the declining importance of the rooms in the library as places of knowledge given the increasing availability of e-books and the option to work at home. Both the library and the slide library are in need of a new role.

In the digital age accessing records can take place anywhere where Wi-Fi is available. But still there is a need for rooms in real space for meeting and discourse, exchange and mutual inspiration. Moreover, a world so virtual is in need of hardware. Cutting edge hardware that is especially needed in art history (large calibrated displays, 3D scanners and printers, VR headsets, etc.) is still beyond what the average researcher and student can afford. There needs to be a place in which such equipment can be used. Similar to the former slide library, departments of art history should open laboratories for experience and collaboration, where all equipment is accessible and free to try, where students can develop their own research projects, and seek advice and exchange with other students. Examples of such emerging facilities are the Wired! Lab and the Co-Lab Studio at Duke University.[30]

In order to manage the lab, organize the infrastructure and consult digital projects, replacing the former head of the slide library, a Chief Technology Officer (CTO) has a key role if departments are serious with their digital strategy. This employee oversees administrators trained in specific functions: maintaining small infrastructure such as Wi-Fi and large infrastructure such as running servers. There is no way around a permanent annual budget for hardware and software and staff.

Enhanced virtual teaching and research environments are also necessary. In order to avoid the need to install software on individual computers with limited specifications and different OS versions, universities need to offer services that give access to cloud storage and cloud computing. With a university login, collaboration in software development and the exchange of data among groups within a teaching or research context becomes possible. An example of such a system is the virtual research platform *DHVLab* developed at the LMU Munich.[31]

As departments are now devoid of slide libraries, on an interdepartmental level data infrastructures are being built and art-historical data is increasingly stored in science clouds, which researchers can access and to which they can contribute. These systems are not limited to collection data, but can comprise any data that is part of an art-historical project. In addition, virtual research databases are needed that specify a meta-structure (i.e. how digital data can be organized). On the basis of the preceding, a research infrastructure can be built that allows data analysis on a user level (without the need to dig deep into software development) and facilitates collaboration on an international level if necessary.

Fourth, the discipline is changing. All of the preceding cannot be accomplished without a strong focus on interdisciplinary collaboration. Art historians and, in particular, information scientists (also statisticians, etc.) are already working together in order to develop new solutions for both disciplines: new tools for art history and a better understanding of images for information science. An emerging example is the Focus Program by the German Research Foundation called *The Digital Image* that combines art-historical approaches with solutions from information science in mixed method approaches.[32] Another example is the international and interdisciplinary Hackathon for Art History and Information Science *Coding Dürer* that took place in 2017 and brought together art historians and information scientists to work on data.[33] In order to make such collaborations possible and successful, art historians have to understand the fundamental principles of information science. Conversely, information scientists have to understand the core principles, goals, and methods of the visual humanities. This requires joint curricula, projects, summer schools, and collaborative experiences. Only together will we be able to tackle the challenges and opportunities that 3D, augmented and virtual reality, artificial intelligence, and machine learning pose to the discipline. Interdisciplinarity or rather transdisciplinarity will change the discipline more than anything else and, by extension, the impact of the discipline on society.

Fifth, our understanding of the history of art is changing. With Big (Image) Data and the computer as a tool to help get from data to knowledge, the epistemic process of how science produces knowledge is transforming. Distant viewing interfaces in recommender (or filtering) systems that predict user preferences, as just described, are just the beginning. The computer will not replace reading and examining objects, but act as a companion that can store and compute infinite numbers of records, process them (e.g. via visual computing), and compare everything to everything else. It will make it easier to take into account lesser known, lesser described, and lesser-published artists and artworks. It will come closer to the original idea of the "museum without walls"—this time with digital means. Its possibilities make it easier to tell other art histories, take new views, and to include the "long tail" of objects in the narrative.[34] This opens up to yet uncharted territories and maybe, thus, a "democratization" of art history (i.e. the total inclusion of every visual artifact).[35] Distant viewing, in the end, is not a means in itself but allows finding that single relevant object that could not be found without the help of the computer—and then potentially visit its original for close inspection.

Sixth, the art-historical researcher is changing. With the use of digital technology in the research process, a new skill in demand has to be what could be called "data literacy." This concerns how to access information and tools as well as how to use them in order to gain the knowledge needed for the research field. But more than that, it needs a critique of sources in a broader understanding:

1. A critique of data concerns how the information was generated, by whom, for what reason, in what context, from which institution, with what bias and gaps.
2. A critique of algorithms is needed in order to evaluate the relevance of results by an understanding of how that result was calculated and under which premises it was generated.
3. A critique of data visualizations allows researcher to understand the seemingly obvious evidence in a context of other possible visualizations.
4. Critical computer literacy is needed in order to stay focused on the goals of a research project among the abundance of data and tools.

Today it seems that the computer is still a new medium, and often the medium seems to be the message. It will probably take a generation until the medium fades into the background as a mostly useful but familiar tool, just like the slide projector in the past.

Still, the question remains, what digital art history really is. There are several options for the future:

1. It is a methodological extension of art history, an addition to the syllabus, the opportunity to new possibilities. And as soon as we are accustomed to it, we drop the prefix "digital" that connotes that it is new and just call it "art history." One could describe this as an evolution.
2. It is a revolution, and what we call digital art history today will be the art history of the future. Then we also drop the "digital" prefix. Like astronomy (and most other natural sciences) there is no "analogue" astronomy anymore. Astronomers, today, look at computer screens instead of through the telescope.[36]
3. It is a transdisciplinary field *between* art history and information science (and possibly other subjects). This means it is unlike the digital humanities that struggle to be, on the one hand, the future of the respective disciplines and, on the other hand, do not wish to be distinguished from them.
4. It is something completely new. With its innovative methods, strong focus on interdisciplinarity, and the potential of new views on the cultural history of visual heritage, it could fall under a term such as "cultural analytics" that cuts off all roots to traditional disciplines in order freely to explore new opportunities.

Now is the time to discuss what kind of future we desire for our discipline and to take steps to realize it. That means creating a new, critical understanding of what it means to do art history in the digital era.

## Notes

1. For this chapter I am indebted to Liska Surkemper as well as to Justin Underhill for numerous consultations and inspirations.
2. Diane M. Zorich, "Transitioning to a Digital World: Art History, Its Research Centers, and Digital Scholarship," A Report to the Samuel H. Kress Foundation and the Roy Rosenzweig Center for History and New Media George Mason University (June 2012), accessed December 26, 2019, www.kressfoundation.org/uploaded-Files/Sponsored_Research/Research/Zorich_TransitioningDigitalWorld.pdf
3. Digital Art History Lab Committee, Frick Art Reference Library, Art History in Digital Dimensions (February 2017), http://dah-dimensions.org/wp-content/uploads/2017/03/Art-History-in-Digital-Dimensions-White-Paper.pdf
4. For a discussion, see the "Critical Section" in the *International Journal for Digital Art History* no. #3, https://journals.ub.uni-heidelberg.de/index.php/dah/issue/view/3471.
5. Heinrich Wölfflin, *Kunstgeschichtliche Grundbegriffe: Das Problem der Stilentwicklung in der neueren Kunst* (Munich: Bruckmann, 1915).
6. Erwin Panofsky, "Ikonographie und Ikonologie," in *Bildende Kunst als Zeichensystem. Ikonographie und Ikonologie*, ed. Ekkehard Kaemmerling, Vol. 1: Theorien—Entwicklung—Probleme (Cologne: DuMont-Buchverl, 1994), 207–25.
7. See Wiebke Ratzeburg, "Mediendiskussion im 19. Jahrhundert. Wie die Kunstgeschichte ihre wissenschaftliche Grundlage in der Fotografie fand," in *Kritische Berichte* 30, no. 1 (2002): 22–40; Ingeborg Reichle, "Fotografie und Lichtbild. Die unsichtbaren Bildmedien der Kunstgeschichte," in *Sichtbarkeit und Medien: Austausch, Verknüpfung und Differenz von naturwissenschaftlichen und ästhetischen Bildstrategien*, ed. Anja Zimmermann (Hamburg: Hamburg University Press, 2004), 177–91.
8. Martin Treml, Sigrid Weigel, and Perdita Ladwig, eds., *Aby Warburg. Werke in einem Band* (Berlin: Suhrkamp Verlag, 2010).
9. André Malraux, *Psychologie de l'Art: Le Musée Imaginaire* (Paris: Skira, 1947).
10. Claude E. Shannon, "A Mathematical Theory of Communication," *The Bell System Technical Journal* 27 (July, October 1948): 379–423, 623–56.

11. Gottfried Wilhelm Leibniz, "Explication de l'Arithmétique Binaire," *Histoire de l'Académie Royale des Sciences* (1703, printed 1705): 85–89.
12. Johanna Drucker, "Doing Art History Digitally/Doing Digital Art History," Digital Art History Lab, Getty Research Institute (March 5, 2013), http://digitalarthistory.weebly.com/uploads/6/9/4/3/6943165/johannadrucker_remarks_gettydah-lab_2013.pdf. On the history of digital art history, see Benjamin Zweig, "Forgotten Genealogies: Brief Reflections on the History of Digital Art History," *International Journal for Digital Art History*, no. 1 (June 2015), https://doi.org/10.11588/dah.2015.1.21633.
13. See Franco Moretti, in Ruben Hackler and Guido Kirsten, "Distant Reading, Computational Criticism, and Social Critique: An Interview with Franco Moretti," *Le foucaldien* 2/1 (2016): 6, doi:10.16995/lefou.22.
14. Franco Moretti, "Conjectures on World Literature," *New Left Review* 1 (January–February 2000): 57, https://newleftreview.org/II/1/franco-moretti-conjectures-on-world-literature.
15. Ted Underwood, "A Genealogy of Distant Reading," *Digital Humanities Quarterly* 11, no. 2 (2017), www.digitalhumanities.org/dhq/vol/11/2/000317/000317.html.
16. Ibid.
17. For this paragraph I am indebted to the replies to one of my twitter post, in particular to the contribution made by Benjamin Zweig: https://twitter.com/HxxxKxxx/status/1064915014514077696.
18. Both in the versions of Riegl's manuscript from 1897/98 and 1899. See Alois Riegl, *Historische Grammatik der bildenden Künste*, ed. Karl M. Swoboda and Otto Pächt (Cologne: Böhlau, 1966), 130, 290.
19. Alois Riegl, *Historical Grammar of the Visual Arts*, trans. Jacqueline E. Jung; foreword by Benjamin Binstock (New York: Zone Books, 2004).
20. Franco Moretti, "A Response," *PMLA* 132, no. 3 (May 2017): 686.
21. Alan Archibald Campbell-Swinton, "Distant Electric Vision (first paragraph)," *Nature* 78 (June 18, 1908): 151, doi:10.1038/078151a0.
22. "Distant Viewing Lab," www.distantviewing.org/dv-tv.
23. K. Bender, "Statistics in Art History (I): The Devil in Paradise," http://kbender.blogspot.com/2013/02/statistics-in-art-history-i.html.
24. K. Bender, "Distant Viewing: A Pact With the Devil in the Paradise of Art History," http://kbender.blogspot.com/2014/02/distant-viewing-pact-with-devil.html.
25. K. Bender, "Distant Viewing in Art History: A Case Study of Artistic Productivity," *International Journal for Digital Art History*, no. 1 (June 2015), https://doi.org/10.11588/dah.2015.1.21639.
26. Harald Klinke, "Big Image Data Within the Big Picture of Art History," *International Journal for Digital Art History*, no. 2 (October 2016), https://doi.org/10.11588/dah.2016.2.33527.
27. See Matthew L. Jockers, *Macroanalysis: Digital Methods and Literary History* (Urbana, Chicago, and Springfield: University of Illinois Press, 2013), 23.
28. Margaret Cohen, *The Sentimental Education of the Novel* (Princeton: Princeton University Press, 1999), 23.
29. See, for example, the project *Artigo.org* that collects tagging data via a crowdsourcing and gamification approach: www.artigo.org/.
30. Co-Lab Studios, https://colab.duke.edu/studio; Wired! Lab, www.dukewired.org/.
31. Harald Klinke, "Datenanalyse in der Digitalen Kunstgeschichte. Neue Methoden in Forschung und Lehre und der Einsatz des DHVLab in der Lehre," in *#DigiCampus. Digitale Forschung und Lehre in den Geisteswissenschaften*, ed. Harald Klinke (München, 2018), 19–34, https://doi.org/10.5282/ubm/epub.41218.
32. DFG-Schwerpunktprogramm, "Das digitale Bild" (SPP 2172), www.kunstgeschichte.uni-muenchen.de/forschung/digitalekg/digitales-bild1/.
33. Harald Klinke, "A Five Days International and Interdisciplinary Hackathon for Art History and Information Science, March 13–17, 2017, Munich, Germany," http://codingdurer.de/.
34. For the meaning of the term, see Chris Anderson, "The End of Theory: The Data Deluge Makes the Scientific Method Obsolete," *Wired Magazine* (July 16, 2008), www.wired.com/2008/06/pb-theory/.
35. Lev Manovich, "Manifesto for Democratic Art History," http://lab.softwarestudies.com/2016/02/manifesto-for-democratic-art-history.html.
36. See Roger Malina, "Yes Again to the End of the Digital Humanities! Please!" (August 6, 2015), http://malina.diatrope.com/2015/08/06/yes-again-to-the-end-of-the-digital-humanities-please/.

## Bibliography

Anderson, Chris. "The End of Theory: The Data Deluge Makes the Scientific Method Obsolete." *Wired Magazine*, July 16, 2008. Accessed February 25, 2019. www.wired.com/2008/06/pb-theory/.

Bender, K. "Distant Viewing in Art History: A Case Study of Artistic Productivity." *International Journal for Digital Art History*, no. 1 (June 2015). Accessed January 27, 2019. https://doi.org/10.11588/dah.2015.1.21639.

———. "Distant Viewing: A Pact with the Devil in the Paradise of Art History." Accessed February 25, 2019. http://kbender.blogspot.com/2014/02/distant-viewing-pact-with-devil.html.

———. "Statistics in Art History (I): The Devil in Paradise." Accessed January 27, 2019. http://kbender.blogspot.com/2013/02/statistics-in-art-history-i.html.

Campbell-Swinton, Alan Archibald. "Distant Electric Vision (first paragraph)." *Nature* 78 (June 18, 1908). doi:10.1038/078151a0.

Cohen, Margaret. *The Sentimental Education of the Novel*. Princeton: Princeton University Press, 1999.

Digital Art History Lab Committee, Frick Art Reference Library. *Art History in Digital Dimensions* (February 2017). Accessed February 25, 2019. http://dah-dimensions.org/wp-content/uploads/2017/03/Art-History-in-Digital-Dimensions-White-Paper.pdf

Drucker, Johanna. "Doing Art History Digitally/Doing Digital Art History." *Digital Art History Lab*, Getty Research Institute (March 5, 2013). Accessed February 25, 2019. http://digitalarthistory.weebly.com/uploads/6/9/4/3/6943163/johannadrucker_remarks_gettydah-lab_2013.pdf

Hackler, Ruben, and Guido Kirsten. "Distant Reading, Computational Criticism, and Social Critique. An Interview with Franco Moretti." *Le foucaldien*, 2/1 (2016). doi:10.16995/lefou.22.

Jockers, Matthew L. *Macroanalysis: Digital Methods and Literary History*. Urbana, Chicago and Springfield: University of Illinois Press, 2013.

Klinke, Harald. "Big Image Data within the Big Picture of Art History." *International Journal for Digital Art History*, no. 2 (October 2016). Accessed February 25, 2019. https://doi.org/10.11588/dah.2016.2.33527.

———. "Datenanalyse in der Digitalen Kunstgeschichte. Neue Methoden in Forschung und Lehre und der Einsatz des DHVLab in der Lehre." In *#DigiCampus. Digitale Forschung und Lehre in den Geisteswissenschaften*, edited by Harald Klinke, 19–34. Munich, 2018. Accessed February 25, 2019. https://doi.org/10.5282/ubm/epub.41218.

Leibniz, Gottfried Wilhelm. "Explication de l'Arithmétique Binaire." *Histoire de l'Académie Royale des Sciences* (1703, printed 1705): 85–89.

Malina, Roger. "Yes Again to the End of the Digital Humanities! Please!" (August 6, 2015). Accessed February 25, 2019. http://malina.diatrope.com/2015/08/06/yes-again-to-the-end-of-the-digital-humanities-please/.

Malraux, André. *Psychologie de l'Art: Le Musée imaginaire*. Paris: Skira, 1947.

Manovich, Lev. "Manifesto for Democratic Art History." Accessed February 25, 2019. http://lab.softwarestudies.com/2016/02/manifesto-for-democratic-art-history.

Moretti, Franco. "Conjectures on World Literature." *New Left Review* 1 (January–February 2000). Accessed February 27, 2019. https://newleftreview.org/II/1/franco-moretti-conjectures-on-world-literature.

———. "A Response." *PMLA* 132, no. 3 (May 2017): 686.

Panofsky, Erwin. "Ikonograph5e und Ikonologie." In *Bildende Kunst als Zeichensystem. Ikonographie und Ikonologie*, edited by Ekkehard Kaemmerling, vol. 1, Theorien—Entwicklung—Probleme. Cologne: DuMont-Buchverl, 1994.

Ratzeburg, Wiebke. "Mediendiskussion im 19. Jahrhundert. Wie die Kunstgeschichte ihre wissenschaftliche Grundlage in der Fotografie fand." *Kritische Berichte* 30, no. 1 (2002): 22–40.

Reichle, Ingeborg. "Fotografie und Lichtbild. Die unsichtbaren Bildmedien der Kunstgeschichte." In *Sichtbarkeit und Medien: Austausch, Verknüpfung und Differenz von naturwissenschaftlichen und ästhetischen Bildstrategien*, edited by Anja Zimmermann, 177–91. Hamburg: Hamburg University Press, 2004.

Riegl, Alois. *Historische Grammatik der bildenden Künste*. Edited by Karl M. Swoboda and Otto Pächt. Cologne: Böhlau, 1966.

———. *Historical Grammar of the Visual Arts*. Translated by Jacqueline E. Jung; foreword by Benjamin Binstock. New York: Zone Books, 2004.

Shannon, Claude E. "A Mathematical Theory of Communication." *The Bell System Technical Journal* 27 (July, October 1948): 379–423 and 623–56.

Treml, Martin, Sigrid Weigel, and Perdita Ladwig, eds. *Aby Warburg. Werke in einem Band*. Berlin: Suhrkamp Verlag, 2010.

Underwood, Ted. "A Genealogy of Distant Reading." *Digital Humanities Quarterly* 11, no. 2 (2017). Accessed February 25, 2019. www.digitalhumanities.org/dhq/vol/11/2/000317/000317.html.

Wölfflin, Heinrich. *Kunstgeschichtliche Grundbegriffe: Das Problem der Stilentwicklung in der neueren Kunst*. München: Bruckmann, 1915.

Zorich, Diane M. "Transitioning to a Digital World: Art History, Its Research Centers, and Digital Scholarship." A Report to the Samuel H. Kress Foundation and the Roy Rosenzweig Center for History and New Media George Mason University, May 2012. Accessed February 25, 2019. www.kressfoundation.org/uploaded-Files/Sponsored_Research/Research/Zorich_TransitioningDigitalWorld.pdf
Zweig, Benjamin. "Forgotten Genealogies: Brief Reflections on the History of Digital Art History." *International Journal for Digital Art History*, no. 1 (June 2015). Accessed February 25, 2019. https://doi.org/10.11588/dah.2015.1.21633.

# 4
# FEMINIST DIGITAL ART HISTORY

*Kathryn Brown and Elspeth Mitchell*

One of the questions posed in the present volume is whether the use of digital technologies in the field of art history can generate new models for the analysis and interpretation of art, its socio-cultural contexts, and institutional frameworks. If that question is answered in the affirmative, what new knowledge is generated, and how do computational methods impact on the discipline of art history itself? These questions seem particularly pertinent to feminist engagements with artworks, museology, and histories of creative production. If feminism has sought to understand—and typically to challenge—the role played by gender in structuring narratives of art history, do methodologies proposed by the digital humanities assist or hamper the realization of that ambition? More specifically, is it possible to identify a branch of "digital art history" as specifically "feminist" and, if so, what might this mean? The aim of this chapter is to debate these issues in light of recent research and exhibition projects and to examine the possibilities and limitations of what might be termed "feminist digital art history."

Before proceeding, it is worth bearing in mind that bringing together the terms "digital," "feminism," and "art history" is itself a task that is fraught with prior assumptions. Each of these terms has links to diverse histories, methods, socio-political contexts, and cultural frameworks that demand scrutiny. As Amelia Jones has noted in her approach to the study of feminism and visual culture, when analyzing the intersection of such fields, it is necessary to remain alert to their respective "modes of thinking, making, doing or strategizing" in order to understand how they may inflect each other.[1] Equally, the notion of a "feminist digital art history" is one that demands a high level of terminological self-reflection on the part of the researcher—including as to different possible meanings depending on what the term "feminist" means and where it appears in the formulation. In the following discussion, we will use "feminist" as a modifier of "digital art history" and will consider the various implications of so doing in the final section of the chapter.

## Virtual Encounters

In her 2007 book *Encounters in the Virtual Feminist Museum*, Griselda Pollock proposes a feminist mode of reading "against the grain" of art history's classificatory systems by means of a central concept: the virtual feminist museum.[2] In developing this idea, Pollock stresses that such a museum is not virtual in the sense of an online platform. Rather, it is a space of encounter that allows individuals to trace new "critical relations" among artworks and, ultimately, between each other.[3] This would be, Pollock argues, a forward-looking, experimental museum that brings together artworks assembled by a feminist (as opposed to phallocentric) logic. At the time of writing the book, Pollock considered such a museum to be unrealizable under then current capitalist and patriarchal conditions:

> It signals a museum that could never be actual. The dominant social and economic power relations that govern the museum make feminist analysis impossible. What corporation would sponsor a feminist intervention which challenges the assumptions of class, race and gender that underpin the current social system despite gestures of inclusiveness and minor corrections to its histories of discrimination?[4]

"Feminism," according to Pollock, is a critical interrogation of patriarchal culture that imagines different forms of sociality and culture. Described as a "research laboratory" and "exhibition" in book form, the virtual feminist museum aims to counter the tendency toward mastery, classification, and definition that Pollock argues has been favored by both the modernist museum and dominant discourses of art history.

As a "*poïesis* of the future," Pollock's project seeks to stage encounters in which to think through, and intervene in, art's histories by staging "transformative interactions between the images differently assembled in conversations framed by feminist analysis and theory."[5] Pollock critically works through images in differential encounters that rupture established conventions and networks. Thus, the virtuality of her feminist museum is inscribed philosophically rather than technologically. Drawing on Elizabeth Grosz's notion of "becoming feminist" as a work of constant analysis and conceptual innovation, the virtual feminist museum must remain, for Pollock, a potentiality.[6]

Why introduce "feminist digital art history" through a concept that Pollock seeks specifically to distance from the online platforms and digital tools that have become the familiar frameworks and methodologies of digital art history? Our reasons are twofold: first, "feminism" is understood in Pollock's analysis as a political stance. Her desire to imagine encounters in the virtual feminist museum addresses some of the key issues at stake in exploring connections between "feminism" and "art history," and it is necessary to unpack those debates in order to understand what "feminist digital art history" is or might be. Second, Pollock employs vocabulary and concepts that have become pillars of the digital humanities: networks and mapping. Her discussion does, therefore, anticipate some of the methodologies that inform digital art history and its desire to unearth hitherto underappreciated or unseen patterns and associations. Indeed, Pollock's discussion of Aby Warburg's *Mnemosyne Atlas* and *Pathosformel* are models that have been taken up and developed through a variety of digital techniques and to different ends, as discussed in Chapters 27 and 28 of the present volume. The question that arises is whether the political ambitions of feminist art history are met by the digital tools that appear to give its proposals visible form. Put differently, what happens when a "*poïesis* of the future" is realized in a technological present?

We might initially compare feminist art history and digital art history in the following way. Pollock presents a feminist reconceptualization of ways in which audiences experience and study the visual arts by proposing new concepts with which to examine and intervene in art's histories. Digital art history, as a field that uses computational and analytical methods enabled by new technology, also aims to reconceptualize the way in which we experience and study the visual arts and thus also challenges traditional discourses that have shaped the discipline.[7]

"Feminism" and "digital" are thus two qualifiers that modify the study and writing of "art history." Feminism, on the one hand, is a politics and theory that problematizes gender, sex, sexual difference, and sexuality in ways that can be used to inform art practice and scholarship. Digital art history, on the other hand, is a method and set of tools. According to Susan Elizabeth Gagliardi and Joanna Gardner-Huggett, art historians tend to conflate theory and method:

> When art historians characterize their approaches as feminist, iconographic, Marxist, or something else, they explain how their evidence coincides with or challenges certain concepts or interventions rather than clarify how they obtained their evidence or analyzed it. This foregrounding of theory over method results in presentations and publications that eschew the iterative nature of research.[8]

Theory only offers a way of organizing or transforming information and is often undertaken with an end point in mind (for example making visible the ideological basis of the erasure of certain artists). In consequence, Gagliardi and Gardner-Huggett stress the need to account for the "how" of art-historical research, an approach that entails exploring more fully the interaction between different methodological models and underlying data.[9] How, then, can feminism challenge the ways in which digital art history formulates its key questions or wrestles with issues such as the limits of data?

## Overview of Principal Strategies

In order to begin to answer these questions, it is necessary to locate our discussion in an overview of some recent art-historical projects and approaches that have taken place at the intersection of the digital humanities and feminism. In the following discussion, the "field" of feminist digital art history is taken broadly to mean computational methods, analytical technologies, and digitization strategies that are related to the lives and careers of female artists, artworks by women, or that otherwise problematize interactions between gender and the canons of art history, including the methodologies used to study the latter.

### *Remapping the Terrain*

Mapping is a mainstay of digital art history. As discussed in Chapter 7, research groups such as Artl@s promote and develop new tools to support this method of investigation. Artl@s specifically positions its mapping work as an attempt to disturb art history's grounding in nationalistic narratives and monographic studies.[10] It argues that digital mapping is a key method for adding to knowledge about art, but also for transforming the way such knowledge is employed in dominant art-historical narratives. If Pollock encouraged researchers to read "against the grain" of art history, the mapping strategies promoted by Artl@s have a similar transformative ambition.

Joanna Gardner-Huggett and Michelle Moravec have each used mapping as a tool for art-historical research on feminist artists.[11] Writing in 2017, Gardner-Huggett argues, following Lucy Lippard's writing on feminist art practices, that the digital mapping of artistic networks is part of an important genealogy of art-historical research into feminist art networks.[12] Her research traces histories of women's collaborative practice (in this case two Chicago-based collectives: ARC Gallery and Artemisia Gallery) and uses digital techniques, such as Geographic Information Systems (GIS), to visualize networks according to location.[13] The digital methods produced results that offered a corrective to her previous research findings, suggesting earlier research had overvalued national engagement in an attempt to insert the collectives into existing narratives of feminist art.

Michelle Moravec has led two digital humanities projects that use social network analysis for research on feminist artists. In both, Moravec was concerned with testing the use and limits of social network analysis for feminist artists who had been marginalized within dominant discourses. Describing the research in 2017, she outlines how *Visualizing Schneemann* sought to explore American artist Carolee Schneemann's artistic relationship with other women through analysis of correspondence collected in the edited volume *Correspondence Course*, edited by Kristine Stiles.[14] The second project examined the manifesto in feminist art as a means of circulating ideas.[15] Moravec describes how both projects failed to produce the results for which she had hoped. The results demonstrated that network analysis has limited use if artworks and archival materials relating to female artists remain under-processed in comparison to that of their male counterparts:

> Even in the case of Schneemann, among a handful of the most celebrated female artists of her generation, network analysis proved quite difficult. Her archived letters are less processed than her male peers, making it impossible to create a thorough correspondence network of her extant letters.[16]

Digital art history research on artists who are women has been constrained by a scarcity of archives, insufficient amounts of machine-readable materials, and limited (or biased) metadata attached to images and artifacts.[17] This situation is a symptom of broader systemic and structural issues that have failed adequately to account for the contributions of artists who are women and/or people of color, working class, disabled, trans, or queer. It is precisely these ideological and cultural structures that have been addressed by feminist, queer, and decolonial critiques of art history. The digitization of artworks and texts by feminist artists, women, and marginalized or oppressed individuals—and the forging of an adequate vocabulary for the meta-data attaching to such works—is an important part of building a feminist digital art history.

In the projects discussed previously, mapping is used to make visible the histories of feminist artists and art collectives for the purpose of examining interactions between individuals and groups. Moravec, in particular, is concerned with testing the use and limits of social network analysis for research on feminist artists who have been marginalized in dominant discourses. Another approach is to examine how a feminist perspective might shape GIS digital methods in art-historical research. Gardner-Huggett's research is informed by the ideas of feminist geographer Mei-Po Kwan.[18] Kwan examines the limitations of GIS methods and considers how they may be reoriented in the light of feminist epistemologies and politics. By "deconstructing the dualist understanding of geographical methods (as either quantitative or qualitative)" and by enacting a "feminist visualization" that undermines the objectifying gaze of the "master subject," Kwan argues for a new kind of critical engagement between researcher and subject matter.[19] Taking up this point, Gardner-Huggett points out that digital mapping does not, in and of itself, offer a radically different form of feminist research within its art-historical application. Rather than simply replace analogue with digital methods, she argues that digital mapping complements the former and "makes the art historian more accountable to historical sources."[20]

## *Online Encounters*

Online platforms and exhibitions are a significant form of digital art history and have become important sites of feminist activity. Broadly, these take the following forms: online indices of female artists and feminist exhibitions; exhibitions of work by women realized solely on online platforms; websites that are constructed to accompany feminist exhibitions; and social media platforms created for the presentation and discussion of art by women.

Three examples of the first category include AWARE (Archives of Women Artists, Research and Exhibitions), Art + Feminism, and N.paradoxa. Co-founded in 2014 by Camille Morineau, AWARE is a website that seeks to restore "the presence of 20th-century women artists in the history of art."[21] It does so by compiling an online, searchable index that profiles the biographies of female artists born between 1860 and 1972 regardless of their country of origin or the media in which they worked. The index draws from the *Dictionnaire universel des créatrices*, an online encyclopedia developed by *Éditions des femmes* and Antoinette Fouque, a key figure in the French Women's Liberation Movement.[22] The index is continually updated and is accompanied by paper and online publications, research events, and reviews of exhibitions by female artists.

AWARE is a collaborative project that solicits contributions from the public for its content. In this regard it is similar to Art + Feminism that describes itself as "a campaign improving coverage of gender, feminism, and the arts on Wikipedia."[23] By organizing edit-a-thons, Art + Feminism leads events (both virtual and physical) that mobilize members of the public to collaborate in the production and dissemination of knowledge about the relationship between gender and art.

The website N.paradoxa, run from the UK by feminist art historian Katy Deepwell, is an online repository of links to research on feminism and contemporary art. The website, launched in 1996, catalogues feminist research on post-1970 art and aims "to promote understanding of women artists and their work" through a database of more than 5,000 links.[24] The material represented concerns feminism's relation to contemporary art and ranges from archives and exhibitions to books and theses.[25] While each of these projects seeks to redress imbalances in publicly available information, they also use technology to encourage discussion and to foster collaborative practices designed to have a broader impact on the artworld.

Inevitably, social media play an important role in realizing the activist potential of online audiences. Social media accounts that specifically engage with artworks made by women or that question the canon of art history have emerged and grown in popularity over the past five years. While the Guerilla Girls have long been noted for their feminist interventions at museums, art fairs, and other events, their web page is now an important source of information and archive of projects, and their Instagram account (@guerillagirls), launched in 2012, showcases their various activities and posters.[26] Similar social media accounts that raise awareness about the relationship between gender and the artworld include #WOMENSART (@womensart1), launched in January 2016 by PL Henderson, which shares artwork by women in different media; and on Instagram, @thegreatwomenartists, an account run by Katy Hessel since October 2015, which describes its aim as "celebrating female art daily." At the time of writing #WOMENSART has amassed over 220,000 followers on Twitter, @guerillagirls 70,000 followers on Instagram, and @thegreatwomenartists 66,500 followers.

Presence and visibility online is essential for artists and institutions. Consequently, dedicated websites that accompany museum exhibitions have been a key output in the realization of major feminist survey exhibitions. These "blockbuster" feminist shows, as Hilary Robinson has noted, had a surge of popularity in major Western museums between 2005 and 2011.[27] Reesa Greenberg, writing in 2015, draws attention to the social and historical significance of dedicated websites for such exhibitions:

> Most exhibition websites are not produced as history but become history. After exhibitions are over, the websites remain online as "permanent," accessible alternatives to existing print format exhibition histories. Moreover, because of the expanded

> possibilities of what can be recorded and presented online, exhibition websites offer viable models for documenting and analyzing exhibitions differently.[28]

Constructing dedicated websites for temporary feminist exhibitions organized by museums is an important tool, she argues, for challenging the patriarchal structures of the artworld.[29] Greenberg concludes that by leaving a trace of the exhibition online, such websites can counter the erasure of women from printed histories.

Roszika Parker and Griselda Pollock have argued that the erasure of women from histories of art is symptomatic of ideological assumptions about sexual difference that have structured the development of the discipline.[30] Greenberg diagnoses a similar issue in the more recent field of exhibition histories, but suggests that the medium of the website can produce content that resists the categorizations and hierarchies of earlier discourses and practices. A website's multimedia capabilities is especially well suited to the types of feminist artwork pioneered in the 1970s such as performance and video art.

Greenberg's optimism is countered, however, by the lifespan and legacies of online projects. Maura Reilly, for instance, has reflected on her ambitions as the founding curator of the Elizabeth A. Sackler Center for Feminist Art (part of the Brooklyn Museum, USA) for a website to accompany the inaugural exhibition of the center, *Global Feminisms: New Directions in Contemporary Art*, in 2007:

> The web is the greatest educational tool, so, from the outset, I set the goal of developing an extensive, interactive website, housed within the Brooklyn Museum site. [. . .] I also designed the Feminist Art Base, the first online digital archive dedicated solely to feminist art. It was meant to be an ever-growing database that offered multimedia profiles from the most prolific contributors to feminist art from the 1960s to the present. [. . .] the goal was to make this ground breaking searchable archive a comprehensive resource for artists, curators, scholars, and the general public. It was meant to be continually expanding. When it was launched in 2007 there were 550 profiles. Today, there are only 320, and the profiles no longer feature videos or performance clips, only 2D works.[31]

Although Reilly's aims align with Greenberg's conceptualization of the positive function of the website as an "accessible alternative" to print, the project was not sustained with the energy with which it was initiated. Reilly also notes that important features of the online database, including the inclusion of video clips, are now defunct. Within a decade, the website not only failed to expand, but actually diminished. If Greenberg is right, should such projects be sustained and, if so, how are they to be adequately supported both technologically and financially? Part of a feminist digital art history is the need to create, maintain and search for visual and archival material. Three key practical issues that arise in this context are: first, the effective tagging of existing material (i.e. metadata that adequately reflects and contextualizes the gendered biographies of artifacts and exhibitions); second, the digitization of a broad range of resources as discussed previously; and third, the creation and implementation of strategies to maintain born-digital materials (including the preservation of relevant software and hardware).

## *Exhibitions, Gender, and Cyberfeminism*

Beginning in March 2019, the Richard Saltoun Gallery, a commercial gallery in London, dedicated a year of programming to female artists. Titled "100% Women," the program included gallery exhibitions, art fair presentations, talks, external collaborations, and digital exhibitions on a new online platform hosted on the gallery's website.[32] As press materials highlighted, several of the online exhibitions featured unrepresented and emerging artists, thus serving as "part of its [the gallery's] commitment to nurturing greater inclusivity."[33] That the launch of the online exhibition platform coincided with the 100% Women initiative not only acknowledges gender-based inequalities in the art market, but optimistically suggests that online exhibitions may be one strategy for addressing the issue.[34]

The Saltoun Gallery is not alone in its use of the internet to exhibit and promote the work of women artists and, indeed, most artists now have their own sophisticated online presences.[35] Yet, the key issue in this case is not simply one of visibility. Rather it concerns how technology relates to institutional frameworks that have been shaped by gendered power relations. This is a topic with which artists, activists, and "cyberfeminists" have long grappled. While it would go beyond the scope of this chapter to discuss the long and complex history of the relationship between art, technology, and gender, it is worth positioning the present discussion against the background of a few key examples that have a bearing on institutional power structures in the artworld. The first is the *Art and Technology* project run between 1967 and 1971 by the Los Angeles County Museum of Art that was intended to demonstrate emerging connections between art, engineering, science, and other technologies. No women were included in the initiative.[36] In her discussion of the project and the formation of the Los Angeles Council of Women Artists (LACWA) in its wake, Jennifer Way discusses LACWA's criticism of the museum and of the ways in which a combination of technology and gender reinforced prevailing patriarchal power structures: technology was gendered as masculine, women were cast as cultural consumers rather than producers, and these ideas were understood as normative elements of social (and museum) organization.[37]

Judy Wajcman's studies of the gendering of technology provide important overviews of the development of women's relationship to science and computing from the 1970s to the present. She notes that while feminists of the 1980s remained largely "pessimistic about the prospects for women offered by the microelectronic revolution, there was a much more enthusiastic response to the dawn of the digital age."[38] Fueled by ideas that cyberspace had the possibility to overturn notions of biological difference, the figure of the cyborg (as proposed by Donna Haraway) and the liberating prospects of virtual realities seemed to offer new possibilities for the subversion of traditional notions of gender, embodied experience, and power relations.[39] As Wajcman notes:

> A common argument [. . .] is that the digital revolution heralds the decline of traditional institutional practices and power bases including patriarchal power. The virtuality of cyberspace is seen to spell the end of naturalized, biological embodiment as the basis for gender difference.[40]

The limitations of the impact of the digital revolution on the practices of art institutions was brought to the fore, however, by Cornelia Sollfrank in 1997 in a work titled *Female Extension*. The artist famously hacked a competition of net art run by the Hamburg Kunsthalle.[41] By creating fake submissions by 127 female artists, she sought to test and disrupt ideologies that underpinned the museum's processes of selection and reward. Although the institution approvingly noted the high submission rate by women, none of them won a prize in the competition. As Merle Radtke puts it: "By occupying the net art competition. Sollfrank questioned long-established institutional structures and practices at various levels, and revealed invisible but thoroughly influential power relations."[42]

Various collectives and research groups have arisen over the past decade that interrogate contemporary technologies from a feminist perspective and create communities that share resources about relationships between technology, pedagogy, arts, and culture. FemTechNet describes itself as a "cyberfeminist praxis: we recognize that digital and other technologies can both subvert and reinscribe oppressive relations of power and we work to make these complex relations of power transparent."[43] It seeks to do so through a range of initiatives including research projects social media postings, online courses, and publications. Groups with similar aims and a focus on encouraging diversity in technology and research include Deep Lab, MzTek, Mz Baltazar's Lab and the Fembot Collective.[44]

Online exhibitions have become part of contemporary, everyday culture and often seek to make visible the work and ideas of artists who are underrepresented in major museum collections. Having regard to the issues just discussed, it is important to consider the relationship between online and physical exhibitions. On the one hand, online exhibitions seem to have the power to alter the ways in which gender has shaped narratives of art history. By bringing to light works that have not been incorporated into museums and by giving voice to underrepresented artists, they can enhance artworld diversity. On the other hand, however, web exhibitions risk falling into the realm of digital ephemera as discussed previously and, in consequence, may reinforce existing canons by failing to provide a lasting platform for individuals who have been excluded from those canons. Having regard to the ideas underpinning Pollock's virtual feminist museum, an online exhibition is not a simple corrective to an historic lack of visibility. Rather, the strategic importance of such initiatives lies in their ambition to provoke change that extends beyond virtual reality and that impacts on institutional practices and wider social behavior (including the greater presence of women and minorities in both the arts and technology).

Unsurprisingly, feminist online projects range from the individual (e.g. Les Femmes Folles: Women in Art) to the institutional.[45] As an example of the latter, Google Arts & Culture (formerly Google Art Project) has been used as a platform for developing media projects, online exhibitions and photo stories (often in collaboration with arts and culture organizations and collections) to present work that examines relationships between gender, culture, and society.[46] Clearly, a key aim of these media projects is to give wider access to works of art and material culture from the contributing partners. In 2011, Nancy Proctor discussed the significance of these kinds of initiatives in terms of access and experience:

> High-resolution images and high-definition video are a good example of how the Web and digital media can be used to complement, rather than imitate, the encounter with the artwork in the gallery. Nelson Mattos, vice-president of engineering at Google, celebrates the access that the Internet provides for those who cannot physically travel to distant museums. The Google Art Project promises to enrich that online art experience both informationally and emotionally.[47]

The significance is not just more visibility for artworks but the promotion of a unique form of engagement and access: High-resolution images and high-definition video allow the close scrutiny of objects alongside a different way of searching the collection catalogue and encountering curated online exhibitions. Proctor captures the excitement of this new kind of art experience: "Watch the technophobes zoom into a gigapixel painting for the first time, and see the scales fall from their eyes when they realize they can't get this close to the art even in the gallery."[48]

Although Google offers such engagement through its Arts & Culture interface there remains a risk of creating a skewed image of art history through uneven access to collections due to high reproduction fees, partnership obligations, and copyright obstacles. Other practical difficulties arise: What about artworks that resist digitization because of their material composition? What criteria will organizers use to decide what is worth reproducing? Extending Wajcman's skepticism about the utopian promise of the digital revolution, limits attaching to the creation of online platforms may simply reinstate the patriarchal logic that has, to date, informed art-historical canons. This risks once again dismissing artwork made by women or other marginalized groups in the structure of newly created digital collections and exhibitions.[49] One might also add that there is a need to look beyond the interface to the structure of the corporation that funds and maintains the relevant site. Just as museums are coming under pressure to be more transparent and accountable as regards their governance and funding, it is reasonable to consider the corporate culture of Google itself—including the sexism scandals in which was embroiled in 2018—when considering the extent to which the Google Arts & Culture platform is, in fact, a tool for advancing gender equality.[50]

## Potential and Limitations

Many of the examples just discussed optimistically suggest that digitization, the strategic use of computer technologies, and shared approaches to learning and online activities can offer the possibility of disrupting conventional art-historical narratives by foregrounding issues of gender and diversity. Echoing the positive rhetoric that surrounded the advent of the internet and of computer art in the 1990s, digital humanities methodologies have seemed to promise a similar democratization of research culture: greater access to materials through digitization, the creation of search and mapping tools to unearth hidden histories, increased collaboration and publication of open access resources, and the creation of platforms that showcase the creativity of individuals who have been omitted from traditional artworld institutions.

Critics of the digital humanities have, however, pointed out the limitations of many approaches that have developed in the field to date. In 2014, Martha Nell Smith debated the consequences of studying "frozen social orders when they are made to seem like objective features of intellectual life."[51] While her discussion focused on the challenges of working in digital archives, she also opened wider questions about humanities research, namely, how to "transform the digital humanities so that innovations are sociological and not only technical."[52] Developing this point, Roopika Risam has argued for an intersectional digital humanities—one that "asks us to begin with the specificities of a data set, identify the layers of difference that intersect within it, and use that knowledge as a basis for project design."[53] In a similar vein, scholars including Kim Gallon and Angel Nieves have called for increased interaction between Africana/Black Studies and the digital humanities. In Gallon's view a "black epistemology will generate questions about the relationship between the racialization of humanity and the digital as power, ultimately fostering new inquiries and deeper understandings about the human condition."[54]

While the authors cited here query the composition of data sets and the kinds of questions posed about them, issues relating to who undertakes (or is able to undertake) a project in the digital humanities are also important in this context. Attention has been drawn to gender and identity formation when examining the diversity of scholars in the digital humanities. Moya Z. Bailey notes that the "ways in which identities inform both theory and practice in digital humanities have been largely overlooked. Those already marginalized in society and the academy can also find themselves in the liminal spaces of this field."[55] One could add to this the need to confront even more basic issues of inequality. As digital humanities projects are reliant on adequate infrastructure (including access to sophisticated computing equipment, software, and technology training), only a limited range of institutions around the world are able to support such research.

The questions raised by these branches of scholarship are relevant to debates about what might constitute feminist digital art history and how it is practised. This involves debating the role that technology plays in determining both the kinds of questions posed by digital projects and the ways in which the latter relate to the goals of humanities research and to notions of academic community. In this vein, Janneke Adema and Gary Hall have called for a style of digital humanities that is essentially "disruptive" in nature. They identify two major threats to the functioning and development of the digital humanities. They argue that the discipline remains within the boundaries of the traditional humanities and is, therefore, simply a transposition of its key tenets and ideas into a digital realm. Furthermore, they worry that research relies too heavily on the approaches and methodologies of computing science and business technologies.[56] Their suggestion is a more radical overhaul of approaches to humanities research as a general matter, including critical re-assessments of the methodologies, aesthetics, and dissemination of research and of the institutions in which that research takes place. Adema and Hall's call to arms aligns with conceptions of feminist scholarship that view the remit of the field as extending beyond issues of methodology and to encompass practices of protest culture. Viewed from this angle, one aspect of feminist digital art history may consist in developing research strategies that do not simply mobilize new scholarly approaches to intersections of art history and technology, but that do so with the ambition of provoking wider social change.[57]

The issues raised in this context are also relevant to more general debates about the gendering of technologies and algorithms that underpin digital humanities research. In *Artificial Knowing*, Alison Adam examines "the ways in which gender, in the form of concepts of masculinity and femininity, is inscribed, in implicit ways" in artificial intelligence (AI).[58] Key to her examination of the relationships between gender and AI is an increased focus on the subject of the knowledge—the "knower." Locating her analysis against the background of feminist epistemology and, in particular, the work of Lorraine Code, Adam highlights the need to maintain focus on the cultural contexts and status of knowers themselves and to be wary of AI that privileges a traditional epistemological model based on "knowing that" as opposed to "knowing how."[59] Her discussion is relevant to the subject of this chapter as it encourages researchers to reflect critically on the algorithms used to undertake digital humanities projects and to test the assumptions on which they are built.

Adam's focus on epistemological self-reflection in computing also suggests an overlap with feminism and the ways in which it relates to the field of art history. As Griselda Pollock has noted, terms such as "race," "gender," "sexuality," and "class" are not "descriptions of given conditions of human beings or inert categories. They are dynamic social signs. They signify materially lived sets of differential and asymmetrical and intersecting relations. [. . .] They are terms in the making of cultural meanings, and thus in the making of the subjects of such meaning: subjectivity."[60] Taking up the debate about terminology with which we opened this chapter, reflection on the cultural complexity of category distinctions that structure both feminism and digital humanities is crucial to determining both the field of feminist digital art history and the role of the researcher within it.

In his discussion of the role of the imagination in the age of computing, Ed Finn makes a comment that is important to the relationship between technology, the humanities, and the lens through which we comprehend the world:

> Ambiguity, dissonance, interpretation, affect: these are the playing fields of humanistic and artistic inquiry. The subject position of the reader becomes increasingly important when the algorithmic portal through which we are accessing the universe of knowledge is itself an active agent, shaping the framing and the tenor of our gaze.[61]

Finn's comment aligns with concerns enunciated by Adam and, as discussed previously, by Kwan, but emphasizes a term that is central to art history: the gaze. An interrogation of the gaze—whether as a perspective embedded in an artwork or the view of an actual spectator—has been central to twentieth- and twenty-first-century art history and has motivated powerful and enduring debates about gendered looking. If, in some measure, digital art history is a delegation of the gaze to an algorithm—a new lens through which one looks at an artwork—feminist digital art history calls for renewed attention to the implications of this act. Rather than understanding feminist digital art history as simply a range of methodologies or exhibition projects pertaining to gender that use computer technologies as new means of analysis and visualization, this field of study calls for a more fundamental inquiry into how such technologies are reshaping the gaze of the researcher/viewer. This not only includes consideration of the gendered premises that are built into search engines or that shape databases and online collections. Rather, it also requires attention to the socio-cultural contexts of knowing more generally. If this debate has been undertaken primarily in media and literary studies and in science and technology, art historians have much to offer by bringing their own conceptions and critiques of the gaze to the fore. It is not simply the case that digital technologies can reshape art history, but rather that art history has the analytical tools to question key concepts that have driven the emergence of those technologies and the implications they have for structuring relationships of power between observer and subject.

## Notes

1. Amelia Jones, "Introduction," in *The Feminism and Visual Culture Reader*, ed. Amelia Jones, 2nd ed. (London and New York: Routledge, 2010), 1–2.
2. Griselda Pollock, *Encounters in the Virtual Feminist Museum: Time, Space and the Archive* (Abingdon: Routledge, 2007).
3. Ibid., 13.
4. Ibid., 9–10.
5. Ibid., 10–11.
6. Elizabeth Grosz, *Time Travels: Feminism, Nature, Power* (Durham and London: Duke University Press, 2005).
7. The Artl@s project, for example, explicitly positions itself as redefining art history "by embracing the theories and methods of the spatial, global, and digital turns that have challenged humanities over the past decades." Béatrice Joyeux-Prunel, Catherine Dossin, and Sorin Adam Matei, "Spatial (Digital) History: A Total Art History? The ARTL@S Project," *Visual Resources* 29, no. 1–2 (2013): 47–58.
8. Susan Elizabeth Gagliardi and Joanna Gardner-Huggett, "Spatial Art History in the Digital Realm," *Historical Geography* 45, no. 1 (2017): 23.
9. Ibid.
10. Joyeux-Prunel et al., "Spatial (Digital) History," 48.
11. Joanna Gardner-Huggett, "Extrapolating Influence: The Challenge of Mapping the History of ARC and Artemisia Galleries, Chicago (1980–1985)," *Historical Geography* 45, no. 1 (2017); Michelle Moravec, "Network Analysis and Feminist Artists," *Artl@s Bulletin* 6, no. 3 (2017).
12. Gardner-Huggett, "Extrapolating Influence."
13. Ibid., 46.
14. Kristin Stiles, *Correspondence Course* (Durham and London: Duke University Press, 2010).
15. Moravec examined digitized U.S. women's liberation movement periodicals to discover which feminist art manifestos had been reprinted, cross referencing the periodicals with the anthology *Feminist Art Manifestos*, ed. Katy Deepwell (2014). See Katy Deepwell, *Feminist Art Manifestos: An Anthology* (London: KT Press, 2014).
16. Moravec, "Network Analysis and Feminist Artists," 80.
17. Ibid.
18. Mei-Po Kwan, "Feminist Visualization: Re-envisioning GIS as a Method in Feminist Geographic Research," *Annals of the Association of American Geographers* (December 2002): 645–61.
19. Ibid., 656.
20. Gardner-Huggett, "Extrapolating Influence," 58.

21. Accessed August 27, 2019, https://awarewomenartists.com/en/a_propos/.
22. Accessed September 3, 2019, www.dictionnaire-creatrices.com/en/.
23. Accessed August 27, 2019, www.artandfeminism.org/.
24. Accessed September 5, 2019, www.ktpress.co.uk/.
25. Accessed September 5, 2019, www.ktpress.co.uk/feminist-art-observatory.asp.
26. Accessed August 27, 2019, www.guerrillagirls.com/our-story.
27. Hilary Robinson, "Feminism Meets the Big Exhibition: Museum Survey Shows Since 2005," *OnCurating*, 29 (May 2016): 29–41.
28. The exhibitions discussed are: *WACK! Art and the Feminist Revolution*; *Global Feminisms*; *elles@centrepompidou*. Reesa Greenberg, "Museums, Women, and the Web," in *The International Handbooks of Museum Studies: Museum Transformations*, ed. Annie E. Coombes and Ruth B. Phillips (Hoboken, NJ: John Wiley & Sons, 2015), 472.
29. Greenberg, "Museums, Women, and the Web," 471.
30. Roszika Park and Griselda Pollock, *Old Mistresses: Women, Art and Ideology* (London and New York: I.B. Tauris, 2013), 49.
31. Maura Reilly, "Foreword," in *Feminism and Museums: Intervention, Disruption and Change*, ed. Jenna C. Ashton (Edinburgh: MuseumsEtc, 2017).
32. Accessed September 5, 2019, www.richardsaltoun.com/online-exhibition/.
33. Accessed September 5, 2019, www.richardsaltoun.com/exhibitions/70/overview/.
34. See research conducted by Freelands Foundation: Marijke Steedman, "Representation of Female Artists in Britain in 2017," accessed September 5, 2019, https://freelandsfoundation.co.uk/research/representation-of-female-artists-in-britain-2017.
35. Other examples include The National Association of Women Artists Inc, www.nawaonlinegallery.org/home; Fusion.art, https://fusionartps.com/; Art Gallery Online, www.contemporaryartgalleryonline.gallery/2019-art-competition-all-women; LightSpaceTime, www.lightspacetime.art/all-women-art-exhibition-january-2018/.
36. See Maurice Tuchman and Jane Livingston, *A Report on the Art and Technology Program of the Los Angeles County Museum of Art 1967–1971* (Los Angeles: Los Angeles County Museum of Art, 1971). In his Introduction, Tuchman notes that a high proportion of female artists submitted unsolicited proposal for the project, but that none of these were accepted (19).
37. Jennifer Way, "Digital Art and the Interface of Technology and Feminism," in *A Companion to Digital Art*, ed. Christiane Paul (Malden, MA and Oxford: Wiley Blackwell, 2016), 181–202 (185–86).
38. Judy Wajcman, "Feminist Theories of Technology," *Cambridge Journal of Economics* 34 (2010): 141–52 (147).
39. Donna Haraway, "A Cyborg Manifesto: Science, Technology, and Socialist-Feminist in the Late Twentieth Century," in *Simians, Cyborgs and Women: The Reinvention of Nature*, ed. Donna Haraway (New York: Routledge, 1991), 149–81.
40. Judy Wajcman, *TechnoFeminism* (Cambridge: Polity Press, 2004), 7.
41. For a discussion of this and similar cyberfeminist works, see Charlotte Frost, *Art Criticism Online: A History* (Canterbury: Gylphi, 2019), 97–98.
42. Merle Radtke, "Female Extension: A Cyberfeminist Intervention," in *Feminism and Museums: Intervention, Disruption and Change*, ed. by Jenna C. Ashton, vol. 1 (Edinburgh: Museums Etc, 2018), 537–47 (545).
43. Accessed August 30, 2019, https://femtechnet.org/publications/manifesto/.
44. Accessed August 30, 2019, www.deeplab.net/#home; https://mztek.org/; www.mzbaltazarslaboratory.org/about/; https://fembot.adanewmedia.org/.
45. *Les Femmes Folles: Women in Art*, https://femmesfollesnebraska.tumblr.com/about, accessed August 30, 2019.
46. Examples include *Road to Equality*, a platform exploring stories to celebrate one hundred years of women's rights in the UK through a curated assemblage of visual and textual material. Others are *Women in Culture*, exploring the impact of women in culture across arts, humanities and sciences, and *Faces of Frida*, a project that looks at Frida Kahlo's life, art, and legacy.
47. Nancy Proctor, "The Google Art Project: A New Generation of Museums on the Web?" *Curator: The Museum Journal* 54, no. 2 (2011): 215–16.
48. Ibid., 218.
49. Ibid., 216.
50. For reports on this issue, see Daisuke Wakabayashi and Katie Benner, "How Google Protected Andy Rubin, the 'Father of Android,'" *The New York Times*, October 25, 2018, www.nytimes.com/2018/10/25/

technology/google-sexual-harassment-andy-rubin.html; Amy Nelson, "Google and the Structural Sexism of the American Workplace," *Forbes*, October, 30, 2018, accessed August 30, 2019, www.forbes.com/sites/amynelson1/2018/10/30/google-and-the-structural-sexism-of-the-american-workplace/#411b73052d70.

51. Martha Nell Smith, "Frozen Social Relations and Time for a Thaw: Visibility, Exclusions, and Considerations for Postcolonial Digital Archives," *Journal of Victorian Culture* 19, no. 3 (2014): 403–10 (404).
52. Ibid.
53. Roopika Risam, "Beyond the Margins: Intersectionality and the Digital Humanities," *DHQ: Digital Humanities Quarterly* 9, no. 2 (2019), www.digitalhumanities.org/dhq/vol/9/2/000208/000208.html. See also Elizabeth Losh, Jacqueline Wernimont, Laura Wexler, and Hong-An Wu, "Putting the Human Back into the Digital Humanities: Feminism, Generosity, and Mess," in *Debates in the Digital Humanities*, Ch. 10 (Minneapolis: University of Minnesota Press, 2016), https://dhdebates.gc.cuny.edu/read/65be1a40-6473-4d9e-ba75-6380e5a72138/section/cfe1b125-6917-4095-9d56-20487aa0b867#ch10.
54. Kim Gallon, "Making a Case for the Black Digital Humanities," in *Debates in the Digital Humanities 2016*, ed. Matthew K. Gold and Lauren F. Klein (Minneapolis, MN: University of Minnesota Press, 2016), https://dhdebates.gc.cuny.edu/read/65be1a40-6473-4d9e-ba75-6380e5a72138/section/fa10e2e1-0c3d-4519-a958-d823aac989eb#ch04.
55. Moya Z. Bailey, "All the Digital Humanists Are White, All the Nerds Are Men, but Some of Us Are Brave," *Journal of Digital Humanities* 1. no. 1 (2011), http://journalofdigitalhumanities.org/1-1/all-the-digital-humanists-are-white-all-the-nerds-are-men-but-some-of-us-are-brave-by-moya-z-bailey/.
56. Janneke Adema and Gary Hall, "Posthumanities: The Dark Side of 'The Dark Side of the Digital,'" *Journal of Electronic Publishing* 19, no. 2 (Fall 2016), doi:10.3998/3336451.0019.201.
57. See Hilary Robinson, "Introduction," in *A Companion to Feminist Art*, eds. Hilary Robinson and Maria Elena Buszek (Hoboken, NJ: Wiley Blackwell, 2019), 6. See also Hester Baer, "Redoing Feminism: Digital Activism, Body Politics, and Neoliberalism," *Feminist Media Studies* 16, no. 1 (2016): 17–34.
58. Alison Adam, *Artificial Knowing: Gender and the Thinking Machine* (London and New York: Routledge, 1998), 1.
59. Ibid., 30.
60. Griselda Pollock, "Essentialism, Feminism, and Art: Spaces Where Woman 'Oozes Away,'" in *A Companion to Feminist Art*, eds. Robinson and Buszek, 261–82 (270).
61. Ed Finn, *What Algorithms Want: Imagination in the Age of Computing* (Cambridge, MA: The MIT Press, 2017), 195–96.

## Bibliography

Adam, Alison. *Artificial Knowing: Gender and the Thinking Machine*. London and New York: Routledge, 1998.

Adema, Janneke, and Gary Hall. "Posthumanities: The Dark Side of 'The Dark Side of the Digital.'" *Journal of Electronic Publishing* 19, no. 2 (Fall 2016). doi:http://dx.doi.org/10.3998/3336451.0019 201

Art+Feminism. Accessed August 27, 2019. www.artandfeminism.org/.

AWARE: Archives of Women Artists, Research & Exhibitions. "Our programmes." Accessed August 27, 2019. https://awarewomenartists.com/en/a_propos/.

Baer, Hester. "Redoing Feminism: Digital Activism, Body Politics, and Neoliberalism." *Feminist Media Studies* 16, no. 1 (2016): 17–34.

Bailey, Moya Z. "All the Digital Humanists Are White, All the Nerds Are Men, But Some of Us are Brave." *Journal of Digital Humanities* 1. no. 1 (2011). http://journalofdigitalhumanities.org/1-1/all-the-digital-humanists-are-white-all-the-nerds-are-men-but-some-of-us-are-brave-by-moya-z-bailey/. Charlotte Frost. *Art Criticism Online: A History*. Canterbury: Gylphi, 2019.

Contemporary Art Gallery Online. "2019 All Women Art Exhibition and Competition Prospectus." Accessed October 15, 2019. www.contemporaryartgalleryonline.gallery/2019-art-competition-all-women.

Deep Lab. Accessed August 30, 2019. www.deeplab.net/#home.

Deepwell, Katy. *Feminist Art Manifestos: An Anthology*. London: KT Press, 2014.

Donna Haraway. "A Cyborg Manifesto: Science, Technology, and Socialist-Feminist in the Late Twentieth Century." In Donna Haraway, *Simians, Cyborgs and Women: The Reinvention of Nature*, 149–81. New York: Routledge, 1991.

Gardner-Huggett, Joanna. "Extrapolating Influence: The Challenge of Mapping the History of ARC and Artemisia Galleries, Chicago (1980–1985)." *Historical Geography* 45, no. 1 (2017): 37–65.

Fembot Collective. Accessed August 30, 2019. https://fembot.adanewmedia.org/.
FemTechNet. "Manifesto." Accessed August 30, 2019. https://femtechnet.org/publications/manifesto/.
Finn, Ed. *What Algorithms Want: Imagination in the Age of Computing*. Cambridge, MA: The MIT Press, 2017.
Fusion.art. Accessed October 15, 2019. https://fusionartps.com/.
Gagliardi, Susan Elizabeth, and Joanna Gardner-Huggett. "Spatial Art History in the Digital Realm." *Historical Geography* 45, no. 1 (2017): 17–36.
Gallon, Kim. "Making a Case for the Black Digital Humanities." In *Debates in the Digital Humanities 2016*, edited by Matthew K. Gold and Lauren F. Klein. Minneapolis: University of Minnesota Press, 2016. https://dhdebates.gc.cuny.edu/read/65be1a40-6473-4d9e-ba75-6380e5a72138/section/fa10e2e1-0c3d-4519-a958-d823aac989eb#ch04.
Greenberg, Reesa. "Museums, Women, and the Web." In *The International Handbooks of Museum Studies: Museum Transformations*, edited by. Annie E. Coombes and Ruth B. Phillips, 471–88. Hoboken: John Wiley & Sons, 2015.
Google Arts and Culture. "Faces of Frida." Accessed October 15, 2019. https://artsandculture.google.com/project/frida-kahlo
———. "Road to Equality." Accessed October 15, 2019. https://artsandculture.google.com/project/road-to-equality
———. "Women in Culture." Accessed October 15, 2019. https://artsandculture.google.com/project/women-in-culture.
Grosz, Elizabeth. *Time Travels: Feminism, Nature, Power*. Durham and London: Duke University Press, 2005.
Guerilla Girls. "Our Story." Accessed August 27, 2019. www.guerrillagirls.com/our-story.
Jones, Amelia, ed. *The Feminism and Visual Culture Reader*, 2nd ed. London and New York: Routledge, 2010.
Joyeux-Prunel, Béatrice, Catherine Dossin, and Sorin Adam Matei. "Spatial (Digital) History: A Total Art History?—The ARTL@S Project." *Visual Resources* 29, no. 1–2 (2013): 47–58.
KT press/ n.paradoxa. "Feminist Art Observatory." Accessed August 27, 2019. www.ktpress.co.uk/feminist-art-observatory.asp.
Kwan, Mei-Po. "Feminist Visualization: Re-envisioning GIS as a Method in Feminist Geographic Research." *Annals of the Association of American Geographers* (December 2002): 645–61.
Le Dictionnaire universel des Créatrices. Accessed August 27, 2019. www.dictionnaire-creatrices.com/en/.
Les Femmes Folles. "About." Accessed August 30, 2019. https://femmesfollesnebraska.tumblr.com/about.
LightSpaceTime. "'All Women' Art Exhibition—January 2018." Accessed November 15, 2019. www.lightspacetime.art/all-women-art-exhibition-january-2018/.
Losh, Elizabeth, Jacqueline Wernimont, Laura Wexler, and Hong-An Wu. "Putting the Human Back into the Digital Humanities: Feminism, Generosity, and Mess." In *Debates in the Digital Humanities*, Ch. 10. Minneapolis, MN: University of Minnesota Press, 2016. https://dhdebates.gc.cuny.edu/read/65be1a40-6473-4d9e-ba75-6380e5a72138/section/cfe1b125-6917-4095-9d56-20487aa0b867#ch10
Moravec, Michelle. "Network Analysis and Feminist Artists." *Artl@s Bulletin* 6, no. 3 (2017).
Mz Baltazar's Lab. "About." Accessed August 30, 2019. www.mzbaltazarslaboratory.org/about/.
MzTEK. "A Community of Technologists." Accessed August 30, 2019. https://mztek.org/.
National Association of Women Artists, Inc. "NAWA Online Exhibitions." Accessed October 15, 2019. www.nawaonlinegallery.org/home.
Nelson, Amy. "Google and the Structural Sexism of the American Workplace." *Forbes* October 30, 2018.
Parker, Roszika, and Griselda Pollock. *Old Mistresses: Women, Art and Ideology*. London and New York: I.B. Tauris, 2013.
Pollock, Griselda. *Encounters in the Virtual Feminist Museum: Time, Space and the Archive*. Abingdon: Routledge, 2007.
———. "Essentialism, Feminism, and Art: Spaces Where Woman 'Oozes Away.'" In *A Companion to Feminist Art*, edited by Hilary Robinson and Maria Elena Buszek, 261–82 (Hoboken, NJ: Wiley Blackwell, 2019).
Proctor, Nancy. "The Google Art Project: A New Generation of Museums on the Web?" *Curator: The Museum Journal* 54, no. 2 (2011): 215–21. doi:10.1111/j.2151-6952.2011.00083.
Radtke, Merle. "Female Extension: A Cyberfeminist Intervention." In *Feminism and Museums: Intervention, Disruption and Change*, edited by Jenna C. Ashton, vol. 1, 537–47. Edinburgh: Museums Etc., 2018.
Reilly, Maura. "Foreword." In *Feminism and Museums: Intervention, Disruption and Change*, edited by Jenna C. Ashton, 16–41. Edinburgh: Museums Etc., 2017.

Richard Saltoun Gallery. "Online Exhibition." Accessed September 5, 2019. www.richardsaltoun.com/online-exhibition/.

Risam, Roopika. "Beyond the Margins: Intersectionality and the Digital Humanities." *DHQ: Digital Humanities Quarterly* 9, no. 2 (2019). www.digitalhumanities.org/dhq/vol/9/2/000208/000208.html.

Robinson, Hilary. "Feminism Meets the Big Exhibition: Museum Survey Shows since 2005." *On Curating* 29 (May 2016): 29–41.

Robinson, Hilary, and Maria Elena Buszek, eds. *A Companion to Feminist Art*. Hoboken, NJ: Wiley Blackwell, 2019.

Smith, Marsha Nell. "Frozen Social Relations and Time for a Thaw: Visibility, Exclusions, and Considerations for Postcolonial Digital Archives." *Journal of Victorian Culture* 19, no. 3 (2014): 403–10.

Stiles, Kristin. *Correspondence Course*. Durham and London: Duke University Press, 2010.

Tuchman, Maurice, and Jane Livingston. *A Report on the Art and Technology Program of the Los Angeles County Museum of Art 1967–1971*. Los Angeles: Los Angeles County Museum of Art, 1971.

Wajcman, Judy. "Feminist Theories of Technology." *Cambridge Journal of Economics* 34 (2010): 141–52.

Wakabayashi, Daisuke, and Katie Benner. "How Google Protected Andy Rubin, the 'Father of Android.'" *The New York Times*, October 25, 2018.

Way, Jennifer. "Digital Art and the Interface of Technology and Feminism." In *A Companion to Digital Art*, edited by Christiane Paul, 181–202. Malden, MA and Oxford: Wiley Blackwell, 2016.

Wilson, Judith. "One Way or Another: Black Feminist Visual Theory." In *The Feminism and Visual Culture Reader*, edited by Amelia Jones, 19–23. 2nd ed. London and New York: Routledge, 2010.

# 5

# SLOW DIGITAL ART HISTORY AND *KUBISM*

## Or, Situation Awareness and the Promise of Open-World Games

*Koenraad Brosens, Bruno Cardoso, and Fred Truyen*

In late April 2019 an international group of art historians convened at The Clark, Williamstown, Massachusetts, to discuss one of the "Grand Challenges of Art History," namely "Digital/Computational Methods and Social Art History."[1] The workshop, followed by a public conversation, accentuated a familiar distrust in, and even dislike for, digital approaches. These were voiced by a number of workshop participants and audience members. Powerful ideological criticism was often interwoven with a nostalgic "hostile worlds" view, claiming, for example, that speedy computers allowing big(gish) data querying fundamentally disrupt the slow, yet highly effective, traditional relational research practices and human ways of archival feeling and thinking so typical of the humanities.

In this chapter we acknowledge that the tenacious refusal to embrace new–old digital art history is to a certain extent justifiable. A majority of digital platforms are goal-oriented algorithmic black boxes that cause a critical loss of "situation awareness," meaning that art historians no longer have a proper understanding (or any understanding at all) of the data and information highways and landscapes they are increasingly forced to navigate. Framing the problem within the conceptual architecture of situation awareness is useful, as it can guide art historians and technologists in their collaborative attempts to develop better tools that allow researchers to regain what is lost. These new tools are badly needed, as art history is still struggling with "the fundamental paradigm shift from a culture of scarcity to a culture of abundance."[2] The field thus faces a crucial challenge, that is "the implementation of what might be called rich connectivity [and] the transformation of recently available and interoperable data into meaningful new relationships enabled by digitization."[3] We argue that video games, and in particular open-world games such as the hugely popular *Minecraft*, can show the way. To support this claim, we present *KUbism*, an open-world game of data, and discuss the results of user tests. *KUbism* forms part of the *Project Cornelia* research agenda that is driven by the premise that in the still amorphous field of digital art history, *slowness* is a sine qua non for the production of, and fruitful engagement with, complex data and information.[4]

### The Loss of Situation Awareness and the Promise of Open-World Video Games

Since the 1990s situation awareness (hereafter SA) has been widely adopted by human factors scientists as a foundation for successful decision making and performance in dynamic (and often safety critical) contexts such as aviation, nuclear power systems, and emergency medical dispatch.[5] Mica Endsley's three-level model of SA (i.e., perception, comprehension, and projection) provides a clear framework for understanding SA as a human-centered design approach that aims to integrate users with (new) technologies.[6] Perception refers to awareness of the attributes, dynamics, and status of data and information in a given context and situation. Comprehension refers to the integration and interpretation of the data and information to explain what is actually *happening* in that situation. Projection, finally, expresses the prediction of a future state provided the situation continues. Thus, SA, which is achieved through many channels simultaneously (including the senses), is about a profound understanding of context and situation, allowing users to evaluate, plan, and decide on the next course of action.[7] It is a process of continuous assessment that is achieved and perfected through learning and practice.

Though decision making and performance in art-historical research is obviously by no means safety critical, SA provides a useful lens through which to explain the persistent resistance to digital art history that goes hand in hand with nostalgic yearning for research practices before the computer. Art historians working in the predigital age always had a clear and concise mental map or "picture in the head" of their research settings and strategies.[8] They had a thorough understanding of both the intellectual and physical tasks they had to perform to find, compare, and integrate data and information. They were deeply familiar with the mechanics and organization of their natural "databases" (i.e., archives, libraries, museums, and research centers), as well as with the operating systems and interfaces that allowed access to data and information (such as the bibliography and the library catalogue). The design of the personal workspace was also geared toward SA, as physical items forming data and information subsets (such as books and Xeroxed articles), often organized in an idiosyncratic manner, were always within sight and easy reach. To a large extent *doing* art-historical research was a routine operation shaped by multiple iterations and shared by many generations of art historians. While following the beaten path, however, art historians also had the ability to tune in to background noise, that is peripheral data and information. They recognized the importance of serendipity. In fact, chance findings often modified the course of action by triggering new questions. In sum, *doing* art-historical research in data repositories *avant la lettre* was a slow and time-consuming, yet also truly rewarding and satisfying, intellectual and physical process. It fostered creativity and curiosity that fueled adventurous exploration. It never put the researcher at risk of falling off the map. Art historians were in constant control. They had SA. When lost, they knew how to regain it quickly.

In the digital age, however, achieving and maintaining SA have become challenging due to a combustible combination of data abundance—if not data overload—and technologically centered system designs that often do not adequately support users entering uncharted territory.[9] Traditional data management systems, for instance, are developed to support our data needs, as they allow us to store, manipulate and retrieve data efficiently. However, these systems are primarily designed for static use scenarios in which querying users are believed to have a sound understanding of the schema, meaning, and contents of the databases.[10] In addition, these traditional scenarios assume that users know exactly what they are looking for. However, computer scientists have stressed that these assumptions are deeply problematic.[11] It is safe to say that almost all art historians would concur with this view. These concerns inspired computer scientists to develop more intuitive search platforms, such as SQLSUGG, AIDE and SeeDB.[12] However, powerful and promising as these and similar tools might be, in providing users with (visually) recommending queries, they still are, in essence, goal-oriented and mostly utilitarian tools focused on the discovery of data patterns. Consequently, they do not cater to the ingrained liking for slow-paced research, serendipity, and the incidental shared by most art historians.[13]

Therefore, we need to conceptualize platforms for data exploration that, at least to a certain degree, reflect the traditional intellectual *and* physical tasks typical of our search practices and that thus guarantee SA. This means we have to shift the focus from the data to the researcher whose creativity, curiosity, and attempts to make sense of an environment (be it objects in the physical world or entities and relations in a network of archival records and publications) are the very drivers of art-historical research.[14] Given this agenda, we argue that video games can be used as an inspiration and a model.[15]

It is a truism that video games, in particular games designed for a primary purpose other than entertainment, are very effective tools in both education and research as they enable high levels of immersion and devotion that traditional learning approaches and utilitarian computer systems cannot offer.[16] "Serious games," also known as "applied games," for example, aim to train or educate players about a certain topic at levels appropriate for individual participants. Serious games have been used successfully in fields as diverse as cultural heritage,[17] defense,[18] health care,[19] and history.[20] "Games with a purpose," also known as "human-based computation games," challenge players to perform tasks that people tend to do better than computers,[21] such as improving the suggestions of collection recommender systems,[22] annotating music and sound,[23] or deriving social information from text.[24]

We believe that a third group of games, that is "open-world games," can be used to develop SA-friendly search and exploration platforms. For open-world games focus primarily on *exploration*, as they allow players to explore worlds and objectives creatively and intuitively, instead of tying them to linear and scripted scenarios.[25] Arguably the best-known open-world game is *Minecraft*, "a game about placing blocks and going on adventures."[26] Indeed, the core gameplay of this sandbox block-based game revolves around the exploration of 3D procedurally generated worlds of blocks that players can pick up and place freely in order to build (and destroy) basic or complex structures.[27] Given its user-centered philosophy and gameplay, it may not come as a surprise that *Minecraft* has already been used as a learning tool to teach a wide range of topics, including project management and artificial intelligence.[28] *Minecraft* has also inspired the development of *OPERAcraft*, an arts and technology education platform that supports live performances of a hybrid art form combining gaming, telematics, machinima, and opera.[29]

Though it may seem slightly strained at first sight, we believe we can draw an analogy between *Minecraft*'s first-person perspective and its explicit focus on free decision making and creative performance in dynamic situations, on the one hand, and doing art-historical research in the archive and the library on the other. We can think of *Minecraft* blocks as archival records, books or journals—as containers of data and information. When put in the *Minecraft* world, these containers become a virtual archive or library. We could enter and leave the datascape whenever we like. We could wander where we please. We could explore the contents of the blocks. We could pick them up, open them, and evaluate the nature, provenance, and quality of the data and information they contain. We could decide to put a block back where we found it or somewhere else—as if we were checking items out of the library. We could group blocks in one or more places, thus creating our own data structures. Ideally, we would be able not only to copy blocks, but also to generate new ones containing data that results from our interactions with existing blocks. A new block could have data, for example, that we extracted from different blocks. The data structure(s) we are building would be our personal and highly flexible workspace(s), with data and information readily at hand and supporting us while we develop our arguments and claims. It deserves emphasis that exploring the datascape, taking, opening and evaluating the containers of data, and reshaping the world by building new containers and structures would be, in essence, a slow process that would force us to think continuously about the ever-changing situation we are in. Put differently, in this open-world game of data, we would have an opportunity to achieve and maintain SA.

The analogy between playing *Minecraft* and exploring and using the archive and library inspired us to build a prototype of a *Minecraft*-like platform to test the hypothesis that art historians and other humanities scholars can indeed benefit from a game-based approach to an engaging exploration of complex data sets. This is a pioneering approach. The closest parent is *Onto-Frogger* (2010), "a single-player, arcade style game for scientific images, their annotations and the connections established by these annotations," that uses elements of the classic game *Frogger* (1981).[30] However, *Onto-Frogger* is focused on exploring the *structure* of graph-based data repositories, while our tool, called *KUbism*, emphasizes the exploration of the data itself.

## KUbism

We used *Terasology*, a *Minecraft*-inspired, open-source, voxel-based game engine implemented in Java that is developed and maintained by a supportive community of software developers, designers, game testers, graphic artists, and musicians to build our open-world game of data.[31] *KUbism* is a desktop application that communicates with a database server, acting as a client in a standard client-server architecture. This way, it stands as an interface between the user and the data contained in the remote *Cornelia* database.

*Cornelia* is a MySQL database that contains a wide array of archival data about the seventeenth-century "art worlds" in Antwerp and Brussels.[32] The data is extracted from a myriad of archival sources, including parish records (i.e., baptism, marriage, and funeral records), notarial deeds (which include a wide array of documents, such as declarations of debt, leases, and wills), and registers of guilds and corporations. *Cornelia* includes *all* of the actors recorded in these documents as they engaged in one or more events and played one or more roles that link them to one or more actors; groups (i.e. cultural, economic, political, social, and/or religious bodies), places (i.e. countries, town, parishes, streets, and/or houses), and/or works of art. As a result, *Cornelia*'s data model is quite complex. In addition, depending on the point of view, the database is rich (at this point, it contains more than 12,000 people and over 300,000 time-dependent relations linking the elements of the database) or poor, as *missing* data is omnipresent.

*KUbism* assumes its data support to be modeled according to the Entity-Relationship (ER) model that "adopts the more natural view [in contrast to the network model, the relational model, and the entity set model] that the real world consists of entities and relationships."[33] True to the ER model, entities and relations in *KUbism* can have attributes that characterize them. In *KUbism*'s user interface, entities ("things that can be distinctly identified"[34]) are represented as blocks—*Minecraft*'s fundamental gameplay element. As they have a more subtle and flexible nature, relationships between entities do not have the same visual presence as entities, and they become explorable only after related entities become part of a new entity set. *KUbism* has six block types, each serving a specific purpose (Figure 5.1).

1. *Entity Block* (Figure 5.1, b, c, and d). Entity Blocks (EB) represent one or more entities of the same type. Users can pick up the blocks and place them anywhere in the world. They can explore the entities and their relations using the other *KUbism* blocks. EBs can be attached to other EBs containing entities of different types. The resulting group may be explored for entities and relations, as if it were a single EB. As a simple example, consider two EBs, $EB_1$ and $EB_2$, and five entities of the same type, $A$, $B$, $C$, $D$ and $E$, such that $EB_1 = \{A, B, C\}$ and $EB_2 = \{A, D, E\}$. Or, to make it more concrete, Block 1 contains three painters and Block 2 contains three painters; one painter belongs to both blocks. (It could also be

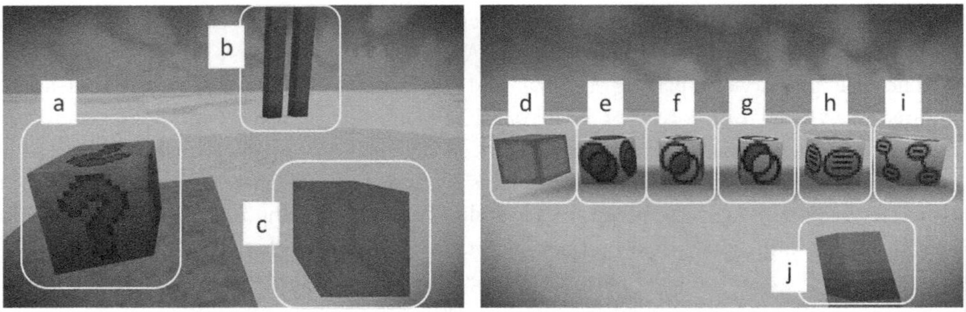


*Figure 5.1* The world of *KUbism*, (left) scenario for user testing and (right) *KUbism* blocks side by side: (a) the "question" block used to ask questions and verify answers; (b) two columns of vertically aligned Entity Blocks, the left column contains a block for each Place and the right column a block for each Actor; (c) Entity Block held by the player's avatar; (d) another Entity Block (e) Union Block; (f) Intersection Block; (g) Difference Block; (h) Entity Exploration Block; (i) Relation Exploration Block; and (j) the player avatar's empty hand.

*Source*: © The authors, 2019.

tapestry producers, parishes, religious paintings—anything that can be distinctly identified.) If a user attaches Block 1 to Block 2 (or vice versa), the result will be a two-EB group. This group would be equivalent to having one single EB referencing the unique entities of both blocks, that is $\{A, B, C, D, E\}$.

2. *Intersection Block* (Figure 5.1, f). The Intersection Block (IB) implements the set intersection operation ($\cap$). When users attach an IB to two or more groups of EBs and activate the IB the IB generates a new EB containing all entities *shared* by the attached groups of EBs, e.g. $EB_1 \cap EB_2 = \{A\}$—the one painter that Block 1 and Block 2 have in common.
3. *Union Block* (Figure 5.1, e). The Union Block (UB) implements the set union operation ($\cup$). It works just like the IB, but instead of the common entities, the resulting EB contains all the entities in all attached groups, without repetitions, e.g. $EB_1 \cup EB_2 = \{A, B, C, D, E\}$
4. *Difference Block* (Figure 5.1, g). In the same fashion as the IB and the UB, the Difference Block (DB) will apply the set difference operation ($\setminus$) on the entities of all attached groups of EBs. This operation is directional, meaning that users have to select a "main" group in a window that pops up when users activate the block before the operation executes. The resulting EB will contain the subset of entities that belongs exclusively to the "main" set, e.g. $E1 \setminus E2 = \{B, C\}$. Or, the newly generated EB will only contain the painters that do not make part of Block 2.
5. *Entity Exploration Block* (Figure 5.1, h). The Entity Exploration Block (EXB) operates like a filter: It browses through the entities in an attached group of EBs and creates a new EB containing the entities with attributes defined by the user. Users can write the conditions in a window that pops up when they activate the EXB. The syntax for writing the conditions is similar to that of the "where" clause of SQL queries. For example, imagine attaching an EXB to two EBs containing entities of type <T> ("painter," for example) with properties Name and Surname. Upon activation, the EXB will show a form where users could write an expression like [<T>.Name] = "John" AND [<T>.Surname]! = "Doe" to obtain a new EB containing the entities of type <T> in the attached EBs with property Name equal to "John," and Surname other than "Doe." As an alternative to creating a new EB, the EXB also allows users to export the entities' data to a comma-separated values (CSV) file that can

be used in other data management and data visualization tools, such as Excel, Gephi, and OpenRefine.

6. *Relation Exploration Block* (Figure 5.1, i). The Relation Exploration Block (RXB) works like the EXB but focuses on the *relationships* between the entities instead of on the individual entities themselves. Upon activation, the RXB displays a form where users can define which relations they want to explore and, optionally, conditions for the related entities. Imagine attaching an RXB to a set of <T>-typed entities sharing a relationship Parenthood that defines the Parent and Child roles. Upon activation, the RXB will display a form where users could ask, for example, to retrieve entities related by Parenthood and the following condition: [Parent.Name]! = [Child.Name]. The resulting EB contains all entities related by Parenthood where the Parent entities have a different Name than their related Child entities. Like the EXB, the RXB allows users to export the retrieved data to a CSV file.

It should be emphasized that *KUbism* is a prototype: It is a functional demo that was designed to evaluate its overall viability, both as a software that supports productive data exploration and as a hedonic-motivation system able to make data exploration a comfortable and compelling experience for users. Therefore, *KUbism* is stripped to its bare essentials. For instance, *KUbism*'s world is empty, featuring only a sky and an endless flat ground. We also limited *KUbism*'s data model to two entities, *actors* and *places*, and two relations, *parenthood* and *baptism*. *Parenthood* is a relation between two *actors* (parent and child), and *baptism* is a relation between an *actor* and their *place* of baptism. We arranged the entities of our simple data model in two columns readily available for participants to interact with, one for the *actors* and the other for the *places* (Figure 5.1, b). Though simplified, *KUbism*'s model is complete enough to test user behavior and experience.[35]

Forty-one users (nineteen male, twenty-two female) participated in the study, which was voluntary and not compensated. Ages ranged from fourteen to fifty-eight years, averaging twenty-nine years old. Regarding education level, one of our participants was a middle-schooler, fifteen were undergraduate students, three had a Bachelor's degree, twelve had a Master's degree, and ten had a PhD. Twenty-six participants worked in the humanities (art history and cultural studies), fourteen in the field of science and technology (computer science and biology)—the one remaining participant is the middle-schooler. Only three participants had any previous (limited) contact with the *Cornelia* database. When questioned about gameplaying frequency on a five-point scale, seventeen participants reported "never" playing video games, eleven played "rarely," three played "monthly," six did so "weekly," and four participants played "daily." As the gameplaying frequency responses are of particular interest to this work, we split our participants in two groups, "Player" and "Non-Player." The former group includes those participants that reported daily, weekly, or monthly playing habits ($n$ = 13) and the latter is composed of those who declared never or rarely playing video games ($n$ = 28).

Before starting the test, we asked participants to read a three-page document that explained the general ideas behind *KUbism*. We then invited the participants to try the controls and ask any questions they might have. Usually, it took less than a couple of minutes before all participants felt comfortable enough to start the test by activating the "question mark" block (Figure 5.1, a). This block presented participants with a form intended to gather their profile data.

Participants were then presented with the first task of the test. We asked users to follow a task-based protocol containing seven challenges or questions about the entities or the relationships in *KUbism*'s data model (Figure 5.2). *KUbism* automatically recorded the time it took for participants to execute each and every challenge in an event log, together with in-game actions like block activation and block placing.

After the test, participants answered two complementary questionnaires to assess their overall user experience with *KUbism*: the System Usability Scale (SUS) and the Hedonic-Motivation System Adoption Model (HMSAM).[36] The SUS is a widely used, technology agnostic model for assessing system usability. The HMSAM aims to evaluate hedonism-oriented systems like video games, focusing on the more intrinsic factors that influence the experience with such systems. It models user experience based on eight constructs: joy, control, focused immersion, temporal dissociation, curiosity, perceived ease of use, perceived usefulness, and, finally, behavioral intention to use. We decided to apply these two questionnaires because of the hybrid nature of our approach, as *KUbism* aims to enhance a utilitarian purpose (data exploration) via a hedonic activity (gameplay).

All participants completed the study's seven tasks successfully. This shows that *KUbism* empowers people with diverse backgrounds to explore data in an accessible and flexible way. This claim is further supported by analysis of the task execution times across participants. The average time was 886 seconds (00:14:46).[37] The only task that took statistically significantly longer to execute was task 6. As this task required participants to explore a *relationship* between entities for the first time (i.e., *parenthood*), it seems there is a learning curve associated with the

| Task | Challenge | Possible Steps to a Solution |
|---|---|---|
| **1** | Find all actors named "Marcus." | 1. Attach an Explore Entities block to the set of all Actors;<br>2. Activate the Explore Entities block with the condition: First Name = "Marcus." |
| **2** | Find all actors with surname "Auwercx." | 1. Attach an Explore Entities block to the set of all Actors;<br>2. Activate the Explore Entities block with the condition: Last Name = "Auwercx." |
| **3** | Find all actors named "Marcus Auwercx." | 1. Connect the blocks produced in tasks 1 and 2 via an Intersection block;<br>2. Activate the Intersection block. |
| **4** | Find all actors with first name "Marcus" or surname "Auwercx." | 1. Connect the blocks produced in tasks 1 and 2 via a Union block;<br>2. Activate the Union block. |
| **5** | Find all actors named "Marcus" without the "Auwercx" surname. | 1. Connect the blocks produced in tasks 1 and 2 via a Difference block;<br>2. Activate the Difference block setting the Task 1 block as the main. |
| **6** | Who were the children of Marcus Auwercx? | 1. Attach an Explore Relations block to the set of all Actors;<br>2. Attach the block produced in task 3 to the Explore Relations block;<br>3. Activate the Explore Relations block imposing a Parenthood relation between the task 3 block (Parents) and the set of all actors (Children). |
| **7** | Where were the children of Marcus Auwercx baptized? | 1. Attach an Explore Relations block to the set of all Places;<br>2. Attach the block produced in task 6 to the Explore Relations block;<br>3. Activate the Explore Relations block imposing a Baptism relation between the task 6 block (Baptized) and the set of all places (Places of Baptism). |

*Figure 5.2* The seven challenges of the authors' task-based user study, along with an efficient path to a solution, in terms of number of steps.

*Source:* The authors, 2019.

exploration of relationships. Interestingly, however, the next task also required the exploration of a relationship (i.e., *baptism*), and there is no significant difference between its execution time and that of tasks 1 to 5. This strongly suggests that the concept and process of exploring relations between entities in *KUbism* is quickly learned and that subsequent exploration of relationships becomes more straightforward.

When we compare task times between the Player and Non-Player groups, quite predictably the former had systematically lower median times for all tasks. However, that difference was only statistically significant for tasks 1, 4, and 6. We can contextualize and explain this as follows. Task 1 was the first time Non-Players interacted with an open-world game, so they felt more hesitant. However, it took Non-Players the shortest amount of time to execute Task 4, which means they learned quickly. As explained previously, task 6 again took them out of their comfort zone. This all suggests that while Players are quicker than Non-Players in learning and applying *KUbism*'s data exploration mechanics, this difference tends to get smaller after the first engagements with the mechanics.

The overall scores for both the SUS and the HMSAM questionnaires are also very encouraging. The median SUS score of eighty across all participants indicates that our participants tended to regard *KUbism*'s usability between "good" and "excellent."[38] Players scored *KUbism*'s usability higher than Non-Players. All of HMSAM's eight dimensions received high median scores across all participants, with *joy* and *curiosity* receiving the highest scores. As *joy* refers to the hedonic quality of the interaction experience and *curiosity* is a precursor of exploratory behavior, we consider this result very important, for *KUbism*'s main goals is to foster search and exploration by making it a positive and curiosity-arousing experience. Unsurprisingly, the Player group had statistically significant higher scores for *joy*, *control*, and *ease of use*, meaning that this group felt more in control of the interaction and had a more pleasurable experience overall. This is in line with the group's higher SUS usability score. Given the widely acknowledged importance of control-related and use-related factors for overall user experience,[39] it is not surprising that people with better gameplay skills find the use of gameplay-based interfaces more pleasurable. The difference between the groups was not statistically significant for the remaining constructs of the HMSAM, i.e. *focused immersion*, *temporal dissociation*, *perceived usefulness*, *behavioral intention to use*, and, of particular importance for our study, *curiosity*. Gaming frequency did *not* appear to have so strong an influence on these dimensions, suggesting that both the more and less experienced players found *KUbism* to be immersive, useful, likely to use in the future, and curiosity-arousing.

*KUbism*'s datascape is scalable, of course, and the *Terasology* engine offers far more interesting design possibilities to enhance user experience. For example, we could think of ways to model networks as (automatically) rendered forests of block-based trees representing family ties. Another interesting line of future development would be to appeal to our drive for social interaction by offering multiplayer gaming modes. Multiple players could engage in collaborative (or even competitive) data exploration. Together, they could discover, generate, and share data subsets. They could also compete toward a goal, such as the construction of data structures that help to address complex research questions.

## Conclusion

Both objective measures (such as completion rate and task time) and the subjective evaluations of the *KUbism* experience, seen from both the SUS's utilitarian perspective and the HMSAM's hedonic perspective, show that *KUbism* is usable, useful, and pleasant to use. With *joy* and *curiosity* as the highest-scoring HMSAM constructs, our open-world game of data explicitly associates data exploration with these dimensions, thus reinforcing the users' innate drive for exploration.

Put differently, *KUbism* can be regarded as a good example of how we can reimagine digital search in an SA-friendly environment. As they leverage our motivation to engage fully with data, the mechanics of open-world gameplay can help us to derive the most value out of the data sets that institutions and individual researchers produce and make digitally accessible—and even add value to them by generating new data containers and data structures in our new datascape

## Acknowledgment

We wish to thank Anne Helmreich, Sandra van Ginhoven and Johanna Drucker for their comments and suggestions that helped to sharpen our thoughts.

## Notes

1. The symposium (April 26th–27th) was organized by Anne Helmreich (Getty Research Institute) and Paul B. Jaskot (Duke University); for a list of the participants, see www.clarkart.edu/ImportedEvents/1415-43656.
2. Roy Rosenzweig, "Scarcity or Abundance? Preserving the Past in a Digital Era," *The American Historical Review* 108, no. 3 (2003): 739.
3. Deb Verhoeven, "As Luck Would Have It: Serendipity and Solace in Digital Research Infrastructure," *Feminist Media Histories* 2, no. 1 (2016): 12.
4. Koenraad Brosens et al., "Slow Digital Art History in Action: Project Cornelia's Computational Approach to 17th-Century Flemish Creative Communities," *Visual Resources (Special Issue on Digital Art History)* 35, no. 1–2 (2019): 105–24, doi:10.1080/01973762.2019.1553444.
5. For a concise introduction to SA and its importance, see Mica R. Endsley, "Situation Awareness: Operationally Necessary and Scientifically Grounded," *Cognition, Technology & Work* 17, no. 2 (2015): 163–67.
6. Mica R. Endsley, "Toward a Theory of Situation Awareness in Dynamic Systems," *Human Factors: The Journal of the Human Factors and Ergonomics Society* 37, no. 1 (1995): 32–64.
7. Ibid., 165.
8. For a discussion of this important metaphor in SA research, see Ann Blandford and B.L. William Wong, "Situation Awareness in Emergency Medical Dispatch," *International Journal of Human-Computer Studies* 61 (2004): 438–42.
9. Mica R. Endsley and Esin O. Kiris, "The Out-of-the-Loop Performance Problem and Level of Control in Automation," *Human Factors: The Journal of the Human Factors and Ergonomics Society* 37, no. 2 (1995): 381–94; Mica R. Endsley and D.G. Jones, *Designing for Situation Awareness: An Approach to Human-Centered Design*, 2nd ed. (London: Taylor and Francis, 2012).
10. Stratos Idreos, Olga Papaemmanouil, and Surajit Chaudhuri, "Overview of Data Exploration Techniques," *Proceedings of the 2015 ACM SIGMOD International Conference on Management of Data* (2015): 277–81, doi:10.1145/2723372.2731084.
11. E.g. Chris Snijders, Uwe Matzat, and Ulf-Dietrich Reips, "*Big Data:* Big Gaps of Knowledge in the Field of Internet Science," *International Journal of Internet Science* 7, no. 1 (2012): 1–5; Idreos et al., "Overview," 277–81.
12. Ju Fan, Guo Liang Li, and Lihzou Zhou, "Interactive SQL Query Suggestion: Making Databases User-Friendly," *Proceedings of the 2011 IEEE 27th International Conference on Data Engineering* (2011), doi:10.1109/ICDE.2011.5767843; Kyriaki Dimitriadou, Olga Papaemmanouil, and Yanlei Diao, "Explore-by-Example: An Automatic Query Steering Framework for Interactive Data Exploration," *Proceedings of the 2014 ACM SIGMOD International Conference on Management of Data* (2014), doi:10.1145/2588555.2610523; Manasi Vartak et al., "SeeDB: Efficient Data-Driven Visualization Recommendations to Support Visual Analytics," *Proceedings of the VLDB Endowment—Proceedings of the 41st International Conference on Very Large Data Bases* (2015): 2182–93, doi:10.14778/2831360.2831371.
13. Verhoeven, "As Luck Would Have It," 16.
14. Abdul Wasay, Manos Athanassoulis, and Idreos Stratos, "Queriosity: Automated Data Exploration," *Proceedings of the 2015 IEEE International Congress on Big Data (BigData Congress)* (2015): 716–19, doi:10.1109/BigDataCongress.2015.116.

15. Jane McGonigal, *Reality Is Broken: Why Games Makes Us Better and How They Can Change the World* (London: Jonathan Cape, 2008).
16. Rosemary Garris, Robert Ahlers, and James E. Driskell, "Games, Motivation, and Learning: A Research and Practice Model," *Simulation & Gaming* 33, no. 4 (2002): 441–67; Juho Hamari, Jonna Koivisto, and Harri Sarsa, "Does Gamification Work? A Literature Review of Empirical Studies on Gamification," in *47th Hawaii International Conference on System Science* (2014), doi:10.1109/HICSS.2014.377; Sara de Freitas, "Are Games Effective Learning Tools? A Review of Educational Games," *Journal of Educational Technology & Society* 21, no. 2 (2018): 74–84.
17. Fotis Liarokapis et al., "Multimodal Serious Games Technologies for Cultural Heritage," in *Mixed Reality and Gamification for Cultural Heritage*, ed. Marinos Ioannides, Nadia Magnenat-Thalmann, and George Papagiannakis (Cham: Springer, 2017), 371–92.
18. E.g. Randall W. Hill et al., "Pedagogically Structured Game-Based Training: Development of the ELECT BILAT Simulation," in *25th Army Science Conference, Orlando, FL* (2006), doi:10.13140/2.1.2902.7520.
19. Francesco Ricciardi and Lucio Tommaso De Paolis, "A Comprehensive Review of Serious Games in Health Professions," *International Journal of Computer Games Technology* (2014): Article No. 9, doi:10.1155/2014/787968.
20. William R. Watson, Christopher J. Mong, and Constance A. Harris, "A Case Study of the In-Class Use of a Video Game for Teaching High School History," *Computers & Education* 56, no. 2 (2011): 466–74, doi:10.1016/j.compedu.2010.09.007. See also Fedwa Laamarti, Mohamad Eid, and Abdulmotaleb El Saddik, "An Overview of Serious Games," *International Journal of Computer Games Technology* (2014): Article No. 11, doi:10.1155/2014/358152.
21. Luis von Ahn, "Games with a Purpose," *Computer* 39, no. 6 (2006): 92–94, doi:10.1109/mc.2006.196.
22. Greg Walsh and Jennifer Golbeck, "Curator: A Game with a Purpose for Collection Recommendation," *Proceedings of the SIGCHI Conference on Human Factors in Computing Systems* (2010): 2079–82, doi:10.1145/1753326.1753643.
23. Edith Law et al., "Tagatune: A Game for Music and Sound Annotation," *Proceedings of the 8th International Conference on Music Information Retrieval* (2007): 361–64.
24. Lisa Pearl and Mark Steyvers, "Identifying Emotions, Intentions, and Attitudes in Text Using a Game with a Purpose," *Proceedings of the NAACL HLT 2010 Workshop on Computational Approaches to Analysis and Generation of Emotion in Text* (2010): 71–79.
25. Amalia Kallergi and Fons J. Verbeek, "Video Games for Collection Exploration: Games For and Out of Data Repositories," *Proceedings of the 14th International Academic MindTrek Conference: Envisioning Future Media Environments* (2010): 143–46, doi:10.1145/1930488.1930518. See also Douglas Heaven, "The Gamers Who Only Want to Explore Virtual Worlds," *NewScientist*, July 23, 2015, www.newscientist.com/article/dn27946-buttonmasher-the-gamers-who-only-want-to-explore-virtual-worlds/.
26. www.minecraft.net/en-us/what-is-minecraft/.
27. *Minecraft* was inspired by *Infiniminer*, a 2009 video game (Windows) created by independent developer Zachary Bart.
28. Darrel M. West and Joshua Bleiberg, "Education Technology Success Stories," *Governance Studies at Brookings* (2013), doi:10.1097/MEG.0b013e32833bce39; Daisuke Saito, Akira Takebayashi and Tsuneo Yamaura, "Minecraft-Based Preparatory Training for Software Development Project," *IEEE International Professional Communication Conference* (2014): 1–9, doi:10.1109/IPCC.2014.7020393; Jessica D. Bayliss, "Teaching Game AI Through Minecraft Mods," *4th International Games Innovation Conference* (2012), doi:10.1109/IGIC.2012.6329841. See also Steve Nebel, Sascha Schneider, and Günter Daniel Rey, "Mining Learning and Crafting Scientific Experiments: A Literature Review on the Use of Minecraft in Education and Research," *Journal of Educational Technology & Society* 19, no. 2 (2016): 355–66.
29. Ivica Bukvic et al., "OPERA*craft*: Blurring the Lines Between Real and Virtual," *Proceedings ICMC|SMC|2014*.
30. www.kallergia.com/projects/pj_of.shtml. Amalia Kallergi and Fons J. Verbeek, "Onto-Frogger: The Making of," *Proceedings of the 6th Nordic Conference on Human-Computer Interaction: Extending Boundaries* (2010): 691–94, doi:10.1145/1868914.1869006.
31. Benjamin Glatzel started the *Terasology* project in early 2011 as an LWJGL-based LightWeight Java Game Library (www.lwjgl.org) Minecraft demo. Later that year Anton Kireev and Rasmus Praestholm connected with Glatzel and together they developed *Terasology* proper.
32. For an introduction to the database, see Koenraad Brosens et al., "MapTap and Cornelia: Slow Digital Art History and Formal Art Historical Social Network Research," *Zeitschrift für Kunstgeschichte* 79 (2016): 315–30.

33. Peter Pin-Shan Chen, "The Entity-Relationship Model: Toward a Unified View of Data," *ACM Transactions on Database Systems (TODS)—Special Issue: Papers from the International Conference on Very Large Data Bases (September 22–24, 1975), Framingham, MA* 1, no. 1 (1976): 9, doi:10.1145/320434.320440.
34. Ibid., 10.
35. For a full discussion and statistical analysis of the tests, see Bruno Cardoso, Koenraad Brosens, and Fred Truyen, "A Game of Data: Kubism, a Block-Based Approach to Data Exploration" (submitted for publication).
36. John Brooke, "SUS—A Quick and Dirty Usability Scale," in *Usability Evaluation in Industry*, ed. P. W Jordan et al. (London: Taylor and Francis, 1996), 189–94; Paul Lowry et al., "Taking 'Fun and Games Seriously: Proposing the Hedonic-Motivation System Adoption Model (HMSAM)," *Journal of the Association for Information Systems* 14, no. 11 (2013): 617–71.
37. The shortest session took 170 seconds (00:02:50) and the longest a total of 1,992 seconds (00:33:12). With the exclusion of tasks 1 and 6, the median time of completion was approximately one minute for all tasks
38. Aaron Bangor, Philip Kortum, and James Miller, "Determining What Individual SUS Scores Mean: Adding an Adjective Rating Scale," *Journal of Usability Studies* 4, no. 3 (2009): 114–23.
39. Ritu Agarwal and Elena Karahanna, "Time Flies When You're Having Fun: Cognitive Absorption and Beliefs About Information Technology Usage," *MIS Quarterly* 24, no. 4 (2000): 665–94; Brooke, "SUS," 189–94; Lowry et al., "Taking," 617–71.

## Bibliography


Agarwal, Ritu, and Elena Karahanna. "Time Flies When You're Having Fun: Cognitive Absorption and Beliefs about Information Technology Usage." *MIS Quarterly* 24, no. 4 (2000): 665–94.

Bangor, Aaron, Philip Kortum, and James Miller. "Determining What Individual SUS Scores Mean: Adding an Adjective Rating Scale." *Journal of Usability Studies* 4, no. 3 (2009): 114–23.

Bayliss, Jessica D. "Teaching Game AI Through Minecraft Mods." In *4th International Games Innovation Conference* (2012). doi:10.1109/IGIC.2012.6329841.

Blandford, Ann, and B. L. William Wong. "Situation Awareness in Emergency Medical Dispatch." *International Journal of Human-Computer Studies* 61 (2004): 421–52.

Brooke, John. "SUS—A Quick and Dirty Usability Scale." In *Usability Evaluation in Industry,* edited by P. W. Jordan et al., 189–94. London: Taylor and Francis, 1996.

Brosens, Koenraad et al. "MapTap and Cornelia: Slow Digital Art History and Formal Art Historical Social Network Research." *Zeitschrift für Kunstgeschichte* 79 (2016): 315–30.

———. "Slow Digital Art History in Action: Project Cornelia's Computational Approach to 17th-Century Flemish Creative Communities." *Visual Resources (Special Issue on Digital Art History)* 35, nos 1–2 (2019): 105–24. doi:10.1080/01973762.2019.1553444.

Bukvic, Ivica et al. "OPERA*craft* : Blurring the Lines between Real and Virtual." *Proceedings ICMC | SMC | 2014*, http://hdl.handle.net/2027/spo.bbp2372.2014.036.

de Freitas, Sara. "Are Games Effective Learning Tools? A Review of Educational Games." *Journal of Educational Technology & Society* 21, no. 2 (2018): 74–84.

Dimitriadou, Kyriaki, Olga Papaemmanouil, and Yanlei Diao. "Explore-by-example: An Automatic Query Steering Framework for Interactive Data Exploration." *Proceedings of the 2014 ACM SIGMOD International Conference on Management of Data* (2014). doi:10.1145/2588555.2610523.

Endsley, Mica R. "Toward a Theory of Situation Awareness in Dynamic Systems." *Human Factors: The Journal of the Human Factors and Ergonomics Society* 37, no. 1 (1995): 32–64.

———. "Situation Awareness: Operationally Necessary and Scientifically Grounded." *Cognition, Technology & Work* 17, no. 2 (2015): 163–67.

Endsley, Mica R., and D. G. Jones. *Designing for Situation Awareness: An Approach to Human-Centered Design*. 2nd ed. London: Taylor & Francis, 2012.

Endsley, Mica R., and Esin O. Kiris. "The Out-of-the-Loop Performance Problem and Level of Control in Automation." *Human Factors: The Journal of the Human Factors and Ergonomics Society* 37, no. 2 (1995): 381–94.

Fan, Ju, Guo Liang Li, and Lihzou Zhou. "Interactive SQL Query Suggestion: Making Databases User-Friendly." *Proceedings of the 2011 IEEE 27th International Conference on Data Engineering* (2011). doi:10.1109/ICDE.2011.5767843.

Garris, Rosemary, Robert Ahlers, and James E. Driskell. "Games, Motivation, and Learning: A Research and Practice Model." *Simulation & Gaming* 33, no. 4 (2002): 441–67.

Hamari, Juho, Jonna Koivisto, and Harri Sarsa. "Does Gamification Work?—A Literature Review of Empirical Studies on Gamification." In *47th Hawaii International Conference on System Science* (2014). doi:10.1109/HICSS.2014.377.

Heaven, Douglas. "The Gamers Who Only Want to Explore Virtual Worlds." *NewScientist*, July 23, 2015. www.newscientist.com/article/dn27946-buttonmasher-the-gamers-who-only-want-to-explore-virtual-worlds/.

Hill, Randall W. et al. "Pedagogically Structured Game-Based Training: Development of the ELECT BILAT Simulation." In *25th Army Science Conference*, Orlando, FL, 2006. doi:10.13140/2.1.2902.7520.

Idreos, Stratos, Olga Papaemmanouil, and Surajit Chaudhuri. "Overview of Data Exploration Techniques." *Proceedings of the 2015 ACM SIGMOD International Conference on Management of Data* (2015): 277–81. doi:10.1145/2723372.2731084.

Kallergi, Amalia, and Fons J. Verbeek. "Onto-Frogger: The Making Of." *Proceedings of the 6th Nordic Conference on Human-Computer Interaction: Extending Boundaries* (2010): 691–94. doi:10.1145/1868914.1869006.

———. "Video Games for Collection Exploration: Games For and Out of Data Repositories." *Proceedings of the 14th International Academic MindTrek Conference: Envisioning Future Media Environments* (2010): 143–46. doi:10.1145/1930488.1930518.

Laamarti, Fedwa, Mohamad Eid, and Abdulmotaleb El Saddik. "An Overview of Serious Games." *International Journal of Computer Games Technology* (2014): Article No. 11. doi:10.1155/2014/358152.

Law, Edith et al. "Tagatune : A Game for Music and Sound Annotation." *Proceedings of the 8th International Conference on Music Information Retrieval* (2007): 361–64.

Liarokapis, Fotis et al. "Multimodal Serious Games Technologies for Cultural Heritage." In *Mixed Reality and Gamification for Cultural Heritage*, edited by Marinos Ioannides, Nadia Magnenat-Thalmann, and George Papagiannakis, 371–92. Cham: Springer, 2017.

Lowry, Paul et al. "Taking 'Fun and Games' Seriously: Proposing the Hedonic-Motivation System Adoption Model (HMSAM)." *Journal of the Association for Information Systems* 14, no. 11 (2013): 617–71.

McGonigal, Jane. *Reality is Broken: Why Games Makes Us Better and How They Can Change the World*. London: Jonathan Cape, 2008.

Nebel, Steve, Sascha Schneider, and Günter Daniel Rey. "Mining Learning and Crafting Scientific Experiments: A Literature Review on the Use of Minecraft in Education and Research." *Journal of Educational Technology & Society* 19, no. 2 (2016): 355–66.

Pearl, Lisa, and Mark Steyvers. "Identifying Emotions, Intentions, and Attitudes in Text Using a Game with a Purpose." *Proceedings of the NAACL HLT 2010 Workshop on Computational Approaches to Analysis and Generation of Emotion in Text* (2010): 71–79.

Pin-Shan Chen, Peter. "The Entity-Relationship Model: Toward a Unified View of Data." *ACM Transactions on Database Systems (TODS)—Special Issue: Papers from the International Conference on Very Large Data Bases (September 22–24, 1975)*, Framingham, MA 1, no. 1 (1976). doi:10.1145/320434.320440.

Ricciardi, Francesco, and Lucio Tommaso De Paolis. "A Comprehensive Review of Serious Games in Health Professions." *International Journal of Computer Games Technology* (2014): Article No. 9. doi:10.1155/2014/787968.

Rosenzweig, Roy. "Scarcity or Abundance? Preserving the Past in a Digital Era." *The American Historical Review* 108, no. 3 (2003): 735–62.

Saito, Daisuke, Akira Takebayashi, and Tsuneo Yamaura. "Minecraft-Based Preparatory Training for Software Development Project." *IEEE International Professional Communication Conference* (2014): 1–9. doi 10.1109/IPCC.2014.7020393.

Snijders, Chris, Uwe Matzat, and Ulf-Dietrich Reips. "*Big Data:* Big Gaps of Knowledge in the Field of Internet Science." *International Journal of Internet Science* 7, no. 1 (2012): 1–5.

Vartak, Manasi et al. "SeeDB: Efficient Data-Driven Visualization Recommendations to Support Visual Analytics." *Proceedings of the VLDB Endowment—Proceedings of the 41st International Conference on Very Large Data Bases* (2015): 2182–93. doi:10.14778/2831360.2831371.

Verhoeven, Deb. "As Luck Would Have It. Serendipity and Solace in Digital Research Infrastructure." *Feminist Media Histories* 2, no. 1 (2016): 7–28.

von Ahn, Luis. "Games with a Purpose." *Computer* 39, no. 6 (2006): 92–94. doi:10.1109/mc.2006.196.

Walsh, Greg, and Jennifer Golbeck. "Curator: A Game with a Purpose for Collection Recommendation." *Proceedings of the SIGCHI Conference on Human Factors in Computing Systems* (2010): 2079–82. doi:10.1145/1753326.1753643.

Wasay, Abdul, Manos Athanassoulis, and Idreos Stratos. "Queriosity: Automated Data Exploration." *Proceedings of the 2015 IEEE International Congress on Big Data (BigData Congress)* (2015): 716–19. doi:10.1109/BigDataCongress.2015.116.

Watson, William R., Christopher J. Mong, and Constance A. Harris. "A Case Study of the In-Class Use of a Video Game for Teaching High School History." *Computers & Education* 56, no. 2 (2011): 466–74. doi: 10.1016/j.compedu.2010.09.007.

West, Darrel M., and Joshua Bleiberg. "Education Technology Success Stories." *Governance Studies at Brookings* (2013). doi:10.1097/MEG.0b013e32833bce39.

# PART II

# Archives, Networks, and Maps

# 6

# TANGLED METAPHORS

## Network Thinking and Network Analysis in the History of Art

*Matthew D. Lincoln*

The rhetoric of networks holds a particular attraction for art historians.[1] Implicit discussions of networks span a wide spectrum of specialties and methodologies within the discipline, and it is quite possible to write productively about art-historical networks without even touching on data, computing, or mathematics. The flow of both technical know-how and academic theory from individual to individual is a central subject of discussions about artistic studios, academies, and kinship networks of artist families. Likewise, the connections between individual artists, patrons, and viewers, and the network concepts of prestige, influence, and of reciprocal versus one-way relationships are central to how art historians discuss patronage and gift-giving.[2] Trade in material goods in the art market; the strategies of artists, buyers, and dealers; and the history of collecting also touch on network concepts of brokerage and community formation.[3] The concept of the network has also been mustered in studies of art historiography to structure narratives about the evolution and spread of disciplinary methodologies, and of central versus peripheral scholars and movements.[4]

As productive as these non-quantitative studies are, computational network analysis—a systematic approach to studying the structures, or networks, that emerge from the interactions of individuals—can further empower this kind of network thinking in two cases that are difficult or impossible to understand *without* computation:

1. When the scales of evidence go beyond what one scholar can keep in his or her head; and/or
2. When the particular research questions require measuring multiple interdependent relationships, in circumstances where even a small number of individuals or links between them can result in complex and often unintuitive results.

As this chapter will demonstrate, art historians focusing on several different periods and cultures have already deployed computational network analysis to explore, analyze, and understand complex patterns in accumulated troves of primary and secondary art-historical sources. The most successful of these attempts have closely engaged with theoretical considerations of network mathematics, treating method as equally important as art-historical questions.[5] To navigate this relationship between method, evidence, and research question means grappling with guidelines for expressing assumptions, manipulating sources, and formulating hypotheses in ways that can seem alien, if not inimical, to those of art historians.

There are wide gaps to bridge between the informal or colloquial understandings of networks as they have been used in earlier art-historical literature and the requirements and outputs of computational network analysis. Miriam Kienle and Stephanie Porras, among others, have outlined the particular opportunities and pitfalls that *visualizations* of network structures present for art historians.[6] However, while it is crucial to understand how different visual idioms shape the construction and interpretation of network visualizations, I will not be retreading this well-covered ground here.

Rather, in this chapter I aim to shift attention to art-historical work that has engaged with the most fundamentally transformative aspects of networks: that measurements one can make of a network transcend the mere sum of its individual constituents and their interconnections These are studies that directly engage concepts from network mathematics, using computation as a way to evaluate evidence in ways not accessible through argumentation via case study or even non-network-based quantitative approaches like counting and averaging. I will identify early prototypes for this type of more formalized art-historical network thinking, and then point to a few recent examples of network analysis that push these methodological boundaries in useful ways.

## Progenitor Networks

Perhaps no art-historical project is more enmeshed in network concepts than the charting of stylistic influence from artist to artist, period to period, and culture to culture. While its favor has waxed and waned, stylistic history is one of the foundational projects of the discipline and still guides much of our practice today. Heinrich Wölfflin himself referred to networks of artistic influence in reference to Albrecht Dürer, albeit in order to argue that Dürer transcended such influences:

> Even if the whole network were visible and we could see what influences he came under we still would not find an answer because genius cannot be explained by an addition of influences.[7]

Rare, though, are the historians who have tried to describe these networks in an explicit and formalized way. The exception that may infamously prove the rule is Alfred Barr's *Diagram of Stylistic Evolution from 1830 until 1935*, a network-like genealogical visualization generated for the Museum of Modern Art's 1936 exhibition *Cubism and Abstract Art* (Figure 6.1).[8] Likely the first image that comes to mind when hearing the term "art-historical network," Barr's diagram has proven to be both a trenchant image as well as an enduring magnet for criticism.[9]

Barr's contemporary Meyer Schapiro expressed his disappointment that the curator had approached the genealogy of Cubism and abstraction solely as a question of style, with no interest in the effects of historical events or social change.[10] More recently, Astrit Burkhardt has interrogated how the schematic clarity of the diagram acts as a screen concealing Barr's politics.[11] For Schapiro, the network paradigm was acceptable; Barr's version of it was merely incomplete. Burkhardt argues, though, that even conceiving of this history as a formalized network was to enforce a teleological and limited view of history. That Barr rendered this network visually, on the cover of a seminal catalogue no less, fortified this reification.

For all its compelling visual clarity, though, Barr's *Diagram* is not a network suitable for mathematical analysis.[12] It is unpredictably multimodal; that is, its constituents have inconsistent

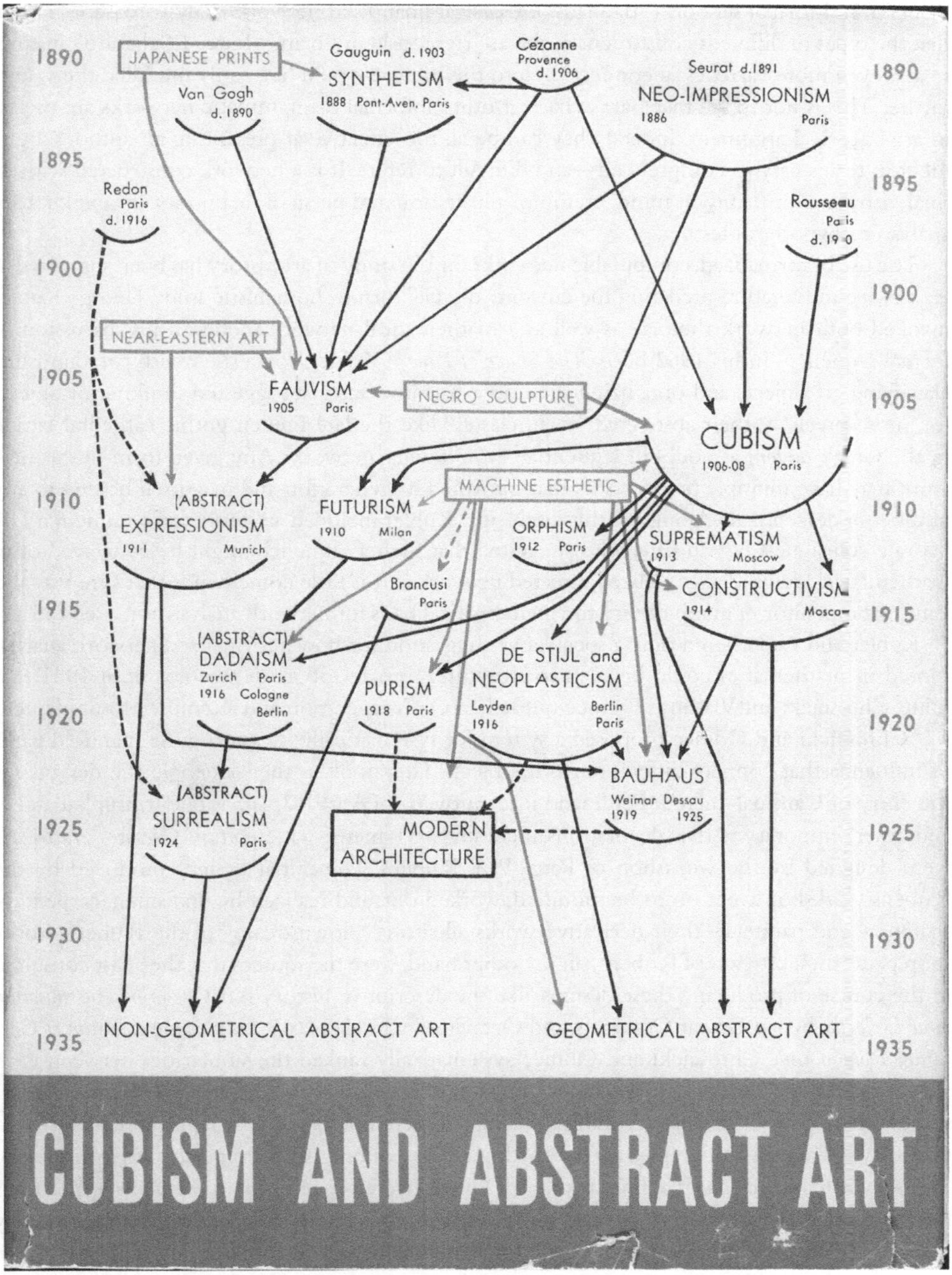


*Figure 6.1* Alfred H. Barr, Jr., "Diagram of Stylistic Evolution from 1830 until 1935," in *Cubism and Abstract Art* (1936), reprint (New York: Museum of Modern Art, 1966).

*Source*: Digital Image © The Museum of Modern Art/Licensed by SCALA/Art Resource, NY.

types, and therefore inconsistent relationship types as well. Its many "isms" ("Fauvism," "Futurism," "Purism," etc.) commingle with named artists ("Cézanne"), media categories ("Japanese Prints"), and formal schools ("Bauhaus"). Classical quantified network analysis requires, rather, that the types of different constituent nodes are rigorously uniform.[13] Indeed, Schapiro's instinct to add even more varieties of connection into this picture would have only muddied the waters further. This is not to say that Barr's chart or other informal diagrammatic networks are useless in art-historical argument. Indeed, they can be all too effective at presenting an author's argument in terms easy to comprehend—and difficult to refute. It is a network constructed with its final visualization firmly in mind, useful for illustration and persuasion, but not for exploratory analysis or hypothesis testing.

The use of formalized, computable networks for the study of art history has been suggested at least twice in literature predating the current "digital" turn in humanistic study. George Kubler invoked both network rhetoric as well as a mathematical network model in his discussion of formal sequences in his 1962 book *The Shape of Time*.[14] Kubler, concerned with paradigms for classifying art objects and organizing them in a narrative history, suggested thinking of objects (or, more precisely, their abstracted "form classes" like the late French gothic cathedral façade or the Greek *rhyton*) as nodes in sequential, evolutionary networks. Any given form in this network may have multiple predecessors that informed its generation and may itself be tied to any number of descendants. Alongside this discussion, Kubler included an illustrated commentary by his Yale colleague Øystein Ore, who suggested that such a sequence might be conceived of in mathematical terms as a formalized directed network.[15] It is little coincidence that Ore was also a major progenitor of graph theory, the mathematical basis for network analysis as it used today.[16]

Kubler and Ore offered only a speculative suggestion for how a formalized network analysis rooted in mathematics could be used to structure histories of art. It was not until 1981 that Julius Chrościcki and Vladimir Odinec unearthed Ore's suggestion and attempted to implement it.[17] Chrościcki and Odinec proposed a system for systematically measuring the manifold paths of influence that connect different artistic objects. They took as their example the designs for the entry of Cardinal-Infante Ferdinand into Antwerp of April 17, 1635. The triumphal arches and other temporary festival decorations, including a 31-meter-wide *Porticus Caesarea-Austriacae*, were designed by the workshop of Peter Paul Rubens. The initial designs produced by the Rubens workshop went on to be modified, worked out, and realized by draftsmen, carpenters, sculptors, and painters—their derivative works all sitting "downstream" of the Rubens workshop patterns. Upstream of Rubens, on the other hand, were the sources that the artist consulted in the course of producing these designs, like the descriptive history *XII Caesarum Austriacorum vitae et elogiae* by Jan Gaspar Gevartius, and Octavius de Strada's 1615 *De vitis imperatorum et Caesarum Romanorum*. Chrościcki and Odinec systematically ranked the similarities between each artwork and their literary/visual sources, generating similarity scores based on a clearly stated (if somewhat arbitrary) formula accounting for shared medium, shared geographical region, shared visual style, shared iconography, and so forth. As if responding to Meyer Schapiro's critique of Barr's stylistic history chart, Chrościcki and Odinec layered much more information into their formulae, adding in semantic, spatial, and political information. But while they exhaustively detailed their method, they offered little in the way of interpretation, presenting only a synthetic overview of the wide array of sources tangential to many artistic projects. And while based on a systematic method, their visualizations, were, to put it mildly, convoluted (Figure 6.2). What would it mean to try and compare two paintings' respective influence networks, and how could those comparisons speak to the histories of those objects? How could one use this approach to characterize entire œuvres or compare the integration or dissolution of influence across different

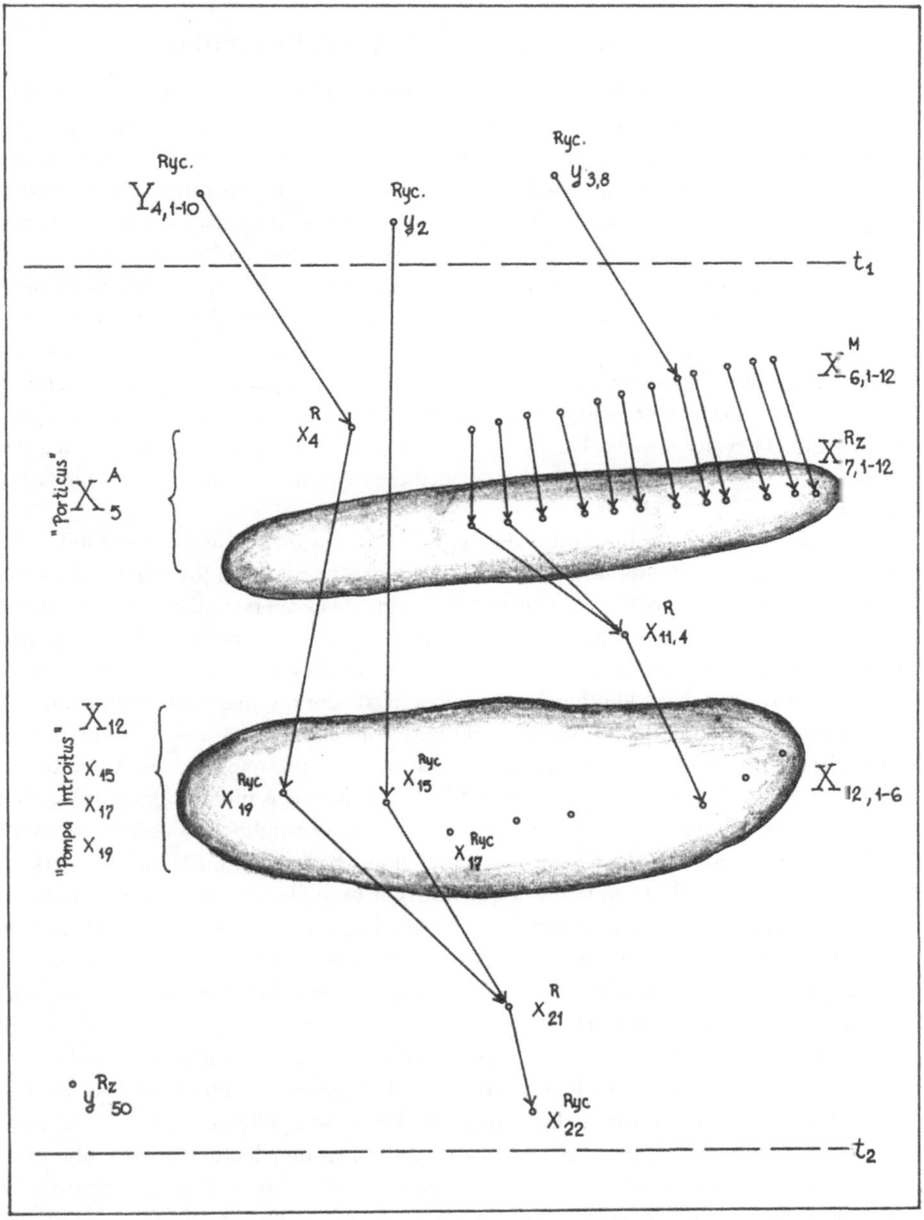


*Figure 6.2* Stanisław Karłowski, “A Graph of Influences on Peter Paul Rubens,” in Juliusz A. Chrościcki and Vladimir P. Odinec, “On Directed Graph Models on Influences in Art Theory,’ *Artibus et Historiae* 2, no. 3 (January, 1981), fig. 19.

*Source*: Artibus et Historiae and IRSA.

regions and periods? Chrościcki and Odinec offered no answers for this. Their approach would draw few imitators.[18]

## From Network Thinking to Network Computing

Much has changed in the last three decades. The formal mathematics of network analysis have moved with force from the realm of theory into that of concrete application. This approach is grounded in the proposition that analyzing the patterns of relations between actors, whether they are people, business firms, biological proteins, or computer circuits, can be just as important as analyzing the individual attributes of those actors.[19] By formalizing data about these relations in a mathematical, and thus computable, model, we can begin to describe and measure patterns of interaction in ways that are difficult or impossible to do manually. Originating in theoretical mathematics and computer science, network analysis was soon adapted by social scientists as a way to bring statistical rigor to models of social interaction.[20] Today, network science comprises a theoretical discipline in its own right that enjoys widespread application in sociology, political science, business management, engineering, computer and information science, neurology, and epidemiology.[21] They are now backed by more user-friendly computational tools, and a much larger variety of data sets, which in turn has opened the field to historians, literary scholars, and art historians.[22]

Formal methods for describing generally fall into two categories: on the one hand, metrics for clarifying the roles and importance of individual nodes or edges; on the other hand, metrics that characterize properties of the entire network.[23] Individuals can be ranked on their centrality, or number of immediate connections; on their relative proximity or peripherality to the rest of the network; on their strength as "brokers" because they hold key positions connecting large sections of the network that would otherwise be unconnected; or on their reach within and across highly connected communities. Entire networks have corollary metrics, among them their relative centralization or diffusion; their degree distribution (how unevenly ties are shared between different members); their density, or number of connections versus number of constituents; the overall propensity of their constituents to cluster into smaller neighborhoods; their transitivity, or tendency for friends of friends to make connections. Both individual- and network-level metrics have little meaning when taken in isolation. For example, a single number representing a network's centralization is uninterpretable outside a larger context. It is in the *comparison* of nodes or networks to one another that the real strength of these measures shines through.

An early example of computational network analysis in art history demonstrates the utility of individual-level metrics: Anne Helmreich's research on the art market networks of the late nineteenth-century firms Goupil & Cie/Boussod and Valadon & Cie analyzed networks formed by the connections of buyers and sellers described by the business records of these dealers. It had commonly been understood that the London art market grew rapidly in size during this period, but the nature of its importance to the global art market, Helmreich argues, is not fully evident without considering the art trade as a dynamic network of artists, dealers, and buyers. Using network visualization techniques to parse the Getty databases, Helmreich discovered that, by the 1870s, the London branches of each of these firms were acting as intermediaries between a surprisingly international range of artists and buyers. Measuring the "betweenness" centrality of individuals, or the number of times that an individual served as a connecting point between two other individuals, made these brokerage roles clear. The London market had not only grown in size, but had become highly central to an international network connecting Britain, continental Europe, and the United States, uniting these regional markets in a way that no city had done before.[24]

Many other studies have followed this pattern by focusing on the individual-level insights derived from network analysis. Marten Jan Bok and Harm Nijboer developed a database of kinship, professional, and geographic relationships between Dutch painters in the sixteenth and seventeenth centuries.[25] Their database is part of a larger umbrella research group dedicated to compiling a wide array of network-like data on early modern northern Europe.[26] Koenraad Brosens, Klara Alen, Astrid Slegten, and Fred Truyen have begun to construct a network model of the seventeenth-century Brussels tapestry industry. They argue that the colloquial understanding of the "network" of tapestry producers in Brussels is, at present, too fragmentary and ill-defined to support the contention that the tapestry industry was largely driven and shaped by patterns of trust and distrust in personal relationships.[27] To augment episodic case studies, Brosens et al. propose mining the rich archives documenting the layers of kinship, artistic, and financial ties that connected tapestry makers in this period.

## Networks Beyond the Sum of Their Parts

Network analysis methods are most impactful, however, for their ability not only to characterize individual positions with networks, but also to describe entire topologies and to show how they can change over time. These measures, such as network density and strength, centralization versus distribution, and assortativity, describe facets of entire communities and represent a distinct shift in art-historical argumentation.

One compelling example is Martin Papenbrock and Joachim Scharloth's work examining shifts in artist exhibitions in Germany as the Nazis began to enforce their cultural policies. By measuring the overall state of networks of artists linked by co-exhibition both before and after 1937, Papenbrock and Scharloth identified a shift from a relatively distributed and locally clustering network in which the same regional groups of artists were commonly exhibited together with little crossover to other regional artists. After 1937, they find a far more centralized exhibition landscape, with a few major artists showing up in many different exhibitions and exerting a homogenizing effect.[28]

Maximilian Schich has also demonstrated how inferring networks from *secondary* sources, that is, mining our own troves of past scholarship, can also produce new insights focused on the overall structure of networks. Schich has analyzed the 1947 *Census of Antique Works of Art and Architecture Known in the Renaissance* as a way of determining which antique sites and monuments tended to be mentioned together.[29] At the large-scale, he has looked at large biographical databases such as the *Allgemeines Künstlerlexikon* and the Getty Union List of Artist Names as proxies for understanding general properties of human cultural networks. Schich et al. found differences between "winner-takes-all" countries such as France, where Paris was far and away the greatest attractor of notable cultural figures, and more distributed countries like Germany, where cultural competition was multi-centric.[30]

Such gestalt measurements of these national cultural networks are not visible from the ground level comparing a handful of individual links at a time, but can only come from looking at the entire network.[31] Here it is not scale alone that provides these new insights, but rather the complex nature of interdependent network structures where often unexpected patterns and behavior emerge once independent links are considered in aggregate. These methods are particularly powerful when used to contrast networks defined by different types of connections between their members. Sometimes these networks may converge: for example, artists coming out of the same studio may also cluster around shared styles. At other times, however, we might expect these communities to form independently of each other, or to even oppose each other (depending on the nature of your workplace, you may actively try to ensure that your network of close friends does *not* overlap with your networks of coworkers!). Network analysis offers several tools for measuring the extent to which one set of relationships parallels or diverges from another. Such a multidimensional analysis is difficult or impossible to do without resorting to some kind of data-based approach.

Yael Rice has productively deployed this approach in a study on the studio networks of illustrators for Mughal manuscripts.[32] She assembled multiple networks of illustrators connected by virtue of having illustrated the same segment of a manuscript. The links assembled from an entire manuscript project resulted in networks connecting a dozen or more named illustrators. Rice hypothesized that family relationships would have explained many of these network connections. Surprisingly, though, the manuscript networks defied this expectation, instead suggesting that familial relationships had a far weaker connection to manuscript projects. Moreover, the instability of the network from project to project—with very few relationships between illustrations persisting from one manuscript to the next—complicated the assumption that that workshops were long-lived or influential organizers.

The study of collaborative production in early modern Dutch and Flemish printmaking has also benefited from a network perspective. Drawing on two major corpora of artistic etchings and engravings, I have analyzed the professional relationships of print designers, plate cutters and publishers from 1550 to 1750 in order to understand how printmaking collaborations aligned (or did not) with regional and national borders, and how those dynamics changed over the course of the sixteenth through the eighteenth centuries.[33] Rather than naively accepting modern catalogers' national labels, this analysis compared those labels against the communities described by the surviving artworks themselves, charting a history in which the cohesion of different printmaking communities ebbed and flowed and offering a distinct alternative to existing narratives structured around national and regional schools.

These approaches show how data-driven, quantitative approaches can be used to clarify and characterize fuzzy and complex social relations, rather than speciously flatten them. As Rice demonstrates, by accepting complicated categories *provisionally*, and counting and computing on those categories in order to interrogate their validity and strength over historical time, network analysis can introduce nuance and complexity rather than suppress it.[34]

## Identifying Productive Limits

Like any research methodology, network analysis has important limitations. Kienle and Porras have written eloquently on the drawbacks of network analysis in the study of the history of art in particular.[35] Network analyses are constrained by how one chooses to define the nodes belonging to the network and the edges that interconnect them. As noted previously, classical approaches to network analysis require that nodes must be of one type (e.g. all people or all artworks) and the edges between them must similarly have the same ontological status (e.g. a network of people may have edges that all represent kinship relations, or correspondence, or co-membership in organizations) in order for the aforementioned metrics such as centrality and clustering to have any meaning. Any quantitative measure derived from that data structure is, obviously, governed by those original decisions. An inappropriately formulated research question will still return network metrics, but they may mean very little indeed.

Deciding how to reshape selected archival and material evidence into network data is, therefore, a heavily loaded activity. Nonsensical decisions made during this construction will lead to nonsensical results. For example, if one constructs a network of all the correspondence to an individual from that person's preserved papers, that person will appear to be extremely central in the resulting network—a disappointing result if one had hoped to gain insight into a larger social network. But such a skewed view is inevitable when the constructing principles—trying to use one person's archive to understand a larger social network—was fundamentally flawed.

That said, the process of attempting to formalize and operationalize a research question into a strict framework like network analysis can be quite productive, even when it fails. Michelle Moravec has written about this phenomenon in her work on networks of feminist art texts.[36] In part of her project, Moravec sought to trace the reprinting of key manifestos within a large corpus of American periodicals from 1969 to 2013. However, the resulting network of reprintings was extremely sparse, with evidence of only two manifestos reprinted within the corpus of periodicals she was studying. Rather than dismissing this as a case of insufficient data, Moravec instead focused on the information communicated by this absence; "on a deeper level," she writes, "the very premise that feminist periodicals circulated manifestos turned out to be flawed."[37] Delving further into a textual analysis of the words in the corpus, she discovered that the term "manifesto" was, itself, used only rarely, and decreased over the period she studied. Expecting a very rich network of republishing and re-citation in printed periodicals, Moravec instead found much subtler and unexpected connections and paths for transmission of feminist ideas. In this case, it was not the quantitative results of network analysis that supported new interpretations but instead the very process of constructing the analysis that led to new insights. Its rigid methodological confines compelled Moravec to examine her sources and the assumptions underlying her research more closely.

## Conclusion: Networking, Creatively

For all the recent attention that art historians have accorded network analysis, most still view it with trepidation. Part of this discomfort may stem from the explicit distancing from the individual object that network analysis, or any other kind of quantitative analysis, enforces. Kubler voiced this concern in *The Shape of Time*:

> It is disturbing to those who value the individuality of a thing to have that individuality diminished by classifications and generalizations. We are caught between difficulties: single things are extremely complicated entities, so complicated that we can pretend to understand them only by generalizing about them. One way out is frankly to accept the complexity of single things. Once their difficulty is conceded, it is possible to find aspects that can be used in comparisons. No such trait now known is unitary or fundamental: every trait of a thing is both a cluster of subordinate traits as well as a subordinate part of another cluster.[38]

Kubler's sentiments are hardly revolutionary. Yet it is still necessary to acknowledge this inevitable distancing in the context of computationally aided studies, which are often challenged (sometimes fairly; often not) as un-nuanced.[39] It is true that objects, artistic ones particularly so, resist both the structured description and the abstraction that computational methods rely upon. Compared to structured data for libraries' generally homogeneous collections of books, for example, museums do not yet have interoperable standards for describing their heterogeneous collections of unique objects. While library data is generally produced through broad consensus about the facts of a book's publication and classification, knowledge about historical objects tends to be advanced through iterative and conflicting scholarly argumentation—a difficult (though not impossible) process to represent in a database.[40]

The contingency of image and physical object in art-historical interpretation further complicates efforts to integrate analogous methods into our discipline. Certainly, not all art-historical questions ought to be expressed as structured data. The precision that would be required for certain types of description—for example, how the artist manipulated a particular pigment in a certain section of a painting, and the interplay between that technique and its visual effect—recalls the specter of Jorge Luis Borges' impossibly mimetic 1:1 map.[41]

Even facing this, network analysis has much to offer in sifting these stockpiles of art-historical knowledge. Art history tends to privilege an individualist perspective that, in its best instances, results in compelling and detailed accounts of artists' personal circumstances and influences. In its worst instances, however, this individualist perspective constructs the artist as a genius who transcends all material and social circumstances.[42] At times when we do wish to characterize larger movements (one is again reminded of Barr's *Diagram*), we sometimes struggle to reconcile the wealth of material evidence with comprehensible, synthetic theories that still account for the place of the individual artist.

Network analysis offers a bridge between these micro-scales and macro-scales because its representations are explicitly constructed from information about individual people, objects, actions, and ideas. We will retain the ability to drill into a particular connection and identify the physical objects that are being used to justify it. Frequent reference back to this micro-scale view will be necessary to avoid losing the trees for the forest, as it were.[43] This multi-scalar approach often reveals how varied both networks, and the positions and choices of individuals that constitute them, can appear based on one's frame of reference.

While art historians have long thought about networks in a colloquial sense, I hope to have made clear that formalized, computational network analysis presents an excellent opportunity for new research, even as it challenges our current usage of the term. Quantitative techniques do demand a certain level of abstraction. As we have seen, often the mere act of abstracting can itself compel us productively to generalize, identifying important commonalities and categories within our subject of study. At the same time, these approaches also require practitioners to be particularly precise in their assumptions, hypotheses, and descriptions of evidence. Yet the examples of network analysis both in art history as well as in other humanistic fields presented here demonstrate that these considerations are not all that far removed from the same concerns in "traditional" art history. While this approach has garnered attention when used on data sets of thousands or millions of records, we have seen that it can also hold useful surprises when applied to much smaller data sets, such as Rice's manuscript data that spanned just a few hundred links. In that case, it was not scale of evidence, but rather the nuance of the question—trying to characterize gestalt differences between networks of relationships—that made computational network analysis invaluable. Framed as such, networks and their measurement are not a means for cordoning off open-ended questions, but instead serve as a way to further them with new evidence, making more explicit the process of humanistic modeling that art historians are already doing.

## Notes

1. In network analysis, the terms "network" and "graph" are often used interchangeably when referring to an information structure comprising nodes and interconnections between them. For the sake of consistency, this chapter will use the term "network." However, note that some cited articles may use the term "graph" instead.
2. Network rhetoric is particularly frequent in scholarship on patronage in the Italian Renaissance: F.W. Kent, "Individuals and Families as Patrons of Culture in Quattrocento Florence," in *Language and Images of Renaissance Italy*, ed. Alison Brown (Oxford: Clarendon, 1995); Evelyn S. Welch, "Women as Patrons and Clients in the Courts of Quattrocento Italy," in *Women in Italian Renaissance Culture and Society*, ed. Letizia Panizza (Oxford: European Humanities Research Centre, 2000); on networks

in gift-giving, see Michael Zell, "The Gift Among Friends: Rembrandt's Art in the Network of His Patronal and Social Relations," in *Rethinking Rembrandt*, eds. Alan Chong and Michael Zell (Boston: Isabella Gardner Stewart Museum, 2002); Michael Zell, "Rembrandt's Gifts: A Case Study of Actor-Network-Theory," *Journal of Historians of Netherlandish Art* 3, no. 2 (2011); Carrie Anderson, "Material Mediators: Johan Maurits, Textiles, and the Art of Diplomatic Exchange," *Journal of Early Modern History* 20, no. 1 (January 2016): 63–85, https://doi.org/10.1163/15700658-12342489.

3. Lea Saint-Raymond and Antoine Courtin, "Enriching and Cutting: How to Visualize Networks Thanks to Linked Open Data Platforms," *Artl@s Bulletin* 6, no. 3 (November 2017), http://docs.lib.purdue.edu/artlas/vol6/iss3/7.
4. See in particular Elizabeth Mansfield, ed., *Art History and Its Institutions: The Nineteenth Century* (Routledge, 2002), pt. II; network rhetoric has been especially relevant to discussions of feminist art and art history: Mary D. Garrard, "Feminist Politics: Networks and Organizations," in *The Power of Feminist Art: The American Movement of the 1970s, History and Impact*, eds. Norma Broude and Mary D. Garrard (New York: H. N. Abrams, 1994); Michelle Moravec, "Toward a History of Feminism, Art, and Social Movements in the United States," *Frontiers: A Journal of Women Studies* 33, no. 2 (2012): 22–54, https://muse.jhu.edu/journals/frontiers/v033/33.2.moravec.html.
5. Broader issues surrounding method-borrowing in a humanities context are explored by Willard McCarty, "Becoming Interdisciplinary," in *Proceedings of Digital Humanities 2013* (Lincoln: University of Nebraska, 2013), http://dh2013.unl.edu/abstracts/ab-107.html.
6. Miriam Kienle, "Between Nodes and Edges: Possibilities and Limits of Network Analysis in Art History," *Artl@s Bulletin* 6, no. 3 (November 2017), http://docs.lib.purdue.edu/artlas/vol6/iss3/1; Stephanie Porras, "Keeping Our Eyes Open: Visualizing Networks and Art History," *Artl@s Bulletin* 6, no. 3 (November 2017), http://docs.lib.purdue.edu/artlas/vol6/iss3/3.
7. Heinrich Wölfflin, *The Art of Albrecht Dürer (1905)*, trans. Alastair Grieve and Heide Grieve (New York: Phaidon, 1971), 41–42.
8. Alfred H. Barr Jr., *Cubism and Abstract Art [1936]*, Reprint (New York: Museum of Modern Art, 1966).
9. MoMA revisited the diagram in digital form (www.moma.org/interactives/exhibitions/2012/inventingabstraction) as an online companion for Leah Dickerman and Matthew Affron, *Inventing Abstraction, 1910–1925: How a Radical Idea Changed Modern Art* (New York: Museum of Modern Art, 2012).
10. Meyer Schapiro, "The Nature of Abstract Art (1937)," in *Modern Art: 19th & 20th Century: Selected Papers*, vol. 2 (New York: George Braziller, 1978), 189.
11. Astrit Schmidt Burkhardt, "Shaping Modernism: Alfred Barr's Genealogy of Art," *Word & Image* 16, no. 4 (October 2000): 387–400, https://doi.org/10.1080/02666286.2000.10435694.
12. For one experimental attempt to use formal analysis on the Barr chart, see Yanan Sun, "From Diagram to Network: A Multi-Mode Network Approach to Analyze Diagrams of Art History," in *Social Informatics*, ed. Akiyo Nadamoto et al., Lecture Notes in Computer Science, vol. 8359 (Berlin and Heidelberg: Springer, 2014), 100–9.
13. There are methods in network analysis for measuring and comparing "multimodal" networks containing heterogeneous node and edge types; see, for example, John Frederick Padgett and Walter W. Powell, "The Problem of Emergence," in *The Emergence of Organizations and Markets*, eds. John Frederick Padgett and Walter W. Powell (Princeton, NJ: Princeton University Press, 2012), 1–31; and the review paper Mikko Kivelä et al., "Multilayer Networks," *Journal of Complex Networks* 2, no. 3 (September 2014): 203–71, https://doi.org/10.1093/comnet/cnu016; however classic measures used in most art-historical network analysis literature to date, such as varieties of node- or network-level centrality, do require a strictly unimodal network.
14. George Kubler, *The Shape of Time: Remarks on the History of Things* (New Haven, CT: Yale University Press, 1962).
15. Ibid., 33–34, note 3.
16. Øystein Ore, *Theory of Graphs* (Providence, RI: American Mathematical Society, 1962).
17. Juliusz A. Chrościcki and Vladimir P. Odinec, "On Directed Graph Models on Influences in Art Theory," *Artibus et Historiae* 2, no. 3 (January 1981): 113–30, https://doi.org/10.2307/1483105.
18. A variation on Chrościcki's and Odinec's work can be found in Günther Korbel, "Eine Typologie von Portweinflaschen mit Hilfe eines Dreieckdiagramms: der methodologische Aspekt," *Zeitschrift Für Archäologie Des Mittelalters* no. 11 (1983): 109–14.
19. Robert A. Hanneman and Mark Riddle, *Introduction to Social Network Methods* (Riverside: University of California, Riverside, 2005), 15, http://faculty.ucr.edu/~hanneman/nettext/.

20. For a concise and eminently readable historiography of social network analysis, see Christina Prell, *Social Network Analysis: History, Theory and Methodology* (Los Angeles: Sage, 2011), Ch. 2.
21. A landmark paper in historical network analysis comes from historical sociology: John F. Padgett and Christopher K. Ansell, "Robust Action and the Rise of the Medici, 1400–1434," *American Journal of Sociology* 98, no. 6 (May 1993): 1259–319.
22. The wider field of historical network analysis is far too broad to survey here, however Charles Wetherell, "Historical Social Network Analysis," *International Review of Social History* 43, no. S6 (December 1998): 125–44, https://doi.org/10.1017/S0020859000115123; Claire Lemercier, "12. Formal Network Methods in History: Why and How?" in *Social Networks, Political Institutions, and Rural Societies*, vol. 11, Rural History in Europe 11 (Brepols Publishers, 2015), 281–310, www.brepolsonline.net/doi/10.1484/M.RURHE-EB.4.00198 offer vital overviews in the discipline of history.
23. Outside the scope of this chapter are predictive network models; methods intended not only to describe networks as measured but to attempt to find generalizable rules for predicting the existence of relationships between any two nodes based on those nodes' own attributes as well as their connective patterns to neighbors. Predictive graph models are a promising frontier for art-historical network analysis, but are as-yet untapped by scholars in this field. For a cogent application of these models, see S.J. Cranmer and B.A. Desmarais, "Inferential Network Analysis with Exponential Random Graph Models," *Political Analysis* 19, no. 1 (January 2011): 66–86, https://doi.org/10.1093/pan/mpq037.
24. See Anne Helmreich, "The Global: Goupil & Cie/Boussod, Valadon & Cie and International Networks," in *Local/Global: Mapping Nineteenth-Century London's Art Market*, ed. Pamela M. Fletcher and Anne Helmreich, *Nineteenth-Century Art Worldwide* 11, no. 3 (2012), www.19thc-artworldwide.org/index.php/autumn12/fletcher-helmreich-mapping-the-london-art-market.
25. Marten Jan Bok and Harm Nijboer, "ECARTICO: Linking Cultural Industries in the Early Modern Low Countries, c. 1475–c. 1725," 2014, www.vondel.humanities.uva.nl/ecartico/.
26. Charles van den Heuvel and Leonor Álvarez Francés, "Report Knaw Project: Mapping Notes and Nodes in Networks," November 2014, www.huygens.knaw.nl/wp-content/uploads/2015/05/EndReportMNN.pdf
27. Koenraad Brosens et al., "MapTap and Cornelia: Slow Digital Art History and Formal Art Historical Social Network Research," *Zeitschrift Für Kunstgeschichte* 79 (2016): 1–14.
28. Martin Papenbrock and Joachim Scharloth, "Datengeleitete Analyse kunsthistorischer Daten am Beispiel von Ausstellungskatalogen aus der NS-Zeit: Musteridentifizierung und Visualisierung," *Kunstgeschichte* (May 2011): esp. 17–18, www.kunstgeschichte-ejournal.net/248/.
29. Maximilian Schich, "Netzwerke von Komplexen Netzwerken in Der (Kunst) Wissenschaft," in *Die Dynamik Sozialer Und Sprachlicher Netzwerke Konzepte, Methoden Und Empirische Untersuchungen an Beispielen Des WWW*, ed. Barbara Frank-Job, Alexander Mehler, and Tilmann Sutter (Wiesbaden: Springer, 2013), 161–78.
30. Maximilian Schich et al., "A Network Framework of Cultural History," *Science* 345, no. 6196 (January 2014): 558–62, https://doi.org/10.1126/science.1240064.
31. It is important to acknowledge, however, that extremely macro views such as that pursued by Schich et al. have come under criticism for overly simplifying their subject matter, making claims about human culture writ large based on biographical databases restricted largely to figures from Western history. See Mark Byrnes, "What We Can and Can't Learn from 2,000 Years of Migration Data for 'Western Intellectuals,'" *The Atlantic: CityLab* (blog), August 2014, www.citylab.com/tech/2014/08/what-we-can-and-cant-learn-from-2000-years-of-migration-data-for-western-intellectuals/375485/; Kienle, "Between Nodes and Edges," 5.
32. Yael Rice, "Workshop as Network: A Case Study from Mughal South Asia," *Artl@s Bulletin* 6, no. 3 (November 2017), http://docs.lib.purdue.edu/artlas/vol6/iss3/4.
33. Matthew Lincoln, "Continuity and Disruption in European Networks of Print Production, 1550–1750," *Artl@s Bulletin* 6, no. 3 (November 2017): Article 2, http://docs.lib.purdue.edu/artlas/vol6/iss3/2.
34. On this use of provisional categorization, see Leslie McCall, "The Complexity of Intersectionality," *Signs: Journal of Women in Culture and Society* 30, no. 3 (March 2005): 1771–800, https://doi.org/10.1086/426800.
35. Kienle, "Between Nodes and Edges"; Porras, "Keeping Our Eyes Open."
36. Michelle Moravec, "Network Analysis and Feminist Artists," *Artl@s Bulletin* 6, no. 3 (November 2017), http://docs.lib.purdue.edu/artlas/vol6/iss3/5.

37. Moravec, "Network Analysis and Feminist Artists," 74.
38. Kubler, *The Shape of Time*, 36.
39. For a provocative take on this critique, see Kieran Healy, "Fuck Nuance," in *Annual Meetings of the American Sociological Association* (Chicago, 2015), http://kieranhealy.org/files/papers/fuck-nuance.pdf
40. Diane M. Zorich, "Library and Museum Information: Beauty and the Beast," *Spectra* 18, no. 4 (1991): 3.
41. Jorge Luis Borges, *A Universal History of Iniquity*, trans. Andrew Hurley (New York: Penguin, 2004).
42. The classic critique of the (male) genius artist construct is found in Griselda Pollock, *Vision and Difference: Femininity, Feminism, and Histories of Art* (New York: Routledge, 1988).
43. On this critique of network analysis, see Mustafa Emirbayer and Jeff Goodwin, "Network Analysis, Culture, and the Problem of Agency," *American Journal of Sociology* 99, no. 6 (May 1994): 1415, www.jstor.org/stable/2782580.

## Bibliography


Anderson, Carrie. "Material Mediators: Johan Maurits, Textiles, and the Art of Diplomatic Exchange." *Journal of Early Modern History* 20, no. 1 (January 2016): 63–85. https://doi.org/10.1163/15700658-12342489.

Barr, Alfred Jr., H. *Cubism and Abstract Art [1936]*. Reprint. New York: Museum of Modern Art, 1966.

Bok, Marten Jan, and Harm Nijboer. "ECARTICO: Linking Cultural Industries in the Early Modern Low Countries, ca. 1475-ca. 1725." 2014. www.vondel.humanities.uva.nl/ecartico/.

Borges, Jorge Luis. *A Universal History of Iniquity*. Translated by Andrew Hurley. New York: Penguin, 2004.

Brosens, Koenraad, Klara Alen, Astrid Slegten, and Fred Truyen. "MapTap and Cornelia: Slow Digital Art History and Formal Art Historical Social Network Research." *Zeitschrift Für Kunstgeschichte* 79 (2016): 1–14.

Burkhardt, Astrit Schmidt. "Shaping Modernism: Alfred Barr's Genealogy of Art." *Word & Image* 16, no. 4 (October 2000): 387–400. https://doi.org/10.1080/02666286.2000.10435694.

Byrnes, Mark. "What We Can and Can't Learn from 2,000 Years of Migration Data for 'Western Intellectuals.'" *The Atlantic: CityLab* (blog), August 2014. www.citylab.com/tech/2014/08/what-we-can-and-cant-learn-from-2000-years-of-migration-data-for-western-intellectuals/375485/.

Chrościcki, Juliusz A., and Vladimir P. Odinec. "On Directed Graph Models on Influences in Art Theory." *Artibus et Historiae* 2, no. 3 (January 1981): 113–30. https://doi.org/10.2307/1483105.

Cranmer, S. J., and B. A. Desmarais. "Inferential Network Analysis with Exponential Random Graph Models." *Political Analysis* 19, no. 1 (January 2011): 66–86. https://doi.org/10.1093/pan/mpq037.

Dickerman, Leah, and Matthew Affron. *Inventing Abstraction, 1910–1925: How a Radical Idea Changed Modern Art*. New York: Museum of Modern Art, 2012.

Emirbayer, Mustafa, and Jeff Goodwin. "Network Analysis, Culture, and the Problem of Agency." *American Journal of Sociology* 99, no. 6 (May 1994): 1411–54. www.jstor.org/stable/2782580.

Fletcher, Pamela M., and Anne Helmreich. "Local/Global: Mapping Nineteenth-Century London's Art Market." *Nineteenth-Century Art Worldwide* 11, no. 3 (2012). www.19thc-artworldwide.org/index.php/autumn12/fletcher-helmreich-mapping-the-london-art-market.

Garrard, Mary D. "Feminist Politics: Networks and Organizations." In *The Power of Feminist Art: The American Movement of the 1970s, History and Impact*, edited by Norma Broude and Mary D. Garrard. New York: H. N. Abrams, 1994.

Hanneman, Robert A., and Mark Riddle. *Introduction to Social Network Methods*. Riverside: University of California, Riverside, 2005. http://faculty.ucr.edu/~hanneman/nettext/.

Healy, Kieran. "Fuck Nuance." Chicago, 2015. http://kieranhealy.org/files/papers/fuck-nuance.pdf

Kent, F. W. "Individuals and Families as Patrons of Culture in Quattrocento Florence." In *Language and Images of Renaissance Italy*, edited by Alison Brown. Oxford: Clarendon, 1995.

Kienle, Miriam. "Between Nodes and Edges: Possibilities and Limits of Network Analysis in Art History." *Artl@s Bulletin* 6, no. 3 (November 2017). http://docs.lib.purdue.edu/artlas/vol6/iss3/1.

Kivelä, Mikko, Alex Arenas, Marc Barthelemy, James P. Gleeson, Yamir Moreno, and Mason A. Porter. "Multilayer Networks." *Journal of Complex Networks* 2, no. 3 (September 2014): 203–71. https://doi.org/10.1093/comnet/cnu016.

Korbel, Günther. "Eine Typologie von Portweinflaschen mit Hilfe eines Dreieckdiagramms: der methodologische Aspekt." *Zeitschrift Für Archäologie Des Mittelalters*, no. 11 (1983): 109–14.

Kubler, George. *The Shape of Time: Remarks on the History of Things*. New Haven: Yale University Press, 1962.

Lemercier, Claire. "12. Formal Network Methods in History: Why and How?" In *Social Networks, Political Institutions, and Rural Societies*, vol. 11, 281–310. Rural History in Europe 11. Brepols Publishers, 2015. www.brepolsonline.net/doi/10.1484/M.RURHE-EB.4.00198.

Lincoln, Matthew. "Continuity and Disruption in European Networks of Print Production, 1550–1750." *Artl@s Bulletin* 6, no. 3 (November 2017): Article 2. http://docs.lib.purdue.edu/artlas/vol6/iss3/2.

Mansfield, Elizabeth, ed. *Art History and Its Institutions: The Nineteenth Century*. Abingdon: Routledge, 2002.

McCall, Leslie. "The Complexity of Intersectionality." *Signs: Journal of Women in Culture and Society* 30, no. 3 (March 2005): 1771–1800. https://doi.org/10.1086/426800.

McCarty, Willard. "Becoming Interdisciplinary." In *Proceedings of Digital Humanities 2013*. Lincoln: University of Nebraska, 2013. http://dh2013.unl.edu/abstracts/ab-107.html.

Moravec, Michelle. "Network Analysis and Feminist Artists." *Artl@s Bulletin* 6, no. 3 (November 2017). http://docs.lib.purdue.edu/artlas/vol6/iss3/5.

———. "Toward a History of Feminism, Art, and Social Movements in the United States." *Frontiers: A Journal of Women Studies* 33, no. 2 (2012): 22–54. https://muse.jhu.edu/journals/frontiers/v033/33.2.moravec.html.

Ore, Øystein. *Theory of Graphs*. Providence: American Mathematical Society, 1962.

Padgett, John F., and Christopher K. Ansell. "Robust Action and the Rise of the Medici, 1400–1434." *American Journal of Sociology* 98, no. 6 (May 1993): 1259–319.

Padgett, John Frederick, and Walter W. Powell. "The Problem of Emergence." In *The Emergence of Organizations and Markets*, edited by John Frederick Padgett and Walter W. Powell, 1–31. Princeton: Princeton University Press, 2012.

Papenbrock, Martin, and Joachim Scharloth. "Datengeleitete Analyse kunsthistorischer Daten am Beispiel von Ausstellungskatalogen aus der NS-Zeit: Musteridentifizierung und Visualisierung." *Kunstgeschichte*. May 2011. www.kunstgeschichte-ejournal.net/248/.

Pollock, Griselda. *Vision and Difference: Femininity, Feminism, and Histories of Art*. New York: Routledge, 1988.

Porras, Stephanie. "Keeping Our Eyes Open: Visualizing Networks and Art History." *Artl@s Bulletin* 6, no. 3 (November 2017). http://docs.lib.purdue.edu/artlas/vol6/iss3/3.

Prell, Christina. *Social Network Analysis: History, Theory and Methodology*. Los Angeles: Sage, 2011.

Rice, Yael. "Workshop as Network: A Case Study from Mughal South Asia." *Artl@s Bulletin* 6, no. 3 (November 2017). http://docs.lib.purdue.edu/artlas/vol6/iss3/4.

Saint-Raymond, Lea, and Antoine Courtin. "Enriching and Cutting: How to Visualize Networks Thanks to Linked Open Data Platforms." *Artl@s Bulletin* 6, no. 3 (November 2017). http://docs.lib.purdue.edu/artlas/vol6/iss3/7.

Schapiro, Meyer. "The Nature of Abstract Art (1937)." In *Modern Art: 19th & 20th Century: Selected Papers*, vol. 2. New York: George Braziller, 1978.

Schich, Maximilian. "Netzwerke von Komplexen Netzwerken in Der (Kunst) Wissenschaft." In *Die Dynamik Sozialer Und Sprachlicher Netzwerke Konzepte, Methoden Und Empirische Untersuchungen an Beispielen Des WWW*, edited by Barbara Frank-Job, Alexander Mehler, and Tilmann Sutter, 161–78. Wiesbaden: Springer, 2013.

Schich, Maximilian, Chaoming Song, Yong-Yeol Ahn, Alexander Mirsky, Mauro Martino, Albert-László Barabási, and Dirk Helbing. "A Network Framework of Cultural History." *Science* 345, no. 6196 (January 2014): 558–62. https://doi.org/10.1126/science.1240064.

Sun, Yanan. "From Diagram to Network: A Multi-Mode Network Approach to Analyze Diagrams of Art History." In *Social Informatics*, edited by Akiyo Nadamoto, Adam Jatowt, Adam Wierzbicki, and Jochen L. Leidner, 100–9. Lecture Notes in Computer Science 8359. Berlin and Heidelberg: Springer, 2014.

van den Heuvel, Charles, and Leonor Álvarez Francés. "Report Knaw Project: Mapping Notes and Nodes in Networks." November 2014. www.huygens.knaw.nl/wp-content/uploads/2015/05/EndReport MNN.pdf

Welch, Evelyn S. "Women as Patrons and Clients in the Courts of Quattrocento Italy." In *Women in Italian Renaissance Culture and Society*, edited by Letizia Panizza. Oxford: European Humanities Research Centre, 2000.

Wetherell, Charles. "Historical Social Network Analysis." *International Review of Social History* 43, Supplement S6 (December 1998): 125–44. https://doi.org/10.1017/S0020859000115123.

Wölfflin, Heinrich. *The Art of Albrecht Dürer (1905)*. Translated by Alastair Grieve and Heide Grieve. New York: Phaidon, 1971.

Zell, Michael. "The Gift Among Friends: Rembrandt's Art in the Network of His Patronal and Social Relations." In *Rethinking Rembrandt*, edited by Alan Chong and Michael Zell. Boston: Isabella Gardner Stewart Museum, 2002.

———. "Rembrandt's Gifts: A Case Study of Actor-Network-Theory." *Journal of Historians of Netherlandish Art* 3, no. 2 (2011).

Zorich, Diane M. "Library and Museum Information: Beauty and the Beast." *Spectra* 18, no. 4 (1991): 2–8.

# 7

# DIGITAL HUMANITIES FOR A SPATIAL, GLOBAL, AND SOCIAL HISTORY OF ART

*Béatrice Joyeux-Prunel*

Digital spatial technologies are contributing to a dramatic renewal of global and social approaches to art history. They help to answer questions that have persisted owing to a lack of large, global, or representative sources or because of the amount of time needed to gather and process data. One of the serendipitous effects of such methods is a broadening of art-historical interests. Research has become more global and includes the "peripheries" as well as the traditional "centers"; more social, insofar as it takes into account groups and populations as opposed to canonical artists; and more art historical in its tracing of the circulation of artifacts and images in diverse contexts. Digital spatial methods can even help renew and refresh old, but too little questioned issues in art history such as "influence," "diffusion," or "style." It becomes all the more interesting for teaching and museography.

To better illustrate the usefulness of cartography for art history, this chapter will begin by situating spatial approaches to the discipline. It will present striking results that only spatial and digital methods could achieve. It will then provide a methodological and theoretical framework for considering and using spatial art history. This will include discussions of how to map (including collecting and organizing data), how to georeference spatial information, and how to analyze the results.

## The Geography of Art: An Ambiguous Legacy

"We have museum catalogues, not artistic atlases,"[1] wrote historian Fernand Braudel in 1949. Today, most available art history "atlases" contain few maps. Instead, they utilize large, colorful chronologies to compare the evolution of artistic trends in different areas and cultures. If some books are exceptions, they appear dated; they are static and not very explicit; the content of the cartographies and that of the articles often diverge.[2]

However, art historians' interest in identifying and analyzing the relationship between place and style is old. Since Vasari, they have frequently linked a style to a local or national school. In the theories of the eighteenth century, climate was supposed to explain the differentiation of artistic productions. The tendency to build a relationship between place and style was encouraged in the nineteenth century by the international influence of Hippolyte Taine (1828–93). In his courses at the École des Beaux Arts de Paris (1864–69), he reported on works according to race, environment, place, and time.[3]

This approach was ambiguous. It was part of a vivid trend where the national criterion guided the discourse on art works; the notion of "school" is its interesting avatar.[4] The geographical history of art helped to justify insidious political theories—first and foremost nationalism, which dismissed the idea of possible exchanges between artistic "languages."[5] Artistic geovisualization could even justify land claims, as was the case with the work of the Germans Josef Strzygowski (1862–1941) and Dagobert Frey (1883–1962). Frey participated in the Nazi looting of artworks in Poland. He justified them with his writings on art in Poland, an art presented as German, underestimating the presence of Jewish and Polish cultures.[6] In cases such as this, cartography was primarily invented to wage war.[7]

Is this the reason why the "spatial shift" of art history in the 1990s occurred without geomapping?[8] At that time, European art historians settled their scores with nationalism;[9] North American art historians were passionate about the theory of forms; neither continent had particular interest in social and geographical logic. If a "spatial shift" was taking place in aesthetics, following Denis Cosgrove's work on landscape,[10] it intended rather to deconstruct artists' relationships to the landscape and socio-cultural spaces of their time.

Since the mid-2000s, however, there has been a renewed interest in artistic geography. Some art historians have called for a better formulation of the geographical approach that had long remained an undertheorized part of the discipline.[11] Art geographers have encouraged us to abandon traditional notions of center, periphery, capitals, and places of art, terms that have often been used without a critical and historical perspective. This awareness of the weight of words, and of their underlying geopolitics, went along with the postcolonial awareness of the discipline.[12] It has accompanied the global turn of art history and its new interest in artistic globalization.[13]

Art geographers took their vocabulary, and on occasion their concepts, from geographers. They did not, however, take the step of mapping.[14] Nevertheless, the entry of digital methodologies into art history in the late 2000s sparked the interest of another community of art historians in cartography—often scholars intrigued by sociology, economics, and their multiple modes of data visualization such as network analysis, factor analysis, or geomapping. The results of their work illustrate the now widespread interest of the digital geographical approach to art history.

## From Geography to Art History

Historical mapping presented a major challenge to art history: it asked researchers to consider space and time as constructed, while also recognizing the reality of what used to be called *facts*. In a way, digital cartography contributes to the material turn in art history: an artifact is an object and, as a material, is subject to the categories of space (in which it circulated) and time. Cartography enjoins us to start by questioning the "where" and "when" of any object of study.

Questions emerged that had been buried for a long time, either because they could be embarrassing (such as the place of origin of a style, too often understood as a "center of influence"), or the geopolitics of art, or because they could not be given satisfactory answers: Is there a geography of art and, if so, what is its evolution? How do styles circulate? How did the use of certain materials such as gold, lapis lazuli, copper, or even oil spread in art? Where do artists live, where do they produce, and where do their works end up? Questions such as these can be re-addressed more successfully because digital mapping facilitates the analysis of massive amounts of data. The map makes it possible to visualize scattered or serial information synoptically. It highlights spatiotemporal relationships between objects or events. It indicates distributions that are not always identifiable from textual sources or that are even less visible when working at a formalist and/or microstorial scale. This approach is particularly useful for the social and economic history of art, as well as for the history of artistic circulation and globalization.

All types of artifacts and places related to art can be situated: works and objects of art, reproductions of images, magazines, exhibition spaces, galleries, studios, museums, and art schools. It is possible to map them in "stocks" (at a given date) or in "flows" (from one date to another). The cartographic approach can also help to trace the places and circulation of individuals—places of birth, study, activity, death, addresses of patrons, daily trajectories, international trips, successive moves, and so on. All that is required is a list of dated and georeferenced items—the first fundamental step in cartographic work.

## Mapping Art History's Usual Sources

Some pre-existing lists provide art historians with ideal sources for developing a cartographic approach to their subject: catalogues raisonnés, exhibition catalogues, auction catalogues, museum collections, biographical directories, gallery directories, and art journals. These directories provide information that is both dated and locatable (e.g. addresses of exhibitions or places where works are made or stored). Such sources are particularly interesting for art historians since they remain consistent over time and contain vast and varied quantities of information that can be useful for many research topics. Exhibition catalogues, for instance, represent a plentiful source of literature, dating back to their invention in 1673.[15] Today, they crisscross the global art market. An exhibition catalogue is a book that gives—or claims to give—information as to the existence of an exhibition, its address, its dates, its title; it lists—or claims to list—the artists who participated and often the works that they exhibited. In consequence, catalogues provide a rich source of social, commercial, geographical or even political data. The titles that are listed may reveal recurring patterns of words or themes and are sometimes accompanied by texts written by artists and selection committees, as well as illustrations and reproductions, or even advertisements. What happens when we geovisualize this kind of data?

Digital cartographies of galleries and exhibitions can help the specialist on an artist to better situate that individual in the places where she or he worked. The project developed by Pamela Fletcher and Anne Helmreich on the nineteenth-century London art market; the Paris art market historical map of the Artl@s team developed by Léa Saint-Raymond, Félicie de Maupeou, and Julien Cavero; and Nadine Oberste-Hetbleck's project on the Cologne art market can be used to locate the activities of an artist, merchant, or patron.[16] These projects use a geographic information system (GIS) to organize, visualize, and analyze dated lists of gallery addresses. They make available these maps and the precise descriptions of the places represented. The exhibition catalogue database of the Artl@s project that I lead (https://artlas.huma-num.fr/map/#/) permits the chronological visualization of a series of exhibitions with a common theme. It also enables users to situate an artist's exhibition places or addresses, or to examine where certain artworks described by these catalogues have circulated, been produced, and collected (Figure 7.1).

"Distribution mapping" is available to beginners with their own data. After measuring the occurrences of an item (e.g. certain artistic activities or artistic populations, etc.) at several locations over a specific period, it is possible to map these locations and to identify spatial patterns of, for example, production and reception. For instance, Figure 7.2 shows the international distribution of exhibitions devoted to Amedeo Modigliani between 1951 and 1960. We can see a remarkable international reception, particularly in Northern Europe and on the East Coast of the United States. The list of all exhibitions was gathered with the help of monographs on Modigliani, but the same can be done with a catalogue raisonné, when available.

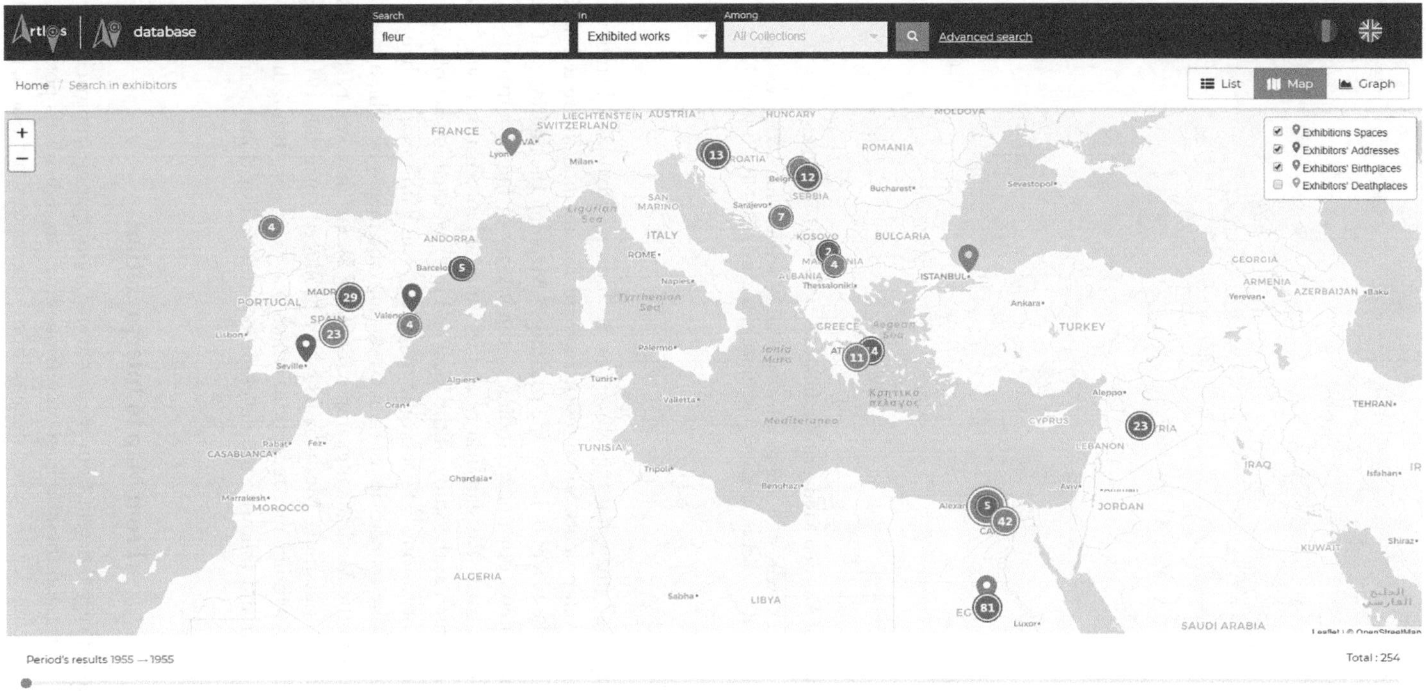


*Figure 7.1* Première Biennale de la Méditerranée—Alexandria, 26 July 1955–15 September 1955. Birthplaces and addresses of exhibitors.

*Source*: © The Artl@s Project, dir. Béatrice Joyeux-Prunel (www.artlas.huma-num.fr). Data contributor: Solène Amice.

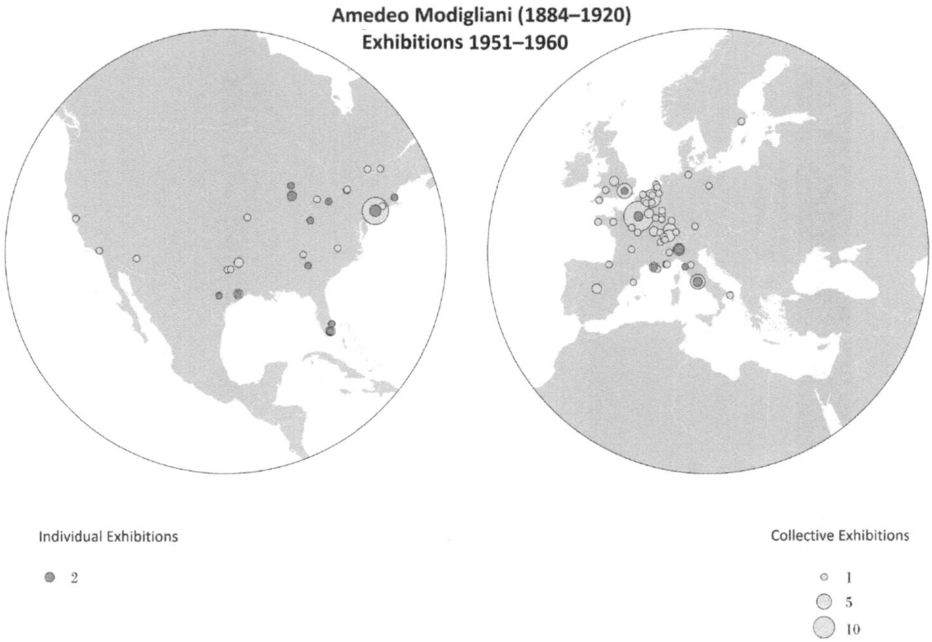


*Figure 7.2* Distribution of Amedeo Modiglian's exhibitions from 1951 to 1960.

*Source*: Map created by Julien Cavero, with data gathered by Béatrice Joyeux-Prunel. This work has received support of TransferS (laboratoire d'excellence, program "Investissements d'avenir" ANR-10-IDEX-0001–02 PSL* and ANR-10-LABX-0099).

"Synchronic mapping" (mapping trajectories or evolutions) provides a better understanding of certain artistic developments. Some researchers are, for instance, interested in the role of travel in painting or in the places of landscape painting.[17] Mapping the addresses of the artists at the Salon d'automne renews our understanding of the history of the Montparnasse district, as well as that of the avant-garde Parisian history and its supposed internationalism.[18] Some maps are of political interest, such as the study of the local and international impact of museums, collections, and heritage institutions.[19] Synchronic mapping is also important when it comes to analyzing artists' careers, the trajectories of their works, and the means by which their work was mediated.[20] To return to the Modigliani example (Figure 7.2), this map was part of a series that mapped all exhibitions containing Modigliani's work produced since the 1910s (Figure 7.3). The series showed how Modigliani's reception, which was very low during his life, suddenly increased after his death and followed the development of a transnational market for classical modern painting.[21]

## From Map to Interpretation

Map-based reasoning is very different from the traditional monographic approach that works on sources related to an artist and these sources only. It questions an individual's position in a larger space and enjoins us to consider his or her distance from other actors and places, the influence of which is not neutral. Moreover, a digital map that allows navigating, zooming, and searching invites the reader to consider possible encounters or proximities (whether an artist lived near a particular

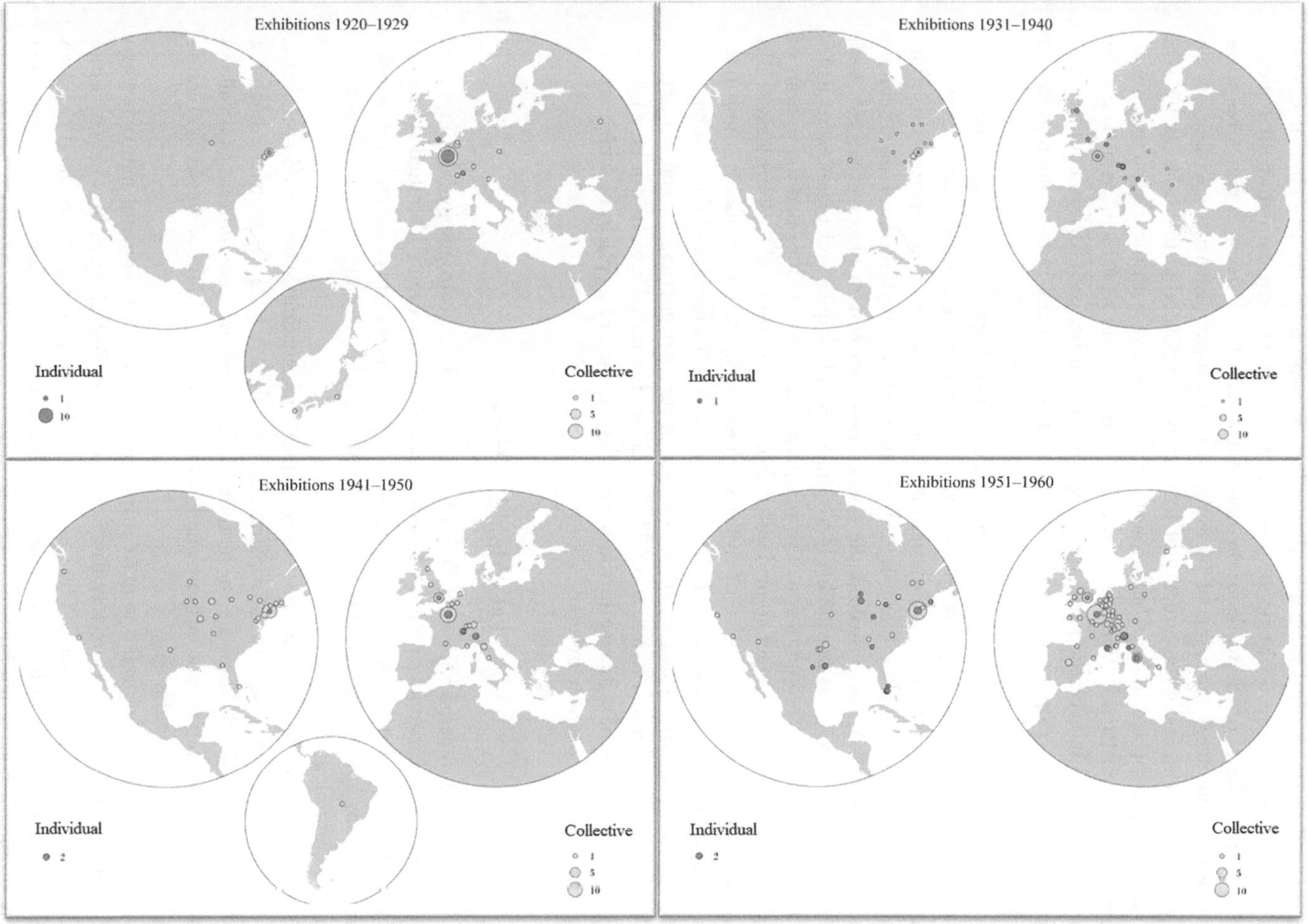


*Figure 7.3* The diffusion of Amedeo Modigliani's work in individual and collective exhibitions over time (1920–1960).

*Source*: Map created by Julien Cavero, with data gathered by Béatrice Joyeux-Prunel. This work has received support of TransferS (laboratoire d'excellence, program "Investissements d'avenir" ANR-10-IDEX-0001-02 PSL* and ANR-10-LABX-0099).

café, gallery, collector, museum). Digital mapping also highlights traffic channels and unsuspected connections, as well as borders that require further investigation on other scales of analysis.

In the Artl@s group, several researchers have worked to map artists' trajectories in ways that have broadened the traditional biographical practices. Starting from the mapping of Claude Monet's exhibitions, Félicie de Maupeou researched the artist's own exhibition strategies.[22] Studying the trajectories of the works of the conceptual artist On Kawara, Sophie Cras questioned claims to the decentralization of New York-based Conceptual Art.[23] Focusing on the places where the members of the Situationist International circulated in the 1950s and 1960s, Emmanuel Guy put the aesthetics of Situationism into perspective with the student and immigrant spaces of central Paris.[24] Working on the global trajectories of African artists and their works, Olivier Marcel showed the permanence of connections between African countries and their former colonial metropolises, as well as the importance of living in these metropolises to escape local careers.[25]

Mapping is a research process rather than an outcome. Geographical questions underpin an interest in the structures on, or against which, artistic creation has developed. Cartography also encourages us to take into account the social dimension of art spaces, from a perspective affiliated with the work promoted by Pierre Bourdieu, and with the work of historians of culture and the literary field.[26] A map visualizes the concentration of certain places of artistic assets (patrons, academies, merchants) that are likely to attract symbolic capital and, therefore, struggles for or against such and such domination. This perspective leads to the idea that the notions of "center" and "periphery" no longer coincide with those of innovation and backwardness. It asks us to analyze the art world as a place of rivalries whose challenge was symbolic domination. Artistic geography then takes on a more dynamic dimension. "Centers" and their protagonists can be perceived as predators of the artistic heritage of the "peripheries," as well as places of reception, or even as vectors of circulation. The so-called dominated regions can be analyzed through their capacities of resistance to the norm of the center, or as places in which artistic languages were invented and reinvented.[27]

## Let's Map! But How?

Along with the need to begin with a detailed chronology, a detailed cartography is an important prerequisite for digital mapping projects. All historical objects or events identified should be linked at least in a simple table to specific locations. Maps can illuminate connections, networks, trends, circulations, and non-circulations that can be missed when reading information as a text, table, list, or chronology (Figure 7.4).

The use of digital mapping software—Geographical Information System (GIS)—makes it possible to map large quantities of information. Starting from a table or database containing addresses and their geolocalization (i.e. the latitude and longitude of these addresses), GIS allows the researcher to superimpose one or more graphical representations of the addresses in question on one or more background maps.

Another more recent approach is to make maps directly from texts—a useful approach when the art historian has abundant sources available in text format. Digital algorithms help to locate automatically all the places mentioned by the author and to map them. This method based on named entity recognition (NER), or sometimes on Text Encoding Initiatives (TEI), may seem relatively simple for users when NER and TEI are mastered, since the corpus to be mapped is immediately circumscribed and does not have to be converted into a database.[28] However, the following discussion will focus more on GIS as it is productive and can be used for any possible art-historical sources, including images and objects.

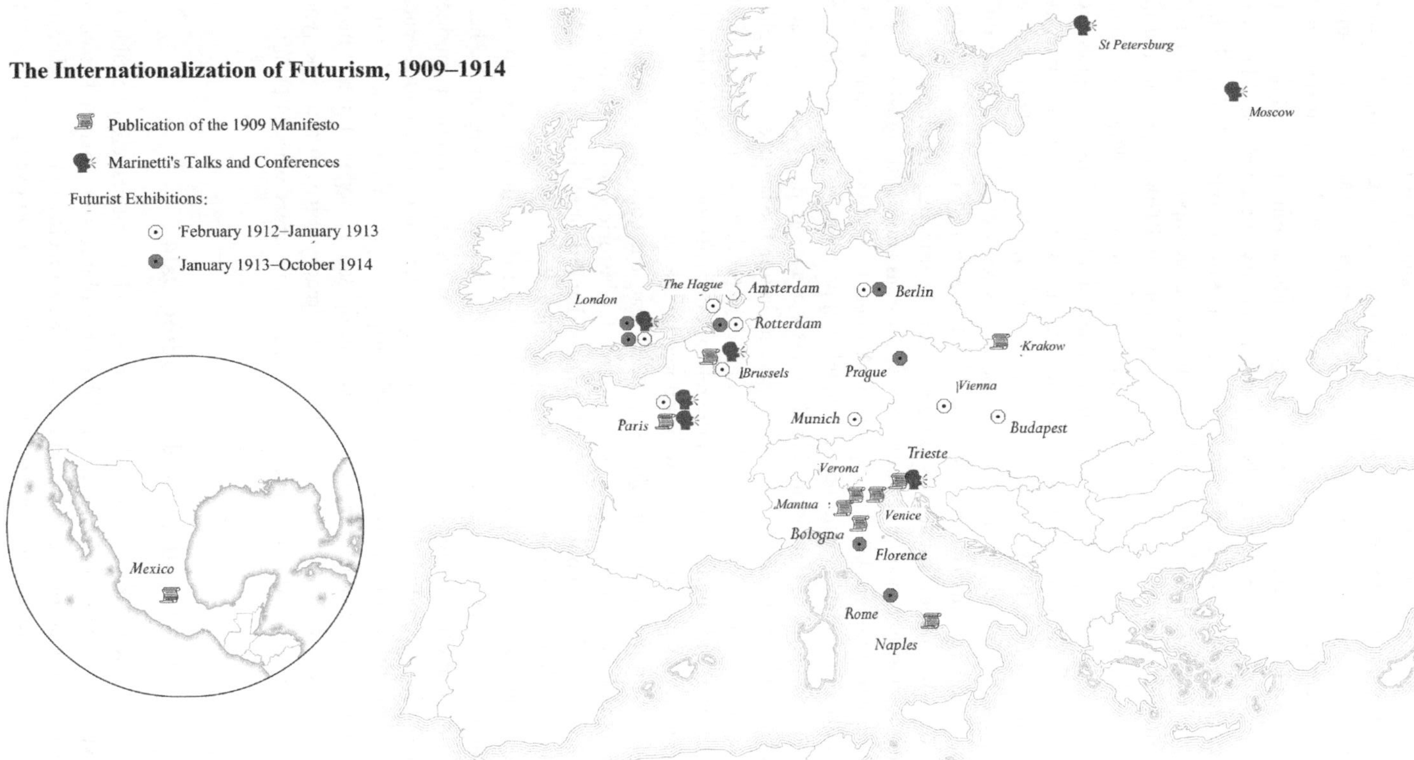


*Figure 7.4* The internationalization of Futurism (1909–1914).

*Source*: Map realized by Julien Cavero with data gathered by Béatrice Joyeux-Prunel. This work has received support of TransferS (laboratoire d'excellence, program "Investissements d'avenir" ANR-10-IDEX-0001-02 PSL* and ANR-10-LABX-0099).

## Sources and Objects of Analysis

The first question to ask concerns the sources and objects of analysis. What do I want to map? Has it been mapped by others? Do I have sufficient sources to create a digital map? Starting with sources put online by other projects (and quoting their provenance) or using existing mapping tools can be a good starting point for art historians who are new to digital cartography. Since 2009, the Artl@s team has constructed a database of geographical and historical data extracted from catalogues produced worldwide from the eighteenth century to the present.[29] The database was conceived to encompass catalogues from a diverse range of regions and periods, ranging from Europe in the eighteenth and nineteenth centuries to contemporary sub-Saharan Africa and Asia; from European biennials of the 1950s to exhibitions in 1970s Argentina and Cuban contemporary biennials. All available addresses found in the relevant catalogues are georeferenced, including those addresses that have long since vanished. The Artl@s catalogues database thus establishes the basis for a broad study of artistic circulation in the contemporary period and of the social spaces of art: It shows where artists were born, where they lived, and where they worked, amongst many other parameters. It also allows researchers to compare different geographies, according to particular filters (Figure 7.5). The Artl@s project is also interesting because it allows users to add new catalogues in cases where the information sought is not yet in the database. The integration process is supported with tutorials and multilingual Labs (Artl@s seminar and mapping training weeks). Participating in Artl@s also allows individuals to become part of a community of researchers who use cartographic approaches, to exchange ideas about good practices, and to generate discussion. Finally, users can export data as. csv spreadsheets which contain all the information stored in the database, including the latitude and longitude of addresses. We train researchers to work with these. csv files to produce their own visualizations. The Artl@s spreadsheets indicate the source of the relevant information, including the name of the person who retrieved it, and can therefore be quoted by the reuser.

Collecting one's own data is also possible—provided that it is copied and structured correctly in tables that indicate a date, a place, and a source for historical information relating to each object. This is where the computing historian realizes that distant reading can be, when the researchers gather data themselves, the closest reading possible.[30]

The researcher will need to consider the representative nature of his or her sources. Have I succeeded in doing an exhaustive search? Is there any information missing and where can I find it? Is the information collected homogeneous? This is where you should consider the categories in which the selected items may fall: for example, the address of a studio, gallery, or exhibition space. If you want to produce a quantitative map, it is essential to ensure that the elements counted come from the same source and fall within the same category. It is also necessary to make sure that data will only be grouped in the same category if it is of the same type and homogeneous (for example, we do not put exhibition spaces and artists' workshops in the same category).

## Organizing and Geocoding Data

The next question is: How to organize your data? The researcher will first create a table (.calc,. csv,. calc or. xls type) divided into columns that indicates the objects to be mapped. Each object must be described at least according to an indicative title, a precise address, the date of this address, and the source of the information concerned. Figure 7.6 is an example of information taken from the catalogue of the first Kassel documenta in 1955, displayed from the paper catalogue to a spreadsheet. Here, exhibitors are listed according to their name, gender, city, year and

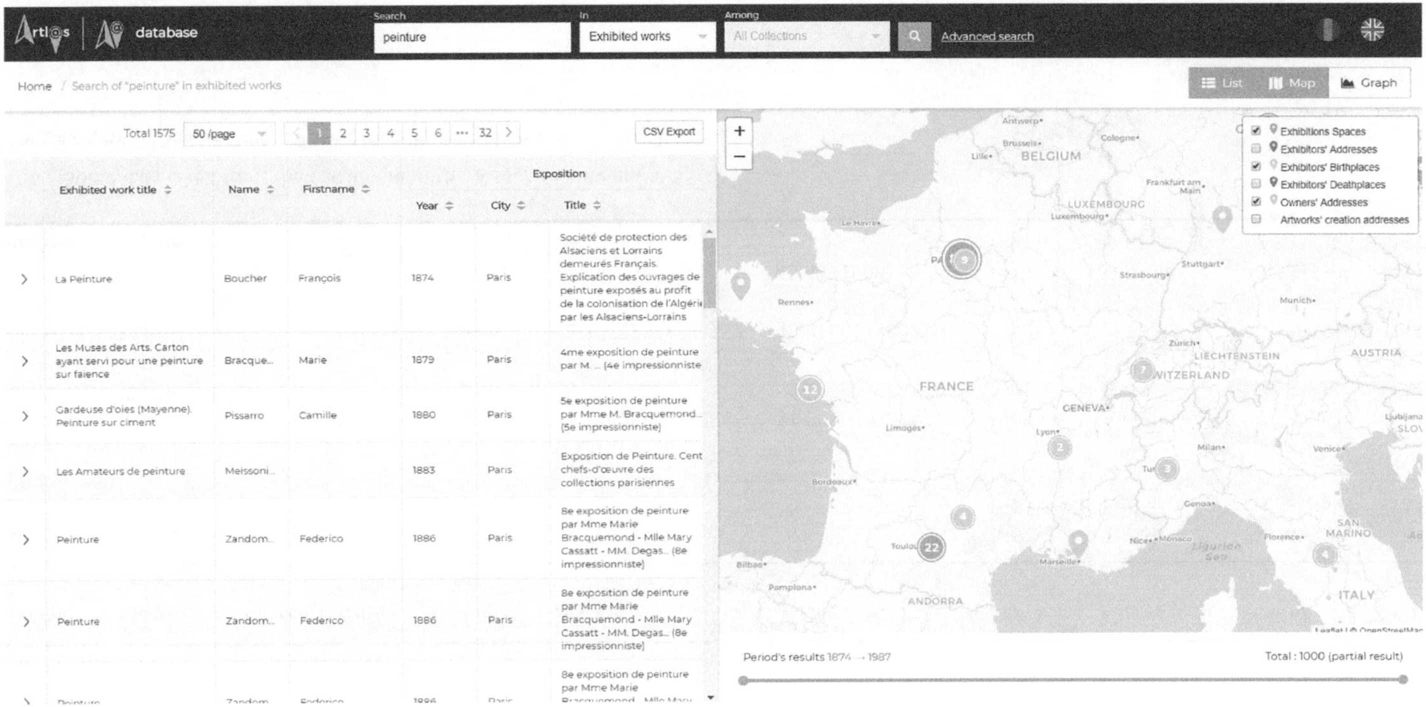


*Figure 7.5* Screenshot of a request result on the Artl@s Exhibition Catalogue Database.

*Source*: Artl@s Project, dir. Béatrice Joyeux-Prunel (www.artlas.huma-num.fr). Accessed January 2020.

| *Artist's Name* | *First Name* | *Gender* | *Artist's Country* | *City* | *X City* | *Y City* | *Birth Year* | *City of Birth* | *X Birth* | *Y Birth* |
|---|---|---|---|---|---|---|---|---|---|---|
| von Jawlensky | Alexej | M | 0 | 0 | 0 | 0 | 1864 | Torjok | 34.9690756 | 57.0359338 |
| Wols (Wolfgang Schulze) | 0 | M | 0 | 0 | 0 | 0 | 1913 | Berlin | 13.3888599 | 52.5170365 |
| Winter | Fritz | M | Germany | Kassel | 9.4762890359284 | 51.3090404274005 | 1905 | Altenbögge | 7.7392844 | 51.598077 |
| Wiemken | Walter Kurt | M | 0 | 0 | 0 | 0 | 1907 | Basel | 7.5878261 | 47.5581077 |
| Vieira da Silva | Marie-Helene | F | France | Paris | 2.35222345196757 | 48.8566148607216 | 0 | Lisbonne | -9.1380056 | 38.7130574 |
| Vedova | Emilio | M | Italy | Venice | 12.3345899 | 45.4371908 | 1919 | Venedig | 12.3345899 | 45.4371908 |
| Taeuber-Arp | Sophie | F | 0 | 0 | 0 | 0 | 1889 | Davos | 9.8237266 | 46.7961744 |

*Figure 7.6* Some data taken from the Catalogue of the Kassel documenta, 1955.

*Source*: Source copied by Solène Amice for the Artl@s Project, dir. Béatrice Joyeux-Prunel.

city of birth. The two kinds of addresses available have been georeferenced, adding a column X for latitude and a column Y for longitude.

This kind of data enables us to visualize, for instance, the different places where the Documenta I exhibitors were born—and how many were born in each place; or the places where they lived in 1955 when they took part in the exhibition, and how many were concentrated in particular locations (Figure 7.7).

Georeferencing addresses is often the most annoying step in geomapping. It is not really a problem when mapping aims to point to cities, whose parameters are preregistered in the most common GIS. It is a problem when you want to map in a fine way—at the street, neighborhood, or city level.

- In the case of contemporary addresses, it is sufficient to register the address list in a geocoding system (several free systems are available online, usually using the geocoding APIs of Googlemap and Openstreetmap, e.g. www.gpsvisualizer.com/geocoding.html). This way, it is possible to obtain the latitude and longitude that will be easy to use in software such as QGis.
- The exercise is more complex when the addresses no longer exist. Some projects allow the longitude and latitude of obsolete addresses to be retrieved—such as the Paris GIS project or the Artl@s project (which has included such information for addresses since the beginning of the nineteenth century). The researcher has to be patient and to accept that these first steps can be messy.

All the columns in the table that describe the data can be used to divide items into groups that can be represented in maps—for example, men/women, paintings/sculptures, nationalities, place of birth, etc. It is at this point that it is advisable to use a powerful GIS to multiply cartographic representations as much as possible by regularly changing the display criteria to see which are the most interesting distributions and evolutions.

As for the transition to the static map—the one that will be published in a potentially paper format (or on a website, or in pdf)—three questions of scale arise:

- Quantity. What is the numerical scale available to me? Do I have more than fifty pieces of data? More than two hundred? More than a thousand? Depending on the quantity of information, different cartographies are preferable. A table that contains fewer than fifty different addresses will likely be translated into a point map (Figure 7.8, left). A spreadsheet with more than two hundred geolocated items will be more easily mapped quantitatively, so it will be necessary to count the frequency, for a given period, of the items belonging to a single category and location (gallery/neighborhood/city/country) at the same time (Figure 7.8, right and Figure 7.7). This aggregated data will be represented in points of different sizes, depending on the quantity concerned.
- Time. Is the data spread over a long or short period? Can a map consistently represent locations separated by ten, twenty, thirty, or even two hundred years? It is clear that an artist's address in 1890 is not comparable with an artist's address in 2020. The researcher must therefore consider how to distribute data according to consistent periods—for example, by ten-year batches (Figure 7.3), by five-year batches, or by years if there is enough data. This separation will involve either making several maps (one per period, as in Figure 7.3) or representing each period with a different color on the same map—preferably with a significant color gradation: from grey to black, from older periods to more recent periods.

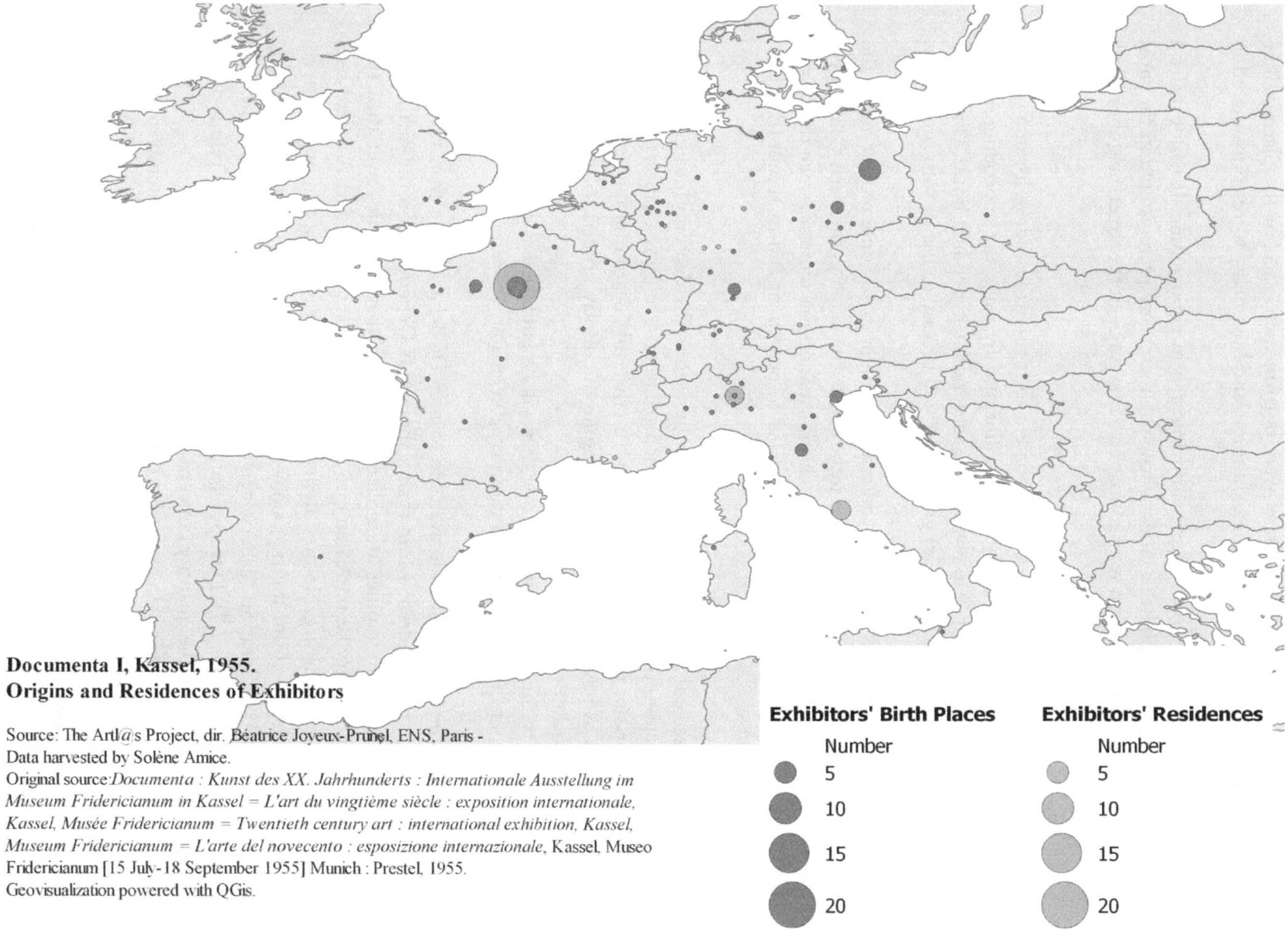


*Figure* 7.7 Birth places and residences of the 114 painters exhibiting at documenta 1, Kassel, 1955.

*Source*: The Artl@s Project, dir. Béatrice Joyeux-Prunel. Data harvested by Solène Amice. *Original Source*: Documenta: Kunst des XX. Jahrhunderts: Internationale Ausstellung im Museum Fridericianum, 1955. Map created by Béatrice Joyeux-Prunel.

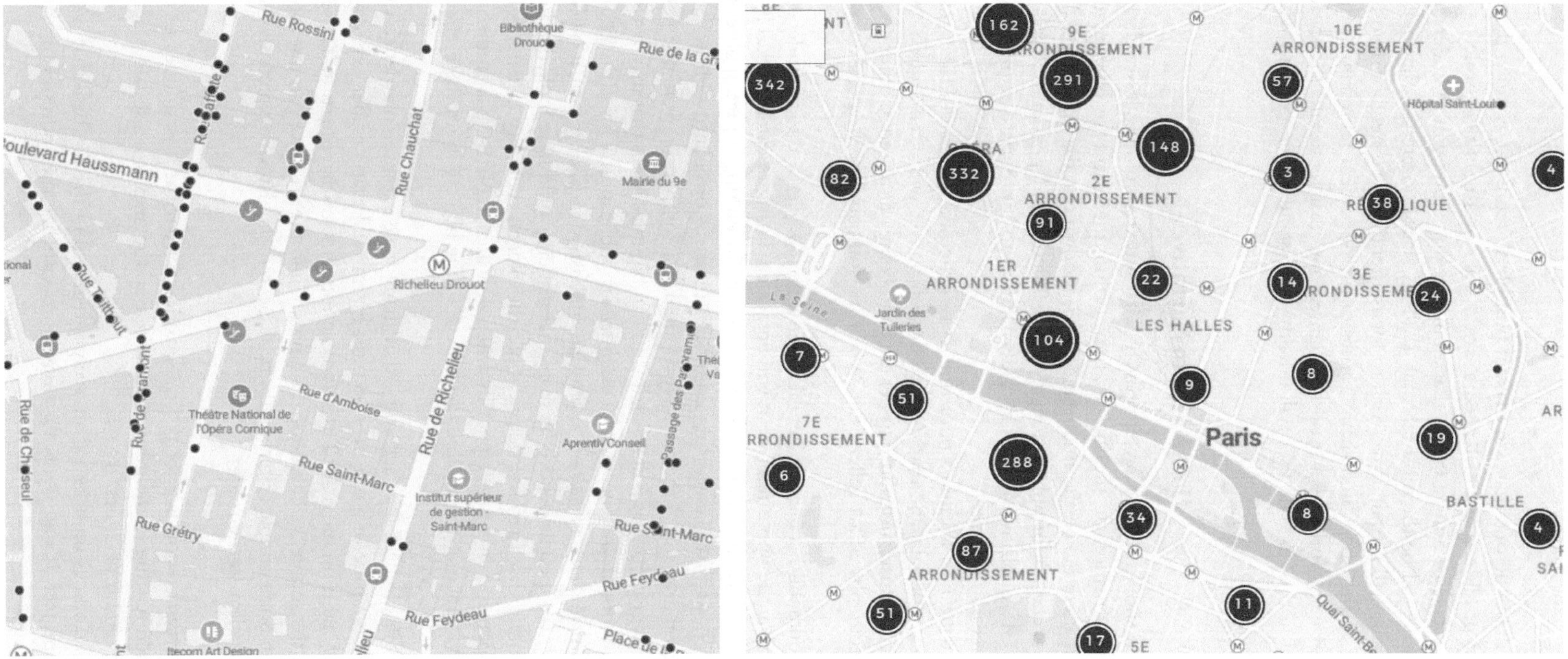


*Figure 7.8* What quantities? Left (a): point map; Right (b): a quantitative map. GEOMAP screenshots.

*Source*: Screenshot details from the project GEOMAP (Julien Cavero, Félicie Faizand de Maupeou and Léa Saint-Raymond) (https://paris-art-market.huma-num.fr/).

- Space. This will be the one that will make it possible to represent as much data as possible in the clearest possible way: Do I need a world scale or a continent-scale to display the data? The advantage of using a GIS is that a quick zoom allows you to understand in little time which scale will be the most relevant. If all my data is located in Berlin, it is obvious that the city scale will prevail. If we wish to focus attention on a neighborhood, we would advise adding, in the upper right-hand corner of the document representing the activities mapped in this neighborhood, a small highlighted map that represents the location of the neighborhood in the city. The user will quickly understand which city and which district is concerned.

## From Map to Narrative

A map in an article should help to say effectively what a text would say less well. It must also provide accurate information on the sources, their origin, the map base represented, and the method of analysis used; hence the importance of a good title and a good legend. However, even when a map is chosen for publication, it cannot function independently. Explanatory text is essential. Even a GIS, published a priori for external users to appropriate, requires explanations of its method, sources, and results.

A single geovisualization is often a poor one. This is the disadvantage of the transition from GIS to the two-dimensional static map. A good demonstration will often require several comparative maps. Specific artistic distributions benefit from being compared to other geographies—for instance the geography of art galleries in New York compared to the geography of income tax in that city.

Finally, when you publish a map, be careful about what it *might* seem to say. Indeed, a map can sometimes seem to say the opposite of what you perceived during research work. The following maps for instance quantify the exhibitions of modern art in European metropolises from 1900 to 1914 (Figure 7.9). At first glance, Paris dominates in terms of quantity. However, the maps show above all a great diversity of the cities represented. If a comparison from one period to the other may help better catch what is at stake, it is still ambiguous. Maps that may have been very useful for research work are not necessarily essential for publication. This is the choice I made for the volumes *Histoire transnationale des avant-gardes* published in pocket format by Gallimard.[31] It was too risky to make people believe, by maps that readers would have looked at before reading the book, in things that I refuted (for example, the alleged centrality of Paris before 1945). Maps can reify a dogmatic discourse, especially when they are circulated to an audience unaware of their symbolic violence or too inclined to believe in the objectivity of these effective visual representations.

Taking this powerful effect into account—that many have ex ante confidence in the maps or the charts seen on a page or a screen—we must be mindful that a reader expects data to be clearly described. What is on the map? Titles and captions answer that question. These must give a clear idea about the source, its definition, its amount, and the trust we can put into what we can see at first sight. Some simple criteria must be respected: the dates, completeness, and quality of the data must be clear to the reader.

- Dating. A geovisualization is poor if the user does not have at least an idea of the decade or of the period relating to the items represented on the map. It is also bad practice to mix different times and time-scales.
- Completeness. Sources must be exhaustively integrated in the database that will serve for the mapping project. If one wants for instance to visualize the addresses of artists from a

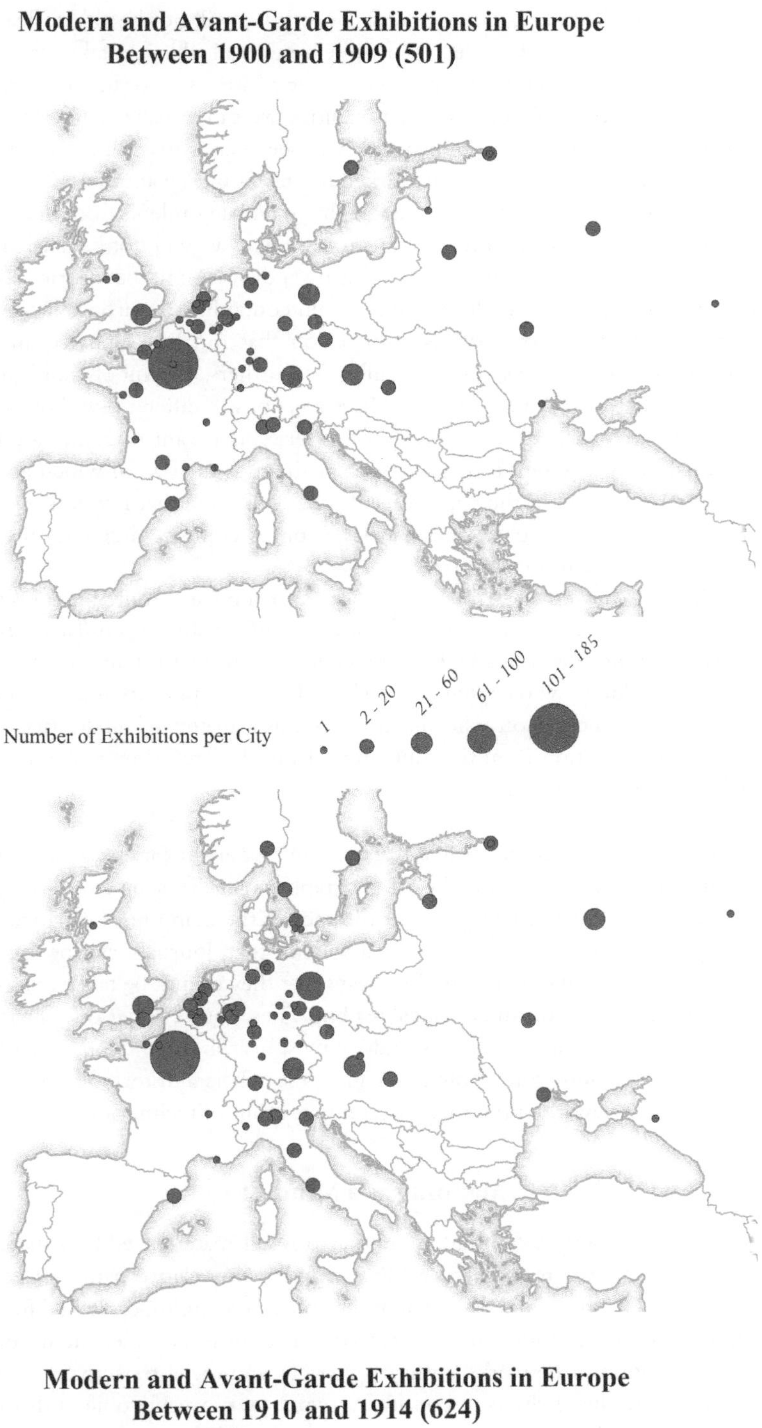


*Figure 7.9* Two unpublished maps created by Julien Cavero with data gathered by Béatrice Joyeux-Prunel.

*Source*: This work has received support of TransferS (laboratoire d'excellence, program "Investissements d'avenir" ANR-10-IDEX-0001–02 PSL* and ANR-10-LABX-0099).

particular art school at a certain moment in history, we will not be able to learn anything from the map if we are not sure that the map represents all addresses taken from the source at that date. Only then, will we be able to compare addresses according to distinct criteria. For instance, if we know about artists' nationalities, we can visualize addresses with several colors according to nationality. Perhaps we will see that artists from a same country or talking a common language lived and worked not far from one another. If we know about artists' genders we might compare the geography of female students from the geography of their male counterparts, etc. If the source is incomplete, we will not be able to assert with intellectual honesty that "men lived in this district and women in that district." Missing data could significantly alter the results of the map and contradict its purported conclusions.

- Homogeneity. Homogeneous data is information that can be compared and subsumed into a single category. If one set of data differs from others, its symbols and legends on the map must be different. For instance, I will have to choose a different symbol to map artists studios and another to map the locations of galleries. If I want to gather a given sum of information and to represent it quantitatively with a dot the size of which accords to the number of items located in the same place, I have to be sure that my dots represent items derived from the same category. Thus, I will be able to compare different dots in different places according to their different sizes.
- Data quality. This means that I know the origin of the data. Sourcing is essential to art history, and this simple criterion can prevent using information from databases where the primary source is not mentioned. Data quality also means that if I am not the producer of the data, I should know who copied it or collected it from a primary source. Not only must I quote and credit the person who did this work as a matter of intellectual honesty, but I also must get protection from that quotation: I can declare in my academic publication that I rely on this scholar's work.

To address comprehensible and foreseeable reactions among art historians against the symbolic violence of numbers, charts, and maps, the art geographer will also keep a critical eye on every step of the geomapping process. The source at the root of the map must be criticized, and this historical critique must be clearly demonstrated in your text. Journals, catalogues, repertories, and dictionaries are historical documents; this means that they cannot be taken at face value, but rather demand contextualization and a critical reading. These sources offer only a partial view of the history of art locations and circulations, and we must bear in mind the fact that the absence of catalogues in some regions could potentially give researchers a distorted historical picture.[32] Finally, one must also be aware of the theoretical implications of technical choices.

## Mapping as a Mindset

Mapping is an approach, a state of mind, more than a result materialized by a map. It is at the heart of this process that the researcher becomes aware of the relative nature of certain terms long considered obvious in art history—centers, peripheries, margins, capitals; diffusions, influences, hegemony; originality, individuality, etc. Maps invite us to consider the history of artists as a complex articulation of networks, affinities, carriers, and social trajectories, conscious and unconscious strategies. They help us to consider artworks as moveable objects that circulate in different contexts and times and encourage us to study their different receptions as well as the multiple actors and mediators involved in these receptions. They also open new research chapters in receptions studies such as the adaptation and resemanticization, or reinterpretation of artworks in their circulation.[33] Once we begin investigating and mapping the circulation of art, we go beyond the dichotomy of center and the periphery; any place can potentially be a center or a periphery depending on the chosen point of view. What counts is circulation, and how objects, people, and ideas circulate.[34]

Merging a historical and aesthetic grounding with new kinds of methodologies enables us to apprehend the traditional objects of art-historical study in new ways. Practiced as a heuristic use, spatial art history opens up new horizons. It also encourages interdisciplinarity and collective work. Digital spatial technology requires us to work differently on a human level: to share, collaborate, learn from others, publish in groups, cite those who code and not only those who "think." It is a history of art that is not traditional, but that is no less fruitful. Integrating into a community will be always rewarding for those who choose this way of doing research: Training will be easier and access to information better; data reuse will be optimized; data management plans better conceived; data standards will be known, accepted, and applied.

Paradoxically, spatial digital art history also brings us back to the roots of art history, asking questions that seemed to be abandoned at a new cost. Thanks to the time saved by digital tools, it is possible to invest much more time in archival research, but also, paradoxically, in classical methods of art history that are currently posing new challenges. How do images circulate, for instance? Until now, only textual descriptions of images have been used to track and trace digitally the circulation of artifacts, and we are still relying on the good old connoisseurial methodologies to reconstitute the circulation of styles and the diffusion of artistic movements.[35] However, why not try to add more objectivity to this work, thanks to visual digital methods? Can spatial digital methods help us to treat formal and stylistic issues? Can computer vision specialists develop solutions to compare circulating images according to their formal content and not only according to their textual metadata? These challenges will advance the history of art as much as the technologies of artificial vision.[36] They will also encourage us to read with a new eye the intuitions of some great art historians of the past, such as Aloïs Riegl and Aby Warburg.[37]

## Notes

1. Fernand Braudel, *La Méditerranée et le Monde méditerranéen à l'époque de Philippe II* (Paris: Armand Colin, 1949), 613.
2. Two exceptions, the *Atlas of Western Art* edited by Antony White and John Steer and the *Atlas of World Art* edited by John Onians crossed more directly geographical and historical issues; but the maps were not made by the authors themselves.
3. Jean-Rémy Mantion, "Le lieu du génie. Remarques sur la géographie de l'art," *Annales Économies, Sociétés, Civilisations* 38, no. 5 (1983): 1084–96; Thomas Da Costa Kaufmann, *Towards a Geography of Art* (Chicago: University of Chicago Press, 2004); Hippolyte Taine, *De l'idéal dans l'art: leçons professées à l'École des beaux-arts* (Paris: G. Baillière, 1867) and *Philosophie de l'art* (Paris: Hachette, 1901[9] (1867[1])), 2 vols. See also *Relire Taine* (Paris: musée du Louvre, École nationale supérieure des Beaux-Arts, 2001).
4. Christine Peltre and Philippe Lorentz, eds., *La Notion d'école* (Strasbourg: Presses universitaires de Strasbourg, 2007).
5. Béatrice Joyeux-Prunel, *'Nul n'est prophète en son pays?' L'internationalisation de la peinture avant-gardiste parisienne* (Paris: Musée d'Orsay/N. Chaudun, 2009), Ch. 1.
6. For instance Dagobert Frey, *Krakau* (Berlin: Deutscher Kunstverlag, 1941). More generally, see Jonathan Petropoulos, *The Faustian Bargain: The Art World in Nazi Germany* (Oxford: Oxford University Press, 2000).
7. Yves Lacoste, *La Géographie, ça sert d'abord à faire la guerre* (Paris: Maspero, 1976; 2nd ed., La Découverte, 1986).
8. Angelo Torre, "Un 'tournant spatial' en histoire? Paysages, regards, ressources," *Annales. Histoire, Sciences Sociales* 63, no. 5 (2008): 1127–44.
9. Béatrice Joyeux-Prunel, "Ce que l'approche mondiale fait à l'histoire de l'art," *Romantisme*, 163, no. 1 (2014): 63–78.

10. Denis Cosgrove, *The Iconography of Landscape: Essays on the Symbolic Representation, Design and Use of Past Environments* (Cambridge: Cambridge University Press, 1989).
11. DaCosta Kaufmann, *Towards a Geography of Art.*
12. Béatrice Joyeux-Prunel, "Art History and the Global: Deconstructing an Already Canonic Narrative," *Journal of Global History* 14, Special Issue 3 (Historicizing the Global: An Interdisciplinary Perspective) (November 2019): 413–35. Cambridge University Press.
13. Kitty Ziljmans and Wilfried van Damme, "Art History in a Global Frame: World Art Studies—Introduction," in *Art History and Visual Studies in Europe: Transnational Discourses and National Frameworks*, ed. Matthew Rampley (Leyden: Brill, 2014), 217–48.
14. There are no maps for instance in DaCosta Kaufmann, *Towards a Geography of Art.* See also Thomas Da Costa Kaufmann and Elizabeth Pilliod, eds., *Time and Place: Essays in the Geohistory of Art* (Burlington: Ashgate, 2005).
15. See Béatrice Joyeux-Prunel and Olivier Marcel, "Exhibition Catalogues in the Globalization of Art: A Source for Social and Spatial Art History," *Artl@s Bulletin* 4, no. 2 (2016): Article 8, https://docs.lib.purdue.edu/artlas/vol4/iss2/8/.
16. Pamela Fletcher, Anne Helmreich, David Israel, and Seth Erickson, "Local/Global: Mapping Nineteenth-Century London's Art Market," *19th Century Art Worldwide* 11, no. 3 (Autumn 2012), www.19thc-artworldwide.org/autumn12/fletcher-helmreich-mapping-the-london-art-market; GeoMAP: A Geography of the Parisian Art Market Between 1815 and 1955 (Soon Expanded to 2015), Developed by Léa Saint-Raymond, Félicie de Maupeou, and Julien Cavéro, the Artl@s Project, https://paris-art-market.huma-num.fr/; Nadine Oberste-Hetbleck, ed., *Art | Gallery GIS | Cologne, Art Cologne* Catalogues, 1967–97, www.aggc.uni-koeln.de/.
17. For instance Richard Brettell, *Pissarro et Pontoise. Un peintre et son paysage* (Paris: Editions du Valhermeil, 1991) and *Sisley*, exh. cat. (Paris: RMN, 1992), 26.
18. Béatrice Joyeux-Prunel, "L'art de la mesure. Le Salon d'Automne (1903–1914), l'avant-garde, ses étrangers et la nation française," *Histoire et mesure* XXII-1 (2007): 145–82.
19. For instance Teodoro Gilabert, "La géographie de l'art contemporain en France" (PhD diss., Espaces géographiques et sociétés (ESO), CNRS: UMR6590—Université de Caen—Université d'Angers—Université du Maine—Université de Nantes—Université Rennes 2-Haute Bretagne, 2006), http://halshs.archives-ouvertes.fr/halshs-00008949/fr/.
20. Béatrice Joyeux-Prunel, *'Nul n'est prophète en son pays.'*
21. See Béatrice Joyeux-Prunel, "La revanche d'un mort? Modigliani sur le marché international de l'art moderne, 1906–1960," in *Modigliani. L'œil intérieur* (Villeneuve d'Ascq: Musée d'art moderne/LaM Livres d'Art; Paris: Gallimard, 2016),158–65.
22. Félicie Faizand de Maupeou, *Claude Monet et l'exposition. Une stratégie de carrière à l'avènement du marché de l'art* (Rouen: Presses universitaires de Rouen en du Havre, 2018).
23. Sophie Cras, "Global Conceptualism? Cartographies of Conceptual Art in Pursuit of Decentering," in *Circulations in the Global History of Art*, eds. Thomas DaCosta Kaufmann, Catherine Dossin, and Béatrice Joyeux-Prunel (London: Routledge, 2015), 167–82.
24. Emmanuel Guy and Laurence Le Bras, eds., *Guy Debord. Un art de la guerre*; exh. cat. (Paris: Bibliothèque Nationale de France (BNF), 2013).
25. Olivier Marcel, "Filling the Blank Space of Global Art Peripheries: Measurements of Art Mobility and Their Ambivalence in Nairobi, Kenya," *Artl@s Bulletin* 2, no. 2 (2013): Article 6, https://docs.lib.purdue.edu/artlas/vol2/iss2/6/.
26. For instance Christophe Charle, "Situation spatiale et position sociale—L'économie des biens symboliques," *Actes de la recherche en sciences sociales* 13 (February 1977): 45–59; Enrico Castelnuovo and Carlo Ginzburg, "Domination symbolique et géographie artistique," *Actes de la Recherche en Sciences sociales* 40 (November 1981): 51–72.
27. See Béatrice Joyeux-Prunel, *Les avant-gardes artistiques. Une histoire transnationale*, vol. 1, 1848–1918; vol. 2, 1918–1945; vol. 3, 1945–1970 (Paris: Gallimard, 2016, 2017), and Béatrice Joyeux-Prunel, *Naissance de l'art contemporain 1945–1970. Une histoire mondiale* (Paris: Éditions du CNRS, forthcoming).
28. David Joseph Wrisley, "Locating Medieval French, or Why We Collect and Visualize the Geographic Information from Texts?" *Speculum* 92, no. S1 (2017): S145–S169.
29. Artl@s (https://artlas.huma-num.fr) is financed by the Ecole normale supérieure, the Agence nationale pour la Recherche (ANR Jeunes-Chercheurs 2011–2016), PSL—Paris Sciences Lettres Research University, the labex TranferS, and Purdue University.

30. So far I do not agree with Franco Moretti's short opposition between "distant reading" and "close reading"—Franco Moretti, "Conjectures on World Literature," *New Left Review* 1 (2000), accessed September 28, 2018, https://newleftreview.org/II/1/franco-moretti-conjectures-on-world-literature.
31. Béatrice Joyeux-Prunel, *Les avant-gardes artistiques*.
32. See, for example, Marcel, "Filling the Blank Space of Global Art Peripheries."
33. Béatrice Joyeux-Prunel, "Circulation and Resemanticization: An Aporetic Palimpsest," *Artl@s Bulletin* 6, no. 2 (Summer 2017): 4–17, http://docs.lib.purdue.edu/artlas/vol6/iss2/13.
34. Thomas DaCosta Kaufmann, Catherine Dossin, and Béatrice Joyeux-Prunel, eds., *Circulations in the Global History of Art* (New York: Ashgate, 2015; New York: Routledge, 2017).
35. For instance *Pointillisme. Sur les traces de Seurat* (Lausanne: Fondation de l'Hermitage, 2008); or *Le Néo-impressionnisme: de Seurat à Paul Klee* (Paris: RMN, 2005).
36. Béatrice Joyeux-Prunel, "Visual Contagions, the Art Historian, and the Digital Strategies to Work on Them," *Artl@s Bulletin* 8, no. 3 (2019): Article 8, 128–44. Online at https://docs.lib.purdue.edu/artlas/vol8/iss3/8/.
37. Aloïs Riegl, *Stilfragen: Grundlegungen zu einer Geschichte der Ornamentik* (Berlin, 1893). English translation by Evelyn Kain, *Problems of Style. Foundations for a History of Ornament* (Princeton, NJ: Princeton University Press, 1992).

## Bibliography

Artl@s (https://artlas.huma-num.fr).

Braudel, Fernand. *La Méditerranée et le Monde méditerranéen à l'époque de Philippe II*, 613. Paris: Armand Colin, 1949.

Brettell, Richard. *Pissarro et Pontoise. Un peintre et son paysage*. Paris: Editions du Valhermeil, 1991.

Budde, Rainer (ed.) *Pointillisme. Sur les traces de Seurat*. Lausanne: Fondation de l'Hermitage, 2008.

Castelnuovo, Enrico, and Ginzburg, Carlo. "Domination symbolique et géographie artistique." *Actes de la Recherche en Sciences sociales* 40 (November 1981): 51–72.

Charle, Christophe. "Situation spatiale et position sociale—L'économie des biens symboliques." *Actes de la recherche en sciences sociales* 13 (February 1977): 45–59.

Cosgrove, Denis. *The Iconography of Landscape: Essays on the Symbolic Representation, Design and Use of Past Environments*. Cambridge: Cambridge University Press, 1989.

Cras, Sophie. "Global Conceptualism? Cartographies of Conceptual Art in Pursuit of Decentering." In *Circulations in the Global History of Art*, edited by Thomas DaCosta Kaufmann, Catherine Dossin, and Béatrice Joyeux-Prunel, 167–82. London: Routledge, 2015.

Da Costa Kaufmann, Thomas. *Towards a Geography of Art*. Chicago: University of Chicago Press, 2004.

DaCosta Kaufmann, Thomas, Dossin, Catherine, and Joyeux-Prunel, Béatrice, ed. *Circulations in the Global History of Art*. New York: Ashgate, 2015, Routledge 2017.

Da Costa Kaufmann, Thomas, and Elizabeth Pilliod, ed. *Time and Place: Essays in the Geohistory of Art*. Burlington: Ashgate, 2005.

Faizand de Maupeou, Félicie. *Claude Monet et l'exposition. Une stratégie de carrière à l'avènement du marché de l'art*. Rouen: Presses universitaires de Rouen en du Havre, 2018.

Fletcher, Pamela, and Helmreich, Anne, with David Israel and Seth Erickson. "Local/Global: Mapping Nineteenth-Century London's Art Market." In *19th Century Art Worldwide*, vol. 11, 3. Autumn, 2012. www.19thc-artworldwide.org/autumn12/fletcher-helmreich-mapping-the-london-art-market

Frey, Dagobert. *Krakau*. Berlin: Deutscher Kunstverlag, 1941.

GeoMAP: A geography of the Parisian art market between 1815 and 1955, developed by Léa Saint-Raymond, Félicie de Maupeou, and Julien Cavéro, the Artl@s Project. https://paris-art-market.huma-num.fr/

Gilabert, Teodoro. "La géographie de l'art contemporain en France." PhD diss., Espaces géographiques et sociétés (ESO, CNRS: UMR6590—Université de Caen — Université d'Angers—Université du Maine—Université de Nantes—Université Rennes 2-Haute Bretagne, 2006). http://halshs.archives-ouvertes.fr/halshs-00008949/fr/.

Guy, Emmanuel, and Laurence Le Bras, eds. *Guy Debord. Un art de la guerre*; exh. cat. Paris: Bibliothèque Nationale de France (BNF), 2013.

Joyeux-Prunel, Béatrice. "Art History and the Global: Deconstructing the Latest Canonical Narrative." *Journal of Global History* 14, Special Issue 3 (Historicizing the Global: An Interdisciplinary Perspective, November 2019):

413–35. Cambridge University Press. URL: https://www.cambridge.org/core/journals/journal-of-global-history/article/art-history-and-the-global-deconstructing-the-latest-canonical-narrative/CB46EC03FC653BDB091EBC9E709BA1E4.

———. "Ce que l'approche mondiale fait à l'histoire de l'art." *Romantisme* 163, no. 1 (2014): 63–78.

———. "Circulation and Resemanticization: An Aporetic Palimpsest." *Artl@s Bulletin* 6, no. 2 (Summer 2017): 4–17. URL: http://docs.lib.purdue.edu/artlas/vol6/iss2/13.

———. "L'art de la mesure. Le Salon d'Automne (1903–1914), l'avant-garde, ses étrangers et la nation française." *Histoire et mesure* XXII-1 (2007): 145–82.

———. "La revanche d'un mort? Modigliani sur le marché international de l'art moderne, 1906–1960." In *Modigliani. L'œil intérieur*, 158–65.Villeneuve d'Ascq: Musée d'art moderne/ LaM Livres d'Art, Paris: Gallimard, 2016.

———. *'Nul n'est prophète en son pays?' L'internationalisation de la peinture avant-gardiste parisienne*. Paris: Musée d'Orsay/N. Chaudun, 2009.

———. *Les avant-gardes artistiques. Une histoire transnationale*, vol. 1, 1848–1918, vol. 2, 1918–1945. Paris: Gallimard, 2016, 2017.

———. " Visual Contagions, the Art Historian, and the Digital Strategies to Work on Them." *Artl@s Bulletin* 8, no. 3 (2019): Article 8, 128–44. URL: https://docs.lib.purdue.edu/artlas/vol8/iss3/8/.

———. *Naissance de l'art contemporain, 1945–1970. Une histoire mondiale*. Paris: Editions du CNRS, 2020.

Joyeux-Prunel, Béatrice, and Marcel, Olivier. "Exhibition Catalogues in the Globalization of Art. A Source for Social and Spatial Art History." *Artl@s Bulletin* 4, no. 2 (2016): Article 8. https://docs.lib.purdue.edu/artlas/vol4/iss2/8/.

Lacoste, Yves. *La Géographie, ça sert d'abord à faire la guerre*. Paris: Maspero, 1976; 2nd edition La Découverte, 1986.

Lemoine, Serge, Marina Ferretti Bocquillon, Erich Franz, and Dominique Lobstein. *Le Néo-impressionnisme: de Seurat à Paul Klee*. Paris: RMN, 2005.

Mantion, Jean-Rémy. "Le lieu du génie. Remarques sur la géographie de l'art." *Annales. Économies, Sociétés, Civilisations* 38, no. 5 (1983): 1084–96.

Marcel, Olivier. "Filling the Blank Space of Global Art Peripheries: Measurements of Art Mobility and their Ambivalence in Nairobi, Kenya." *Artl@s Bulletin* 2, no. 2 (2013): Article 6. https://docs.lib.purdue.edu/artlas/vol2/iss2/6/

Moretti, Franco. "Conjectures on World Literature." *New Left Review* 1 (2000). Accessed September 28, 2018. https://newleftreview.org/II/1/franco-moretti-conjectures-on-world-literature.

Nadine Oberste-Hetbleck, ed. ART | GALLERY GIS | COLOGNE. *Art Cologne* catalogues, 1967–[illegible]7. www.aggc.uni-koeln.de/.

Onians, John, ed. *Atlas of World Art*. London: Laurence King Publishing, 2005.

Peltre, Christine, and Lorentz, Philippe, eds. *La Notion d'école*. Strasbourg: Presses universitaires de Strasbourg, 2007.

Petropoulos, Jonathan. *The Faustian Bargain: The Art World in Nazi Germany*. Oxford: Oxford University Press, 2000.

Riegl, Aloïs. *Stilfragen: Grundlegungen zu einer Geschichte der Ornamentik*. Berlin: 1893. English translation by Evelyn Kain. *Problems of Style: Foundations for a History of Ornament*. Princeton: Princeton University Press, 1992.

Steer, John, and White, Antony, ed. *Atlas of Western Art History: Artists, Sites and Movements from Ancient Greece to the Modern Age*. London: Facts on File, 1994.

Stevens, MaryAnn (ed.) *Sisley*, exh. cat, 26. Paris: RMN, 1992.

Taine, Hippolyte. *De l'idéal dans l'art: leçons professées à l'École des beaux-arts*. Paris: G. Baillière, 1867.

———. *Philosophie de l'art*, 2 vol. Paris: Hachette, 1901[9] (1867[1]).

Torre, Angelo. "Un 'tournant spatial' en histoire? Paysages, regards, ressources." *Annales. Histoire, Sciences Sociales* 63, no. 5 (2008): 1127–44.

Waschek, Matthias (ed.), *Relire Taine*. Paris: musée du Louvre, École nationale supérieure des Beaux-Arts, 2001.

Wrisley, David Joseph. "Locating Medieval French, or Why We Collect and Visualize the Geographic Information from Texts?" *Speculum* 92, no. S1 (2017): S145–S169.

Ziljmans, Kitty, and van Damme, Wilfried. "Art History in a Global Frame: World Art Studies—Introduction." In *Art History and Visual Studies in Europe: Transnational Discourses and National Frameworks*, edited by Matthew Rampley, 217–48. Leyden: Brill, 2014.

# 8

# MAPPING PAINTINGS, OR HOW TO BREATHE LIFE INTO PROVENANCE

*Jodi Cranston*

The Isabella Stewart Gardner Museum in Boston houses the extraordinary collection of Mrs. Gardner in a purpose-built Venetian-style palace. Observing the artworks in exactly the same arrangement as Mrs. Gardner experienced them allows visitors to situate themselves physically in the early twentieth century and to imagine a kind of kinship with the world of Fenway Court, as Mrs. Gardner referred to her house. This type of house museum arguably nudges us into the edges of history a bit more easily and effectively than the galleries of a traditional purpose-built museum: the wallpaper, the furnishings, the absence of wall labels. But how much of the lives of these artworks still remains lost to us as we stand before them? How much of the life of any artwork remains lost to us when we look at it in a museum?

Wall labels can help to provide context—up to a point. We can learn about the technical details of the object: the title, the artist, the dimensions, and the medium. Often we find a brief description of the style and meaning of the artwork, and possibly its function—although not usually for autonomous paintings. Mention is usually made of the funding source or the donor's name. And usually there is a brief note of a famous person who owned the artwork, who, because of his or her social position, is mentioned to establish the artificial moment when this artwork became a "work of art" worthy of being purchased for the museum.

But so many questions emerge between these lines of text. And so many questions remain unanswered. What exactly were the paths taken by these artworks to get here? What did these artworks witness? Who also stood before these objects? What, if anything, happens to our understanding of, for example, Leonardo's *Mona Lisa* (Musée du Louvre, Paris), if we discover that Napoleon decided to place the portrait in his bedroom? And, what if we know that the picture adorned the wall of a thief's Paris apartment and returned to Italy for a short time before it was returned to the Louvre? Or, that the picture traveled from Paris again during World War II to prevent its seizure by the Nazis? This information is usually available in catalogue entries and museum object files, and many museums—although not all—now share with the public on museum websites as much information as they possess.

Consider, for example, the overwhelmingly detailed provenance record from the website of the National Gallery of Art in Washington, DC, of Sébastien Bourdon's 1652 portrait of *Ebba Sparre*.[1] Hiding within this string of names and semi-colons and dates are fascinating stories of sales, of bequests, and of relocations. The portrait traveled with Queen Christina of Sweden on her way to Rome, where it spent its first seventy-five years available to Italian viewers before returning to Bourdon's native France and eventually spending the bulk of its life in the United Kingdom. Just as fascinating, although for different reasons, are those entries with startlingly little information to share, with gaps that reveal how selective and limiting and Western biased art-historical archives can be; how the structure of these archives prioritizes artists and collectors—or the proper name. What does the archival silence tell us?

The lists, whether long or almost nonexistent or somewhere in between, effectively flatten the objecthood of these artifacts—as the influence of anthropology on art history has reinforced.[2] The people, rather than the artworks, take precedence, and the relationship between people (and places) and artworks recedes if not disappears. But sometimes the objects reveal their own biography by showing their provenance in a different format from a list of text. The reverse side of a canvas, for example, might indicate the movement of the painting with labels and stamps that state the dates of possession and the addresses, as well as places and dates of exhibitions.[3] Not in chronological order, but appearing randomly, more like stamps in a passport, labels can inadvertently convert provenance information from a list into a kind of diagram, and, in the process, take an unintentional step toward visualizing this information.

This chapter focuses on two digital projects that visualize through geographic mapping the stories that have been trapped within lists of people and places in provenance records. My first project *Mapping Titian* (www.mappingtitian.org), which concerns the paintings by the sixteenth-century Venetian artist, and, more recently, *Mapping Paintings* (www.mappingpaintings.org) allow users to visualize through geographic mapping one of the central concerns of art history, namely, the changing contexts of an artwork throughout the course of its life. Geographic maps can be made with the filter of artwork, artist, medium, genre, owner, patron, dates, and/or location, with the goal of deepening the user's experience of the artwork's biography. Compare, for example, the processes of reading a provenance entry and of seeing the geographic visualization of that entry. The map makes the itinerary of this artwork more impactful, and also allows multiple objects to be compared simultaneously (Figures 8.1 and 8.2).[4]

All of the provenance data for the works included in the aforementioned projects has been available for decades and, in some cases, centuries. However, the database assembled to create these geographic maps allows the information to be collated, compared, and searched within seconds, rather than years, and now the years can be spent making sense of the answers to a variety of new questions. If the lists of provenance information told a rudimentary history of things, then the visualization of that same information pushes that history toward the history *in* things, to borrow the terminology of thing theory. The visualization flips the perspective of the story, so that we see history through the lens of the object rather than through the lens of the human protagonists.

The nature of provenance data makes it an easy fit for geographic mapping over time. The term "provenance," which was first used in relation to artworks in the mid-eighteenth century, means to "come from." Museums still think of provenance in similar terms: for example, the website of the Museum of Fine Arts, Boston, states that "the provenance of a work of art is its history of ownership, from the time of its creation to the present."[5] Each unique object can usually be defined by a specific owner with a date range in years and with a location that can be translated into longitude and latitude points. The sequential and transferable nature of provenance adapts easily to the computational requirements for data structure. But the data requirements also strip the subjective layers of taste and value that have accumulated around the concept of provenance, especially the idea that an artwork has a certain pedigree solely because of its association with certain privileged individuals. Spreadsheets require consistent entries and remove all biased cachet from a name and related concerns about what constitutes authenticity.

Geographic mapping of provenance data carries over this foregrounding of time and place at the expense of pedigree and, in the process, offers a different perspective on known information

### Itinerary Points

Venice (45.442482, 12.34005), *Owner: Titian, Dates: 1560 — 1562*

Madrid (40.416775, -3.70379), *Owner: Philip II, Dates: 1562 — 1626*

Alcazar of Madrid (40.418, -3.7143), *Owner: Spanish Royal Collection, Dates: 1626 — 1704*

Paris (48.856613, 2.35222), *Owner: Antoine, 4th Duc de Gramont, Dates: 1704 — 1706*

Palais Royal (48.863335, 2.336944), *Owner: Duc d'Orleans, Dates: 1706 — 1792*

Paris (48.856613, 2.35222), *Owner: Eduoard de Walckiers, Dates: 1792 — 1792*

Rue d'Artois (48.87333, 2.307123), *Owner: Francois-Louis-Joseph de Laborde-Mereville, Dates: 1792 — 1793*

London (51.508514, -0.125487), *Owner: Francois-Louis-Joseph de Laborde-Mereville, Dates: 1793 — 1798*

Higham House (51.608376, -0.02072), *Owner: Jeremiah Harman, Dates: 1798 — 1798*

Savile Row (51.51095, -0.140307), *Owner: Michael Bryan, Dates: 1798 — 1798*

Cleveland House (51.504345, -0.139535), *Owner: Lord Francis Egerton, 3rd Duke of Bridgewater; Frederick Howard, 5th Earl of Carlisle; and George Granville Leveson-Gower, 1st Duke of Sutherland (Bridgewater Syndicate), Dates: 1798 — 1798*

Attingham Hall (52.68507, -2.667016), *Owner: Lord Berwick, Dates: 1798 — 1824*

Cobham Hall (51.394444, -0.418611), *Owner: Earl of Darnley, Dates: 1824 — 1896*

144/6 New Bond Street (51.51049, -0.142684), *Owner: Colnaghi, Dates: 1896 — 1896*

152 Beacon Street (42.354572, -71.07574), *Owner: Isabella Stewart Gardner, Dates: 1896 — 1903*

Fenway Court (42.338318, -71.09876), *Owner: Isabella Stewart Gardner, Dates: 1903 — 1924*

Fenway Court (42.338318, -71.09876), *Owner: Isabella Stewart Gardner Museum, Dates: 1924 — Present Day*

*Figure 8.1* Itinerary points for Titian's *Europa*.

*Source*: See www.mappingpaintings.org/vk1fz6fh (accessed 26 June 2019) © The author, 2019.

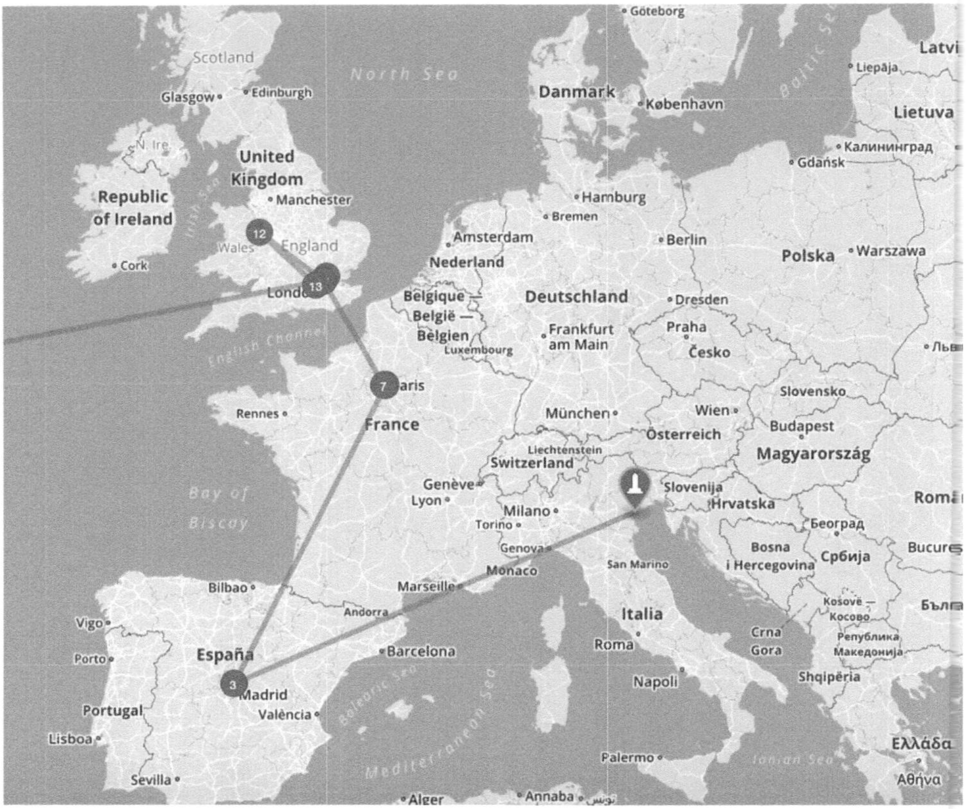


*Figure 8.2* Provenance map for Titian's *Europa*.

*Source*: See www.mappingtitian.org/paintings/europa/provenance (accessed 26 June 2019) © The author, 2019.

and highlights archival incompleteness. Visualizing the data changes it. We might look at a provenance list and see that a painting, such as Titian's *Europa*, was in England for several centuries, but not realize until it is mapped that the picture was not easily accessible for over a half century. How would limited accessibility affect our understanding of its influence? What, for example, is the impact of seeing that, after being at least five days' travel by coach outside of London (265 kilometers), Titian's *Europa* was a repeat visitor to a particular London neighborhood before coming to Mrs. Gardner's collection?[6] We might see in a catalogue entry that Titian's portrait of *Admiral Giovanni Moro* was lost in a fire in Berlin, but when the map ends in Berlin in 1945, at the former site of Flakturm II, a Nazi repository of artworks, it is horribly breathtaking.[7] The maps function as a tool that shifts our perspective on, and affective response to, provenance data. But we still have to work to understand what we are seeing and figure out how to interpret the maps that we can make on these platforms.

*Mapping Paintings* and *Mapping Titian* were designed to allow the research question to be the primary initiator and generator of the maps. Unlike many computational humanities projects to date, these platforms are intended to be open-ended and to foster the projects of many users rather than to present the research conclusions of one user. I collected from scholarly print publications the data for all of the paintings attributed to Titian for the *Mapping Titian* project, and users can manipulate that data to create custom maps for their own research purposes.[8] That

Titian data has become the "seed data" for the *Mapping Paintings* platform, which is designed to receive data from users who are willing to share in a scholarly variant of a crowd-sourced environment. Anyone can upload provenance data for private projects, but can also publish that data to the group of registered users once it has been verified by the site administrator. *Mapping Paintings* is not limited to the work of a single artist, to a known artist, to a specific geographic area, or even to the medium of painting. The platform also recognizes that often there are unknown elements in provenance data—that specific locations, dates, and owners are frequently unknown—and it allows for the visualization of those various information gaps. We ask contributors to include citations of their data sources and to include notes that capture scholarly debates and hypotheses to assist in their own research and to enhance the user experience of the platform.

Since the platform was designed to encourage multiple users to develop their own projects, it is not limited by a single set of research questions generated by a small group of researchers. Provenance data generated by the platform hopefully will inaugurate further interpretative projects that potentially extend to and incorporate multiple disciplines: these projects can be a powerful demonstration of the ways in which artworks become casualties and shapers of history, such as the Nazi theft of objects and Allied efforts to save and return artworks in World War II. Provenance maps can also initiate a consideration of how non-art-related events, such as widespread disease, migration, or piracy affect the movement of artworks. But the potential projects can also deepen the field of art history. Which kinds of artworks travel most often? Which artworks stay together in collections? Which cities are most closely connected through the exchange and sale of artworks and how do those relationships change over time? How does the geographic mapping of provenance data affect traditional art-historical narratives of artistic influence and emulation? Do artistic styles in fact travel and spread in the ways that art history has suggested?

I developed the platforms because I have asked many of these questions in my own research and felt as though I was hazarding answers based on anecdotal evidence or an excessively limited group of artworks or on intuition. For much of the remainder of this chapter, I will focus on three different research projects that were supported by the geographic maps that I made on the *Mapping Titian* platform.

## Project 1

My first project to use the platform was related to lingering questions that I had from my dissertation research on Italian Renaissance portraiture, which I had completed some fifteen years prior to the development of *Mapping Titian*. My question centered on the reception of painted portraits by viewers in subsequent generations. Did portraits remain in the families of the sitters who originally commissioned the artworks? Did portraits leave those commissioning families at a similar, specific moment in the lives of the objects? How would our conception of portraiture change if subsequent viewers collected and displayed portraits of individuals whom they had never seen or known? Were there any consistent answers to these questions?

I can now answer these questions with some degree of certainty for portraits attributed to Titian and hope at some point to answer this for many more Italian Renaissance artists once more data populates the *Mapping Paintings* platform. There are approximately sixty-five portraits attributed to Titian between 1510 and 1576, the years accepted as those spanning the artist's career.[9] When we shift the time frame of the provenance map from 1576–1650, there are a significant number of portraits that have left Venice and many that have left Italy.[10] However, the comparison effected by these maps is not totally revelatory especially when limited to static maps with a fixed scale. The exercise also indicates how there can be too much data for a map to bear. However, this is also an example of how valuable the collation of data for a geographic mapping project can be (even if the maps are not always immediately so), because we can see more clearly that nearly 75% of the portraits passed into a different family within one generation of their completion. This result aligns with what art historians who study the seventeenth century and the rise of art collections have long suspected: that portraits were collected less for the identity of the sitter and more for the name of the artist.[11] But knowing that this sale of the portraits occurred even earlier than suspected further compromises the importance of ideas about resemblance and likeness. Portraits seem to have functioned more as allegories of personhood and identity as early as the sixteenth century.

## Project 2

My second project to use the *Mapping Titian* platform was for an afterword to an anthology of essays that discussed the long shadow of influence of sixteenth-century Venetian art.[12] The contributions to the printed volume explored how Titian's paintings in particular exerted a measurable influence on artists outside both Venice and Italy throughout the centuries that followed. I wanted to determine exactly which paintings by Titian were in Venice in the seventeenth century and to explore how we define the idea of regional stylistic influence if and when a majority of those influential artworks had left their home city.

We know well from earlier scholarly contributions that visits to Italy were made by artists such as the Flemish painter Peter Paul Rubens and that seventeenth-century artists were exposed to Venetian artworks in European collections. Sales by collectors became the good fortune of others, as groups of paintings were obtained (through the help of agents in Venice) by Cardinal Scipio Borghese, Cardinal Leopoldo de'Medici, Charles I, the Duke of Hamilton, and Archduke Leopold Wilhelm, among others.[13] The *Mapping Titian* platform confirmed that within the first few decades of the seventeenth century, almost half of Titian's pictures had left the Republic, joining those that had already been sent outside Venice—especially to Spain—by Titian himself upon their creation. Most of the paintings remaining in Venice were immovable altarpieces or ceiling painting canvases or *scuole* pictures. But those that were portable and remained in Venice nearly always changed location at some point (if not multiple times) before the end of the seventeenth century. In a very short space of time, less than fifty years after Titian's death in 1576, many of his pictures were scattered throughout Europe and found new groups of viewers in places where the artist himself had never visited.[14] Occasionally some of the pictures remained in one location for an even shorter span of time (ten to twenty years) before being sold again and moving to a new location. This market activity heightened the broader interest in Titian's work that many traveling artists had already begun to cultivate through their early seventeenth-century visits to important pre-sale sites for seeing Titian's works, such as Madrid, Rome, and, of course, Venice.

Venice remained an important home to collections, totaling almost forty in the lagoon in 1700, but the migration of so many important sixteenth-century artworks to locations outside Venice created an impossible demand in the following century for original sixteenth-century pictures. Seventeenth-century painters created repetitive works that addressed this demand not only by giving acquisitive European collectors the "Giorgione" or the "Titian" that they otherwise could not obtain, but also by creating a collecting culture that appreciated repetitive artworks precisely for the ways in which these later pictures approximated and deviated from their sources.

The compressed time frame for these mobile sixteenth-century pictures and the evidently lengthy impact that they had on subsequent generations of artists meant that, contrary to prevailing scholarly conclusions, the signs of influence were not necessarily or solely evidence of stagnation for a particular artist or of clever business strategies to capitalize on market demands within Venice. There were certainly examples of these situations. But with so many Venetian pictures departing for other cities, one wonders not only how diluted those sixteenth-century Venetian artistic traditions had become for on-site observers, or how available in Venice these traditions were to newly arriving painters. Consider, for example, just one branch of influential pictures by Titian that had long resided outside of the city: his *Danaë* (Museo del Prado, Madrid), the Farnese *Danaë* (Museo di Capodimonte, Naples), the *Venus of Urbino* (Gallerie degli Uffizi, Florence), and multiple versions of *Venus and Adonis* (Museo del Prado, Madrid; Getty Museum, Los Angeles, CA; Metropolitan Museum, New York; National Gallery of Art, Washington, DC) all began their early lives somewhere other than Venice. Moreover, by 1650 related pictures, such as the *Sacred and Profane Love* (c. 1515, Villa Borghese, Rome) and *Nymph and Shepherd* (c. 1570, Kunsthistorisches Museum, Vienna), had departed for locations north and south of Venice. The *Sleeping Venus* (c. 1510, Gemäldegalerie, Dresden) left comparatively late, saying goodbye to Venice's shores by 1700. And, of course, the focus on these departures disregards not only the arrival to Venice of artworks made elsewhere and collected by Venetians, but also the role of prints in creating increasingly unprecedented access to artworks without the overlapping of territorial and stylistic boundaries.[15] There are times when cities that are geographically distant are much closer because of the movement of artworks, and, consequently, we need to look more closely at what we mean by a regional influence. Digital mapping on a platform that facilitates the simultaneous mapping of multiple objects recalibrates through the displayed density of exchanges between two cities the actual geographical distances between those cities.

## Project 3

The third and final project included in my book *Green Worlds of Renaissance Venice* concerns the creation and imagination of green spaces and places in sixteenth-century Venice.[16] A central thread in the book is the development and legacy of Venetian pastoral painting, and at which point in time the pastoral art made by Venetian artists in the sixteenth century leaves the lagoon city for other locations. What is the broader impact of the physical location of these artworks on contemporary pastoral literary culture? Or is this a case of the visual arts detaching from the literary tradition that first inspired them, of leaving that literary tradition behind in Venice?

The map (Figure 8.3) shows that a few pastoral-type pictures remained in Venice, but that many more left the city for new homes in collections throughout Europe.[17] The departures were hardly specific to pastoral artworks, as we have already seen. Entire collections of diverse holdings were sold to or confiscated by newly emerging collectors in Rome, Madrid, Paris, London, Brussels, and Amsterdam.[18] But the relocation of the majority of Venetian pastoral artworks certainly affected the reception of the pastoral in Venice. Consider, for example, the chronology in order of departure date from Venice of Titian's pastoral paintings that had not been (or were not known to have been) commissioned by patrons living outside of Venice: *Three Ages of Man*, 1550 (National Gallery of Scotland, Edinburgh); *Sacred and Profane Love*, before 1608 (Villa Borghese, Rome); *Flaying of Marsyas*, 1620 (National Museum in Kroměříž, Czech Republic); *Pastoral Concert*, 1623 (the Musèe du Louvre, Paris); *Nymph and Shepherd*, 1638 (Kunsthistorisches Museum, Vienna); *Venus With Organist and Dog*, 1639 (Museo del Prado, Madrid); *Gypsy Madonna*, 1657 (Kunsthistorisches Museum, Vienna); *Noli me Tangere*, before 1690 (National Gallery, London); and *Sleeping Venus* (if we accept Titian's participation with Giorgione), no later than 1699 (Gemäldegalerie, Dresden). Giorgione's paintings, which I have not included in this map view, have less certain provenance information, which contributes to uncertain attributions, but even

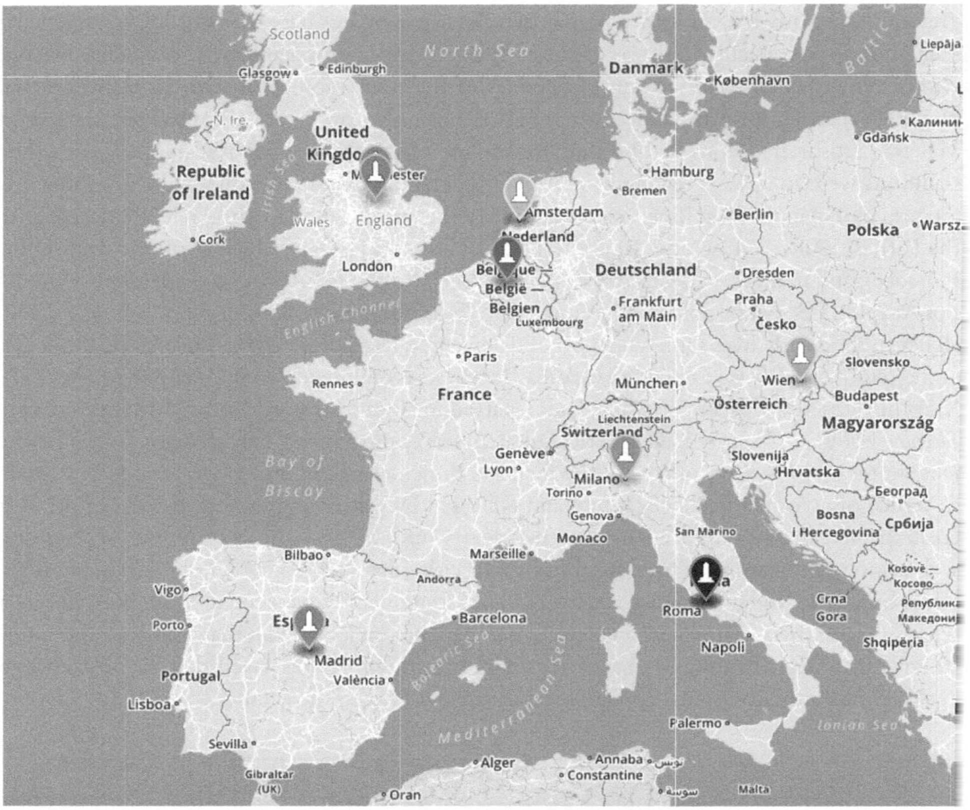


*Figure 8.3* Locations of Titian's pastoral paintings in 1650.

*Source*: See www.mappingtitian.org/map/?map_id=74 (accessed 26 June 2019) © The author, 2019.

the generally accepted works follow the same chronology as that for Titian's paintings.[19] Drawings are also difficult to track because of the limited provenance information, but we know that artists, such as Rembrandt and, later, Watteau, had direct access to many Venetian pastoral drawings, as well as prints.[20]

The cities that received the most Venetian pastoral artworks were also those that around the same time began to produce their own painted, drawn, printed, and written variations of the pastoral mode. The geographic center for the pastoral, as has been well charted by art and literary historians, first shifts southward toward Rome, and then northward toward France, Holland, and England. Venice, and all that it nurtured and cultivated for the pastoral mode, remained in the forefront of cultural production in these other places, whose inhabitants continued to focus their attention on, if not idealize, this city as the locus of artistic inspiration and creativity. Many seventeenth-century Venetian artists seemed to take a similarly distanced or external position by visualizing their world as its visitors experienced it, as an urban island set apart from the green landscapes of the countryside. The pastoral was no longer lived in Venice and was never lived again in exactly the same way.

These three projects were motivated by specific research questions, but I have also found interesting case studies of individual paintings solely from compiling the provenance data. The act of attaching specific longitudes and latitudes to the provenance data, which I at first thought would be a yeoman's task, has unexpectedly resulted in bringing that provenance to life. Titian's *Charles V With Hound* (Museo del Prado, Madrid) was gifted by Philip IV of Spain to Charles I of England in the hope of inspiring the beleaguered British ruler; but upon Charles I's beheading, the Spanish monarchy bought back the painting. Henry Clay Frick wanted to purchase important old master paintings to add to his collection and, upon hearing that the well-known collector Sir Hugh Lane had died in the sinking of the ship, the Lusitania, bought several pictures, including Titian's *Portrait of a Man With a Red Cap* (Frick Collection, New York), because of the steeply discounted prices. These stories have been available, but they become all the more vivid when we lift them out of the lists and out of the endless semi-colons and periods symbolizing different types of ownership. Our attention can be refocused on new questions, such as the diverse motivations of ownership, for example.

The ambition of this project is to collaborate with museums and to bring the provenance of museum collections to visitors with interactive kiosks and/or wall labels with QR code links to entries on the platform or possibly through scanning the artwork with a smartphone. But this has proven to be a challenging part of the project, with museums voicing objections to having technology in the galleries or wanting to develop their own proprietary projects. The questions and concerns about the platform itself that have been voiced by museum curators relate to citing sources for the data and including exhibition histories. But I also think that some of the resistance comes from the politics of provenance itself. Provenance often reveals some of humankind's worst actions toward cultural heritage and toward individuals and communities. Shameful pasts are easier to conceal in a list of text. Gaps in provenance are far more obvious when noted in a map where there is no place for a pin to land or where a painting essentially disappears from history because of the incompleteness of archival information that is typically relied upon to guarantee authenticity and originality. If the operating assumption is that the recording of a noteworthy object guarantees its status as an artwork, then the unknown or the inhumane compromises the preciousness of that artwork and leaves spaces for users to invent connections that make the archives comprehensible.

As an academic, I see those gaps not as barriers but as invitations for interpretation and as symptoms of some related, yet distinct, historical event or moment. An object can slip out of historical consciousness because of some obstructing event, such as war, or because the named owner matters less, or because the structure of the archive has changed, even if for a short time, such that the identity of the owner or artwork, or both, does not matter. Provenance is a way of writing history and, just like maps, tells a particular story replete with its own limitations. But to map provenance, like mapping anything, offers a new perspective. Our questions can shift from "who owned this?" to "what did this object witness?" and " what was the agency of the object?"

My hope for my digital mapping project—and, indeed, for any computational humanities project—is that the different medium offers new perspectives on the questions that we ask of the material that we study and on how that material has come to us. Jacques Derrida talks about precisely these possibilities of electronic media in his 1995 lecture, "Mal d'Archive" (which was published as a long essay and then translated into English as "Archive Fever") in which he discusses the notion of archives in Freud's writings. Derrida raises the concern that new technologies impact not only on the conservation of psychoanalysis, but also transform it in its very practices. Derrida says:

> The technical structure of the archiving archive also determines the structure of the archivable content even in its very coming into existence and in its relationship to the future. The archivization produces as much as it records the event. [. . .] The archiving technology . . . inform[s] . . . the conception of the future and possibly the future itself.[21]

No longer constrained to a paragraph of text, the digital provenance archive can affect how we manage information and how we think about provenance as a concept. Digital geographic mapping of the lives of artworks is just one step in how art historians can consider how (and even if) we archive these lives in the future and what unforeseen impacts provenance can have on the types of digital archives that are developed.

## Notes

1. For the provenance, consult www.nga.gov/collection/art-object-page.41646.html, accessed June 7, 2018. See also Anne Higonnet, "Afterword: The Social Life of Provenance," in *Provenance: An Alternate History of Art*, ed. Gail Feigenbaum and Inge Reist (Los Angeles: Getty Research Institute, 2012), 197.
2. One of the seminal texts in this regard has been Arjun Appadurai, "Introduction: Commodities and the Politics of Value," in *The Social Life of Things: Commodities in Cultural Perspective*, ed. Arjun Appadurai (Cambridge: Cambridge University Press, 1986), 3–63.
3. See, for example, the exhibition "Provenance: A Forensic History of Art," organized by Nancy Karrels in 2017, which explored the stamps and labels on the backs of paintings: accessed June 11, 2018, https://kam.illinois.edu/exhibition/provenance-forensic-history-art.
4. Accessed June 7, 2018, www.mappingpaintings.org/u44r93sx.
5. Accessed June 7, 2018, www.mfa.org/collections/provenance.
6. Accessed June 7, 2018, www.mappingtitian.org/paintings/europa/provenance.
7. Accessed June 7, 2018, www.mappingpaintings.org/jpj43bjs.
8. Much of the provenance information collected to create the platform came from Harold E. Wethey, *The Paintings of Titian*, 3 vols. (London: Phaidon, 1969–75).
9. Accessed June 7, 2018, www.mappingtitian.org/map/?map_id=70.
10. Accessed June 7, 2018, www.mappingtitian.org/map/?map_id=71.
11. Krzysztof Pomian, *Collectors and Curiosities: Paris and Venice, 1500–1800*, trans. Elizabeth Wiles-Portier (Cambridge: Polity Press, 1990), 107; Simona Savini Branca, *Il collezionismo veneziano nel '600* (Florence: Leo S. Olschki, 1965).
12. Andaleeb Badiee Banta, ed. *The Enduring Legacy of Venetian Renaissance Art* (New York: Routledge, 2016). My contribution is "Quick to Say Good-bye, Hard to Forget: The Long Lives of *Cinquecento* Venetian Pictures," 169–78.
13. There are many studies on these individual collectors. A helpful introduction is Jonathan Brown, *Kings and Connoisseurs: Collecting Art in Seventeenth-Century Europe* (New Haven, CT: Yale University Press, 1995).
14. Accessed June 7, 2018, www.mappingtitian.org/map/?map_id=72.
15. Northern European artworks and prints were already being collected in the fifteenth and sixteenth centuries. See, for example, the inventory of the Vendramin collection (published and discussed by Jaynie Anderson, "A Further Inventory of Gabriel Vendramin's Collection," *Burlington Magazine* 121 [1979]: 639–48), which includes both types of objects in the sixteenth century.
16. Jodi Cranston, *Green Worlds of Renaissance Venice* (University Park, PA: Penn State University Press, 2019).
17. Accessed June 7, 2018, www.mappingtitian.org/map/?map_id=74.
18. For a helpful survey of these transactions, see Brown, *Kings and Connoisseurs*. Christina Anderson, *The Flemish Merchant of Venice: Daniel Nijs and the Sale of the Gonzaga Art Collection* (New Haven and London: Yale University Press, 2015) offers an in-depth profile of an art dealer who resided in Venice.
19. The same contours in provenance can be found by considering the provenance information offered by Anderson (*Giorgione*, 294–308) for the generally accepted attributions.
20. Robert C. Cafritz, "Reverberations of Venetian Graphics in Rembrandt's Pastoral Landscapes," in *Places of Delight: The Pastoral Landscape*, ed. Robert Cafritz, Lawrence Gowing, and David Rosand (Washington, DC: Phillips Collection, 1988), 131–47; Robert C. Cafritz, "Rococo Restoration of the Venetian Landscape and Watteau's Creation of the Fête Galante," in *Places of Delight*, 149–81.
21. Jacques Derrida, *Archive Fever: A Freudian Impression*, trans. Eric Prenowitz (Chicago and London: The University of Chicago Press, 1996), 17. Originally published as *Mal d'Archive: une impression freudienne* (Paris: Éditions Galilée, 1995).

## Bibliography

Anderson, Christina. *The Flemish Merchant of Venice: Daniel Nijs and the Sale of the Gonzaga Art Collection.* New Haven and London: Yale University Press, 2015.

Anderson, Jaynie. "A Further Inventory of Gabriel Vendramin's Collection." *Burlington Magazine* 121 (1979): 639–48

———. *Giorgione: The Painter of Poetic Brevity.* Paris: Flammarion, 1997.

Appadurai, Arjun. "Introduction: Commodities and the Politics of Value." In *The Social Life of Things: Commodities in Cultural Perspective*, edited by Arjun Appadurai, 3–63. Cambridge: Cambridge University Press, 1986.

Branca, Simona Savini. *Il collezionismo veneziano nel '600.* Florence: Leo S. Olschki, 1965.

Brown, Jonathan. *Kings and Connoisseurs: Collecting Art in Seventeenth-Century Europe.* New Haven: Yale University Press, 1995.

Cafritz, Robert C. "Reverberations of Venetian Graphics in Rembrandt's Pastoral Landscapes." In *Places of Delight: The Pastoral Landscape*, edited by Robert Cafritz, Lawrence Gowing, and David Rosand, 131–47. Washington, DC: Phillips Collection, 1988.

———. "Rococo Restoration of the Venetian Landscape and Watteau's Creation of the Fête Galante." In *Places of Delight: The Pastoral Landscape*, edited by Robert Cafritz, Lawrence Gowing, and David Rosand, 149–81. Washington, DC: Phillips Collection, 1988.

Cranston, Jodi. "Quick to Say Good-bye, Hard to Forget: The Long Lives of *Cinquecento* Venetian Pictures." In *The Enduring Legacy of Venetian Renaissance Art*, edited by Andaleeb Badiee Banta, 169–78. New York: Routledge, 2016.

Derrida, Jacques. *Archive Fever: A Freudian Impression.* Translated by Eric Prenowitz. Chicago and London: The University of Chicago Press, 1996. Originally published as *Mal d'Archive: une impression freudienne.* Paris: Èditions Galilèe, 1995.

Higonnet, Anne. "Afterword: The Social Life of Provenance." In *Provenance: An Alternate History of Art*, edited by Gail Feigenbaum and Inge Reist, 196–209. Los Angeles: Getty Research Institute, 2012.

Pomian, Krzysztof. *Collectors and Curiosities: Paris and Venice, 1500–1800.* Translated by Elizabeth Wiles-Portier. Cambridge: Polity Press, 1990.

Wethey, Harold E. *The Paintings of Titian*, 3 vols. London: Phaidon, 1969–75.

# 9

# QUALITATIVE APPROACHES TO NETWORK ANALYSIS IN ART HISTORY

## Research on Contemporary Artists' Networks

*Sanja Sekelj*

Network analysis is based on the assumption that certain social phenomena cannot be explained solely by the characteristics of an individual or of specific social groups but rather by their roles in structured social relations. Its focus is, therefore, on the relations between different types of participants (individuals, groups, institutions), the totality of which forms a structure that simultaneously allows and limits their activity.[1] This kind of network mapping of relations of collaboration or co-attendance of actors in the cultural field has received substantial attention in the field of digital humanities and (digital) art history in recent years. The often-emphasized trait of the new methods is their potential to represent the participation of marginalized groups in the art world (such as women) or to highlight the role of those actors whom traditional art history has not valued or included in the art-historical canon. The logic behind such thinking is based on the conviction that a computerized processing of large amounts of data may reveal previously unseen structural patterns in which the hitherto omitted actors may come to occupy prominent positions owing to the "objectivity" of data and digital analytical tools.

The previously described automation bias, often present in the field of digital humanities and digital art history, has already been subject to criticism which emphasizes that data sets are not neutral or natural phenomena, but involve a certain level of interpretation. Modern data visualization methods may not only conceal the assumptions on which the relevant data sets have been constructed, but also reinforce social and cultural mechanisms of marginalization, thus reproducing the universalizing tendency of traditional art history.[2] Moreover, critics have emphasized the need to produce more complex visualizations which would allow for the presentation of the multifaceted and constructed nature of the data.[3] They have also made efforts to provide tools that would make it possible to document the process of manipulating visualizations. Such techniques would, therefore, help to achieve greater transparency in the research process.[4]

However, when speaking of network analysis in the field of art history, can we address the activity of a specific actor based only on the position and number of relations that he or she enters within a network? Alternatively, is it more important to ask how these relations were established in the first place? What is the content of communication that has been facilitated through these relations? How has the communication evolved and what have been its consequences, both for the observed phenomenon and for the wider social and cultural context? In other words, how should one approach the modeling, visualization, and interpretation of data in a contextual way?

This chapter is an effort to tackle the issue of mediating between quantitative and qualitative data analysis based on the example of contemporary artists' networks in Croatia. Since our research was conducted with the help of custom-made digital tools and on relatively small data samples, the construed character of visualizations soon became evident, especially with regard to pre-defining the relations between various entities. If a specific number of artists participate in the same exhibition, does it automatically imply a sort of relation between them? Or, how do the artists participating in a program of the same institution relate to each other? This chapter describes attempts to achieve deep interdisciplinarity between art history and social network analysis. While agreeing with the aforesaid opinions that visualization is always already interpretation, and that in order critically to approach visualizations one should have at least a basic knowledge of the mechanisms by which digital tools operate, we also wish to emphasize the need to acquire a more thorough knowledge of the disciplinary context in which certain methods have emerged and evolved. Is there a critique of what Johanna Drucker has called "realist approaches" within the tradition of social network analysis?[5]

## Organization and Communication Models of Artists' Networks in the Twentieth Century

The question of how to reconcile quantitative data analysis with the theoretical preoccupations and methodological paradigms of the humanities lies, according to Johanna Drucker, at the heart of the reflection on digital art history.[6] The general emphasis is on the need to cultivate an approach to the analysis of network visualizations that will simultaneously take into consideration the macro and micro perspectives, that is, a combination of distant and close reading.[7] The ways in which this has been tackled so far differ depending on the nature of the art-historical phenomenon and the nature and quantity of the analyzed data. Furthermore, according to the latter, one can roughly differentiate between two approaches.

In the first option, quantitative analysis is conducted on the basis of a large amount of data that has been taken from the relevant museum or archival institutions in an already systematized form. Visualizations and quantitative analyses serve to achieve additional spatial and temporal contextualization of the phenomenon in question. They perform the function of detecting structural patterns at the macro level, but include critical consideration of possible inconsistencies arising from the data set, as well as from the multiple social or cultural factors that may have affected them. These structural patterns are then compared with the already existing or new micro case studies.[8]

The second option involves the autonomous collecting, sorting, and modeling of data, and is most often accompanied by the independent conceptualization and development of digital tools adapted to a specific field of research. The parallel process of art-historical research and deduction of research results as quantifiable metadata contributes to the development of an open and flexible infrastructure (adaptable by means of simple changes depending on the future research), while simultaneously integrating the quantitative and qualitative reading levels of the material. Such a process leads to reflection on the art-historical material *through* digital tools and preserves the relation to the original material, encouraging constant relocation from close to distant reading and vice versa.[9] Since autonomous data collection and data modeling is a painstaking and time-consuming process, it is still difficult to speak of big data analyses, although the amount of data is such that the analysis may still indicate certain structural patterns. This option will often result in positive interaction between art history and network analysis, as it has been developed within sociology, which requires an initial reflection on a particular art-historical phenomenon as a network phenomenon, and consideration of the usefulness and adaptation of certain sociological concepts and methods in its interpretation.

One such initiative has been the project *Modern and Contemporary Artists' Networks, Art Groups and Art Associations. Organisation and Communication Models of Artists' Collaborative Practices in the 20th and 21st Century—ARTNET*, conducted at the Institute of Art History in Zagreb.[10] Gathering an interdisciplinary team of experts in the fields of art history, history of architecture, sociology, and information technology, the project dealt with artistic networks in modern and contemporary art, with the aim of detecting and describing the organizational and communicational models in their background as analytical samples.[11] According to the model just described, the Croatian Artists' Network Information System (CAN_IS) relational database was developed and linked to a complementary visualization interface in which all entities/nodes (persons, events, objects) and their interrelations were defined during the intense collective discussions of the team members. Simultaneously, the process of building the database included downloading previously assembled data sets, as well as manual collection and addition of data, which had to be systematized and double-checked.[12]

In addition to addressing individual entities and their possible relations, the discussion included: the differences between network phenomena from different time periods in the twentieth century; ways in which networking practices depended on their socio-political context and technologies; discussions of factors that facilitated or limited the formation and operation of particular networks (for example, differences in networking between institutional and non-institutional contexts); or the wider consequences that the activity of a particular network had for the art world. The art network phenomena and the quantitative analyses of network visualizations were observed in their contexts. This meant that certain participants and their relations were interpreted within the network structure as a whole and also within the specific spatial and temporal context in which they operated. In this respect, it is important to emphasize that many discussions were devoted precisely to the problem of network dynamics, that is, to the ways in which the development of a network over time can be presented. This, in fact, turned out to be among the central theoretical and methodological issues of the project and one that challenges claims that network analysis in digital art history threatens to ruin historical thinking.[13]

Within the project, there were minor differences among individual researchers concerning their approach to network analysis and the interpretation of results depending on the nature of the observed art phenomenon and the question raised, the current state of research, and the type and quantity of the available data. In most cases, however, researchers studied formal sociability by generating affiliation networks in which participants were linked through common participation in events such as exhibitions, discursive events, or professional bodies. In this case, joint participation in an event was viewed as a context that offered a possibility for creating a social relation (whereby common participation could also result from a pre-existing relation),[14] and the primary role of a network participant was predetermined by the institutional context in which he or she entered (e.g. as a curator, member of the jury, participant of a discursive event). Although primarily serving the study of mechanisms of institutional cooperation and the role of participants occupying prominent positions in the network, almost all research analyses within these and related networks emphasized the importance of informal sociability for the self-organization of participants in general or for structural changes within the network over time.[15] In other words, the network visualizations thus generated were also used as datascapes to observe the multiplexity of relations between individual participants.[16]

## Researching Networks of Contemporary Art

The methodology described was also used in researching artists' networks related to the Croatian context from 1990 onwards.[17] The process of collecting and processing data for this particular period and place raised specific issues: in addition to the fact that there was still no systematic art-historical research of the period, the socio-political context of Croatia in the 1990s caused stagnation in artistic production in public cultural institutions. New generations of participants had emerged who approached the task of organizing artistic events without an institutional background. As a result, a considerable amount of archival material is still privately owned by these individuals, and some of this had disappeared or had not even been produced at the time of the event organization. The process of data collection was also influenced by rapid developments in information and communication technologies. Communication among the participants in the Croatian art world of the period often took place through various local and international mailing lists and BBS systems, many of which have been deleted and lost. For these reasons, compiling the database was preceded by a lengthy process of mapping the relevant local and international organizations, initiatives, individuals, and their means of communication. On the one hand, the problem was the absence of ready sources of information. On the other, due to the fact that the period under investigation was very recent, a large amount of data still had to be found, systematized, and turned into metadata that could enter the database.

Taking into account that there was no proper overview of post-1990 art practices, the quantitative analyses focused on network practices within the institutions, that is, on creating egocentric networks in which individuals working at these institutions played a central role. In the design of network visualizations we typically used the "nominalist strategy."[18] Since we aimed to remove—as much as possible—confirmation bias at the level of data entry, we decided to enter all the programs of each institution and all those with whom they collaborated.

An example of this approach is the local network of the Soros Center for Contemporary Art Zagreb (SCCA), which emerged from organizing annual exhibitions between 1993 and 1998 (Figure 9.1).[19] A multifaceted, complex network involved subjects who participated in the organization of exhibitions as exhibitors or catalogue authors, or in various administrative-organizational bodies of SCCA. Quantitative analysis indicated the basic features of the network structure and singled out the key protagonists. Since we were interested in the positions of actors within the network, and relations among them, we decided to transform this multifaceted and complex network into a single-mode, co-affiliation network (Figure 9.2). This visualization would have allowed us to make certain conventional calculations, such as calculating network density. However, it became clear that the annual exhibition held in 1998 did not, as was usual, include a public call to artists according to a pre-defined concept; instead, SCCA's employees decided to make a retrospective exhibition of the Group of Six Artists, an art group from the time of the Yugoslav New Art Practice.[20] Since the calculation of network density indicates a discrepancy between the relations that could have been achieved within the network and those actually achieved, and most subjects in the SCCA network could not participate in one of the exhibitions because they did not belong to the specified art group, quantitative analysis would not have faithfully reflected the interrelations between the participants within the network, and may have even led to wrong conclusions.

Art-historical research in interpreting the results served as a corrective that enabled us to situate the SCCA network within a specific historical and temporal context, and to suggest reasons why some actors (besides the SCCA employees) took on multiple roles or prominent positions within the network. In conjunction with the arrangement of specific annual exhibitions in the network topology, it also led to the conclusion that, in the local community, the SCCA did

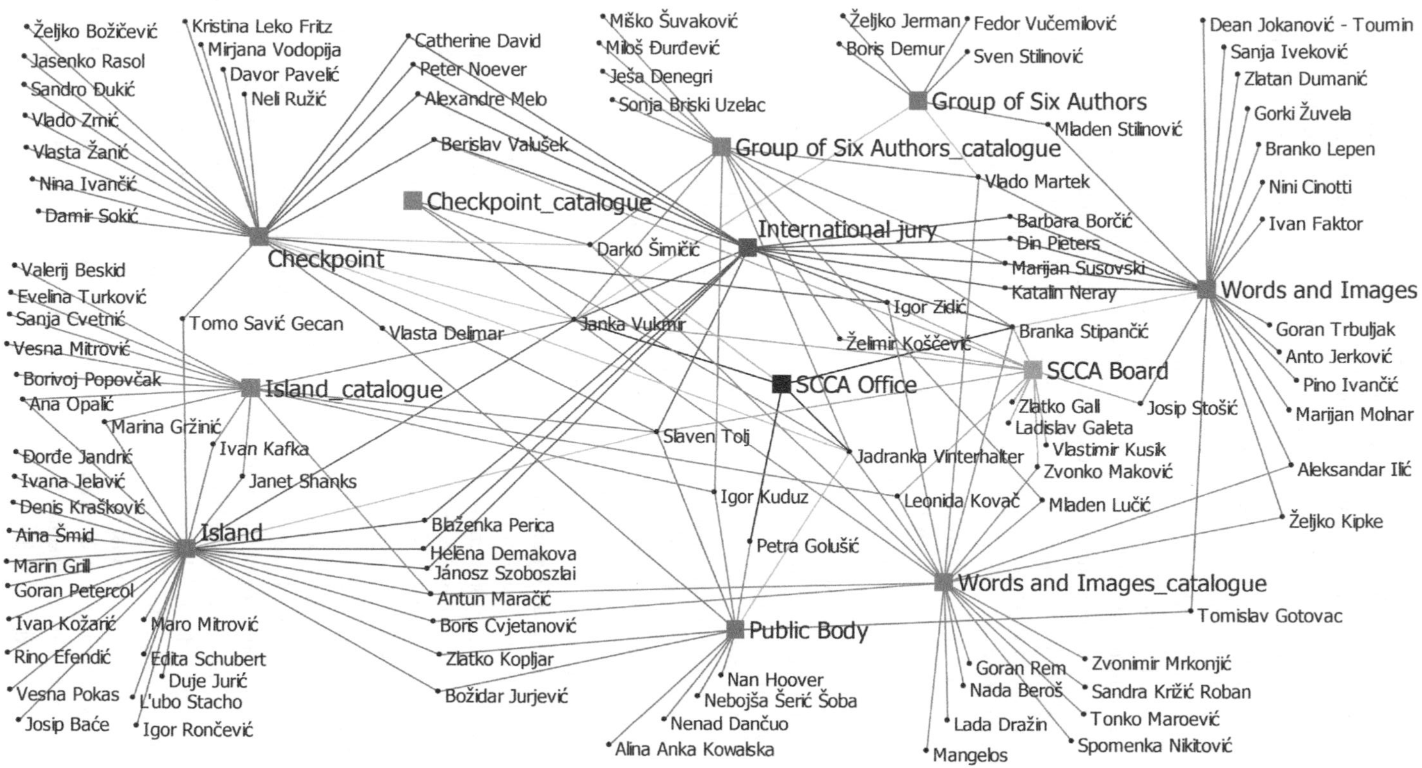


*Figure 9.1* Organizational and collaborative structure of the SCCA-Zagreb Annual Exhibitions, 1993–1998.

*Source*: Željka Tonković, Sanja Sekelj.

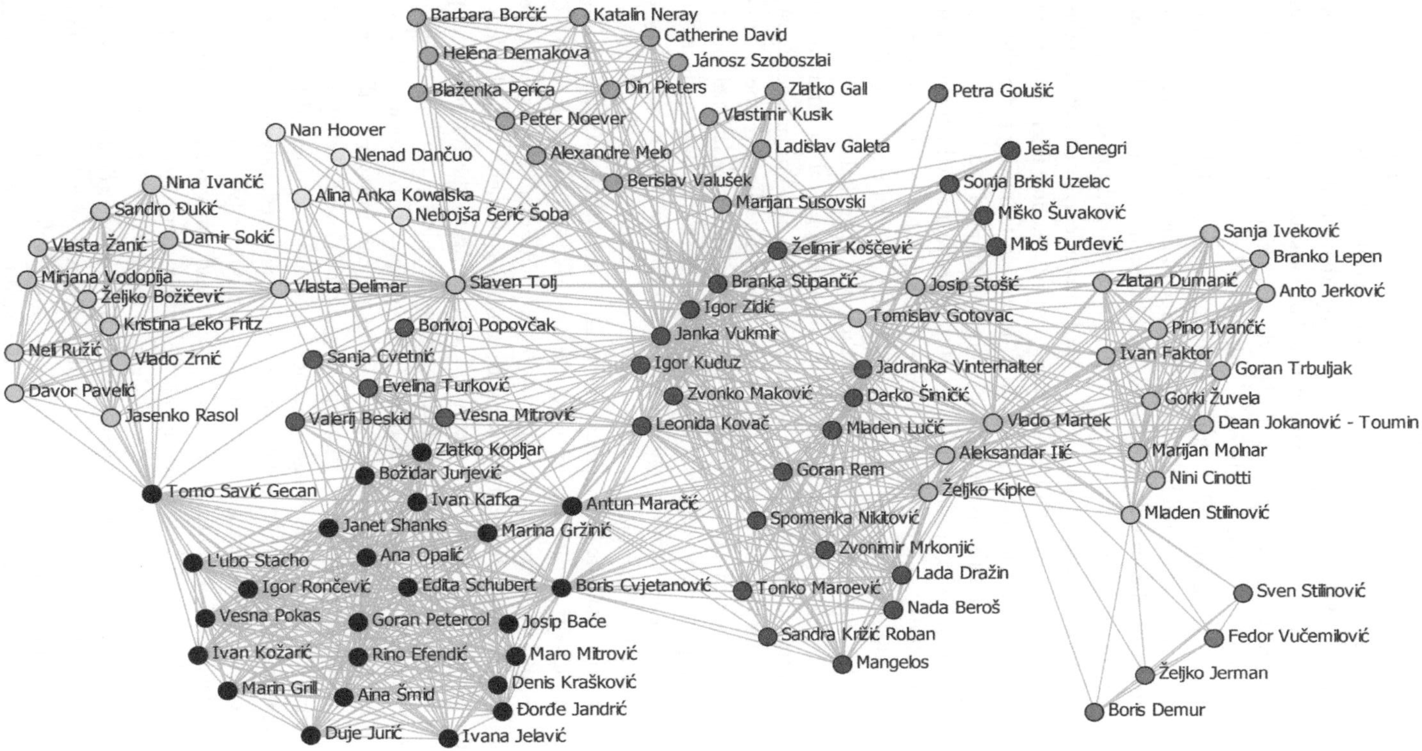


*Figure 9.2* Visualization of cohesive groups of members of the SCCA-Network, 1993–1998.

*Source*: Željka Tonković, Sanja Sekelj.

not function as a new place of art networking; instead, the network depended on the personal connections of individuals who were actively involved in its work.[21] The quantitative analysis indicated, therefore, the multiplexity of relations that were important for the formation of the SCCA network, and the persistence of certain informal social relations formed back in the 1980s. It did not, however, offer answers about the meanings that circulated within the network, or about the conscious action of individual participants. The visualization did not provide information on network dynamics and included neither those participants who cooperated with the Center in a more informal way, nor the rich international network of the Center created through the SCCA's joint programs and meetings at the European level. It also failed to provide an answer to the questions whether and how the structure of the network influenced the artistic production of its subjects or the art field in general. Such deficiencies in the application of analytical tools are the reason why the discrepancy between the empirical and supposedly objective approach of social sciences and that practiced within the humanities is often noted in the field of digital art history. It also points to why, following such comparison, there is a need for theoretical reflection on the basic concepts, tools, and methods.[22] However, following the earlier assertion that the methods of other scholarly disciplines should not be adopted too lightly, we would like to add that it is also necessary to consider the disciplinary context in which certain analytical methods have been developed, and how they have been used to solve certain problems. In other words: is network analysis, as argued by Ann Mische, merely a set of techniques for analyzing social structures, or is it a wider conceptual basis and theoretical paradigm?[23]

As yet, there is no consensus in the social sciences on the theoretical basis for an analysis of social networks, or on the correlation between structure, culture, and human agency, or on the structuralist bias often present in network analysis. These topics have, however, been approached productively, on both theoretical and practical levels, from the angle of relational sociology.[24] It has emerged from critiques of the approach in which social phenomena are reduced solely to structural patterns, taking into account both structure and culture (that is, according to relational sociology, structure and culture can be separated only at the analytical level). Moreover, the structure itself is relational: the arrangement of elements within the structure and its emergence depend on the activity of the participants, the historical context, and the cultural patterns that are at their disposal at a given moment. New configurations in the structure, resulting from interconnections between different participants, can also yield new cultural values, which in turn affect the network structure. In other words, according to the relational perspective, the network presupposes an interrelation between structure, culture, and human agency, and emphasizes their dynamism and fluidity over time.[25] The complexity of the described system is further enhanced by the fact that the participants always take part in several different networks simultaneously, with their own specific cultural patterns, and that consequently a change within one structure can cause a cascade of changes in other, more or less connected networks. Since studying historical networks from this perspective necessarily involves analyzing various cultural narratives that co-exist and interact at a given historical moment (which Mustafa Emirbayer and Jeff Goodwin have termed "cultural structure"),[26] network analysis in relational sociology necessarily involves additional qualitative research (conducting interviews, historiographical and ethnographic research).[27] Moreover, according to Betina Hollstein, the best results are obtained precisely by *combining* quantitative and qualitative methods. Qualitative data collection and analysis make it possible to address some of the recurrent problems in social network analysis, such as the interpretation of human agency or the emergence and development of social networks.[28]

It is based on these theoretical insights that we addressed the issue of network practices in Croatian contemporary art in the framework of the ARTNET project. The focus was on the cultural hub that is today most often referred to as the "independent scene," its basic structure made up of organizations linked through the legal framework of civic associations and the common values reflected in their way of working (horizontality, solidarity, encouragement of local and international cooperation) and their artistic production (inclination to experimentation, participation, social engagement).[29] It is a complex and under-researched phenomenon that attracts different types of participants (organizations, artists, curators, activists, etc.), whose activities span several fields of action (contemporary art, human rights, labor rights, women's rights, green economy, etc.), brought together precisely by the previously mentioned common values. We studied the independent scene by conceptualizing it—following Harrison White—as "netdom," that is, a specific social structure (network) whose agents are linked through shared stories (domain).[30] In addition to describing and analyzing the network's structure, we were also interested in the way this network comprising the independent scene developed during the 1990s and transitioned to the new millennium. What were the changes and what triggered them? What specific actions of individual actors brought about changes in the network's structure, and by which political and cultural discourses were they, in turn, triggered? How were the common values and stories of these participants generated within the network? Did the socio-political and cultural context influence their spread, and how? What was the significance of the network for the actors involved, and for the cultural field in general, and in what way did the "cultural structure" change with the consolidation of the independent scene network after 2000?

In order to answer these questions and to describe the interdependence of structure, culture, and human agency, a research segment—along with the archival one—also included semi-structured interviews with key participants in the independent scene in the 1990s.[31] These interviews resulted in qualitative data in which the participants themselves reflected on their own networking practices, and it was already at the level of designing the interviews that we tried to reconcile the analysis of the aforementioned three segments. The sequentially divided protocol required that the participants reflect on their own activities, the key agents, sites, projects, and events that were important for networking, and the issues of socio-political context, cultural policies, and financing.[32] The participants themselves defined their own social and cultural environment and determined the significance of individual elements in both structures for the formation of the independent scene network.

We used qualitative structural analysis (QSA) for analyzing the interviews—a methodological approach based on the aforementioned critiques of social network analysis, which approaches the analysis of the qualitatively collected data in a structural manner; in other words, the analysis of qualitative material was performed with the help of concepts developed within the tradition of social network analysis.[33] The analysis of interviews was therefore focused on the structure, the actors, and the relations, as well as the related concepts (e.g. network density for the structure, centrality for the actors, or strong and weak ties for the relations).[34]

For example, for the structure of the network and its dynamics, but also for the ways in which connections were formed among the participants, the relevance of the socio-political context (the disintegration of Yugoslavia, war, rising nationalism and conservatism in the field of cultural policies) was emphasized, as it directly influenced the disappearance of some former places of networking. This explains why the artistic and cultural scene of the 1990s mainly developed in smaller, informal social circles. The gathering of participants with similar ideologies ultimately resulted in the formalization of cooperations through the establishment of new structures in the independent scene after 2000 (the founding of civic associations, linking them together in platforms, the emergence of financial resources intended exclusively for the civil sector). The altered context and logic of organizing the participants after 2000 also influenced the emergence of concentrators within the network, i.e. nodes with an exceptionally high number of relations.[35] The role of concentrators was taken by the newly established associations and platforms, which meant that civic associations were the structure of the scene and its main actors at the same time. Relations within the Croatian independent scene were established on the basis of mechanisms of status and value homophily and transitivity, and were often multifold: They included mixed professional and friendship relations and elements of "recognition" in terms of similar aesthetic and ideological values.[36]

Conclusions about the social structure of the independent scene obtained in this way could be paired with qualitative definitions provided by the participants themselves, whereby they contextualized their actions with regard to the social and cultural structures that were available to them at that moment. In this case especially, qualitative analysis contributed to the analysis of certain relations within the network. It helped us to make conclusions about the existence of strong or weak links within the network, to determine whether certain relations were made spontaneously or intentionally, and to establish the reasons for their creation. The following is an example of qualitative data obtained from the analysis of the interviews: one of the research participants, who was actively involved in the formation of the independent scene, described it after 2000 in the following way:

> We were following a different kind of logic, one of self-organization. [...] In the 2000s, efforts were made to connect all of these cultural NGOs with the aim of strengthening and providing a lasting framework for cultural activities. One of the guiding principles was for networks to serve as a foundation for a new cultural center, a new type of institution for contemporary cultural practices. I believe that is the key difference between the alternative scene of the 80s and the independent scene that originated in the 90s, because the scene that took hold in the 2000s did not accept the label of alternative culture, unlike the one formed in the 80s.[37]

The results of qualitative analysis could then be supplemented or compared with the results of classical quantitative analysis of social networks. For example, the collaborative networks of the curatorial collective WHW, one of the hubs of the independent scene at the beginning of the new millennium, served as a datascape to describe the collective's individual collaborations with other institutions from the public and civil sector and its changed networking logic after they took over the Nova Gallery in Zagreb in 2003 (Figure 9.3). The visualized networks also enabled us to describe the structure of their program and their most common collaborators (Figure 9.4).[38] The visualization of the entire collaboration network of the WHW collective also confirmed one of the results of qualitative structural analysis: the fact that the role of concentrators in the independent scene after 2000 was taken over by the newly established civic associations. While the strong links of the WHW collective with some other civic associations can be inferred from the frequency of collaboration over a longer period of time, the individuals involved in the work of these associations are poorly represented or invisible in the visualization, which is a consequence of the collective signing of individual programs.

## Conclusion

This chapter has offered an overview of some of the complex issues that arise from the use of digital tools and social network analysis in interpreting art-historical phenomena. Testing the new tools and methods on small data samples has shown to what extent (still experimental phase) one still needs a solid knowledge of the material itself and the ways in which its data is structured, but also of the analytical methods elaborated within the tradition of social network analysis. The examples discussed show that both an injudicious use of methods borrowed from

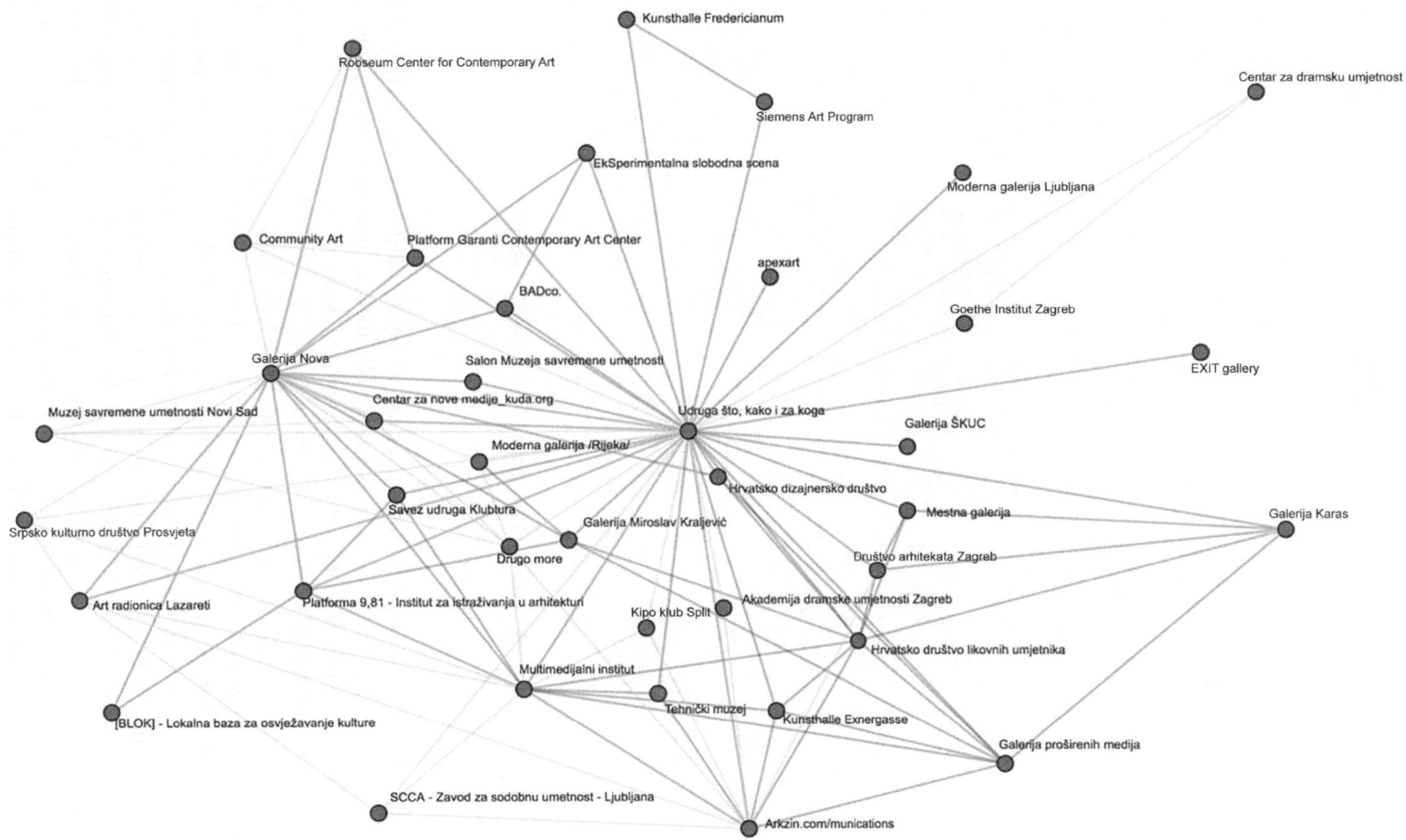


*Figure 9.3* Institutional collaboration of the WHW curatorial collective between 2000 and 2006.

*Source*: Željka Tonković, Sanja Sekelj.

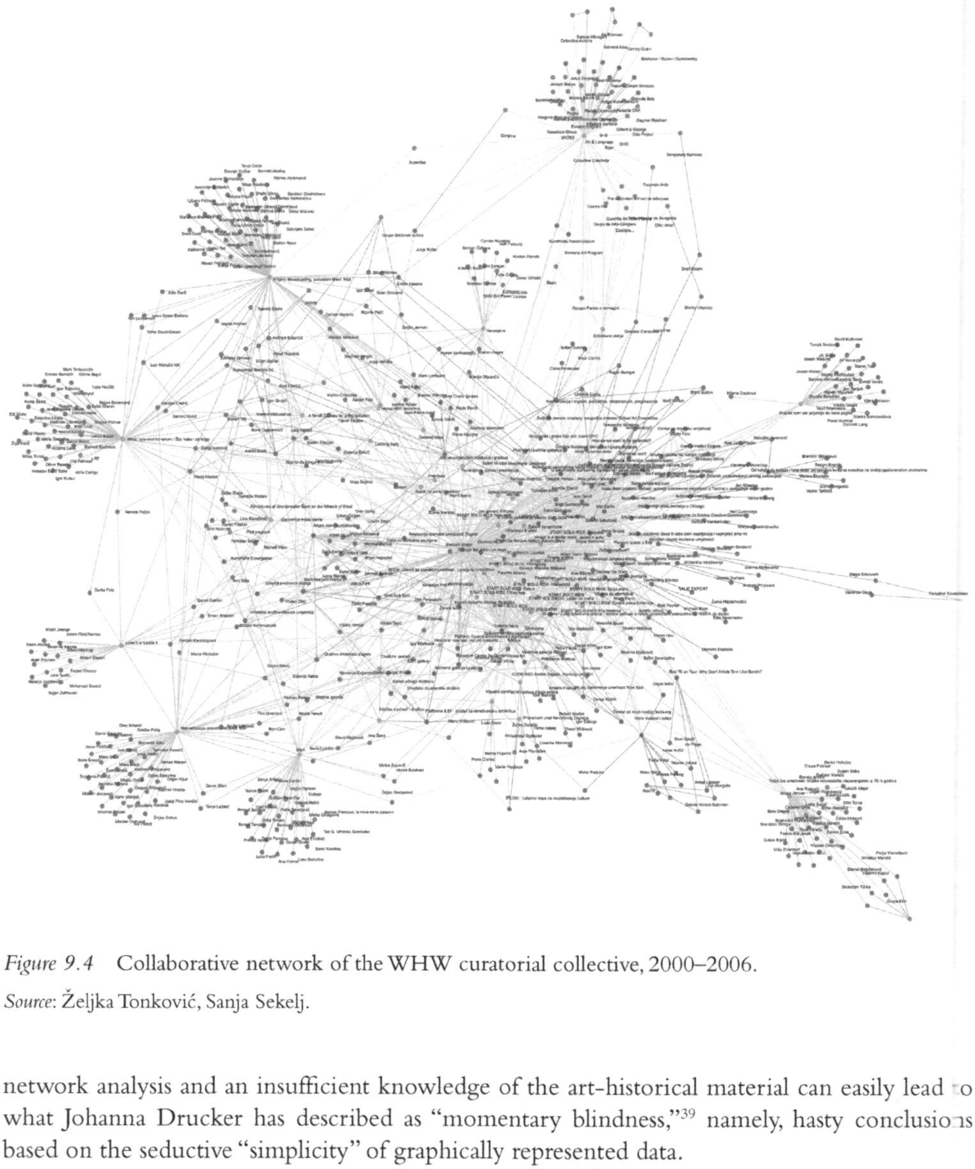

*Figure 9.4* Collaborative network of the WHW curatorial collective, 2000–2006.

*Source*: Željka Tonković, Sanja Sekelj.

network analysis and an insufficient knowledge of the art-historical material can easily lead to what Johanna Drucker has described as "momentary blindness,"[39] namely, hasty conclusions based on the seductive "simplicity" of graphically represented data.

Take, for example, the WHW collaborative network: Since after 2000 the role of concentrators in the independent scene was taken over by collectives (which also signed their programs collectively), a quantitative network analysis in which one looks for relations between individuals would actually rule out the most active collaborators from the WHW collaborative network. This proves to what extent the results of quantitative network analysis can be misleading and why they should be used only as one step in the research process when interpreting art-historical phenomena. The example of the SCCA network and the calculation of network density additionally highlights the need to have a solid knowledge of the analytical methods developed within the tradition of social network analysis, which should not be used merely because they are at our disposal, but because their use may offer relevant answers to our research questions. In this sense, even a simple description of the generated datascape may offer significant insights into the relations between data and encourage further art-historical research. Although the construction of a method that would reconcile quantitative and qualitative levels of data interpretation is still in its infancy, the solution should be sought in profound interdisciplinarity within research teams, familiarity with the current knowledge from other scientific disciplines, and a common articulation of languages and methods for digital art history.

## Notes

1. Among the abundant scholarly literature on the basics of social network analysis and methodology overviews, see, for example, Alain Degenne and Michel Forse, *Introducing Social Networks*, trans. Arthur Borges (London, Thousand Oaks, and New Delhi: Sage Publications, 1999); John Scott and Peter J. Carrington, *The Sage Handbook of Social Network Analysis* (London, Thousand Oaks, and New Delhi: Sage Publications, 2011); Stanley Wasserman and Katherine Faust, *Social Network Analysis: Methods and Applications* (New York: Cambridge University Press, 2009). As for the popular scientific production, see Albert László Barabási, *Linked: The New Science of Networks* (Cambridge, MA: Perseus Publishing, 2002); Guido Caldarelli and Michele Catanzaro, *Networks: A Very Short Introduction* (Oxford: Oxford University Press, 2012).
2. Cf. Miriam Kienle, "Between Nodes and Edges: Possibilities and Limits of Network Analysis in Art History," *Artl@s Bulletin* 6, no. 3 (2017): 5–6, 11–13; Miriam Kienle, "Digital Art History 'Beyond the Digitized Slide Library': An Interview with Johanna Drucker and Miriam Posner," *Artl@s Bulletin* 6, no. 3 (2017): 123–24.
3. Johanna Drucker, "Humanities Approaches to Graphical Display," *Digital Humanities Quarterly* 5, no. 1 (2011).
4. Maranke Wieringa, Daniela van Geenen, Karin van Es, and Jelmer van Nuss, "The Fieldnotes Plugin: Making Network Visualization in Gephi Accountable," in *Good Data*, ed. Angela Daly, S. Kate Devitt, and Monique Mann (Amsterdam: Institute of Network Cultures, 2018).
5. Drucker, "Humanities Approaches to Graphical Display."
6. Kienle, "Digital Art History 'Beyond the Digitized Slide Library,'" 122–23.
7. Kienle, "Between Nodes and Edges," 9.
8. A fine example of this approach is found in Matthew D. Lincoln, "Continuity and Disruption in European Networks of Print Production, 1550–1750," *Artl@s Bulletin* 6, no. 3 (2017): 23–40.
9. Members of the project team *MapTap* termed this working model "slow digital art history." Cf. Koenraad Brosens, Klara Alen, Astrid Slegten, and Fred Truyen, "MapTap and Cornelia: Slow Digital Art History and Formal Art Historical Social Network Research," *Zeitschrift für Kunstgeschichte* 79 (2016): 315. A similar approach is cultivated in the *E.A.T. Datascape* project at the Sciences Po Media Lab, in which Christophe Leclercq and Paul Girard have been emphasizing the role of researcher/art historian in the entire process, from data modeling to data visualization and further to analysis. Cf. Christophe Leclercq and Paul Girard, "The Experiments in Art and Technology Datascape," in *Keys for Architectural History Research in the Digital Era* ("Actes de colloques"), ed. Juliette Hueber and Antonio Mendes da Silva (Paris: Publications de l'Institut national d'histoire de l'art, 2014), 50–65.
10. The project took place from 2014 to 2018 with the financial support of the Croatian Science Foundation. The project team included Ljiljana Kolešnik (project leader), Tamara Bjažić Klarin, Nikola Bojić, Sanja Horvatinčić, Irena Kraševac, Ivana Meštrov, Dalibor Prančević, Petar Prelog, Sanja Sekelj, Artur Šilić, and Željka Tonković. For additional information, please refer to the project's website: "Project ARTNET," ARTNET, accessed May 30, 2019, www.art-net-hrzz.org/home.
11. For a description of the initial premises of the project, see Ljiljana Kolešnik, "Digitalna povijest umjetnosti—obilježja, problemi, perspektive = Digital Art History—Features, Problems, and Prospects," *Život umjetnosti* 99 (2016): 9–17.
12. Thus, at the time of writing this chapter, the CAN_IS database included 33,115 persons, 2,716 exhibitions, and 1,030 institutions.
13. Cf. Kienle, "Between Nodes and Edges," 11.
14. Stephen P. Borgatti and Daniel S. Halgin, "Analyzing Affiliation Networks," in *The Sage Handbook of Social Network Analysis*, eds. John Scott and Peter J. Carrington (London, Thousand Oaks, and New Delhi: Sage Publications, 2011), 420. The difference between the method described in this article and the ARTNET approach was that, in the latter, most researchers considered participations in various

types of parallel events and different types of participation, which generated complex networks; archival research, in turn, proved the creation of very strong social ties in certain cases.

15. For the analyses of specific cases within the project, see Ljiljana Kolešnik and Sanja Horvatinčić, eds., *Modern and Contemporary Artists' Networks. An Inquiry into Digital History of Art and Architecture* (Zagreb: Institute of Art History, 2018).
16. The difference with regard to the described approach is also evident in an article by Ljiljana Kolešnik, Nikola Bojić, and Artur Šilić, based on the systematic research and quantification of informal social relations of Almir Mavignier from 1960, which explained the development and later structure of formal sociability in the New Tendencies movement. Ljiljana Kolešnik, Nikola Bojić, and Artur Šilić, "Rekonstrukcija personalne mreže Almira Mavigniera i njezina relacija prema prvoj izložbi Novih tendencija. Primjer primjene mrežne analize i mrežne vizualizacije u povijesti umjetnosti = Reconstruction of Almir Mavignier's Personal Network and its Relation to the First New Tendencies Exhibition. The Example of the Application of Network Analysis and Network Visualisation in Art History," *Život umjetnosti* 99 (2016): 57–77.
17. In the ARTNET project, I conducted my research of networking practices after 1990 in collaboration with Željka Tonković.
18. The "nominalist strategy" implies that it is the researcher who defines the network boundaries according to certain pre-defined criteria. The opposite approach is the "realist strategy" which implies that the network boundaries are determined by network actors themselves. Cf. Stephen P. Borgatti and Daniel S. Halgin, "On Network Theory," *Organization Science* 22, no. 5 (September–October 2011): 1170.
19. For a description of the foundation and activity of SCCA, the cultural and socio-political context in which it operated, and a more detailed network analysis, see Željka Tonković and Sanja Sekelj, "Godišnje izložbe Soros centra za suvremenu umjetnost Zagreb kao mjesto umrežavanja = Annual Exhibitions of the Soros Center for Contemporary Art Zagreb as a Place of Networking," *Život umjetnosti* 99 (2016): 79–93.
20. The Group of Six Artists was active in Zagreb between 1975 and 1981. Members of the group were Boris Demur, Željko Jerman, Vlado Martek, Mladen Stilinović, Sven Stilinović, and Fedor Vučemilović.
21. Tonković and Sekelj, "Annual Exhibitions of the Soros Center for Contemporary Art Zagreb as a Place of Networking," 90.
22. Cf. Kienle, "Digital Art History 'Beyond the Digitized Slide Library,'" 122.
23. Ann Mische, "Relational Sociology, Culture, and Agency," in *The Sage Handbook of Social Network Analysis*, eds. Scott and Carrington, 80.
24. For a brief overview of the genesis of relational perspective in sociology, see Mische, "Relational Sociology, Culture, and Agency," 80–84.
25. For a detailed critique of "structural determinism" and a description of the relational perspective in terms of interrelation between structure, culture, and human agency, see Mustafa Emirbayer and Jeff Goodwin, "Network Analysis, Culture, and the Problem of Agency," *American Journal of Sociology* 99, no. 6 (1994): 1411–54.
26. Ibid., 1440–42.
27. See, for example, Mische, "Relational Sociology, Culture, and Agency," 90.
28. Bettina Hollstein, "Qualitative Approaches," in *The Sage Handbook of Social Network Analysis*, eds. Scott and Carrington, 404.
29. Additional information in, for example, Dea Vidović, "Nezavisna kultura u Hrvatskoj (1990–2010)," in *Dizajn i nezavisna kultura*, eds. Maroje Mrduljaš and Dea Vidović (Zagreb: Savez udruga Klubtura—UPI 2M PLUS d.o.o.—KURZIV, 2010), 9–39; Marko Golub, "Obrnuto ispričana priča: uzorci urbane scene Zagreba = A Story Told in Reverse: Patterns in the Urban Scene of Zagreb," *Život umjetnosti* 73 (2004): 30–39.
30. Harrison C. White, *Identity and Control: How Social Formations Emerge* (Princeton: Princeton University Press, 2008).
31. Interviews within the ARTNET project were initiated by sociologist Željka Tonković.
32. From November 2015 until July 2017, we conducted thirty interviews, with the average duration of ninety minutes. Along with Željka Tonković and Sanja Sekelj, interviews were conducted by the ARTNET members Ivana Meštrov, Sanja Horvatinčić, and Dalibor Prančević.
33. This approach was developed by Andreas Herz, Luisa Peters, and Inga Truschkat. For a detailed description of the method, see Andreas Herz, Luisa Peters, and Inga Truschkat, "How to Do Qualitative Structural Analysis: The Qualitative Interpretation of Network Maps and Narrative Interviews," *Forum: Qualitative Social Research* 16, no. 1 (2015).

34. The first research results were published in the final book of the ARTNET project. For a detailed description of the method and the results, see Željka Tonković and Sanja Sekelj, "Duality of Structure and Culture: A Network Perspective on the Independent Cultural Scene and the Formation of the WHW Curatorial Collective," in *Modern and Contemporary Artists' Networks: An Inquiry into Digital History of Art and Architecture*, ed. Ljiljana Kolešnik and Sanja Horvatinčić (Zagreb: Institute of Art History, 2018), 164–90.
35. Cf. Barabási, *Linked*, 55–64.
36. For a detailed description of the first research results, see Tonković and Sekelj, "Duality of Structure and Culture."
37. Interview 18, conducted by Sanja Sekelj and Željka Tonković on December 6, 2016. More examples of qualitative data in Tonković and Sekelj, "Duality of Structure and Culture."
38. For a detailed description of the visualizations, see Tonković and Sekelj, "Duality of Structure and Culture."
39. Drucker, "Humanities Approaches to Graphical Display."

## Bibliography


ARTNET. "Project ARTNET." Accessed May 30, 2019. www.art-net-hrzz.org/home.

Barabási, Albert László. *Linked: The New Science of Networks*. Cambridge, MA: Perseus Publishing, 2002.

Borgatti, Stephen P., and Daniel S. Halgin. "Analyzing Affiliation Networks." In *The Sage Handbook of Social Network Analysis*, edited by John Scott and Peter J. Carrington, 417–33. London, Thousand Oaks, and New Delhi: Sage Publications, 2011.

———. "On Network Thery." *Organization Science* 22, no. 5 (September–October 2011): 1168–81.

Brosens, Koenraad, Klara Alen, Astrid Slegten, and Fred Truyen. "MapTap and Cornelia. Slow Digital Art History and Formal Art Historical Social Network Research." *Zeitschrift für Kunstgeschichte* 79 (2016): 315–30.

Caldarelli, Guido, and Michele Catanzaro. *Networks: A Very Short Introduction*. Oxford: Oxford University Press, 2012.

Degenne, Alain, and Michel Forse. *Introducing Social Networks*. Translated by Arthur Borges. London, Thousand Oaks and New Delhi: Sage Publications, 1999.

Drucker, Johanna. "Humanities Approaches to Graphical Display." *Digital Humanities Quarterly* 5, no. 1 (2011). www.digitalhumanities.org/dhq/vol/5/1/000091/000091.html#d57570e220

Emirbayer, Mustafa, and Jeff Goodwin. "Network Analysis, Culture, and the Problem of Agency." *American Journal of Sociology* 99, no. 6 (1994): 1411–54.

Golub, Marko. "Obrnuto ispričana priča: uzorci urbane scene Zagreba = A Story Told in Reverse: Patterns of the Urban Scene of Zagreb." *Život umjetnosti* 73 (2004): 30–39.

Herz, Andreas, Luisa Peters, and Inga Truschkat. "How to Do Qualitative Structural Analysis: The Qualitative Interpretation of Network Maps and Narrative Interviews." *Forum: Qualitative Social Research* 16, no. 1 (2015).

Hollstein, Bettina. "Qualitative Approaches." In *The Sage Handbook of Social Network Analysis*, edited by John Scott and Peter J. Carrington, 404–16. London, Thousand Oaks, and New Delhi: Sage Publications, 2011.

Kienle, Miriam. "Between Nodes and Edges: Possibilities and Limits of Network Analysis in Art History." *Artl@s Bulletin* 6, no. 3 (2017): 4–22.

———. "Digital Art History 'Beyond the Digitized Slide Library': An Interview with Johanna Drucker and Miriam Posner." *Artl@s Bulletin* 6, no. 3 (2017): 121–25.

Kolešnik, Ljiljana. "Digitalna povijest umjetnosti—obilježja, problemi i perspektive = Digital Art History—Features, Problems, and Prospects." *Život umjetnosti* 99 (2016): 9–17. www.ipu.hr/content/zivot-umjetnosti/ZU_99-2016_010-019_Kolesnik.pdf

Kolešnik, Ljiljana, Nikola Bojić, and Artur Šilić. "Rekonstrukcija personalne mreže Almira Mavigniera i njezina relacija prema prvoj izložbi Novih tendencija. Primjer primjene mrežne analize i mrežne vizualizacije u povijesti umjetnosti = Reconstruction of Almir Mavignier's Personal Network and its Relation to the First New Tendencies Exhibition. The Example of the Application of Network Analysis and Network Visualisation in Art History." *Život umjetnosti* 99 (2016): 57–77. www.ipu.hr/content/zivot-umjetnosti/ZU_99-2016_058079_Kolesnik_Bojic_Silic.pdf

Kolešnik, Ljiljana, and Sanja Horvatinčić, ed. *Modern and Contemporary Artists' Networks. An Inquiry Into Digital History of Art and Architecture*. Zagreb: Institute of Art History, 2018.

Leclercq, Christophe, and Paul Girard. "The Experiments in Art and Technology Datascape." In *Keys for Architectural History Research in the Digital Era* ("Actes de colloques"), edited by Juliette Hueber and Antonio Mendes da Silva, 50–65. Paris: Publications de l'Institut national d'histoire de l'art, 2014 Accessed January 10, 2019. https://journals.openedition.org/inha/4926

Lincoln, Matthew D. "Continuity and Disruption in European Networks of Print Production, 1550–1750." *Artl@s Bulletin* 6, no. 3 (2017): 23–40.

Mische, Ann. "Relational Sociology, Culture, and Agency." In *The Sage Handbook of Social Network Analysis* edited by John Scott and Peter J. Carrington, 80–97. London, Thousand Oaks, and New Delhi: Sage Publications, 2011.

Scott, John, and Peter J. Carrington, ed. *The Sage Handbook of Social Network Analysis.* London, Thousand Oaks, and New Delhi: Sage Publications, 2011.

Tonković, Željka, and Sanja Sekelj. "Duality of Structure and Culture: A Network Perspective on the Independent Cultural Scene in Zagreb and the Formation of the WHW Curatorial Collective." In *Modern and Contemporary Artists' Networks. An Inquiry Into Digital History of Art and Architecture*, edited by Ljiljana Kolešnik and Sanja Horvatinčić, 164–90. Zagreb: Institute of Art History, 2018.

———. "Godišnje izložbe Soros centra za suvremenu umjetnost Zagreb kao mjesto umrežavanja = Annual exhibitions of the Soros Center for Contemporary Art Zagreb as a place of networking." *Život umjetnosti* 99 (2016): 79–93. www.ipu.hr/content/zivot-umjetnosti/ZU_99-2016_080-095_Tonkovic_Sekelj.pdf

Vidović, Dea. "Nezavisna kultura u Hrvatskoj (1990–2010)." In *Dizajn i nezavisna kultura*, edited by Maroje Mrduljaš and Dea Vidović, 9–39. Zagreb: Savez udruga Klubtura—UPI 2M PLUS d.o.o.—KURZIV, 2010.

Wasserman, Stanley, and Katherine Faust. *Social Network Analysis: Methods and Applications.* New York: Cambridge University Press, 2009.

White, Harrison C. *Identity and Control: How Social Formations Emerge.* Princeton: Princeton University Press, 2008.

Wieringa, Maranke, Daniela van Geenen, Karin van Es, and Jelmer van Nuss. "The Fieldnotes Plugin: Making Network Visualization in Gephi Accountable." In *Good Data*, edited by Angela Daly, S. Kate Devitt and Monique Mann, 277–96. Amsterdam: Institute of Network Cultures, 2019.

# 10

# *MAPPING SENUFO*

## Mapping as a Method to Transcend Colonial Assumptions

*Susan Elizabeth Gagliardi*

What might research and the publication of results look like if scholars producing them integrated decades of theories about the construction of cultural or ethnic groups and the politics of knowledge production into their work on arts of Africa once considered "traditional"? *Mapping Senufo*—an in-progress, collaborative, born-digital publication project that I initiated and now co-direct with Constantine Petridis—offers a model for joining such theories with research practice.[1] It also contributes to my larger effort to forge a range of alternate possibilities for how scholars study "traditional" or "classical" arts of Africa and present their findings with attention to specificity.

*Mapping Senufo* will highlight different stories and perspectives, each one linked to particular objects, images, people, places, or events, rather than insisting on a single, all-encompassing narrative. The approach reflects the project team's resolve to take seriously the long-established understanding that a marker of identity, like the labeling of an art style or knowledge itself, is historically constituted, fluid, and positional. The multimodal, digital publication that the project team is developing will exemplify in its form the contingent nature of identities, style labeling, and knowledge production.

In 1908, French colonial administrator Maurice Delafosse published an early description of a West African cultural or ethnic group regarded as Senufo. A map showing what he considered to be the geographic extent of Senufo country accompanies his text (Figure 10.1). The area Delafosse designated as Senufo spans the borders of present-day Burkina Faso, Côte d'Ivoire, and Mali, a region that was subject to French colonial rule from the late nineteenth century to the mid-twentieth century. A small part of the area identified as Senufo on Delafosse's map extends into part of present-day Ghana. A dotted line at the upper boundary of Delafosse's Senufo country reflects uncertainty about how far north the so-called country extends. In his accompanying text, Delafosse acknowledges that he applies the term *Senufo* to people who did not necessarily use the label to identify themselves.[2] The uncertainty in the map and Delafosse's admission in the text point to the colonial construction of the term *Senufo* as a discrete cultural or ethnic marker locatable to a specific geographic area, an area that is now and has historically been culturally, linguistically, and religiously diverse.

By the 1910s and 1920s, art historians and other art enthusiasts began applying the term *Senufo* to select objects from Africa entering European and North American collections. Art

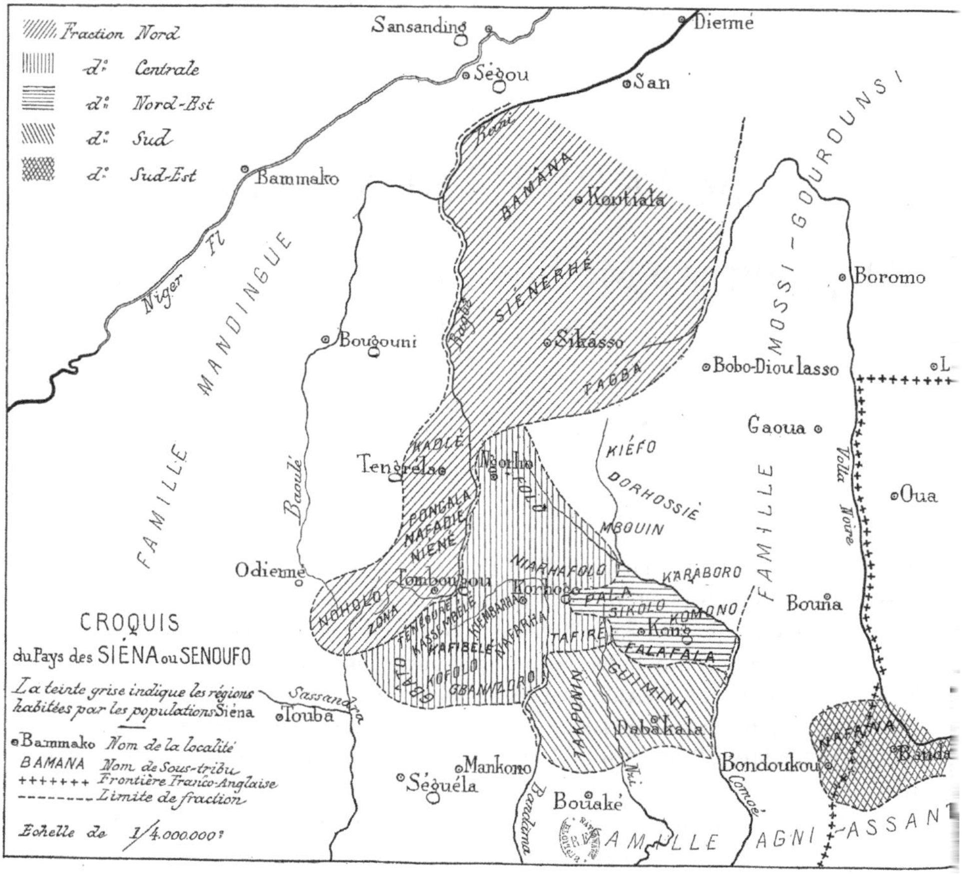


*Figure 10.1* Sketch of the country of the Siéna or Senufo.

*Source*: From Delafosse 1908, pl. 1.

connoisseurs assumed that the distribution of artistic form overlapped neatly with the distribution of timeless cultural or ethnic groups, and they relied on the correspondence to explain art.[3] But scholars have for decades recognized that framing analysis of art or other phenomena in terms of timeless cultural or ethnic groups obscures historical complexity.[4] Curators, dealers, collectors, and other art enthusiasts nevertheless find the categories convenient for organizing art and explaining it. Through caveats in an introduction or other glosses, they may acknowledge colonial assumptions embedded in the approach. But presentations of African art still often imply the existence of timeless groups on the African continent.

As I see it, curators and other scholars of African arts have engaged in circular logic, identifying a corpus of art with a particular cultural or ethnic group on the basis of form and then using that corpus to confirm the existence of the group. They often rely on vocabularies that reinforce ideas about discrete groups even when they acknowledge theories pointing to historical dynamism and exchange.[5] One goal of *Mapping Senufo* is to create a publication that illustrates rather than merely tells readers how the term *Senufo* and the corpus of art it names are intimately connected to, instead of separate from, the colonial and postcolonial contexts in which Senufo identities and arts have flourished.

Petridis and I recognize colonial histories undergirding the collection and study of classical African arts as well as the changing nature of knowledge. Through *Mapping Senufo*, we also aim to show multiple possibilities for understanding what *Senufo* means and how the term relates to a corpus of arts. Previous studies of African arts have focused on capturing cultural essences. But as Kwame Anthony Appiah explains, identities and labels emerge in particular historical contexts and depend on changing narratives. They do not reflect stable essences.[6] Using the Senufo corpus as a case study, we shift attention to particular historical contexts and changing narratives surrounding the term *Senufo* and its application to the arts. We demonstrate the impossibility of arriving at any single, all-encompassing definition of what the term *Senufo* means or what Senufo arts are.

The multimodal, digital publication format will allow us to heighten readers' awareness of their own involvement in the making of meaning. A key advantage of the format is its ability to harness the interactivity of digital environments to render readers active participants in knowledge construction.[7] *Mapping Senufo* will exploit such potential. It will permit readers to isolate and investigate particular objects, images, people, places, and events integral to the ongoing definition of a single category of art. It will map connections among different elements as well as indicate certain absences in the historical record. *Mapping Senufo* will thus embody complexity and contingency at the core of identities, style labels, and knowledge construction.

Through their attention to various elements, readers will establish their own understandings of the term *Senufo*, the corpus of art it names, and specific histories embedded in the label and objects it encompasses. Readers will also experience silences in the historical record that result from different observers' decisions about what information to record, thereby illuminating power structures embedded in knowledge production. *Mapping Senufo* will make evident the subjectivity, selectivity, partiality, and processes inherent in the identification of Senufo art as a distinct category. It will transform decades of theories about the contingent nature of culture-based classifications and the study of classical African arts into actual practice within a publication.

Significantly, the multimodal, digital format for *Mapping Senufo* we are currently developing echoes aspects of knowledge transmission prevalent in the area spanning the borders of present-day Burkina Faso, Côte d'Ivoire, and Mali from at least the late twentieth century to the present. Reflecting on how his paternal grandfather, the late Lamina (Tientigui) Traoré from Bougoula, Mali, relayed local knowledge to him, Ibrahim Traoré Banakourou explained that the elder often told a riddle but did not immediately explain its significance. The elder Traoré expected the younger Traoré to reflect on the riddle and to arrive at his own conclusions. Over time, the elder Traoré offered additional bits of information or insight that allowed the younger learner to expand his knowledge through contemplation and the embodiment of understanding. Rather than articulating a clear argument at the outset and supplying evidence to support it the elder posed a question in the form of a riddle, directed the grandson to certain evidence, and allowed the latter to discover his own findings.[8] The approach, like the design for *Mapping Senufo*, highlights the time-based and subjective nature of knowledge acquisition.

This chapter reflects my own perspectives, developed through extensive field-based, archival, and museum research. I conclude that in order to transcend colonial assumptions, scholars must engage with colonial and postcolonial contexts of knowledge production rather than use colonial and postcolonial sources to recapture an imagined precolonial past. This chapter also addresses the iterative nature of our work, which relies on digital methods, and demonstrates how art-historical research in the digital realm prompts scholars to grapple with and write about their processes in generative ways.[9] For example, when we first turned to digital technologies to map locations and evaluate other information about specific objects, we realized that the technologies favor precision. However, we could not always determine exact coordinates or otherwise confirm reported information, so we decided to avoid plotting points that appear to confirm locations. The ambiguity in location information we encountered prompted us to re-evaluate the subjectivity inherent in any person's collection or analysis of information, including our own.

We are also experimenting with the form of scholarly publication in the digital era. With the recent addition of a visual artist to the project team, we are aiming to move from positivist approaches to digital mapping and data visualization to more conceptual renderings in our final publication design. While our digital monograph remains in development, research and design processes involved in its making have already prompted the *Mapping Senufo* team to examine what we think we know, how we know it, and what we may never be able to know in ways we did not anticipate when we launched the project.

## Operative Fictions and the Organization of Knowledge

The term *Senufo* and other cultural or ethnic group labels offered early twentieth-century admirers of African arts ready categories for objects then entering European and North American collections. The approach was grounded in then common anthropological conceptions of the distribution of people on the African continent. As Delafosse's efforts to locate and define a Senufo group suggest, colonial officials imagined that cultural or ethnic labels pertained to specific geographic areas, each one considered the domain of a "race" or "tribe" and thought to encompass its own language, religion, social organization, and art style. A 1972 map of the continent reflects the tenacity of such logic, although the lengthy note accompanying the map admits controversy and contradictions in the approach (Figure 10.2). By the end of the twentieth century, anthropologists acknowledged that peoples on the African continent defied ready categorization into ahistorical groups.[10]

Even while museum curators and other scholars recognize complexities in the application of cultural or ethnic group markers to the arts, they continue to attribute individual works to entire groups of people when they have little information about specific artists, patrons, or audiences. For example, the Art Institute of Chicago identifies as Senufo the maker or makers of a wooden drum from Africa (Figure 10.3). At least one person whose name we do not know made the drum before 1957, when French art dealer Charles Ratton owned it and the object reportedly appeared in an exhibition in Cannes, France. By contrast, the Art Institute identifies a specific person—Pablo Picasso—as the maker of a bronze figure in the form of a standing woman from Europe (Figures 10.4 and 10.5). The museum specifies that Picasso made the work before 1957, and more precisely in 1945.[11]

Seen together, the museum's records for the two objects suggest that identification of the wooden drum's maker or makers as Senufo is akin to identification of the bronze figure's maker as Picasso. Yet identifying an object with a cultural or ethnic group does not yield the same insight into the production, meaning, or circulation of the work as identifying an object with a named person. What exactly does it mean to identify a work's maker or makers only as Senufo? And does the identification acknowledge the maker as a particular person, one with a specific history and specific connections to particular places and other people, including people who might not have spoken a Senufo language or otherwise identified as Senufo?

Linguistically, the area that Delafosse designates as Senufo is more complicated than the 1908 map suggests. Today, as in the past, people in areas that many maps designate as Senufo speak dozens of unrelated languages, and their own histories and their families' histories may connect them to multiple geographic locations. People within a single town recognize different, and

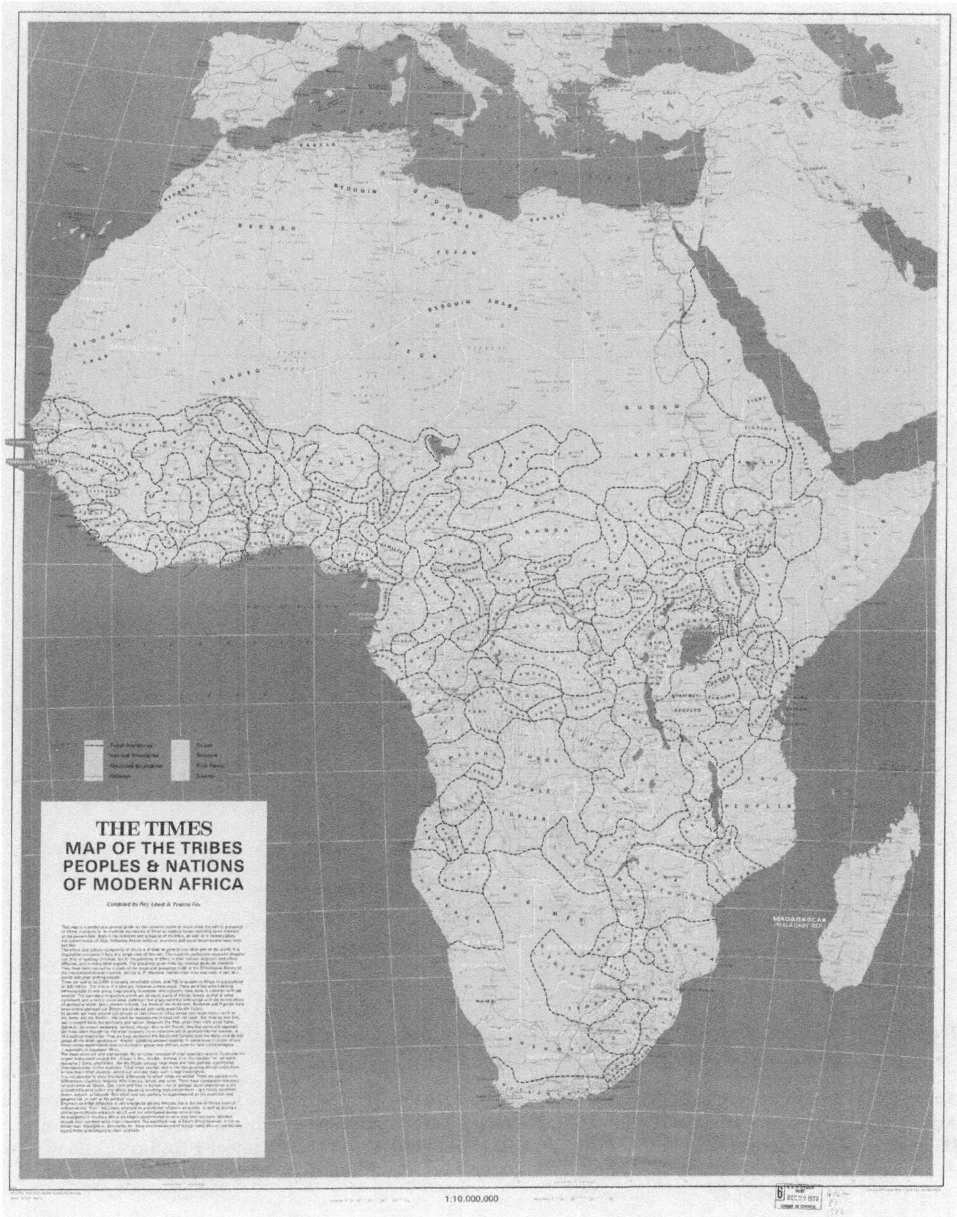


*Figure 10.2* *The Times* map of the tribes, peoples, and nations of modern Africa. Cartography by John Bartholomew & Son Ltd. London, 1972.

*Source*: Library of Congress Control Number 73691651.

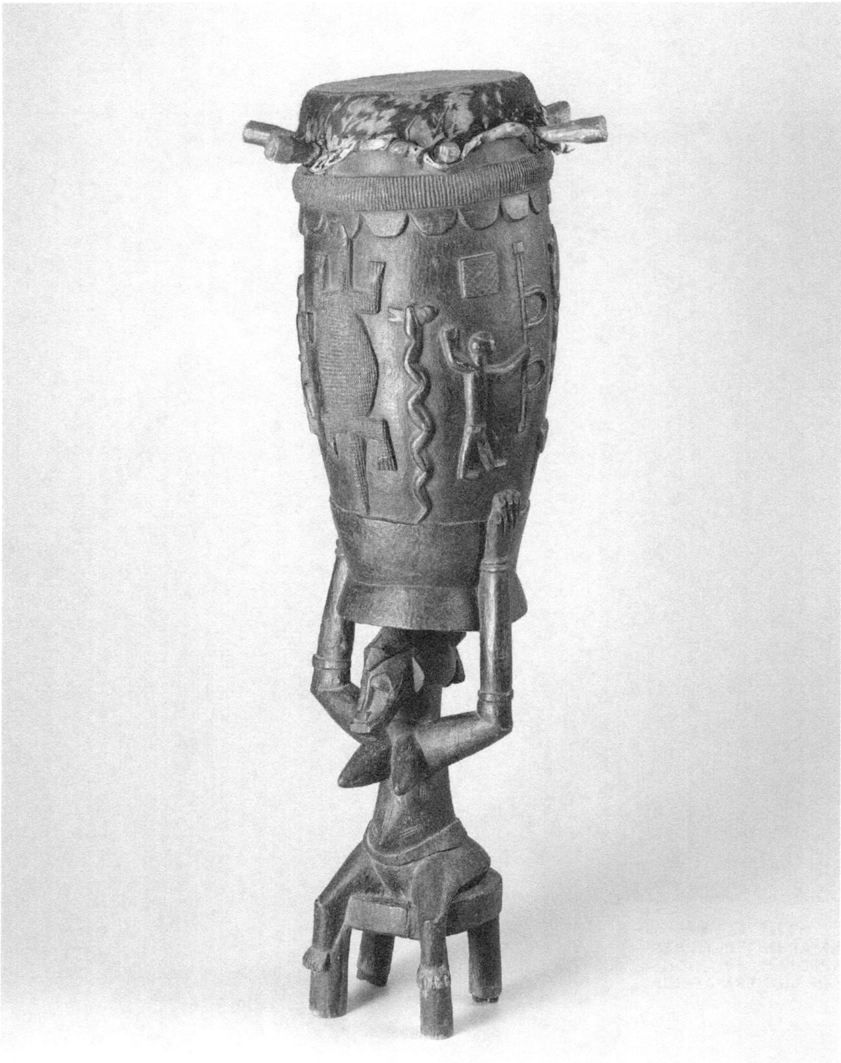

*Figure 10.3* Unrecorded maker(s). Drum in a style identified as Senufo, by 1957. Wood, hide, and applied color, 122.9 × 49.2 cm.

*Source*: The Art Institute of Chicago, Robert J. Hall, Herbert R. Molner Discretionary, Curator's Discretionary, and African and Amerindian Art Purchase funds; Arnold Crane, Mrs. Leonard Florsheim, O. Renard Goltra, Holly and David Ross, Departmental Acquisitions, Ada Turnbull Hertle, and Marion and Samuel Klasstorner endowments; through prior gifts of various donors, 1990.137.

unrelated, languages as their first languages. Mapping town-to-town linguistic data from the present or a past moment would result in a map that pixelates, breaking apart the solid shape that often delimits a discrete Senufo area or a Senufo area divided into Senufo subgroups.[12]

Study of the region's history further demonstrates the complexity of identities prior to European colonization of the area Delafosse designated as Senufo.[13] Certain identities, including ones historically expressed by variants of the term *Senufo*, marked occupational or linguistic

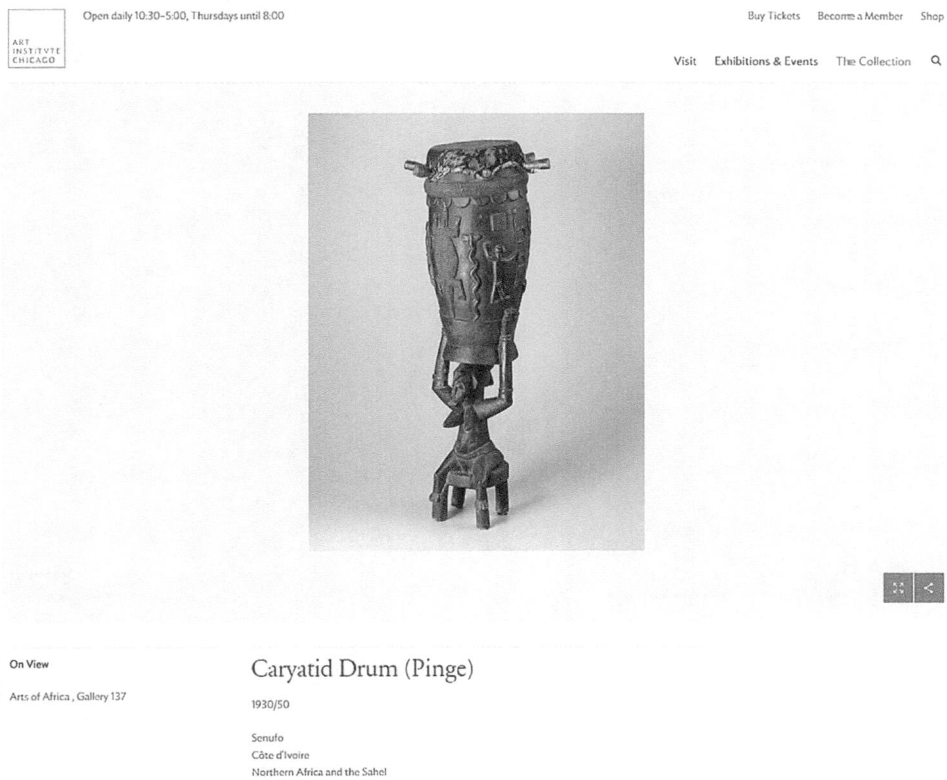


*Figure 10.4* Screenshot of the Art Institute of Chicago's "About This Artwork" page for a drum in its collection (ARTIC 1990.137), captured March 11, 2019.

difference. Other identities distinguished people who had converted to Islam from people who had not, so *Bamana*—a term applied to another corpus of art—described individuals who had not converted to Islam. Identities overlapped and shifted as people changed occupations, converted to Islam, or abandoned Islam.[14] However, European colonial officials and other observers misconstrued the multiple and ever-shifting identities they encountered. They imagined finding "races" or "tribes" and found them, often disregarding or flattening historical, locational, or situational specificity. Delafosse's efforts to define a Senufo country and identify characteristics of Senufo people provided a foundation for subsequent studies of Senufo populations and arts.[15] Within the colonial context, the meaning of the term *Senufo* changed, and Senufo identity became important in different ways to colonial officials and other people living in the colonies.

Objects from Africa traveled to Europe and North America through colonial channels, and they began to capture the attention of European and American artists in the early twentieth century. Few details about the objects' making, use, or circulation in Africa accompanied works when they entered European and American collections. In order to classify and explain art, dealers and collectors began associating the objects with particular cultural or ethnic groups.[16] They also attempted to refine their categories, and in some cases, a single object received different labels at different moments.[17] When in 1963, modernist art historian Robert Goldwater opened the influential exhibition *Senufo Sculpture from West Africa* at New York's now-defunct Museum

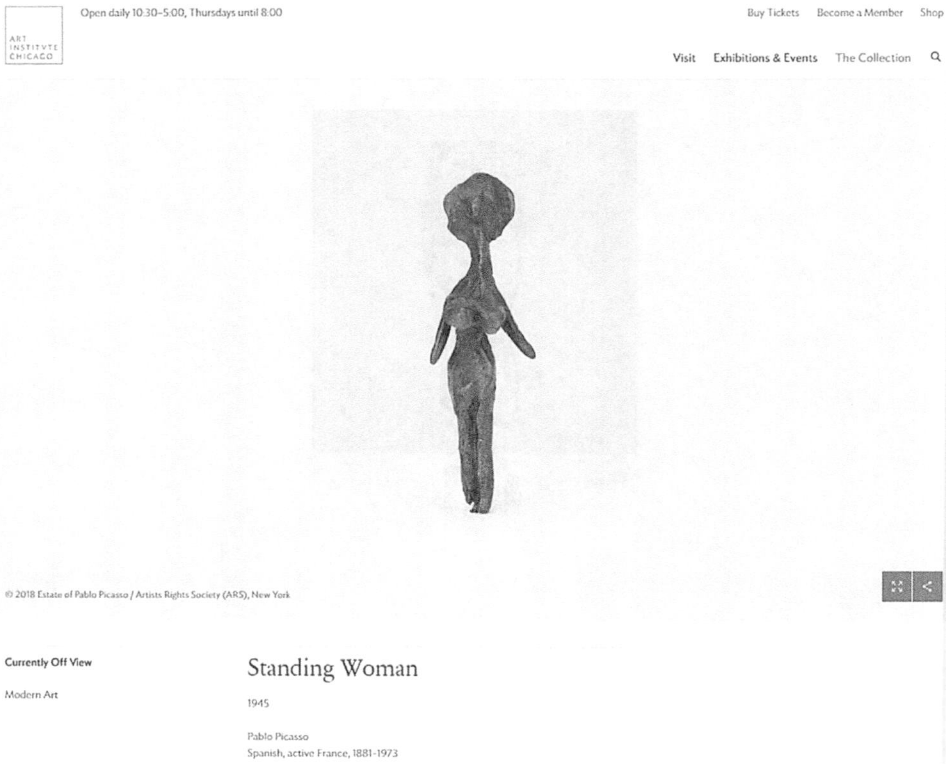


*Figure 10.5* Screenshot of the Art Institute of Chicago's "About This Artwork" page for a bronze figure in its collection (ARTIC 1967.688), captured March 11, 2019.

*Source*: Picasso's *Standing Woman* © 2018 Estate of Pablo Picasso/Artists Rights Society (ARS), New York.

of Primitive Art, he presented to museumgoers arts that Goldwater, who never traveled to West Africa, attributed to "the Senufo people." He also solidified parameters of a Senufo style.

As Stephan Palmié observes, culture-based classifications—what, in recognition of their constructed nature, he calls "operative fictions"—serve to help people organize information about the world.[18] But the existence of a category in the present neither confirms colonial and postcolonial imaginings about the category nor denies recognition of it as an historical construction. I argue that in order to transcend colonial assumptions, we must acknowledge in publications and other presentations about African arts that culture-based classifications and the arts they circumscribe developed within specific historical and geographical contexts. The idea of a bounded Senufo identity emerged in tandem with colonization. Furthermore, as Senufo identity acquired new meanings and importance in the colonial period, people who identified or were identified as Senufo contributed in different ways to the definition of the identity. Similarly, the labeling of a corpus of art as Senufo developed in conjunction with colonization of the area, even if artists in the area had a long history of artistic production prior to colonization. And once artists, patrons, and other people in western West Africa recognized foreign demand for objects and knowledge, they likely contributed to the production of art and information about it with the desires and expectations of their foreign audiences in mind. Indeed, by the 1930s, foreign observers referred to a foreign market for Senufo arts in northern Côte d'Ivoire.[19] Recognition of colonial-era artists' responses to foreign demands for particular kinds of objects and stories about them, even if extant documentation provides us with scant details, further complicates the idea that the arts capture precolonial cultural essences.

In a 2001 reflection on the state of scholarship on Africa, Achille Mbembe explains that "almost universally, the simplistic and narrow prejudice persists that African social formations belong to a specific category, that of simple societies or of traditional societies."[20] The notion is still apparent in scholarly conventions for writing about classical arts of Africa that continue to label and describe an object in terms of its connection to a cultural or ethnic group on the basis of the object's form. While some admirers of African arts may cling to such colonial understandings of the continent, other people desire more information. Artist, curator, and scholar Nana Oforiatta Ayim told *Vogue* reporter Alex Frank: "At the Hermitage in St. Petersburg, in one room there would be some random masks and in another room some amazing Picassos, with so much more about the Picassos than the neglected masks. I remember being young and thinking, *I want there to be more*."[21] *Mapping Senufo* begins with a commitment to providing readers with more information about individual works and labels attached to them. It uncovers specific details and makes apparent the historical construction and contingencies of a name applied to people, a name applied to arts, and knowledge about them.

## Data and Mapping

Palmié explains that "as one scales downward from ostensible typological clarity, pesky detail increases, boundaries desolidify, and complexities proliferate on different levels."[22] There are various ways to scale downward, and efforts to maintain certain typologies may nevertheless persist. When Goldwater organized *Senufo Sculpture From West Africa*, he posited a geographic distribution of substyles on the basis of form. Anita Glaze, who conducted fieldwork in northern Côte d'Ivoire in the late 1960s and 1970s, questions Goldwater's understanding of the geographic distribution of objects. She starts with the idea that art styles and typologies reflect boundaries of larger or smaller language groups and subgroups. She also considers how different occupational identities or different ethnicities within a broader Senufo group contribute to the distribution of styles. And she identifies other factors that impact style, including a maker's occupation, a maker's particular networks of personal relations, and a patron's or user's additions of other elements to a work.[23] Despite her attention to such "pesky" details and historical complexities, Glaze states that her primary goal is the elucidation of "the traditional framework of Senufo art."[24] Her writing thus often vacillates between keen attention to detail and an effort to make such detail fit within broad claims about Senufo art.

Like Glaze, Till Förster, who began to study Senufo arts in northern Côte d'Ivoire in the late 1970s, considers the importance of different artisan groups to the production of arts across the region recognized as Senufo. Förster also explains that people who did not necessarily identify themselves with a Senufo group have created objects that connoisseurs label as Senufo. He notes that the term *Senufo* has encompassed people who in the past differentiated themselves from their neighbors, often on the basis of occupation. And he explains that the idea of a shared Senufo identity developed in the twentieth century. Förster recognizes centuries of migration and exchange within and beyond the area that Delafosse recognized as Senufo. But while Förster acknowledges such dynamism, he still seeks to define a discrete Senufo worldview, thereby maintaining rather than desolidfying boundaries.[25]

When Petridis and I began to work on *Mapping Senufo*, we wondered what would happen if we shifted focus away from a single framework and toward complex details. We decided to set aside the broader Senufo classification or smaller subgroup classifications to see what, if any, geographic or other patterns emerged through examination of the distribution of objects based on firsthand location data. We considered the corpus of art labeled as Senufo an ideal case study due to the existence of field-based documentation for specific objects dating from the nineteenth century to the present day. Since the end of the nineteenth century, government officials, missionaries, scholars, and other observers, including art collectors and dealers, have traveled through the region that corresponds with the area Delafosse designated as Senufo. The observers often recorded seemingly specific information about individual objects. We endeavored to scour records in public and private repositories in Africa, Europe, and North America in order to identify location information for individual objects. We imagined plotting location data on a map to reveal where particular objects were made, documented, or acquired. We also sought to track change over time. We aimed to determine if complexities would proliferate and lead us to develop more nuanced understandings.

As we gathered names of locations and dates attached to particular objects, we realized that we had to differentiate reliable, primary-source data from specious interpretations in order to plot accurate points. In an analysis of the use of archival photographs as historical evidence, Carolyn Keyes Adenaike warns that "replacing data with interpretations or failing to distinguish between the two, amounts to destroying primary evidence."[26] She adds that such replacement or conflation undermines subsequent research. Adenaike's plea for scholars to separate data from interpretation extends to documents other than photographs. Unfortunately, scholars of African arts and other art enthusiasts have often replaced data with interpretations or glossed over differences between the two. For example, scholars have recently suggested that because a sculpture was photographed in the town of Lataha in northern Côte d'Ivoire at some moment before July 1953, the sculpture must be the work of a Master of Lataha. Even if the scholars acknowledge that the location of documentation does not necessarily equate to the location of origin, the naming of an artist as the "Master of Lataha" as a matter of convenience obscures recognition of the mobility of people and objects or the history of a particular place.[27]

We have concluded that even when we can find the name of a place associated with an object, we must determine if the particular place is linked to the site of the object's making, documentation of use, or acquisition, or if the place is otherwise linked to the reported maker of the object. And the identification of a place requires additional assessment. In some cases, different geographic locations may be identified with the same place name. The Danish collector Carl Kjersmeier designates a place called Niena as the provenance for a Senufo sculpture that he acquired in West Africa in the early 1930s and that Man Ray subsequently photographed (Figure 10.6).[28] A place-name database links the name Niena to four different geographic locations in present-day Mali.[29] We need to know more about Kjersmeier's itinerary, his acquisition methods, his documentation methods, and historical locations of places known as Niena in order to pinpoint the Niena associated with the figure and locate the sculpture to a particular place with its own specific history. And even if we could determine the Niena Kjersmeier references, we still need to assess whether he acquired the sculpture in Niena, or someone else told him that the sculpture was linked to the place, or he had another reason for linking the sculpture to Niena.

Scholars and art enthusiasts have tried for decades to track down specific information about individual European artists and particular works they produced in the early twentieth century, probably the same period when West African artists created many of the objects we now recognize as Senufo.[30] Importantly, but not surprisingly, scholars and art enthusiasts have paid less attention to specific information attached to individual works produced in Africa during the same time period. According to Christopher Steiner, specificity in descriptions of classical African arts may disrupt European and American audiences' "'authentic' communion" with the

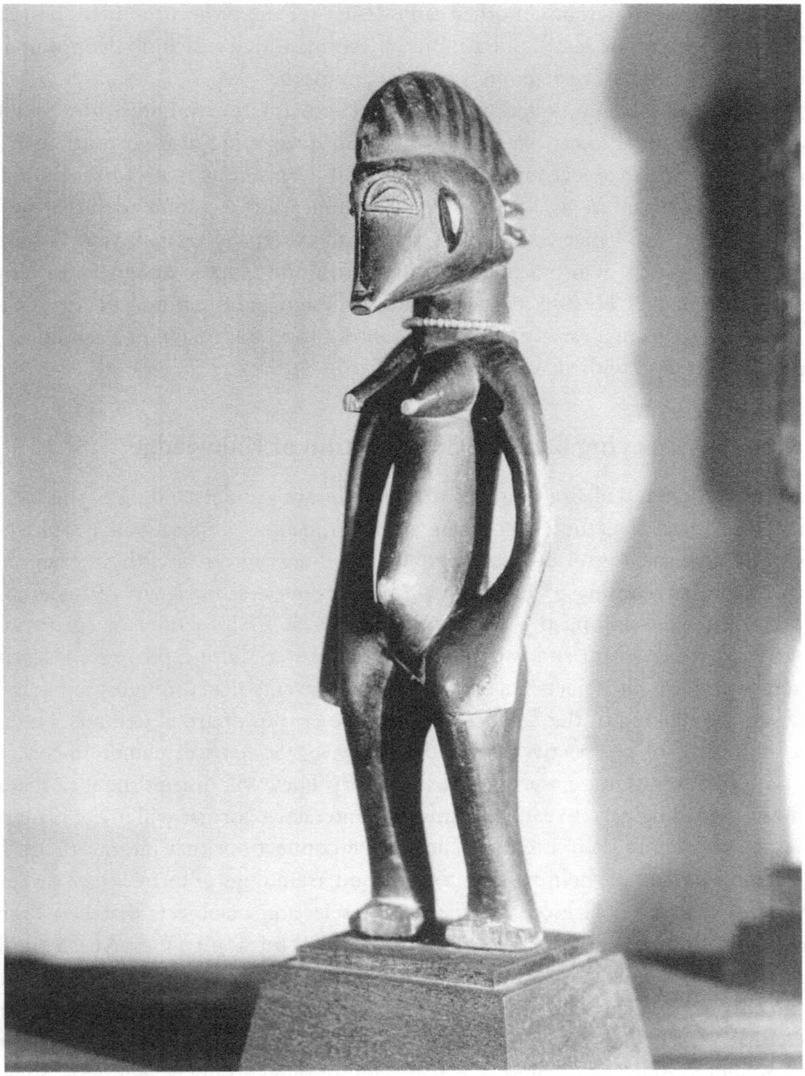

*Figure 10.6* Man Ray [Emmanuel Radnitzky], Untitled, 1933/34. Gelatin silver print, 11.2 × 8.1 cm, private collection.

*Source*: © Man Ray 2015 Trust/Artists Rights Society (ARS), NY/ADAGP, Paris.

works and deny audiences a sense of "discovery." He explains the approaches "emerge out of the intellectual void created by cycles of collective amnesia."[31] Through its emphasis on specific details, *Mapping Senufo* aims to fill an intellectual void, unsettle colonial assumptions, and assess African arts with a rigor and attention to detail that parallels the rigor and attention to detail that scholars have used to study arts of Europe.

However, due to the unreliability and uncertainty of information we have been able to recover, the *Mapping Senufo* monograph as we currently conceive it no longer aspires to map all available place-based information for objects identified as Senufo. We became concerned that such a map would mislead readers, appearing to confirm information that we have determined is ambiguous rather than certain. Another early design for the project focused on evaluation of the quality and character of data about art. But objects identified as Senufo disappeared from the data-driven design, and we have adopted another approach.[32]

Following August 2018 consultations with Erik Steiner, Creative Director of Stanford University's Spatial History Project, we are working on developing a conceptual map, one that examines how particular objects, images, people, and events contribute to the historical construction of a category of art we know as Senufo. Steiner also recommended that we engage a visual artist. Petridis and I met with several artists and eventually invited Mark Addison Smith to work with us. Smith's own practice as a visual artist and graphic designer involves translating narrative into images. He also teaches electronic design and multimedia courses. Smith thus brings to the project team a variety of skills to contribute to our design of a nonlinear structure for a digital monograph with an argument.

## Laying Bare the Construction of Knowledge

Our monograph design will aim to manifest Bruno Latour's understanding of the social. Latour argues that the social does not encompass a set of qualities imposed on people, but rather emerges from various interrelations. As people and things interrelate, they create and recreate a social group. According to Latour, an "on-going process made up of uncertain, fragile, controversial, and ever-shifting ties" constitutes the social.[33] An identity or corpus of art, like a social group, emerges from and is defined by similar ever-shifting processes. *Mapping Senufo* will present stories about objects, images, people, and events that through their interrelations contribute to the making of the Senufo label and the corpus of arts it delimits. The presences, absences, and range of perspectives covered in *Mapping Senufo* will evince uncertain, fragile, controversial, and ever-shifting aspects of the category. They will disrupt the idea that there is a single, all-encompassing narrative. The multimodal, interactive format will invite readers to focus on elements that capture their attention and pursue connections that interest them. The readers will become authors of their own contingent understandings of term *Senufo* or Senufo arts.

One section of the publication will focus on a selection of objects that Leo Frobenius or members of his research team drew during a 1907–1909 mission to West Africa and linked to specific locations. Some of the objects the research team identified as Senufo correspond with the Senufo corpus as we currently know it. In other cases, the research team applied other labels to objects that present-day connoisseurs regard as Senufo. And in still other cases, the team identified as Senufo objects that present-day art connoisseurs do not recognize as Senufo. Some drawings feature multiple labels, causing further confusion (Figure 10.7). *Diulla*, or Jula appears in ink near the drawing of a staff, suggesting someone linked the object to the Jula label. But *Senufo* written in pencil at the paper's edge indicates another person identified the staff with the Senufo label. The Jula and Senufo identifications for the same object raise questions about who labeled the objects as Jula or Senufo, when, and on what basis.

Our preliminary evaluations of some firsthand observers' documentation have also led us to the troubling confirmation of observers' lack of attention to specific details about particular people, places, or events in West Africa. In 2014, French Catholic missionary Pierre Boutin characterized the now-closed Musée Africain in Lyon, France, as a significant repository for arts identified as Senufo. He reported that the museum then held as many as 760 Senufo objects. Boutin also emphasized the importance of missionaries' firsthand documentation of works in the museum's collection.[34] When Petridis and I traveled to the museum in early March 2016, we identified 344 catalog cards containing some kind of place-based information for objects in the museum's collection labeled as Senufo. But we could not always determine if the location

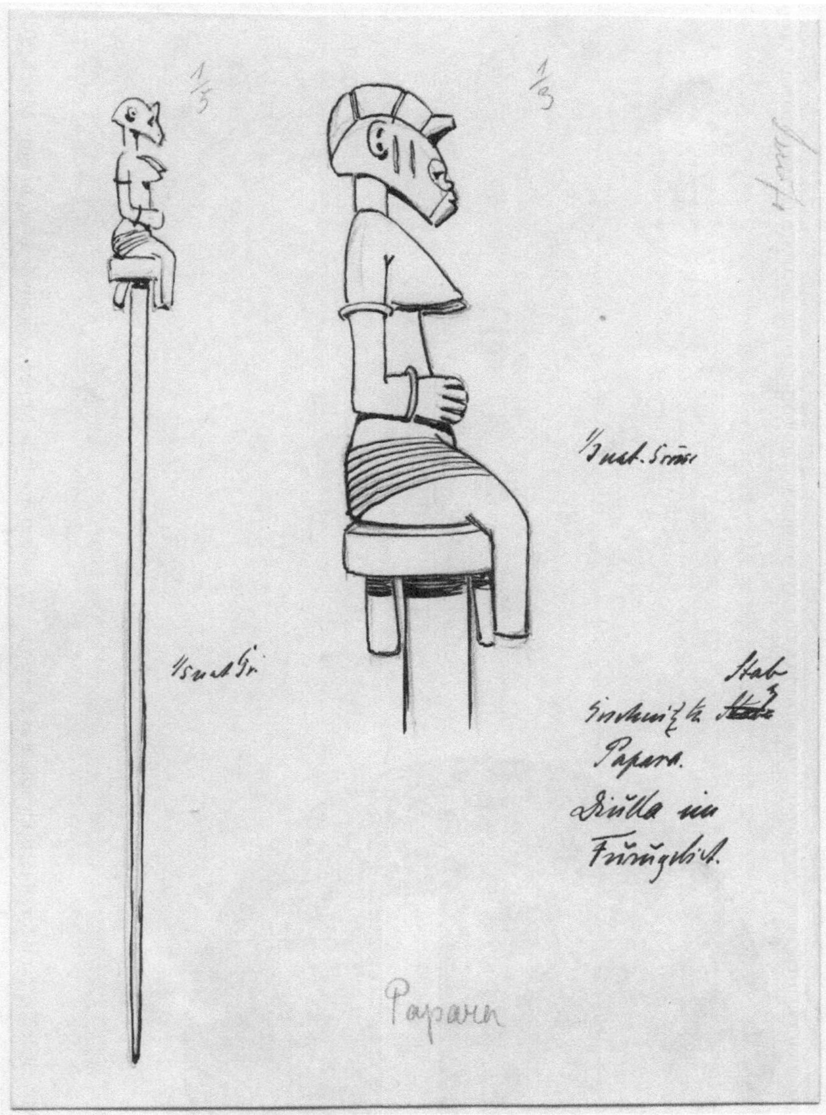


*Figure 10.7* Wooden staff labeled as "Papara. Diulla [Jula] in area of Furru [probably Fourou, Mali]." Ink drawing on paper possibly by Reinhard Hugershoff, 12.7 × 16.8 cm.

*Source*: Frobenius-Institut an der Johann Wolfgang, Goethe-Universität Frankfurt/Main, KBA 10416.

information came from a source written at the time of an object's acquisition in West Africa, if it came from Boutin's memory, or if came from Boutin's assessment of an object's form. We had also imagined that the museum's records might contain firsthand information about particular West African makers and patrons or about specific contexts for the works' production and use. However, we found it difficult to recover such detail or to distinguish between firsthand information and interpretation.

Based on her analysis of the cards, *Mapping Senufo* graduate research assistant Caitlin Glosser reports that while 318 cards attribute objects to an unrecorded maker, 209 cards recognize Boutin

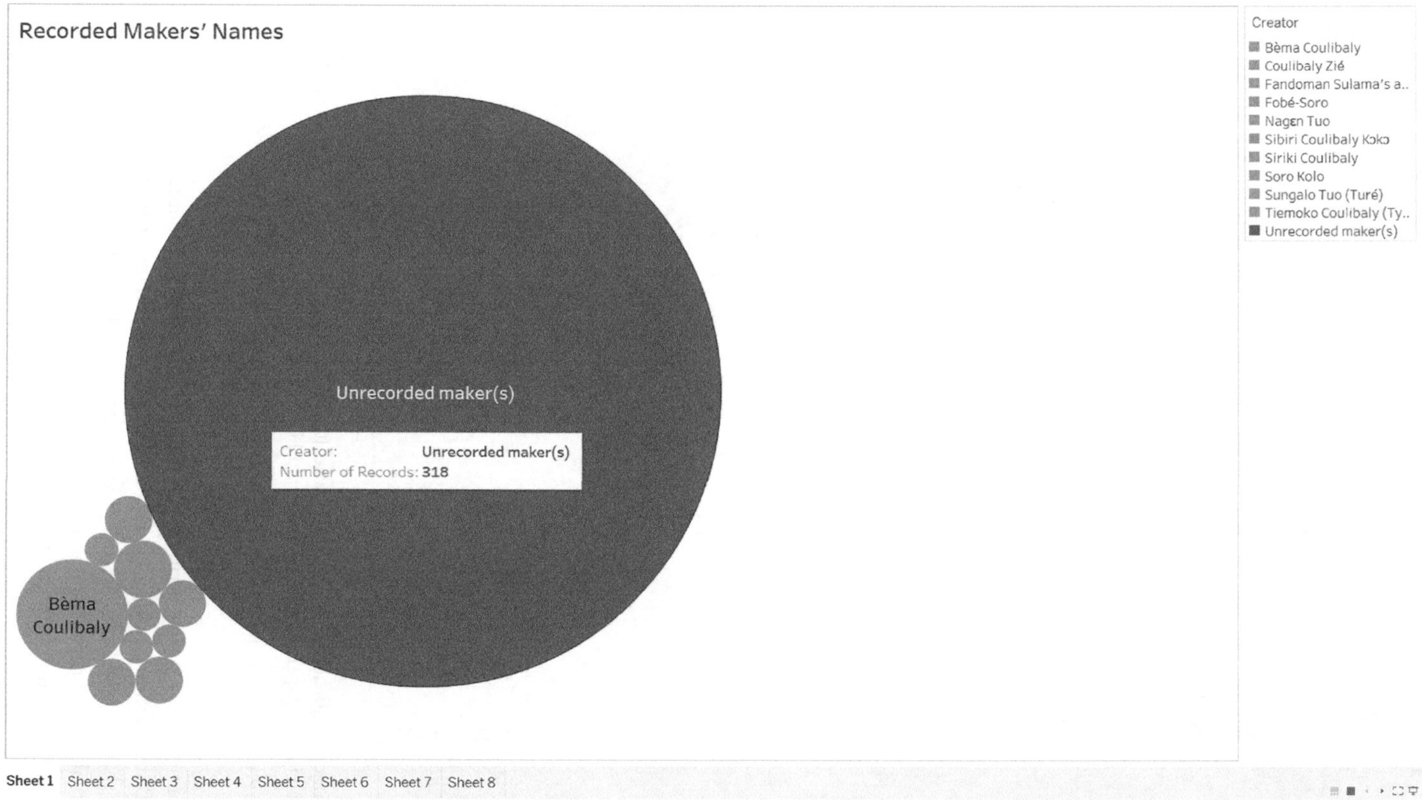


*Figure 10.8* Names of makers recorded on 344 catalogue cards for objects identified as Senufo in the collection of the Musée Africain de Lyon in early March 2016.

*Source*:Visualization by Caitlin Glosser, following Erik Steiner, 27 September 2018.

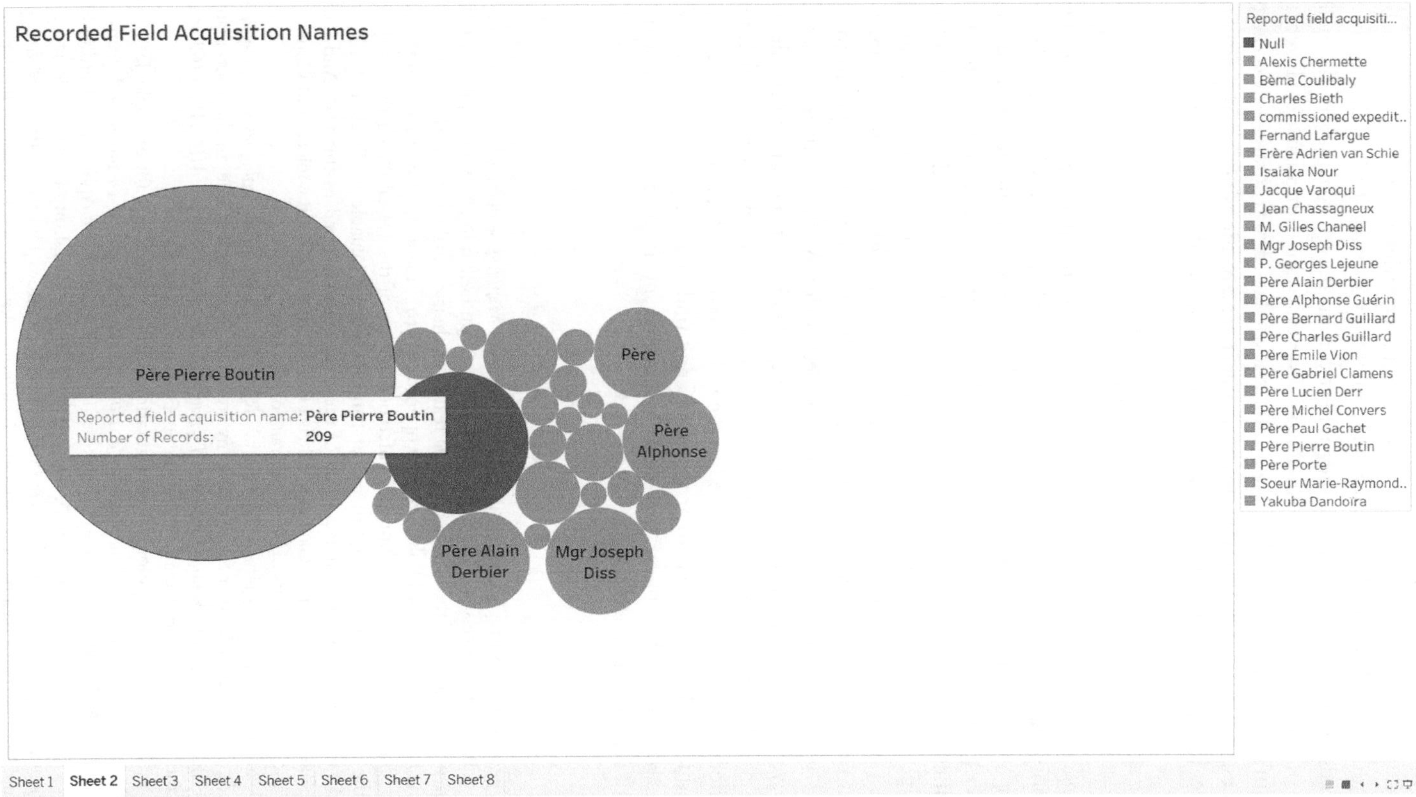


*Figure 10.9* Names of people who acquired objects in the field recorded on 344 catalog cards for objects identified as Senufo in the collection of the Musée Africain de Lyon in early March 2016.

*Source*: Visualization by Caitlin Glosser, following Erik Steiner, 27 September 2018.

as the person who acquired an object (Figs 10.8 and 10.9).[35] Her analysis reveals that Boutin appears ever-present in the archive because he acquired or documented hundreds of objects, but the people who made the objects Boutin and other missionaries acquired are largely absent from the records. As Michel-Rolph Trouillot demonstrates in *Silencing the Past*, the absences in historical records are not neutral. Rather, they reflect certain power dynamics in the making and remaking of history.[36] Or as Glosser explained, citing Christine Borgman, details recorded on the museum's cards are data that "exist within a knowledge infrastructure—an ecology of people, practices, technologies, institutions, material objects, and relationships."[37] *Mapping Senufo* aims to uncover and illustrate such knowledge infrastructures related to Senufo arts.

## Conclusion

The term *Senufo* exists, and it has variously referred to occupation, language, geography, culture, or other phenomena. But the term's meaning neither is stable nor refers to a singular, fixed entity. *Mapping Senufo* began with the desire to recover lost perspectives and focus on the specificity of single objects in order to undermine colonial assumptions. Our first efforts to identify and map specific locations linked to objects labeled as Senufo led us to realize that place names attached to different objects provide different kinds of information. Locations may relate to places where an object was reportedly made, documented, or acquired. We also concluded that the verifiability or reliability of information varies, even when the information appears to come from observers with firsthand experience of arts in West Africa. At this point in the project's development, we have determined that in order to understand the range of objects identified as Senufo and available information about them, we must "reassemble the social." Our embrace of digital methods has led us to unanticipated findings. The multimodal, digital monograph we eventually produce will allow readers to arrive at different understandings through their selection of stories about particular objects, images, people, and events involved in the construction of a category of art known as Senufo.

## Notes

1. For a list of people contributing to the project, see "People," in *Mapping Senufo* (Atlanta: Emory Center for Digital Scholarship), accessed March 17, 2019, www.mappingsenufo.org/public-people. I thank past and present members of the *Mapping Senufo* team for their contributions to the project. I also thank Tatiana Reinoza and Kailani Polzak for the opportunity to present an early version of this paper at the 2018 College Art Association annual conference as part of the Destabilizing the Geographic panel that they co-organized. They and the other panelists offered valuable feedback. I thank André Dombrowski for a comment that fueled some of the thinking developed in this text. And I thank Yaëlle Biro, Kathryn Brown, Marcia Gagliardi, Chris Higa, Linda Kim, Sarah McKee, and Constantine Petridis for their helpful comments on various drafts of this text.
2. Maurice Delafosse, "Le peuple siéna ou sénoufo," *Revue des études ethnographiques et sociologiques* 1 (1908): 16–32. I thank Erik Steiner for drawing my attention to the dotted line on the 1908 map.
3. See Susan Elizabeth Gagliardi, *Senufo Unbound: Dynamics of Art and Identity in West Africa* (Cleveland: The Cleveland Museum of Art; Milan: 5 Continents Editions, 2015), 42–44.
4. For critical evaluations of anthropological configurations of the "native," see for example, Jean Bazin, "À chacun son Bambara," in *Au coeur de l'ethnie: Ethnies, tribalisme, et état en afrique*, ed. Jean-Loup Amselle and Elikia M'Bokolo (Paris: La Decouverte, 1985), 87–127; Arjun Appadurai, "Putting Hierarchy in Its Place," *Cultural Anthropology* 3, no. 1 (1988): 36–49; Jean-Loup Amselle, *Mestizo Logics: Anthropology of Identity in Africa and Elsewhere* (Stanford, CA: Stanford University Press, 1998 [1990]); Lila Abu-Lughod, "Writing Against Culture," in *Recapturing Anthropology: Working in the Present*, ed. Richard Fox (Santa Fe, NM: School of American Research Press, 1991), 137–62; Achille Mbembe, *On the Postcolony* (Berkeley: University of California Press, 2001); Michel-Rolph Trouillot, "Anthropology

and the Savage Slot: The Poetics and Politics of Otherness," in *Global Transformations: Anthropology and the Modern World* (New York: Palgrave Macmillan, 2003), 7–28. For assessments of what Sidney Kasfir referred to as the "one tribe-one style" model for the study of African arts, see, for example, Pieter Jan Vandenhoute, *Classification stylistique du masque Dan et Guéré de la Côte d'Ivoire Occidentale (A. O. F.)* (Leiden: E. J. Brill, 1948); Roy Sieber and Arnold Rubin, *Sculpture of Black Africa: The Paul and Ruth Tishman Collection* (Los Angeles: Los Angeles County Museum of Art, 1968); Sidney Littlefield Kasfir, "One Tribe, One Style? Paradigms in the Historiography of African Art," *History in Africa* 11 (1984): 163–93; Marla Berns, Richard Fardon, and Sidney Littlefield Kasfir, eds., *Central Nigeria Unmasked: Arts of the Benue River Valley* (Los Angeles: Fowler Museum at UCLA, 2011).

5. Cf. Amselle, *Mestizo Logics*; Trouillot, "Anthropology and the Savage Slot."
6. Kwame Anthony Appiah, *The Lies that Bind: Rethinking Identity* (New York: Liveright Publishing Corporation, 2018), 199.
7. For example, see Nicholas Bauch, *Enchanting the Desert* (Stanford, CA: Stanford University Press, 2016), accessed March 17, 2019, www.enchantingthedesert.com/home/; Samuel Liebhaber, *When Melodies Gather: Oral Art of the Mahra* (Stanford: Stanford University Press, 2018), accessed March 17, 2019, www.whenmelodiesgather.org/; Thomas S. Mullaney, ed., *The Chinese Deathscape: Grave Reform in Modern China* (Stanford, CA: Stanford University Press, 2019), accessed March 17, 2019, http://chinese deathscape.org/. See also Cheryl E. Ball, "Show, Not Tell: The Value of New Media Scholarship," *Computers and Composition* 21 (2004): 403–25; Lauren Klein, "The Image of Absence: Archival Silence, Data Visualization, and James Hemings," *American Literature* 85, no. 4 (2013): 668, 672.
8. Ibrahim Traoré Banakourou, pers. comm., September 16, 2018.
9. For a discussion of how digital mapmaking impacts art-historical research and focuses scholars' attention on process, see Susan Elizabeth Gagliardi and Joanna Gardner-Huggett, "Introduction to the Special Issue: Spatial Art History in the Digital Realm," *Historical Geography* 45 (2017): 17–36.
10. See references listed in note 4.
11. See the Art Institute of Chicago's online entries for Caryatid Drum (ARTIC 1990.137) and Standing Woman (ARTIC 1967.684), www.artic.edu/artworks/111401/caryatid-drum-pinge; www.artic.edu/artworks/28418/standing-woman (both accessed March 11, 2019).
12. Geographer Anne Kelly Knowles suggested such a map that dissolves rather than reinforces boundaries of a Senufo area during the 2014 Kress Summer Institute on Digital Mapping and Art History at Middlebury College. Petridis and I have attempted to gather data necessary to create such a map, but we have not yet obtained them.
13. Amselle, *Mestizo Logics*, 43–57.
14. For example, see Louis-Gustave Binger, *Du Niger au golfe de Guinée par le pays de Kong et le Mossi, 1887–1889* (Paris: Hachette, 1892), 215; Robert Launay, *Traders Without Trade: Responses to Change in Two Dyula Communities* (Cambridge: Cambridge University Press, 1982); Till Förster, *Die Kunst der Senufo, Museum Rietberg Zürich, aus Schweizer Sammlungen* (Zurich: Museum Rietberg, 1988), 9; Anja Veirman, "The Art of Living: Some Aspects of the Art and Culture of the Senufo," in *Forms of Wonderment: The History and Collection of the Afrika Museum, Berg en Dal*, ed. Jan-Lodewijk Grootaers and Ineke Eisenburger (Berg en Dal: Afrika Museum, 2002), 110. See also Gagliardi, *Senufo Unbound*, 41–49.
15. Till Förster, *Zerrissene Entfaltung: Alltag, Ritual und künstlerische Ausdrucksformen im Norden der Côte d'Ivoire* (Cologne: Rüdiger Köppe, 1997), 94–95.
16. Yaëlle Biro, *Fabriquer le regard: Marchands, réseaux et objets africains à l'aube du XX^e siècle* (Dijon and Paris: Les presses du réel, 2018). See also John Warne Monroe, "Surface Tensions: Empire, Parisian Modernism, and 'Authenticity' in African Sculpture, 1917–1939," *American Historical Review* 117, no. 2 (2012): 445–75.
17. For example, see Gagliardi, *Senufo Unbound*, 44–45.
18. Stephan Palmié, *The Cooking of History: How Not to Study Afro-Cuban Religion* (Chicago and London: The University of Chicago Press, 2013), 6.
19. For example, see Carl Kjersmeier, *Centres de style de la sculpture nègre africaine*, vol. 1 (Paris: éditions Albert Morancé; Copenhagen: Illums Bog-Afdeling, 1935), 29; Frédéric-Henri Lem, *Sculptures Soudanaises* (Paris: Arts et Métiers Graphiques, 1948), 38.
20. Mbembe, *On the Postcolony*, 3.
21. Nana Oforiatta Ayim quoted in Alex Frank, "Nana Oforiatta Ayim's Open-Source Encyclopedia of African History Starts with Ghana," *Vogue*, October 20, 2017, accessed August 26, 2018, www.vogue.com/article/ghana-africa-art-cultural-encyclopedia, emphasis in the original.
22. Palmié, *The Cooking of History*, 6. See also Amselle, *Mestizo Logics*, 30.

23. Anita J. Glaze, *Art and Death in a Senufo Village* (Bloomington: Indiana University Press, 1981), 1–45, 194.
24. Ibid., xi.
25. Förster, *Die Kunst der Senufo*, 10.
26. Carolyn Keyes Adenaike, "Contextualizing and Decontextualizing African Historical Photographs," *History in Africa* 23 (1996): 429–37.
27. For example, see Eberhard Fischer and Lorenz Homberger, eds., *Afrikanische Meister: Kunst der Elfenbeinküste* (Zurich: Scheidegger & Spiess, 2014), 157–64.
28. Kjersmeier, *Centres de style*, vol. 1, "Liste des Illustrations II," fig. no. 39.
29. A search for "Niena" in the present-day country of Mali in the National Geospatial Intelligence Agency (NGA) GEOnet Names Server (GNS) yielded four populated places. They are: Niéna (13.6322 N, -4.9959 W), Niéna (11.425157 N, -6.348808 W), Niéna (11.457527 N, -5.32556 W), and Nièna (13.147232 N, -6.081274 W). See NGA GEOnet Names Server (GNS), updated May 30, 2017, accessed June 1, 2017, http://geonames.nga.mil/namesgaz/.
30. For example, see Joshua I. Cohen, "Fauve Masks: Rethinking Modern 'Primitivist' Uses of African and Oceanic Art, 1905–8," *The Art Bulletin* 99, no. 2 (2017): 135–63.
31. Christopher Steiner, "Discovering African Art . . . Again?" *African Arts* 29, no. 4 (1996): 1, 4, 6, 8, 93.
32. I thank Gesa Kirsch for drawing our attention to the disappearance of objects from *Mapping Senufo* during the June 2018 From Prototype to Published KairosCamp, an Institute for Advanced Topics in the Digital Humanities funded by the National Endowment for the Humanities and hosted by the Digital Publishing Institute, West Virginia University.
33. Bruno Latour, *Reassembling the Social: An Introduction to Actor-Network-Theory* (Oxford and New York: Oxford University Press, 2005), 28. See also Appiah, *The Lies That Bind.*
34. Pierre Boutin, "Comment se constituent les collections: l'exemple sénoufo," *Afrique: Archaéologie & Arts* 10 (2014): 43–66.
35. Caitlin Glosser used the project database developed by Joanna Mundy and Sara Palmer to organize data on the catalog cards, and Glosser used Tableau software to visualize data. For information about the project database, see Joanna Mundy and Sara Palmer, "About Database Design," in *Mapping Senufo* (Atlanta: Emory Center for Digital Scholarship, September 23, 2016), accessed September 23, 2018, www.mappingsenufo.org/database-design.
36. Michel-Rolph Trouillot, *Silencing the Past: Power and the Production of History* (Boston: Beacon Press, 1995), 48–49.
37. Christine L. Borgman, *Big Data, Little Data, No Data: Scholarship in the Networked World* (Cambridge, MA: MIT Press, 2015), 4. See also Glosser, unpublished analysis of research on the 344 catalog cards from the Musée Africain de Lyon, November 3, 2017.

## Bibliography


Abu-Lughod, Lila. "Writing against Culture." In *Recapturing Anthropology: Working in the Present*, edited by Richard Fox, 137–62. Santa Fe: School of American Research Press, 1991.

Adenaike, Carolyn Keyes. "Contextualizing and Decontextualizing African Historical Photographs." *History in Africa* 23 (1996): 429–37.

Amselle, Jean-Loup. *Mestizo Logics: Anthropology of Identity in Africa and Elsewhere*. Stanford, CA: Stanford University Press, 1998[1990].

Appadurai, Arjun. "Putting Hierarchy in its Place." *Cultural Anthropology* 3, no. 1 (1988): 36–49.

Appiah, Kwame Anthony. *The Lies that Bind: Rethinking Identity*. New York: Liveright Publishing Corporation, 2018.

Ball, Cheryl E. "Show, Not Tell: The Value of New Media Scholarship." *Computers and Composition* 21 (2004): 403–25.

Bauch, Nicholas. *Enchanting the Desert*. Stanford: Stanford University Press, 2016. Accessed March 17, 2019. www.enchantingthedesert.com/home/.

Bazin, Jean. "À chacun son Bambara." In *Au coeur de l'ethnie: Ethnies, tribalisme, et état en afrique*, edited by Jean-Loup Amselle and Elikia M'Bokolo, 87–127. Paris: La Decouverte, 1985.

Berns, Marla, Richard Fardon, and Sidney Littlefield Kasfir, eds. *Central Nigeria Unmasked: Arts of the Benue River Valley*. Los Angeles: Fowler Museum at UCLA, 2011.

Binger, Louis-Gustave. *Du Niger au golfe de Guinée par le pays de Kong et le Mossi, 1887–1889.* Paris: Hachette, 1892.

Biro, Yaëlle. *Fabriquer le regard: Marchands, réseaux et objets africains à l'aube du XX^e siècle.* Dijon and Paris: Les presses du réel, 2018.

Borgman, Christine L. *Big Data, Little Data, No Data: Scholarship in the Networked World.* Cambridge: MIT Press, 2015.

Boutin, Pierre. "Comment se constituent les collections: l'exemple sénoufo." *Afrique: Archaéologie & Arts* 10 (2014): 43–66.

Caillié, René. *Travels through Central Africa to Timbuctoo and Across the Great Desert to Morocco, 1824–1828.* London: Henry Colburg & Richard Bentley, 1830.

Cohen, Joshua I. "Fauve Masks: Rethinking Modern 'Primitivist' Uses of African and Oceanic Art, 1905–8." *The Art Bulletin* 99, no. 2 (2017): 135–63.

Delafosse, Maurice. "Le peuple siéna ou sénoufo." *Revue des études ethnographiques et sociologiques* 1 (1908): 16–32.

Fischer, Eberhard, and Lorenz Homberger, eds. *Afrikanische Meister: Kunst der Elfenbeinküste.* Zurich: Scheidegger & Spiess, 2014.

Förster, Till. *Die Kunst der Senufo, Museum Rietberg Zürich, aus Schweizer Sammlungen.* Zurich: Museum Rietberg, 1988.

———. *Zerrissene Entfaltung: Alltag, Ritual und künstlerische Ausdrucksformen im Norden der Côte d'Ivoire.* Cologne: Rüdiger Köppe, 1997.

Frank, Alex. "Nana Oforiatta Ayim's Open-Source Encyclopedia of African History Starts with Ghana." *Vogue,* October 20, 2017. Accessed August 26, 2018. www.vogue.com/article/ghana-africa-art-cultural-encyclopedia.

Gagliardi, Susan Elizabeth. *Senufo Unbound: Dynamics of Art and Identity in West Africa.* Cleveland: The Cleveland Museum of Art; Milan: 5 Continents Editions, 2014.

Gagliardi, Susan Elizabeth, and Joanna Gardner-Huggett. "Introduction to the Special Issue Spatial Art History in the Digital Realm." *Historical Geography* 45 (2017): 17–36.

Glaze, Anita J. *Art and Death in a Senufo Village.* Bloomington: Indiana University Press, 1981.

Kasfir, Sidney Littlefield. "One Tribe, One Style? Paradigms in the Historiography of African Art." *History in Africa* 11 (1984): 163–93.

Kjersmeier, Carl. *Centres de style de la sculpture nègre africaine,* vol. 1. Paris: éditions Albert Morancé; Copenhagen: Illums Bog-Afdeling, 1935.

Klein, Lauren. "The Image of Absence: Archival Silence, Data Visualization, and James Hemings." *American Literature* 85, no. 4 (2013): 661–88.

Latour, Bruno. *Reassembling the Social: An Introduction to Actor-Network-Theory.* Oxford and New York: Oxford University Press, 2005.

Launay, Robert. *Traders without Trade: Responses to Change in Two Dyula Communities.* Cambridge: Cambridge University Press, 1982.

Lem, Frédéric-Henri. *Sculptures soudanaises.* Paris: Arts et Métiers Graphiques, 1948.

Liebhaber, Samuel. *When Melodies Gather: Oral Art of the Mahra.* Stanford: Stanford University Press, 2018. Accessed March 17, 2019. www.whenmelodiesgather.org/.

Mbembe, Achille. *On the Postcolony.* Berkeley: University of California Press, 2001.

Monroe, John Warne. "Surface Tensions: Empire, Parisian Modernism, and 'Authenticity' in African Sculpture, 1917–1939." *American Historical Review* 117, no. 2 (2012): 445–75.

Mullaney, Thomas S, ed. *The Chinese Deathscape: Grave Reform in Modern China.* Stanford: Stanford University Press, 2019. Accessed March 17, 2019. http://chinesedeathscape.org/.

Mundy, Joanna, and Sara Palmer. "About Database Design." In *Mapping Senufo.* Atlanta: Emory Center for Digital Scholarship, September 23, 2016. Accessed September 23, 2018. www.mappingsenufo.org/database-design.

Palmié, Stephan. *The Cooking of History: How Not to Study Afro-Cuban Religion.* Chicago and London: The University of Chicago Press, 2013.

Sieber, Roy, and Arnold Rubin. *Sculpture of Black Africa: The Paul and Ruth Tishman Collection.* Los Angeles: Los Angeles County Museum of Art, 1968.

Steiner, Christopher. "Discovering African Art . . . Again?" *African Arts* 29, no. 4 (1996): 1, 4, 6, 8, 93.

Tautain, Louis Frédéric Emile. "Le Diouladougou et le Senefo." *Revue d'ethnographie* 6 (1887): 395–99.

Trouillot, Michel-Rolph. "Anthropology and the Savage Slot: The Poetics and Politics of Otherness." In *Global Transformations: Anthropology and the Modern World*, 7–28. New York: Palgrave Macmillan, 2003.
———. *Silencing the Past: Power and the Production of History*. Boston: Beacon Press, 1995.
Vandenhoute, Pieter Jan. *Classification stylistique du masque Dan et Guéré de la Côte d'Ivoire Occidentale (A.O.F.)*. Leiden: E. J. Brill, 1948.
Veirman, Anja. "The Art of Living: Some Aspects of the Art and Culture of the Senufo." In *Forms of Wonderment: The History and Collection of the Afrika Museum, Berg en Dal*, edited by Jan-Lodewijk Grootaers and Ineke Eisenburger. Berg en Dal: Afrika Museum, 2002.

# 11
# X-RECEPTION
## Re-mediating Trans- Feminist and Queer Performance Art

*T.L. Cowan*

What does it mean to move performance art, its archives, and repertoires—in this case the archives and repertoires of Trans- Feminist and Queer (TFQ) performance art—from a small stage with a limited, friendly, mostly insider audience to online platforms that offer a far wider audience?[1] What are the possible consequences of these translocations and remediations, and what do these questions have to do with scholarly activities in the digital humanities?

In order to think through these questions I begin, perhaps anachronistically, with H.R. Jauss's *Toward an Aesthetic of Reception*, particularly his influential essay "Literary History as a Challenge to Literary Theory."[2] I consider Jauss's conceptions of historically contingent reception aesthetics, how audiences make meaning based on previous experience with like or unlike works, and how they create meaning through what Jauss calls a "horizon of expectation."[3] I extend Jauss's reception aesthetics to my study of TFQ performance art and digital humanities as a means of understanding how horizons of expectation and reception aesthetics of expressive culture change over time. I am particularly interested in how such practices and possibilities change based on historical context, platform scale, and culture (potential size, character, values, and reception behaviors of a platform's audience), and how digital humanities practices of the trans- and re-mediation (cross-platform transfer) of performance art materials, are, ultimately, experiments in what I shall call "X-reception." This builds upon Beth Coleman's paradigm-shifting framing of "X-reality" as "a continuum of exchanges between virtual and real spaces" and as an "extension of agency."[4] Echoing Irit Rogoff's call, a theory of X-reception urges both performance studies scholars and digital humanists to think with humility and criticality; that is, to inhabit the conditions and contexts of offline and online research environments.[5] I shall argue that X-reception theory helps us to conceptualize the responsibilities, research ethics, accountabilities, and managed risk that need to become part of how we understand, express, and evaluate rigor as practiced at the intersection of digital humanities and performance studies.

### TFQ Cabaret

In the first instance, a clarification is necessary about the subject matter of this chapter, the archives and repertoires of TFQ performance art. In this case, I am considering one of the great and centrally important forms of TFQ performance art: the small-scale, very local, grassroots, satirical variety show known as the cabaret. TFQ scenes are those driven by, and oriented centrally toward, an ever-shifting intersectional trans- feminist and queer aesthetic, politics, and ethics that rejects the aesthetic, political, and economic supremacy of "Pride" capitalism. Instead, TFQ scenes tend to occur in small and inexpensive spaces and to feature sets of short performances of five to fifteen minutes across genre and form (dance, spoken word, music, drag, installation, visual art, sound art, stand-up, sketch or improv comedy, video art, film, and much more) that explicitly work against forms of supremacy in contemporary culture. This may target, for example, forms of racism and misogynoir,[6] transphobia and transmisogyny, sexism, fat phobia and lezbophobia, ongoing settler and neo-colonial violence, extractive capitalism, or discrimination through other lived experiences of poverty, migration and immigration, disability, and mental illness. Significantly, while this list of oppressive realities is what TFQ performance often responds to, it is as much about creating and reveling in joy as it is about exposing the existence of pain. That is, TFQ cabaret performance is as much about fashioning meaningful spaces in which participants can take risks with each other, as it is about the danger of being exposed to an unfriendly world. It is, most centrally, about intimacy, and the ways that performers and audiences (and most performers are also audience members) create a provisional kind of trust in whatever configuration they find themselves. It is almost always the job of the MC to bring the audience and the performers together and to create the imaginative, speculative-pragmatic, fantastical, transformed, and transformative space in which the cabaret takes place.

Because of its usually small anticipated and cultivated audience (rarely more than a few hundred people at one show and often less than one hundred), TFQ cabarets and other performance happenings tend to take place in multipurpose spaces: community centers and bookstores, small, low-tech stage spaces in galleries, living rooms, basements, and sex-shops, as well as schools, cafeterias, strip clubs, gymnasiums, banquet halls, and queer bars (if any exist) but often as the early show or on a weeknight.[7] Usually the organizers of the event will attempt a surface transformation of the space in order to create a room conducive for a show—with makeshift sound and stage equipment, a bar, some snacks, curtains, decorations, tables and chairs, and a hacked together projection rig. TFQ cabaret happens where it can, when it can, how it can. It is necessarily, and has always been, mobile. And with this mobility comes a whole range of skills, warnings, and labors that cabaret organizers, producers, curators, performers, and audiences have come to understand.

In addition to the kinds of performers and performances that tend to be highlighted and researched as the central figures of a TFQ cabaret, the element that really makes or breaks a show is the audience and its capacity to fabulate along with the MC and the performers, to do the work of creating a shared space of intimacy and risk. If an audience does not understand and appreciate the codes of the show, refuses to produce an enthusiastically raucous dynamic, or cannot be trusted with the performers, aesthetics, ethics, politics, and erotics of the show, then the cabaret not only flops, but also becomes a potential site of harm.

This chapter attends to the importance of building infrastructures of and for TFQ cabarets across platforms in order to host the cabaret's mobility, and the conditions of vulnerability and risk that emerge for trans- feminist and queer performers and audiences with each new physical and online venue. While much digital humanities design and scholarship works toward building template-driven platforms to increase end-user accessibility, the kinds of online spaces that might work best for repositories of TFQ live performance, especially of cabaret, will require a versatile approach that allows the people whose materials are collected within an archive, repository, or online exhibition to customize accessibility (who can access the materials), longevity (how long the materials are available), and description (metadata and context) functions.

## Networked Research Scenarios

Moving performance materials online creates the potential for entirely new audiences and modes of reception. Online platforms for hosting and circulating performance materials are increasingly familiar sites of digital humanities and performance studies inquiry in the mutually informing processes of research-creation and research-reception. Online archives, collections, exhibitions, publications, and repositories housed institutionally or on DIY sites hosted by CMS applications like WordPress or Omeka, and semi-institutional sites housed by university- or library-funded initiatives like SCALAR are what Michelle Moravec calls "digital archival environments."[8] The process of digital creation requires researchers to experiment with how to remediate performance materials across platforms and how to responsibly account for, and attend to, potentially massively different levels of access, opportunity, and risk. The latter arise as the performance-circulation shifts from small-scale performance scenarios, with infrastructures of intimate reception, to the scenario of potentially open-access online platforms.

Accepting that "digital archival environments are here to stay," Moravec argues that "we must shift the focus from debates over their appropriateness or the utility of them to discussion of how our research practices require rethinking in light of them."[9] In particular, she notes that we need to focus on "human relationships and experiences that are mediated by these environments."[10] In building and using digital environments, she asks researchers to ask themselves questions including:

- "What consent has been given by individuals who are visible in a digital archival environment and what controls exist to mitigate that exposure?"[11]
- Who labored, and under what conditions, to create materials in a digital archival environment?[12]
- What are the "absences, both those created technologically, as well as those that flow from decisions about content and context in a given digital archival environment?"[13]

Because TFQ cabaret and its reception are structured by relationships (both long-standing and temporary intimacies), the remediation of its performance requires attention as to how those intimacies (and the nature of the intimacy) shift across media.

Performance research is increasingly invested in, and reliant on, digitized networked performance archives which are often remediated multiple times (i.e. from a performance to a video file stored on a cassette or DVD perhaps screened by one or two people at a time, to a digital video uploaded and made available to a potentially infinite audience). Rather than rendering the remediation process invisible, we need to engage with what modes of reception each step of the remediation process enables and disables. Sarah Bay-Cheng, Jennifer Parker-Starbuck, and David Saltz contend that "[c]riticism of performance across digital domains and subsumed within media networks require new forms of criticism and modes of scholarship that can account for a dynamic, changing, and increasingly collaborative field" of performance studies and creation.[14] They argue that we need a "multidimensional approach to the field of media-performance intersections that can attend not only to the individual instances of performance, but also respond to the changing dynamics of media, technology and performance.[15] The digital archival environment is central to these changing dynamics. Indeed, as Gabriella Giannachi, Nick Kaye, and Michael Shanks note in *Archaeologies of Presence*, "new strategies for documentation [. . .] have increasingly come to emphasize the reader or viewer's relationship with that which remains over the reconstruction of past events or the transparency of one medium, context and time to another."[16] Rather than focus purely on a "live performance/documentation" binary, performance studies scholars are creating methods that attend to the multiply mediated and networked experiences of both and to the "processes by which a performance constitutes mediates, and is mediated by networks of digital exchange and to trace our own engagement within those networks."[17] The hybrid disciplinary space of digital humanities-performance studies offers a challenging ethico-methodological site for the kinds of entangled thinking and experimentation that we need as more and more performance materials (especially those from minoritized scenes) are captured for online circulation.

In my mind, the leaders in the field of online reception theory, praxis, and the protection of sensitive cultural heritage materials are the collaborators involved the Content Management System (CMS) Mukurtu[18] and the research site Local Contexts,[19] namely, Warumungu community members, the Penobscot Nation, the Passamaquoddy Nation and other research partners working with project directors Kimberly Christen and Jane Anderson. Mukurtu and Local Contexts are designed to facilitate critical engagements with the ways that Indigenous cultural heritage materials have historically been collected by colonial institutions and how they have been placed online by these institutions, generally on open-access sites. The Mukurtu CMS is largely predicated on thinking about audience and, according to cultural protocols, about which (inside-community and/or outside-community) audiences should or should not have access to the materials in their collections. The Traditional Knowledge (TK) Labels is a system that continues to be shaped by the co-researchers and developers of these projects in order to provide context for the materials that are being circulated online. The description is worth quoting in full:

> The TK Labels are a tool for Indigenous communities to add existing local protocols for access and use to recorded cultural heritage that is digitally circulating outside community contexts. The TK Labels offer an educative and informational strategy to help non-community users of this cultural heritage understand its importance and significance to the communities from where it derives and continues to have meaning. TK Labeling is designed to identify and clarify which material has community-specific restrictions regarding access and use. This is especially with respect to sacred and/or ceremonial material, material that has gender restrictions, seasonal conditions of use and/or materials specifically designed for outreach purposes. The TK Labels also can be used to add information that might be considered "missing," including the name of the community who remains the creator or cultural custodian of the material, and how to contact the relevant family, clan or community to arrange appropriate permissions.[20]

Ultimately, the Mukurtu and Local Contexts projects and the TK Labels system are motivated by an anti-colonial belief that not all people should have access to the materials of cultures that are not their own, and that people should know the cultural protocols of the material they are being given access to; it is a fundamental rejection of extractive and possessive colonial principles and practices, as well as a challenge to online, open-access principles and practices. In her chapter "Relationships, Not Records: Digital Heritage and the Ethics of Sharing Indigenous Knowledge Online," Christen explains the ETHICS guidelines that shape the working relationships between university-based researchers and researcher-participants from beyond the university. Christen writes that "[t]aken together, these steps comprise an ETHICS (Engage, Talk, Help, Invest, Create, Support) for archival practices. Choosing to follow this path will not guarantee success, but ETHICS does set a framework for respectful digital archiving projects that create not just records, but relationships."[21] It is centrally important for digital humanists and performance studies scholars to follow the lead of the knowledge and practices emerging from Indigenous digital archival environments and the activities that produce and sustain them. My goal here in theorizing the unpredictability of online reception using the framework of X-reception—as an ethical methodology for TFQ (and other) online archival, repository, and exhibition projects—is to emphasize why we need to think, act, build, and maintain research-driven online environments with care for the pasts, presents, and futures of the people, knowledge, and relationships that have produced the materials that have become our research artifacts.

## Reception/X-Reality/X-Reception/X$^\infty$-Reception

In this section I offer the example of TFQ cabaret performance events as a way into thinking about how reception—offline and online—hinges on the experiences of the performers and audiences, and their relationships with each other. Drawing on Jauss's theory of the "horizon of expectations," we can imagine that the reception the work receives from an intended TFQ cabaret audience "in the historical moment of its appearance" is produced through that audience's "pre-understanding of the genre, from the forms and themes of already familiar works."[22] In Jauss's terms, reception "comes to light at the intersections of diachrony and synchrony," the intersection of its historical moment and the audience's pre-understanding or familiarity with the genre; reception is historically contingent, shaped in a present moment by the "constant and variable factors" of past and future experiences that build an audience's understanding of a genre.[23]

Conventionally, the "horizon of expectations" has been understood as an axis, with the synchronic moment as a vertical "slice" through a long diachrony of chronological time. What happens when we introduce the virtual dimension into this horizon of expectations? Beth Coleman's theory of X-reality as the simultaneous "interlacing of virtual and real experiences" helps us to answer this question.[24] Coleman takes "the x of X-reality to stand for an x-factor or variable, as it would in an equation."[25] In positing an X-reality, Coleman "advocate[s] for multidirectional and multivalent understanding of the nature of pervasive media."[26] I shall use the term "X-Reception" to refer to a reception practice that traverses online, virtual, or augmented critically restored documentation, ephemera, and other "remains" and the live performance they index.[27] I propose the term "X$^\infty$-Reception" to emphasize Coleman's attention to the multidirectional and multivalent nature of X-reality. For a theory of reception, X$^\infty$ attends to how the infinite variables of context, intimacy, and reception shift and collapse in the virtual dimension. The online condition of endless possibilities needs to be anticipated and accounted for both in the process of platform design and development and in the responsible maintenance once the platform goes "live." While the factor of infinite variables is already present in Coleman's theory, I propose that the infinity sign of X$^\infty$-Reception urges us to ethical action. This is the ethical attention to the infinite variables of reception (and circulation) opened by bringing performance materials—especially minoritized materials—online.

## Cabaret's Context: Horizons of Gay Expectations

Small-world cabarets are networks: each performer brings five to ten friends, and friends of friends.[28] If there are ten artists, you can expect fifty to one hundred people to attend a show, plus whoever comes because they know the work of one or more of the performers, are a fan of the cabaret series or the regular at bar or other place the show is taking place, have a crush on or want to hook up with someone else who is going, or found the event through a listserv, newsletter, looking through free weekly event listings, social media event postings, a poster on the street or in a café, and are looking for TFQ events. Cabaret functions as a reception network as each audience member is potentially seeing the work of nine artists (everyone who is not their friend) for the first time.[29] In all likelihood, these friends are familiar with most or all of the performers, but there are plenty of cabarets in which the audience friends of one performer do not very much like the work of another. While each performer brings an *integral audience*, there may be the odd accidental audience situation from time to time. But, importantly, this is within the reception context of mixed and overlapping integral audiences, and the reception context is influenced by the ethics, affects, and behaviors of the majority integral audience.

An online archive or publication venue for cabaret performance brings a different sort of reception context, even if the initial reach is still to an insider audience. If each person posts their piece or exhibit to a social media site like Facebook or Twitter, that means the whole site is exposed to at least—and this is a modest number—fifty "friends" or "followers" (plus re-postings). The reception variables become infinite and multiply mediated, not only for the material that was posted, but for all other material on the site as well. Each performer and performance becomes vulnerable to the connections of the largest and most heterogeneous friend or follower. This is obvious social media and network theory. But it is worth stating here, as we consider what it means to build online, open-access TFQ performance archives.

Jauss notes that a new work (or, in this case, a new performance):

> does not present itself as something absolutely new in an informational vacuum, but predisposes its audience to a very specific kind of reception, by announcements, overt and covert signals, familiar characteristics, or implicit allusions. It awakens memories of that which was already [seen], brings the [audience] to a specific emotional attitude, and with its beginning arouses expectations for the 'middle and end,' which can then be maintained intact or altered, reoriented, or even fulfilled ironically in the course of the reading according to the specific rules of the genre or type of [performance].[30]

The performer can only predispose her audience if she anticipates who that audience will be and what their horizon of expectations will be: "the interpretive reception of a [performance] always presupposes the context of experience of aesthetic perception."[31] Furthermore, Jauss explains that "the question of the subjectivity of the interpretation and of the taste of different [audiences] can be asked meaningfully only when one has first clarified which transubjective horizon of understanding conditions the influence of the [performance]."[32] This is the classic entanglement of reception: The performer must know her audience in order to offer context-appropriate cues for interpretation. Interpretive reception is always habituated by the contextual knowledges of the audience and this shapes their aesthetic perception. We can only gauge how different audience members interpret or receive a performance once we know the horizon of aesthetic understandings that shaped the performance (i.e. what is the performer's reference set for the reception cues she gives to the audience?).

When we think of "onlining" (i.e. placing performance materials online), what do we do with the creation-reception context just described? How do we work toward "X-reality design that purposefully exploits the experience of intersecting levels of information, engagement, and agency"?[33] In particular, how do we contend with the fact that the imagined (and actual) audience for most TFQ performances are those in the know? In Jauss's terms, these audiences are predisposed; and, in Richard Schechner's terms this is the integral audience—"people who know each other, are involved with each other, support each other," whose information, engagement, and agency is intimately tied to the performer's.[34] Importantly, TFQ performance is often not only produced for its predisposed and supportive audience, but also only exists within a performance scene conditioned by the assumed or assured absence of hostile (or even indifferent) audiences. It is not only who is in the room, but also who is not (allowed) in the room that permits the kind of work that happens on TFQ stages.

## Architectures of Collapse

The general rule in the digital humanities has been to use the affordances of digital technologies to circulate materials once "hidden" and to bring them into the open-access light for all to see and know. The digital humanities hope, as Jennifer Guiliano and Carolyn Hietman argue in their essay "Difficult Heritage and the Complexities of Indigenous Data," has been for the ways that public-facing projects bring context and critique to colonial sources. However, they note that

> [c]oncerns about reproducing colonialized collections are heightened when the historical record is digital. Digital assets, including digital archives, exposed via the web are subject to endless and unanticipated refraction or what anthropologist Michael Wesch has called the endless remix. While images and documents may be carefully contextualized within a given web-based project domain, those images and documents are susceptible to infinite and unanticipated refraction . . . the endless internet remix and or misuse.[35]

This possibility (and expectation) of endless remix contributes to what scholars of digital culture call "context collapse." Writing about teens and social media in her book *It's Complicated*, danah boyd states that "a context collapse occurs when people are forced to grapple simultaneously with otherwise unrelated social contexts that are rooted in different norms and seemingly demand different social responses."[36] Jenny L. Davis and Nathan Jurgenson make a potentially important distinction about the point of collapse: Context collusion is the process whereby social actors *intentionally* collapse, blur, and flatten contexts, especially using various social media. However, the instance that, perhaps rightfully, garners more attention is context collisions, in which different social environments unintentionally and unexpectedly come crashing into each other.[37] Sarah L. Buglass et al. note that context collapse and online vulnerability are linked, with vulnerability increasing with network size and network heterogeneity, meaning that the larger the network and the more diverse it is in terms of mingling individuals and groups from different social spheres, particularly those of different life stages (i.e. family, classmates from elementary, high school, college friends, current friends) and environments (i.e. colleagues, party friends), the more vulnerable the individual is to risk of harassment and/or attack.[38]

Research on context collapse and the complex experiences of, and exposure to, online vulnerability and violence tend to focus on social media networking sites like Facebook, Twitter and Instagram (and earlier studies on Friendster, etc.) I want to suggest that, while social networking platforms are arguably different from the digital humanities projects undertaken by research teams—speculative and realized online scholarly archives, collections, repositories, publications, etc.—we nonetheless have much to learn from social media scholars and much to account for in terms of the ways that heterogenous and diverse audiences (those whom we seek out and promise to our grant agencies in order to reach audiences beyond the university) function.

Michael Wesch notes that putting yourself (or someone else) on YouTube means entering into a performance-reception media environment comprising

> an infinite number of contexts collapsing upon one another into that single moment of recording. The images, actions, and words captured by the lens at any moment can

> be transported to anywhere on the planet and preserved (the performer must assume) for all time. The little glass lens becomes the gateway to a black hole sucking all of time and space—virtually all possible contexts—in on itself.[39]

Social media scholarship has largely elided the question of the intentional YouTube performance, versus the *unintentional* performance video posted with or without permission of the performers. Wesch writes about students and other Youtubers who are actively, agentially performing on "the biggest and the smallest stage—the most public space in the world."[40] It is, however, centrally important for performance studies, media studies, and social media scholars to consider the case of those millions of performance videos that are recorded by someone with a phone or a handheld camera who then post to the same reception situation of "virtually all possible contexts." While arguably the audience for a digital humanities open-access archive may not initially have the same built-in audience as a YouTube video, putting anything online means that it has the same *potential* audience.

What are our responsibilities to anticipate and be accountable for the vulnerabilities (and opportunities) of $X^{\infty}$-reception for the people whose materials we collect and circulate online? For many years digital humanities projects were understood *de facto* as necessarily "open access," and many such projects predicate their scholarly significance and knowledge-mobilization plans on their increased capacities to initiate and sustain the very conditions of context collapse that have social media scholars issuing a warning signal. Returning to boyd's study of teens online, "intended audience matters, regardless of the actual audience";[41] thus when we think of designing performance studies archival environments in the digital humanities, it becomes our responsibility to design for intended and potential actual audiences ($X^{\infty}$-audiences).

Most scholarship on context collapse has focused on the experiences of social media users, but when we take into consideration the massive potential collapse of performance contexts in open access online archives, it becomes necessary to consider the ethical responsibilities of the creators and managers of these sites. Unlike social media where users have some agency and awareness of what is happening in their feeds and can drive the content that they post and respond to, performers whose materials make up performance archives do not have a similar level of control. As "stewards"[42] of the materials in our digital archival environments, we have to consider $X^{\infty}$-reception factors in our sustainability plans.

I see at least three salient points to note for the digital humanities. The first is that context collapse (the convergence of heterogenous audiences) is a scenario that, while it may positively democratize information, also puts people at risk. This is something for us to be attentive to as we fall for and into open-access collections of minoritized materials. The second is that, while we may not be building the next Twitter or Facebook, the materials that we post in our online archives, repositories, exhibitions, and so on, very well may circulate through these network and social media platforms; thus, whatever circulation and refraction is true for materials posted on these platforms, is potentially also true for scholarly, archival and other open access research platforms. The third is that online archives run by scholars or scholarly institutions are not self-driven social media sites in which the account holder signs up, logs in and monitors their own social media traffic, retweeting, reposting and comment threads. The duty of monitoring, of paying attention to how materials on our scholarly sites are being used, arguably becomes the job of the researchers and archivists who built the site and who have solicited materials. Thus, insofar as we can learn from the scholarship about context collapse in social media scenarios, we need to come up with our own reception-action theories and ethico-methodologies for dealing with the technologies we build in the interests of science, the humanities, and the arts. As we engineer new ways for new audiences to experience new and old materials, we need methods that ethically manage the risks we create for the people whose materials we circulate, and for the heritage integrity of those materials themselves.

What is appropriate for one social sphere is not appropriate in another. TFQ people know this extremely well. In fact, TFQ performance spaces are highly context-specific aesthetic-political-social-sexual spheres; they are networks with their own internal logics, values, and norms. This makes the risks involved with the potential context collapses initiated by an online archive, collection, exhibition, publication, or other form of remediation and cross-platform transfer very real.

⋆ ⋆ ⋆

In this chapter I have proposed a theory of X$^{\infty}$-reception that operates as an ethico-methodology for the digital humanities, especially for the creation, study, and use of online archives, repositories, exhibitions, collections, and publications of materials emerging from small-world, subcultural, minoritized, and/or marginalized grassroots performance events. This theory of reception is based not only on an historical understanding of the genres and forms of TFQ performance, but also on the centrality of intimacy and relationships in the reception of TFQ performance.

My theory of reception and proposed methods for online platform research and creation are predicated upon a need to be attentive to uneven distributions of vulnerability (to attack) based on oppressive relations of power and reception-action based on ideological norms and social values that are antithetical to the existence, let alone the joyful thriving, of trans- feminist, and queer people and our worlds. In *Updating to Remain the Same*, Wendy Hui Kyong Chun asks, "How can we understand publicity not in terms of a need for safety and protection, which is neither safe nor protecting, but rather the fight for a space in which one can be vulnerable and not attacked?" I believe that a praxis of X$^{\infty}$-reception is both the fight for these spaces of vulnerability free from attack; it is also, the fight that we know so well, when TFQ materials get into the hands of those who will use our work against us.[43] The thing about creating TFQ work in a phobic world is that *the mere fact* of people making the work—without even getting on stage or bringing the cabaret to the street—is enough to shock and arouse the hateful speech and actions of a very large portion of the world. That is, the form of the performance may not be new to an experienced TFQ audience, but the "explicit [TFQ] body in performance"[44] might be shockingly new when seen online as proof that trans- feminist and queer people, exist, create, and thrive. What does it mean to move TFQ utopian performatives which "in their doings, make palpable an affective vision of how the world might be better," to the X$^{\infty}$-reception venue of the internet?[45] Remediating performances that take place in the utopian spaces of TFQ nightlife makes them accessible to both the utopian *and* dystopian realities of the internet. It's great to bring life-affirming TFQ materials to those who need them and do not otherwise have access. But what happens if your online archive becomes a site of transgender or queer bashing, baiting, trolling, or doxxing?

In all likelihood, a small online archive of materials about TFQ cabaret may in practice have an audience very similar in size and character to its inaugural audience. But there is the possibility of something very different happening, an eventuality in which all the bad things that the paranoid perspective tells us to think about occur: reprints, screenshots, and other image and content captures recirculating in or through anti-TFQ sites, feeds or threads, instrumentalized either for the purpose of causing harm or for LOLs (the two are often not unrelated).

The ethical responsibilities toward the works and artists that we re-mediate and re-circulate in our exhibits, publications, and archives cannot end at copyright, permission, and take-down policies. A failed aesthetic reception framework in a TFQ performance scenario is frequently informed by androcentrism, homophobia, fat phobia, ableism, transphobia and transmisogyny, misogynoir, misogyny, racism, and white supremacy. The fear—beyond the very real fear of online and physical violence and harassment—is that the restrictions we face on virtual platforms perversely make their way to brick and mortar performance platforms either through cultural censorship, renewed attacks on TFQ artists by funding agencies, and/or through self-censorship in what artists will and will not do on stage, anticipating what will and will not be programmable on a virtual platform.

## Notes

1. *The Archive and the Repertoire: Performing Cultural Memory in the Americas* (Durham, NC: Duke University Press, 2003).
2. Hans Robert Jauss, "Literary History as a Challenge to Literary Theory," in *Toward an Aesthetic of Reception*, trans. Timothy Bahti (Minneapolis: University of Minnesota Press, 1982), 3–45.
3. Ibid., 22.
4. B. Coleman, *Hello Avatar: Rise of the Networked Generation* (Cambridge, MA: MIT Press, 2011), 3–4.
5. Irit Rogoff, "'Smuggling'—An Embodied Criticality," *Eipcp.net*, 2006, www.curatorial.net/resources/Rogoff_Smuggling.pdf. Accessed January 13, 2019.
6. Moya Bailey, "They Aren't Talking about Me. . .," www.crunkfeministcollective.com/2010/03/14/they-arent-talking-about-me/. Accessed March 15, 2010.
7. For a discussion of how and why queer women's nightlife is often relegated to weeknights, see Islandia, "Looking back at Lesbifiesteras and Burlesquimeras: Queer Women Searching for Space in Mid-2000's Mexico City," *The Helix Queer Performance Network*, http://helixqpn.org/post/159981257402/looking-back-atlesbifiesteras-and-burlesquimeras. Accessed April 25, 2017.
8. Michelle Moravec, "Feminist Research Practices and Digital Archives," *Australian Feminist Studies* 32, no. 91–92 (April 2017): 187.
9. Ibid., 196.
10. Ibid.
11. Ibid., 195.
12. Ibid.
13. Ibid., 195–96.
14. Sarah Bay-Cheng, Jennifer Parker-Starbuck, and David Z. Saltz, *Performance and Media: Taxonomies for a Changing Field* (Ann Arbor: University of Michigan Press, 2015), 8.
15. Ibid., 8–9.
16. Gabriella Giannachi, Nick Kaye, and Michael Shanks, "Introduction: Archaeologies of Presence," in *Archaeologies of Presence: Art, Performance and the Persistence of Being*, ed. Gabriella Giannachi, Nick Kaye, and Michael Shanks (London: Routledge, 2012), 8.
17. Sarah Bay-Cheng, "Theater Is Media: Some Principles for a Digital Historiography of Performance," *Theater* 42, no. 2 (May 2012): 40.
18. See Mukurtu's work at http://mukurtu.org/. Accessed June 3, 2019.
19. See the Local Context site here, http://localcontexts.org/. Accessed June 3, 2019.
20. See http://localcontexts.org/tk-labels/. Accessed June 3, 2019.
21. Kimberly Christen, "Relationships, Not Records: Digital Heritage and the Ethics of Sharing Indigenous Knowledge Online," in *The Routledge Companion to Media Studies and Digital Humanities*, ed. Jentery Sayers (Abingdon: Routledge Handbooks Online, 2018), 411, https://www-routledgehandbooks-com.myaccess.library.utoronto.ca/doi/10.4324/9781315730479. Accessed April 21, 2019.
22. Jauss, "Literary History," 22.
23. Ibid., 37–38.
24. Coleman, *Hello Avatar*, 19.
25. Ibid.
26. Ibid.
27. Rebecca Schneider, *Performing Remains: Art and War in Times of Theatrical Reenactment* (London: Routledge, 2011).
28. I discuss cabaret as a "small-world" phenomenon in my essay "The Internet of Bawdies: Transmedial Drag and the Onlining of Trans-Feminist and Queer Performance Archives, a Workshop Essay," *First Monday* 23, no. 4 (July 2018). https://doi.org/10.5210/fm.v23i7.9256. Accessed January 28, 2020.

29. I discuss this cabaret reception phenomenon in my chapter "'I Remember . . . I Was Wearing Leather Pants': Archiving the Repertoire of Feminist Cabaret in Canada," in *Basements, Attics, Closets and Cyperspace: Explorations in Canadian Women's Archives*, eds. Linda Morra and Jessica Schagerl (Ontario: Wilfred Laurier University Press, 2012).
30. Jauss, "Literary History," 23.
31. Ibid.
32. Ibid.
33. Coleman, *Hello Avatar*, 147.
34. Richard Schechner, *Performance Theory* (New York: Routledge, 2004), 220.
35. Jennifer Guiliano and Carolyn Heitman, "Difficult Heritage and the Complexities of Indigenous Data," *Journal of Cultural Analytics* (August 2019). https://culturalanalytics.org/article/11041-difficult-heritage-and-the-complexities-of-indigenous-data, accessed January 28, 2020; Michael Wesch, "An Anthropological Introduction to YouTube," *YouTube* [online]." Accessed October 15, 2009.
36. danah boyd, *It's Complicated: The Social Lives of Networked Teens* (New Haven, CT: Yale University Press, 2014), 31.
37. Jenny L. Davis and Nathan Jurgenson, "Context Collapse: Theorizing Context Collusions and Collisions," *Information, Communication & Society* 17, no. 4 (March 2014): 480.
38. Sarah L. Buglass, Jens F. Binder, Lucy R. Betts, and Jean D.M. Underwood, "When 'Friends' Collide: Social Heterogeneity and User Vulnerability on Social Network Sites," *Computers in Human Behavior* 54 (January 2016): 5–6.
39. Michael Wesch, "YouTube and You: Experiences of Self-Awareness in the Context Collapse of the Recording Webcam," *Explorations in Media Ecology* 8, no. 2 (January 2009): 23.
40. Ibid., 22.
41. boyd, *It's Complicated*, 30.
42. Christen, "Relationships, Not Records," 405.
43. Wendy Hui Kyong Chun, *Updating to Remain the Same: Habitual New Media* (Cambridge: MIT Press, 2016), 158.
44. Rebecca Schneider, *The Explicit Body in Performance* (New York: Routledge, 2013).
45. Jill Dolan, *Utopia in Performance: Finding Hope at the Theater* (Ann Arbor: University of Michigan Press, 2005), 6.

## Bibliography


Bailey, Moya. "They Aren't Talking About Me . . ." March 15, 2010. Accessed February 3, 2019. www.crunkfeministcollective.com/2010/03/14/they-arent-talking-about-me/.

boyd, danah. *It's Complicated: The Social Lives of Networked Teens*. New Haven: Yale University Press, 2014.

Bay-Cheng, Sarah. "Theater Is Media: Some Principles for a Digital Historiography of Performance." *Theater* 42, no. 2 (May 2012): 27–41.

Bay-Cheng, Sarah, Jennifer Parker-Starbuck, and David Z. Saltz. *Performance and Media: Taxonomies for a Changing Field*. Ann Arbor: University of Michigan Press, 2015.

Buglass, Sarah L., Jens F. Binder, Lucy R. Betts, and Jean D. M. Underwood. "When 'Friends' Collide: Social Heterogeneity and User Vulnerability on Social Network Sites." *Computers in Human Behavior* 54 (January 2016): 62–72.

Christen, Kimberly. "Relationships, Not Records: Digital Heritage and the Ethics of Sharing Indigenous Knowledge Online." In *The Routledge Companion to Media Studies and Digital Humanities*, edited by Jentery Sayers, 403–12. Abingdon: Routledge Handbooks Online, 2018. Accessed April 21, 2019. https://www-routledgehandbooks-com.myaccess.library.utoronto.ca/doi/10.4324/9781315730479.

Chun, Wendy Hui Kyong. *Updating to Remain the Same: Habitual New Media*. Cambridge: MIT Press, 2016.

Coleman, B. *Hello Avatar: Rise of the Networked Generation*. Cambridge, MA: MIT Press, 2011.

Cowan, T. L. "'I Remember . . . I Was Wearing Leather Pants': Archiving the Repertoire of Feminist Cabaret in Canada." In *Basements, Attics, Closets and Cyperspace: Explorations in Canadian Women's Archives*, edited by Linda Morra and Jessica Schagerl, 65–86. Ontario: Wilfred Laurier University Press, 2012.

———. "The Internet of Bawdies: Transmedial Drag and the Onlining of Trans-Feminist and Queer Performance Archives, a Workshop Essay." *First Monday*, 23, no. 7. (July 2018). https://firstmonday.org/ojs/index.php/fm/article/view/9256 doi:10.5210/fm.v23i7.9256. Accessed Feburary 28, 2020.

Davis, Jenny L., and Nathan Jurgenson. "Context Collapse: Theorizing Context Collusions and Collisions." *Information, Communication & Society* 17, no. 4 (March 2014): 476–85.

Dolan, Jill. *Utopia in Performance: Finding Hope at the Theater.* Ann Arbor: University of Michigan Press, 2005.

Giannachi, Gabriella, Nick Kaye, and Michael Shanks. "Introduction: Archaeologies of Presence." In *Archaeologies of Presence: Art, Performance and the Persistence of Being*, edited by Gabriella Giannachi, Nick Kaye, and Michael Shanks, 1–25. London: Routledge, 2012.

Guiliano, Jennifer, and Carolyn Heitman. "Difficult Heritage and the Complexities of Indigenous Data." *Journal of Cultural Analytics* (August 2019).

Islandia. "Looking back at Lesbifiesteras and Burlesquimeras: Queer Women Searching for Space in Mid-2000's Mexico City." *The Helix Queer Performance Network.* April 25, 2017. Accessed April 27, 2017. http://helixqpn.org/post/159981257402/looking-back-atlesbifiesteras-and-burlesquimeras.

Jauss, Hans Robert. "Literary History as a Challenge to Literary Theory." In *Toward an Aesthetic of Reception.* Translated by Timothy Bahti, 3–45. Minneapolis: University of Minnesota Press, 1982.

Moravec, Michelle. "Feminist Research Practices and Digital Archives." *Australian Feminist Studies* 32, no. 91–92 (April 2017): 186–201.

Rogoff, Irit. "'Smuggling'—An Embodied Criticality." *Eipcp.net.* 2006. Accessed January 13, 2019. http://eipcp.net/dlfiles/rogoff-smuggling

Schechner, Richard. *Performance Theory.* New York: Routledge, 2004.

Schneider, Rebecca. *Performing Remains: Art and War in Times of Theatrical Reenactment.* London: Routledge, 2011.

Wesch, Michael. "YouTube and You: Experiences of Self-Awareness in the Context Collapse of the Recording Webcam." *Explorations in Media Ecology* 8, no. 2 (January 2009): 19–34.

# 12

# DIGITAL METHODS AND THE STUDY OF THE ART MARKET

*Pamela Fletcher and Anne Helmreich*

The history of the art market is almost ideally suited for digital approaches and computational analysis. Immense amounts of potential data relevant to the art market exists in auction records, dealers' stock books, exhibition catalogues, collectors' inventories, museum object files, and artists' personal papers. Until relatively recently such sources were largely isolated and, if aggregated, overwhelmed scholars' ability to locate, extract, and synthesize data; concomitantly, the narrative case study model has largely prevailed. However, over the past decade, museums, libraries, and archives have worked to make their collection data available in digital form, prompted in part by the larger move to digitization across all fields, but also by ethical and legal questions about the provenance of individual art objects. Major collaborative research projects have also helped to open up the archives and translate primary sources into shareable data that can be compiled.

The field of art market studies is just beginning to reckon with the new possibilities afforded by these data sets and databases and the potential they offer for transcending the case study. For example, digital and computational methods allow art historians to visualize networks of artists, dealers and collectors; map the circulation of individual art objects; and conduct statistical analyses of patterns in the prices, titles, and exhibition histories of objects. The latter inquiries reflect, in many ways, a dominant view of art market studies as focused on questions of price, taste, and other mechanisms of the market. The first section of this chapter aims to provide a short overview of the questions and possibilities of this kind of work in the digital field, while also suggesting what it might mean for the discipline to move beyond the case study model. The chapter also aims, however, to complicate the perhaps too-seductive fantasy of a perfect correspondence between econometric digital methods and the study of the art market. On the one hand, significant work in economics and art history uses price data and numerical measures of the market in ways that fall outside what we usually mean when we refer to "digital art history."[1] On the other hand, and more significant for our purposes here, is that fact that the "art market" is not just a set of economic mechanisms for buying and selling art. It is simultaneously a set of relationships, experiences, expectations, memories, and shared understandings of the evolving definition of art and its shifting cultural values. Therefore, in the second section of the chapter we turn our attention to how digital and computational methods might aid us in understanding the art market as an experiential field.

## Data and the Definition of the "Art Market"

The study of the art market was, of course, well established before digital and computational methods were introduced, and that historiography has fundamentally shaped the terrain into which current studies venture. The scholarship has often been equated with studies of taste, particularly in light of economist William J. Baumol's dictum that the buying and selling of art does not behave in accordance with any specific underlying law or theory; it is "inherently rudderless."[2] So how can taste be measured and tracked over time? For the art historian and pioneering scholar of the art market Gerald Reitlinger, price could be used as "a yardstick of taste," and thus an index to "a whole system of aesthetic values."[3] While Reitlinger's data, published in the early 1960s, has been critiqued for distortions,[4] his concern with prices as a means of measuring taste has been extended in more recent scholarship.[5] The application of economic concepts and econometric techniques to the history of the art market has also become far more sophisticated and complex as represented by the work of such scholars as J. Michael Montias, Neil de Marchi, Hans van Miegrot, Thomas Bayer, and John Page.[6]

In the decades succeeding Reitlinger's publication, scholars have also argued that the history of the art market comprises more than prices and statistics. As historian Filip Vermeylen explains, whereas economists have tended to focus on prices (largely with the framework of supply and demand), economic sociologists (and we would add here art historians) have examined the market as "a societal phenomenon rather than a purely commercial one."[7] David Ormrod's observation in 1999 that the "new art history," referring to an engagement with the socio-historical context in which a work of art was embedded, has produced an "accumulation of local studies"—or what he also describes as "research at a microsocial level" concerned with "the social background, status, and training of artists, guild and civic regulation of the art trade, the shift from patronage to market mechanisms, the growth of actions and the rise of the art dealer"—remains true today.[8] Case studies of these more contextualized aspects of the market have greatly expanded our knowledge of the specific mechanisms of particular markets, with a focus on the production and sale of objects.

Over the past decade, the potential sources and uses of data for both economic and social histories of the art market have expanded dramatically, offering new possibilities but also conceptual and methodological challenges. Scholars have worked to expand the definition of primary source material for the study of the market beyond price and sales data. Commissions and contracts hold information about the negotiations of value between artists and patrons; inventories record the symbolic and fiscal capital invested in works of art, and the accompanying legal structures of ownership; and exhibition and auction catalogues, dealer stock, sale, and commission books, as well as museum records all help to track the complicated pathways for the display, circulation, and exchange of objects. As art history becomes a more global discipline and we learn more about the mobility and exchange of works of art in other geographic and temporal contexts, we anticipate that the notion of the accompanying archival record—that is, what constitutes the trace of the market's activity and what constitutes the market itself—will expand still further.

In recent decades, access to many of these archival sources has been transformed as museums, libraries and archives have embraced principles of open access, making research materials freely available online, and have invested heavily in digitization and accompanying metadata generation programs. For example, the Metropolitan Museum of Art has digitized 898 catalogues and checklists produced by the New York based Knoedler Art Gallery between 1869 and 1946, and in 2017 adopted the policy of making "all images of public-domain works in its collection available under Creative Commons Zero." It is one of an increasing number of art museums making a commitment to open access or open content.[9] Furthermore, the Metropolitan's API (application programming interface) allows users to access all of the institution's open access data, including the record for a valid object and the open access data about that object.[10] By opening up, in effect, their databases, museums are providing the community with instantly machine-readable information.

Scholars and research institutions have also worked to gather and render accessible relevant data. For example, the Getty Provenance Index, drawing on such sources as archival inventories, sales catalogs, and dealer stock books, allows scholars to trace the provenance of a work of art as well "to illustrate a wide variety of collecting patterns, including those related to consumer behavior, market trends, dealer networks, and modes of display."[11] Project Cornelia brings together attribution and relational archival data to support investigation into the dynamic interchange between the creative industries in the cities of Antwerp and Brussels in the seventeenth century;[12] and Artl@s, which aims to advance the study of a global art history, currently makes three databases publicly available: a global database of exhibition catalogues, a georeferenced map of Parisian art dealers between 1815 and 1955, and a database relating to the French Academy in Rome.[13]

This promising work faces several challenges. First, while many archival sources have been digitized and made discoverable online, they are not yet fully machine readable. Optical character recognition (OCR) technology has made significant advances in recent years, but it is most effective against typeset text (enabling searches across digitized newspapers and books, for example), but far less effective for hand-writing, particularly for challenging paleography. The recently developed Transkribus service platform, an outcome of the e-infrastructure project READ (Recognition and Enrichment of Archival Documents) funded by the European commission, has made significant breakthroughs in teaching computers to read hand-written documents.[14] Even for those sources that might be responsive to OCR, considerable human intervention is often required not only to confirm that the transcription is accurate but also, and equally significantly, that the appropriate data is extracted and structured for subsequent research use. Second, countless archival records have yet to be digitized or even made physically accessible in a reliable or regularized manner to researchers. Third, these sources—contracts, inventories, catalogues, etc.—are not just inert lists but rather complicated narratives that should be understood as acts of representation in need of contextualization and interpretation. Thus the translation of this material into "data" is a complex undertaking.[15] Finally, there is another question of access that is harder to quantify and perhaps to solve: the large number of databases that have been compiled by individual scholars in the course of their research but remain private intellectual property. While there can be good intellectual as well as practical reasons for keeping databases private, the field would greatly benefit from thinking about protocols for sharing underlying data sets as part of the publication process and adopting corresponding practices of sustainability.

What do these newly abundant digitized resources and data sets, along with increasingly powerful and accessible computer processing tools, mean for the study of the art market? It is already evident that using data about prices, provenance, the regulations and norms of the market and its practices (including taxes, tariffs, insurance, transportation, and commission), the emergence of specializations and professions, the development of new markets, and the incentives and disincentives that shaped the activities of artists, agents, and buyers allows art historians to tell new and richer histories of taste, the critical fate of individual objects, the circulation and cultural transfer of goods, the larger ecosystem of the market(s), and processes of transculturation as well as resistance to them.[16] Yet, the new scale of the data involved in this history may have more profound implications. In the field of literary studies, Franco Moretti has argued for a transformation in literary history by shifting one's gaze from a relatively small pool of exceptional texts to a large body of work, described as "a collective system, that should be grasped as such, as a whole."[17]

What would it mean for the larger discipline of art history to take up Moretti's challenge, and take seriously the question of working at scale? One of the most pressing challenges is this: across geographic and temporal fields, new data sets repeatedly reveal that there is far more art being produced, exhibited, sold, and presumably enjoyed, than art history even imagines accounting for. Describing the annual Royal Academy exhibitions in nineteenth-century London, where thousands of works were on display each year, Martin Myrone recently invoked Franco Moretti's phase "the slaughterhouse" of (art) history to describe these vast scores of forgotten—and often untraceable—works of art.[18] Similarly, recent work on the art market of the low countries in the early modern period has established this as a mass market and, as Bruno Blondé and Veerle De Laet have observed, "paintings were owned right across the population."[19] What is our responsibility to this vast material? How does it shape our understanding of the works that have survived to become the objects of substantial study and attention? How might the digital inform how we move between distant and close reading and the questions we ask as we do so?

## Expanding the Model

New computational tools and methods also hold the promise of expanding the definition of the "art market" beyond questions of price, circulation, and the institutions and identities of market actors. In practice, the art market is a less easily quantifiable set of relationships between people, objects, spaces, and social practices, as well as a set of experiences and assumptions. An example from our own field of nineteenth-century British art helps draw out what we mean by art market studies in an expanded field. What did it feel like to see a large oil painting protected by a railing and two policemen managing the crowds, to catch glimpses of it over other people's shoulders and while hearing a cacophony of voices? How did this compare to standing alone in front of a small framed watercolor in a small private gallery? What difference did it make to be standing in a crowd of strangers, or pigeon-holed by a dealer trying to persuade you of a picture's merits? How might other factors—such as your memories of previous viewings in the same space, the ambience of the surroundings, your sense of which works are and are not for sale, the gossip circulating about an artist or work of art, the verbal inflections of critics—impact your experience of the work and decision to enter into a financial transaction? How might artists have shaped their work with the foreknowledge of these viewing contexts and experiences? These intangibles are all equally important aspects of the market for art and the ways it might shape production, reception, interpretation, value, and consumption. How might digital and computational methods, which obviously lend themselves to statistical analysis, help scholars to reveal and understand these more experiential aspects of the art market?

We begin with a speculative example that can likely be realized soon. Dealers are often described as the eyes of the market or as possessing an exceptional eye, meaning an ability to perform acts of connoisseurship and discernment visually. While such anecdotal descriptions often suggest an unusual capacity to remember and to see critically, in fact, we know that many dealers and connoisseurs have been aided by photographs, often building their own collections in support of their commercial activities. In the case of Bernard Berenson, who worked closely with dealers such as Robert Langton Douglas and the Duveen Brothers, his photo archive was eventually donated to Villa I Tatti, the Harvard University Center for Italian Renaissance Studies.[20] As photo archives such as this advance their work in digitization, computer-driven algorithms will make it possible to find patterns across such collections, even matching images.[21] This approach has already aided scholars in making attributions and might help realize Berenson's ambition, which shaped his "homeless" paintings project, to locate works of art whose ownership was unknown to him.[22] Using computer vision techniques to identify dealer's stamps and perhaps even render hand-written annotations machine readable may help to situate Berenson more fully within his network of dealers, agents, and collectors. In other words, while we can never fully reconstitute Berenson's memory and his accumulation of knowledge that informed his "eye," we can recover traces of his activity through the archive he assembled and relied upon and by examining how he deployed that in pursuit of his activities as an advisor and intermediary between dealers, buyers, and sellers.

Computer-aided reading of texts also holds promise in this context. Digital humanities approaches that can surface word frequencies and patterns within segments of texts, as well as to model topics have been fruitfully applied in literary studies. Given the art market's reliance on the written word, in the form of object descriptions and inventories, exhibition and auction catalogues, correspondence, stock books, and art criticism, what questions might text analysis allow us to ask at a larger scale than close reading allow? How, for example, did the language of connoisseurship evolve over time? What descriptive language is associated with the processes of creating fiscal value? What trends might large-scale analysis of titles and other supplementary material in exhibition catalogues reveal?[23] Text mining can also direct us to new sources, now digitized and discoverable. A recent study of the Old Bailey Proceedings, the trial records of the city of London, rethought indictments of theft as a new kind of inventory detailing exchanges of goods and relative values. The study then applied computational analysis or distant reading approaches, focusing on term frequency, to discover the most frequently stolen items in the second half of the eighteenth century, decades that witnessed the rise of the Industrial Revolution.[24]

Shifting from techniques of computer vision and text analysis, which rely on forms of optical recognition, social network analysis has proven to be a useful method for conceptualizing the market as a set of relationships between people, objects, spaces, and social practices. While network analysis is discussed more fully in this volume by Matthew Lincoln, given its growing significance within art market studies, we wish to address it through this particular lens for the purposes of this chapter. As we have previously argued, network analysis, the study of relationships between entities, is particularly well suited to both modeling the market and tracking its historic behavior. For example, in the case of studying the buying and selling patterns of the Goupil/Boussod & Valadon art firm in the nineteenth century, it was fairly straightforward to translate the agents of artist, buyer, and dealer (or their geographic locations of activities) into nodes and their transactions into edges.[25] Likewise, Christine Howald and Léa Saint-Raymond, in their study of looting and subsequent dispersal of the objects originally located at the Chinese government seat of Yuanmingyuan in the 1860s, investigated the behavior of auctioneers, experts, and sellers through network analysis.[26] Johannes Gramlich, in his recent overview of new developments in provenance research, an essential component of art market studies, has observed that the study of the networks, and more specifically the personal relationships that sustained the art market, complements the socio-economic approach.[27]

Despite the evident benefits of social network analysis, it must be approached with caution, as a number of scholars have recently reminded us.[28] Networks cannot be isolated from their socio-historical conditions and scholars should guard against replicating such distorting paradigms as "center-periphery." As Miriam Kienle and Stephanie Porras observe, network analysis can make it difficult to recognize where and how actors are situated in time and space and, perhaps even more significantly, with respect to dynamics of power and access to knowledge and its expression.[29] Nevertheless, we should avoid whole-scale condemnation of "the digital" for revealing such patterns in our sources. Indeed, Joanna Gardener-Huggett's recent study demonstrates how digital methods can act as a corrective: Her use of digital mapping led her to rewrite her analysis of the networks in which the Chicago-based women artists' collectives ARC Gallery (1973 to the present) and Artemesia Gallery (1973–2003) were embedded, now recognizing that these entities were operating largely within a midwestern context rather than a national framework.[30]

Mapping and geospatial analysis can help visualize other aspects of the market. For example, scholars have mapped the changing cultural geographies of modern London and Paris, locating art galleries, auction houses, artists' studios and residences, and other retail and exhibition spaces in an attempt to reconstitute the meanings conveyed by spatial proximity, distance, neighborhood, and topography.[31] While the subject of mapping in art history is well covered by other chapters in this volume, our point here is the ways in which spatial visualizations can convey meaningful information about the lived experience of markets, allowing viewers to grasp patterns and clusters quickly. This might include the intersection of other features of the city—including transportation networks, other retail markets, sites of leisure and entertainment, neighborhood boundaries, and real estate values—with the spaces for seeing and selling art.

Moving inside these spaces, scholars have begun to model artists' studios, art galleries and other exhibition spaces in an attempt to understand the physical and even aural contexts in which art was made, viewed, and sold. The process is challenging, as there is often only fragmentary data about these sometimes ephemeral spaces. The very uncertainty built into the process of reconstruction, however, can be the site of productive scholarly debate, as is made clear by the multiple recreated versions of the Joshua Reynolds exhibitions at the British Institution in 1813 and 1823. The versions created by a literary historian and an art historian differed significantly in their use of period images and textual sources and, as a result, offered the opportunity for scholarly reflection not only on digital best practices, but also on early nineteenth-century exhibition norms.[32]

Sophie Raux's reconstructions of art dealer Edme-François Gersaint's shop developed out of multiple approaches aided by digital technology. These included tracking change over time in housing picture dealers on the Pont Notre-Dame, where Gersaint was located, a computer model of the bridge, and three-dimensional visualizations of the shop interior and shopfront. The latter is presented to the reader as a series of proposals which are then tested against known evidence and visual logic before reaching a final conclusion, allowing the reader to engage with the intellectual debate that informed the final outcome.[33] Sally Webster and David Schwittek, working primarily from historic photographs, have reconstructed the Lenox Library Picture Gallery as it appeared in the 1880s, when it was open to visitors, as a means of both reconstituting this experience virtually and exploring the collector's curatorial strategies. Usefully, the authors include a project narrative that documents the various steps taken to achieve the reconstruction and its accompanying analysis.[34] A provocative possibility for future projects might involve incorporating other sensory material and kinetic experiences into reconstructions, for example, measuring the impact that crowds of viewers have on sightlines or on the aural experience of the space.[35]

## Conclusion

In sum, the "digital turn" allows for two critical shifts in art market studies. The first, predicated on the scale of data now available in tandem with advances in structuring and querying data as well as easier access to computer processing and computational analysis applications, is the opportunity to move away from the case study. This is a direction that has been anticipated by leading art market scholars who have bridged art history and economics. The second recognizes the ability of computational tools to help us answer questions that focus on the experiential qualities of the market and requires that scholars creatively use quantitative data to address the qualitative. While these two shifts may seem to point in opposing directions, in our view it is precisely this intellectual expansiveness that testifies to the promise that digital and computational methods have for expanding our understanding—and even our definitions—of the art market.

## Notes

1. For a larger discussion of this term, see Pamela Fletcher, "Reflections on Digital Art History," *caa. reviews*, June 18, 2015, www.caareviews.org/reviews/2726.
2. As quoted in Neil de Marchi, "Introduction," in *Economic Engagements with Art*, eds. Neil De Marchi and Craufurd D.W. Goodwin (Durham, NC and London: Duke University Press, 1999), 4.
3. Gerald Reitlinger, *The Economics of Taste: The Rise and Fall of Picture Prices 1760–1960* (London: Barrie and Rockliff, 1961), xi–xii.
4. Guido Gerzoni, "Reflections on Historical Series of Art Prices: Reitlinger's Data Revisited," *Journal of Cultural Economics* 19, no. 3 (1995): 251–60.
5. For example, Thomas M. Bayer and John R. Page, *The Development of the Art Market in England: Money as Muse, 1730–1900* (London: Pickering & Chatto, 2011).
6. See, for example, J.M. Montias, *Art at Auction in Seventeenth-Century Amsterdam* (Amsterdam: Amsterdam University Press, 2002); J.M. Montias, "Socio-Economic Aspects of Netherlandish Art from the Fifteenth to the Seventeenth Century: A Survey," *The Art Bulletin* 72, no. 3 (September 1990): 358–73; Louisa Wood Ruby, "The Montias Database: Inventories of Amsterdam Art Collections," in *In His Milieu: Essays on Netherlandish Art in Memory of John Michael Montias*, eds. A. Golahny, M. M. Mochizuki, and L. Vergara (Amsterdam: Amsterdam University Press, 2006), 395–401; Neil de Marchi and Hans J. Van Miegroet, eds., *Mapping Markets for Paintings in Europe 1450–1750* (Turnhout, Belgium: Brepols, 2006); Bayer and Page, *The Development of the Art Market in England*.
7. Filip Vermeylen, *Painting for the Market, Commercialization of Art in Antwerp's Golden Age* (Turnhout, Belgium: Brepols, 2003), 6.
8. David Ormrod, "Art and Its Markets," *The Economic History Review* 52, no. 3 (August 1999): 545, 546.
9. "Open Access at the Met," www.metmuseum.org/about-the-met/policies-and-documents/open-access. One of the first museums in the United States to adopt an open-access policy was the Walters Art Museum, in 2012 ("The Walters Art Museum, Year in Review 2011–2012," Annual Report). For an overview of the state of open access around this time, see Kristin Kelly, *Images of Works of Art in Museum Collections: The Experience of Open Access. A Survey of 11 Museums*, prepared for the Andrew W. Mellon Foundation (Washington, DC: Council on Library and Information Services, 2013). Not included as a case study in the CLIR report was the Rijksmuseum, which began to release its public domain images online in 2011. For more about the work of the Rijksmuseum in this domain, see, Joris Pekel and Europeana Foundation, "Democratising the Rijksmuseum," Europeana Report, August 27, 2014, https://pro.europeana.eu/post/democratising-the-rijksmuseum.
10. "The Metropolitan Museum of Art Collection API," https://metmuseum.github.io/.
11. "Using the Databases," The Getty Research Institute, www.getty.edu/research/tools/provenance/faq.html.
12. https://projectcornelia.be/.
13. Artl@s brings together a collection of research projects sharing a desire to globalize art history and advance digital applications under one umbrella. https://artlas.huma-num.fr/en/. The databases are available at: https://artlas.huma-num.fr/en/artlas-bases-de-donnees-en-acces-public/.
14. Richard Dunley, "Machines Reading the Archive: Handwritten Text Recognition Software," March 19, 2018, https://blog.nationalarchives.gov.uk/blog/machines-reading-the-archive-handwritten-text-recognition-software/.
15. Francesco Freddolini and Anne Helmreich, "Inventories, Catalogues and Art Historiography: Exploring Lists Against the Grain," *Journal of Art Historiography* no. 11 (December 2014): 1–14. For more on data preparation, see Anne J. Gilliand, "Setting the Stage," in *Introduction to Metadata,* ed. by Murtha Baca (Los Angeles: The Getty Research Institute, 2016), www.getty.edu/publications/intrometadata/setting-the-stage/.
16. See, for example, the database and visual applications published by "Mapping Art Markets in Europe," www.artmarkets.eu/presentation/?lang=en, which also relate to the publication *Moving Pictures, Intra-European Trade in Images, 16th–18th Centuries*, ed. Neil De Marchi and Sophie Raux (Turnhout Belgium: Brepols,

2014). See also the forthcoming, Sandra van Ginhoven, Christian Huemer, and Matthew Lincoln, *Data-Based to Data-Driven: New Avenues for Research in the History of Collecting and Art Markets* (Los Angeles: Getty Publications/Getty Research Institute, n.d.); Claartje Rasterhoff and Sandra van Ginhoven, eds., "Art Markets and Digital Histories," special issue, *Arts* 8, nos. 2 and 3 (2019). Their introduction, "Art Markets and Digital Histories," *Arts* 8, no 3 (2019): 105; https://doi.org/10.3390/arts8030105. For more on circulation, see Béatrice Joyeux-Prunel, "Circulation and the Art Market," *Journal for Art Market Studies* 1, no. 2 (2017), www.fokum-jams.org/index.php/jams/article/view/13.

17. Franco Moretti, "Graphs, Maps, Trees—Abstract Models for Literary History 1," *New Left Review* 24 (November, December 2003): 68.
18. Martin Myrone, "1845: The Slaughterhouse of Art History," in *The Royal Academy of Arts Summer Exhibition: A Chronicle, 1769–2018*, ed. Mark Hallett, Sarah Victoria Turner, and Jessica Feather (London: Paul Mellon Centre for Studies in British Art, 2018), https://chronicle250.com/1845.
19. Bruno Blondé and Veerle De Laet, "Owning Paintings and Changes in Consumer Preferences in the Low Countries, Seventeenth-Eighteenth Centuries," in *Mapping Markets for Paintings in Europe 1450–1750*, eds. Neil de Marchi and Hans J. Van Miegroet (Turnhout, Belgium: Brepols, 2006), 77.
20. Alexandra Provo, "Surrogates and Intermediaries: The Informational Role of Photographs in the Art Market," *Dealing Art on Both Sides of the Atlantic, 1860–1940*, ed. Lynn Catterson (Leiden and Boston: Brill, 2017), 269–88.
21. John Resig, "Using Computer Vision to Increase the Research Potential of Photo Archives," https://services.tineye.com/solutions/JohnResigComputerVisionResearchPaperMatchEngine. The Frick photo archive, used in Resig's analysis, is among a group of fourteen institutions in the process of digitizing their photo archives and aiming to create a digital research platform for their study as part of the work of the Pharos Consortium.
22. "Homeless Paintings of the Italian Renaissance," http://itatti.harvard.edu/berenson-library/collections/photograph-archives/homeless-paintings.
23. Béatrice Joyeux-Prunel and Olivier Marcel, "Exhibition Catalogues in the Globalization of Art, A Source for Social and Spatial Art History," *Artl@s Bulletin* 4, no. 2 (Fall 2015): Article 8, https://docs.lib.purdue.edu/cgi/viewcontent.cgi?article=1084&context=artlas.
24. Anne Helmreich, Tim Hitchcock, and William J. Turkel, "Rethinking Inventories in the Digital Age: The Case of the Old Bailey," in *Inventories and Catalogues: Material and Narrative Histories*, guest ed. Francesco Freddolini and Anne Helmreich, *Journal of Art Historiography* 11 (December 2014), https://arthistoriography.files.wordpress.com/2014/11/helmreich_hitchcock_turkel.pdf
25. Pamela Fletcher, Anne Helmreich, David Israel, and Seth Erickson, "Local/Global: Mapping Nineteenth-Century London's Art Market," *Nineteenth-Century Art Worldwide* 11, no. 3 (Autumn 2012), www.19thc-artworldwide.org/autumn12/fletcher-helmreich-mapping-the-london-art-market.
26. Christine Howald and Léa Saint-Raymond, "Tracking Dispersal: Auction Sales from the Yuanmingyuan Loot in Paris in the 1860s," *Journal of Art Market Studies* 2, no. 2 (2018), www.fokum-jams.org/index.php/jams/article/view/30.
27. Johannes Gramlich, "Reflections on Provenance Research: Values—Politics—Art Markets," *Journal of Art Market Studies* 1, no. 2 (2017), www.fokum-jams.org/index.php/jams/article/view/15.
28. See, for example, Thomas Skowronek, "Anamorphosis of Unexpected Results, on the Epistemological Culture of Art Market Visualizations," *Journal of Art Market Studies* 1, no. 2 (2017), www.fokum-jams.org/index.php/jams/article/view/12.
29. Miriam Kienle, "Between Nodes and Edges: Possibilities and Limits of Network Analysis in Art History," *Artl@as Bulletin* 6, no. 3 (2017): Article 1, https://docs.lib.purdue.edu/cgi/viewcontent.cgi?article=1152&context=artlas; Stephanie Porras, "Keeping Our Eyes Open: Visualizing Networks and Art History," *Artl@s Bulletin* 6, no. 3 (2017): Article 3, https://docs.lib.purdue.edu/cgi/viewcontent.cgi?article=1121&context=artlas. See also Léa Saint-Raymond and Antoine Courtin, "Enriching and Cutting: How to Visualize Networks Thanks to Linked Open Data Platforms," *Artl@s Bulletin* 6, no. 3: Article 7, https://docs.lib.purdue.edu/artlas/vol6/iss3/7/.
30. Joanna Gardner-Huggett, "Extrapolating Influence: The Challenges of Mapping the History of ARC and Artemisia Galleries, Chicago (1980–1985)," *Historical Geography* 45 (2017): 37–65.
31. See, for example, Pamela Fletcher and David N. Israel, *The London Gallery Project* (2007), Revised September 2012, http://learn.bowdoin.edu/fletcher/london-gallery/; Michelle Greet, "Mapping Cultural Exchange: Latin American Artists in Paris Between the Wars," in *Circulations in the Global History of Art*, eds. Thomas DaCosta Kaufmann, Catherine Dossin, and Béatrice Joyeux-Prunel, Studies in Art Historiography Series (Farnham: Ashgate, 2015), 133–47; Léa Saint-Raymond, Félicie de Maupeou,

and Julien Cavero, "Les rues des tableaux: The Geography of the Parisian Art Market 1815–1955," *Artl@s Bulletin* 5, no. 1 (2016): Article 10, https://docs.lib.purdue.edu/artlas/vol5/iss1/10/; Hannah Williams, "Artists' Studios in Paris: Digitally Mapping the 18th-Century Art World," *Journal 18* no. 5, Coordinates (Spring 2018), www.journal18.org/issue5_williams/.

32. Janine Barchas, *What Jane Saw*, www.whatjanesaw.org/1813/; Janine Barchas, "Digitally Reconstructing the Reynolds Retrospective Attended by Jane Austen in 1813: A Report on E-Work-in-Progress," *ABO: Interactive Journal for Women in the Arts, 1640–1830* 2, no. 1 (2012): Article 13, https://scholarcommons.usf.edu/abo/vol2/iss1/; Catherine Roach, "Rehanging Reynolds at the British Institution: Methods for Reconstructing Ephemeral Displays," *British Art Studies* no. 4, https://doi.org/10.17658/issn.2058-5462/issue-04/croach.
33. Sophie Raux, "Virtual Explorations of an 18th-Century Art Market Space: Gersaint, Watteau, and the Pont Notre-Dame," *Journal 18* no. 5, Coordinates (Spring 2018), doi:10.30610/5.2018.3, www.journal18.org/2542.
34. Sally Webster and David Schwittek, Carlo Diego, Cara Jordan, Lauren Ritz, Leonidas Maliokas, and Bruce Weber, "A Digital Recreation of the Lenox Library Picture Gallery: A Contribution to the Early History of Public Art Museums in the United States," *Nineteenth-Century Art Worldwide* 17, no. 2 (Autumn 2018), www.19thc-artworldwide.org/autumn18/webster-on-a-digital-recreation-of-the-lenox-library-picture-gallery.
35. Dianne Favro and Christopher Johanson argue for how digital technologies can support investigations into sensorial and kinetic understandings of experiences of the built environment in "Death in Motion, Funeral Processions in the Roman Forum," *Journal of the Society of Architectural Historians* 69, no. 1 (March 2010): 12–37.

## Bibliography


Barchas, Janine. "Digitally Reconstructing the Reynolds Retrospective Attended by Jane Austen in 1813: A Report on E-Work-in-Progress." *ABO: Interactive Journal for Women in the Arts, 1640–1830* 2, no. 1 (2012): Article 13. https://scholarcommons.usf.edu/abo/vol2/iss1/.

Bayer, Thomas M., and John R. Page. *The Development of the Art Market in England: Money as Muse, 1730–1900*. London: Pickering & Chatto, 2011.

Blondé, Bruno, and Veerle De Laet. "Owning Paintings and Changes in Consumer Preferences in the Low Countries, Seventeenth-Eighteenth Centuries." In *Mapping Markets for Paintings in Europe 1450–1750*, edited by Neil de Marchi and Hans J. Van Miegroet, 69–84. Turnhout, Belgium: Brepols, 2006.

de Marchi, Neil. "Introduction." In *Economic Engagements with Art*, edited by Neil De Marchi and Craufurd D.W. Goodwin, 1–30. Durham and London: Duke University Press, 1999.

de Marchi Neil, and Hans J. Van Miegroet, eds. *Mapping Markets for Paintings in Europe 1450–1750*. Turnhout, Belgium: Brepols, 2006.

Favro, Dianne, and Christopher Johanson. "Death in Motion, Funeral Processions in the Roman Forum." *Journal of the Society of Architectural Historians* 69, no. 1 (March 2010): 12–37.

Fletcher, Pamela, Anne Helmreich, David Israel, and Seth Erickson. "Local/Global: Mapping Nineteenth-Century London's Art Market." In *Nineteenth-Century Art Worldwide,* vol. 11, no. 3 (Autumn 2012). www.19thc-artworldwide.org/autumn12/fletcher-helmreich-mapping-the-london-art-market.

———. "Reflections on Digital Art History." *caa.reviews*, June 18, 2015. www.caareviews.org/reviews/2726

Freddolini, Francesco, and Anne Helmreich. "Inventories, Catalogues and Art Historiography: Exploring Lists Against the Grain." *Journal of Art Historiography*, no. 11 (December 2014): 1–14.

Gardner-Huggett, Joanna. "Extrapolating Influence: The Challenges of Mapping the History of ARC and Artemisia Galleries, Chicago (1980–1985)." *Historical Geography* 45 (2017): 37–65.

Gilliand, Anne J. "Setting the Stage." In *Introduction to Metadata*, edited by Murtha Baca. Los Angeles: The Getty Research Institute, 2016.

Gerzoni, Guido. "Reflections on Historical Series of Art Prices: Reitlinger's Data Revisited." *Journal of Cultural Economics* 19, no. 3 (1995): 251–60.

Gramlich, Johannes. "Reflections on Provenance Research: Values—Politics—Art Markets." *Journal of Art Market Studies* 1, no. 2 (2017). www.fokum-jams.org/index.php/jams/article/view/15.

Greet, Michelle. "Mapping Cultural Exchange: Latin American Artists in Paris between the Wars." In *Circulations in the Global History of Art*, edited by Thomas DaCosta Kaufmann, Catherine Dossin, and Béatrice

Joyeux-Prunel, Studies in Art Historiography Series, 133–47. Farnham, Surrey, England; Burlington, VT Ashgate Publishing, 2015.

Helmreich, Anne, Tim Hitchcock, and William J. Turkel. "Rethinking Inventories in the Digital Age: The Case of the Old Bailey." In *Inventories and Catalogues: Material and Narrative Histories*, edited by Francesco Freddolini and Anne Helmreich *Journal of Art Historiography* 11 (December 2014). https://arthistoriography.files.wordpress.com/2014/11/helmreich_hitchcock_turkel.pdf

Howald, Christine, and Léa Saint-Raymond. "Tracking Dispersal: Auction Sales from the Yuanmingyuan Loot in Paris in the 1860s." *Journal of Art Market Studies* 2, no. 2 (2018). www.fokum-jams.org/index php/jams/article/view/30

Joyeux-Prunel, Béatrice. "Circulation and the Art Market." *Journal for Art Market Studies* 1, no. 2 (2017). www.fokum-jams.org/index.php/jams/article/view/13.

Joyeux-Prunel, Béatrice, and Olivier Marcel. "Exhibition Catalogues in the Globalization of Art, A Source for Social and Spatial Art History." *Artl@s Bulletin* 4, no. 2 (Fall 2015): Article 8. https://docs.lib.purdue edu/cgi/viewcontent.cgi?article=1084&context=artlas.

Kelly, Kristen. *Images of Works of Art in Museum Collections: The Experience of Open Access, A Survey of 1: Museums*, prepared for The Andrew W. Mellon Foundation. Washington, DC: Council on Library and Information Services, 2013.

Kienle, Miriam. "Between Nodes and Edges: Possibilities and Limits of Network Analysis in Art History." *Artl@s Bulletin* 6, no. 3 (2017): Article 1. https://docs.lib.purdue.edu/cgi/viewcontent.cgi?article=1152&context=artlas.

Montias, J. Michael. *Art at Auction in Seventeenth-Century Amsterdam*. Amsterdam: Amsterdam University Press, 2002.

———. "Socio-Economic Aspects of Netherlandish Art from the Fifteenth to the Seventeenth Century: A Survey." *The Art Bulletin* 72, no. 3 (September 1990): 358–73.

Moretti, Franco. "Graphs, Maps, Trees—Abstract Models for Literary History 1." *New Left Review* 24 (November, December 2003): 67–93.

Myrone, Martin. "1845: The Slaughterhouse of Art History." In *The Royal Academy of Arts Summer Exhibition: A Chronicle, 1769–2018*, edited by Mark Hallett, Sarah Victoria Turner and Jessica Feather. London: Paul Mellon Centre for Studies in British Art, 2018. https://chronicle250.com/1845.

Ormrod, David. "Art and its Markets." *The Economic History Review* 52, no. 3 (August 1999): 544–51.

Porras, Stephanie. "Keeping our Eyes Open: Visualizing Networks and Art History." *Artl@s Bulletin* 6, no. 3 (2017): Article 3. https://docs.lib.purdue.edu/cgi/viewcontent.cgi?article=1121&context=artlas.

Provo, Alexandra. "Surrogates and Intermediaries: The Informational Role of Photographs in the Art Market." In *Dealing Art on Both Sides of the Atlantic, 1860–1940*, edited by Lynn Catterson, 269–88. Leiden and Boston: Brill, 2017.

Raux, Sophie. "Virtual Explorations of an 18th-Century Art Market Space: Gersaint, Watteau, and the Pont Notre-Dame." *Journal 18* no. 5, Coordinates (Spring 2018). doi:10.30610/5.2018. www.journal18.org/2542.

Reitlinger, Gerald. *The Economics of Taste, The Rise and Fall of Picture Prices 1760–1960*. London: Barrie and Rockliff, 1961.

Roach, Catherine. "Rehanging Reynolds at the British Institution: Methods for Reconstructing Ephemeral Displays." *British Art Studies* 4. https://doi.org/10.17658/issn.2058-5462/issue-04/croach.

Ruby, Louisa Wood. "The Montias Database: Inventories of Amsterdam Art Collections." In *his Milieu: Essays on Netherlandish Art in Memory of John Michael Montias*, edited by A. Golahny, M. M. Mochizuki and L. Vergara, 395–401. Amsterdam: Amsterdam University Press, 2006.

Saint-Raymond, Léa, and Antoine Courtin. "Enriching and Cutting: How to Visualize Networks Thanks to Linked Open Data Platforms." *Artl@s Bulletin* 6, no. 3: Article 7. https://docs.lib.purdue.edu/artlas/vol6/iss3/7/.

Saint-Raymond, Lea, Félicie de Maupeou, and Julien Cavero. "Les rues des tableaux: The Geography of the Parisian Art Market 1815–1955." *Artl@s Bulletin* 5, no. 1 (2016): Article 10. https://docs.lib.purdue.edu/artlas/vol5/iss1/10/

Skowronek, Thomas. "Anamorphosis of Unexpected Results, On the Epistemological Culture of Art Market Visualizations." *Journal of Art Market Studies* 1, no. 2 (2017). www.fokum-jams.org/index.php/jams/article/view/12.

Van Ginhoven, Christian Huemer, and Matthew Lincoln. *Data-Based to Data-Driven: New Avenues for Research in the History of Collecting and Art Markets*. Los Angeles: Getty Publications/Getty Research Institute, forthcoming.

Van Ginhoven, Sandra, and Claartje Rasterhoff, eds. "Art Markets and Digital Histories." A special issue of *Arts* 8, nos. 2 and 3 (2019).

Vermeylen, Filip. *Painting for the Market, Commercialization of Art in Antwerp's Golden Age*. Turnhout, Belgium: Brepols, 2003.

Webster, Sally, David Schwittek, Carlo Diego, Cara Jordan, Lauren Ritz, Leonidas Maliokas, and Bruce Weber. "A Digital Recreation of the Lenox Library Picture Gallery: A Contribution to the Early History of Public Art Museums in the United States." *Nineteenth-Century Art Worldwide* 17, no. 2 (Autumn 2018). www.19thc-artworldwide.org/autumn18/webster-on-a-digital-recreation-of-the-lenox-library-picture-gallery.

Williams, Hannah. "Artists' Studios in Paris: Digitally Mapping the 18th-Century Art World." *Journal 18* no. 5, Coordinates (Spring 2018). www.journal18.org/issue5_williams/.

# 13

# NOISE MANAGEMENT IN THE ARCHIVAL ECOSYSTEM

## Debating Principles for Classification*

*Anna Dot and Pablo Santa Olalla*

Incalculable amounts of data are collected at every second, in real time, by a huge number of sensors placed everywhere. Most of this data is stored and classified in different kinds of archives and databases. Despite the apparently objective nature of this information gathering, the task of archiving is a process of communication that involves both a distance between the source of knowledge and the knower and a long-term relationship with uncertainty: A message is extracted from an information source and is kept as a signal for a future, unknown recipient. The transmission of this message across time and space is, however, imperfect and unstable. On the one hand, according to Claude E. Shannon, any general communication system is affected by "noise," which generates a series of transformations in the message that is transmitted.[1] On the other, as Diana Taylor argues, "the value, relevance, or meaning of the archive, how the items it contains get interpreted, even embodied" are also subject to change over time.[2]

Inevitably, many sources of "noise" surround archival procedures. Based on the idea of the archive as an evolving channel, the aim of this chapter is to reconsider the role of archival noise. Advocating against the common drive toward noise cancellation, our hypothesis advocates for the need to interpret and value the meanings of noise. We shall argue that interruptions that occur in archival procedures have the potential to add meaning to the archive. First, an examination of the "dead," "living," and sometimes "reanimated" condition of archives will allow us to devise a provisional classification of archival noises. Second, a reflection on the relation between modern, Western notions of history and the origin of noise within the archive will be discussed. Third, the status of the document will be analyzed as a metaphorical "sponge" that absorbs both noises and valued information. Finally, glitch, anarchives, and redirected cyberattacks will be considered as examples of contemporary approaches to archival procedures that take into account noises as constitutive elements.

### Archival Typologies

In this section, we distinguish between two different archival typologies: *dead* and *living* archives. The term "dead" has been used to designate those archives that are completed collections of data circumscribed by a closed field that does not generate new information in and of itself. An example would be a set of documents and materials that a political party produced during its lifetime and retained after its dissolution. It could be said that such an archive is complete insofar as the archive stores files that are no longer in use.[3] Celia Ramírez López, who coordinated the UNAM (Universidad Nacional Autónoma de México) Historical Archive throughout the 1990s, has addressed the issue of dead archives, pointing out an "incapacity to communicate" as one of their characteristics. Nevertheless, she also remarks that the use of the term "dead archive" is "censored by the modern [meaning 'contemporary'] archivistics."[4] Arguably, "censorship" is too strong a term in this context: The "dead" archive is not literally "censored," but is typically *discussed* through acknowledgment of the continuous need of archives to be updated. Recent studies on the archive have challenged traditional myths that still link it to its etymological Greek definition, namely as "a public building" and "a place where records are kept."[5] While the practice of archiving exists from the moment when certain objects are recognized as items "supposedly resistant to change," it is common to witness the transformation, corruptibility, subversion, and political manipulation of archives.[6]

For example, Maria Eichhorn's *Rose Valland Institute* (2017), presented at Documenta 14, addressed the issue of the Nazi looting of the European Jewish population through archival research, academic discussion, and artistic methodologies, thus restoring the capacity to communicate [and interpret?] material from the Hessisches Hauptstaatsarchiv in Wiesbaden and the Bundesarchiv in Koblenz. Other reflections on this theme can be found in Simone Osthoff's research. She has considered archives "as, almost literally, 'live' entities."[7] In her book *Performing the Archive: The Transformation of the Archive in Contemporary Art from Repository of Documents to Art Medium* (2009), Osthoff addresses the work of Lygia Clark, Hélio Oiticica, Paulo Bruscky and Eduardo Kac "who destabilized the archive by creating fluid boundaries between their artworks, their writings, and archives."[8] She describes their artworks as disruptive acts that change the archive's ontology: From "the archive as a repository of documents to the archive as a dynamic and generative medium."[9] The archive remains in a state of latency until it is disrupted by an artist's intervention. In Osthoff's words: "[I]f not alive, the archive in contemporary art is in a state of flux, undead, ghostly";[10] as if it waited for the artist to bring new energy to dead material. In similar terms, Jussi Parikka argues that the archive, as a "key institutional 'site' of memory with an intertwined history with modernity and the birth of the state apparatus,"[11] is abandoning its existence as a static "place of history, memory and power."[12] Instead it is becoming increasingly a "dynamic and temporal network, a software environment, and a social platform for memory—but also for remixing."[13]

Therefore, present research into archives and archival practices suggests that there is always a chance to generate new information from archived documents, whether due to new research approaches to data, or as a consequence of new archival procedures. Technological transliteration and the digitization of paper archives may open new research perspectives by allowing further accessibility as well as possibilities for remix. The digital transformation of the archive is like the lightning bolt that strikes Frankenstein and brings him into a new existence. Such a "reanimation" of archives may be achieved through curatorial procedures. Daniel García Andújar's *Postcapital Archive (1989–2001)* (2004–present) is an exceptional study case of the latter: It is conceived as a corpus of items to discuss drifts of capitalism between the fall of the Berlin Wall and the attacks of 9/11. It is an accumulation of items within a closed period. However, the archive is revived in each new exhibition in which new ways of displaying and arranging the elements are found and the installation itself responds to site specificities. Such examples challenge the notion of the permanently "dead" archive. However, it must be acknowledged that before dying and being reborn, archives used to be alive.

By referring to the "living" condition, we signal those archives that relate to an open field that generates new data and that regularly receive materials and documentation. An example might be the local archive of a city, continually recording deaths, births, weddings, divorces, traffic accidents, pollution levels, cultural events, etc. The project *The File Room* (1994) by Antoni Muntadas is a good example of this category. It is an online database of artistic censorship where users can add details about new cases of prohibited artworks.[14] A further example is Christian Boltanski's *Les Archives du Cœur* (2008–present), in which the French artist records an ever-increasing archive of heartbeats and that has a permanent storage site on the Japanese island of Ejima.

## Classifying Archival Noises

The way in which a living archive relates to time differs from the way dead archives do so: Whereas for the former the storage of data is an ongoing process that needs to be (re)thought every now and then, for the latter this process is a fixed and stable with a concrete beginning and end. Although both types of archives are affected by the presence of noise, living ones have additional layers of complexity given the high volume of data that they have to handle. The most surprising internal or external item may disrupt the expected performance of the archival mechanisms. Consider, for example, the body of a dead moth that the engineer Grace Murray Hopper found stuck in a relay which prevented the computer Mark II from its normal functioning in 1947 at Harvard University.[15] In the case of Muntadas' *The File Room*, deviations generated by internet bots and trolls act as noises, eventually leading to false entries in the censorship database. These are easily recognizable because of their content, including commercial key words such as product names and terms like "buy" and "online."[16]

One of the consequences of this kind of noise in *The File Room* is the difficulty for the user to navigate sea of excessive data and to find the information that he or she seeks. There, as Hito Steyerl has put it: "The focus moves from acquisition to discerning, from scarcity to overabundance, from adding on to filtering."[17] These and other noises relating to the creation, capture, and storage of data are vivid in living archives which become noisy ecosystems. What can be said about these noises? Real-time, living archives and databases are expected periodically to store amounts of new, raw data. In order to do so, however, protocols relating to collecting and importing information have to be implemented. These steps are prone to generate noises of different kinds, including the excesses or omissions derived from sifting real-world, bad or loose categorizations or the incommensurability between reality outside the archive and the archival structure. These noises appear because the archival procedure depends on the abstraction of the real world into information by means of categories and typologies, thus implying a characterization of the data producers and a consequent hierarchization of the data. In digital archives, the abstraction process is even stricter and generates higher levels of noise. The categorized specifications have to be converted into a binary code through a series of translations that go through the different languages and codes used by the human and non-human agents (archivists, programmers, users, computers, databases, spreadsheets or display devices). By contrast, dead archives are noiseless, since no new data is generated, captured, harvested, and inserted until the archive is reanimated.

Beyond noises generated by the importation and collection of data, there is another important source of archival noise: Misunderstanding. Translation is an essential and transversal procedure of the archival process. Different bodies of information need to be translated into specific formats; the archivist's lexicon has to fit into the programmer's language; the programmer's language into the digital code; the code into the user interface, and so on.

An archivist may eliminate any errors in collecting, categorizing and importing data; may avoid any translation errors and misunderstandings in the communication flows between the agents; and may even look for dead moths in the computer relays. Yet despite this work, he or she may eventually find faults in the resulting data accumulation. There are many chances of encountering noises within the archive, even after cleaning up the structural archival procedures. When this happens, the archivist has the duty to double or triple-check the whole process, generating not only temporal delay but also potential dismay.

The source of the problem may not be in the archival procedures, but in the data itself. Data may come from uncontrolled sources, provoking a lack of formal coherence within the different stages of abstraction—categories, files, code—in which it is compiled. However, for the information to be searchable, to flow, and to perform well within the archival context, data need to be uniform in each step. The archivist has to design a proper stylesheet that accords with the archival material and the purposes of the archive and needs to check, filter and edit the data to ensure style appropriateness. Wrong data, or bad stylizations—such as an out-of-place comma—can be perceived as errors in an archive search engine or database: They are elements of disruption that interrupt the expected functioning of the archival ecosystem.

We have so far discussed different kinds of noise generated by the movement of materials and data through time. This includes *blinking noises* which appear when an error is found in particular information. These are then reported, checked, corrected, and eliminated. There are also *cyclical noises*. The misplacement of commas within text strings of a CSV file is a common example. As "CSV" means "comma-separated values," when a comma acts as a traditional comma rather than as a separator between different pieces of information, algorithms will interpret it as a separator regardless of its real purpose. Then, these misplaced commas can disrupt the proper functioning of an archival procedure. Finally there are *continuous noises* that are inherent in certain archives. For example, we can imagine a persistent sense of discomfort for archivists working with images of war or violence. Feeling the archivist not in the best conditions, discomfort can cause him or her distractions, demotivation and a will to evade the task at hands. At the same time, however, we propose a tentative classification of archival noises determined by their location in the archive:

- *Personal/contextual/cultural noises*. Present-day doubts about the historical past or the future usefulness of an archive may stimulate a drive to preserve everything, thus resulting on an overabundance of stored data that may be interpreted as noise. According to Steyerl, separating noise from information is a political act "of conscious decoding."[18] Therefore, the impact that subjective, emotional traits attributed to information may have on the performance of the archive depend on the archival agents' culture, political bias, and/or identity. Individual prejudices, biases, assumptions, and ethical dilemmas have consequences for both the management of data and the archive's structure.
- *Environmental noises*. As in the case of the dead moth that Grace Murray Hopper found in the computer's circuits, environmental facts and agents can damage the archive or influence the way the archival procedures take place. This includes the impact of weather, ambient conditions, dust, bugs, fungus, background sound interferences in and around the archival space, or even lack or excess of space. Physical degeneration of the archived data can also bring noises to the archival system. This includes the aging of historical documents, but also the environmental conditions that affect the archivist's work and impact on the correct interpretation of the archived data.
- *Intrinsic archival noises*. First, this kind of noise may be generated by the content of the archive itself e.g. misplaced or absent elements, wrong information, and the absence or overabundance of content. Second, intrinsic noise can exist within the structure of the archive. This includes wrong categorizations and hierarchies, errors in code and algorithms, and recursion. Third, there are noises generated during archival procedures, including errors

produced in the moment of capturing data, data importation, display errors, and the wrong selection of data.

- *Noises in archival communications.* This category includes miscommunications between archival agents, such as archivists, programmers, and other human or non-human agents who contribute documents, information, and metadata. Such errors can also arise in the translation or transcription of data. The potential for this kind of noise is particularly acute when a particular file or document is transposed into a different technological environment, for example with digitization or the storage of analogical/material items into digitally "dematerialized" databases.

A taxonomy of archival noise emerges from the combination of classifications based on duration and location. Nevertheless, when classifying the traits of an archive, a recursive issue develops and undermines the stability of the classificatory system itself as apparently unclassifiable noises start to emerge. From this perspective, any attempt to establish an exhaustive classification of archival noises suffers from the very noises it wants to classify. What consequences could this recursive noise have? Is it necessary to eliminate noise from a classification of archival noises? Or does noise generate useful information about the cultural frame and specificities of the classifications in and of the archive?

## Archives as Noise Generators

"Our contemporary experience of time is in crisis," the Catalan philosopher Fina Birulés argued in 2018.[19] Birulés recalled François Hartog's introduction of the anthropological concept of "regime[s] of historicity" into critical theory in order to grasp the transformations between the end of the modernist idea of time and "presentism."[20] Departing from the *Querelle des anciens et des modernes* in the seventeenth-century French Academy, and particularly in the centuries after the Enlightenment, Western conceptions of historical time do not seek to learn from the past. The modernist experience of rupture, prominent in the avant-gardes of the twentieth century such as Futurism or Dada, is not suitable for our time experience either. It has been argued that this notion of time based on a sequence of ruptures derived largely from the Western belief in the possible construction of the future through social labor.[21] In the wake of postmodernist reappropriations of history, we are surrounded by an experience of time that points neither backwards nor forwards, but is centered on the only cult of the present.[22] Such "presentism" not only has an effect on the intergenerational transmission of knowledge, but also on the tasks of design and production of new media. According to Jay Bolter and Richard Grusin, "our culture wants both to multiply its media and to erase all traces of mediation."[23] This is why an archivist may feel the need to eliminate noise while simultaneously struggling with questions about what information should be eliminated or preserved, not for the future, but as an antidote to the implications of presentism.

Nowadays archival science, and particularly information capture and storage for big data, have the utopian ambition of preserving everything. Yet this drive for completeness is neither directed to the past nor fueled to the future: We preserve everything in response to current doubts, well summarized by the expression "just in case." What will be the implications of deciding whether or not to register on, or erase information from, specific archival systems over time? The ecosystem of the living archive is complex and requires all of its agents to engage in a long-term relationship with uncertainty. The contemporary archivist cannot know what queries will challenge the archival device after his or her work; he or she is obliged to make predictions about the future, and these predictions are themselves a source of noise within the archive. The boom of the archival impulse in the twentieth century plays an important role in historical methodologies. François Hartog identifies a transition from the "witness" to the "document" within the Western discipline of history. In his view, history proclaimed itself as a "science of the past," under the domain of the "document" as an objective piece of evidence. Its authenticity was then more related to the provenance of the document than to its content. As Hartog writes: "History is the science of the written traces. From the shoreline of the present, the absent historian is no more than an eye which reads the archives."[24] The document has become one of the Historian's main tools. Nevertheless, it is not a noiseless, clear, clean, quiet, scientifically objective piece of truth, but a collection of traces that, ultimately, can be artificially created. As Parikka writes:

> The documents of the past are such concrete instances of pasts present but even more so of the way in which technical media records time and acts as a time machine between current times and the past [. . .] technical media record not only meanings but also noise and the physicality of the world outside our human intentions or signifying structures.[25]

What once was "information" can later be erased or lost as the medium deteriorates. Alternatively, something that was unintentionally saved or accidentally recorded on a document could be a source of unexpected information. According to Wolfgang Ernst, even trash data has the potential of being useful.[26] Nevertheless, despite the present archival drive that seeks to preserve as much information as possible, archives are often "less concerned with memory than with the necessity to discard, erase, eliminate," as Ernst reflects quoting the art historian and theoretician Sven Spieker.[27] In this regard, an archive is not simply determined by what it stores, but also by what it discards. In consequence, not only documents, but also archival records themselves, can be read as a mere channels, communicative media between past and present, loss and retrieval. Archival negotiation selects only the documents that are expected to work better as mediators between past and future. Filled with noisy entities, the archive acts as a *hub* of connections from distant points in time. In this vein, an archive stores information as an electronic capacitor stores electricity. Within a generator, a dielectric material sorts positive and negative electric charges, that are physically retained and can be retrieved later. An archive does the same with "positive" information and "negative" noises. Nevertheless, no one knows whether positive or negative charges will be useful once the informational spark of the archive is released. Questions arise: Is noise a bad thing? Is it mandatory to eliminate noise from the archive?

## Reconsidering Noise

Michel Foucault's comments with regard to medicine become pertinent when thinking of the archive as a power device that is complicit with social control. According to him, the task of modern medicine is to "listen and interpret" the "'organ's non-silence' [. . .] 'constituted by' or at least 'carrying' various discontinuous elements, i.e. isolable from each other by certain criteria."[28] Foucault's analysis is based on the assumption that the body has an acoustic code to send messages: When the organs are not quiet, illness appears. To Foucault, this explains why modern, Western medicine reached a consensus on how to distinguish a useful body's message from noise. Illness-generated noises are selected and classified by the clinical experience which translates them from raw data to a diagnostic that allows noise cancellation, either through the suggestion of a cure or through the announcement of imminent death. Accordingly, the doctor needs to identify one specific sound from other noises that can distract him or her from making the correct diagnosis. The archivist has to perform a similar task: In his or her hands, raw data from the empirical world is codified, classified, and stored. The world may sometimes be a chaotic and noisy entity in the eyes of the archivist, who seeks to *cure* it from the disease of disorder and misunderstanding. But, as posited earlier, following Ernst, noises and accidental data might not be useless at all.

Aside from silence, another two antonyms to noise could be cleanliness and clarity, which would ideally allow thought clearness. As Julia Kristeva has argued: "It is thus not the lack of cleanliness or health that causes abjection but what disturbs identity, system, order, what does not respect borders, positions rules, the in-between, the ambiguous, the composite."[29] A sound recording is said to be clean when it has no background noises. In a similar way, we speak of clear or defined images when their limits and contours are not blurred, but sharp. An archivist looks forward to eliminating "abject" elements from the archival structure, but also from its content, context, and participating agents. These abject elements may correspond to the different noise categories that have been proposed previously: From environmental and material conditions to the archivist's personal prejudices; from temporary errors in display to embedded, unconscious, social biases. These can interrupt the normal workflow of an archive and even generate further noises. Archival abjections simultaneously carry "deviated data" which challenge the distinction between relevant and irrelevant archived or archivable items. Taking into account the will to eliminate noise, archives are often interpreted as repressive devices.[30] They stop the free circulation of things in the name of order, forbidding the disruptive capacities of abjection. However, Rosa Menkman, glitch artist and author of *The Glitch Moment(um)* (2011), warns of the impossibility of finding a noiseless channel. She argues that "what makes every medium specific is *how* it fails to reach a state of complete transparent immediacy."[31] Thus noise can be discovered not only in the origin of the medium's failures, but in its specificities too. With this in mind, Menkman uses the word "glitch" to describe

> a (actual and/or simulated) break from an expected or conventional flow of information or meaning within (digital) communication systems that results in a perceived accident or error. A glitch occurs on the occasion where there is an absence of (expected) functionality, whether understood in a technical or social sense. Therefore, a glitch [. . .] is not always strictly a result of a technical malfunction.[32]

Glitch, as the product of noise that can generate more noise, is a social matter that escapes any unequivocal cultural definition. It can "reflexively stage a reconsideration or re-view its opposite—the world of meaning, norms and regulations, goodness, or beauty";[33] that is to say, the world of silence, cleanliness and clarity. Menkman's notion of glitch is a synonym for noise and a cause of abjection. It has a political and critical dimension, which potentially can shed light on the repressive mechanisms of each medium and, therefore, of the archive. With this term, she has also named an art genre: So-called *glitch art*, represented by the products of contemporary artistic practices that not only search for a certain kind of design and aesthetics, but that also convey issues such as "planned obsolescence, built-in nostalgia, critical media aesthetics and the gentrification and continuing development of a glitch art genre."[34] In her "Glitch Studies Manifesto," Menkman advocates using glitches "to bring any medium into a critical state of hypertrophy, to (subsequently) criticize its inherent politics."[35]

As is clear by now, within the frame of contemporary thinking, where postmodern and postcolonial theories are cornerstones of debate, noise—as a source of difference, otherness, and disorder—has to be taken into account. If noisy elements blur distinctions, rules or categories, however, how can an archivist proceed in his or her task? A solution might be to accept the noisy elements as glitches and to use and decode the meanings and epistemological *détournements* that they carry. There is no a single answer to this conundrum, but a plethora of them. One good example is the *anarchive*. As an experimental archival device, it allows processes, themes and materials usually ignored by traditional archives, such as the continuous development of the archival structures and awareness of politics, affect, and care. *Anarchivo SIDA* (2012-present) is a research-based anarchive conducted by Equipo Re (Aimar Arriola and Nancy Garin) within which documents of "the aesthetic practices, representations, collective experiences, and performative tactics that have shaped HIV/AIDS politics" are collected and curated departing from a non-Western framework.[36] Arriola and Garin place special attention on the sensitivity of the materials compiled. Some of them have been donated by individuals and they carry personal memories, such as memories of loved ones who died from AIDS.

Other example of tactics to internalize and use noise within archival devices could be the appropriation of noise. An example is *Queering the map* (2017—present), which consists of an interactive map that allows users to geolocate a queer experience. The map was released by the Canadian designer Lucas LaRochelle. In February 2018 a troll bot attacked the map by inserting messages with the text "Make America Great Again, Donald Trump best president!" Thus, giving it a "glitch art" appearance. LaRochelle withheld the map and asked for help online. A community of users created a collaborative and open-source code repository in order to fix the security issues of the initial release.[37] Now the project is active, content-moderated, and supported by a community. It has not only recovered, but also further developed from a sudden attack of noise.[38]

## Conclusion: The Impossibility of Classifying Noise

In his speech "Some Reflections on the Present Outlook for High-Quality Machine Translation" (1971), Yehoshua Bar-Hillel shared some arguments against the possibility of developing what was called a "Fully Automatic High Quality Translation." This was supposed to be achieved by machine translation technologies that purported to provide perfect translations. Bar-Hillel stated:

> A translation which is of good quality for a certain user in a certain situation might be of lesser quality for the same user in a different situation or for a different user whether in the same or in a different situation. What is satisfactory for one need not be satisfactory for another.[39]

In our view, the same logic works for archives. It is impossible to find a stable classification for noise because what might be noisy to one person or situation, might not be noisy to another. Glossing Bar-Hillel's discussion of machine translation, we argue that: "An input which is noisy for a certain archivist in a certain situation might be less noisy for the same archivist in a different situation or for a different archivist whether in the same or in a different situation. What is satisfactory for one need not be satisfactory for another." This adapted quotation assumes that noise is contingent. It depends on its contextual and cultural causality. Useful data is always present in archives, but the same can be said about noise, regardless of its duration or location. It is not possible to remove noise completely from archival ecosystems. Instead, because archives are the result of negotiations, dealing with the noises within them demands a flexible approach. An attempt to classify noises is also an attempt to insert them into the humanized order of the archive. Nevertheless, if noise is the drive of a medium to escape from its internal order, a classification of noises must necessarily remain incomplete: Even if media adapt to noises, new noises will appear in old, new, and renewed mediums.

In this chapter, we have proposed possible classifications of archival noise, but we have come to the conclusion that any such taxonomy will itself be rendered obsolete by the recursive logic of noise. Simply said: Classificatory order does not sit well with the very nature of noise. This is why we advocate a reconsideration of the origins of noises and their epistemological usefulness, rather than insisting on an exhaustive classification that would be quickly outdated. A classification of noises is an oxymoron; a device programmed for its self-destruction.

In summary, we defend that those who take part in the complex rhizome of an archive participate in its evolving ecosystem: A complex body of relationships between human and non-human agents that escapes any attempt at total control. The task of the archivist is to negotiate between the fluidity of living agents and the apparent fixity of archival structures. Upcoming research on programming for archival science should approach the way in which machines deal with noise and complexity. Furthermore, the positive recognition and acceptance of unclassifiable noises in the archival ecosystem should play a significant role in determining those expectations and uncertainties that condition the evolution of the archive.

## Notes

* This chapter is the result of work by the consolidated research group "Gender Studies Research Group: Translation, Literature, History and Communication" (GETLIHC) (2017, SGR 136) of the University of Vic–Central University of Catalonia (UVic-UCC) (C. de la Laura, 13, 08500, Vic, Spain). Author's ORCID number: 0000-0001-9132-0138.

1. Claude E. Shannon, "A Mathematical Theory of Communication," *The Bell System Technical Journal* 27 (July–October 1948): 379–423, 623–56.
2. Diana Taylor, *Archive and the Repertoire: Performing Cultural Memory in the Americas.* (Durham, NC: Duke University, 2003), 19.
3. According to the Society of American Archivists, these non-useful files are usually known as "noncurrent records": "Noncurrent records are often stored out of the office of creation in a records center or on offline media. Either they may be destroyed when their frequency of use falls so low that they have lost all value or they may be transferred to an archival repository for permanent retention." See https://www2.archivists.org/glossary/terms/n/noncurrent-records. Accessed June 16, 2018.
4. Celia Ramírez López, "La archivística: un viejo oficio, una nueva profesión," in *Teoría y práctica arhivística I*, ed. Gustavo Villanueva Bazán (México: UNAM, 2000), 16.
5. Taylor, *Archive and the Repertoire,* 19.
6. Ibid.
7. Simone Osthoff, "Simone Osthoff. Interview," *Neural* 58 (Autumn 2017): 7.
8. Simone Osthoff, "Performing the Archive and Vilém Flusser," *Flusser Studies* 24 (2017): 2.
9. Ibid., 1.
10. Ibid., 7.
11. Jussi Parikka, *What Is Media Archaeology?* (Cambridge: Polity Press, 2012), 15.
12. Ibid.
13. Ibid.
14. See www.thefileroom.org/. Accessed June 20, 2018.
15. An explanation of the "First Actual Case of Bug Being Found," written by Grace Murray Hopper, can be found in the American History Museum's website: http://americanhistory.si.edu/collections/search/object/nmah_334663. Accessed June 20, 2018.
16. See an example of this in www.thefileroom.org/documents/dyn/DisplayCase.cfm/id/1589. Accessed July 6, 2019.
17. Hito Steyerl, *Duty Free Art. Art in the Age of Planetary Civil War* (London: Verso, 2017), 55.
18. Ibid., 44.
19. Fina Birulés, "Arxius temporals (I). Crisi contemporània i temps," Filmed April 2018 at La Virreina Centre de la Imatge, Barcelona, Video, 1:41:43, www.youtube.com/watch?v=rDh2r7c_-jE. Accessed June 21, 2018.
20. François Hartog, *Regimes of Historicity: Presentism and Experiences of Time* (New York: Columbia University, 2016).

21. Zygmunt Bauman, *Liquid Modernity* (Cambridge and Malden, MA: Polity Press, 2000), 131.
22. Ibid.
23. Jay Bolter and Richard Grusin, *Remediation: Understanding New Media* (Boston, MA: MIT, 2000), 5.
24. Our translation from "La historia es la ciencia de las trazas escritas. Desde la orilla del presente, el historiador ausente no es más que un ojo lector de los archivos." François Hartog, "El testigo y el historiador," *Estudios sociales* 21 (2nd Semester, 2001 [2000]): 23.
25. Jussi Parikka, "Archival Memory Theory: An Introduction to Wolfgang Ernst's Media Archaeology," in *Digital Memory and The Archive*, ed. Jussi Parikka (Minneapolis: University of Minnesota, 2013), 9.
26. Wolfgang Ernst, *Digital Memory and The Archive*, ed. Jussi Parikka (Minneapolis: University of Minnesota, 2013), 140.
27. Wolfgang Ernst, "Archive Rumblings: Interview with German Media Archaeologist Wolfgang Ernst," Interview by Geert Lovink, *nettime*, February 26, 2003, www.nettime.org/Lists-Archives/nettime-l-0302/msg00132.html. Accessed July 28, 2018.
28. Our translation from "«non-silence des organes» [. . .] «constitué par» ou du moins «porteur de» divers éléments discontinus, c'est-à-dire isolables les uns des autres par des critères certains." Michael Foucault, "Message ou bruit?" in *Dits et écrits 1954–1988, I (1954–1969)*, eds. Daniel Defert, François Ewald, and Jacques Lagrange (París: Gallimard, 1994), 558.
29. Julia Kristeva, *Powers of Horror: An Essay on Abjection* (New York: Columbia University, 1982), 4.
30. See Rodney G. S. Carter, "Of Things Said and Unsaid: Power, Archival Silences, and Power in Silence," *Archivaria. The Journal of the Association of Canadian Archivists* 61, (Spring 2006): 215–33. Carter expresses a critique of silence as a repressive phenomenon within archives by tracing back contemporary and feminist archival theory until Michel Foucault and Jacques Derrida.
31. Rosa Menkman, *The Glitch Moment(um)* (Amsterdam: Institute of Network Cultures, 2011), 65.
32. Ibid., 9.
33. Ibid., 28.
34. Ibid., 8.
35. Ibid., 11.
36. See www.anarchivosida.org/index_en.php. Accessed June 24, 2019.
37. See https://github.com/SekhmetDesign/phacks18-queeringmap1. Accessed June 24, 2019.
38. Mathew Rodriguez and Lucas LaRochelle, "Post-Cyberattack Queering the Map Argues That Anywhere Can Be a Queer Space," *Into* 3 (April 2018).
39. Yehoshua Bar-Hillel, "Some Reflections on the Present Outlook for High-Quality Machine Translation," *Feasibility Study on Fully Automatic High Quality Translation* (Austin: Linguistics Research Center of the University of Texas, 1971), 75–76.

## Bibliography


Bar-Hillel, Yehoshua. "Some Reflections on the Present Outlook for High-Quality Machine Translation." In *Feasibility Study on Fully Automatic High Quality Translation*, 73–76. Austin: Linguistics Research Center of the University of Texas, 1971.

Bauman, Zygmunt. *Liquid Modernity*. Cambridge and Malden, MA: Polity Press, 2000.

Birulés, Fina. *Arxius temporals (I). Crisi contemporània i temps*. Filmed April 26, 2018 at La Virreina Centre de la Imatge, Barcelona. Video, 1:41:43. Accessed June 21, 2018. www.youtube.com/watch?v=rDh2r7c_-jE.

Bolter, Jay, and Richard Grusin. *Remediation: Understanding New Media*. Boston, MA: MIT, 2000.

Carter, Rodney G. S. "Of Things Said and Unsaid: Power, Archival Silences, and Power in Silence." *Archivaria: The Journal of the Association of Canadian Archivists* 61 (Spring 2006): 215–33.

Ernst, Wolfgang. "Archive Rumblings: Interview with German Media Archaeologist Wolfgang Ernst." Interview by Geert Lovink. *nettime*, February 26, 2003. Accessed July 28, 2018. www.nettime.org/Lists-Archives/nettime-l-0302/msg00132.html.

———. *Digital Memory and The Archive*. Minneapolis: University of Minnesota, 2013.

Foucault, Michael. "Message ou bruit?" In *Dits et écrits 1954–1988, I (1954–1969)*, edited by Daniel Defert, François Ewald and Jacques Lagrange, 557–60. París: Gallimard, 1994.

Hartog, François. "El testigo y el historiador." *Estudios sociales* 21 (2nd Semester 2001): 11–30

———. *Regimes of Historicity: Presentism and Experiences of Time*. New York: Columbia University, 2016.

Kristeva, Julia. *Powers of Horror. An Essay on Abjection*. New York: Columbia University, 1982.

Menkman, Rosa. *The Glitch Moment(um)*. Amsterdam: Institute of Network Cultures, 2011.

Osthoff, Simone. "Performing the Archive and Vilém Flusser." *Flusser Studies* 24 (2017): 1–7.
———. "Simone Osthoff. Interview." *Neural* 58 (Autumn 2017): 7–9.
Parikka, Jussi. "Archival Memory Theory: An Introduction to Wolfgang Ernst's Media Archaeology." In *Digital Memory and The Archive*, edited by Jussi Parikka, 1–21. Minneapolis: University of Minnesota, 2013.
———. *What Is Media Archaeology?* Cambridge: Polity Press, 2012.
Ramírez López, Celia. "La archivística: un viejo oficio, una nueva profesión." In *Teoría y práctica arhivística I* edited by Gustavo Villanueva Bazán. México: UNAM, 2000.
Rodriguez, Mathew, and Lucas LaRochelle. "Post-Cyberattack Queering the Map Argues That Anywhere Can Be a Queer Space." *Into* 3 (April 2018). Accessed July 25, 2019. www.intomore.com/culture/postcyberattack-queering-the-map-argues-that-anywhere-can-be-a-queer-space.
Shannon, Claude. E. "A Mathematical Theory of Communication." *The Bell System Technical Journal* 27 (July–October 1948): 379–423, 623–56.
Steyerl, Hito. *Duty Free Art. Art in the Age of Planetary Civil War*. London: Verso, 2017.
Taylor, Diana. *Archive and the Repertoire: Performing Cultural Memory in the Americas*. Durham: Duke University, 2003.

# PART III

# Museums

## Real, Virtual, and Augmented

# 14

# DIGITAL IMAGING PROJECTS FOR ASIAN ART AND VISUAL CULTURE

## Transcultural Mediations and Collaborations

*Katherine R. Tsiang*

Art historians struggle to interpret works of art and visual culture the content of which has acquired multiple meanings rooted in religious concepts, political ideologies, and artistic imagination. Social, geographical, architectural, cultural, and technological factors, among others, impact on the reception of images both at the time of their creation and in later periods. In the last century, the visual imaging technology of photography was crucial for the development of art history and archaeology as fields of study and profoundly influenced approaches to research and teaching. Recent historiographic studies of the photographic records of ancient sites and monuments reveal the kinds of choices photographers made to construct their images and show how these images were shaped by individual and institutional preconceptions, research agendas, and other cultural and social biases.[1] The photographic records made of cultural sites has had a great impact on the preservation and, at times, the ruin of these sites, as well as on scholars' understanding of these sites and their significance in historical and modern contexts.

Similarly, recent digital technologies now widely used for recording, managing and displaying art are enhancing and reshaping historical disciplines. The ultimate effect of these developments remains to be determined, but it is already evident that computer-based tools enable researchers to create new methodologies and invent new perspectives. Such developments must be integrated with traditional scholarship so the knowledge they create can be shared more effectively than before. Digital methods for recording, curating, and displaying two and three-dimensional art and artifacts make possible major innovations in the use of such materials for teaching and research. For the past fourteen years the Center for the Art of East Asia in the Department of Art History, Division of Humanities, at the University of Chicago (henceforth CAEA) has been developing digital technologies for archiving and viewing collections of East Asian paintings and sculptures. It has undertaken two initiatives using different kinds of technology to gather information and create websites for displaying and sharing the results. In the process, the projects have resulted in innovative viewing software built on existing cyberinfrastructure that allows interactive access to works of art to simulate the viewing of actual objects. The websites and digital installations for exhibition reconstruct traditional viewing practices and restore broken sculptures and ruined sites in ways that static photos cannot. This chapter outlines the digital strategies that the CAEA has devised and implemented over these fourteen years to analyze and communicate research into traditional East Asian painting and sculpture. It introduces the digital imaging technologies and open-source software that we have used and developed for interactive viewing of paintings and sculptures that make them more fully and widely accessible than in the past. The digital images and metadata offer new perspectives on traditional art forms and works of art that are now removed from their former contexts and widely dispersed. They compile and reassemble fragmented materials in ways that offer new kinds of knowledge for further analytical study.

Established in 2003, the CAEA began with a mission to serve the growing interest in, and widespread teaching of, the arts of Asia, undertaking projects that extended beyond the classrooms and libraries of the university. The CAEA collaborates with institutions around the world to organize conferences and research projects. Its digital painting and sculpture imaging projects were designed to address the challenges facing academic teaching and research given the difficulty of viewing artworks in museums or remote sites around the world. Books and slide libraries provide limited photographic images of art works, and museum collections are widely scattered and not readily accessible for study. The CAEA's digital imaging projects offer effective visual access to works of East Asian art, providing accurate information and interactive capabilities so as to facilitate insights into their material, spatial, and visual characteristics in historical contexts.[2]

## The Scroll Paintings Project

One of the major formats for traditional East Asian painting is the handscroll, or horizontal scroll, first produced more than fifteen hundred years ago. Paintings in this format are generally much greater in width than in height, so they are difficult to publish as photographs in printed media. One must choose sections in order to show these works in PowerPoint presentations, or even to display them in museums. Handscrolls entail temporal and participatory aspects of viewing that cannot be readily experienced today. The historical scrolls are seldom exhibited because of their fragile nature when unrolled and their sensitivity to light exposure. In recent times, art history students and specialists study them primarily through fragmentary photographic images that do not show the scrolls in their entirety. Although the internet now enables greater accessibility to images of many important works of art, most sites still show only sections of painted scrolls. The East Asian Scroll Paintings website (https://scrolls.uchicago.edu) provides viewers with a much better understanding of the horizontal scrolling format and gives scholars fuller access to the contents of the paintings, including both their images and texts.[3]

To create handscroll paintings, artists painted with Chinese ink and water-based pigments on long strips of silk or sheets of paper that could be joined together and extended to any desired length. When completed, the painted sections were mounted on long horizontal sheets of paper as backing and reinforced with silk borders. Blank sheets of paper at the end, or left edge, of the scroll, lengthen the scroll and attach it to a wooden roller. The beginning, the right edge of the scroll, typically has a silk cover and silk cord attached for rolling and tying the painting for storage. Because the paintings were not on constant display, but were brought out for occasional viewing, many of these relatively fragile works have been preserved over the centuries.

Traditional viewing of a handscroll painting was an interactive experience that could be purely personal or shared with friends and family members, as depicted in historic paintings. A painting required careful handling, placing the scroll on a flat surface for viewing section by section. Viewing would begin at the far right side by unrolling toward the left while rolling up the right side in order to move on to the next section. In this way the viewer usually would see only a section about shoulder-width at any time. This kind of viewing provides a sense of spatial and temporal movement through painted scenes of landscape or narrative or figural subjects, and allows close examination of details. A host could invite a few friends, frequently members of a community of educated connoisseurs and collectors, to view a painting and to write their comments, poems, and signatures, or to stamp their seals on the extra lengths of paper attached to the end of the painting. The added materials became a meaningful part of the scroll, a work of art that included a historical record of the collectors and those who had seen it.

Viewing scroll paintings on the East Asian Scroll Painting website (https://scrolls.uchicago.edu) imparts a sense of the traditional viewing experience. For each scroll displayed, the project has acquired high-resolution photographic images of the paintings from museums along with an agreement that permits the project to use them. Once acquired, the images are processed for interactive viewing. Though initially we scanned images from books and reproduction scrolls for classroom teaching, we transitioned to using original photographs so that the site could be more widely accessed. Overlapping photographs of the entire scroll that are digitally "stitched" together produce a single, long horizontal image. This image file image is converted with special software to produce a "zoomable" tile image format, currently the DZI (deep zoom image) format.[4] The HandscrollViewer is a custom extension of OpenSeadragon developed by Charles Crable and is located at https://github/charlescrable/HandscrollViewer-OpenSeadragon-Extension. This viewer software allows detailed and effective interactive viewing of the scroll painting, but at the same time is secure in that the full image of the painting cannot be downloaded for reuse.

The website's viewing window displays a portion of the current scroll at different zoom levels chosen by the viewer. Any part of the painting can be viewed in greater or lesser detail by zooming—using a number of interface features including mouse double click, button clicks, or scroll wheel manipulation. Additional functions allow the website user to pan or navigate back and forth through the painting—dragging the cursor on the image, clicking on a new portion of the painting, pressing on any arrow keys, etc. Furthermore, a navigation control that moves a rectangular window on a thumbnail image of the current painting allows the user to reposition the scroll image in the main viewing window. Full screen viewing can be toggled on and off.

Custom viewing features include an initial, home image position at the right edge of the scroll, mimicking the traditional scroll viewing method. Implementing toggle buttons causes the painting to scroll continuously slowly to the left or right, which is useful in a teaching environment. Two scroll paintings can be displayed in independent viewing windows, one above the other, for comparison purposes. Finally, optional annotations can be included that highlight particular areas of narrative or thematic interest, or that draw attention to an artist's signature or seals. Clicking an annotation opens a small text window containing a comment, translation, or historical information. Additionally, the website features intuitive search capability based on metadata fields specific to East Asian scroll paintings, including title, artist, museum or repository, culture, dynasty/period, or theme/subject. The search interface relies on carefully edited data entered for each work of art.

The website's interactive high-resolution presentation of an artist's brushwork and application of colors, calligraphy, viewer's comments, and stamped seals, rivals the information obtainable by seeing the actual work of art and allows for repeated viewing, comparative study, and further analysis. Details of the materials used in the painting or the mounting also provide important historical information. The information made visible, as well as the metadata display, have the potential to stimulate new approaches and insights into traditional questions of authorship, authenticity, or the development of artistic styles, and facilitate the sharing of research. The ease of panning, close looking, and ability to compare one scroll or section of a scroll to another provides perspectives on the paintings as multimedia constructions created over time. Though the actual paintings cannot be handled, their viewing on the website offers an awareness of their materiality that becomes an integral part of the viewing experience.

Because of the time-consuming and difficult nature of acquiring photographs, processing and researching them, as well as negotiating permissions for use from museums, the CAEA is working on a new initiative to invite other institutions to collaborate by creating their own websites that could display the handscroll paintings in their collections with technology similar to that already developed. The software and defined protocols for the organization of materials comprise a working model that can serve as a prototype for others. In addition to its use for teaching East Asian painting history and historiography, the software also has the potential for application to other kinds of art and media, such as scrolling texts, ornamental friezes, mural paintings, and other horizontal formats.

## The Chinese Buddhist Caves Temple Projects and 3D Imaging

The CAEA conceived of the Chinese Buddhist Caves Project to promote further understanding of the art and visual culture of medieval Chinese Buddhist cave temple sites—complexes of caves carved into mountainsides or rocky riverbanks as religious shrines—many of which are currently in severely damaged condition. Their important historical contents include sculptural images of Buddhist divinities as well as engraved dedicatory inscriptions and Buddhist scriptural texts. Widely distributed in China, the cave sites are part of a broader cultural landscape of Buddhist cave shrines whose production began in India and extended across Central Asia into China. The creation of Buddhist caves in China began in the fourth century and peaked in the fifth through ninth centuries. Many continued to serve as religious centers for monastic communities and lay worshippers up to the twentieth century. Buddhist sites suffered serious damage in the early part of the twentieth century after they drew the attention of art collectors outside of China. Scholars first took interest in the historical, religious, and fine sculptural contents of caves and published them. Edouard Chavannes' groundbreaking study, *Mission archéologique dans la Chine septentrionale*, published in Paris in 1909, was among the first to focus on the engraved inscriptions at the Buddhist cave complex of Longmen and to include photographs of the sculptures in the caves.[5] These photographs attracted the attention of art dealers and collectors and led to the widespread defacement of many carved sculptures at Longmen and other Buddhist cave sites. Art collectors in China traditionally did not consider the stone images of divinities in Buddhist caves to be collectible works of art, though many were of high artistic quality. However, Western collectors had been interested in ancient European stone carvings for centuries, and Japanese buyers associated the sculptures with their own Buddhist artistic traditions. The colonial presence of Europeans and the political upheavals of the late nineteenth and early twentieth centuries in China led to the export and sale of enormous quantities of Chinese cultural properties abroad.[6]

The CAEA conducted research projects on sculptures originating in two cave complexes in northern China, Xiangtangshan in Hebei province (https://xts.uchicago.edu)[7] and Tianlongshan in Shanxi province (https://tls.uchicago.edu).[8] In 2004 the CAEA, in collaboration with Humanities Computing at the University of Chicago, began research on these cave shrines, undertaking, in addition, the digital imaging of the many sculptures now located in collections around the world. The components and goals of the Cave Projects include (1) research on the history of the caves—historical records, inscriptions, and modern evidence of the removal of the sculptures; (2) locating the sculptures that are now widely scattered in museum collections around the world and identifying them with their former cave locations; (3) traveling to museums to record the sculptures using high resolution digital photography and 3D scanning;

(4) photographing and scanning the caves themselves; and (5) presenting the resulting data in bilingual websites, exhibitions, and digital restorations of the caves.

Previous historical studies conducted on the caves assembled much of the scant documentation remaining in traditional sources along with the existing inscriptional evidence used for dating the cave sites. Recent archeological examination of the sites, together with published reports in China, has provided additional information on the sites, their contents, and the condition of the caves. Accurately dating the caves and their sculptures and associating the sculptures now outside China with individual caves is the primary aim of the Caves Projects.

The Xiangtangshan caves are mainly the product of artists of the Northern Qi dynasty (550–577) created at two principal sites in the vicinity of the Northern Qi capital. The earlier and larger caves of the Northern Xiangtangshan site, associated with the patronage of the Northern Qi ruling house, are situated on the side of a mountain one hundred meters above a broad valley. They are of bold design with sculptures of monumental scale that are impressive in spite of their damaged state. Even the smallest of the three main caves at this site once displayed larger-than-life-sized carved figures around three walls of a square chamber as well as engraved texts of Buddhist scriptures. The sculptures were carved from dense limestone, with finely finished surfaces. Xiangtangshan sculptures began to appear on the art market around 1914. The earliest published photographs of Xiangtangshan show the caves already damaged, with rather clumsy attempts to repair them. Local artisans carved new figures from stone or shaped them from clay, and they fitted new heads on the bodies of headless statues so that worshippers could continue their observances at the site.[9]

The Tianlongshan cave complex, situated in the mountains west of the city of Taiyuan, includes more than twenty caves carved from rather soft coarse sandstone from the sixth to eighth centuries (including the Eastern Wei, Northern Qi, Sui, and Tang dynasties). The caves are mostly modest in scale with the exception of one very large-scale group of colossal sculptures carved on a cliff face during the eighth century. The sponsorship and dating of the caves is uncertain, as little documentation remains. One partially preserved inscription carved outside Cave 8 from the year 584 in the Sui, provides dated material for comparison with other caves at Tianlongshan. Later sculptures, widely believed to be from the eighth century in the Tang dynasty, are distinctive in having sensuously modeled contours and relaxed standing and seated poses, as seen in Cave 18. Early photographs taken in the 1920s drew robbers to the site, resulting in the removal of many of the sculptures (Figures 14.1 and 14.2).

The CAEA participated in producing a report of a group of caves at Xiangtangshan in collaboration with Chinese experts and with the office in charge of preservation and management of the caves. Published in 2013, the report includes findings concerning the sculptures now outside China, identifying their original locations, together with a report on the scanned 3D imaging of the caves and sculptures.[10] In the case of Tianlongshan, historical photographs taken around 1920, though incomplete, show many of the sculptures largely intact in the caves and serve as valuable evidence of the former contents and layout of the caves.[11] Previous scholarly work referring to the early photographs of the caves and comparing them with photographs of sculptures in museums and private collections outside China had identified the location of many of the sculptures in the caves.[12] Our research on the records from scholars' visits, art gallery and auction sale catalogues, and museum acquisitions has further documented the recent history of the sculptures and their circulation in the art market from the 1920s to the present day.

The collection of information on sculptures from both the Xiangtangshan and Tianlongshan sites that found their way into many museum and private collections around the world has relied on museum visits, previous scholarly work, and, most recently, museum websites. In some museums the original sculptures are prominently displayed in the galleries. In other locations, they are

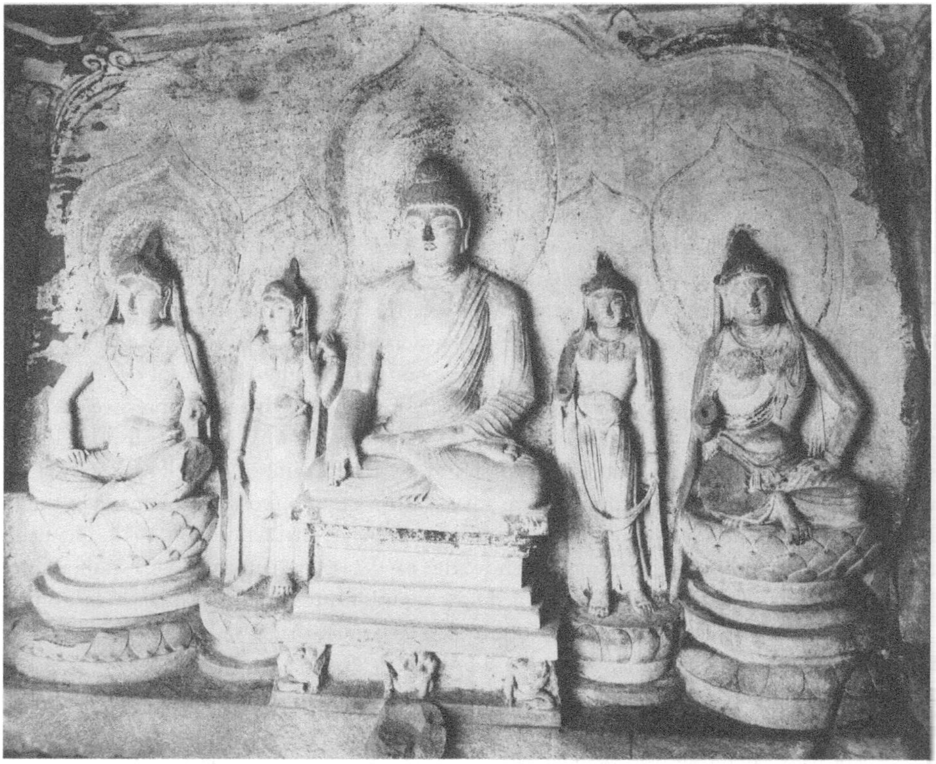

*Figure 14.1* Historical photograph of Tianlongshan Cave 18, north wall.
*Source:* Tomura, 1922, pl. 75.

hidden away in storage and have seldom, if ever, been exhibited. As a consequence of our efforts to identify and record these sculptures, some have been brought out from storage while others are now exhibited with more complete information.

A small team based at the CAEA traveled to numerous museums in Europe, North America, and Japan to photograph and 3D scan the sculptures from the cave sites. The team recorded the Xiangtangshan sculptures from 2005–2008 and the Tianlongshan sculptures from 2014–2017 with high-resolution color photographs and 3D scans of each sculpture. In both projects, we were able to collect the digital data for most of the known sculptures.[13] The final sculpture photos were cropped to a standard aspect ratio with a black background. The team performed 3D scanning using the best and most practical technology available at the time. The resulting 3D models from both cave projects are dimensionally accurate, multi-million triangle meshes with sub-millimeter resolution. The earlier scanning of the Xiangtangshan sculptures used a rather unwieldy Konica-Minolta laser scanner and processed the raw data using RapidForm software. The Konica scanner did not include photography for mapping sculpture color onto the surface of the models. The Tianlongshan sculptures were scanned using much more convenient portable handheld Artec Spider and Eva scanning devices with post-processing using Artec Studio software. The Artec technology used with the Tianlongshan sculptures also included automatic photo capture for application of full color textures with the 3D model geometry. The color photographs, in addition to serving as an archival record, were valuable for correcting the textures

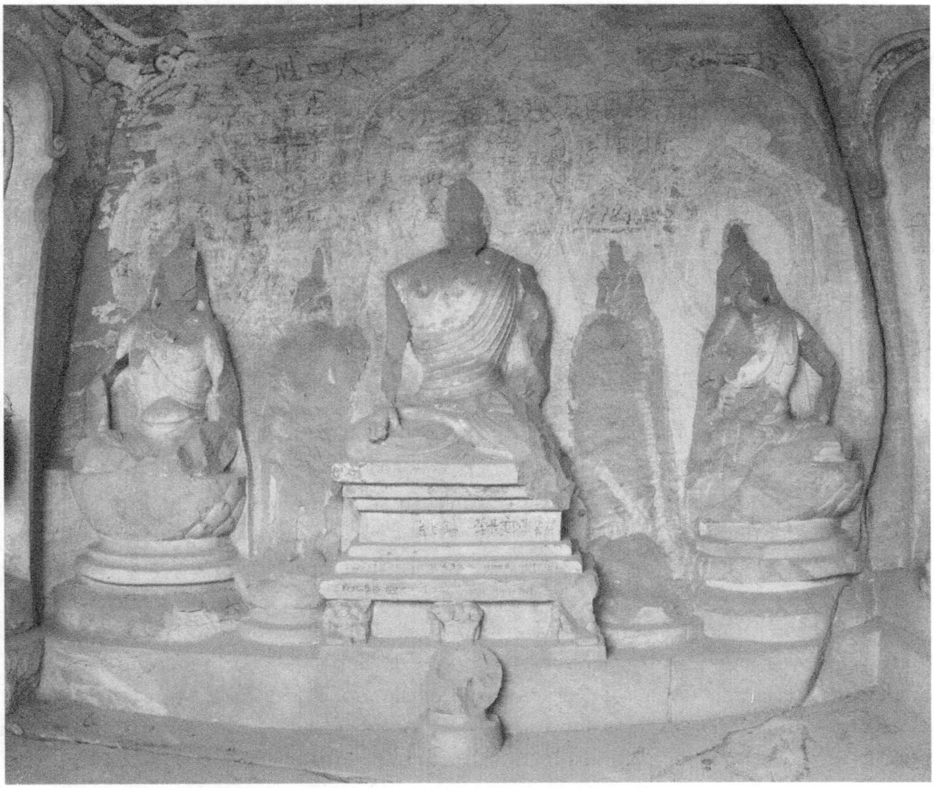

*Figure 14.2* Recent photograph of Tianlongshan Cave 18, north wall.

*Source*: Photo courtesy of Li Yuqun.

applied to the 3D models of the Tianlongshan sculptures. The final 3D models of both cave projects are stored in either the standard PLY or OBJ file format.

The digital photographs and 3D models of more than eighty Xiangtangshan sculptures are particularly revealing as there was no photographic record of the Xiangtangshan caves before removal of the sculptures. High-resolution imaging assisted in identifying sculptures from specific caves and matching them with traces remaining at their former locations in the caves. Some types of figures—Buddhas, bodhisattvas, disciples, and other attendant divinities—in a single cave often exhibit shared features, such as details of modeling, poses, garments, hands, and facial features. At the same time, variations can also appear from one part of a cave to another, as well as between different caves. Viewing the images and 3D models of these widely scattered artworks shows clearly the distinctive characteristics of different types of statuary and styles of carving for comparative study. These features can be associated with historical workmanship, patronage, and different groups of crafts persons that decorated the caves over time.

Viewing the Tianlongshan Caves Project imaging material for more than one hundred sculptures taken from the site has also facilitated better understanding of the distinctive styles of carvings in the different caves. Compiling this data also enabled us to reconstruct broken sculptures, including those whose heads and bodies had been separated because of their removal from the caves at different times.

The CAEA photographed the cave sites and worked together with institutions in China that conducted 3D scanning of selected caves. The 3D information from the caves places numerous scanned sculptures back into their former locations in the caves with greater accuracy than would have been possible with photographic evidence alone. In China numerous organizations are now conducting 3D scanning of Buddhist cave sites and other cultural and historical materials. We are looking into future possibilities for further collaborative efforts.

Presenting the results of the research and digital imaging data makes possible the creation of websites, exhibitions, and digital restorations of the caves. We developed bilingual (English and Chinese) websites for both the Xiangtangshan and Tianlongshan Caves Projects to show the images of caves and to provide interactive displays of sculptures through both high-resolution 2D images and 3D models. The design of the website interface allows the visitor to navigate and access the information via a list of categories or according to the current location of sculptures. Viewers who opt to search by category can choose from sculptural figure type, specific cave, dynastic period or date. See project websites at https://xts.uchicago.edu and https://tls.uchicago.edu.

Viewing high-resolution 3D models is possible on any computer with appropriate software that is now widely available, but it is not readily shared on a website. Our interactive 3D sculpture model viewer employs a unique software library developed by Charles Crable to display 3D models remotely across the internet. Using this unique software provides a safe and effective interface. During model manipulation, the software renders a low-resolution data set using the browser's WebGL functionality (see www.khronos.org/webgl/). When model manipulation is not taking place, a high-resolution 2D rendering of the model is displayed from the server side. The high-resolution 3D model is not downloaded to the viewer's device, ensuring the security of the model. Model manipulation functions include rotation, zooming in and out, panning, and changing the light position. This high-resolution 3D sculpture model viewing software has potential for uses in many fields of study that require publishing high-resolution single object 3D models.

The bilingual websites were designed to reach the widest possible audience. Analytics show that, in the past year, 50% of the viewers of the Tianlongshan Caves Project site were in the United States, 25% were in China, and 8% in Japan. Viewers in South Korea, the United Kingdom, and Canada totaled 16%.[14]

Another important result of the Caves Projects was the creation of exhibitions to display the sculptures and caves in gallery spaces and to reconstruct their former appearance. The exhibition resulting from the Xiangtangshan Caves Project organized by the University of Chicago Smart Museum of Art together with the Arthur M. Sackler Gallery, Smithsonian Institution was entitled "Echoes of the Past: the Buddhist Cave Temples of Xiangtangshan." This show opened at the Smart Museum of Art and traveled to four other museums from 2010–2013. The exhibition included a selection of stone sculptures from the caves together with digital installations. Interactive computer stations provided information about the types of sculpted figures and their former arrangements in the caves.[15] A rendering of a 3D digital cave reconstruction was a major feature of the exhibition. A video recording of the cave reconstruction installation is viewable at https://xts.uchicago.edu/content/exhibitions.

The Tianlongshan project resulted in an exhibition created for the OCAT Institute in Beijing that was on display from September through December, 2017. "The Buddhist Cave Temples and Sculptures of Tianlongshan—Historical Photographs and New Imaging Technology" opened as half of a larger collaborative exhibition at the OCAT Institute, Beijing.[16] Like the Tianlongshan Caves Project website, the CAEA-designed exhibition of the Tianlongshan caves featured historic photographs of the caves together with new digital imaging technology. This exhibition did not include any actual sculptures. The CAEA's specially designed digital installations for the exhibition included compilations of data from selected caves, 3D models and restorations of broken sculptures, and historical timelines, along with displays to show the global distribution of the sculptures. Special displays explained the technology underlying the 3D models. In addition, the exhibition featured installations created by the Institute of Art at the Taiyuan University of Technology, that scanned the cave site in its current condition. One installation combined a 3D cave model with 3D models of sculptures outside China to reconstruct the former appearance of the cave. Another featured a VR experience of the cave interior. Unlike the Xiangtangshan exhibition that was shown in multiple venues in the United States, the Tianlongshan exhibition appeared only at one location in China. The latter, predominantly digital exhibition, however, can travel with relative ease to other sites.

## Future Goals

The Center for the Art of East Asia has developed the means to display art-historical information on the internet in unprecedented ways and has created the foundational websites to facilitate viewing high-resolution imagery for an international audience. As we continue our efforts, we are eager to enable other institutions to build on our existing technologies and to develop their own archives of images and models to be made publicly accessible. We are developing other projects in which we can act as a coordinating center for facilitating imaging and data compilation projects that work with technology specialists, museums, and other institutions around the world.[17]

In the bigger picture, we foresee the creation of a dispersed network of sites that offer vivid and realistic interactive engagement with scroll painting, sculpture, and cave temples and various other kinds of works of art. The network of users can assist with software development and support, based on their own particular needs, and can individually customize the viewing interface in their own archive sites. Through interaction between diverse institutions and the integration of computer technology into humanities scholarship, new possibilities can emerge for the understanding of art production throughout human history.

To implement this vision, we are developing publicly available software libraries and high-level APIs to make handscroll painting images and 3D sculpture models effectively viewable in websites of universities, museums, and other institutions. Also, we will work with outside collaborators on continuing to develop software for local, real-time interactive display of 3D sculpture models in an exhibition environment. The new initiative will extend the CAEA's current in-house technologies for viewing scrolling images and 3D models of sculptures remotely across the internet. With these viewer interfaces, archived scrolls and sculptures can become more widely accessible than our limited resources and manpower can facilitate. We are releasing code for this unique software with accompanying documentation to ensure that users can successfully implement the systems on their own. Furthermore, we will develop and support open project infrastructures for the technologies. The aforementioned open projects should allow outside developers and users to participate in the continuing design and support of the technologies in order to create, augment, and maintain web-based high-resolution images and 3D model archives with content that can be successfully shared.

The principal open project technologies will allow (1) secure and effective viewing of high-resolution images of East Asian handscrolls and other wide horizontal images within a website application; (2) secure and effective viewing of very high-resolution 3D models of sculptures within a website application; and (3) interactive display of very high-resolution sculpture 3D models in an exhibition environment.[18]

## Conclusions

The release of this technology to interested outside users benefits our Center as well as other institutions that will be able to share their research materials. Implementing good open-source technology has the potential to save expenditure of time and funds for purchasing software or building a system from scratch, as well as extensive traveling. Additionally, we have designed these as tools specifically for use by humanists and museum professionals. Through research and experience, we understand the advantages of small group-based projects and explicitly designed systems as opposed to trying to use software designed by computer specialists who have little understanding of the users' special professional interests, expertise, and needs. While we would like to believe that we have produced prototypes for other similar projects, the evidence gathered in each of these projects is unique and has unique original contexts. The display of the results in digital databases is dependent on the kinds of images and information to be accessed. To promote the sharing of information and technologies with colleagues at other institutions the CAEA recently hosted a workshop at the University of Chicago that invited participants working on digital imaging projects to discuss techniques and approaches to enable greater connectivity among our various experts, resources, and results.[19]

The analysis of art—form, space, materials, color, style, historical dating, authenticity, and so on—can all be enhanced through digital quantification and display. By expanding our current efforts, and by encouraging sharing digital technology with others engaged in related work at other institutions, we hope to increase access to art-historical resources that can more fully harness the potential of the internet for teaching and research, allowing scholars, students, and enthusiasts around the world to engage with East Asian art to develop new kinds of knowledge and a deeper understanding of their cultural and historical contexts.

## Notes

1. Jas Elsner, "The Excavated Object: Time, Change and Archaeology in the History of Art," and Sally Crawford and Katharina Ulmschneider, "Archeologists, Early Photography, and the Search for Time," in *Sites and Images: Two Research Projects of Oxford University and the University of Chicago*, eds. Wu Hung and Guo Weiqi (Beijing: OCAT Institute, 2017), 46–67.
2. The current chapter has benefited from recent extensive studies of digital humanities theories and practices. These include *Our Cultural Commonwealth: The Report of the American Council of Learned Societies Commission on Cyberinfrastructure for the Humanities and Social Sciences* (Washington, DC: American Council of Learned Societies, 2006); Anne Burdick et al., *Digital Humanities* (Cambridge, MA and London, UK: The MIT Press, 2012); David M. Berry and Anders Fagerjord, *Digital Humanities: Knowledge and Critique in a Digital Age* (Cambridge, UK and Malden, MA: Polity Press, 2017); Agiatis Benardou et al., eds., *Cultural Heritage Infrastructures in Digital Humanities* (London and New York: Routledge, 2018).
3. The acquisition of images of the scrolls initially began with scanning from books and reproductions to create a website that offered an interactive experience for students for Wu Hung's Chinese art history classes. Because many publications do not show handscroll paintings in their entirety, the Center began approaching museums to request photographs specifically for the purpose of viewing on our website. Acquisition of museum photographs for the scrolls website began 2006 with support from the University of Chicago Provost Office, followed by the George Walsh Award, a grant from the Blakemore Foundation in 2008, from Women's Board of the University of Chicago in 2010.
4. Image tiling refers to the loading of image pixels only when a tile section comes into view through panning. The East Asian Scroll Painting website uses a custom extension of the open-source OpenSeadragon javascript viewer library (see https://openseadragon.github.io).
5. Edouard Chavannes, *Mission archéologique dans la Chine septentrionale* [*Archaeological Mission to Northern China*] (Paris: Imprimerie nationale, 1909).
6. Recent studies of this phenomenon include James L. Hevia, "Plunder, Markets, and Museums: The Biographies of Chinese Imperial Objects in Europe and North America," in Jan Mrázek and Morgan Pitelka,

eds., *What's the Use of Art? Asian Visual and Material Culture in Context* (Honolulu: University of Hawai'i Press, 2008), 129–41; Karl E. Meyer and Shareen Blair Brysac, *The China Collectors: America's Century-Long Hunt for Asian Art Treasures* (New York: Palgrave Macmillan, 2015); Michael St. Clair, *The Great Chinese Art Transfer: How So Much of China's Art Came to America* (Madison, NJ: Fairleigh Dickinson Press, 2016).

7. The Xiangtangshan Caves Project was carried out with the support of generous grants from the E. Rhodes and Leona Carpenter Foundation, the J. Paul Getty Trust, and Leon Levy Foundation.
8. The Tianlongshan Caves Project received the support of the Bei Shan Tang Foundation, the Luce Foundation, the Acorn Foundation, the Tang Research Foundation, and private donors.
9. Mizuno Seiichi and Nagahiro Toshiō, *Kyōdōsan sekkutsu* [The Buddhist Cave-Temples of Hsiang-t'ang-ssu on the Frontier of Honan and Hopei] (Kyoto: Tōhō bunka gakuin Kyoto kenkyujo, 1937). Several free-standing sculptures from the caves, published in the *Burlington Magazine* in 1914, are among the first taken from the caves. "Early Chinese Sculpture," *The Burlington Magazine* 25 (1914): 40.
10. Fengfeng Mining District Office of Protection and Management of Cultural Relics, and Center for the Art of East Asia University of Chicago. *The Cave of the Engraved Scriptures at Northern Xiangtangshan: Caves 1, 2, and 3 in the Southern Sector* (Beijing: Wenwu Publishing House, 2013).
11. Tomura Tajirō, *Tenryūzan sekkutsu* (Tokyo: Kaneo Bun'endō, 1922).
12. Harrie A. Vanderstappen and Marylin Rhie, "The Sculpture of T'ien-lung-shan: Reconstruction and Dating," *Artibus Asiae* 27, no. 64–65 (1966): 189–220; Li Yuqun and Li Gang, *Tianlongshan shiku* [The Tianlongshan Caves] (Beijing: Kexue chubanshe, 2003).
13. Though successfully acquiring full information on most known sculptures from these sites, conducting digital photographs and 3D scans has not been universally feasible. Many known sculptures that are in private collections are inaccessible, and the situation of other previously published examples is now unknown.
14. Google Analytics, "XTS Caves Project (UA-399913-27)," Property of the Google Analytics account 'UofC Humanities (UA-399913),' accessed July 13, 2018, http://analytics.google.com/analytics/web/. This is not accessible to the general public.
15. See the exhibition catalog. Katherine Tsiang et al., *Echoes of the Past: The Buddhist Cave Temples of Xiangtangshan* (Chicago: Smart Museum of Art, University of Chicago, 2010). For the 3D rendering of the cave we worked with Tianyuan 3D corporation in Beijing to scan the cave and create the 3D model of the cave in its current condition. Together with historical photographs and 3D models of the missing sculptures, the artist Jason Salavon rendered the cave model into a large digital installation nearly the size of the actual cave for the exhibition.
16. The show was accompanied by the aforementioned catalog. Hung and Weiqi, *Sites and Images*. (See note 1.)
17. The CAEA hosted a workshop at the University of Chicago on October 26–27, 2018, entitled "Digital Asian Art History." For more information, see the website at https://voices.uchicago.edu/caeatest/.
18. I am very grateful to Charles Crable for his input and advice on technical details in writing this chapter, for his work on these projects and creation of the resulting websites that would not have been possible without his singular programming skills and his commitment.
19. The "Digital Asian Art History Workshop" organized by the CAEA was held in the Department of Art History at the University of Chicago on October 26–27, 2018. It included museum curators, and technical experts, scholars and students who work with digital imaging of Asian works of art. https://voices.uchicago.edu/caeatest/2018/09/17/digital-asian-art-workshop-october-26-27-announcement/.

## Bibliography

Benardou, Agiatis, Erik Champion, Costis Dallas, and Lorna M. Hughes, eds. *Cultural Heritage Infrastructures in Digital Humanities*. London and New York: Routledge, 2018.

Berry, David M., and Anders Fagerjord. *Digital Humanities: Knowledge and Critique in a Digital Age*. Cambridge, UK and Malden, MA: Polity Press, 2017.

Burdick, Anne, Johanna Drucker, Peter Lunenfeld, Todd Presner, and Jeffrey Shnapp. *Digital Humanities*. Cambridge, MA and London, UK: The MIT Press, 2012.

Edouard Chavannes. *Mission archéologique dans la Chine septentrionale* (*Archaeological Mission to Northern China*). Paris: Imprimerie nationale, 1909.

Fengfeng Mining District Office of Protection and Management of Cultural Relics, and Center for the Art of East Asia University of Chicago. *The Cave of the Engraved Scriptures at Northern Xiangtangshan: Caves 1, 2, and 3 in the Southern Sector*. Beijing: Wenwu Publishing House, 2013.

Hevia, James L. "Plunder, Markets, and Museums: The Biographies of Chinese Imperial Objects in Europe and North America." In *What's the Use of Art? Asian Visual and Material Culture in Context*, edited by Jan Mrázek and Morgan Pitelka. Honolulu: University of Hawai'i Press, 2008.

Li Yuqun, and Li Gang. *Tianlongshan shiku [The Tianlongshan Caves]*. Beijing: Kexue chubanshe, 2003.

Meyer, Karl E., and Shareen Blair Brysac. *The China Collectors: America's Century-long Hunt for Asian Art Treasures*. New York: Palgrave Macmillan, 2015.

Mizuno Seiichi, and Nagahiro Toshiō. *Kyōdōsan sekkutsu* [The Buddhist Cave-Temples of Hsiang-t'ang-ssu on the Frontier of Honan and Hopei]. Kyoto: Tōhō bunka gakuin Kyoto kenkyujo, 1937.

*Our Cultural Commonwealth: The Report of the American Council of Learned Societies Commission on Cyberinfrastruture for the Humanities and Social Sciences*. Washington, DC: American Council of Learned Societies, 2006.

St. Clair, Michael. *The Great Chinese Art Transfer: How So Much of China's Art Came to America*. Madison: Fairleigh Dickinson Press, 2016.

Tsiang, Katherine et al. *Echoes of the Past: The Buddhist Cave Temples of Xiangtangshan*. Chicago: Smart Museum of Art, University of Chicago, 2010.

Vanderstappen, Harrie A., and Marylin Rhie. "The Sculpture of T'ien-lung-shan: Reconstruction and Dating." *Artibus Asiae* 27, no. 64–65 (1966): 189–220.

Wu Hung and Guo Weiqi, eds. *Sites and Images: Two Research Projects of Oxford University and the University of Chicago*. Beijing: OCAT Institute, 2017.

# 15

# A FIELD GUIDE TO DIGITAL SURROGATES

## Evaluating and Contextualizing a Rapidly Changing Resource

*Emma Stanford*

Between 1844 and 1846, William Henry Fox Talbot, the British inventor of calotype photography, published *The Pencil of Nature*, a series of fascicles of photographs intended to showcase "application[s] of the photographic art."[1] Viewed now, with almost two hundred years of hindsight, this series constitutes a bold statement on what Talbot perceived to be the role of his brand new invention. Among the wide range of objects photographed, from Oxford buildings to scraps of lace, are two of particular interest to the digital humanist: a sketch of a Francisco Mola painting and a marble bust of Patroclus. Beside the photograph of the Mola sketch, Talbot wrote that "Fac-similes can be made from original sketches of the old masters, and thus they may be preserved from loss, and multiplied to any extent."[2] Beside the photograph of the bust, he noted that the many possible angles and lighting conditions demonstrated "how very great a number of different effects may be obtained from a single specimen of sculpture."[3] He hit upon, in other words, the great strengths and weaknesses of photographic reproductions of art: their reliability, their detail, and their inherent subjectivity. While our standards for photographic reproductions have changed since Talbot's day—we would not be satisfied with a photograph of a sketch of a painting—those central themes have not.

The importance of early photography in the art world was immediate. Of the three cameras pictured in the 1846 photo of Talbot and Nicolaas Henneman's outdoor studio, two are pointed at works of art (Figure 15.1). In 1848, Sir William Stirling Maxwell published the world's first photographic art book, *The Annals of the Artists of Spain*, featuring paintings by Goya, Velasquez, and others. Stirling is credited with popularizing Spanish art in Britain, although in fact, every subject in his book was itself a reproduction: most commonly an engraving, but occasionally a watercolor or oil copy if a print could not be found or commissioned.[4] Art photography began in earnest in 1856, when the Victoria and Albert Museum in London established its own photography studio, producing more than ten thousand photonegatives of collection items at the V&A and elsewhere.[5]

Today, it is difficult to imagine researching art without using facsimiles. While printed art books are still important—particularly as introductions or surveys—the giant of art reproduction is now the digital facsimile or digital surrogate. It is increasingly common for cultural heritage institutions to make large numbers of images available online, more than could ever be displayed in a museum at one time: 30,000 at the Getty Museum,[6] 375,000 at the Metropolitan Museum of Art,[7] 637,000 at the Rijksmuseum,[8] a million at the British Museum.[9] While it is

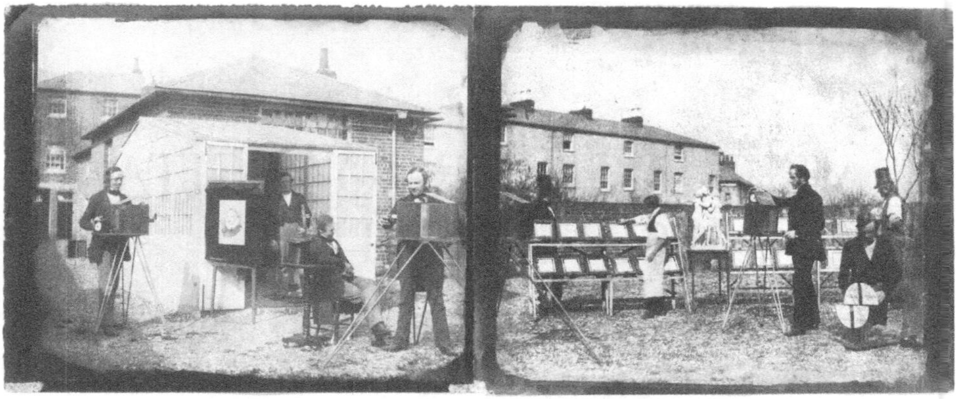

*Figure 15.1* The "Reading Establishment" of William Henry Fox Talbot and Nicolaas Henneman, where the prints for *The Pencil of Nature* were produced.

*Source:* The Metropolitan Museum of Art, New York (public domain).

difficult to estimate the number of institutionally held art reproductions online, it is certainly in the tens of millions, if not the hundreds of millions, and the number is growing. A recent survey of 214 museum staff by Nik Honeysett of the Balboa Park Online Collaborative found that while the percentage of museum collections available online is still low (half of respondents had digitized less than 10% of their collections), more than 60% of respondents planned to digitize their entire collections in the long term.[10]

So what exactly are these initiatives creating? What is a digital surrogate of an art object? There is a long-standing tendency to misunderstand art facsimiles—to view them either as a perfect substitute or as a threat to the original's authenticity. In the early 1800s, in the heyday of fine art engraving, print collectors imagined that the items in their collections might eventually replace their deteriorating originals.[11] In 1935, Walter Benjamin worried that the ubiquity of art photography detracted from the "aura" of the originals, with the implication that the photographic reproductions of the time were accurate enough to devalue the experience of seeing an artwork in person.[12] In 1995, at the dawn of digital photography, Douglas Davis claimed that all "handmade images or words that [could] be scanned" could now be "endlessly reproduced without degradation, always the same, always perfect."[13] Recent thinking about digital facsimiles has been more cautious, casting them as related but distinct entities that hold their own expressive power and occupy their own place in the world of scholarship.[14] Shoji Yamada explicitly links digital surrogates to their printed and handmade predecessors, likening digital art reproductions to *utsushi*, a Japanese term for an art copy that "may itself gain prestige in Japanese art history, becoming a masterpiece in its own right."[15] Although we are closer now to understanding what a digital surrogate is, digitization has progressed so quickly that the creators and users of digital surrogates lack clear and well-established metrics for evaluating them. This chapter will explore the potential and the limitations of digitized art objects, and provide some guidelines for creating and assessing high-quality digital surrogates.

## Mind the Gaps: What Gets Digitized and Why

For cultural heritage institutions, selection—what is acquired, what is catalogued, what is displayed, and now what is digitized—is an old problem. The Bodleian Libraries' Hebraica curator at the University of Oxford, César Merchán-Hamann, tells the story of his nineteenth-century predecessor Adolf Neubauer, who, given the opportunity to buy items from a newly discovered collection of Hebrew manuscript fragments, chose about two thousand fragments of particular scriptural or historical importance and left the remainder of household receipts and family letters. Over the course of the twentieth century, historians began to take greater interest in ephemeral and mundane artifacts, and those rejected fragments—happily bought by Cambridge University Library—are now of the greatest importance to research.

Digitization amplifies this problem. An object is selected for digitization based on a complex set of interdependent criteria. Is the object robust enough to hold up to prolonged handling during digitization? Is the object of an appropriate size and type to be photographed or scanned using equipment that the institution already owns? Is the object already catalogued? Finally, will the digitized object have *impact*? This last criterion is perhaps most treacherous. In attempting to maximize the potential impact of a proposed digitization project, an institution may focus on the "important" parts of its collection, but importance is an extremely subjective measure dependent on many variables. Something may seem unimportant now only because it has not been catalogued or made available to the public; if it were catalogued and digitized, it might be more widely researched. As digitization money follows cataloguing money, long-standing Euro-centric biases in European and North American institutions are reinforced.[16]

The selection decision is further complicated by the question of how digitization is paid for. Neubauer had an acquisition budget to spend at his own discretion. For the most part, curators today choosing items to digitize do not have the same luxury. Digitization of art objects requires top-of-the-line, often bespoke equipment. A 100-megapixel camera, suitable for large-format items such as paintings or maps, might cost £40,000; a lens and a cradle or mount for the object might cost as much again. Each of these might need to be replaced every three to five years. Added to this is the cost of the technical infrastructure for delivery and preservation; the time of the photographers, conservators, cataloguers, software engineers and system administrators; and any licensing or support fees for software used during the digitization process. If an institution is particularly wealthy and particularly dedicated, it may fund digitization itself. The majority of institutions, however, seek government grants, private donations, or support from philanthropic organizations.

This results in digitization disparities due to geographic and political factors; Germany, the Netherlands, and the countries of Scandinavia, for example, lead the field thanks to their governments' heavy investment in digitization and cultural programs in general.[17] Even where external funding is available, it introduces complications, as what is digitized depends on the priorities of the donor or funding body. While the impact requirements of philanthropic institutions' grant boards may lead to more innovative and collaborative project proposals, externally steered projects run the risk of overlooking institutional knowledge of considerations that are difficult to quantify: what is rare, what is vital to current research, what would especially benefit from digital tools, and what is uncatalogued and consequently underrepresented in assessments of impact. For example, the Bodleian Libraries at the University of Oxford, as of 2020, have digitized approximately 900,000 images of rare books, manuscripts and other special collections. Of these, roughly two-thirds were funded by The Polonsky Foundation, a UK-based philanthropic organization with a particular interest in digitizing Hebrew materials, pre-modern manuscripts, and entire collections rather than one-off items. As a result, the Bodleian's digital collection is dominated by Hebrew manuscripts, and to a lesser extent by Greek manuscripts, medieval German manuscripts and early printed books. Meanwhile, the library's other collections—of Asian manuscripts, maps, music, and post-1500 materials, to name a few—are relatively unrepresented, and less than a quarter of the items on the manuscript curators' top-priority lists have been digitized. Maintaining balance in an externally funded digital collection requires careful internal assessment and proactive grant-seeking, which themselves require money that many institutions do not have.

It is to be hoped that, as time passes, more institutions will make room for digitization in their own budgets. In the meantime, they have a responsibility publicly to document the financial and institutional factors influencing what gets digitized, proactively to seek funding for projects that fill gaps in their digital collections, and to devote as much money as possible to electronic cataloguing, so that even if the digital image collection does not accurately reflect the physical one, the digital catalogue does.

## The Weaknesses of the Digital Surrogate: What's Added, What's Missing

With twenty years of digital photography behind us, and fifty or sixty years of microfilm and slide scans, it is growing easier to see the inadequacies of the present technology—and indeed of any future technology. Even the terms we use for digital reproductions—facsimile, surrogate, avatar,[18] prosthesis,[19] minion[20]—emphasize the distance between original and copy. This distance can be seen plainly in a museum shop, where postcards and prints contradict our memory of the color and brightness of the originals. With a digitized reproduction, the contrast may not always be obvious, as the viewer may not have access to the original,[21] but it is still there. Camera sensors and color calibration tools are improving by the year, and in many digital collections it is possible to see sharp differences in resolution, color temperature and brightness between twenty-year-old and five-year-old images (Figure 15.2).

For the most part, however, the deficiencies of digital surrogates are things that even a state-of-the-art camera cannot rectify. A digital surrogate may capture only select aspects of the

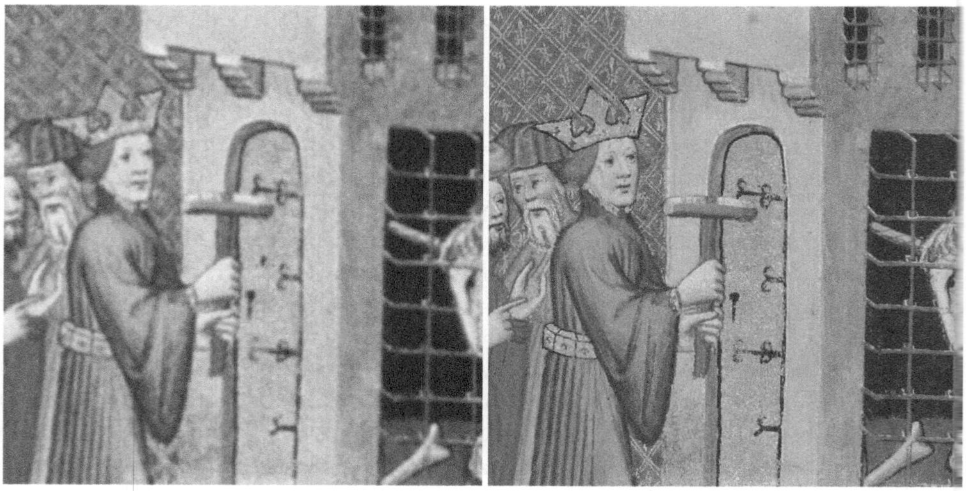

*Figure 15.2* Two facsimiles of Bodleian Library MS. Bodl. 264, fol. 2v. Left: a 2007 scan of a c. 1970 35mm slide. Right: a 2013 photo captured on a 40-megapixel digital camera.

*Source*: http://bodley30.bodley.ox.ac.uk:8180/luna/servlet/detail/ODLodl~24~24~140038~145421, Bodleian Libraries.

original, on the rationale that only those aspects are of interest. For example, a surrogate of an illuminated manuscript might omit the undecorated pages; a surrogate of a printed book might omit flyleaves and boards; a conventionally lit surrogate might omit textural details that can only be captured with raking light. Reflective, responsive surfaces such as gold leaf are notoriously difficult to capture; a Kyoto temple that had digitized its screen paintings applied actual gold leaf to the printed-out copies displayed in the temple in order to preserve the play of light on gold.[22] There are also non-visual contextual clues that feed our interpretations of art: the frame, the item's place on a shelf, its position in a gallery, its weight and size, even the number of people crowded around it. Asked if one of her paintings could be reproduced in a book, an artist told Susan Bielstein, "45 ft. paint on canvas? 12 in. ink on paper. Forget it."[23]

At the heart of this issue is the fact that a digital art surrogate forces a particular interpretation of an object.[24] This is most obvious in a restorative digitization, where the supposed original condition of a damaged object is simulated digitally. The Kyoto screen painting reproductions, for example, were adjusted to represent what conservators thought had been the paintings' original colors. Similarly, software has been developed that removes the cracks from images of old paintings.[25] The purpose of this kind of surrogate is to allow viewers to step back in time and see the object as it once was, although of course what they are actually seeing is an artistic rendering of one specific idea of what the object might once have looked like. Such a rendering is almost certainly significantly different from the original state of the object. Yamada notes that in the case of the screen paintings, some paint pigmentation was removed from the copies in the mistaken belief that it was dirt.[26] Even if such a surrogate were accurate in its simulation, however, it would still be unsuitable for viewers interested in the progress of decay, the history of use, and the dirt itself.[27]

Unless we create a full three-dimensional simulation (and perhaps even then), when we digitize a painting or a manuscript, we are digitizing an interpretation.[28] An object in three-dimensional space can be inspected and handled in any number of ways; a two-dimensional digital surrogate of that object is frozen at a particular angle, under a particular light, and presented with a particular viewing experience in mind. When it comes to sculpture and other types of art that are obviously three-dimensional, this is as plain to us as it was to Talbot. Yet because we so often think of drawings and manuscripts as conveyors of two-dimensional information, we forget about their three-dimensional qualities.[29] Some of these qualities are the results of artistic intention: a painter's impasto technique, for example, or gold leaf applied to gesso in order to create texture on the page of a manuscript, or the rough back of a sculpture intended to be displayed in a niche. Other three-dimensional details—like the warping of water-damaged parchment, or a signature on the back of a canvas—may not have been present when the object was created, but nevertheless illuminate its history. We lose that history when we digitize the object in two dimensions. Modern digitization conventions often exacerbate this problem, as, in order to obtain a clear, crisp image, a painting may be unmounted or its frame cropped out or a page may be held at an angle to reduce curvature and interleaved with black cloth. A digital collection may come to resemble a series of butterflies mounted in a case.

Careful study of users' habits when consulting an art object can mitigate this problem, as specific three-dimensional handling procedures can be reproduced digitally. After observing that researchers working with cuneiform tablets tended to lift the tablets in the air and tilt them back and forth to catch different angles of light, Ségolène Tarte and her team turned this interpretive model into a Flash-based viewer that allows users to rotate and apply raked light to the tablets' digital surrogates.[30] The difficulty with this approach is that there is no single model for viewing an art object. Given the opportunity to consult a decorated manuscript, a codicologist and an art historian will proceed very differently, and a model that carefully mimics the procedure of one may not meet the other's needs at all. It may also be argued that the more closely a digital surrogate tries to mimic the experience of handling the original, the more jarring its differences become. Dot Porter has likened this principle to the "uncanny valley" phenomenon of computer animation, wherein an animation that very closely mimics a real person is more unsettling and distracting than one that does not.[31] A page-turning animation in a digitized manuscript does not meaningfully enhance the user's experience; it merely wastes time and—because it is unlikely to resemble the actual experience of turning the manuscript's pages—introduces inaccuracy.[32]

In lieu of bespoke viewing tools, many cultural heritage institutions are moving toward the open-source, community-driven software of the International Image Interoperability Framework (IIIF),[33] which aims to increase the versatility and utility of digitized collections by minimizing institutional overhead and enabling collaboration. Rather than building several new image viewers to accommodate the different needs of their users, an institution can simply borrow from a range of IIIF-based viewers, including Mirador, which simulates a scholarly workspace for the comparison and annotation of image resources;[34] the Universal Viewer, which accommodates audio and video content as well as images; and Diva.js, which combines PDF-style scrolling with zoom-and-pan detail viewing. Newer tools specifically designed for art interpretation include Cogapp's "slow looking" tool, which slowly pans around an image,[35] and the Victoria and Albert Museum's Compariscope, which allows the user to overlay and align images for detailed comparison.[36]

The widespread adoption of these tools lessens the burden on any single institution's software developers, as well as the burden on researchers to familiarize themselves with multiple complex user interfaces unique to specific institutions. The potential for interoperability and resource-sharing, meanwhile, opens up new opportunities for research. Scholars can use IIIF tools to reassemble the dispersed fragments of a medieval Qu'ran and to overlay Rembrandt van Rijn's *The Night Watch* with the artist's preliminary sketches: things that are impossible in the physical world, but potentially effortless in the digital world. It is important to keep in mind, however, that the existence and usage of these tools are essentially arbitrary. The facilitation of a particular research technique through software, like the digitization of a particular object, is conditional on various stakeholders' perhaps erroneous assessments of its importance and feasibility. In order for a digital art research tool to exist, software developers must know that it is needed; in order for it to be used, researchers must know that it exists. These factors preference researchers at wealthy institutions practicing widely used research techniques. Moreover, digital tools are being created and refined all the time, and the newer a digital tool or digitized resource, the less likely it is that the researchers to whom it might be useful will know about it. Art scholarship, and humanities scholarship in general, are traditionally slow-moving fields that are being rapidly accelerated by technology. Teaching and dissemination methods have not yet caught up with these changes. In fact, given the rapid improvements in cultural heritage photography and image delivery tools over even the past ten years, it is possible to feel paralyzed: Why digitize anything right now? Why not wait, knowing that in five years the technology will have improved again?

The first reason is, of course, that while digital surrogates may not be perfect, they are better than nothing, and the need for them is urgent. Choosing to put off digitization of a particular object means that fewer researchers will have access to that object, and consequently that less research will be conducted on it. The second reason is that while there are unavoidable losses and risks in digitization, it is possible to mitigate them.

## Building an Effective Digital Surrogate

### *Cataloguing for Discoverability*

A record without an image is more valuable than an image without a record.

—*Chris Edwards*[37]

Digitization holds enormous potential for increasing global access to art, as a digitized artwork is theoretically accessible to anyone with an internet connection. Making a digital surrogate available online does not ensure that anyone will actually use it, however, or that the people who do use it will constitute a wider audience than would have viewed the original in person. This is, in fact, where many institutions' digital collections fall down. Many collections are hidden in websites with query-based page URLs that cannot be indexed by search engines. This means that many users' first port of call, Google, returns no results. Many collection websites also have unintuitive user interfaces that can be discouraging and frustrating, especially to the researcher who has to visit several in succession.

Significantly increasing access to digital collections requires dedicated cataloguing and dissemination efforts. Museums and libraries struggle to fund cataloguing, meaning that information about collection items is often extremely brief and held only in printed or handwritten catalogues. Moreover, traditional cataloguing practices, tailored to the needs and skills of curators and advanced researchers, often obfuscate what is important to a less experienced user. Marie Thompson puts it this way:

> An engraving of birds by Buffon can be of interest to a scholar, a student, a pupil or an historian. It is capable of being read at several different levels. . . [which] should be reflected in the cataloguing and caption data: a scientific level which would for example identify the persons represented by a manuscript illumination and a level of wider interest which would describe a castle or a four-poster bed for the pupil or the iconographer. Such an approach still causes debate in cataloguing circles. Reaching a wider public with the web means adapting our cataloguing habits.[38]

One experiment in adapting cataloguing habits was the Bodleian Libraries' Medieval and Renaissance Manuscript Illumination project, which in the late 2000s described and digitized twenty-five thousand 35mm slides of manuscript illuminations, including searchable descriptive captions created over decades through a combination of amateur and expert input. The slide images are relatively low-quality, and for each manuscript, only a handful of images of illuminations are available, rather than a complete facsimile.[39] Nevertheless, the digital collection is hugely popular among researchers as well as casual browsers thanks to the captions Another example of discovery-oriented metadata is SFMOMA's Send Me project, which used curator-generated subject tags ("dog," "high heels," "love," "people of color") to identify and send out images of collection items in response to user requests.[40] Such tags would rarely be included in a traditional catalogue, but they are immensely useful.

A distinction can usefully be made here between catalogue metadata and discovery metadata. Discovery metadata is the information users need in order to find an item relevant to their search, and catalogue metadata is what they might want to look at after they find it. For example, even an experienced scholar, searching for the Gutenberg Bible, might type "Gutenberg Bible" into the search field of the Bodleian or Vatican Library's website, rather than a shelfmark or catalogue identifier. This search would return no results, because these libraries do not currently include colloquial names for items in their catalogues.

Adding discovery metadata is a tall order, as different users come to a digital collection with different questions, and consequently need different metadata. "Gutenberg Bible" might be enough for some; others might look for "pen flourishing" or "rubrication" or "Mainz" or "marbled pastedowns"—and they might look for these terms in any number of languages. Creating metadata of this kind requires not only time, but knowledge of the institutional audience, which is prone to change. In order to reduce the burden on staff and to ensure that the created metadata meets user needs, some institutions are turning to crowdsourcing platforms like Zooniverse and From The Page, which have worked with Tate Britain, the British Library, and Stanford University, among others, to create public transcription and tagging projects. These new projects are promising, but it remains to be seen whether they have a significant effect on discoverability.

## *Designing for Usability*

The hallmark of a bad digital surrogate is that its badness cannot be gauged, because important contextual details are missing. Put another way, there are no bad digital surrogates—only misleading and poorly described ones. The Bodleian's Early Manuscripts at Oxford, for example, a landmark digitization project of the mid-1990s, features relatively low-resolution, dim, poorly color-calibrated images of medieval manuscripts. With clear information about the date of capture, equipment and color processing, these weaknesses would be manageable; without it, the manuscript surrogates are potentially enormously misleading.

As digital collections age and the disparity between old and new surrogates increases, bringing technical metadata into the foreground becomes more important, as it allows users to make an informed choice about how much to trust a given surrogate. Including color charts and rulers in the image is a good place to start; this is something many institutions currently do. The next step is to make the image metadata available alongside the image, or at least a subset of it: date of capture most importantly, but also capture equipment and color profile if possible, and a citation of any digitization standard adhered to (for example, a four-star FADGI rating).[41] Ideally, an institution should also provide an explication of the digitization equipment used, the routine post-processing activities, and the thinking behind the choice of a particular standard. At the moment, no institution provides anything close to this level of detail, meaning that users must make their own assumptions about the quality of the surrogate without formal training in how to do so.

There are also technical and legal obstacles to usability. A particular problem for global access are the demands many digital collections make on the user's computer processor and internet connection. In the last ten years, most collections have switched from high-resolution static images, which can be easily downloaded, to tiled-zoom image formats such as JPEG2000. By breaking a single image up into tiles that are served up individually and stitched together in the browser, JPEG2000 mitigates the network burden while also providing reassurance to institutions worried about unlicensed downloading of full-resolution images. For users with slow connections, however, even a tiled image can be extremely frustrating to view in-browser. While many institutions argue that because they allow free access to their online images, there is no need to provide a high-resolution download option, this attitude ignores not only the continued prevalence of low-speed internet in many parts of the world but also the fact that many researchers—particularly those conducting heavily image-based research—prefer to download images to print out, view offline, or edit using desktop software. Institutions that do not permit download and reuse of their digital collections, or whose reuse guidelines are not clear, are likely to find that their collections are passed over in favor of others that are easier to use.

## *Capturing the Uncapturable and Leveraging Difference*

Virtually every article on art digitization has had to reckon with Benjamin's question of aura: what is threatened, and perhaps lost, through mechanical reproduction. Several have argued convincingly that ubiquitous reproductions only augment the aura of the original object by establishing its presence more firmly in our minds.[42] People still flock to see the *Mona Lisa* in person. In fact, even though medium- and high-resolution photos of the *Mona Lisa* are readily available online, many visitors take their own phone-camera pictures, out of an impulse to capture the profound experience of having shared physical space with the painting.

It is impossible to capture this experience with a universally available digital surrogate. Through creative tools and rich metadata, however, it is possible to approximate many aspects of it. Burns argues that during digitization, "the materiality of the original object is not 'lost'; it is only translated into metadata and digital information."[43] For example, in order to capture the feeling of connection to the artist and early owners and viewers of a painting, the surrogate can be displayed alongside images of objects from the artist's lifetime, or a simulation of the room in which the painting might have been originally displayed. Provenance information, such as an owner's signature, a child's doodle, or evidence of early damage and repairs, can be captured in the digitization and analyzed in the metadata. To communicate the physical substance of the object, meanwhile—its three-dimensionality—museums and libraries can use virtual modeling tools such as Sketchfab;[44] they can provide data about the object's dimensions and weight, or an image of it next to an object of familiar size for scale; and they can create images and videos of the pages being turned or of the object from different angles. With these peripheral resources, the digital surrogate becomes something closer to a critical edition: an enriched extension of the original object.[45]

The nature of the gap between original and surrogate may change as technology improves, but it can never be entirely closed. In fact, the strengths of digital surrogates lie in their differences: their versatility, their independence from time and place, their potential for creative interaction. The most effective digital surrogates leverage these traits. The Kyoto Culture Association's Tsuzuri project addresses the diaspora of Japanese art by creating detailed digital reproductions of Japanese artworks held by American and European institutions and displaying them in situ;[46] the ReACH project at the Victoria and Albert Museum, inspired by Henry Cole's 1867 initiative to share plaster casts among museums, is working to establish best practices for creating and sharing digital facsimiles;[47] using IIIF tools, Biblissima has restored the miniatures cut out of a medieval manuscript;[48] *Jheronimus Bosch, the Garden of Earthly Delights* turns a famously complex painting into an interactive series of text and video annotations.[49] While the bedrock of the modern digital surrogate is responsible image capture and high-quality metadata, its higher potential lies in its creators' ability to imagine new modes of delivery and interpretation for cultural heritage content.

## Notes

1. William Henry Fox Talbot, *The Pencil of Nature*, facsimile ed. (London: KWS, 2011), Plate XXIII.
2. Ibid.
3. Ibid., Plate V.
4. Hilary Macartney and José Manuel Matilla, eds., *Copied by the Sun: Talbotype Illustrations to the Annals of the Artists of Spain by Sir William Stirling Maxwell* (Madrid: Museo Nacional del Prado, 2016), 60, 63.

5. Anais Aguërre and Brendan Cormier, "Introduction," in *Copy Culture: Sharing in the Age of Digital Reproduction*, ed. Brendan Cormier (London:V&A Publishing, 2018), 23.
6. Rob Sanderson, "30,000 Getty Museum Images Published Online as IIIF," *The Iris, Getty Museum*, accessed June 25, 2018, http://blogs.getty.edu/iris/30000-getty-museum-images-published-iiif/.
7. Metropolitan Museum of Art, "Open Access at the Met," accessed June 25, 2018, https://metmuseum.org/about-the-met/policies-and-documents/open-access.
8. Rijksmuseum, "Rijksstudio," accessed June 28, 2018, www.rijksmuseum.nl/en/rijksstudio.
9. British Museum, "Collection online," accessed June 25, 2018, www.britishmuseum.org/research/collection_online/search.aspx.
10. Nik Honeysett, "CMS in Context," accessed June 25, 2018, https://prezi.com/n3gcej7ijusk/cms-in-context/.
11. Peter Walsh, "Rise and Fall of the Post-Photographic Museum: Technology and the Transformation of Art," in *Theorizing Digital Cultural Heritage: A Critical Discourse (Media in Transition)*, ed. Fiona Cameron and Sarah Kenderdine (Cambridge, MA: MIT Press, 2007), 23.
12. Walter Benjamin, "The Work of Art in the Age of Mechanical Reproduction," in *Illuminations*, ed. Hannah Arendt, trans. Harry Zohn (New York: Schocken Books, 1969).
13. Douglas Davis, "The Work of Art in the Age of Digital Reproduction (An Evolving Thesis: 1991–1995)," *Leonardo* 28, no. 5 (1995): 382.
14. Michelle Warren, "Situating Digital Archives," *Digital Philology* 3, no. 2 (Fall 2014): 173; Jasmine Burns, "The Aura of Materiality: Digital Surrogacy and the Preservation of Photographic Archives," *Art Documentation: Journal of the Art Libraries Society of North America* 36, no. 1 (Spring 2017): 5. Catherine Soussloff et al., "The Aesthetics of Publishing: The Art Book as Object from Print to Digital," *Visual Resources* 24, no. 1 (2008): 47.
15. Shoji Yamada, "Who Moved My Masterpiece? Digital Reproduction, Replacement, and the Vanishing Cultural Heritage of Kyoto," *International Journal of Cultural Property* 24 (2017): 308.
16. Alanna Bayer, "Evangelizing the 'Gallery of the Future': A Critical Analysis of the Google Art Project Narrative and Its Political, Cultural and Technological Stakes" (Electronic Thesis and Dissertation Repository, University of Western Ontario, 2014), 60.
17. Ole Marius Hylland, "Even Better than the Real Thing? Digital Copies and Digital Museums in a Digital Cultural Policy," *Culture Unbound* 9, no. 1 (2017): 66.
18. Ségolène Tarte, "Interpreting Ancient Documents: Of Avatars, Uncertainty and Knowledge Creation," ESF Exploratory Workshop on Digital Palaeography (July 2011).
19. Warren, "Situating Digital Archives," 173.
20. Soussloff et al., "The Aesthetics of Publishing," 47.
21. Jasmine Burns, "Digital Facsimiles and the Modern Viewer: Medieval Manuscripts and Archival Practice in the Age of New Media," *Art Documentation: Journal of the Art Libraries Society of North America* 33, no. 3 (Fall 2014): 166.
22. Yamada, "Who Moved My Masterpiece?" 303.
23. Soussloff et al., "The Aesthetics of Publishing," 47.
24. Walsh, "Rise and Fall of the Post-Photographic Museum," 31; Macartney and Matilla, *Copied by the Sun*, 63.
25. S.D. Desai et al., "Detection and Removal of Cracks from Digitized Paintings and Images by User Intervention," *2013 2nd International Conference on Advanced Computing, Networking and Security* (2013): 51.
26. Yamada, "Who Moved My Masterpiece?" 310.
27. Burns, "Digital Facsimiles and the Modern Viewer," 150.
28. Ibid., 352; Ségolène Tarte, "Digitizing the Act of Papyrological Interpretation: Negotiating Spurious Exactitude and Genuine Uncertainty," *Literary and Linguistic Computing* 26, no. 3 (2011): 350.
29. Emma Stanford, "Booksquashing," The Bodleian Libraries, accessed December 15, 2018, https://medium.com/@bodleian/booksquashing-1d3fa800c253.
30. Ibid., 352.
31. Dot Porter, "Zombie Manuscripts: Digital Facsimiles in the Uncanny Valley," *Dot Porter Digital*, accessed June 25, 2018, www.dotporterdigital.org/zombie-manuscripts-digital-facsimiles-in-the-uncanny-valley.
32. While digital preservation is a separate subject, it is worth noting here that bespoke digital simulations of analogue procedures run the risk of obsolescence, as anyone who has been prompted to enable a Flash plugin can attest.
33. See http://iiif.io.

34. Benjamin Albritton, "Fellow Travelers: The Canterbury Tales and IIIF," *Digital Manuscripts at Stanford*, accessed June 25, 2018, http://web.stanford.edu/group/dmstech/cgi-bin/wordpress/fellow-travelers-the-canterbury-tales-and-iiif.
35. See http://slowlooking.cogapp.com.
36. See https://vanda.github.io/iiif-features/compariscope.html.
37. Annelisa Stephan, "A Conversation with the Getty's New Imaging and Digital Media Architect," *The Iris, Getty Museum*, accessed June 25, 2018, http://blogs.getty.edu/iris/a-conversation-with-the-gettys-new-imaging-and-digital-media-architect.
38. Marie Thompson, "Taking Up the Digital Challenge: Image Digitisation Projects at the Bibliothèque nationale de France," *Art Libraries Journal* 27, no. 3 (2002): 12.
39. Burns, "Digital Facsimiles and the Modern Viewer," 165.
40. Jay Mollica, "Send Me SFMOMA," *SFMOMA*, accessed June 25, 2018, www.sfmoma.org/read/send-me-sfmoma.
41. See www.digitizationguidelines.gov/guidelines/digitize-technical.html.
42. Walsh, "Rise and Fall of the Post-Photographic Museum," 29; Aguërre and Cormier, "Introduction," 21.
43. Burns, "The Aura of Materiality," 5.
44. See https://sketchfab.com/models/62886082c3b144d18ca516b396cf29f5.
45. Warren, "Situating Digital Archives," 173.
46. See https://global.canon/en/tsuzuri/overview.html.
47. See www.vam.ac.uk/research/projects/reach-reproduction-of-art-and-cultural-heritage#outputs.
48. See http://demos.biblissima-condorcet.fr/chateauroux/demo.
49. See https://tuinderlusten-jheronimusbosch.ntr.nl.

## Bibliography

Aguërre, Anais, and Brendan Cormier. "Introduction." In *Copy Culture: Sharing in the Age of Digital Reproduction*, edited by Brendan Cormier, 19–26. London: V&A Publishing, 2018.

Albritton, Benjamin. "Fellow Travelers: The Canterbury Tales and IIIF." *Digital Manuscripts at Stanford*. Accessed June 25, 2018. http://web.stanford.edu/group/dmstech/cgi-bin/wordpress/fellow-travelers-the-canterbury-tales-and-iiif/.

Bayer, Alanna. "Evangelizing the 'Gallery of the Future': A Critical Analysis of the Google Art Project Narrative and Its Political, Cultural and Technological Stakes" (Electronic Thesis and Dissertation Repository, 2014), 2239. https://ir.lib.uwo.ca/etd/2239.

Benjamin, Walter. "The Work of Art in the Age of Mechanical Reproduction." In *Illuminations*, edited by Hannah Arendt, translated by Harry Zohn. New York: Schocken Books, 1969.

British Museum. "Collection Online." Accessed June 25, 2018. www.britishmuseum.org/research/collection_online/search.aspx.

Burns, Jasmine. "The Aura of Materiality: Digital Surrogacy and the Preservation of Photographic Archives." *Art Documentation: Journal of the Art Libraries Society of North America* 36, no. 1 (Spring 2017): 1–8.

———. "Digital Facsimiles and the Modern Viewer: Medieval Manuscripts and Archival Practice in the Age of New Media." *Art Documentation: Journal of the Art Libraries Society of North America* 33, no. 3 (Fall 2014): 148–67.

Davis, Douglas. "The Work of Art in the Age of Digital Reproduction (An Evolving Thesis: 1991–1995)." *Leonardo* 28, no. 5 (1995): 381–86. www.jstor.org/stable/1576221.

Desai, S. D., et al. "Detection and Removal of Cracks from Digitized Paintings and Images by User Intervention." *2013 2nd International Conference on Advanced Computing, Networking and Security* (2013): 51–55.

Honeysett, Nik. "CMS in Context." Accessed June 25, 2018. https://prezi.com/n3gcej7ijuss/cms-in-context/.

Hylland, Ole Marius. "Even Better than the Real Thing? Digital Copies and Digital Museums in a Digital Cultural Policy." *Culture Unbound* 9, no. 1 (2017): 62–84.

Macartney, Hilary, and José Manuel Matilla, eds. *Copied by the Sun: Talbotype Illustrations to the Annals of the Artists of Spain by Sir William Stirling Maxwell*. Madrid: Museo Nacional del Prado, Centro de Estudios Europea Hispánica, 2016.

Metropolitan Museum of Art. "Open Access at the Met." Accessed June 25, 2018. https://metmuseum.org/about-the-met/policies-and-documents/open-access.

Mollica, Jay. "Send Me SFMOMA." *SFMOMA*. Accessed June 25, 2018. www.sfmoma.org/read/send-me-sfmoma.

Porter, Dot. "Zombie Manuscripts: Digital Facsimiles in the Uncanny Valley." *Dot Porter Digital*. Last modified May 12, 2018. www.dotporterdigital.org/zombie-manuscripts-digital-facsimiles-in-the-uncanny-valley.

Rijksmuseum. "Rijksstudio." Accessed June 28, 2018. www.rijksmuseum.nl/en/rijksstudio.

Sanderson, Rob. "30,000 Getty Museum Images Published Online as IIIF." *The Iris, Getty Museum*. Accessed June 25, 2018. http://blogs.getty.edu/iris/30000-getty-museum-images-published-iiif.

Soussloff, Catherine, et al. "The Aesthetics of Publishing: The Art Book As Object from Print to Digital." *Visual Resources* 24, no. 1 (2008): 39–58. https://doi.org/10.1080/01973760801892225.

Stanford, Emma. "Booksquashing." *The Bodleian Libraries*. Accessed December 15, 2018. https://medium.com/@bodleian/booksquashing-1d3fa800c253.

Stephan, Annelisa. "A Conversation with the Getty's New Imaging and Digital Media Architect." *The Iris, Getty Museum*. Accessed June 25, 2018. http://blogs.getty.edu/iris/a-conversation-with-the-gettys-new-imaging-and-digital-media-architect.

Talbot, William Henry Fox. *The Pencil of Nature*, facsimile ed. London: KWS Publishers, 2011.

Tarte, Ségolène. "Digitizing the Act of Papyrological Interpretation: Negotiating Spurious Exactitude and Genuine Uncertainty." *Literary and Linguistic Computing* 26, no. 3 (2011): 349–58.

———. "Interpreting Ancient Documents: Of Avatars, Uncertainty and Knowledge Creation." *ESF Exploratory Workshop on Digital Palaeography* (July 2011). Accessed January 22, 2020. https://tei-c.org/Vault/MembersMeetings/2011/veranstaltungen/digital_palaeography/abstracts/index.html.

Thompson, Marie. "Taking Up the Digital Challenge: Image Digitisation Projects at the Bibliothèque nationale de France." *Art Libraries Journal* 27, no. 3 (2002): 7–12. https://doi.org/10.1017/S0307472200020058.

Walsh, Peter. "Rise and Fall of the Post-Photographic Museum: Technology and the Transformation of Art." In *Theorizing Digital Cultural Heritage: A Critical Discourse (Media in Transition)*, edited by Fiona Cameron and Sarah Kenderdine, 19–34. Cambridge: MIT Press, 2007.

Warren, Michelle. "Situating Digital Archives." *Digital Philology* 3, no. 2 (Fall 2014): 169–77.

Yamada, Shoji. "Who Moved My Masterpiece? Digital Reproduction, Replacement, and the Vanishing Cultural Heritage of Kyoto." *International Journal of Cultural Property* 24 (2017): 295–320. https://doi.org/10.1017/S0940739117000145.

# 16

# A SERVICE-ORIENTATION AND OPEN-SOURCE APPROACH TO DEVELOPING VIRTUAL MUSEUMS

*Martin White and Ben Jackson*

This chapter discusses how modern web technologies can be effectively used to present museums' disparate cultural objects in digital space as aggregated collections in a virtual museum (VM) using service-orientation. We show how innovative open-source technologies and methods, including developing a bespoke application programming interface (API), allow a museum to exploit service-orientation to improve access to its collections. By publishing an API, a museum allows third parties (i.e. the "app community") to create interesting VMs that can bring similar collections from different museums together in digital space. An example of such an aggregated collection is the Reanimating Cultural Heritage collection of Sierra Leone material culture.[1] Another interesting innovation, in the development of VMs, is the integration of 3D in a typical web technology stack to enable interaction with an object "in the round" thereby giving visitors a more interesting experience. The technology for integrating 3D into a website is referred to as a Web3D technology stack.[2]

In this chapter, we describe the technology we use to develop and update two VMs that exploit a model, view, controller (MVC) design pattern. We illustrate how to extract object data from these collections using two different APIs to create a mobile friendly VM experience. In particular, we will show how to access object data from the Reanimating Cultural Heritage collection (http://sierraleone.heritageinformatics.org/) and the Church of Santa Chiara 3D Reconstruction (http://sc.heritageinformatics.org/), which are two VMs we developed recently.[3]

Previous research shows that VMs can provide engaging museum visitor experiences.[4] Here, we demonstrate that although the technology required is readily available open source, creating 3D content for a VM is time-consuming and, hence, costly. As such, a VM exploiting 3D media objects will need to be relatively selective, depending on financial resources available for the project. Further, a museum should also consider how 3D media object enabled VMs will be maintained as digital assets in the future. Discussion of this point is, however, beyond the scope of this chapter. The VMs discussed next provide two different examples of 3D navigation: (1) an example component illustrating navigation of 3D objects, in this case thirteen ivory, wooden, pottery and glazed 3D bowls from the Reanimating Cultural Heritage collection (http://rch.heritageinformatics.org/); and (2) 3D navigation through a 3D reconstruction of the Church of Santa Chiara, Florence (http://sc.heritageinformatics.org/3dtour/).

A VM should render on a mobile device because most museum visitors will have a smartphone with integrated high-resolution cameras and web browsers capable of displaying 3D objects. Smartphones can be used to present sophisticated mobile VMs that can exploit both virtual reality (VR) and augmented reality (AR).[5] One can imagine scenarios whereby AR is used to recognize a physical object on display in the museum. A visitor's mobile AR application then allows the visitor to investigate related objects in the mobile VM.[6] Further, AR is particularly useful for visitors when they want to continue their museum scenario experience at home.[7]

Asking visitors to use their own mobile devices to interact with a museum's objects fits well with current modern web technology stacks and development methods.[8] Having regard to this approach, we are effectively exploiting data as a service APIs, which allows mobile VMs to be rapidly created as single page applications that are both responsive and mobile first focused.[9] Responsive mobile first is, in our opinion, a crucial component in the design of simple user-friendly mobile VMs. This is because, in many cases, it is no longer necessary to install fixed museum interactive installations (such as the Santa Chiara touch screen interactive) in the physical space of the museum. Instead, visitors can simply see the VM, including AR components, on their smartphones.[10]

## The Reanimating Cultural Heritage Collection

The Reanimating Cultural Heritage collection was created as part of a large grant project in the "Beyond Text" strategic program funded by the UK Arts and Humanities Research Council.[11] The collection aggregates around 3,600 COs drawn from the Sierra Leone National Museum, British Museum, Cootje Van Oven Collection, Brighton Museum and Art Gallery, Glasgow Museums, World Museum Liverpool, and the British Library. Figure 16.1 illustrates the desktop RCH browser interface to the various museums' Sierra Leone objects included in the collection. Figure 16.2 illustrates a Sapi-Portugese Ivory Bowl as part of the collection represented in 3D. The interface allows the user to select an image, video, 3D model using the X3D format, audio commentary, or a different image that can be used as the trigger image in an AR application. In addition, other objects that have 3D interfaces can be selected in the Browse Exhibition Objects pane.

The 3D models in Figure 16.2 that were created to augment the Reanimating Cultural Heritage project are individual representations of objects, which in this case are bowls, where navigation is achieved by orbiting the 3D object with a virtual camera. Orbiting and magnification of a 3D object is a simple navigation paradigm that translates easily between desktop and mobile devices without extra development. This means that the mobile first nature of the scene only requires the rendering area to scale according to the allocated screen space, while the complexities of navigation on different devices do not change. More specifically, in this case where we implement the 3D object, we only have to override the objects CSS style class to match the container block element (Media Objects) window and height parameters and they should scale together.

## The Church of Santa Chiara

The Church of Santa Chiara is a Renaissance church originally located in Florence, Italy. It was deconsecrated in 1851 and is currently converted for use as commercial premises and domestic dwellings. The Victoria and Albert Museum rebuilt the Church of Santa Chiara Chancel Chapel, which is now on display in room 50b as part of the Medieval and Renaissance Galleries. The Chancel Chapel has been placed in its "original social and cultural context" so that viewers can

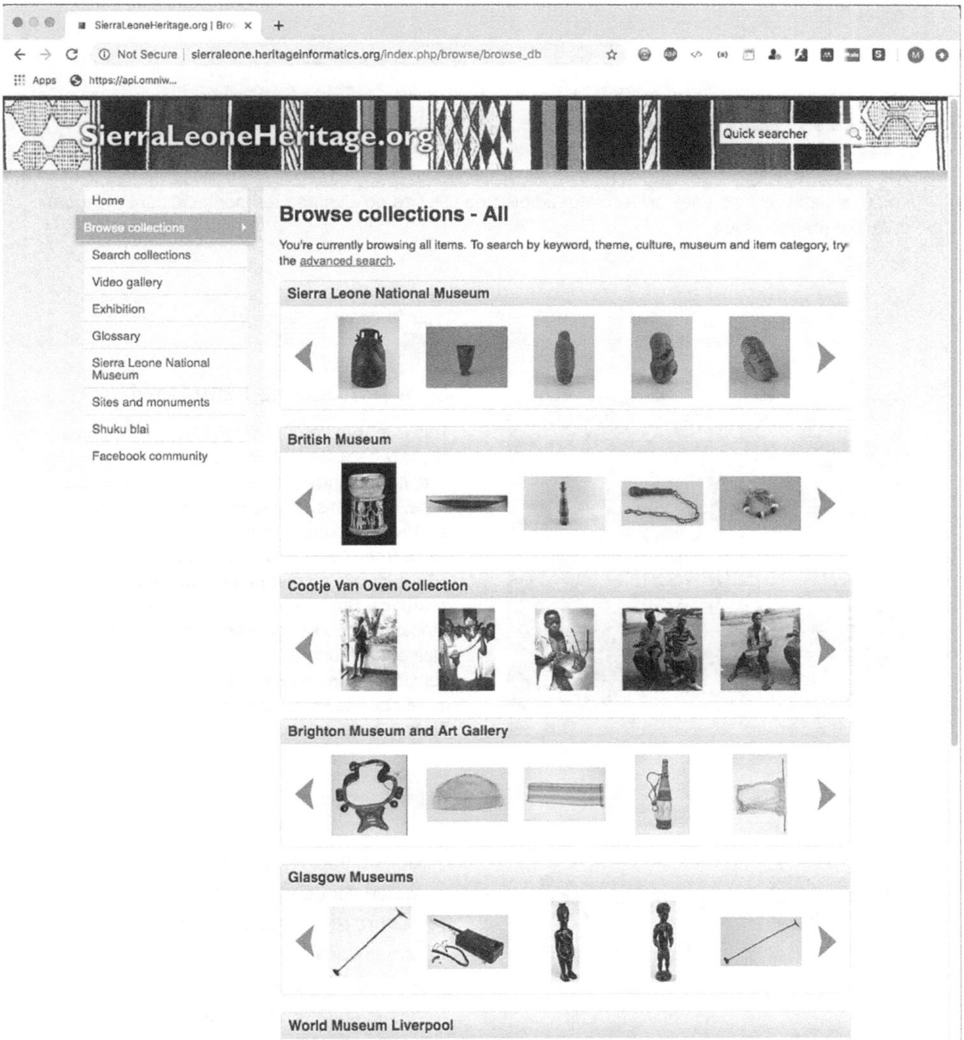


*Figure 16.1* Original desktop interface for browsing the RCH collection.

see the Chancel Chapel, high altar, and the two side altars together. This Chancel Chapel is the only "Italian Renaissance chapel that can be seen outside of Italy. It comes from the Church of Santa Chiara, part of a Franciscan convent dedicated to St Clare that once contained the high altar."[12] Figure 16.3 illustrates the Chancel Chapel with one of the side altars in the Medieval and Renaissance Galleries.

As part of the room 50b gallery, we created a VM comprising a 3D reconstruction of the Church of Santa Chiara, its Chancel Chapel and Side Altars. The original technology components used in creating this VM include the 3D reconstruction of the Church, Chapel, and Altar, a 3D walkthrough of the church rendered into a video, and associated information choreographed into a touch screen-based Flash interactive. A more recently developed VM, see Figure 16.4, using a new Santa Chiara API now includes the ability to navigate around the 3D reconstruction of the Church, Chapel and Altars.

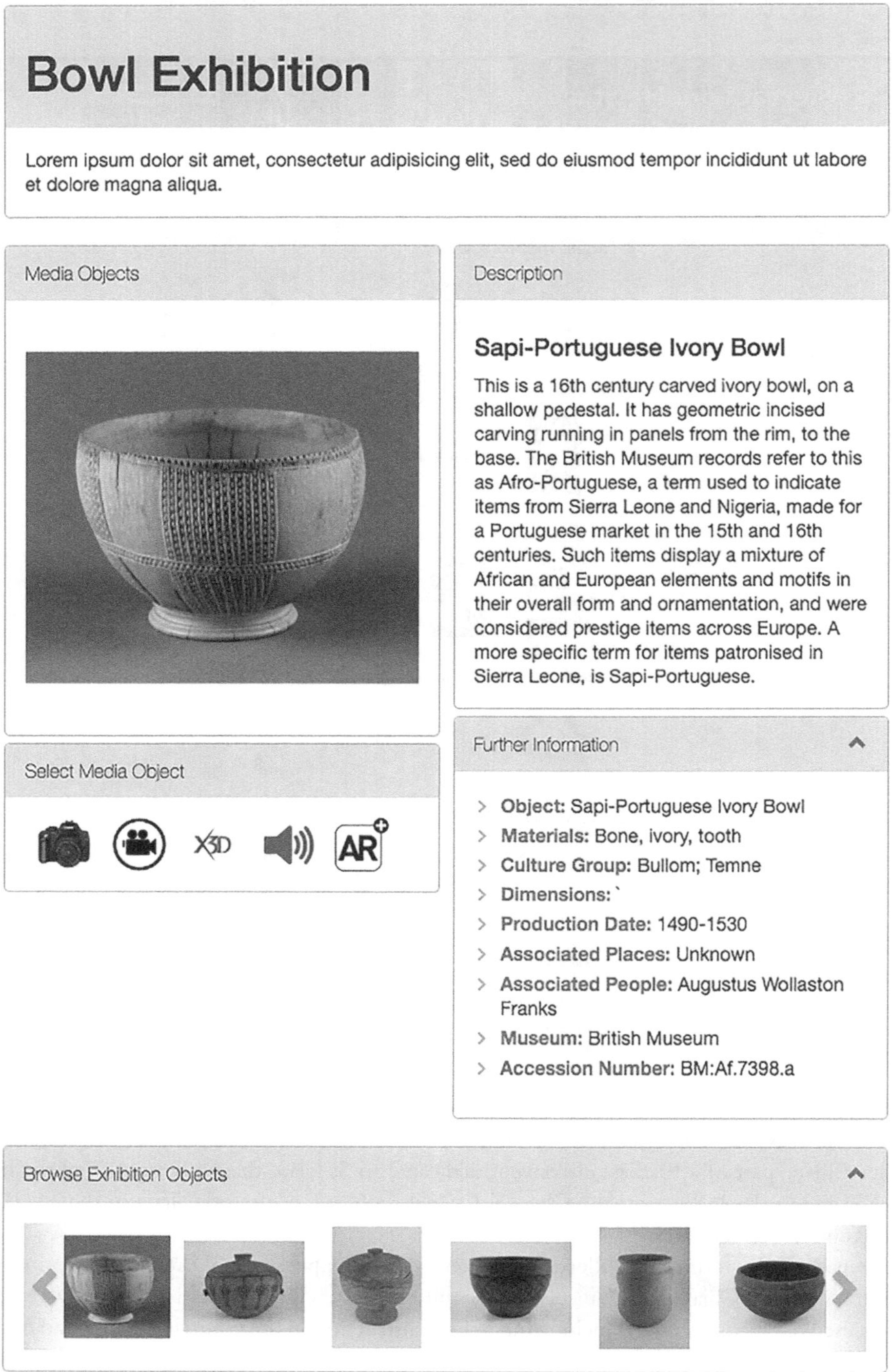


*Figure 16.2* X3D integrated into the Virtual Museum.

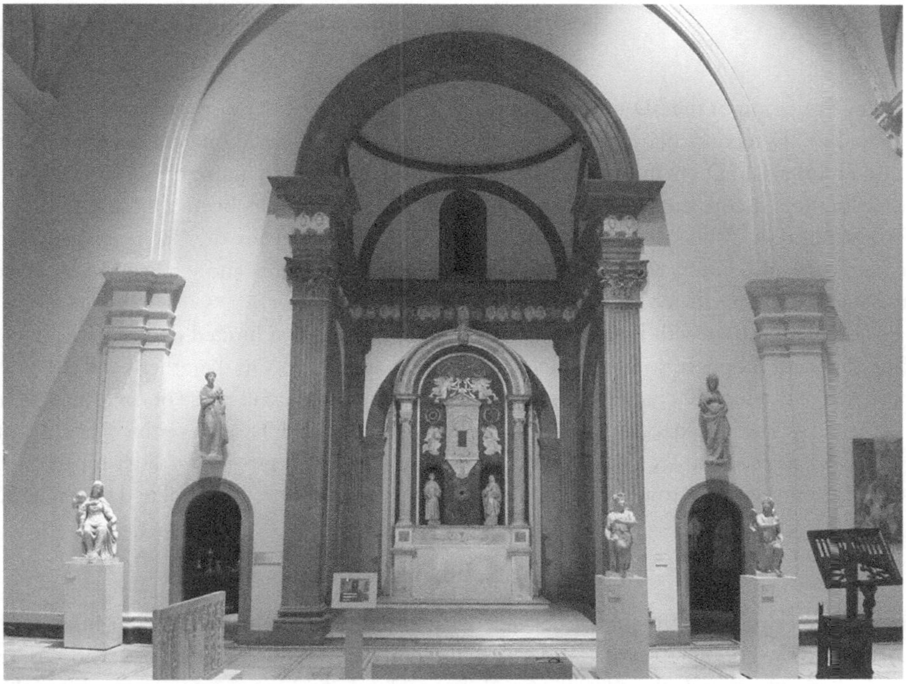

*Figure 16.3* Santa Chiara Chancel Chapel with view of the virtual museum interactive to the bottom front left.

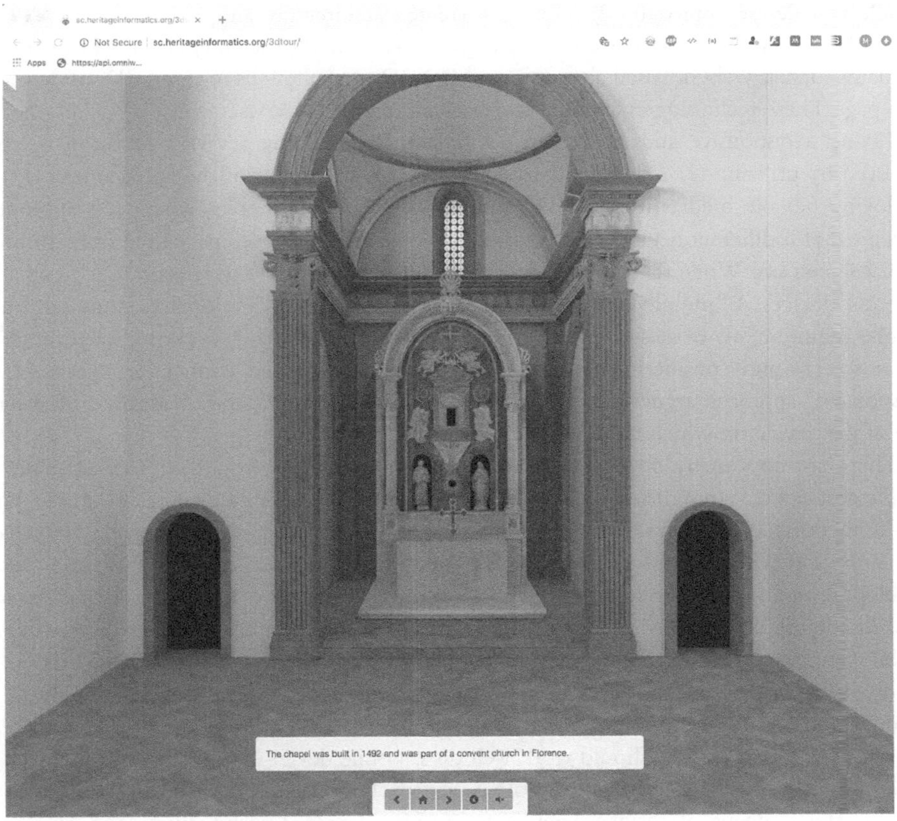


*Figure 16.4* Santa Chiara responsive mobile first design exploiting the 3D reconstruction in X3D.

A key limitation of the 3D walkthrough approach is that the user does not have the ability to navigate the 3D reconstruction. Unlike 3D navigation of a single 3D media object, navigation around an internal 3D environment, like Santa Chiara, raises many more opportunities for user interaction. It is useful, therefore, to restrict options to prevent users becoming lost or confused by the navigation. While developing interaction and navigation for the 3D reconstruction of the Santa Chiara Church we attempted to assist the user's journey and experience by limiting options according to device type and user preferences.

For example, a user with limited 3D gameplay experience or a limited device may prefer the default interaction options to be as simple and intuitive as possible. On the other hand, a user with experience of playing 3D computer games may value access to the full range of navigation options and as few navigation restrictions as possible applied to the model. To achieve this type of control, we can use screen size to set a default interaction mode and then provide facilities for the user to enable features they wish to use. Selection of preference can be stored in cookie data if required.

## Virtual Museum Technologies

Our brief description of the digital heritage projects referred to earlier, does not indicate their limitations in the context of more modern technologies. For example, both live versions of these resources are currently deployed with out of date technology (both were created around 2009). Reanimating Cultural Heritage for example, is designed for the desktop only, and the Santa Chiara Interactive is based on Flash. As a solution to these problems, new versions are currently being designed based on more recent web technologies that largely focus on (1) a responsive mobile first design approach; (2) a service-oriented architecture and APIs to access CO data resources; (3) use of modern web technology stacks; and (4) the integration of 3D through standards such as WebGL based abstractions (e.g. X3D) that allow us to insert 3D models into a web page. These technologies allow us to create more efficient VMs.

Taking a responsive and mobile first approach to designing a VM application is largely achieved by utilizing (1) a fluid grid-based framework for layout of the application (app); (2) deploying flexible media (images, 3D); and (3) CSS3 media queries, which sets appropriate screen sizes for different devices (mobile, tablet, PC, etc.); the VM web page then scales smoothly to that screen size. While there are other approaches, it is important to retarget VM views across different devices. A "mobile first" approach simply requires the developer to consider a user's mobile requirements by designing for the smallest screen first, then working up through the larger screens and considering (e.g. interaction methods, limited connection speed, etc.). A "responsive" approach argues that a single website (or VM) should automatically fit the screen size of the device on which the VM is being viewed.

There are now many new web technologies and front-end (client-side) frameworks that enable cost-effective responsive and mobile first designs.[13] For example, there are simple frameworks focusing on implementing a fluid grid system only, and more complete frameworks like Bootstrap, which is a more complete "popular HTML, CSS, and JavaScript framework for developing responsive, mobile first projects on the web." Frameworks, like Bootstrap, are often used in conjunction with MVC frameworks like AngulaJS. There are too many responsive and mobile first based frameworks to cover in any detail in this chapter. Suffice it to say that unless a native or hybrid approach is used to design a VM, then any of the current frameworks should produce good results for a VM viewed by the user in a museum visitor scenario. However, a key requirement is that the VM should work well on a mobile device.

One of the most interesting technology approaches available to facilitate the design of VMs is the concept of service-orientation, service-oriented architectures and application programming interfaces (API). Service-orientation "is a software design paradigm that partitions software functionality into operational capabilities that can be consumed as a service." As such, a service-orientated architecture (SOA) can be simply described as an "architectural design pattern in which application components provide services to other components via a computer protocol." That protocol could also be described as an API, which, simply put, is a "set of routine definitions and tools for building software applications—a good API will provide all the building blocks needed to develop the application." In the context of this paper the application is a VM.

There are some notable projects that partially follow this approach.[14] The Muse Open Source project, for example, is a "free software platform for publishing native iPad apps for digital libraries with cultural heritage content" that embraces the notion of open-source collections to develop museum apps while also exploiting smart devices. Muse also, supports the OpenGLAM initiative. While these characteristics are laudable, Muse also locks the developer into the iOS platform, in this case an iPad.

The Muse project also exploits the Europeana APIs with an app available for iPad on the Apple App Store, thus demonstrating the advantages of service-orientation through APIs. However, the Muse App also effectively demonstrates a key disadvantage in that the Europeana APIs access already aggregated collections. That is, Europeana based applications use objects stored in the Europeana repository, where such object metadata is very often shallow (i.e. composed of filtered data from the original participating museum rather than the original museum's collection record, which may have more extensive metadata). The Reanimating Cultural Heritage collection suffers from the same problem.

As mentioned previously, a solution would be for museums to publish their own APIs (ideally according to an open standard) to access their object collections data leaving the filtering of metadata to be done at the application design level. Many museums are now doing so with notable examples being the Victoria and Albert Museum and The British Museum.[15] Using "museum APIs" as a Google search term will reveal an interesting collection of museum APIs. While it is clear that there is much current interest in this approach, you can soon get lost in many different approaches! However, the "museums and the machine-processable web" on their museum APIs web page maintains an interesting "collection of museum, gallery, library, archive, archaeology and cultural heritage APIs, machine-readable, linked and open data services for open cultural data."[16] Other APIs can be found on the programmableweb.com website, simply use the search term 'museums' and you will find many museum APIs. Some museums, e.g. Shrewsbury Museum and Art Gallery are basing their API on the Open Search format. While there are many approaches to consider when developing a museum API for exposing collections online, we believe that a museum publishing its own API is a much better approach than the notion of aggregating data from many museums into a single collection maintained by a third party.[17]

Finally, any museum that exposes its collections through an API[18] is already well placed to allow the museum commercial industry to create interesting mobile VMs, especially when such collections can be combined with other interesting associated content such as diaspora knowledge gathered through social plugins and APIs (e.g. comments made on Facebook).

## The Reanimating Cultural Heritage API

The digital repository created for the Reanimating Cultural Heritage is configured as a client-server architecture exploiting an open-source PHP framework called CodeIgnitor. The original API is documented at http://rch.heritageinformatics.org/api/.[19]

This RCH API facilitates the development of an MVC and API based VM for accessing objects from the RCH collection as a service. In principle, a VM thus developed could be extended by merging other museum API calls together with the RCH API to integrate similar objects into the virtual space. If you access the aforementioned API link, you will see that a selection of example API calls are documented together with a method for presenting the results. For example, clicking on the first API call link (e.g. get_item/coid/1/.....) will return a JSON packet with the CO data (for CO ID 1), and installing a JSON viewer on your browser will print the JSON data. Various API calls are documented first as a basic API call example, followed by a description, then another link that returns an example render of the result, which is visible at the bottom of the page. Further, checking the browser URL after making the API call reveals the API call structure:

http://rch.heritageinformatics.org/index.php/api/search_service/get_item/coid/1/format/json

This example indicates that the API call is used as part of a search service, which returns a particular CO with ID 1 in a JSON format. Figure 16.5 illustrates the API documentation interface showing all videos associated with COID 345 being returned.

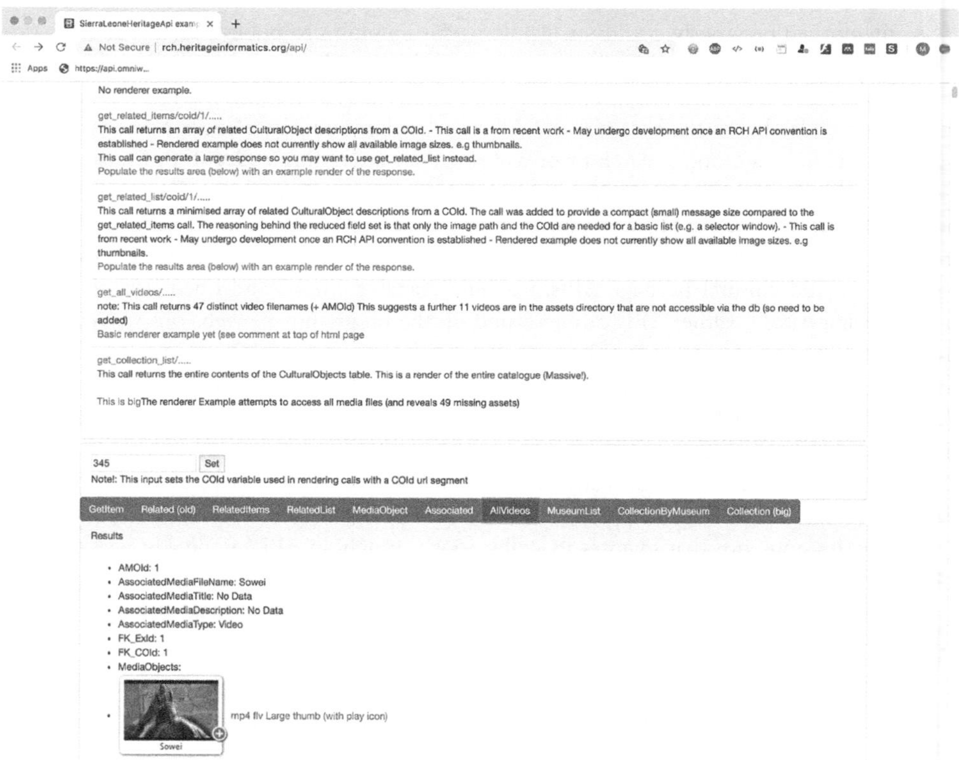


*Figure 16.5* API calls for accessing CO media and metadata for RCH.

*Source*: http://rch.heritageinformatics.org/api/.

## The Church of Santa Chiara API

The Santa Chiara API has around twenty-two basic access API calls, such as get_Database, get_Intro, get_Menu, and so on. Figure 16.6 shows the Santa Chiara API guide, which is simply accessed using the URL: http://sc.heritageinformatics.org/index.php/api. The API documentation is composed of a captured image that shows the call and response of the API call that has been taken from the Restlet Client extension.

You can search and add the Restlet Client extension to your browser and follow the user guide and tutorials to see how it works. Such tools can be used to help you develop a read only API, which for building simple VMs to access objects in single page applications is all you need to build secure VMs with simplified code and reduced need for updates. In this case, the API can be published without requiring passwords—or technically capable administrators.

The get_Menu API call loads all the data required for the home page. If you use the Restlet Client to examine the API calls, you should see a subset of API calls on the left-hand pane with the get_Menu API call selected, the top right-hand pane shows the API request the GET http://localhost:8888/index.php/api/get_Menu, so you can see we are using a localhost to develop the VM. The bottom right-hand pane shows the response, which is a JSON payload in the body.

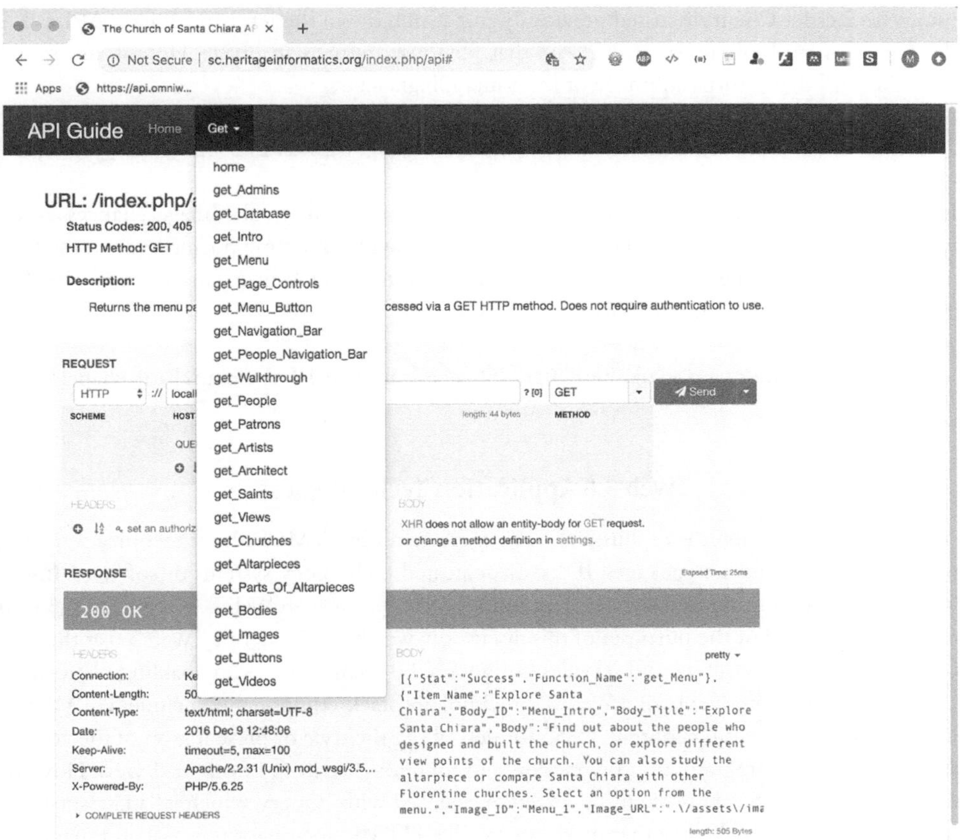


*Figure 16.6* The Santa Chiara API Guide.

## Building Museum APIs: Tutorial

Using a tool like the Restlet Client allows you to examine an existing VM (or website) that uses a service-oriented approach, i.e. an AJAX request and response base protocol. For example, you can use the Chrome Developer Inspect tool to examine "Network" traffic and "Save as a HAR file with Contents" contents returned from the Victoria and Albert Museum website (or VM).

You can try this at home: Open a Chrome browser and type in https://collections.vam.ac.uk/. You should get a page called "V&A Search the Collections" with a set of thumbnail images. Right click your mouse and open the Chrome Inspect panel, and then select one of the images or search for another image (I searched for Santa Chiara to find an image called "Chancel Chapel from Church of Santa Chiara, Florence"). The image will pop up, select details, then in the Network pane you will see a list of GET methods (API calls effectively) that are used to fetch the contents to the browser view. You can now right click in the Network pane and select "Save all as HAR with Contents," and (as shown in the Restlet Client tutorial) you can import this API information into your Restlet Client to examine these GET methods further.

Let's say you were interested in using this image to build into a VM of your own. If you click on the Download Image button, you can clearly agree to terms of use and download the image. However, you may wish to select the actual image from the V&A server using their GET method (API call). All you need to do is find the particular API call, which you can easily do using the Restlet Client discussed previously, just search down the left had panel of API calls in the scenarios tab looking for an API call that obviously returns an image. Here is an example GET API call that returns an image of the Santa Chiara altar:

https://media.vam.ac.uk/media/thira/collection_images/2012FL/2012FL4125_jpg_l.jpg

In reality, if you were building a VM that needed to exploit this particular image, chances are you would want to get more CO data too, so you would spend some time poring over all the GET methods that would be useful to construct your version of the "Santa Chiara," using the V&A information as a guide for your VM:

https://collections.vam.ac.uk/item/O17758/chancel-chapel-from-church-of-chapel/

## Web 3.0 Application Technologies

A key aim of this chapter is to illustrate how to create mobile VMs without recourse to expensive commercial software packages, IDEs, or dedicated technology systems or software. Instead we wish to exploit a typical Web 2.0 technology stack to create a Web 3.0 application, in our case a mobile VM. For the purposes of this discussion, we choose to define "Web 3.0 as the creation of high-quality content and services using Web 2.0 technology as an enabling platform."[20]

Typical core components of a Web 2.0 technology stack components include: HTML5 for structuring and presenting content, CSS3 for describing the style or presentation of the content, and JavaScript for programming interaction and functionality in the front-end view. However, straightforward JavaScript is often supported or replaced with JQuery, which is "a fast, small, and feature-rich JavaScript library that makes things like HTML document traversal and manipulation, event handling, animation, and AJAX (Asynchronous JavaScript and XML) much simpler with an easy-to-use API that works across a multitude of browsers." Another key requirement for responsive and mobile first web applications (e.g. a mobile VM) is that contents should be asynchronously updated to provide rapid update. Fortunately, JQuery provides AJAX functionality with its JQuery.getJSON() and JQuery.ajax() methods.[21]

There are, however, alternative methods for making asynchronous requests, using JavaScript and XMLhttpRequest. With AJAX, we typically use JSON (JavaScript Object Notion), which is a lightweight data-interchange format for exchanging data between the back-end (e.g. web server) and front-end, to replace the XMLHttpRequest. XMLHttpRequest is itself an API call for transferring data between the front-end view and back-end model.[22]

There are also many front-end frameworks (such as Bootstrap, AngulaJS), along with back-end frameworks such as Laravel, CodeIgniter, Zend (based on PHP)—too many to discuss in any detail—that lend themselves to efficient responsive and mobile first VM development. The key point is that there are numerous open-source web technology stacks that a VM developer can exploit to create highly innovative mobile VMs (as a Web 3.0 Application) using standard software and web development skills.

## Integrating 3D Technologies Into the Web Stack

AVM can provide a more interesting experience for the visitor if it incorporates some elements of 3D. This does not need to be restricted to single 3D presentations of an object, but can also be based on a 3D reconstruction of a site or monument to include interesting user interactions. Therefore, a critical development that favors mobile VMs is the ready availability of open-source 3D graphics APIs, such as WebGL, X3DOM, and AR SDKs.[23] WebGL is "exposed through the HTML5 Canvas element as a Document Object Model interface." These, and other AR libraries such as the Metaio AR SDK now acquired by Apple, have accelerated the potential to implement innovative interactive mobile VMs as web or mobile apps, rather than native apps. Furthermore, these mobile VMs can easily exploit 3D reconstructions as part of an object's digital representation, including in an AR context.

It is, however, beyond the scope of this chapter to describe the technologies needed to build 3D models for exploitation in VMs in any detail. While it is often time-consuming and expensive to use traditional technologies such as 3D authoring packages including 3ds Max, Maya, and the open-source Blender.[24] 3ds Max and Maya are both commercial, but museums—many of which are charities—can often acquire cheap licensing when compared to the commercial cost. There are also many excellent online tutorials that accompany these packages as well as their integrated tutorials. Other 3D reconstruction methods include some form of scanning, such as laser and photogrammetry that can produce good results, but invariably require some post-processing in the 3D authoring packages mentioned.[25]

## Santa Chiara VM Architecture

Both the Reanimating Cultural Heritage and Santa Chiara APIs have been discussed, so we shall now turn to the MVC design pattern for these VMs and consider how the APIs are used in the MVC architecture. In the case of Reanimating Cultural Heritage, we used the CodeIgniter PHP framework, which is already based on an MVC design pattern. CodeIgniter is well documented as a PHP based MVC framework, so we will not discuss this further here.[26]

Instead, we will focus on the Santa Chiara MVC architecture as it was developed from scratch. The Santa Chiara VM was created as a very lightweight MVC architecture composed of an application folder, with subfolders containing the VM's model, views, and controller components. It is largely based on PHP (controller and model), JavaScript and JQuery with HTML and CSS3 (Views) exploiting Bootstrap.

As discussed previously, the concepts behind service-orientation and APIs are extremely useful for developing a mobile VM in a simple way. Furthermore, it is not uncommon to build service-orientation into a model, view, controller (MVC) design pattern that has many architectural advantages over a standard JavaScript approach. The main advantage is that MVC encourages us to separate out code concerns and to write more structured, organized code that is easier to maintain. To help us adopt an MVC approach, there are many open-source MVC frameworks available for both server-side (PHP based) and client-side (JavaScript based) that we can exploit. As mentioned, our RCH VM utilizes CodeIgnitor, although there are newer PHP based MVC frameworks like Laravel and many others available.[27]

It is, however, relatively easy to build your own MVC design pattern simply by following the principle of separating the application code into the three MVC components shown in Figure 16.7 and routing all requests to and from the database (model) via the controller (API layer). The key steps to exploiting an MVC design pattern to encode a simple API driven approach are:

- **View**. Create appropriate scripts at the front-end that make AJAX requests to an API call. These scripts can be written in JavaScript that utilize JQuery's AJAX calls (e.g. jQuery.getJSON()) to make the media request via an URL that addresses a PHP based API call method in the controller. The JSON object returned from this request is parsed to extract data in the CO for the front-end view.
- **Controller**. The API can be coded as part of the VM's controller as a PHP class with a set of PHP based methods (or functions) where each method implements the API call. The API methods in the controller can be designed to request the database object (e.g. a COs associated data set (3D, text, metadata, video, etc.)) through the model's data abstraction layer (DAL). The DAL, in this case, is written as PHP data Objects (PDO).[28] The API call then returns the CO data set via a JSON packet to the view where the jQuery.getJSON() handler, which you write, parses the data into appropriate HTML5 block elements, such as a div tag.

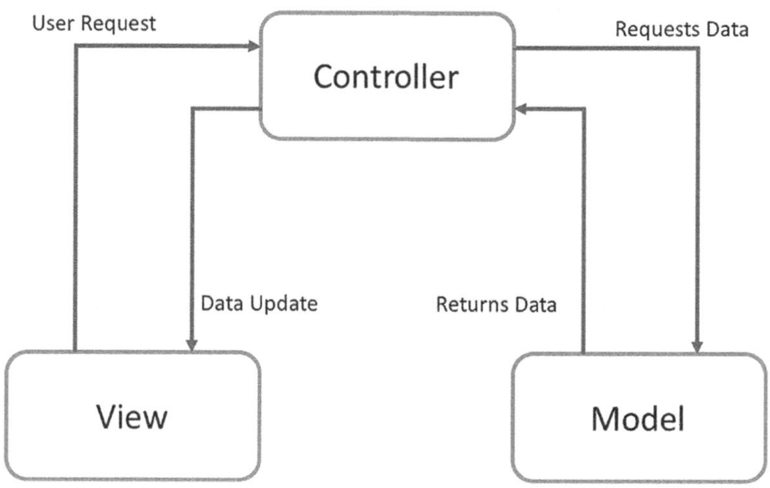


*Figure 16.7* MVC design pattern.

- **Model.** The model is designed as a PHP class with a set of PHP methods or functions using PDO, starting with one that makes the database connection, which match the API call and are implemented as a data abstraction layer. The database holds the appropriate data (or links to data) for the VM.

Of course, there can be many architectural variations to this approach, but the principle should be the same, and in this case the preceding description broadly explains the way CodeIgniter implements an API (in our RCH project). For our Santa Chiara VM, we simplified the CodeIgniter approach to implement an API without using any particular framework.

Figure 16.8 shows the folder structure (LHS) for the Santa Chiara VM and the MVC structure (RHS). You can see that we have developed an API layer in the controller, a model composed of a data abstraction layer (DAL) that can be used to access different models, e.g. MySQL DB, SQLite DB, or a JSON flat file. The ability to swap out different models and views is a particular advantage of MVC. In this case, each model contains a copy of the complete Santa Chiara CO data. In addition, it is possible to use Google's Firebase with built-in API capabilities to access Santa Chiara COs stored in the cloud.

The key code components are those located in the application folder, particularly the model, view, and controller subfolders. There are, of course, other support folders such as an asset folder that contains media files, script folder containing JavaScript files, and so on. The MVC architecture largely works by invoking the index.php page, which instantiates required libraries and files including the mvc.php file. The mvc.php file invokes the page loader called load.php, which loads the views depending on controller methods called. Object data from the model passes through the controller to the view as described previously and shown in Figure 16.7. You will note we have several views; the example view is the response.php file. This is basically an example Santa Chiara VM. A study of the Santa Chiara API documentation view would allow a developer to build many other Santa Chiara VMs. Another Santa Chiara view is the CMS view, which allows the CO and associated data in the three models to be modified. For simple VMs, you do not need to build a full CRUD API capability, a simple read only API is sufficient, as illustrated in Figure 16.6.

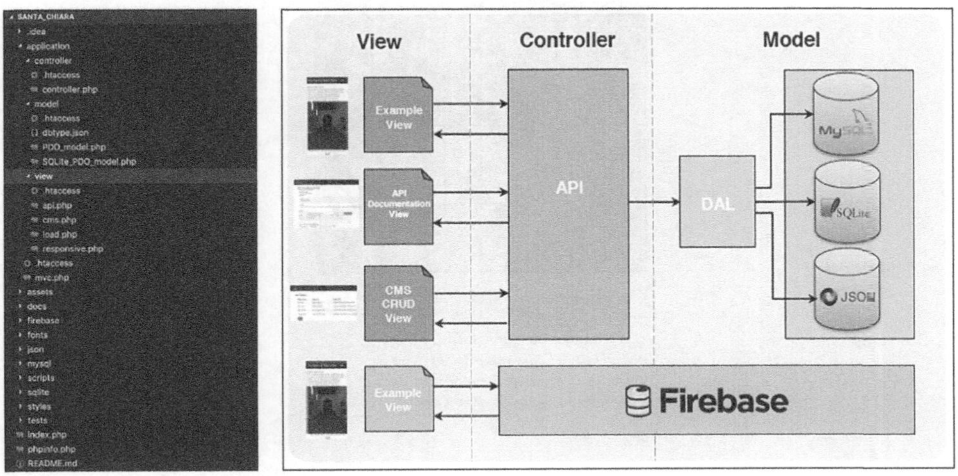


*Figure 16.8* MVC architecture for the Santa Chiara Virtual Museum.

Figure 16.9 illustrates a responsive mobile first view of the Altarpiece in the Church of Santa Chiara for the example Santa Chiara VM in a localhost development environment. Here, we can see six main VM elements:

1. Logo: The Church of Santa Chiara.
2. Navigation menu: Home, People, Views, Altarpiece, Churches in Florence, Walkthrough (the video) 3D Tour (user can navigate freely through the Church—see Figure 16.4).
3. Title: The Altarpiece.
4. Description: A brief description of the page contents.
5. 3D image: 3D image view looking at the Altarpiece, which also has hotspots to further information integrated in the image. You can see St Clair information has been activated.
6. Image caption: Image from the 3D reconstruction of Santa Chiara.

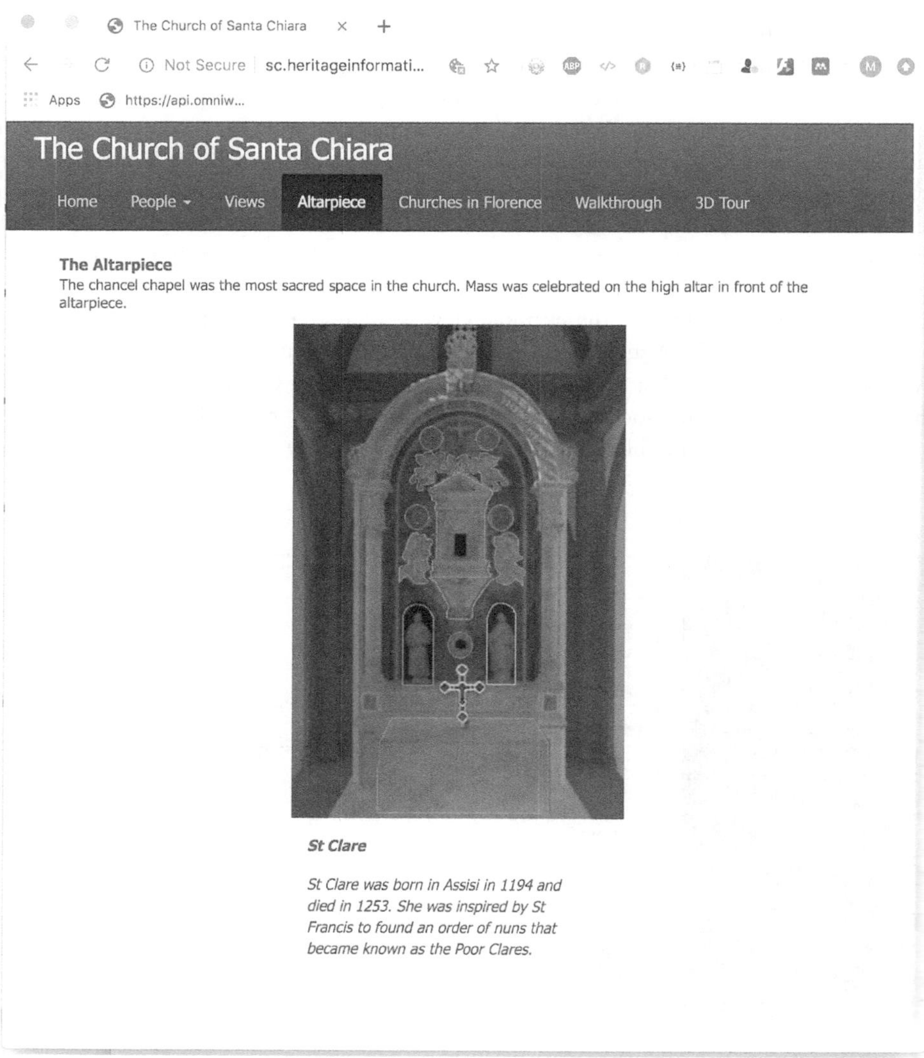


*Figure 16.9* Example mobile response view of Santa Chiara VM created with the API.

*Table 16.1* Example MVC code structure for Santa Chiara.

| Example View code: responsive.php — a container to hold the VM's main navigation elements, e.g. title, description, image and caption |
| --- |

```
<div class="container" id="wrapper">
    <div id="navMainContentsContainer" class="row">
       <div id="mainContents" class="col-sm-12">
           <div id="exploreSantaChiara">
               <div class="mainInfo">
                   <div id="title"></div>
                   <div id="description"></div>
               </div>
               <!--<div class="imageGroup"> -->
               <div id="imageCol" class="text-center">
                   <div class="imageBox">
                       <div id="picture"></div>
                       <!-- A 3D render of one of the views of
looking towards the main Altar is currently used -->
                   </div>
                   <div id="pictureCaption"></div>
               </div>
               <!--</div> -->
           </div>
```

| Example View code: apiSantaChiara.js — AJAX $.getJSON call for the menu data and parses this to get the #title, #description, #picture and #pictureCaption |
| --- |

```
$ (document). ready(function(){
    /**
     * @function get_Menu
     * @param "./index.php/api/get_Menu"
     * @description gets the menu data from API in JSON format.
Then places data into divs
     * @return {jQuery.jqXHR}
     */
    $.getJSON("./index.php/api/get_Menu", function(data){
        //placing content
        $.each(data, function(index) {
            if(data[index].Item_Name == "menu"){
               // Place the title
               // Explore Santa Chiara
               $("#title").html(data[index].Body_Title);

               // Place the description
               //Find out about the people . . .
               $("#description").html("<p>"+data[index].Body+"</p>");

               // Place the picture
               // Insert a 3D image
               $("#picture").html("<img src='"+data[index].Image_
URL+"'>");

               // Place the picture caption
               // Insert a caption for the 3D image
               $("#pictureCaption").html("<p>"+data[index].Image_
Caption+"</p>");
            }
        });
    }) ;
```

(*Continued*)

*Table 16.1* (Continued)

Example Controller code: controller.php — API call get_menu to the PDO_model.php for menu data that is returned to apiSantaChiara.js above

```
    /**
     * Gets menu data
     *
     * @api * * @return void
     */
    function get_Menu()
    {
        $data = $this->model->get_Menu();
        echo json_encode($data);
    }
```

Example Model code: PDO_model.php — the model queries the database for menu data and returns this to the API get_Menu call.

```
    /**
     * Get the menu from database
     *
     * @return array
     */
    function get_Menu()
    {
        try {
            if(isset($this->backendType["JSON"])){
                $result = file_get_contents($_SERVER['DOCUMENT_
ROOT']."/json/menu.json");
                $result = json_decode($result);
            } else {
                $sql = 'SELECT Menu.menuID, Menu.title, Menu.body
AS bodyID, Body.bodyTitle, Body.body, Menu.image, Image.imageURL,
Image.caption FROM Menu Inner Join Body on Menu.body = Body.
bodyName Join Image on Menu.image = Image.imageName';
                $stmt = $this->dbhandle->query($sql);
                $result = null;
                $result[0]['Stat'] = 'Success';
                $result[0]['Function_Name'] = 'get_Menu';
                $i = 1;
                while ($data = $stmt->fetch()) {
                    $result[$i]['Item_Name'] = $data['menuID'];
                    $result[$i]['Title'] = $data['title'];
                    $result[$i]['Body_ID'] = $data['bodyID'];
                    $result[$i]['Body_Title'] = $data['bodyTitle'];
                    $result[$i]['Body'] = $data['body'];
                    $result[$i]['Image_ID'] = $data['image'];
                    $result[$i]['Image_URL'] = $data['imageURL'];
                    $result[$i]['Image_Caption'] = $data['caption'];
                    $i++;
                }
            }
        } catch (PDOException $e) {
            $this->handle($e);
        }
        return $result;
    }
```

Each of these elements can be created using the API calls discussed previously, as can any other page elements that are selected via the navigation menu. The API simply returns data for the front-end view and you have to design the view in HTML5 and CSS3.

Owing to limitations of space, it is not possible to discuss the codebase in detail in this chapter. However, Table 16.1 illustrates some code snippets, including API calls, from the view, controller, and model that built this home page for the Santa Chiara VM.

For the Santa Chiara VM home page we can see the front-end view (responsive.php), and in this code snippet a container holds the main navigation elements to allow users to explore the Santa Chiara VM, the title, description, image and caption already mentioned. Object data now has to be requested through the controller to the back-end model to asynchronously update this home page. This is done using the apiSantaChira.js file, and here we make an AJAX request using JQueries $.getJSON() function to call the get_Menu PHP method in the controller. This returns the required data as a JSON object.

The JSON data object is then parsed in the handler section of the code to extract the title, description picture, and picture caption data, which are then assigned to their respective div tags in the view using the JQuery. html() function. The response.php file then renders it to the browser. In this particular example, the get_Menu API call is invoked in the controller class as a method whereby it simply invokes the get_Menu method in the model class and loads this into a data variable. This is then presented, using the PHP echo language construct, to the original AJAX call in the apiSantaChira.js file. This is the JSON object whose components, i.e. title, description, image, and caption are returned to the front-end view.

Finally, the get_Menu method in the model class simply decides if the back-end CO data is stored in a JSON file or a database. If a database has been pre-selected, it executes a prepared SQL statement to extract the required data from the database (mySQL or SQLite depending on which one has been selected by the user). There are, of course, many API calls designed for the Santa Chiara VM, but in principle they work in the same way as the get_Menu API call.

## Conclusions

In this chapter, we have discussed a method for building simple access-only virtual museums based on mobile first and responsive web technology stacks that incorporate 3D, VR, and AR digital media. While there are many approaches that can be taken, the preceding discussion focuses on exploiting service-orientation through a simple read only API that allows a museum to expose its digital cultural objects for easy access in single page applications. Using this approach takes advantage of the fact that most contemporary museum visitors are likely to have a smartphone and so can easily download an app. This allows the visitor to avoid queues at fixed museum interactive installations, and to enjoy a more rewarding personalized experience that encourages reflection on what they have seen in the museum after their visit.

New Web 3.0 technologies allow virtual museums to be created from a designer's perspective—rather than a technology perspective—making them far easier to develop. The codes required to build a simple virtual museum are not difficult to master and to craft into a template structure that can be reused time and time again.[29] There is no need for a content management system. Rather, it is possible to integrate the contents as a JSON flat file and, when the resulting virtual museum has had its day, a replacement can be built using the same API with a new front end.

## Notes

1. This is an aggregated collection of Sierra Leone material cultural represented in digital space, i.e. the Reanimating Cultural Heritage digital heritage repository, interface recently updated, "SierraLeone-Heritage.Org | Digital Heritage Resource," n.d., accessed August 2, 2018, www.sierraleoneheritage.org/.
2. The Web 3D Consortium maintains an open standard for incorporating 3D objects, which in this case represent museum digital artifacts, in a typical web browser where the web browser is used to host a virtual museum, "Web 3D Consortium—Open Standard for Real-Time 3D Communication," n.d., accessed August 15, 2018, www.web3d.org/.
3. These are two virtual museums, created by the authors, that exploit 3D, VR and AR, "SierraLeone-Heritage.Org | Digital Heritage Resource," n.d., accessed August 2, 2018, www.sierraleoneheritage.org/; Michael Gkion, Zeeshan Patoli, and Martin White, "Museum Interactive Experiences Through a 3D Reconstruction of the Church of Santa Chiara," In *IASTED Computer Graphics and Virtual Reality Conference*. Cambridge, UK: ACTA Press, 2011.
4. The authors and others show that many 3D, VR, and AR can be integrated effectively to create online virtual museums, Gkion et al., "Museum Interactive Experiences through a 3D Reconstruction of the Church of Santa Chiara"; Martin White, Zeeshan Patoli, and Tudor Pascu, "Knowledge Networking Through Social Media for a Digital Heritage Resource," in *Digital Heritage International Congress (DigitalHeritage)*, vol. 2, 389–92 (2013). https://doi.org/10.1109/DigitalHeritage.2013.6744787; Tsutomu Miyashita et al., "An Augmented Reality Museum Guide," *Proceedings—7th IEEE International Symposium on Mixed and Augmented Reality 2008* (ISMAR, 2008): 103–6; Sassithorn Rattanarungrot and Martin White, "A Service-Oriented Mobile Augmented Reality Architecture for Personalized Museum Environments," *Virtual Systems & Multimedia (VSMM)*, 2014 International Conference On, https://doi.org/10.1109/VSMM.2014.7136695; Sasithorn Rattanarungrot, Martin White, and Ben Jackson, "The Application of Service Orientation on a Mobile AR Platform—A Museum Scenario," *International Congress on Digital Heritage—Theme 2—Computer Graphics and Interaction*, eds. Gabriele Guidi, Roberto Scopigno, and Pere Brunet (IEEE, 2015). https://doi.org/TBA; Stella Sylaiou et al., "Exploring the Relationship Between Presence and Enjoyment in a Virtual Museum," *International Journal of Human-Computer Studies* 68, no. 5 (2010): 243–53. http://sro.sussex.ac.uk/24404/.
5. The application of service-orientation combined with Augmented Reality and mobile virtual museums can be particularly effective, Sassithorn Rattanarungrot and Martin White, "A Service-Oriented Mobile Augmented Reality Architecture for Personalized Museum Environments"; Rattanarungrot, White, and Jackson, "The Application of Service Orientation on a Mobile AR Platform—A Museum Scenario".
6. Switching between an AR- and VR-based VM context was first demonstrated in the ARCO project, Rafal Wojciechowski et al., "Building Virtual and Augmented Reality Museum Exhibitions," in *Proceedings of the Ninth International Conference on 3D Web Technology*, 135–44. Web3D '04 (New York, NY: ACM, 2004). https://doi.org/10.1145/985040.985060 in 2004 on the desktop.
7. The use of augmented reality technology lends itself to interesting virtual museum scenarios, including continuing a museum visit in the home, Sassithorn Rattanarungrot, Martin White, and Ben Jackson, "The Application of Service Orientation on a Mobile AR Platform—A Museum Scenario".
8. This is because there is a current trend to "shift the business logic of web application development from the back-end to the front-end where back-end data can be easily accessed via a simple API" Martin Angelov, "The Languages, Frameworks and Tools to Learn in 2017," 2018. https://tutorialzine.com/2016/12/the-languages-frameworks-tools-you-should-learn-in-2017.
9. Single page applications, a mobile first approach and APIs are critical to creating simple virtual museums online, "Create APIs to Power Data Integration and Deliver Data as a Service," n.d., accessed August 1, 2018, http://transform.ca.com/LAC-Data-Integration-through-Creating-REST-APIs.html?mrm=508752&cid=EMEA-SEM-API-ACF-000011–00000947–000000110; "Single-Page Application," https://en.wikipedia.org/wiki/Single-page_application. "SPARQL 1.1 Overview," 2013, www.w3.org/TR/sparql11-overview/; Philipp Steinweber, n.d., "Why 'Mobile First' Is the New 'Responsive,'" accessed August 1, 2018, https://soulfulhustle.com/mobile-first-vs-responsive/.
10. Using a smartphone provides an opportunity for the visitor to reflect upon the physical object in the museum by accessing both it and related objects in more interesting virtual and augmented ways,

Michael Gkion, Zeeshan Patoli, and Martin White, "Museum Interactive Experiences through a 3D Reconstruction of the Church of Santa Chiara".

11. Reanimating Cultural Heritage: Digital Repatriation, Knowledge Networks and Civil Society Strengthening in Post-Conflict Sierra Leone, Paul Basu, "Reanimating Cultural Heritage: Digital Repatriation, Knowledge Networks and Civil Society Strengthening in Post-Conflict Sierra Leone," 2008, http://projects.beyondtext.ac.uk/reanimatingculturalheritage/index.php?i=38&p=Reanimating cultural heritage digital repatriation, knowledge networks and civil society strengthening in post-conflict Sierra Leone.
12. The Chancel Chapel from the Church of Santa Chiara was acquired by the Victoria and Albert Museum, London (formerly the South Kensington Museum) in 1860 by John Charles Robinson. You can access more information about the V&A Medieval and Renaissance Galleries and in particular the Sacred Spaces, here: Meghan Callahan and Donal Cooper, "Sacred Space in the Modern Museum: Researching and Redisplaying the Santa Chiara Chapel in the V&A's Medieval & Renaissance Galleries," *V&A Online Journal*, no. 5 (2013). www.vam.ac.uk/content/journals/research-journal/issue-no.-5-2013/sacred-space-in-the-modern-museum-researching-and-redisplaying-the-santa-chiara-chapel-in-the-v-and-as-medieval-and-renaissance-galleries/; "Video: Medieval and Renaissance Galleries—Victoria & Albert Museum," n.d., accessed August 2, 2018. www.vam.ac.uk/content/videos/m/video-medieval-and-renaissance-galleries/; "Chancel Chapel from Church of Santa Chiara, Florence | Sangallo, Guiliano Da | V&A Search the Collections," n.d., accessed August 2, 2018, http://collections.vam.ac.uk/item/O17758/chancel-chapel-from-church-of-chapel-sangallo-guiliano-da/.
13. Modern front-end libraries that facilitate service orientation and application programming interfaces include Bootstrap, "Bootstrap The World's Most Popular Mobile-First and Responsive Front-End Framework," n.d., accessed August 15, 2016, http://getbootstrap.com/; "Service-Orientation," n.d., accessed August 2, 2018, https://en.wikipedia.org/wiki/Service-orientation; "Service-Oriented Architecture," n.d., accessed August 2, 2018, https://en.wikipedia.org/wiki/Service-oriented_architecture; "Application Programming Interface," n.d., accessed August 2, 2018, https://en.wikipedia.org/wiki/Application_programming_interface.
14. Some museums that partially follow a service-orientation approach include Muse, OpenGLAM and Europeans, where OpenGLAM "promotes free and open access to digital cultural heritage held by galleries, libraries, archives and museums," "Muse Open Source | The Personal Mobile Museum," 2013, http://muse-opensource.org/; "Open Galleries, Libraries, Archives and Museums," 2016, http://openglam.org/; "Introduction to the Europeana APIs," 2015, http://labs.europeana.eu/api.
15. Both the Victoria and Albert Museum and the British Museum are developing their own APIs to access their collections online, "Victoria and Albert Museum API Documentation," n.d., accessed May 6, 2016, www.vam.ac.uk/api/; "Home | The British Museum | British Museum SPARQL Endpoint | RDF Cultural Heritage Data," n.d., accessed May 6, 2016, http://collection.britishmuseum.org/.
16. It is not difficult to find many examples where museums are attempting to adopt APIs to access their collections, "Museum and the Machine-Processable Web," n.d., Accessed May 10, 2016, http://museum-api.pbworks.com/w/page/21933420/Museum APIs; "Museums APIs," 2016, @programmableweb. 2016. www.programmableweb.com/category/museums/apis; "Shrewsbury Museum & Art Gallery Open Data API for Developers," n.d., accessed August 2, 2018, www.shrewsburymuseum.org.uk/api/; "Home—OpenSearch," n.d., accessed May 9, 2016, www.opensearch.org/Home.
17. This is because that third party will only have to create an API to access the aggregated collection. This often leads to so-called shallow metadata being available on the aggregated collection. Any third party can already aggregate many museums collections if those museums publish their own APIs.
18. Such as a REST API or Linked Open Data (LOD), "Linked Data | Linked Data—Connect Distributed Data across the Web," 2016, http://linkeddata.org/; "Europeana Linked Open Data," 2015, http://labs.europeana.eu/api/linked-open-data-introduction, e.g. using a query language such as SPARQL, "SPARQL 1.1 Overview," 2013, www.w3.org/TR/sparql11-overview/; "Home | The British Museum | British Museum SPARQL Endpoint | RDF Cultural Heritage Data," n.d., accessed May 6, 2016, http://collection.britishmuseum.org/.
19. The Reanimating Cultural Heritage repository (Basu 2008) exploits CodeIgnitor, "CodeIgniter Web Framework," 2016, www.codeigniter.com/, which is a web framework based on a MVC design pattern (Dev 2014) and associated MySQL database, and is structured to facilitate development of an API within its MVC architecture.

20. An example Web 3.0 definition, "Web 3.0, the "Official" Definition. | Calacanis.Com," n.d., accessed August 15, 2016, http://calacanis.com/2007/10/03/web-3-0-the-official-definition/.
21. JQuery is a very useful code library that provides an abstraction over JavaScript, while at the same time providing excellent AJAX (Asynchronous JavaScript and XML) functionality that allows web browser components to be updated rather that the whole page, which is a much slower process, "What Is JQuery?" 2018, https://jquery.com/; "JQuery.GetJSON() | JQuery API Documentation," n.d., accessed August 9, 2016, http://api.jquery.com/jquery.getjson/; Zack Bloom, "You Might Not Need JQuery," *HubSpot*. 2018, http://youmightnotneedjquery.com/.
22. A more painful alternative to JQuery is to stick with JavaScript and use XMLhttpRequest to update components in the virtual museum's web page, Bloom, "You Might Not Need JQuery"; Wikipedea Contributors n.d., "XMLHttpRequest," in Wikipedia, accessed August 2, 2018, https://en.wikipedia.org/w/index.php?title=XMLHttpRequest&oldid=846436270.
23. WebGL and abstractions such as X3DOM and some AR SDKs are particularly useful open source technologies for building virtual museums, "WebGL—OpenGL ES 2.0 for the Web," 2016, www.khronos.org/api/webgl/; Johannes Behr et al., "X3DOM: A DOM-Based HTML5/X3D Integration Model," *Proceedings of the 14th International Conference on 3D Web Technology* (Darmstadt, Germany: ACM, 2009). https://doi.org/10.1145/1559764.1559784; "Metaio | Home," 2015, www.metaio.com/index.html; Rattanarungrot, White, and Jackson, "The Application of Service Orientation on a Mobile AR Platform—A Museum Scenario"; Y. Jung, J. Behr, and H. Graf, "X3DOM As Carrier of the Virtual Heritage," *ISPRS—International Archives of the Photogrammetry, Remote Sensing and Spatial Information Sciences* XXXVIII-5 (2012): 475–82. https://doi.org/10.5194/isprsarchives-XXXVIII-5-W16-475-2011; Antonio Baglivo et al., "X3D/X3DOM, Blender Game Engine and OSG4WEB: Open Source Visualisation for Cultural Heritage Environments," *Proceedings of the DigitalHeritage 2013—Federating the 19th Int'l VSMM, 10th Eurographics GCH, and 2nd UNESCO Memory of the World Conferences*, Plus Special Sessions From CAA, Arqueologica 2.0, 2013 et al. 2: 711–18, https://doi.org/10.1109/DigitalHeritage.2013.6744840.
24. Commercial and open-source 3D authoring packages can be used to create 3D representationalism of a museum's physical artifacts, "3ds Max | 3D Modelling & Rendering Software | Autodesk," n.d., accessed August 11, 2016, www.autodesk.co.uk/products/3ds-max/overview; "Maya | Computer Animation & Modelling Software," n.d., accessed August 11, 2016, www.autodesk.co.uk/products/maya/overview; "Blender.Org—Home of the Blender Project—Free and Open 3D Creation Software," n.d., accessed August 11, 2016, www.blender.org/.
25. Laser scanning and photogrammetry are two common techniques used to generate 3D models, but they also often require extensive post processing, "Terrain Surveys—Land Surveyors Laser Scanning Services—Terrain Surveys," n.d., accessed August 11, 2016, www.terrainsurveys.co.uk/services/laser-scanning/?gclid=Cj0KEQjwxLC9BRDb1dP8o7Op68IBEiQAwWggQJKUU0ESjv9ZWJ1tDAFVhuClFBhh7MpTTw-TsIMpCEYaAou38P8HAQ; English Heritage, *3D Laser Scanning for Heritage* (English Heritage, 2011); Jan Heller et al., "3D Reconstruction from Photographs by CMP SfM Web Service," Machine Vision Applications (MVA), 2015 14th IAPR International Conference On, https://doi.org/10.1109/MVA.2015.7153126; "Autodesk 123D Catch | Generate 3d Model from Photos," n.d., accessed August 11, 2016, www.123dapp.com/catch.
26. Model, View, Controller (MVC) is a software design pattern that separates out the view (i.e. the web page from the data in the database, i.e. the model, and the business logic (the controller) that brings data from the model and puts it in the view. This is key because it allow you to make many different views (virtual museums) using the same data (model), for example. In our case we often use CodeIgnitor with its in built MVC design pattern to develop virtual museums, "CodeIgniter Web Framework," 2016, www.codeigniter.com/.
27. There are many MVC frameworks that we can exploit to build our virtual museums, "An Introduction to MVC Frameworks," n.d., accessed August 15, 2016, http://blog.scottlogic.com/2013/12/06/JavaScript-MVC-frameworks.html; "Welcome to the Apache Struts Project," n.d., accessed August 15, 2016, https://struts.apache.org/; "AngularJS—Superheroic JavaScript MVW Framework," n.d., accessed August 15, 2016, https://angularjs.org/; "Laravel—The PHP Framework For Web Artisans," n.d., accessed August 15, 2016, https://laravel.com/; "7 Best PHP Frameworks for 2015 | Winspire Web Solution | Pulse | LinkedIn," n.d., accessed August 15, 2016, www.linkedin.com/pulse/7-best-php-frameworks-2015-winspire-web-solution.
28. The PHP Data Objects (PDO) extension is a lightweight consistent data abstract layer that allows us to easily connect to different databases using the methods to connect to a database, issue queries and

fetch data, "PHP: Introduction—Manual," n.d., accessed August 15, 2016, http://php.net/manual/en/intro.pdo.php.

29. Many of our final year project students have contributed to working on our VM projects, but in particular we would like to thank Sam Jones who developed the full CRUD (Create, Read, Update, Delete) version of the Santa Chiara API under the guidance of the authors. From this full CRUD API version, the authors have stripped out the Create, Update, and Delete API calls along with the CMS view to leave the Read only API discussed and illustrated in Figure 16.6. The reason for this, of course, is that a museum would not want to expose its entire object database by publishing the full API without adequate security. As mentioned in the conclusion, for a museum to develop simple VMs for accessing their CO collections, a read only API is sufficient.

## Bibliography


"3ds Max | 3D Modelling & Rendering Software | Autodesk." n.d. Accessed August 11, 2016. www.autodesk.co.uk/products/3ds-max/overview.

"7 Best PHP Frameworks for 2015 | Winspire Web Solution | Pulse | LinkedIn." n.d. Accessed August 15, 2016. www.linkedin.com/pulse/7-best-php-frameworks-2015-winspire-web-solution.

"An Introduction to MVC Frameworks." n.d. Accessed August 15, 2016. http://blog.scottlogic.com/2013/12/06/JavaScript-MVC-frameworks.html.

Angelov, Martin. "The Languages, Frameworks and Tools To Learn In 2017." 2018. https://tutorialzine.com/2016/12/the-languages-frameworks-tools-you-should-learn-in-2017.

"AngularJS—Superheroic JavaScript MVW Framework." n.d. Accessed August 15, 2016. https://angularjs.org/.

"Application Programming Interface." n.d. Accessed August 2, 2018. https://en.wikipedia.org/wiki/Application_programming_interface.

"Autodesk 123D Catch | Generate 3d Model from Photos." n.d. Accessed August 11, 2016. www.123dapp.com/catch.

Baglivo, Antonio, Francesca Delli Ponti, Daniele De Luca, Antonella Guidazzoli, Maria Chiara Liguori, and Bruno Fanini. "X3D/X3DOM, Blender Game Engine and OSG4WEB: Open Source Visualisation for Cultural Heritage Environments." *Proceedings of the DigitalHeritage 2013—Federating the 19th Int'l VSMM, 10th Eurographics GCH, and 2nd UNESCO Memory of the World Conferences*, Plus Special Sessions From-CAA, Arqueologica 2.0, 2013 et al. 2: 711–18. https://doi.org/10.1109/DigitalHeritage.2013.6744840.

Basu, Paul. "Reanimating Cultural Heritage: Digital Repatriation, Knowledge Networks and Civil Society Strengthening in Post-Conflict Sierra Leone." 2008. http://projects.beyondtext.ac.uk/reanimating culturalheritage/index.php?i=38&p=Reanimating cultural heritage digital repatriation, knowledge networks and civil society strengthening in post-conflict Sierra Leone.

Behr, Johannes, Peter Eschler, Yvonne Jung, Z Michael, #246, and llner. 2009. "X3DOM: A DOM-Based HTML5/X3D Integration Model." *Proceedings of the 14th International Conference on 3D Web Technology*. Darmstadt, Germany: ACM. https://doi.org/10.1145/1559764.1559784.

"Blender.Org—Home of the Blender Project—Free and Open 3D Creation Software." n.d. Accessed August 11, 2016. www.blender.org/.

Bloom, Zack. "You Might Not Need JQuery." *HubSpot*. 2018. http://youmightnotneedjquery.com/.

"Bootstrap The World's Most Popular Mobile-First and Responsive Front-End Framework.' n.d. Accessed August 15, 2016. http://getbootstrap.com/.

Callahan Meghan, and Donal Cooper. "Sacred Space in the Modern Museum: Researching and Redisplaying the Santa Chiara Chapel in the V&A's Medieval & Renaissance Galleries." *V&A Online Journal*, no. 5 (2013). www.vam.ac.uk/content/journals/research-journal/issue-no.-5-2013/sacred-space-in-the-modern-museum-researching-and-redisplaying-the-santa-chiara-chapel-in-the-v-and-as-medieval-and-renaissance-galleries/.

"Chancel Chapel from Church of Santa Chiara, Florence | Sangallo, Guiliano Da | V&A Search the Collections." n.d. Accessed August 2, 2018. http://collections.vam.ac.uk/item/O17758/chancel-chapel-from-church-of-chapel-sangallo-guiliano-da/.

"CodeIgniter Web Framework." 2016. www.codeigniter.com/.

Contributors, Wikipedea. n.d. "XMLHttpRequest." In Wikipedia. Accessed August 2, 2018. https://en.wikipedia.org/w/index.php?title=XMLHttpRequest&oldid=846436270.

"Create APIs to Power Data Integration and Deliver Data as a Service." n.d. Accessed August 1, 2018. http://transform.ca.com/LAC-Data-Integration-through-Creating-REST-APIs.html?mrm=508752&cid=EMEA-SEM-API-ACF-000011-00000947-000000110.

Dev, ExpressionEngine. "Model-View-Controller : CodeIgniter User Guide." 2014. https://ellislab.com/codeigniter/user-guide/overview/mvc.html.
English Heritage. *3D Laser Scanning for Heritage*. English Heritage, 2011.
"Europeana Linked Open Data." 2015. http://labs.europeana.eu/api/linked-open-data-introduction.
Gkion, Michael, Zeeshan Patoli, and Martin White. "Museum Interactive Experiences through a 3D Reconstruction of the Church of Santa Chiara." In *IASTED Computer Graphics and Virtual Reallity Conference*. Cambridge, UK: ACTA Press, 2011.
Heller, J., M. Havlena, M. Jancosek, A. Torii, and T. Pajdla. 2015. "3D Reconstruction from Photographs by CMP SfM Web Service." Machine Vision Applications (MVA), 2015 14th IAPR International Conference On. https://doi.org/10.1109/MVA.2015.7153126.
"Home—OpenSearch." n.d. Accessed May 9, 2016. www.opensearch.org/Home.
"Home | The British Museum | British Museum SPARQL Endpoint | RDF Cultural Heritage Data." n.d. Accessed May 6, 2016. http://collection.britishmuseum.org/.
"Introduction to the Europeana APIs." 2015. http://labs.europeana.eu/api.
"JQuery.GetJSON() | JQuery API Documentation." n.d. Accessed August 9, 2016. http://api.jquery.com/jquery.getjson/.
Jung, Y, J Behr, and H. Graf. "X3DOM As Carrier of the Virtual Heritage." *ISPRS—International Archives of the Photogrammetry, Remote Sensing and Spatial Information Sciences* XXXVIII-5 (2012): 475–82. https://doi.org/10.5194/isprsarchives-XXXVIII-5-W16-475-2011.
"Laravel—The PHP Framework For Web Artisans." n.d. Accessed August 15, 2016. https://laravel.com/.
"Linked Data | Linked Data—Connect Distributed Data across the Web." 2016. http://linkeddata.org/.
"Maya | Computer Animation & Modelling Software." n.d. Accessed August 11, 2016. www.autodesk.co.uk/products/maya/overview.
"Medieval & Renaissance Galleries—Victoria and Albert Museum." n.d. Accessed August 2, 2018. www.vam.ac.uk/page/m/medieval-and-renaissance-galleries/.
"Metaio | Home." 2015. www.metaio.com/index.html.
"Muse Open Source | The Personal Mobile Museum." 2013. http://muse-opensource.org/.
"Museum and the Machine-Processable Web." n.d. Accessed May 10, 2016. http://museum-api.pbworks.com/w/page/21933420/Museum APIs.
"Museums APIs." 2016. @programmableweb. 2016. www.programmableweb.com/category/museums/apis.
Miyashita, T., P. Meier, T. Tachikawa, S. Orlic, T. Eble, V. Scholz, A. Gapel, O. Gerl, S. Arnaudov, and S. Lieberknecht. "An Augmented Reality Museum Guide." *Proceedings—7th IEEE International Symposium on Mixed and Augmented Reality 2008* (ISMAR 2008): 103–6, IEEE Explore Digital Library.
"Open Galleries, Libraries, Archives and Museums." 2016. http://openglam.org/.
Philipp Steinweber. n.d. "Why 'Mobile First' Is the New 'Responsive.'" Accessed August 1, 2018. https://soulfulhustle.com/mobile-first-vs-responsive/.
"PHP: Introduction—Manual." n.d. Accessed August 15, 2016. http://php.net/manual/en/intro.pdo.php.
Rattanarungrot, S., and M. White. "A Service-Oriented Mobile Augmented Reality Architecture for Personalized Museum Environments." Virtual Systems & Multimedia (VSMM), 2014 International Conference On. https://doi.org/10.1109/VSMM.2014.7136695.
Rattanarungrot, Sasithorn, Martin White, and Ben Jackson. "The Application of Service Orientation on a Mobile AR Platform—A Museum Scenario." *International Congress on Digital Heritage—Theme 2 - Computer Graphics And Interaction*, edited by Gabriele Guidi, Roberto Scopigno, and Pere Brunet. IEEE, 2015. https://doi.org/TBA.
"Service-Orientation." n.d. Accessed August 2, 2018. https://en.wikipedia.org/wiki/Service-orientation.
"Service-Oriented Architecture." n.d. Accessed August 2, 2018. https://en.wikipedia.org/wiki/Service-oriented_architecture.
"Shrewsbury Museum & Art Gallery Open Data API for Developers." n.d. Accessed August 2, 2018. www.shrewsburymuseum.org.uk/api/.
"SierraLeoneHeritage.Org | Digital Heritage Resource." n.d. Accessed August 2, 2018. www.sierraleoneheritage.org/.
"Single-Page Application." 2018. https://en.wikipedia.org/wiki/Single-page_application.
"SPARQL 1.1 Overview." 2013. www.w3.org/TR/sparql11-overview/.
Sylaiou, Stella, Katerina Mania, Athanasis Karoulis, and Martin White. "Exploring the Relationship between Presence and Enjoyment in a Virtual Museum." *International Journal of Human-Computer Studies* 68, no. 5 (2010): 243–53. http://sro.sussex.ac.uk/24404/.

"Terrain Surveys—Land Surveyors Laser Scanning Services—Terrain Surveys." n.d. Accessed August 11, 2016. www.terrainsurveys.co.uk/services/laser-scanning/?gclid=Cj0KEQjwxLC9BRDb1dP8o7Op6 8IBEiQAwWggQJKUU0ESjv9ZWJ1tDAFVhuClFBhh7MpTTw-TsIMpCEYaAou38P8HAQ.

"Victoria and Albert Museum API Documentation." n.d. Accessed May 6, 2016. www.vam.ac.uk/api/.

"Video: Medieval & Renaissance Galleries—Victoria and Albert Museum." n.d. Accessed August 2, 2018. www.vam.ac.uk/content/videos/m/video-medieval-and-renaissance-galleries/.

"Web 3.0, the "Official" Definition. | Calacanis.Com." n.d. Accessed August 15, 2016. http://calacanis.com/2007/10/03/web-3-0-the-official-definition/.

"Web 3D Consortium—Open Standard for Real-Time 3D Communication." n.d. Accessed August 15, 2018. www.web3d.org/.

"WebGL—OpenGL ES 2.0 for the Web." 2016. www.khronos.org/api/webgl/.

"Welcome to the Apache Struts Project." n.d. Accessed August 15, 2016. https://struts.apache.org/.

"What Is JQuery?" 2018. https://jquery.com/.

White, M., Z. Patoli, and T. Pascu. "Knowledge Networking through Social Media for a Digital Heritage Resource." In *Digital Heritage International Congress (DigitalHeritage)*, vol. 2, 389–92 (2013). https://doi.org/10.1109/DigitalHeritage.2013.6744787.

Wojciechowski, Rafal, Krzysztof Walczak, Martin White, and Wojciech Cellary. 2004. "Building Virtual and Augmented Reality Museum Exhibitions." In *Proceedings of the Ninth International Conference on 3D Web Technology*, 135–44. Web3D '04. New York, NY: ACM. https://doi.org/10.1145/985040.985060.

# 17

# ART HISTORY, HERITAGE GAMES, AND VIRTUAL REALITY

*Erik Champion and Anna Foka*

Traditionally, art history has been viewed as a concern about the context of creation, curation, critique, and classification of art, but its range and focus is seldom agreed on. A conventional view of art history may suggest that, as a field, it is dedicated to issues of classification and the development of related expertise in curation and critique. Yet, if we follow the arguments of the nineteenth-century philosopher Konrad Fiedler,[1] knowledge of historical form does not necessarily entail a knowledge of art, while knowledge of the history of art does not necessarily give one an understanding of art objects themselves, the material and symbolic qualities of an object of art, or deeper questions relating to the ontology of art.

More recently, the emergence of "new art history" or "the social history of art" has drawn upon critical thinking ranging from Gramsci and the Frankfurt school to postcolonial and gender studies in order to interpret art in relation to its social and historical context. Critical art theory focused on how (through artistic thinking, cognition, and configuration) art history can function either as a form of education, or as a medium of open knowledge production.

However, according to Johanna Drucker contemporary art history faces unique challenges regarding digital practice. While digital repositories have increased access to art-historical corpuses, tools for analysis and for computational processing have not developed as rapidly. Drucker argued that current directions in digital art history are driven by the remediation of images and their availability (and resistance) to techniques of data mining and other computational techniques.[2] Although critically appropriate tools and methods for examining art-historical data are taking shape, a gap remains between audience and practice, between collecting institutes and the specialized needs of researchers and educators, and between the institutional value and history of corpus and the increasingly dynamic changes in technological progress.[3]

This chapter focuses on how the engaging and entertaining medium of virtual reality and serious games has the potential to connect traditional galleries, libraries, archives, and museum (GLAM) sector organizations with contemporary audiences by blending old traditions and new technologies. Following a short definition of virtual reality, we discuss the relevance and increasing intersecting importance of virtual heritage and serious games, especially those dealing with topics and issues in art history. We suggest that while the majority of studies deal with physical or digital maintenance and display of art-historical objects; public engagement can further be achieved with the aid of participatory, sensory, and interactive platforms.[4]

There is also a question here concerning digital research infrastructures themselves. The institutional theory of art holds that an object can only be art in the context of the institution known as "the art world." As Arthur Danto has famously argued, a pile of Brillo cartons in a supermarket is not art, whereas Andy Warhol's *Brillo Boxes* are understood to be artworks in a framework of artistic theory and a knowledge of the history of art.[5] Art is an artifact on which the art world has conferred the status of candidate for appreciation.[6]

Art can, however, now contain its own "intelligence," its own sensors and its own tools, perform functions and queries on a vast scale, incorporate or reject dynamic content, and reconfigure itself according to the environment or the sensitivity of the platform that hosts it. It can also frame not just artworks and aesthetic objects but also present and allow us to explore new and rejuvenated frameworks through which people can experience art, either directly, or through institutions and social frameworks.[7]

We suggest that, broadly speaking, art history games allow the public to achieve four things. They can compel people to classify and judge art; identify art and match art to artists; understand how art is made and conserved as art works; or communicate the spatial, chronological, personal and social context in which art is created and experienced. Virtual reality and computer games are particularly suitable for exploring context, for they can work within their own rules, and convey critical changes in time, space or behavior through interaction and sensory immersion. After all, virtual reality and games, in order to create thematic, conceptual experiences, must create persuasive frameworks in which the experiences themselves are framed by contextual meaning. Rather than just provide a simulated experience of an art encounter directly, could this new technology allow us to understand how others have experienced art? Given the volatile, complex, contested, yet often fragile nature of art and heritage, virtual reality, augmented reality and mixed reality offer fascinating opportunities to explore not only artifacts, but the changing ways in which they are experienced, judged, shared, and valued.

## Alternative Realities in History

The idea of an alternative, "virtual" reality (VR) as a modern concept arguably arose not from science but from exemplars in science fiction: *Pygmalion's Spectacles* (1935), *Typewriter in the Sky* (1940), *I (Professor Corcoran)* (1961), *The Three Stigmata of Palmer Eldritch* (1965), *Neuromancer* (1984), and *Snow Crash* (1992). Another inspiration was sensory cinema. In the 1950s, predating digital computing, a mechanical VR engine was created. Morton Heilig envisaged an "Experience Theatre" that could encompass the senses beyond flat screens.[8] He built a mechanical device, the "Sensorama" in 1962 (Figure 17.1), along with five short films to be displayed in it, designed to engage multiple senses (sight, sound, smell, and touch). In 1968 Ivan Sutherland and Bob Sproull created the first Head Mount Display (HMD) in order to facilitate the immersion of the participant. The HMD was so heavy (and perilous in appearance) that it was named *The Sword of Damocles*.

According to Billinghurst et al., Virtual Reality (VR)

> uses technology to immerse a person in a completely computer generated world and remove them from reality. In this way VR is different from its cousin, Augmented Reality (AR), which aims to seamlessly superimpose virtual imagery over a user's view of the real world.[9]

Billinghurst also follows Milgram and Kishino's famous definition of Mixed Reality, "a particular subclass of VR related technologies that involve the merging of real and virtual worlds."[10]

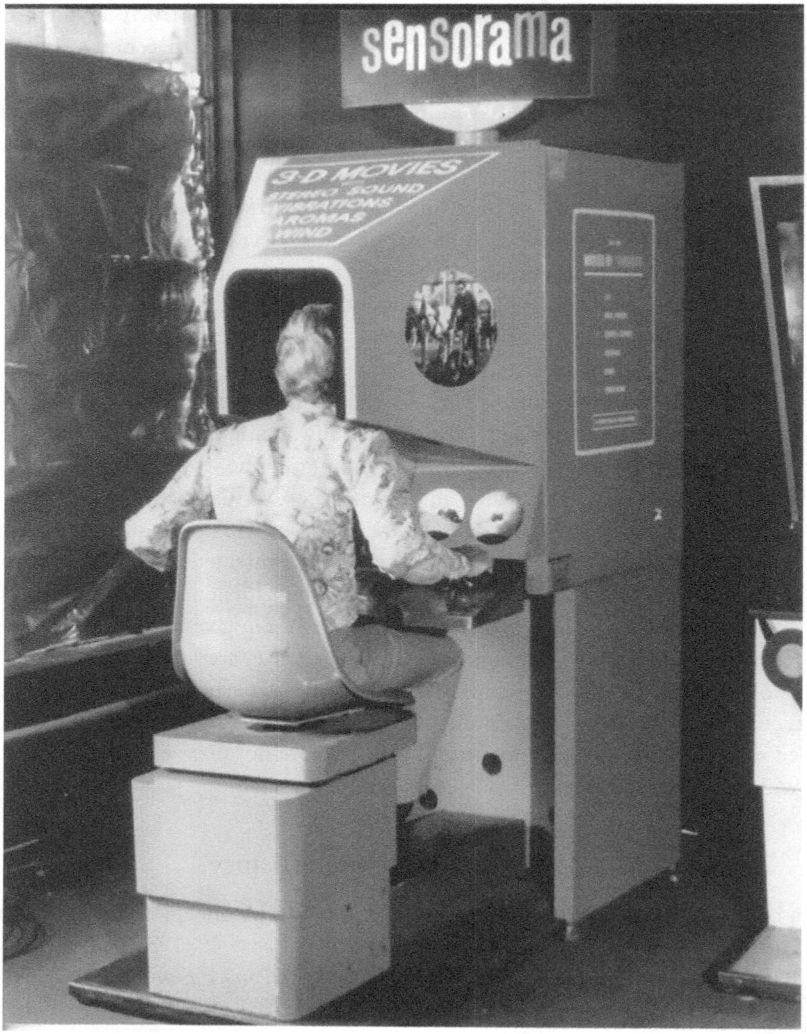


*Figure 17.1* Sensorama by Morton Heilig.

*Source*: CC By-SA 4.0, Wikipedia, created by Minecraftpsyco.

MR, VR and AR are currently platforms used for gaming, film and tourism. VR is expanding its reach to incorporate a number of popular internet applications, such as mapping applications (Google Earth) and online 3D model repositories (Sketchfab). The pedagogical advantages of digitally simulated training environments have found avenues in military projects and in medical research, especially in relation to training, rehabilitation, and physiotherapy research. The platform is also often used (alongside AR) as a knowledge production mechanism within the cultural heritage sector. The benefits of using VR as both a tool and a methodology within overall reconstructions are critical,[11] but require further development owing to their cost, complexity, lack of user-based evaluation, and their as yet inadequate capacity to preserve and maintain content.

Current VR typically utilizes either large-scale displays or an HMD (Head Mounted Display) to generate visual, sonic, and haptic environments and artifacts. VR systems can transmit sensations such as vibrations to the user through haptic systems, game controllers, and ambisonic architectural arrangements.[12] Sensations, in turn, create emotions, so the goal of sensory enhancement of experiences in VR is often to generate emotions that may lead to social change. Recent EU and international projects and related evaluations (such as The CHESS project, [LEAP] LEarning of Archeology through Presence, UShoMe, EMOTIVE and meSCH) have explored the relationship between technology, emotional engagement, and storytelling.

At an institutional level, digital prototypes in the form of 3D visualizations have become increasingly prominent in showcasing humanities research, especially in relation to museums.[13] Intellectual traditions have shown a marked preference (or even ocularcentric bias) for vision as the figure of knowledge.[14] On the other hand, intangible cultural heritage, for example rituals, dance, or music may particularly benefit from the use of immersive and sensory digital platforms. For example, Figure 17.2 captures a 2D rendering caption of 3D VR immersive environment for Roman pantomime dancing, developed as a collaboration between Humlab, Umeå University, The University of Oxford, and Roehampton University, with the purpose of visualizing a genre classified as intangible cultural heritage.[15]

The lack of direct experiential and sensory evidence for digital art history is an issue in much historical research, and the creation of immersive interactive and multimodal environments for knowledge production is still underexplored. While VR or MR (mixed reality) are increasingly popular visualization platforms, they are still sparingly used: this is an issue attributable to the complexities of local infrastructure as well as emerging upgrades that relate to constant platform development and sustainability. The creation of immersive, interactive, and multimodal environments for art history objects is a new field that requires further reflection and exploration.

Unlike standard 3D modeling that is viewed in regular screen environments,[16] VR engines enable participation, observation, and user interaction. These, in turn, afford sensory engagements with virtual environment(s), architecture, and artifacts. Materials and environments are further digitally reconstructed as 3D models within a virtual space. Historical data of sorts are

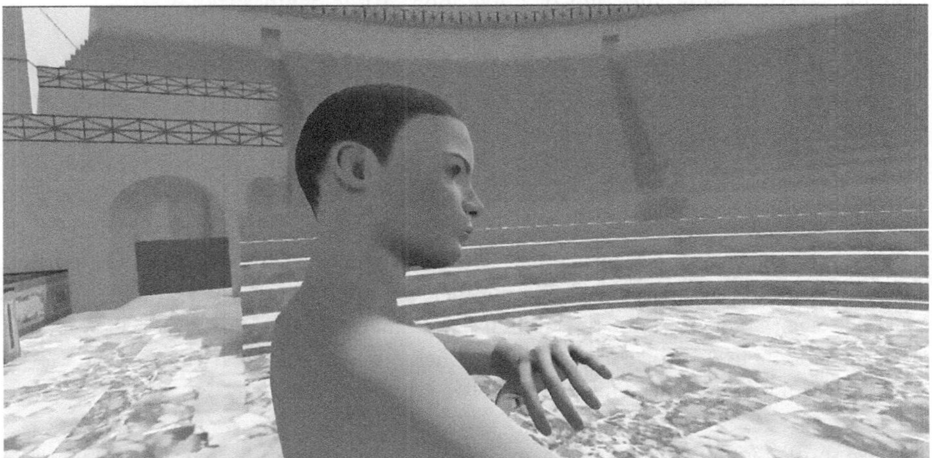

*Figure 17.2* The Virtual Reality environment and avatar in 2D, digitizing ancient dance 2015, Humlab.

currently implemented within gaming platforms;[17] virtual reality, or augmented reality environments as well as, less frequently, within mixed reality environments.[18]

VR platforms afford the possibility of engagement with the sensory sphere and are considered more effective in tandem with narratives evoking emotions and serendipitous connections. Such projects are, however, relatively recent (www.chessexperience.eu/). It is worth noting that the VR/Digital Art pioneer Dr. Char Davies has also criticized the continuing emphasis on Cartesian separation of mind or body in many virtual environments, arguing that we should instead explore more complex concepts of embodiment.

So how can virtual reality afford opportunities for digital art history? Advantages of the digital are replication, calculation, and reconfigurability. Advantages of VR, in particular, include immersion, sensory engagement, and the speed and computing power to respond to the viewer and calculate and visualize responses and answers (be they for quizzes, to load new media or to search databases) across a multitude of senses, at different levels and scales. Many systems, however, fall into disuse. Their content quickly becomes hidden, inaccessible, or incomplete, not degrading gracefully when installed and played on home desktop computers. VR consists of technology, *and* content, *and* requires immersed and engaged users. Yet "the goal of virtual reality is to dominate the senses, taking its users to a place totally disconnected from the real world."[19] This is a strong statement, as AR and MR are generally seen as aspects of virtual reality, but place the augmented or mixed reality experience in or alongside the real world. Should users be totally separated from the real world? Another concern is preservation of content. Content that can only work on a certain technological platform without input, maintenance and care from end-users or specialists is likely to be superseded very quickly. Given the high costs of machinery, few research labs push the sensory potential of the technology itself. If VR is only served by frozen content that is not easily modified, adapted, or reconfigured, one might question whether it will prove to be a consistently useful platform for pioneering forays into digital art history and heritage.

## Virtual Heritage

World heritage sites, according to international organizations like UNESCO (https://whc.unesco.org/en/conventiontext/) and ICOMOS[20] are selected based on their cultural significance (including aesthetic significance, and, by implication, artistic significance):

> Cultural significance means aesthetic, historic, scientific, social or spiritual value for past, present or future generations. Cultural significance is embodied in the place itself, its fabric, setting, use, associations, meanings, records, related places, and related objects.
>
> *(Australia ICOMOS Incorporated International Council on Monuments and Sites, 2013 #24)*

From the start of this century, virtual heritage has generally been viewed internationally as a hybridization of VR and cultural heritage, but there are still relatively few accessible examples of virtual heritage that demonstrate the cultural significance of the original material, or intangible heritage, including live performance (defined earlier as part of cultural heritage). One exception is the definition by Stone and Ojika who declared that virtual heritage is:

> the use of computer-based interactive technologies to record, preserve, or recreate artifacts, sites and actors of historic, artistic, religious, and cultural significance and to deliver the results openly to a global audience in such a way as to provide formative educational experiences through electronic manipulations of time and space.[21]

However, virtual heritage also implies that it is nearly as good as the object or activity it simulates or relives. The question arises, therefore, as to how time and space can be manipulated to convey the recording, preserving, and "recreating" of these artifacts, sites, and actors as a formative educational experience without an overly dry, incomplete, or misleading exposition.

Perhaps this complex challenge is why scholarship tends to emphasize technological developments, new interfaces, and accelerated computational power, enhanced artificial intelligence, or increased graphical resolution over a suitable and engaging user experience and group-based learning. The technological specifications of VR as a heritage visualization platform is a shiny laboratory where humanities content, academic research, and technology are required to act in unison under limited and controlled creative license, however, community engagement and outreach are seldom incorporated.

Given the combination of cultural study, preservation technologies, computational advancements, and the educational aims of cultural institutions, the potential for artistic expression and critique of the friction and frisson between tradition and technology offer fertile ground for critical engagement with culture and art. How can virtual art and heritage be best interactively and immersively experienced in order to evoke critical thinking?

## Art History and Heritage Games

Artgames (digital art games) may have been around since the 1980s. In her article "Towards an Art History for Videogames," Lana Polansky noted that *Deus Ex* (by Automata, 1984)[22] can be considered an artgame, but that the history of artgames has gone unnoticed by many, for early artgames were infrequent commercial successes, and later games lacked unique character or were overly commercialized. That said, there have been recent discussions on how games could be considered to be art (https://smartech.gatech.edu/handle/1853/33113) *Art History of Games Symposium* (Georgia Tech 2009, 2010) and how games can investigate the aims of art history and the issues raised by it.

We suggest that rather than looking at heritage as an ossified dimension of art history, we consider heritage itself as imaginative and inherently forward looking. Heritage does not relate merely to the physical maintenance of objects, but also includes aspects of open citizen science, understanding of, and participation in, the heritage milieu. Here the charms and capabilities of computer games are beguiling, but the dramatically rhetorical and gently persuasive power of VR is still under-explored and under-examined, even though group dynamics, digital technology and engaging interaction are (for many societies) today provided by computer games.

Although the first computer art is over sixty years old ("art" is defined here loosely), exhibitions and installations set up for games and serious games mostly arose in the last couple of decades. There are specific games for topics in art history, and ARTtigo claims to have ninety-five art history computer games on its website. We have not investigated all of them, but most appear to be casual games, where you can write graffiti, identify famous painters and match paintings, take virtual tours around artist quarters, create unusual shapes and patterns, and answer quizzes. Most of the painters are famous (Picasso, Kandinsky, Warhol, Van Gogh, Mondrian, Matisse, etc.), some of the games only seem to be referring to famous artists as tropes, but there may be some interesting game mechanics in there to learn from.

For example, "The Search for Picasso's Studio" (https://artsology.com/search-for-picasso.php) may be of some interest, as you have to find his studio using current photos of Montmartre. Although the interface design is basic, one could imagine applying this idea to phone-based augmented reality and panoramic mapping software like Google Maps, to help people link artists, elements in their paintings, and the places where they lived and the places that inspired them.

For every successful example, there are missing or abandoned games. For instance, the BBC has created fascinating history and art history-related games (www.bbc.co.uk/history/interactive/games/), but many sections are now archived (such as history for kids: www.bbc.co.uk/history/forkids/) without any particular explanation.

In his 2012 paper, "A Curiously Short History of Game Art," J. Sharp argued that the "history of game art is short with a 'relative lack of critical success,'" but from 2012 onwards there have been major art game exhibitions, installations and conferences, including on topics as to whether computer games, or machinima can be considered to be art.[23] Recent papers arguing for this include "Video Games Are One of the Most Important Art Forms in History" and Laura Parker's "A Journey to Make Video Games into Art."[24]

Other writers have explored the possibilities of computer and video games in museums.[25] Famous museums have staged game exhibitions. Sometimes art galleries provide their own free games for exploration purposes, such as the National Gallery of Art in Washington DC and there are dedicated game museums such as The Strong National Museum of Play (New York), The Finnish Museum of Game (Tampere), Computer Game Museum of Berlin (Berlin), Video Game Museum of Rome (Rome), the Nationaal Videogame Museum (Netherlands), or the National Videogame Museum-NVM (Texas).

In terms of art history, academics have explored games where you can "impact the course of art history, make strategic Medici-patronage decisions to support Renaissance's Best Artists or face exile."[26] Wikipedia has a surprisingly interesting article on art games (https://en.wikipedia.org/wiki/Art_game) but with few examples of art history games. One game, that seems to be more pastiche than a serious exploration of art history, was Pac-Mondrian, featured in *The Guardian* (www.theguardian.com/technology/blog/2004/dec/30/pacmondrian) and *The New York Times* (www.nytimes.com/2004/12/27/arts/design/chomp-if-you-like-art.html) and reviewed online in an article entitled *Chomp if You Like Art*, on the blog gamescenes (www.gamescenes.org/2009/10/game-art-price-budget-boys-pacmondrian-2002.html). Unfortunately, "seems to be" is key here because the link to the original game does not work (http://pbfb.ca/pac-mondrian/play.html).

This is a widespread problem; preservation and access are rare commodities in art history and heritage games. For example, consider art history games like ARTournament (Figure 17.3), described as a "A Mobile Casual Game to Explore Art History." There are several papers on it,[27] but we had to contact one of the project team to find the website (http://artournament.info/).

Or consider "Panic in the Gallery" (Figure 17.4). It was described as "An online educational game for art history: Design and evaluation of a matching game" where a new art gallery intern has various quests involving learning about various paintings from different art movements and the lives of their artists in order to catalogue them.[28] The project uses quizzes and other activities to facilitate users' experience and knowledge of art history objects.

Another art history game that no longer works online but can be downloaded, is ThIATRO. You have to travel through a simple city quarter with 3D buildings, find the art galleries, and select the correct paintings according to the clues. The website reads:

> The players are immersed into a 3D virtual world. Their task is to borrow artworks for their own exhibition according to the requirements set forward by ThIATRO's game mechanics. It is interesting to see that the recognition of artworks changed considerably after playing ThIATRO which is an indication of learning taking place while playing.

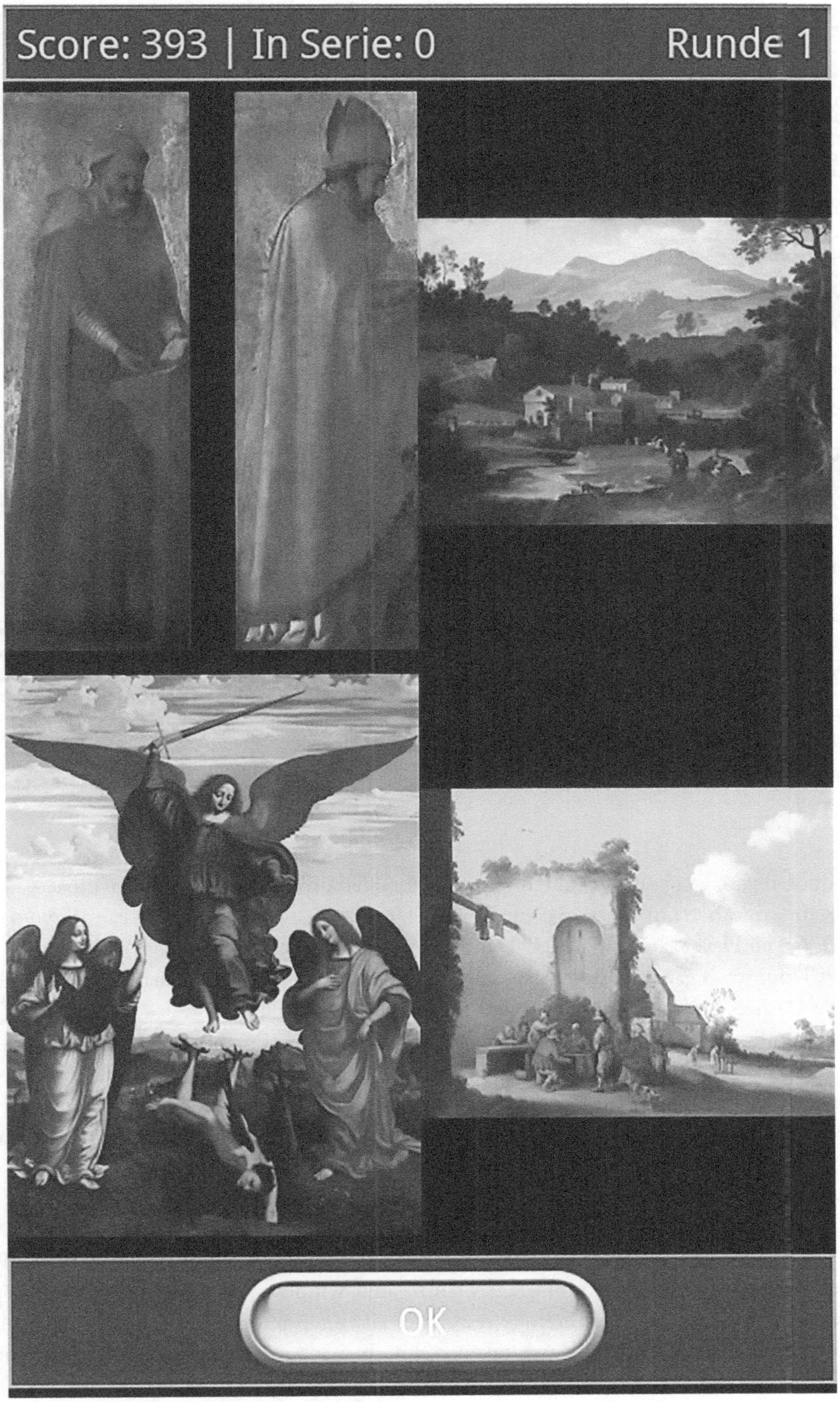


*Figure 17.3* "Artournament."

*Source*: Permission of Dr. Josef Wolfartsberger.

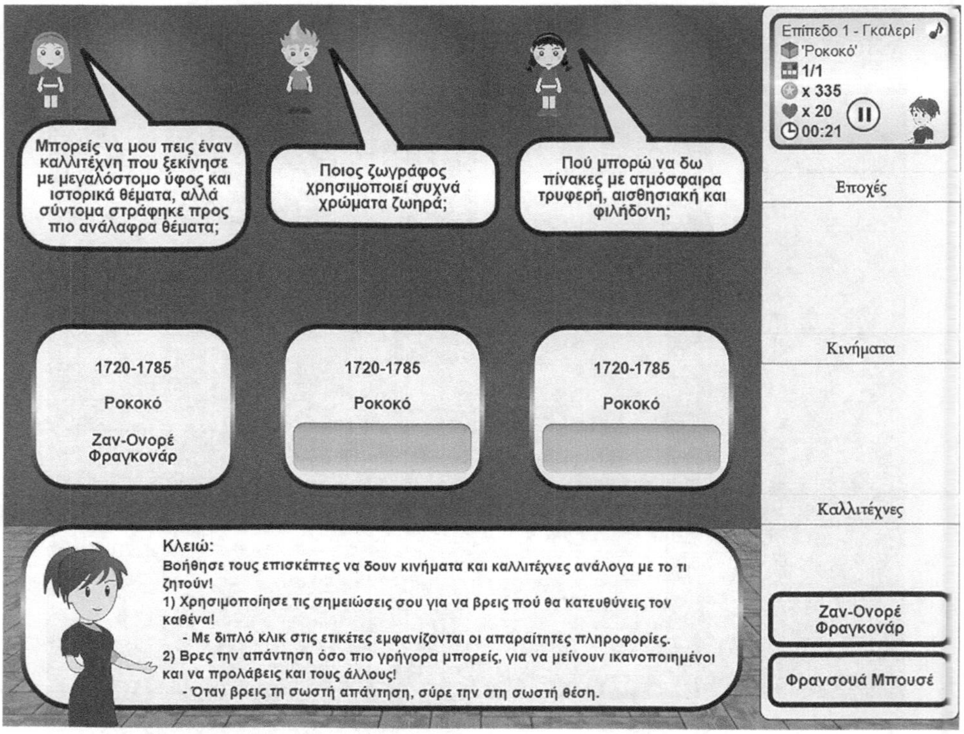


*Figure 17.4* "Panic in the Gallery."Visitor in Room Quiz (Rococo).

*Source*: Permission of Chrysanthi Tseloudi.

The quoted passage about ThIATRO has an embedded link (www.thiatro.info/) that no longer seems to work, but http://vsem.ec.tuwien.ac.at/thiatro/ does work if you can download the UNITY Web Player (and ThIATRO can be played in German or in English).

Art Thief was a game created by students in the fall of 2017 at California Institute of the Arts for the CalArts Game Makers Club and the premise is excellent: "Fresh-faced security guard Olive defends the museum from a nefarious art thief. She must gather clues, solve puzzles, craft items, and listen to the many woes of the museum's colorful cast of employees, artworks, and enemies."[29] Art Thief has the distinctive advantage of still being playable online, many others appear to have been taken down from the web or cannot be found. Unfortunately, the point-and-click 2D online game has many bugs and the gameplay is not highly interactive.

In terms of 3D heritage there was "The Forbidden Palace: Beyond Space and Time," a 3D Second-Life like world written in the Torque engine, described as "an educational game where players can explore the Forbidden City in Beijing, China, as a partnership between the Palace Museum and IBM" (www.mobygames.com/game/windows/forbidden-city-beyond-space-and-time). There was also the carefully researched 3D environment, UCLA's "Rome Reborn" (www.romereborn.org/), which was taken offline but appears to be available again, but as a purchasable product. An alternative recommendation is "Virtual Rome" (https://research.reading.ac.uk/virtualrome/) or further afield but still Roman is the University of Arkansas' "Digital Pompeii Unity" game project (http://tesseract.uark.edu). While the Swedish Pompeii project by the University of Lund (www.pompejiprojektet.se/) offers 3D models. So classical archaeology already has exemplars to work with, and reconstruction lies deeply in the tradition of the discipline itself.[30] However, these examples are more walk-through simulations than richly interactive computer games.

Computer games can be defined as feedback systems or even as persuasion machines with goals, punishments and rewards, imaginative themes and settings (fantasy), competition (in most cases) and dynamic, increasingly difficult but challenges. Games are challenging but also engaging, goal-based, complicitly systematic and ergodic (one works toward the goals). They acknowledge failure and reward effort and success. They are also thematically imaginative, dynamically adaptable to a variety of learning strategies, played individually or in groups, yet typically incomplete in setting or in instruction. As semi-open learning systems, they offer great potential for virtual heritage. But the high failure-to-success ratio of such serious games, and the inability of many such games to foster and develop new cultural knowledge of the past via interaction is concerning.

While there are distinct advantages of games, they have several constraints, particularly in terms of how seriously they are taken: Yet they often feature embodiment and alternate forms of digitally mediated reality, reward systems (leading to in-world tracking), and learning through play, which also means learning from failures. But what are heritage games, and how can they advance digital heritage, let alone virtual heritage? A simple way to distinguish virtual heritage and digital heritage is that the former is typically three-dimensionally immersive it contains both an element of spatial immersion and a sense of cultural inhabitation.[31] Digital heritage games could be two-dimensional or use layered reality (as opposed to genuine spatial depth). However, creating three-dimensionality can add great challenges: more pixels, more content, far more navigation guides, longer training times, more required levels of realism, more care needed to avoid potential nausea and discomfort (especially when deployed on head-mounted displays). That said, 3D environments can be more engaging and can engender a greater sense of place, of cultural inhabitation and an understanding of social roles and spaces.

What are the particular issues of 3D heritage games, especially those focused on areas pertinent to art history? These games take longer to learn, they require advanced technology that must be maintained, and levels of scholarly accuracy are not usually clearly demarcated from the "fun" parts. In addition, the field of appropriate evaluation is still in its infancy. So how would art history both leverage and distinguish itself from virtual heritage? We argue that it does not have to, at least not if it is keen to explore how virtual and augmented reality can explore not just the art object, but also the creation and experience of that artistic object, situated, framed, and enlivened by the cultural constraints of relevant and accessible technology.

In designing museums and art galleries the architectural designer is often forced to make a choice between extroverted and introverted design. They may design a building that is a showpiece in itself and thus risk overwhelming the collection it contains. Alternatively, a building might act as little more than a backdrop. To what extent should the built environment be part of the experience or fade into the background? Arguably, this dilemma is less obvious in game design, for the creation of game space may borrow tips from real world places on the creation of thematic atmosphere. Nevertheless, architecture is often partially integrated into the meaningful game experience. Game designers use power-ups, damaged artifacts, and off-camera cues to both indicate new places of interest and the sense of an external world. Yet there are still some techniques used by architects that may help designers to create more allusive and suggestive thematic pathways and focal areas.

For example, nineteenth-century art historians such as Wölfflin and Burckhardt helped to form a profession that talked of façades and sculptural elements that suggested structure and have risen to empathic feelings on the part of the viewer by virtue of a building's proportion, color, and form. However, they forgot to mention that architecture, unlike other arts, also involves the use of space as a proprioceptive journey.[32]

The skilled design of real-world environments also requires attention to the inter-relation of material between rooms, and the interstitial nature of spatial function. The circulation paths of large buildings can be symbolically linked to allude to new goals without the use of signposts. Indeed, if we need to place signs everywhere, that is a good indication the designer has admitted defeat.

Digital environments are thus not just renditions of infinite space. In *Hamlet on the Holodeck*, Murray defined virtual environments as "digital space."[33] For example, architecture has inbuilt physiological and psychological stimuli and phobic triggers related to sensory notions of proximity and distance. In order to be continually meaningful, digital environments also require paths and centers, focal points, and movement areas that connect spaces and themes. VR can incorporate similar techniques, but digital space, per se, is not digital *place*.

The intangible aspects of heritage sites and objects, even our experience of them, can be portrayed or alluded to using VR technology and game design techniques. Moreover, the processes by which these objects can be compared, by which they were built or used, experienced and critiqued, can also be represented, statically, dynamically, metaphorically, and interactively. A further dimensional possibility seldom mentioned or explored, however, is to also represent or to allow participants to explore historical and cultural experiences and even sensory encounters of these objects, sites, and processes. This, we suggest, is of great use to digital art history.

## The Critical Componentry of Heritage Games

While classifying heritage games may be academically intriguing, there are so few robust and engaging examples of heritage games that comprehensive classification would be premature. The first question to be posed is: Where do heritage art games fit? Are they both virtual heritage and digital heritage? Arguably, virtual heritage is more of a communication tool than a preservation, categorization, or organizational strategy. Due to fast-moving technology, bugs, and the variety of platforms and needs, heritage games are hard to find and harder to maintain, many virtual heritage projects are oxymoronic, they cannot even preserve themselves. Few projects constitute heritage objects or collections because they cannot even save themselves, and some scholars have questioned whether video games themselves can ever be preserved. Given the highly contextual knowledge required in art history, and given many art history departments cannot afford to maintain trained technical staff with expertise in VR, preservation is a major issue.

Second, are there particular case studies that are seen to be exemplars of the field? There are good academic surveys of serious games for cultural heritage. Given the relative lack of access and obsolescence of projects and the range of research fields and countries involved, it is very hard to assess the overall field. A third challenge is how to protect authorship of the game and the interests of the stakeholders in the heritage that is portrayed. How can raw data, fragile artifacts, individual or group participation, creative practice, and scholarly expertise and authority all be catered for within a single platform? The new EU Infrastructure ARIADNE PLUS (https://ariadne-infrastructure.eu/), CrossCult (www.crosscult.eu/) and the Time Machine Project (https://timemachine.eu/) may address these challenges, but some of the answers may already be shown in the commercial 3D model hosting and viewing platform Sketchfab (www.sketchfab.com/), which includes the ability to build online guided tours of 3D models, landscapes, and buildings and to share 3D models via social media (Twitter and Facebook).

A fourth issue is one of aesthetics: We may wish to recreate heritage digitally by using the most impressive and up-to-date aesthetic techniques to hand. However, a desire to demonstrate aesthetic mastery can compete with actual historic incompleteness, fragmented data and gaps in the record. Incompleteness includes our understanding of past cultural perspectives, the "other," how much can be clarified and how much can be bridged. A related problem in archaeology is determining whether a particular discovery represents a turning point in a culture's aesthetic, a typical form practiced by all, or a work by a singular imagination.

## Conclusion

What are the implications of these issues for digital humanities and art history? If digital humanities can harness the scale, calculating power and speed of computation and the analysis of humanities tools, methods and practices, we suggest that there is much more to explore in digital heritage—especially virtual heritage—that is both immersive and engaging. We have suggested that there has been an over emphasis on the quantitative. This has resulted in failure to acknowledge the development and promotion of non-textual media. It has also engendered a fuzzy relationship between VR and the general immersive reality field in relation to contemporary digital research infrastructures for the arts and humanities, which is still to be fully explored at time of writing.[34]

In this chapter, we have outlined major challenges, but we also look forward to the opportunities provided by the continual development of computational technology. The latter includes consideration of how that technology can aid in increasing and enhancing a shared understanding of the aims of virtual heritage, including the involvement and participation of the public, and the leveraging of a robust infrastructure that supports the aims of virtual heritage.

What is needed in this field, we suggest, is a more theoretical and systematic analysis of the purposes and goals of virtual heritage itself and an improved understanding of the varying contexts within which virtual heritage can be developed, modified, maintained, and shared. Aesthetically, there are challenges and opportunities in how technology, art, and user can interact engagingly. There are difficulties in exploring how heritage and arts of the past can or should be portrayed given our remoteness in time, space, and perspective. It is only by probing such issues further that we will be able critically to evaluate the computational tools that have been developed for the study of artworks and their histories, as well as the disciplinary opportunities and challenges that have emerged in response to the use of digital resources and methodologies.

## Notes

1. Conrad Fiedler, *On Judging Works of Visual Art* (Berkeley, Los Angeles, and London: University of California Press, 1978).
2. Johanna Drucker, "Is There a 'Digital' Art History?" *Visual Resources* 29, no. 1–2 (2013): 5–13.
3. Stuart Dunn et al., "Spatial Narratives in Museums and Online: The Birth of the Digital Object Itinerary," in *Museums and Digital Culture: New Perspectives and Research* (London and New York: Springer, 2019), 253–71.
4. For a concept of art history object platforms concerned with the visualization of provenance and GIS, see Dunn et al., "Spatial Narratives in Museums and Online."
5. Arthur Danto, *Beyond the Brillo Box: The Visual Arts in Post-Historical Perspective* (Berkeley and Los Angeles: University of California Press, 1992).
6. George Dickie. "Art and the Aesthetic," *Noûs* 13, no. 1 (1979), 113–17.
7. See https://news.artnet.com/art-world/ai-art-comes-to-market-is-it-worth-the-hype-1352011.
8. Inventor in the Field of Virtual Reality, see http://uschefnerarchive.com/morton-heilig-inventor-vr/.
9. Mark Billinghurst et al., "A Survey of Augmented Reality," *Foundations and Trends in Human-Computer Interaction* 8, no. 2–3 (2014): 73–272.

10. Paul Milgram and Fumio Kishino, "A Taxonomy of Mixed Reality Visual Displays," *IEICE Transactions on Information and Systems* 77, no. 12 (1994): 1321–29.
11. Helen Slaney, Anna Foka, and Sophie Bocksberger. "Ghosts in the Machine: An Experiment in Distributed Reception," in *Digital Humanities Quarterly* (Boston: Northeastern University Press, 2018).
12. Stanford, Virtual Human Interaction Lab, https://vhil.stanford.edu/.
13. Valeria Vitale, "Transparent, Multivocal, Cross-Disciplinary: The Use of Linked Open Data and a Community-Developed RDF Ontology to Document and Enrich 3D Visualisation for Cultural Heritage," in *Digital Classics Outside the Echo Chamber* (London: Ubiquity Press, 2016), 147–68; Erik Champion, *Critical Gaming: Interactive History and Virtual Heritage*, eds. Marilyn Deegan, Lorna Hughes, Andrew Prescott, Harold Short, and Dymphna Evans, Digital Research in the Arts and Humanities (London: Ashgate Publishing, September 2015).
14. Anna Foka and Viktor Arvidsson, "Experiential Analogies: Sonic Digital Ekphrasis as a Digital Humanities Project," *Digital Humanities Quarterly* 10, no. 2 (2016).
15. See, for example, the UNESCO definition: https://ich.unesco.org/en/what-is-intangible-heritage-00003.
16. Vitale, "Transparent, Multivocal, Cross-disciplinary," 147–68.
17. Adam Chapman, Anna Foka, and Jonathan Westin, "Introduction: What Is Historical Game Studies?" *Rethinking History* 1, no. 3 (2017): 358–71.
18. Jonathan Westin, Anna Foka, and Adam Chapman, "Introduction: What Is Historical Game Studies?" Humanising Places: Exposing Histories of the Disenfranchised Through Augmented Reality, *International Journal of Heritage Studies* 24, no. 3 (2018): 283–86.
19. Tom Garner and Mark Grimshaw, "Sonic Virtuality: Understanding Audio in a Virtual World," in *The Oxford Handbook of Virtuality*, ed. Mark Grimshaw (Oxford, UK: Oxford University Press, 2014), 364–77, Ch. 22; Charles E. Hughes and Christopher B. Stapleton, "The Shared Imagination: Creative Collaboration in Augmented Virtuality," Paper presented at the Proc. HCI International, 2005.
20. Via the Australia ICOMOS Charter for Places of Cultural Significance, The Burra Charter, 2013, https://australia.icomos.org/publications/charters/.
21. https://whc.unesco.org/en/conventiontext/.
22. Parker Laura, "A Journey to Make Video Games Into Art," August 2, 2013, www.newyorker.com/tech/annals-of-technology/a-journey-to-make-video-games-into-art.
23. John Sharp, "A Curiously Short History of Game Art," *FDG 12 Proceedings of the International Conference on the Foundations of Digital Games, Raleigh, NC* (May 29–June 1, 2012): 26–32.
24. This chapter will not make the case that video games are art, for many others have already done so. See Scott Steinberg, "Who Says Video Games Aren't Art?" August 31, 2010, http://edition.cnn.com/2010/TECH/gaming.gadgets/08/31/video.games.art.steinberg/; Scott Steinberg, "Who Says Video Games Aren't Art?" August 31, 2010, http://edition.cnn.com/2010/TECH/gaming.gadgets/08/31/video.games.art.steinberg/.
25. Tiia Naskali, Jaakko Suominen, and Petri Saarikoski, "The Introduction of Computer and Video Games in Museums—Experiences and Possibilities," paper presented at the IFIP WG 9.7 International Conference, HC 2013, London, UK, June 17–18, 2013; Eduardo Navas, Owen Gallagher, and Xtine Burrough, *The Routledge Companion to Remix* (New York: Routledge, 2015).
26. Allison Meier, "You're a Medici Can You Support the Renaissance's Best Artists, or Will You Be Exiled?" *Hyperallergic*, March 7, 2017, https://hyperallergic.com/391922/arte-mecenas-game-on-italian-renaissance-art-economies/.
27. Josef Froschauer, Johannes Zweng, Dieter Merkl, Max Arends, Doron Goldfarb, and Martin Weingartner, "Artournament: A Mobile Casual Game to Explore Art History," paper presented at the 12th International Conference on Advanced Learning Technologies, 2012.
28. Chrysanthi Tseloudi and Thrasyvoulos Tsiatsos, "Panic in the Gallery: An Online Educational Game for Art History: Design and Evaluation of a Matching Game," paper presented at the 2015 6th International Conference on Information, Intelligence, Systems and Applications (IISA), Ionian University, Corfu, Greece, July 6–8, 2015.
29. https://calarts-gamemakers.itch.io/art-thief.
30. See www.arktimes.com/arkansas/gaming-the-past-at-ua/Content?oid=4111829 or, for more information, https://classicalstudies.org/scs-blog/david-fredrick/blog-what-classicists-can-do-video-games.
31. Erik Champion, "History and Cultural Heritage in Virtual Environments," in *The Oxford Handbook of Virtuality*, ed. Mark Grimshaw (Oxford: Oxford University Press, 2014), 269–83.

32. See, for example, Evonne Levy, *Baroque and the Political Language of Formalism (1845–1945): Burckhardt, Wölfflin, Gurlitt, Brinckmann, Sedlmayr* (Basel: Schwabe Verlag, 2015).
33. Janet H. Murray, *Hamlet on the Holodeck: The Future of Narrative in Cyberspace* (Boston: MIT Press, 1997).
34. A. Foka, A. Misharina, V. Arvidsson, and S. Gelfgren, "Beyond Humanities Qua Digital: Spatial and Material Development for Digital Research Infrastructures," *Digital Scholarship in the Humanities* 33, no. 2 (2018): 264–78. Oxford: Oxford University Press.

## Bibliography

Anderson, Eike Falk, Leigh McLoughlin, Fotis Liarokapis, Christopher Peters, Panagiotis Petridis, and Sara Freitas. "Developing Serious Games for Cultural Heritage: A State-of-the-Art Review." [In English]. *Virtual Reality* 14, no. 4 (January 12, 2010): 255–75. https://doi.org/10.1007/s10055-010-0177-3.

Antonelli, Paola. "Video Games: 14 in the Collection, for Starters." *Inside/Out. MoMA*, March 7, 2012. www.moma.org/explore/inside_out/2012/11/29/video-games-14-in-the-collection-for-starters/.

"Artigo." Citizen Science Games, Updated 2019. Accessed March 7, 2019. https://citizensciencegames.com/games/artigo/.

Barwick, Joanna, James Dearnley, and Adrienne Muir. "Playing Games with Cultural Heritage: A Comparative Case Study Analysis of the Current Status of Digital Game Preservation." *Games and Culture* 6, no. 4 (2011): 373–90. https://doi.org/10.1177/1555412010391092. http://journals.sagepub.com/doi/abs/10.1177/1555412010391092.

Bekele, Mafkereseb Kassahun, Roberto Pierdicca, Emanuele Frontoni, Eva Savina Malinverni and James Gain. "A Survey of Augmented, Virtual, and Mixed Reality for Cultural Heritage." *Journal on Computing and Cultural Heritage (JOCCH)* 11, no. 2 (2018): 7.

Billinghurst, Mark, Adrian Clark, and Lee Gun. "A Survey of Augmented Reality." *Foundations and Trends® in Human-Computer Interaction* 8, no. 2–3 (2014): 73–272.

Carson, Don. "Environmental Storytelling: Creating Immersive 3d Worlds Using Lessons Learned from the Theme Park Industry." *Gamasutra. com* 1 (2000).

Cepeda, René Alberto García. "Reconciling Art History and Video Games." *iDMAa Journal (International Digital Media and Arts Association)*, no. 11. 23 nOVEMBER 2015. (November 23, 2015): Online. www.idmaajournal.org/2015/11/reconciling-art-history-and-video-games/.

Champion, Erik. "History and Cultural Heritage in Virtual Environments." In *The Oxford Handbook of Virtuality*, edited by Mark Grimshaw, 269–83. Oxford: Oxford University Press, 2014.

———. "Chapter 2: The Role of 3d Models in Virtual Heritage Infrastructures." In *Cultural Heritage Infrastructures in Digital Humanities*, edited by A. Benardou, E. Champion, C. Dallas, and L. Hughes. Digital Research in the Arts and Humanities, 15–35. London, UK: Routledge, 2017.

———. *Critical Gaming: Interactive History and Virtual Heritage*, edited by Marilyn Deegan, Lorna Hughes, Andrew Prescott, Harold Short, and Dymphna Evans, Digital Research in the Arts and Humanities. London, UK: Ashgate Publishing, September, 2015.

Chapman, Adam, Anna Foka, and Westin Jonathan. "Introduction: What Is Historical Game Studies?" *Rethinking History* 1, no. 3 (2017): 358–71.

Danto, Arthur. *Beyond the Brillo Box: The Visual Arts in Post-Historical Perspective*. Berkeley and Los Angeles: University of California Press, 1992.

Davies, Char. "Rethinking Vr: Key Concepts and Concerns." *Hybrid Reality: Art, Technology and the Human Factor, 9th International Conference on Virtual Systems and Multimedia* (2003): 253–62. www.immersence.com/publications/char/2003-CD-VSSM.html.

Dickie, George. *Art and the Aesthetic: an Institutional Approach, Noûs* 13, no. 1 (1979): 113–17.

Drucker, Johanna. "Is There a 'Digital' Art History?" *Visual Resources* 29, no. 1–2 (2013): 5–13.

Dunn, Stuart, Graeme Earl, Anna Foka, and Will Wooton. "*Spatial Narratives in Museums and Online: The Birth of the Digital Object Itinerary*." In *Museums and Digital Culture: New Perspectives and Research*, red. Tula Giannini and Jonathan Bowden, 253–71. London and New York: Springer. 2019.

Fiedler, Conrad. *On Judging Works of Visual Art*. Berkeley, Los Angeles and London: University of California Press, 1978.

Flynn, Bernadette. "Augmented Visualisation: Designing Experience for an Interpretative Cultural Heritage." Paper presented at the 12th International Conference on Information Visualisation (IV'08), London, UK, July 9–11, 2008.

Foka, A., A. Misharina, V. Arvidsson, and S. Gelfgren. "Beyond Humanities Qua Digital: Spatial and Material Development for Digital Research Infrastructures." *Digital Scholarship in the Humanities* 33, no. 2 (2018): 264–78. Oxford: Oxford University Press.
Froschauer, Josef, Johannes Zweng, Dieter Merkl, Max Arends, Doron Goldfarb, and Martin Weingartner. "Artournament: A Mobile Casual Game to Explore Art History." Paper presented at the 12th International Conference on Advanced Learning Technologies, 2012.
"Games as Cultural Heritage: Copyright Challenges for Preserving (Orphan) Video Games in the EU." JIPITEC 6, 2015. Accessed November 28, 2018. www.jipitec.eu/issues/jipitec-6-2-2015/4273.
Garner, Tom, and Mark Grimshaw. "Sonic Virtuality: Understanding Audio in a Virtual World." In *The Oxford Handbook of Virtuality*, edited by Mark Grimshaw, 364–77, Ch. 22. Oxford, UK: Oxford University Press, 2014.
Hanes, L., and R. Stone. "A Model of Heritage Content to Support the Design and Analysis of Video Games for History Education." *Journal of Computers in Education* (2018): 1–26. https://doi.org/10.1007/s40692-018-0120-2.
"History." BBC, 2014. Accessed March 7, 2019. www.bbc.co.uk/history/forkids/.
"Inventor in the Field of Virtual Reality." USC School of Cinematic Arts, Updated October 31, 2018. Accessed April 3, 2019. http://uschefnerarchive.com/morton-heilig-inventor-vr/.
Jenkins, Henry. "Game Design as Narrative." *Computer* 44 (2004): 53.
Meier, Allison. "You're a Medici. Can You Support the Renaissance's Best Artists, or Will You Be Exiled?" *Hyperallergic*, March 7, 2017. https://hyperallergic.com/391922/arte-mecenas-game-on-italian-renaissance-art-economies/.
Milgram, Paul, and Fumio Kishino. "A Taxonomy of Mixed Reality Visual Displays." *IEICE Transactions on Information and Systems* 77, no. 12 (1994): 1321–29.
Mortara, Michela, Chiara Eva Catalano, Francesco Bellotti, Giusy Fiucci, Minica Houry-Panchetti, and Panagiotis Petridis. "Learning Cultural Heritage by Serious Games." *Journal of Cultural Heritage* 15, no. 3 (January 5, 2014): 318–25. https://doi.org/10.1016/j.culher.2013.04.004. www.sciencedirect.com/science/article/pii/S1296207413001349.
Naskali, Tiia, Jaakko Suominen, and Petri Saarikoski. "The Introduction of Computer and Video Games in Museums—Experiences and Possibilities." Paper presented at the *IFIP WG 9.7 International Conference*, HC 2013, London, UK, June 17–18, 2013.
Navas, Eduardo, Owen Gallagher, and Xtine Burrough. *The Routledge Companion to Remix Studies*. New York: Routledge, 2015. www.routledge.com/The-Routledge-Companion-to-Remix-Studies/Navas-Gallagher-burrough/p/book/9781315879994.
Noh, Zakiah, Mohd Shahrizal Sunar, and Zhigeng Pan. "A Review on Augmented Reality for Virtual Heritage System." Paper presented at the International Conference on Technologies for E-Learning and Digital Entertainment, 2009.
Parker, Laura. "A Journey to Make Video Games into Art." *The New Yorker*, August 2, 2013. Accessed July 13, 2019. www.newyorker.com/tech/annals-of-technology/a-journey-to-make-video-games-into-art.
Sharp, John. "A Curiously Short History of Game Art." Paper presented at the Proceedings of the International Conference on the Foundations of Digital Games, 2012.
Steinberg, Scott. "Who Says Video Games Aren't Art?" August 31, 2010. Accessed July 13, 2019. http://edition.cnn.com/2010/TECH/gaming.gadgets/08/31/video.games.art.steinberg/.
Stone, Robert J. "Serious Gaming—Virtual Reality's Saviour?" Paper presented at the Proceedings of the Eleventh International Conference on Virtual Systems and Multimedia: Virtual Reality at Work in the 21st Century: Impact on Society, Belgium, October 3–7, 2005.
Stone, Robert J., and Takeo Ojika. "Virtual Heritage: What Next?" *IEEE Multimedia* 7, no. 2 (2000): 73–74. https://ieeexplore-ieee-org.dbgw.lis.curtin.edu.au/stamp/stamp.jsp?tp=&arnumber=848434.
Summers, David. "The 'Visual Arts' and the Problem of Art Historical Description." *Art Journal* 42, no. 4 (1982): 301–10. https://doi.org/10.2307/776690. www.jstor.org/stable/776690.
"A Thrilling Game Where You Can Impact the Course of Art History." Kotaki. Updated July 20, 2017. Last accessed July 13, 2019.
Thwaites, Harold. "Digital Heritage: What Happens When We Digitize Everything?" In *Visual Heritage in the Digital Age*, edited by Eugene Ch'ng, Vincent Gaffney and Henry Chapman, 327–48. London: Springer, 2013.
Tscheu, Frances, and Dimitrios Buhalis. "Augmented Reality at Cultural Heritage Sites." In *Information and Communication Technologies in Tourism 2016*, 607–19. London: Springer, 2016.

Tseloudi, Chrysanthi, and Thrasyvoulos Tsiatsos. "Panic in the Gallery: An Online Educational Game for Art History: Design and Evaluation of a Matching Game." Paper presented at the 2015 6th International Conference on Information, Intelligence, Systems and Applications (IISA), Ionian University, Corfu, Greece, July 6–8, 2015.

Tussyadiah, Iis P., Timothy Hyungsoo Jung, and Claudia tom Dieck, M. "Embodiment of Wearable Augmented Reality Technology in Tourism Experiences." *Journal of Travel research* 57, no. 5 (2018): 597–611.

Van Krevelen, D. W. F., and Ronald Poelman. "A Survey of Augmented Reality Technologies, Applications and Limitations." *International Journal of Virtual Reality* 9, no. 2 (2010): 1.

"Video Game Preservation: An Impossible Dream?" Technewsworld, TechNewsWorld, Updated May 24, 2017, 2015. Accessed May 24, 2017. www.technewsworld.com/story/81729.html.

Vlahakis, Vassilios et al. "Archeoguide: First Results of an Augmented Reality, Mobile Computing System in Cultural Heritage Sites." *Virtual Reality, Archeology, and Cultural Heritage* 9 (2001).

Westin, Jonathan, Anna Foka and Adam Chapman. "Humanising Places: Exposing Histories of the Disenfranchised Through Augmented Reality." *International Journal of Heritage Studies* 24, no. 3 (2018): 283–86.

"What Is Mixed Reality?" Medium, Medium, Updated March 31, 2017. Accessed March 8, 2019. https://medium.com/@marknb00/what-is-mixed-reality-60e5cc284330.

# 18

# ART WITH A LIFESPAN

## Digital Technologies and the Preservation of BioArt

*Christl Baur*

"It's alive!" This can be a promise or threat, depending on the perspective of the artist involved in the movement that is often referred to as "BioArt."[1] Peter Weibel introduced the term "BioArt" in his essay "Biotechnologie und Kunst" (Biotechnology and Art) in 1981.[2] Here, for the first time, reference was made to the use of biological systems as a means of artistic expression. Since then, however, only a very limited audience has had the opportunity to experience such artistic presentations live in exhibitions or performance situations. Traditional art spaces, such as museums and galleries, still have difficulties in displaying and preserving BioArt. This seems like a contradiction, as *live* is the only way that many of these artworks can be exhibited and observed. As artificial biological systems have increasingly been used as artistic media, a heated controversy has begun as to whether the term "BioArt" should be used to refer to any artistic examination of biotechnological processes and their social consequences or solely to those artistic expressions that emerge from the use of actual biological media.

In this chapter, I shall use the term "BioArt" as a polysemic placeholder that contains its own evolution, as Jens Hauser has put it.[3] With the emergence of BioArt, the means of artistic expression have become richer, and the tools needed to analyze such artworks have become more complex. This chapter will argue that BioArt depends as much on digital methods of dissemination and research as it does on the manipulation of organic material. Although the biological and the technological seem to be different branches of study, they are closely connected in the field of BioArt, and the digital humanities (broadly conceived) have a role to play when considering the development of this field of art production.

New biological media, ranging from transgenic organisms to synthetic DNA, are now familiar materials in artworks. The prospect of producing new creatures in the laboratory has inspired artists to turn to this scientific field since the 1980s. Their works challenge audiences to test future scenarios of life in which biological diversity is no longer created solely by mechanisms of evolution, but specifically by human hands. The recombination of genes across species boundaries, and hence the production of so-called transgenic organisms, leads to a comprehensive re-evaluation of the relationship between art, technology, and nature and thereby becomes the sounding board of BioArt. Although the path from the studio to the laboratory opens a multitude of new artistic means of expressions (including bacteria, cells, tissue cultures, or transgenic organisms), this shift also makes it necessary to become familiar with new epistemologies and the logic of the technical-scientific regime of experimental laboratory settings.[4] In addition, new methods must be found to maintain these art forms in the art world and to bring the art world closer to the challenges they offer.

Museums and galleries—as well as the contemporary art market—often overlook the significance of this type of art because of the difficulty of integrating it into traditional museum structures. Therefore, we must question what changes need to be made in order to exhibit BioArt within the museum and to determine whether the art institution is, in fact, the ideal place to conserve, collect, and present it. As BioArt is *in vivo* it cannot be considered as a purely digital artwork. In most works, however, the digital component plays an important role in both the creation and documentation process. An example is Eduardo Kac's work *Genesis* (2001).[5] In the first phase of the work the artist created a synthetic gene through the online participation of the audience. Then a digital visualization of the three-dimensional structure of the new protein was produced, both in a digital and physical version.[6] The researcher and artist need, therefore, to attend to both the physical production of the work and to the mechanisms of its digital production in order to analyze it. This includes study of the digital techniques used to solicit participation and examination of the ontological difference between the physical and digital objects. Although an artist is not expected to become a scientist, the understanding of the technologies underpinning, for example, the relevant biological manipulations are essential in developing a work at the complex nexus of art and science as well as building a bridge to the audience.

## In the Tradition of "Aliveness"

To some extent, art has always been a reflection on what it means to be "alive."[7] Whether we look at paintings that express nature in as "realistic" a style as possible, or whether an artist tries to uncover invisible emotional states, the "living state of the real"[8] is at the core of the exercise. Indeed, the entire history of art can be described as a history of the living. Starting from the earliest anthropomorphic sculptures and the animation of malleable matter, myths of vivification have surrounded artifacts made by artists.[9] Art has effectively imagined, portrayed, and imitated living beings and ecosystems until, quite recently, manipulation on a cellular and molecular level became possible. Today's artists enter laboratories to use biotechnologies that are especially "close to life,"[10] and the new discipline of synthetic biology is highly suitable to enhance these art-historical paradigms of creation.

Gina Czarnecki's work *Heirloom* (Figure 18.1) is in the tradition of the representation of the living. The artist created a living portrait of her two daughters[11] whose skin cells were collected at the age of eleven and thirteen and then cultivated on glass masks of the two girls' faces. The work extends a long artistic tradition of portraiture but—even though the masks were crafted by means of traditional techniques—the addition of skin cultures and 3D printing takes a new turn.[12] The centerpiece of the installation, which comprised diverse objects, are two incubators with the masks immersed in a red-colored nutrient bath in which cells were growing. Once they have sufficiently grown, the plexiglass masks are taken out of the incubator to dry, at which point the cells stop growing and die. The DNA portraits of the two girls remain and serve as an exploration of the role of genes in identity formation. They can be easily preserved through standard procedures[13] utilized on a daily basis in natural history museums.

## Accessibility and Materialization

It is a fact that the use of biology as a new medium must overcome hurdles that can still inhibit broad artistic use. Unlike photography or video, biological equipment is not readily available outside research institutions. Artists who are willing to explore the use of biological material

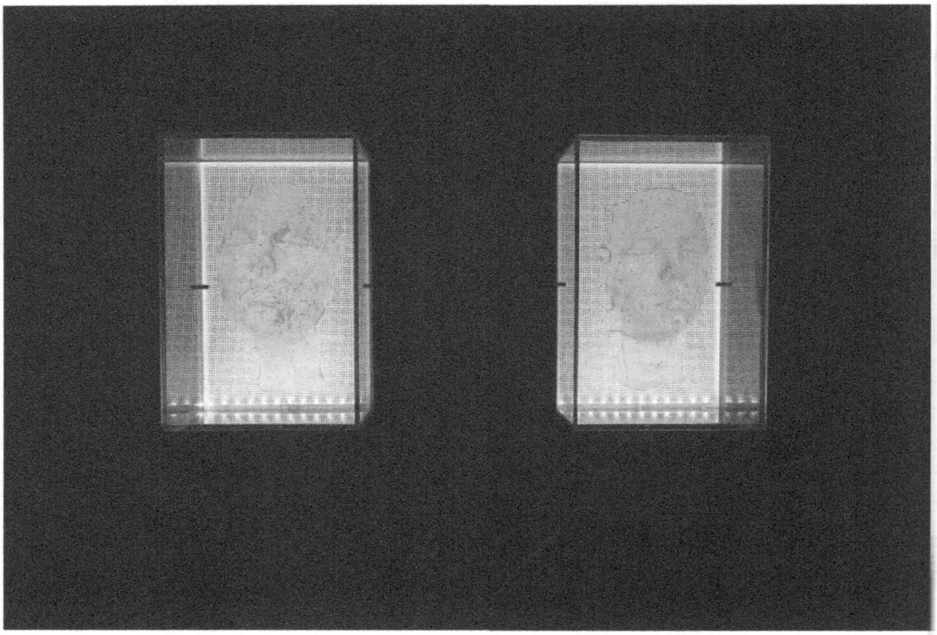

*Figure 18.1* Gina Czarnecki, *Heirloom*.
*Source*: Ars Electronica | Florian Voggeneder.

must therefore collaborate with scientific laboratories. This can be an advantage, as art and science can benefit greatly from each other.[14] More and more museums around the world are establishing fully functioning laboratory environments within their exhibition spaces to help them produce and preserve works with living cells. Since not all living materials are controllable, these living artworks require professional supervision by microbiologists or an adequate scientific team that knows what to do in the case of contamination.

The work *Victimless Leather* (2004) by the artists Oron Catts and Ionat Zurr, was displayed in Tokyo in 2009 at the Mori Art Museum as part of the exhibition *Medicine and Art: Imagining a Future for Life and Love*. It became subject to a foreign fungi invasion, and the organizing museum had to regenerate it from the cellular base materials.[15] This regeneration was necessary, as visitors wanted to see the "actual" work and not a mangled mass of fungal cells. Yet this raises a sensitive issue about the preservation of this kind of art: is the original version of the cells the actual work of art or, as in a performance context, can the work (i.e. the cells) be "re-grown" for every new exhibition? If the former is the case, the only way to keep the artwork is to conserve the actual cell culture and to present the work once, as it is difficult to keep the cells alive for a long period of time. Nor is it possible to transport them over international borders due to laws that limit the "international transfer of recombinant organisms."[16] Most artists will, therefore, define a specific type and number of cells that originate directly from the artist or from other living entities. Under these circumstances, the cells can be exchanged on a regular basis or renewed for a new exhibition. They require food and nurturing as well as a suitable environment so that they stay alive and interact with the rest of the artwork in whatever way the artist intends.

In addition, many artists believe that the process of cell nutrition is an integral part of the artistic experience as it raises "questions about the care and maintenance of all life forms."[17] Guy

Ben-Ary's work *cellF* (Figure 18.2) is a good example that shows how an artwork cannot exist and function without a living cell culture at the core of, in this case, a neural synthesizer. The "brain" of the installation is constructed of biological neural networks that sprout in a petri dish and that monitors the "body" in real time. The latter comprises an array of analogue modular synthesizers that work in synergy with the brain and, together, they improvise music with human musicians.[18] It is an entirely autonomous instrument composed of a neural network, bio-engineered from the artist's own cells, that controls a custom-built synthesizer. As the artist puts it: "There is no programming or computers involved, only biological matter and analogue circuits; a 'wet-analogue' instrument."[19] This very personal approach uses the skin cells of the artist, which are transformed into stem cells and, in the next step, split into neural networks that become the "external brain" of the artist.

If we think about preserving such a work, we find it impossible to come up with ways that the living cells can be conserved, besides keeping them in labs on a constantly nutritious ground. Through this, they are probably able to survive a certain amount of time while continuously dividing. Another option is to keep the pool of cells that was produced for the performance and to preserve it in paraformaldehyde. This method unfortunately leads to the death of the cells and, as a result, the biological material can only be preserved exactly the way it was on the day of the performance. This leads to the necessity that for every single performance, the artist must cultivate his skin cells into a neural network for the work to interact with other musicians. This however raises questions about how the artwork, other than through documentation, can be presented after the artist's passing?

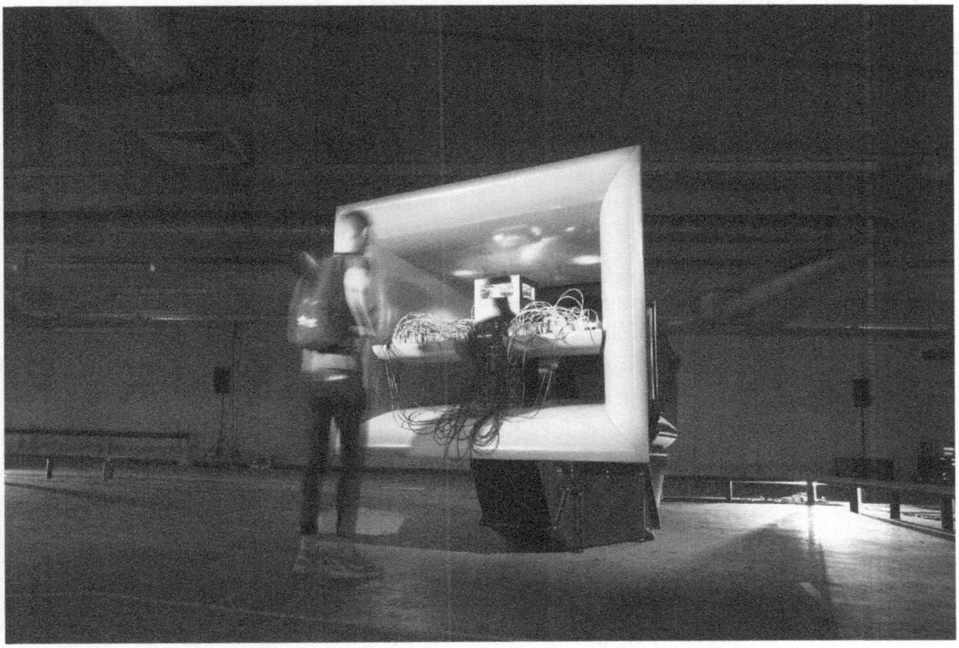

*Figure 18.2* Guy Ben-Ary, *cellF*.

*Source*: Ars Electronica | Christopher Sonnleitner.

## Preservation and Presentation

The life of an artwork's cells usually ends with the termination of the exhibition; they are "autoclaved" in order to comply with policies that prevent the international transfer of living organisms. Hence artworks are usually recreated for every new exhibition. This means, in effect, that a single work exists in numerous versions. Some artists decide, in addition to creating an installation with a limited lifespan, to transform the termination of the artwork into a performance by inviting visitors to a public "execution" of the cells. With their work *Semi-Living Worry Dolls* (2000), Ionat Zurr and Oron Catts "engaged the audience explicitly in the *liveness*" of the dolls by "exposing them to the non-sterile conditions of the world outside of Petri dishes and incubators, allowing audience members to touch them with (gloved) hands."[20] In this way, the killing ritual "forces the artists and the viewers" into an active role in the "cycle of the life/death."[21]

Not all bio artists (or funding sponsors) are content to let their masterpieces rest in peace, however, even if those works have the chance of a glorious funeral. In fact, some try to immortalize their works by using unconventional methods.[22] Julia Reodica's project *hymNext* (2008) involved the artist stopping the growth of artificially grown hymens to "coat them in latex";[23] Tagny Duff's *Living Viral Tattoos* (2008), which used retroviruses and immunohistochemical stains to tattoo skin cultures,[24] were inserted in paraformaldehyde fixate. The conservation of the actual biological material is not so complicated and can be learned and studied from animal preservation and the conservation of human artifacts in natural history museums and bio labs. Most BioArt works, however, do not consist solely of cell cultures but are composed of complex installations with several different hardware and software components. This combination raises more complex issues as we touch conservation practices dealing with mixed media works including digital, conceptual, and physical artifacts such as kinetic and video installations.

Traditional and digital documentation techniques are an essential way to keep both the concept and the artwork alive. Large photographs illustrating BioArt are very common, and works also reach mass audiences through video documentation and online resources. Stelarc's *Ear on Arm* (2008), for example, in which an artificially grown ear was implanted into the artist's forearm by a surgeon, is memorialized with model plaster ear-and-arm "casts"[25] as well as documentation of the surgery. The artist's web page creates an important digital archive of the surgical photography and medical, artistic, and biological engineering involved in the project and makes the work accessible to a global audience. To understand and grasp all aspects of such a work, researchers need to examine all of these different resources in order to have a complete picture of the artist's intentions as well as the physical and contextual quality and complexity of the work. In other words, the biological, medical, and digital need to come together.

Some artists consider that BioArt includes these non-living visual and digital proxies. This method of archiving conservation through transformations of physical media recalls the problem of contradictory BioArt definitions: does BioArt include works that are about the modification of nature? Catts, co-founder of the Tissue Culture & Art Project thinks, "not quite." While he accepts that conservation in glycerol (as done with his *Semi-Living Worry Dolls*) might fall under the heading of BioArt, the assumption of printed paper as "alive" goes too far for him: it defeats the premise of "durational art."[26] Catts regards the solid-state photos of TC&A's tissue-cultured work *Pig Wings* (2000–01) taken by the Museum of Modern Art (New York) as "just the prints."[27] True BioArt, by contrast, "goes through a living cycle."[28] Although Catts defines true BioArt for himself in a narrow sense as to limit it to the living work, others (such as Eduardo Kac) consider the digital form of an artwork as an integral part of their artistic practice. In fact, Kac's widely "publicized photographs and posters of the white bunny as florescent green"[29] (*GFP Bunny*, 2000) are graphically altered, thereby representing a different kind of interaction between the digital, the visual, and the biological.[30] Louis-Marie Houdebine, Kac's scientific partner stated, that the "GFP rabbits in his laboratory do not fluoresce bright green because the gene for fluorescence is not exposed in rabbit fur."[31] It seems that the art piece that captured the imagination of the world and basically invented the entire BioArt field is fake.[32] Or is it? The animal still contained the GFP gene. The concept of genetically modifying the bunny was still being implemented. The photographic prints, photoshopped neon green, still inspired discussions about biological changes.

This story of a groundbreaking artwork gives credibility to Tagny Duff's argument about the "liveliness" of the documentary and the integration of the digital into the physical. As the ancestor of the BioArt field shows, an inanimate piece about biotechnology can, if sufficiently moving, be transformed into a simulacrum of living art itself. "Memory and identity were once understood as inextricably interconnected, and skin, face, and body were imprinted with experiences and memories," wrote Christiane Paul in response to Kac's work. "Now plastic surgery and bioengineering have turned the body into a modifiable sculpture,"[33] and BioArt works can be reincarnated and disseminated through non-biological media. The biological and the digital thus exist in a vital partnership in this branch of art, and researchers need to be alert to the possibilities and limitations of each field in their approach to the study and conservation of BioArt.

Through documentation processes developed over the past thirty years, museums, galleries, and collectors of ephemeral artworks need to combine the tools necessary to respond to the artist's needs. The focus of this practice is typically based on an interview with the artist, which is ideally conducted at the time of acquisition of the work. Such interviews record the artist's views on the various facets of the artwork: its appearance, the significance of its materials; whether (and where) additional parts are available; how the artist defines the possible "decay" of the work; whether and when a restorer should intervene in the work's deterioration; and who (artist, representative of the artist, or conservator) is allowed to preserve or recreate the artwork. It is essential that we understand why artists use their chosen materials and how they understand the associated display and deterioration processes, otherwise we risk losing or distorting material evidence and thus our understanding of a significant branch of twentieth- and twenty-first-century visual culture. The need to document the artist's philosophy in relation to the conceptual and material reconstruction of his or her work therefore becomes indispensable.

While honoring artistic intention plays a key role in the ethical preservation and documentation of BioArt works, decision making based solely on artist testimony is problematic. Intention is neither static nor always conscious; it is both difficult to determine and practically impossible to limit. In addition, the passage of time opens up the potential for the artist to rethink the work both conceptually and materially. Crucially, the passage of time also reminds us that the artist will one day be absent from future consultation, which is why the conservation process needs to be clearly defined and documented.[34] Ultimately, the maintenance of the object becomes a collective responsibility, for in many BioArt works, unhindered decay materially implements the concept of mortality and raises complex questions about the work's longevity.

## The Challenge of the Ephemeral

Similarities can be found in the conservation, preservation, and mediation of ephemeral performance, body art, and BioArt. They survive as film, photo, or video documents, as traces such as posters or flyers, as digital records, or in the form of remaining material or fetishized relics. In the case of BioArt, the question arises whether works that contain living entities (even if these are cellular matter) should be considered as a form of performance art? In a way, the conservation of artworks using living matter deals with problems that performance art has confronted for decades. Contrary to performance art, however, BioArt installations include solid material, such as the installation, as well as the living cells.

In gallery spaces, BioArt is generally presented in three interconnected forms:[35]

1. As an installation that has to be maintained over the period of the presentation. It can take hybrid forms between performance and installation and incorporate biotechnical devices. Gilberto Esparza's work *Plantas Autofotosintéticas* (Figure 18.3) is a symbiotic, self-regulating system for wastewater treatment. The project is an examination of the social question about the handling of precious water resources. The artist uses sewage, and thus man-made pollution, as a source of energy. Micro-organisms, which are part of the installation, not only purify the water, but also generate the light required for the photosynthesis of aquatic plants. In maps, the origin of the polluted water and voltameter show the energy produced. Another instrument translates the light activities of the nucleus (cell nucleus) and the biological processes into sound. The artistic research creates a model of a self-regenerating water system that can actually be applied in cities.[36]
2. As physical marks that relate to the process of the work in the manner of a synecdoche.[37] If we think about the work *May the Horse Live in Me* (2011) by the artist duo Art Orienté Objet, it is hard to determine exactly what the "piece" of art consists of. The blood plasma of a horse and a human are mixed together and the cocktail is injected into the artist's blood stream. Is it the actual performance, the scientific research, the photographs taken of the performance, or the engraved aluminum caskets with the freeze-dried hybridized human-equine blood that synecdochically represents the actual work of art or which turns the work into "art"?[38] It is rather the whole process, which takes places across time and space, that changes an aesthetic object into an experience.

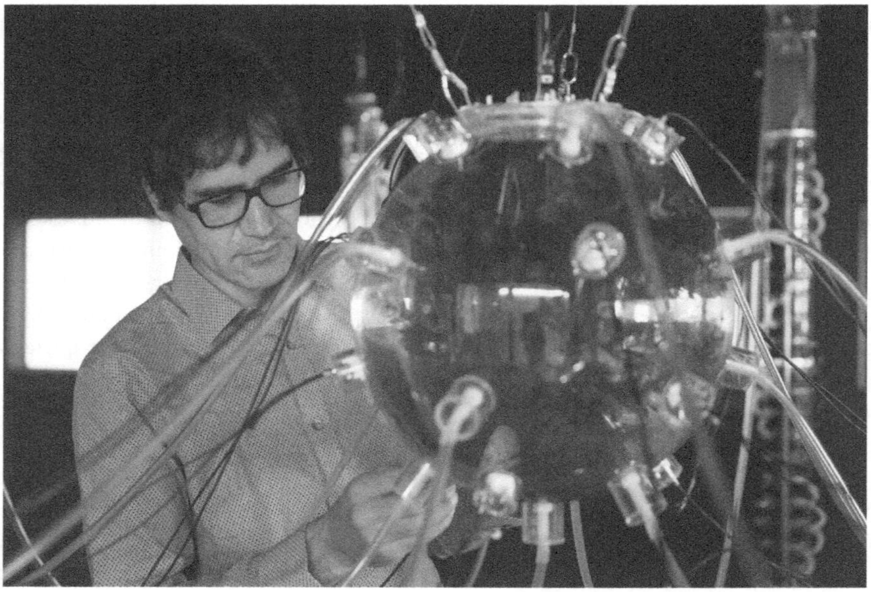

*Figure 18.3* Gilberto Esparza, *Plantas Autofotosintéticas*.

*Source*: Ars Electronica | Tom Mesic.

3. As documents of the work, such as photographs, videos, drawings, and digital resources. Eduardo Kac's *Free Alba!* (2001) photographs, in which the artist presents the press coverage related to the ongoing *GFP Bunny* discussion, are examples of this.[39] Although "art documentation is by definition not art, it merely refers to art," contemporary art at large "has shifted its interest away from the artwork and towards art documentation."[40] According to Boris Groys, this tendency paradoxically shows the living nature of art in general: If one regards life itself as a continuous process that can only be preserved for posterity in the form of documenting the end result, then art is identical with life. As Groys puts it: "Art documentation, by contrast, marks the attempt to use artistic media within art spaces to refer to life itself [. . .]. Art becomes a life form, whereas the artwork becomes no-art, a mere documentation of this life form."[41] Groys considers art today as "biopolitical, because it uses artistic means to produce and document life as a pure activity."[42] A project by the Critical Art Ensemble illustrates this logic. Although the group is best known for its activist strategies, participatory performances, and fieldwork, *Marching Plague* (2005–07), which deals with the theme of biological warfare and the paranoia surrounding bioterrorism, was presented as a site-specific video on the Scottish Isle of Lewis. While the CAE performed a live germ-testing performance on the location, no audience was convened, and the documentary thus became the work itself.

The issues just discussed raise questions about the "unpresentability" of this kind of art. On the one hand, BioArt defies reproducibility. On the other hand, it postulates the significance of direct presence. Therefore, the works are often read and interpreted via a text or paratext. These become a piece of the work as they can no longer be distinguished from the other representational additions and framing devices.[43] The term "BioArt" still describes an unsolved post-digital paradigm and stands for both "biomedia" and "biotopics" by tending to abolish their ontological differentiations. On the one hand, we have art in which the use of biological metaphors and symbols stimulates biopolitical discussions and which is sustained by conventional conservation techniques. On the other hand, there is art that uses biotechnology, but that does not necessarily deal with biological topics. The medium can, but does not necessarily meet the message.[44]

In this context, we need to look at the role of the collector, whether it is a cultural institution or a private individual. What does it mean to own an artwork that will never look the same from one month to the next or that can only be conserved in a certain state (something that often means letting the living parts of the work die)? Moreover, how does an ever-changing, living sculpture alter our preconceptions of what it means to conserve an artwork for posterity?

The questions that we need to ask ourselves are the following: What is the most important part of the work that needs to remain? How can the meaning of the work be conveyed and in which context should it be understood and experienced? Finding answers to those topics requires a new relationship between the collector (the collecting institution) and the artist. It involves a dialogue as well as an understanding of the preserving institution's mission.

The artists Shiho Fukuhara and Georg Tremmel have found a beautiful and very poetic way of preserving a person's DNA long after his or her demise. Their work *Biopresence* (2005) infuses the DNA of recently deceased loved ones into trees, turning the plants into living memorials. "Basically, it can also be seen as a complex pattern of silent mutations,"[45] said Tremmel. Here not only the work of art becomes immortal, but also the humans or living creatures, whose DNA is stored in a single tree cell as a silent mutation or living tombstone.

The presentation of BioArt ex post facto as documentation "could only develop under the conditions of today's biopolitical age, in which life itself has become the object of technical and artistic intervention."[46] But what does this new relationship between life, technology, and art mean as the aspiration of BioArt is no longer to depict, but rather to become life itself? The difficulty is that museum-friendly art documentation turns into a representative symbol that refers to "art as life itself."[47] Thus, despite the difficulties in presenting BioArt live, an increasing number of artists succeed in creating real biological processes that appear to the viewer as "living," or at least as organically authentic—since their essence is based on organic authenticity. By transgressing the semiotic processes of representation and metaphor, this goes beyond creating presence in a face-to-face situation that cannot be conveyed without reducing it to a purely heuristic placeholder of discourses.[48]

## What Should Remain?

In most cases the question of what will or should remain addresses not only the artworks themselves, but also the context (cultural, technological, sociological, and others) from which they derive. In an area where artworks are phenomena rather than objects, the question of what should remain becomes even more pressing. Preserving such works of art is and will become an increasingly complex task. But even when such preservation succeeds, it will be insufficient without knowledge of the context in which the work emerged and developed. This context will give audiences the tools to understand the importance and the relevance of the artwork.

The technological context of the work also has to be taken into account, as works of art using new technologies are increasingly part of a larger system which itself is in constant evolution and exists independently of the artwork. It becomes even more complex when artworks interact with one or many other systems (e.g. installations that link many types of machines and devices). What will be the most difficult aspect to preserve will certainly be these links, particularly in light of the obsolescence of hardware and software. Even with the best preservation strategies, even in the best access conditions, a BioArt work will only exist as a memory without structured documentation. In fact, if we take into account the living aspects of certain works, it is more than likely that this documentation will soon to be the only remaining aspect of the work. It remains to be seen, what documentary structure is the most appropriate. It is also important to experiment with different forms and strategies of dissemination of this documentation, since without this dissemination it is useless. In this field the prospect of digital preservation and dissemination can be particularly useful especially when it comes to creating standards for this process that can, in consequence, be applied globally. Documentary strategies will also have to deal with increasingly complex situations: How to apply methodology constraining documentary practices to an object that is unstable, generative, or collaborative? For these new types of objects, we need new documentary methods and new research tools.[49]

We must document as many aspects as possible of the artistic activities involving new technologies in order to retain traces of the evolution of new art forms. Therefore, documentation strategies must also incorporate the latest technologies and tools. It is ironic that documentation using new technology is also facing the same preservation difficulties as the artworks they intend to document. This documentation is complex and often uses a variety of technologies in design and structure that are similar to those employed by the artworks themselves. This convergence between artworks and their documentation is a new issue that also has an effect on the artistic practice itself as well as on the museum structures as they need to find ways to preserve hardware as well as software if the artists intention is to employ on the original technological items.

We need to be aware that if we do not try to address and solve issues concerning the conservation of ephemeral and living art forms now, these works might be lost for future generations. Since two of the art museum's missions are to collect artworks and to provide a site for educational exploration, it is important that BioArt is also included, so that future generations can learn about it. Collecting, preserving, and presenting BioArt should become a standard process for any contemporary art institution, and adequate physical and digital conditions to accommodate this art form need to be created. Finally, it is also necessary to make BioArt accessible to everyone and to work further on the digitization of this aspect of collections as well as re-staging BioArt works.[50] In this respect, conferences, publications, and online resources in the field of media archeology are very important and can be seen as something like an "afterlife" of the original artwork in its various forms. It is, therefore, crucial to write a media history that is not just a history of images and their reception, but also a history of science, technology, and digital strategies of preservation.[51]

## Notes

1. Robert E. Mitchell, *Bioart and the Vitality of Media* (Seattle: University of Washington Press 2010), 22.
2. Peter Weibel, "Biotechnologie und Kunst," in *Technik und Gesellschaft: Symposion der technischen Universität Wien in Lech am Arlberg (24.-30.08.1980)*, ed. M.E.A. Schmutzer, Schriftreihe der Technischen Universität Wien, Bd. 19 (Wien: Universität Wien, 1981), 158–69.
3. Jens Hauser, "Biomediality and Art," in *Recomposing Art and Science*, eds. Irene von Hediger and Jill Scott (Berlin: de Gruyter, 2016), 201–20.
4. Ingeborg Reichle, "Bio-Art: Die Kunst für das 21. Jahrhundert," *Kunstforum International* 258 (December 2018): 87.
5. Eduardo Kac, "Genesis," accessed April 27, 2019, www.ekac.org/geninfo2.html.
6. Eduardo Kac, "Life Transformation—Art Mutation," in *Signs of Life: Bio Art and Beyond*, ed. Eduardo Kac (Cambridge, MA: MIT Press, 2007), 172.
7. Jens Hauser, "Es gibt keine Bio Art!" *Ars Electronica Blog*, June 2, 2015, accessed January 6, 2019, https://ars.electronica.art/aeblog/de/2015/06/02/es-gibt-keine-bio-art/.
8. Jens Hauser, "Art Between Synthetic Biology and Biohacking: Searching for Media Adequacy in the Epistemological Turn," eds. Lanfranco Aceti, Paul Thomas, and Edward Colless, *Leonardo Electronic Almanac* 22, no. 1 (2017): 128–36. Cambridge, MA: LEA/MIT Press.
9. Ibid., 132.
10. Ibid., 129.
11. Gina Czarnecki, *Heirloom*, accessed January 24, 2019, www.ginaczarnecki.com/heirloom.
12. Annick Bureaud, "Journal Entry: Sleeping Beauties," *Trust Me, I'm an Artist Blog*, July 28, 2016, accessed February 1, 2019, http://trustmeimanartist.eu/journal-entry-sleeping-beauties/.
13. Frances Stracey, "Bio-Art: The Ethics Behind the Aesthetics," *Nature Reviews Molecular Cell Biology* 10 (May 20, 2009): 496–500.
14. Marta de Menezes, "The Laboratory as an Art Studio," in *The Aesthetics of Care?* ed. Oron Catts (Perth: Symbiotica, 2002), 53–58.
15. Marietta Radomska, *Uncontainable Life: A Biophilosophy of Bioart* (Linköping: University Electronic Press, 2016), 163. The relevant incident caused the organizing museum to restart the artwork from the cellular base materials.
16. Ali K. Yetisen, Joe Davis, Ahmet F. Coskun, George M. Church, and Seok Hyun Yun, "Bioart: Trends in Biotechnology," *Cell Press* 33, no. 12 (December 2015): 729.
17. Ionat Zurr and Oron Catts, "The Ethical Claims of Bio-Art: Killing the Other or Self-Cannibalism," *Australian and New Zealand Journal of Art* no. 5 (January 2004): 167–88.
18. Guy Ben-Ary and Gemma Ben-Ary, "Bio-Engineered Brains and Robotic Bodies: From Embodiment to Self-Portraiture," in *Robots and Art—Exploring an Unlikely Symbiosis*, eds. Damith Herath, Christian Kroos, and Stelarc (Singapore: Springer, 2016), 307–25.
19. Guy Ben-Ary, *cellF*, accessed January 10, 2019, http://guybenary.com/work/cellf/.
20. Nora S. Vaage, "What Ethics for Bioart?" *NanoEthics* 10, no. 1 (April 2016): 89.
21. Zurr and Catts, "The Ethical Claims of Bio-Art," 167.
22. Alex J. Maben, "Communicating Meaning in BioArt: The Temporal Strength of Living Media and the Impact of Longevity," *Inquiries Journal* 9, no. 1 (2017), accessed January 21, 2019, www.inquiriesjournal.com/a?id=1518.
23. Anne Byerley and Derrick Chong, "Biotech Aesthetics: Exploring the Practice of Bio Art," *Culture and Organization* 21, no. 3 (2015): 211.

24. Tagny Duff, "Going Viral: Live Performance and Documentation in the Science Laboratory," *Performance Research* 14, no. 4 (2009): 144.
25. Byerley and Chong, "Biotech Aesthetics," 211.
26. Zurr and Catts, "The Ethical Claims of Bio-Art," 170–71.
27. Byerley and Chong, "Biotech Aesthetics," 211.
28. Ibid., 212.
29. Eduardo Kac, accessed July 20, 2019, www.ekac.org/gfpbunny.html.
30. Joe Davis, "Romance, Supercodes, and the Milky Way DNA," in *Ars Electronica 2000—Next Sex*, eds. Gerfried Stocker and Christine Schöpf (Wien: Springer, 2000), 217.
31. Ibid., 217–18.
32. Maben, "Communicating Meaning in BioArt."
33. Christiane Paul, "Time Capsule," *Intelligent Agent* 2, no. 2 (1998): 4–13.
34. Alison Bracker, "When Is the End?" no. 1, October 2012, accessed January 20, 2019, https://frieze.com/article/when-end.
35. Jens Hauser, "Observations on an Art of Growing Interest: Toward a Phenomenological Approach to Art Involving Biotechnology," in *Tactical Biopolitics: Art, Activism, and Technoscience*, eds. Beatriz da Costa and Kavita Philip (Cambridge, MA: MIT Press, 2008), 91–92.
36. Gilberto Esparza, *Plantas Nómadas*, accessed February 2, 2019, www.plantasnomadas.com/.
37. Hauser, "Observations on an Art of Growing Interest," 91–92.
38. Jens Hauser, "Dialogues on 'Bioart' #1: A conversation with Jens Hauser," Interview by Daniela Silvestrin, Digicult, accessed February 2, 2019, http://digicult.it/news/dialogues-on-bioart-1-a-conversation-with-jens-hauser/.
39. Eduardo Kac, *Free Alba!* accessed December 21, 2018, www.ekac.org/freealba.html.
40. Boris Groys, "Art in the Age of Biopolitics: From Artwork to Art Documentation," in *Documenta 11_Platform 5* (Ostfildern-Ruit: Hatje Cantz, 2002), 108.
41. Ibid., 109–10.
42. Ibid., 108.
43. Jens Hauser, "Toward a Phenomenological Approach to Art Involving Biotechnology," in *Evolution Haute Couture: Art and Science in the Post-Biological Age*, ed. Dmitry Bulatov (Kaliningrad: National Centre for Contemporary Art, Baltic Branch, 2013), 339–40.
44. Ibid.
45. David Cohn, "DNA Dose Seeds Living Tombstones," *Wired International*, February 11, 2005, www.wired.com/2005/11/dna-dose-seeds-living-tombstones/.
46. Groys, "Art in the Age of Biopolitics," 110.
47. Hauser, "Observations on an Art of Growing Interest," 91–92.
48. Hauser, "Toward a Phenomenological Approach to Art," 339–40.
49. Ibid., 340.
50. Marta Filipa da Costa Rodrigues, "The Challenges of the Ephemeral: Conserving Performance Art," accessed January 15, 2019, www.academia.edu/16325064/The_Challenges_of_the_Ephemeral_Conserving_Performance_Art?email_work_card=view-paper.
51. Hauser, "Dialogues on 'Bioart.'"

## Bibliography


Byerley, Anne, and Chong, Derrick. "Biotech Aesthetics: Exploring the Practice of Bio Art." *Culture and Organization* 21, no. 3 (2015): 197–216.

Catts, Oron. *The Aesthetics of Care?* Perth: Symbiotica, 2002.

Costa, Beatriz da, and Philip, Kavita. *Tactical Biopolitics: Art, Activism, and Technoscience*. Cambridge, MA: MIT Press, 2008.

Davis, Joe. "Romance, Supercodes, and the Milky Way DNA." In *Ars Electronica 2000—Next Sex*, edited by Gerfried Stocker and Christine Schöpf, 217–35. Wien: Springer, 2000.

Gessert, George. *Green Light: Towards an Art of Evolution*. Cambridge, MA: MIT Press, 2010.

Hauser, Jens. "Biomediality and Art." In *Recomposing Art and Science*, edited by Irene von Hediger and Jill Scott, 201–20. Berlin: de Gruyter, 2016.

———. "Remediating Still Life, Pencils of Nature and Fingerprints." In *Relive: Media Art Histories*, edited by Sean Cubitt and Paul Thomas, 275–307. Cambridge, MA: MIT Press, 2013.

———. "Toward a Phenomenological Approach to Art involving Biotechnology." In *Evolution Haute Couture: Art and Science in the Post-Biological Age*, edited by Dmitry Bulatov, 338–59. Kaliningrad: National Centre for Contemporary Art, Baltic Branch, 2013.

Kac, Eduardo. *Signs of Life: Bio Art and Beyond*. Cambridge, MA: MIT Press, 2007.

Mitchell, Robert E. *Bioart and the Vitality of Media*. Seattle: University of Washington Press, 2010.

———. "Bioart: Media, Evolution, Culture." In *Evolution Haute Couture: Art and Science in the Post-Biological Age*, edited by Dmitry Bulatov, 360–73. Kaliningrad: National Centre for Contemporary Art, Baltic Branch, 2013.

Myers, William. *Bio Art: Altered Realities*. London: Thames & Hudson, 2015.

Reichle, Ingeborg. "Bio-Art: Die Kunst für das 21. Jahrhundert." *Kunstforum International* 258 (December 2018): 86–95.

# 19

# THE EXPANDING ROLE OF DIGITIZED COLLECTIONS

## The Medici Archive

*Alessio Assonitis*

The Medici Archive Project (MAP) was founded in the early 1990s to foster the study of the *Mediceo del Principato*, the epistolary collection of the Medici Grand Dukes, dating from 1537 to 1743 (see bia.medici.org).[1] Comprising more than three million letters and occupying a mile of shelf space at the Archivio di Stato in Florence, this archival corpus should be considered a global, local, and private archive. Penned by an extensive network of Medici diplomats and informants, around two million letters chronicle political and cultural developments in Europe, Asia, Africa, and the Americas. Letters also document the mechanisms that connected the Medici court with its administrative bodies, including the legislative, judicial, financial, and public health branches of government. At the same time, the *Mediceo del Principato* also records the personal vicissitudes of the Medici themselves and the events at their court. We learn of their passions and ambitions, their education and scholarship, their patronage and taste, their physical maladies and religious observance, and their everyday interactions with each other and with the world inside and outside their palaces and villas.

In order to facilitate access to the content of the *Mediceo del Principato*, MAP hired scholars and postdoctoral fellows to enter transcriptions and synopses of these documents into a Microsoft Access database, which was accessible only at MAP's headquarters, located at the Archivio di Stato. Throughout the late 1990s and early 2000s, scholars and students of early modern political, diplomatic, religious, economic, artistic, scientific, military, food, and medical history visited MAP to retrieve primary data essential for their research.

To best serve this expanding scholarly community, MAP constructed BIA, a web-based platform, online since 2012, funded by the Andrew W. Mellon Foundation. In addition to providing a faster and more user-friendly interface for document entry, BIA enables scholars from all over the world to view digitized images of archival documents and to make structured queries to provide targeted results. Members of the BIA community are able to annotate each database item and to link those notes to forum discussions. As of August 2019, BIA's online community stands at almost five thousand registered users—professors, curators, graduate and undergraduate students, independent scholars, and even high school students—who actively contribute to the academic exploration and mapping of the *Mediceo del Principato* directly on this platform.

BIA currently comprises over 25,000 transcribed documentary records; more than 19,000 biographical entries; 87,000 geographical and topographical tags; and more than 700,000 digitized images. For the first time in the history of the Medici Archive, the approach to the collections has not been to replicate an ossified organizational structure that would supplant the many previous ones. Instead, the solution that MAP has adapted bypasses the problem of structure by individually cataloging and tagging each document to facilitate a fluid navigation by means of content-based searches as well as ones utilizing historical archival metadata.

For those scholars who have little or no training in reading early modern Italian scripts—a subject rarely taught in American and British institutions—MAP developed in 2013–14 a teaching module directly connected to BIA. Having recognized the need for instruction in Italian archival practices, online paleography courses that make use of the *Mediceo del Principato* have been offered since 2015. More than three hundred graduate students, professors, and curators have participated at this initiative: one that successfully merged education and community-sourcing and which developed into research trajectories that had not hitherto been contemplated.

The prominent role played in early modern studies by BIA enabled MAP to pursue a variety of focused scholarly endeavors which transformed a small academic start-up into a fully fledged research institute. After its launch, MAP founded five research programs; sponsored over a dozen international conferences in Italy and the United States; set up a predoctoral fellowship program; established an educational program devoted to paleography and archival studies; partnered with Italian, European, and American research institutes; started a peer-reviewed book series with the academic publisher Brepols; and curated exhibitions in Florence and abroad.

## BIA and Early Modern Artistic Discourse

Each document transcribed and contextualized in BIA was entered (and appropriately tagged) according to one or more material culture topic categories, which were determined at the inception of the project.[2] BIA's primary focus on material culture content has enabled scholars to harvest data on the patronage, production, conservation, presentation, and dissemination of a vast variety of artworks, exotica, scientific tools, manuscripts and printed volumes. Aside from straightforward "simple searches" for documents pertaining to artists, objects, and geographical and topographical sites, the index of possibilities for engaging with new research strains has been copious and multifarious.

This digital platform has proven to be an indispensable tool for mapping artistic networks and charting the mobility of artists in Italy and in Europe. Prominent examples are the dense epistolary exchanges directly and indirectly pertaining to Baccio Bandinelli and the complicated commissions for the funerary monument of Leo X and Clement VII in Santa Maria Sopra Minerva in Rome (1536–1541/2) and the tomb of Giovanni dalle Bande Nere (1540–54);[3] reports of Benvenuto Cellini's peregrinations in Rome, Mantua, Ferrara, and Paris;[4] the copious Medici ambassadorial dispatches and *avvisi* (newsletters) detailing Gian Lorenzo Bernini's life and career, including his major commissions in Baroque Rome (e.g. *Fountain of the Four Rivers*, Chigi Chapel at Santa Maria del Popolo, the colonnade and cathedra at the Basilica of Saint Peter) and his close relations with regents, popes, prelates, and nobles, and his travels and sojourns in Tuscany and France.[5]

The activity of artists at court is also documented (and searchable) as well as their personal relations with the ducal and grand ducal entourage. During the first half of Cosimo I's rule, ducal secretaries facilitated and monitored the artistic projects of Bronzino, Pontormo, Bandinelli, Tribolo, and Giovanni Battista del Tasso. A pivotal role was played by Pier Francesco Riccio, who served, among many things, as the duke's artistic and cultural broker. This role was in part taken over by Giorgio Vasari, as many documents record, who devised, supervised, and often executed Cosimo I's artistic program in the last two decades of his rule. Thanks to BIA, scholars can unlock the complex structure of court patronage, the mechanisms of which were seldom regulated by contractual agreements.[6]

Another important BIA feature is the classification of documents related to gift-giving culture. The abundant archival material pertaining to this facet of art history has been overlooked, especially from the diplomatic perspective. Through BIA, Medici letters not only inform scholars of the protocol and reception of gifts of artistic objects but also provide a roadmap for the phenomenology of early modern gift-giving culture based on cultural, religious, and even aesthetic tenets.[7] Also important is the possibility of investigating the relation between "object" (gift) and "language" (letter), the importance of materiality and temporal parameters of gifts; and the understanding of the cultural and geo-political conventions that regulate such exchanges.

Numerous accounts also shed light on modes of artistic display, both within the Medici sphere and at other courts. Likewise, similar inquiry into collecting practices can yield information on cultural brokerage, whether a court secretary shaping the Grand Duke's taste or antiquarian dealers recommending objects from the Mediterranean, Northern Europe, Asia, and the Americas.[8] The Medici either obtained or requested all sorts of oddities: a carcass of a whale, desiccated insects, irregular pearls, phosphorescent stones, tortoise shell, Chinese vases, relics of saints, bezoar stones, skulls of indigenous Americans, byzantine medals, china root, magnifying lens, astrolabes, Indian rackets, and bizarre corals.[9] Thanks to BIA it is also possible to track the discovery, sale, and restoration of antiquities, and the regulations and disputes regarding their import. Clusters of letters document a number of well-known cases, such as the excavation and sale of the *Chimera*, the *Arringatore*, and the *Arrotino*.[10] Diplomatic dispatches from the major European cities, which comprise more than half of the *Mediceo del Principato*, as well as the more than two hundred thousand *avvisi*—five thousand of which are cataloged in BIA—describe the destruction and construction of urban landscapes. Noteworthy in terms of quantity and quality of content are the letters pertaining to seventeenth-century Rome, Paris, and London.[11] Finally, strains of documents, whose connection was only made possible thanks to BIA, illustrate a great variety of themes, including art restoration practices, travel and shipping of artworks, expropriations and frauds, iconoclasms, and travel literature.

## The Problem of the Medici Archives

As the only foreign research center deeply rooted in the "trenches" of Italian archives, MAP is often forced to bridge the gap between Italian public research institutions and the European and American scholars who make use of their resources. This pivotal role has been a challenging one, especially since new generations are now eager to harness the great potential that such vast corpora of data can offer in various fields of research.

MAP has become aware of the difficulties and exigencies of foreign scholars, many of whom can afford little time in Florentine archives and libraries. A great number of researchers have expressed dissatisfaction with the limited availability of manuscripts and the painfully complicated red tape necessary to obtain permission to digitize them. Others are concerned with the lack of proper paleographic training in their home institutions as well as the impressionistic digital projects produced by Italian archives and libraries. They are also frustrated by erratic closures of buildings, the difficulty of getting the assistance of qualified personnel, and the labyrinthine indexing system of archival collections, still fettered to idiosyncratic eighteenth- and nineteenth-century cataloguing criteria. It is not surprising, then, to see graduate students, with little or no archival experience, spending the entire length of their research sojourns taking photographs of documents, the majority of which have little to do with the scope of their project. This new modus operandi has inevitably generated large quantities of digitized archival material which, once scrutinized and harvested by the owner upon returning to their home institutions, will remain in their computers' hard drives and stored under haphazard labeling.

In recent years, scholars have increasingly lamented the fact that there is no available software that can organize digitized Italian medieval and early modern documents—financial, legal, court, state, civic, private, ecclesiastical, etc.—according to standardized archival parameters. In order to solve this problem, some scholars have created rudimentary management databases (much like MAP's 1990s Access database) or jerry-rigged image organizers such as Picasa or Lightroom, with limited data retrieval possibilities. Many scholars came to MAP looking for a solution. They asked if they could donate their "personal archives" of digital images to BIA, hoping to domicile their material here for both the sake of long-term preservation and research utility. MAP had to refuse these offers because BIA was designed only to accept epistolary material from the *Mediceo del Principato*.

Another common desideratum, especially from scholars of younger generations, is a digital workspace for sharing documents and collaborating on transcriptions. Those who enrolled in MAP's online paleography courses—where community annotation, commenting, and transcription of *Mediceo del Principato* documents is permitted—suggested that MAP retool the BIA teaching module for private or commercial use. This operation turned out to be impossible, since this module is closely connected to the BIA system. For lack of alternatives, MAP alumni opened private Facebook profiles devoted solely to collaborative work. However, the architecture of Facebook, though allowing for long strings of comments and basic searches, proved to be impractical for scholarly discourse. Scholars easily lost track of specific thread discussions; they were unable to annotate text; and they found it impossible to organize archival metadata. Within months after its creation, this page was abandoned by almost all of its members.

MAP has been addressing these and other problematic issues voiced by the members of the BIA community. A great number of scholars have been concerned about the difficulty of publishing small-scale archival discoveries in a manner that would receive proper academic accreditation. With over half-a-million digitized letters (and 150,000 new ones being digitized each year), BIA constitutes a vast territory for archival exploration. BIA users continually unearth documents that are crucial for their own research. However, as often happens in archival practice, scholars also discover letters of critical historical importance outside their field. Even though these scholars will not use these discoveries in their own research, they want to make sure that these documents are seen by their peers in the relevant fields. The BIA users who came across these documents outside their field of expertise were faced with three options: (1) donating the discovery to an expert in the field; (2) setting the discovery aside in the hope that they would find time to prepare it for publication in the form of a Short Notice; or (3) entering the discovery into BIA. It should be noted that, although BIA gives full credit to the author, these discoveries are buried among twenty-five thousand document entries.

Responding to the feedback from its community, MAP found itself at a crossroads. It had to decide whether to focus solely on research about the Medici or to broaden its resources on digital access and the preservation of Italian archives. The following section examines the decision taken by MAP and its outcome.

## MIA and the Future of the Medici

The concept of MIA (mia.medici.org) took shape around this time in response to the aforementioned issues. In January 2015, MAP submitted to the Andrew W. Mellon Foundation a prospectus for a universal portal called "My Interactive Archive," which enabled individuals and institutions to house, qualify, share, and even upload—by means of a specifically developed mobile device application—any type of document, originating from any Italian archive, and from any Italian archival collection housed in a foreign institution. Along with this portal, MAP proposed to develop standard protocols for the digital publication of Short Notices, to promote the importance of digital scholarship worldwide, and to establish an accreditation format that would receive proper academic gravitas during job searches and tenure-track reviews. This was an overly ambitious project. An interactive portal that could potentially accept billions of medieval and early modern high-resolution images went well beyond MAP's technical capabilities and human resources.

Thanks to the important feedback from the Mellon staff, this project was recalibrated both in scope and name. In March 2015, MAP submitted a more focused proposal for a prototype web portal named MIA—Medici Interactive Archive—specifically dedicated to uploading, preserving, and cataloging digital documents from a number of Medici collections housed at the Archivio di Stato in Florence, including:

- The *Mediceo del Principato*: the administrative, diplomatic, and private correspondence of the Medici Dukes and Medici Grand Dukes (1537–1743, c. 6,500 volumes).
- The *Miscellanea Medicea*: comprising letters, dispatches, contracts, wills, inventories, horoscopes, maps, etc. that were once an integral part of the *Mediceo del Principato* but were removed in the 1780s (1532–1743, c. 800 volumes).
- The *Guardaroba Medicea*: the documentary material, mostly inventories and account books, recording Medici commission, labor cost, accession, and circulation of raw materials, works of art, and manufactured luxury objects (1532–1743, c. 1,700 volumes).
- The *Scrittoio delle Regie Possessioni*: the administrative and financial documents—mostly payment records, inventories, and ground plans—related to Medici villas, houses, farms, palaces, parks, and the Jewish Ghetto (1530s—1743, c. 4,500 volumes).
- The *Mediceo avanti il Principato*: the private and business papers of the fourteenth-, fifteenth-, and early sixteenth-century Medici family (1370s—1537, c. 165 volumes).

The history of the Medici archival collections can be divided into a series of major milestones: its origins in the late 1370s; its consolidation under Cosimo I de' Medici in the 1540s by ducal archivist Giovanni Grasso; its dispersal by Lorraine archivist Jacopo Riguccio Galluzzi in the 1770s; its attempts at reorganizing and indexing these corpora (especially the *Mediceo del Principato*) in the nineteenth century by ASF archivists Filippo Moisè and Gaetano Milanesi; and its digital renaissance with the Mediceo Avanti il Principato (www.archiviodistato.firenze.it/map/) and BIA platform in the 2000s.

With the launch of MIA in summer of 2020, the Medici Archive will reach another milestone. Thanks to MIA, scholars will be able to upload and store their digitized documents from any of the five Medici archival collections; assign to a Medici digitized document its specific documentary type; qualify Medici digitized documents either with basic metadata (Archival Entities) or advanced metadata (Document Entity); access and work with their libraries of Medici digitized documents anywhere in the world; peruse and study the libraries of Medici digitized documents of other scholars; begin to digitally preserve these archival collections at a time when Italian archives are subject to erratic closures and limited availability of manuscripts; catalogue Medici documents according to a simple and clear indexing methodology; and conduct targeted searches within large quantities of archival material.

Since 2013, BIA has served as a platform uniquely designed for housing digitized images of letters contained in the *Mediceo del Principato*. It permits all users to add textual metadata to the digitized letters, but the uploading of digitized images of documents can only be carried out by

MAP's staff. MIA will resolve the shortcomings of BIA by means of two major innovations. First, it accepts any possible type of document; second, it allows any user to upload digitized images of documents and to add textual metadata to them. Not only will MIA bring universality to the digital archive platform, but it will enable users to influence the criteria used to associate and organize the platform's documents. First, MIA will make it possible to order the documents of the Medici collections according to the way they were once arranged while the Medici regime was in power. Second, it will allow one or more users to experiment with and innovate new models for ordering the documents, according to nearly any analytical criteria. Third, MIA will give users the possibility of drawing attention to important discoveries of documents within the Medici collections.

As such, MIA will resolve a number of pressing issues previously voiced by its community. A scholar's digital library of Medici documents can now be safely saved in a system that is user-friendly, even for those scholars who are not experts with Medici collections or with medieval and early modern documentary types. MIA will allow for the cataloguing of all types of documents, each with a specific template. The structured entry fields for each documentary type template will ensure that scholars enter only the relevant metadata when cataloging an uploaded document. Another advantage of MIA is that it enables scholars to access Medici digitized documents uploaded by others, thus avoiding unnecessary travel to the Archivio di Stato in Florence.

Why reconstruct the Medici archives? One can say that the culture, customs, and events of the early modern period can come to life again thanks to the letters in the *Mediceo del Principato* (and thanks to BIA, which is making them available worldwide). The missives arriving from all corners of the world describe in great detail the hardships, accomplishments, and expectations of early modern men and women, during a period marked by deadly plagues, religious turmoil, political instability, forced migrations, massive segregations, national identities, but also of artistic genius, technological advancements, global awareness, print and news proliferation, medical research, and scientific discoveries.

However, despite the encyclopedic and kaleidoscopic nature of its content, the *Mediceo del Principato* remains an incomplete collection and thus provides only a fragmented reconstruction of this historical period. For instance, in post-Medici Tuscany, archivist Jacopo Riguccio Galluzzi removed a great number of the attachments to letters which later formed another archival collection, called *Miscellanea Medicea*. Just as today's emails arrive with attachments, Medici letters often arrived with *avvisi*, poems, treatises, maps, wills, contracts, recipes, passports, musical scores, inventories, drawings, invoices, war updates, and arrest warrants. Since the structure of BIA was originally designed to accept only epistolary types (minutes, drafts, letters, and copy-letter book entries), all other kinds of enclosures (now in the *Miscellanea Medicea*) had to be left out. Once reunited with its original letter, each attachment will shed light on the history of a person, object, or event.

The preceding example shows the importance of reuniting two Medici documents that were originally produced together. It is also useful to the historian to be able to associate documents with distinct Medici origins but which are thematically related. For instance, to study objects in the Medici collections, it is important to integrate inventories with letters. The great number of inventories and account books included in the archive of the *Guardaroba Medicea* represent an impressive record of their collections over the course of two hundred years. The 1553 inventory of Palazzo Vecchio (*Guardaroba Medicea* 28) is a case in point: chairs, medicine boxes, carpets, mattresses, maps, and scimitars appear alongside Ming vases, Inca masks, sculptures by Michelangelo, pictures by Raphael, printed editions of Dante and Petrarch, and manuscripts by Machiavelli. And yet, the circa seventeen hundred volumes of Medici inventories and payment records tell us very little about the history, patronage, provenance, authorship, condition, creative process, and reception of a given item. To find the answers one needs to examine the letters in the *Mediceo del Principato*. Here is an example: The inventory of Cosimo I de' Medici's library indicates that he owned Andreas Vesalius's *De Humani Corporis Fabrica*. However, a string of letters in the *Mediceo del Principato* complements this inventory entry by relating Cosimo's enthusiasm upon receiving the news that this book had arrived in Florence; his request to have a special stool built for it and to have it bound in leather; his copious annotations on this book; the request for a second copy, since the first was thick with glosses; and, having read it over a number of times, his invitation to Vesalius to perform an anatomy lesson at the University of Pisa.[12]

The *Mediceo del Principato* serves the same contextualizing and enriching function with regard to the *Scrittoio delle Regie Possessioni*. While these architectural and administrative documents give shape to those buildings that made Florence and Tuscany one of Europe's cultural capitals, the letters in the *Mediceo del Principato* animate these spaces with descriptions of the activities that took place inside and outside these walls. This reconstruction can be further enhanced if one incorporates the objects listed in the *Guardaroba Medicea*.

Recently, MAP's staff have brought to light one hundred previously unstudied volumes from the *Scrittoio delle Regie Possessioni* comprising administrative documentation related to the Jewish Ghetto built by Cosimo I in 1570. The written descriptions, blueprints, plans, and drawings included in these volumes meticulously detail the construction and upkeep of Italian and Spanish synagogues, Talmudic schools, private apartments (including the function and furnishing of each room), shops, public spaces, market area, sewage systems, and the water supply. Moreover, there are lists of every single Ghetto inhabitant as well as all the records of leases, expropriations, and confiscations over the course of almost two hundred years. And yet, as detailed as they might be, these documents hardly convey the dynamic activity that took place inside the Ghetto and the intense relationship that the Medici had with Florentine Jews. The thousands of letters in the *Mediceo del Principato* written by or to Jews, or which refer to Jews, allow for a reconstruction of this lost history, even more so since the Ghetto was demolished in the 1880s. One learns about Jewish merchants and antiquarians who connected Florence with Asia and Africa; astrologers and book dealers; families of artisans and tailors; scholars, doctors, and scientists; theatrical impresarios and actors; and important Florentine Jewish dynasties such as the Abravanel.[13] The *Mediceo del Principato* also describes the personal intervention of the Medici, who provided Jews with traveling licenses, tax dispensations, commercial benefits, or legal aid and who blocked unjust confiscations, forced conversions to Christianity, scapegoating, and prohibitions against interfaith relationships.

One of the most drastic interventions that took place during the eighteenth-century dispersal of the Medici collections was the separation of the archive of the late medieval and Renaissance banking and merchant family (*Mediceo avanti il Principato*) from the archive of the early modern Grand Dukes (*Mediceo del Principato*). Reuniting the *Mediceo del Principato* with its earlier counterpart will enable scholars to retrace historical threads that were interrupted by this arbitrary caesura. For instance, the papers of the *Mediceo avanti il Principato* chronicle the origin of the Medici Duchy and Grand Duchy as well as the lives and actions of those historical figures that were instrumental in its creation (e.g. Holy Roman Emperor Charles V, Queen of France Catherine de' Medici, Pope Clement VII de' Medici). This collection also details two centuries of their financial prosperity, from the early mercantile trades to the banking boom under Cosimo the Elder and Lorenzo the Magnificent. Digitally merging both collections will allow scholars to analyze historical phenomena that extended across both archival periods and which have profoundly influenced the course of European history, such as the proliferation of Protestant Reformation, the expansion of the Ottoman Empire, and the exploration of the Americas.

As we have seen in the preceding examples, simultaneous access to these archival collections is a vital objective. Once completed, MIA will enable scholars to perform two fundamental operations: collaborate on the restoration of the original order of the Medici Archive as it was before its dispersal in the 1780s and explore and construct new research trajectories by reorganizing the documents in the Medici Archive according to thematic criteria. In order to facilitate both operations, the completed MIA platform will enable scholars to annotate digital images of Medici documents, comment on any aspect of the metadata related to documents, and receive updates of scholars' recent activities. In addition, MIA will also provide a workspace in which scholars can teach with MIA documents and a dedicated space which will spotlight complete critical editions of documents of historical import. These will be submitted to a peer-review committee composed of two or more members of MAP's Academic Board. Effectively, this space will give prominence to these documents so that the author can receive recognition and the discovery can more readily enter academic discourse.

MAP believes that MIA will ultimately give long overdue recognition to the study of historical archival practice in early modern academic discourse; sensitize the academic community to the importance of both preservation and the accessibility of historical archives during a period when many public institutions are suffering budget cuts and personnel shortages. It will also allow other institutions and/or individuals to make use of the MIA open-source code in order to (re)construct other archival corpora and make them available to the academic community; encourage scholars to explore archival trajectories which may emerge from the work on, and reconstruction of, the Medici Archive, both in Florence or in other Italian, European, and American archives; and create partnerships with other research institutes, universities, archives, and libraries committed to increasing digital access to historical primary source material. Finally, on a scale that far exceeds what the founders imagined possible, MIA will fulfill MAP's foundational mission dating back to the early 1990s, which was to study and valorize the *Mediceo del Principato*. In a very real sense, MIA will enable MAP to evolve from an Italo-centric approach to Renaissance studies to a global approach: with the tools and experience provided by MIA, MAP will be in a position to extend its success with the Medici Archive to nearly any other early modern archive, anywhere in the world.

## Digitization and Self-Archiving

Early modern scholars are now rediscovering archival investigation in Italy to be an indispensable component of historical scholarship. New generations of academics and students—particularly American, British, and German—are eager to harness the great potential that such vast corpora can offer in the fields of research. Italian archives such as the ones in Venice, Florence, and Rome (once the near exclusive data-mining territory of Italian scholars) are now becoming international clearinghouses. This is primarily thanks to the technological resources and digital humanities projects that have been developed.

In accordance with its agreement with the Andrew W. Mellon Foundation, MAP will provide MIA's open-source code to interested parties. Archival institutions housing early modern manuscripts, particularly small, underfunded public ones and family-owned private ones, stand to benefit enormously from MIA's cost-free solution to the expensive problem of developing or applying data-management software for online storage and user accessibility. The MIA interface is designed for the effective and easy use of archives. This means that archivists and librarians, and even lay volunteers with a minimum of training, can customize a MIA profile and preserve their share of the world's cultural patrimony of archival documents.

## Notes

1. The BIA (2010–12; 2013–14) and MIA (2015–17; 2017–19) platforms were constructed by a team of early modern scholars, digital humanists, and software developers from the Medici Archive Project (MAP). Their names do not appear next to that of the author of this chapter and principal investigator of both projects merely for reasons of space. Lorenzo Allori and Sheila Barker were instrumental in devising the architecture and content of both BIA and MIA platforms. Thomas Brownlees, Piergabriele Mancuso, Samuel Morrison Gallacher, and Lorenzo Vigotti, along with the aforementioned scholars, co-wrote the grant proposals for the MIA platform in 2015 and 2017. For their invaluable contributions at various stages of both projects, the author would also like to thank Lorenzo Pasquinelli, Shadab Bigdel, Rose Byfleet, Stefano Dall'Aglio, and Maurizio Arfaioli. A special thanks also goes to Carlotta Paltrinieri who assisted the author on the research for this chapter. Finally, as director of MAP, I am deeply indebted to George Frampton Jr, board chair of this research institute.
2. The categories are Academies; Animals Exotic and Unusual; Antiquities and Antiquarianism; Archives; Arms and Armor; Art Collecting; Art, Legislation; Art Literature; Avvisi (newsletters), Books and Printing; Carriages; Ceramics, Coins and Medals; Costume and Dress; Devotional Objects; Drawings; Food and Wine; Fortifications, Fountains and Hydraulics; Frames, Furniture; Games Toys Sports; Gardens; Gifts from the Medici Court to Gifts not Medici; Gifts to the Medici Court from:, Glassware, Gold and Silverwork; Jews and Jewish Culture; Jewels and Jewelry; Luxury Textiles; Maps and Mapmaking; Medicine; Miraculous Images; Music and Musical Instruments; Natural Sciences; Painting; Pietre Dure; Relics; Sculpture; Tapestries and Hangings; Theater and Festival; and Timepieces.
3. On Bandinelli and his commissions, see BIA documents: DocID#18477 (This letter from Luigi del Riccio to Cosimo I is accompanied by a memoriale written by Bandinelli himself DocID#18479); DocID#18771, DocID#18552, DocID#18553 (Turini and Cybo ask Cosimo I to allow Bandinelli back to Rome to complete the papal tombs); DocID#18735 (a request for black marble for the tombs at Santa Maria sopra Minerva); DocID#23552 (Cardinal Cybo complains against Bandinelli's inappropriate language).
4. On Cellini's mobility and travels: DocID#3502 (Eleonora de Toledo proposes Cellini to the French court); DocID#22012 (mention to his early work in France is made in this avviso from Venice); DocID#6303 (Cellini recorded in Rome; DocID#7282); DocID#19914 (his immatriculation in the *Arte dei Fabbricanti*); DocID#14163, DocID#26649, DocID#18778 (Cellini is mentioned in the Medici household payrolls).
5. See the *avvisi*: DocID#19721; DocID#20816; DocID#19888; DocID#20905; DocID#19961; DocID#22499; DocID#22747; DocID#19959; DocID#8268.
6. On the role of Pierfrancesco Riccio, Giorgio Vasari, and on Medici patronage, see among many: DocID#7050; DocID#2472; DocID#5567; DocID#3076.
7. On the phenomenology of gift-giving culture at the Medici court: DocID#523; DocID#4109; DocID#18682; DocID#6592.
8. On the circulation, collection, and display of objects from the Mediterranean, the Levant, Northern Europe, or the Americas, see DocID#6233; DocID#16555; DocID#8898; DocID#9202; DocID#15651; DocID#7916; DocID#30095; DocID#15581.
9. See BIA documents: DocID#1390 (regarding a unicorn horn); DocID#23702 (Hannibal's elephant bones); DocID#13878 (boxes of corals); DocID#6342 (pearls ordered for Sultan Süleyman the Magnificent); DocID#16179 (an ebony cabinet containing among other objects a Galilean telescope and an astrolabe).
10. On these sales, see documents: DocID#1252; DocID#4725; DocID#281.
11. On urban landscapes and redevelopments: DocID#3126; DocID#19063 and the related letter DocID#16899; DocID#25281 and DocID#25285; DocID#24448; DocID#24289; DocID#24327; DocID#24446; DocID#7855.
12. See BIA's documents: DocID#2412; DocID#2435; DocID#7059; DocID#14746; DocID#19960; DocID#19965.
13. On the Abravanel affair: DocID#28468; DocID#28773; DocID#26847; DocID#26849; DocID#26697.

# 20

# DIGITAL LANGUAGES FOR ART HISTORY

## Audience Engagement, Virtual and Augmented Reality

*Stefania De Vincentis and Luca Nicolò Vascon*

Johanna Drucker has described the difficulties encountered by art history in adapting and adhering to digital techniques for the study of cultural heritage.[1] The main problem, she argues, is "intersemiotic," insofar as digital humanities must transpose sources into language, be they hand-written codices, inventories, archival sources, 3D models, or photogrammetric analyses. In addition to the question of how to rethink art history in light of technologies that can help us decipher and reconstruct artistic data on the basis of their material elements, the other issue to be addressed concerns the effective management of the digital information and communication technology (ICT) resources employed in the treatment and interpretation of an artwork. In this case, the study of digital art history (DAH) raises problems of a methodological nature. Drucker proposes a distinction between "digitized" and "digital" art history, where the former corresponds to "repository building" derived from the use of online resources and the latter comprises "analytic techniques enabled by computational technology."[2] In other words, she distinguishes between existing methods and resources on the one hand and, on the other, developments that influence the evolution and fundamental approaches of art history as a whole.[3]

More recently, Georg Schelbert has moved beyond this dichotomy.[4] He focuses on the need to adopt a different methodological approach by understanding the digital reproduction of artworks (including scanning, modeling, and visualization) as an integral part of DAH. His considerations are far from the usual resistance to the proliferation of digital tools—databases, devices, web platforms—that seem to threaten the aura of the actual artworks, thereby feeding the mistrust of art historians.

More recent studies tend to embrace warnings about the uncritical use of ICT data for the interpretation of sources and texts[5] and adopt a circular model that combines the analysis of formal and measurable features of artworks with analytical, theoretical and critical speculation about their historical context. This process emphasizes the need to gather a large amount of data about context in order to relate it to the artwork's material qualities. The conflict between the simple digitization of the artwork and the danger of analyzing linguistic and morphological data without applying appropriate standards is addressed by combining the work of two kinds of institution active in the study of DAH, namely museums and universities. However, the input of libraries, archives and research institutions is also important in this process.

By initiating a dialogue between the academic study of the history of the artwork and current museum practices, DAH can focus on the purposeful dissemination of research results and configure a novel space of interaction between the artwork, scholars, and visitors. While research institutions have undertaken a number of activities to that effect, the gap between the efficiency of digital resources and the difficulty of making these resources available to the wider public remains to be fully bridged. It is now essential for the discipline of art history to foster a greater connection with kindred institutions such as museums, libraries and archives in order to achieve a more viable definition of DAH as a continuous accumulation of knowledge in digital form that makes artifacts open to various kinds of research.[6]

The two case studies discussed next illustrate different forms of dialogue between cultural heritage technologies and art historical collections. The selected institutions are the Pinacoteca Nazionale of Ferrara, part of the museum complex of the Gallerie Estensi,[7] and the Scuola Grande di San Rocco in Venice, founded in 1478 and managed since 1749 by the eponymous archconfraternity. While the Ferrara museum operates within the Gallerie Estensi's wider line of research on digital humanities[8] (where technology contributes both to institutional communication activities and to art historical research), the Venetian case illustrates a project of augmented reality capable of prompting new critical readings of artworks. Such projects lend themselves to an interconnected and interdisciplinary reading of the artifact and usher in a research methodology inscribed in DAH. Museums and cultural institutions do not simply use technological resources to turn the exhibition space into an attractive environment that is abstracted from their collection: rather, they create a mediated space of investigation and communication in which experts and laypeople can enter into contact with both the actual artwork and its digital elaboration. In this knowledge network, visitors can identify, categorize, and contextualize artifacts within the realm of their own experience, and scholars can validate and compare their research and formulate new hypotheses. The result is the creation of an interactive exhibition venue in which visitors have the opportunity not only to observe but also to participate in the process of artistic interpretation and production.

## The Pinacoteca Nazionale of Ferrara: Digital Reconstruction of the Belfiore *Studiolo*

The exhibition project *Parallel Workshops, the Belfiore Studiolo and Borso's Bible 1447–1463* is part of the Pinacoteca's overhaul of its exhibition system.[9] This case study illustrates how the application of digital technology to museum activities can go beyond didactic functions. The temporary exhibition, curated by Marcello Toffanello in 2018, was devoted to a landmark moment in the history of Ferrara's artistic culture, namely the Estense Renaissance. Its centerpiece was the *Bible* of Borso d'Este (one of the most important Renaissance manuscripts in the world and a masterpiece of the figurative culture of the ancient Estense capital), now held at the Biblioteca Estense in Modena.

Beside the Bible, which could be perused virtually on a dedicated multimedia device, the highlight of the project was the opening of a new room inside the Pinacoteca, dedicated to the Belfiore *studiolo* at Palazzo dei Diamanti. The room had been commissioned in the mid-fifteenth century by Borso's brother, the Marquis Leonello d'Este (1407–1450),[10] and was dedicated to intellectual pursuits and the contemplation of art. The room showcases two of the Pinacoteca's masterpieces: the paintings of the muses *Urania* and *Erato* from the Sacrati Strozzi collection at the Pinacoteca of Ferrara.[11] These were originally part of the decorative cycle of the ancient—and now razed—Belfiore *studiolo*. The exhibition also hosted an additional painting from the original cycle: the Muse *Polhymnia*, lent by the Gemäldegalerie in Berlin.

The *studiolo*, documented in studies on collection history, was intended to represent the virtues of its owner, who thereby affirmed his position in different fields of knowledge.[12] The *studiolo* was not only a "most eclectic example of art at court"[13] but also "an opportunity to disseminate the art-historical heritage after the death of the patron."[14] It was destroyed in the seventeenth century and its artworks are now part of the collections of various museums around the world.

According to Guarino da Verona's iconographic description from 1447,[15] the decorative layout on the walls of the *studiolo* comprised paintings of the nine muses—personifications of the arts and of the works of the intellect, that were supposed to pay homage the Marquis's wisdom and governance skills. The muses identified by Guarino are: Clio, inventor of history; Thalia, of agriculture; Erato, of conjugal ties; Euterpe, of flutes; Melpomene, of song and dance; Polhymnia, of agriculture; Terpsichore, of dance; Urania, of astronomy; and Calliope, "investigator of the sciences and priestess of poetic art."[16]

In his praise of the Marquis's idea to decorate the *studiolo* with depictions of the muses, Guarino da Verona underscores the originality of ascribing civic and cultural virtues to pagan deities, thereby freeing these virtues from Christian hegemony. After Leonello's death, the cycle was completed by his brother Borso, who made a few additions and changed the original layout. The work was commissioned first to the painter Angelo Maccagnino, then (after the latter's death) to Cosmè Tura, but other artists were also involved, including Giuseppe Pannonio.[17] Six paintings of the muses are currently documented: Erato and Urania, at the Pinacoteca of Ferrara; Terpsichore at the Museo Poldi-Pezzoli in Milan; Thalia (attributed to Pannonio), at the Szépmüvészéti Múzeum of Budapest; Calliope (probably painted by Cosmè Tura) at the National Gallery in London; and finally Polhymnia, that the Staatliche Museen, Gemäldegalerie of Berlin, lent to the Pinacoteca for the exhibition (as noted previously).

Historical data, gathered under the supervision of Toffanello, comprised primarily handwritten sources from the Modena State Archives which faithfully described the *studiolo*'s spatial layout. The plausibility of the dimensions reported in these documents was then verified through 3D digital reconstructions. Due to an absence of documentation about the decoration and interior composition of the space, digital technologies were used to formulate hypotheses about the kind of wooden lining on the walls. The final choice fell on a carved partition composed of geometric marquetry[18] thanks to a comparison with better-known *studioli*, including those of Federico da Montefeltro in Urbino and Gubbio. The main focus of the Pinacoteca's digital project, however, was on the reconstruction of the Belfiore's *studiolo* painting cycle.

In addition to providing insight into Estense Renaissance culture,[19] the exhibition project aimed to present the results of the institution's technological and museographic update. This had begun in 2016 with the repositioning of the panels of the Costabili polyptych (painted by Dosso Dossi and Garofalo) during the reorganization of the rooms dedicated to sixteenth-century Ferrarese painting. It continued with the set-up of a new exhibition itinerary from the fourteenth to the eighteenth century. In this framework of reorganization and modernization, the Gallerie Estensi, in collaboration with the Pinacoteca Nazionale of Ferrara[20] and the FrameLab of Bologna University,[21] developed a joint research project on the Belfiore *studiolo*.

The FrameLab follows interdisciplinary criteria that determine the application of digital technologies in the cultural field. It underscores the importance of accessibility and communication for the understanding and dissemination of research, and privileges the narrative aspect of studies and applications associated with the digital cultural heritage. The tools used for the dissemination of cultural heritage include historical 3D reconstructions based on virtual models; the creation of semi-immersive virtual tours; photographic reproductions of art historical artifacts; digital restoration of photographs and documents and their subsequent integration into databases; and the digital elaboration and analysis of manuscripts. The relevance of the project lies in its capacity to satisfy the requirements of art-historical research and of scientific accuracy while also producing a device that is readily accessible and usable.

In a short interview, Toffanello underscored the strong points of the operation and the research opportunities that were opened up by digital reconstruction based on documentary sources. From the beginning, the project stated its intent to suggest, rather than faithfully describe, the environment and cultural program imagined by Leonello d'Este for the *studiolo* where the two works are held inside the now-razed palace known as *Delizia di Belfiore*.[22] The rendering of the *studiolo*'s space in relation to the dimensions of the pictorial cycle suggested new hypotheses about the placement of the paintings and the actual size of the room (too big compared to the canvases). Most importantly, it investigated the very notion of the *studiolo* as a private place designed for personal use, meditation and rest and as a showcase of the nobleman's most treasured collections of objects.

Another important issue concerned the choice of the digital language to be used in the reproduction of a hitherto unreconstructed space. A touch-screen panel was chosen to display, *in situ*, the 3D virtual representation of the *studiolo* and the hypothetical arrangement of paintings on the walls. This solution allowed the audience to move around the virtual space, zoom in on the details of the artworks and obtain historical and iconographical information about the muses represented on each painting. In order to avoid the risk of forgery—a frequent occurrence when working with high-definition computer graphics—the rendering did not show the *studiolo* in every detail. Instead, it was presented as a prototype where the six sufficiently documented canvases had been arranged: "Thus, the user is aware of facing a reconstructed object that suggests and illustrates rather than graphically reproduces an actual environment."[23] The same information displayed on the touch screen were also available on the website with the addition of various further pieces of information.

If, from a scientific standpoint, the initial push for dissemination brought about unexpected results by suggesting new interpretations of existing studies and disclosing further research paths, the project nevertheless suffered from technological shortcomings. Owing to a lack of internet hotspots, the digital apparatus was disconnected from its theoretical counterpart on the website. As a result, the museum could neither communicate with the Lab nor avail itself of technologies that would have allowed it to become a place not only for the preservation and viewing of the cultural heritage but also for research.

After the exhibition, the two muses that belonged to the Pinacoteca (*Erato* and *Urania*) were placed in a dedicated room along with wooden artifacts and objects that evoked the decorations and collections of the original *studiolo*. Beneath the two paintings, a touch-screen device presented viewers with a virtual (hypothetical) reconstruction of the spaces and the history of Renaissance environments. The project confirmed that digital devices inside museums, while often misinterpreted as accessories aimed at making the venue more attractive, can reinforce the position of the museum as a venue for research, active participation, and the fostering of knowledge. The digital reconstruction proved an effective means to rethink the display of the paintings inside the Belfiore *studiolo*, whose size (6.4 m × 8 m) was relatively large when compared to similar cases such as the one in Gubbio. The use of digital technologies also contributed to validating primary source material and encouraged research interest in this environment. Moreover, the video narrative device allowed audiences to become familiar with the space and the story of its walls, thereby enabling them to recognize it as a precursor of the contemporary museum.

## Dynamic Light and Augmented Reality at the Scuola Grande di San Rocco, Venice

The Scuola Grande di San Rocco is the seat and property of an archconfraternity established in 1478 which takes care of the building's preservation and keeps it open to the public. Over the last ten years, the Scuola has been gradually switching to LED light sources, and the architect Alberto Pasetti Bombardella[24] was appointed to design and install the new lighting system. In 2014, he completed the work on the Sala dell'Albergo. This was an important space in the life of the Scuola, as it was where the governing body used to meet. In 1564, Tintoretto won the competition to decorate the room and to execute the ceiling painting of the *Glory of San Rocco* as well as a large wall painting, *The Crucifixion*, completed in 1567.[25]

The Scuola Grande was lit with natural light until 1937, when the Spanish engineer and set designer Mariano Fortuny was asked to illuminate it.[26] Pasetti Bombardella's new lighting system developed the existing infrastructure, including Fortuny's original floor lamps, and included new projectors for spot and scattered light beams designed to enhance the display of Tintoretto's majestic canvases. Pasetti Bombardella's attempt to achieve an entirely hidden lighting design that could mimic the lighting conditions contemporary to Tintoretto's work and highlight the original colors of any part of the paintings led to the creation, development, and production of an array of small individual light sources, and highly specific lenses and components, all controlled by a single computer board (Figure 20.1).

In order to explore the possibility of controlling the lights via a smart and clear interface that could switch between various lighting schemes, Pasetti Bombardella contacted a working group composed of Marco Luitprandi, Chiara Masiero Sgrinzatto, Matteo Tagliatti, and myself,[27] which boasted a cumulative experience in cultural heritage, communication, imaging, and interactive design. Soon we started seeing additional and more interesting possibilities: after preliminary tests, we devised the idea of transforming the highly fragmented lighting system into a new feature that would reveal and develop a narrative that resonated with the paintings in the room. The main guideline was to be as non-intrusive as possible: technology was meant to be an invisible auxiliary to the viewers' understanding of the artworks. The system that we developed provided an enhanced—augmented reality—experience of the space and of the works exhibited in it.

The system connects the dynamic light environment to the director's device, i.e. a tablet in the hands of a guide who can control any light source in the room, whether one by one or by groups. A nearly 4-gigapixel 360° Virtual Reality (360°VR) photographic picture of the room functions both as a straightforward interface and as the main iconographic content of the whole system. During the visit and depending on the subjects on which he or she wants to focus, the guide can dim the lights and use spots to highlight specific parts of a painting, architectural elements, and so forth. But this is not all: the visitors can have—or rent—their own smart device, which can also control the zoom and viewing of the gigapixel image, or reveal related content. The director's tablet can control not only the lighting down to a single element of a painting, but also the specific contents shown on a visitor's smart device (tablets or smartphones) as well as on the smart screens that may be available in the room.

The *Crucifixion* painting is large (more than 5 m × 12 m) and covers the whole front wall of the room (8 m × 13 m). Whereas the viewer can only observe the painting only from a very steep angle, the digital interface provide an orthogonal frontal view, similar to that found in art history books. This makes it possible to overlay notes, sketches, graphics, and so forth under the control of the guide's master tablet.

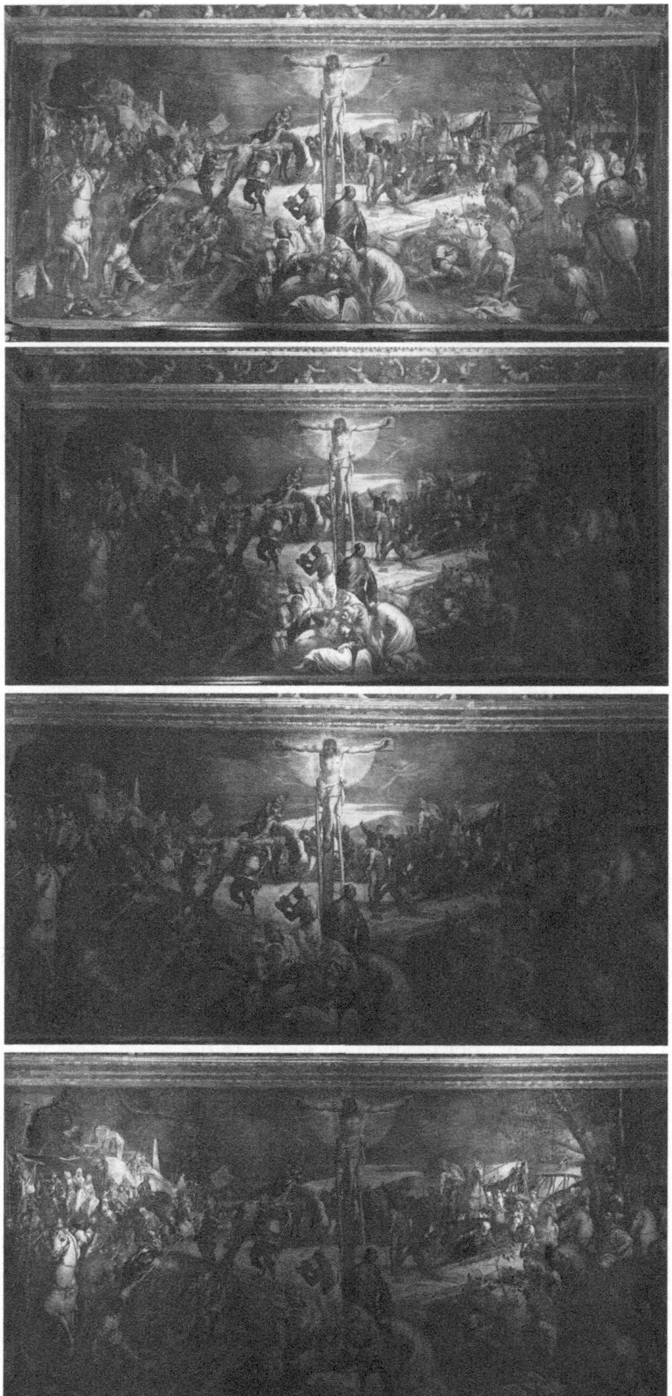

*Figure 20.1* An example of various light scenes on Tintoretto's *Crucifixion* in the Scuola Grande di San Rocco.

*Source*: Officine Panottiche + Nuovostudio.

As the system is based on a web interface over a local network, users are not required to download an app on their own devices, and no data plan is used. The system's flexibility concerns both its mode of operation and buying/renting options: It can be set to work with the devices provided by the museum, with the visitor's personal devices, or both. Moreover, it can function either through a mobile app or by simply logging on to a local network.

In the freest and most comprehensive scenario that we tested, if a group of visitors use their own hardware (tablets or smartphones), they will simply connect to the local Wi-Fi and access a web page. Then their device will be ready for the storytelling and will mimic what the guide sees on the master tablet. This entails following the path and zooming through the high-definition image of the room and exploring additional information that complements details emphasized by the lights in the physical space. The devices can also be used to browse high-resolution pictures at the end of the tour and to compare them with the actual paintings.

In other cases, the system can be used as an automatic guide that allows visitors to connect their devices at given times of the day and to follow a pre-recorded pattern. An even simpler option would be to allow one visitor at a time to act as the director, controlling the lights and contents with the help of a touchscreen without using any other device.

Studying how human beings perceive, react and adapt to a specific situation is the staple of any project involving Augmented Reality (AR), Virtual Reality (VR), Cross Reality (XR) or Mixed Reality (MR) installations, all of which involve, in one way or another, tampering with these cognitive processes. The design, principles of interaction, content, and technology must all be developed consistently with one another and be as transparent as possible, in order to convey the relevant message without interfering with it.

When looking at a work of the scale of Tintoretto's *Crucifixion* in the Sala dell'Albergo, the viewer is usually not standing still. The composition is too monumental for one's field of view and too detailed to be comprehensible at one glance. The painting can only be seen in its entirety just before the viewer enters the room. This is why the audience tends to move around the room, focusing on single details and reconstructing the ensemble in their short-term memory.

The occasional reflections of light that may impair our view of small areas of a painting (impossible to avoid in the case of monumental and non-flat canvases) are typically removed from visual memory because the slightest movement is sufficient to fix the problem: They are perceived, but not registered in our experience. For the same reason, when walking around Sala dell'Albergo, we devise our own viewing pattern, a complex network of movements comprising eyes, head, and body. Although these may vary from one person to the other, such patterns result in a "general" (but incomplete) impression of the room, always focused on the *Crucifixion* painting.

This is where our AR project enables a different, unique experience of the room that disrupts typical viewing patterns and adds a new interpretive layer through a shared itinerary. The lighting design is certainly spectacular, and seeing it fade away and, a moment later, shine on a specific figure, detail or background can be a deeply emotional experience. However, that same lighting is also doing a more important job, insofar as it allows us to make selections within our actual visual experience while also keeping an eye on the complexity that surrounds us. The gigapixel image completes the experience by showing what is inaccessible to the naked eye (Figure 20.2).

From a photographic point of view, gigapixel images in VR360° are not a recent development—nor were they new in 2014, when the project started. However, they were and remain technically challenging and require specialized equipment, competencies, and skills. We needed a sturdy tripod with a special head capable of micrometric positioning in order to shoot with enough precision the 650 and more pictures needed to cover the entire work from the

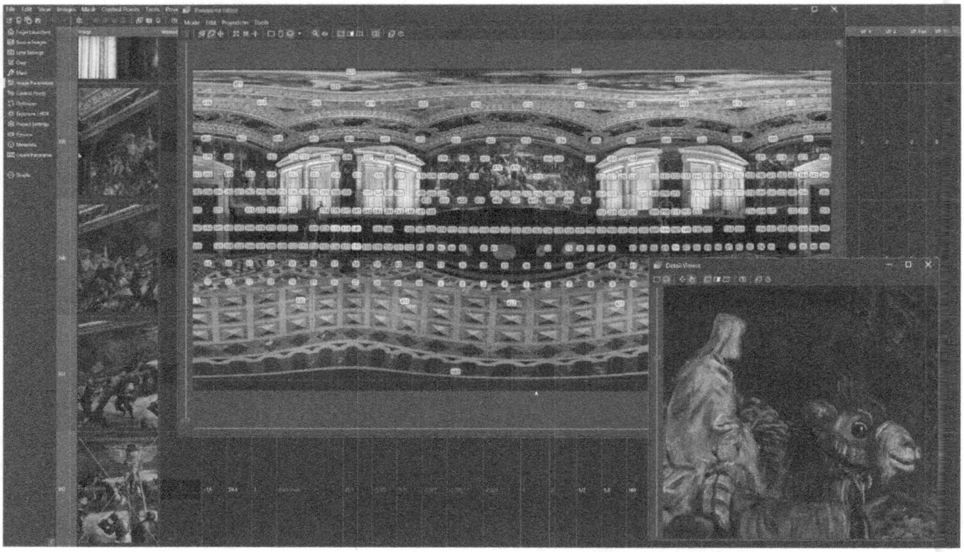

*Figure 20.2* Building the gigapixel image, equirectangular in the background and 100% detail in the front.
*Source*: Officine Panottiche + Nuovostudio.

center of the room.[28] In this case, the task was even more challenging than usual: The space was available only for short photo sessions of one and a half hours maximum. Because we used a telephoto lens, we encountered problems with the focus. Shallow depth of field and angled shots toward a flat surface require focus-stacking techniques. The focusing plane is thin and parallel to the camera sensor, but the room walls and the paintings are not. In consequence, multiple images are taken for each framing with different focus settings; they are then aligned, stacked together, and blended in a completely in-focus image. The available light was also an issue, as photographing a complete 360° scene precludes the use of flash or any additional lighting other than what is available on the premises.

As the monumental *Crucifixion* painting is not perfectly planar, small areas of the canvas inevitably reflect light differently. There was also the even more challenging problem of brush strokes and highly reflective color surfaces that caused shiny white spots to appear on the picture. While good LED lights and the correct lighting arrangement may prevent one from noticing the problem with the naked eye, photography exposes all these issues. We therefore developed new post-production techniques and software filters, and fine-tuned existing ones, in order to achieve a clean image. Once these issues were solved, we ended up with images distributed in an irregular pattern in the "virtual sphere,"[29] and were left with a considerable amount of manual work to complete.

The goal was to obtain the best possible definition so as to allow the viewer to examine the brushstrokes and textures of the canvas. I should also mention that these images do not require a particularly large bandwidth to be browsed and can be easily viewed from an old smartphone or personal computer. In the uploading process, the image is decomposed into smaller tiles, as in the case of Google Maps. Only the requested tiles are actually downloaded and displayed, and even downloading a large amount of data will result in a smooth experience for the user. In order to demonstrate the potential of the system and to develop the controller interface, we created different type of contents (music, text, graphics, and video). The interface was minimal

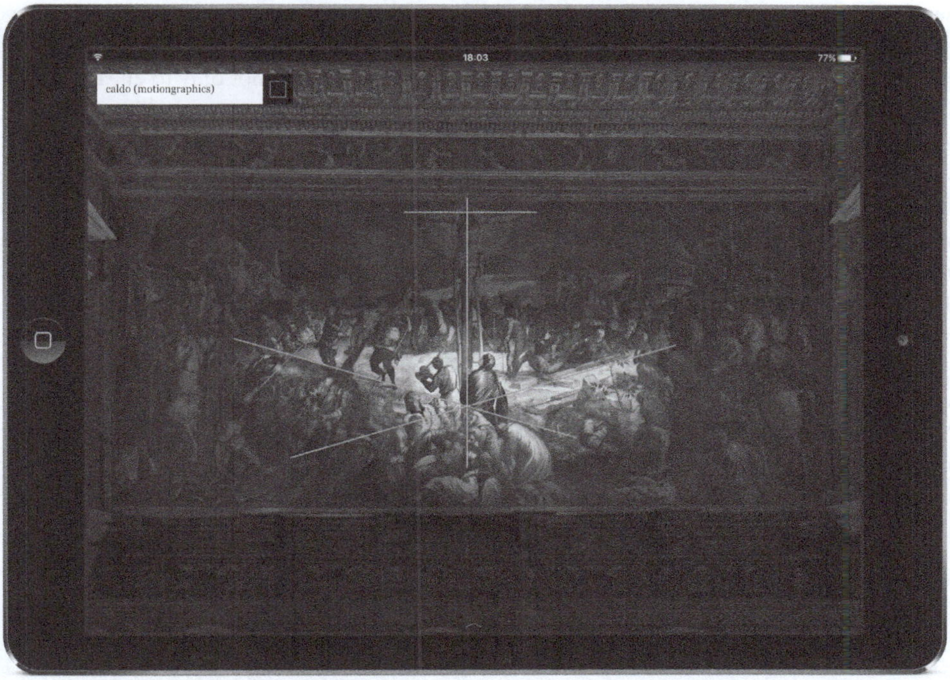


*Figure 20.3* An example of animated graphic contents the guide can show on connected devices.
*Source*: Officine Panottiche + Nuovostudio.

(based on the VR360° image of the space) and transparent for the final users (as they perceive only the change in content on their device (Figure 20.3).

In our tailor-made AR environment, we tried to make technology as inconspicuous as possible and to direct the viewer's attention away from the filter of their own device in order to focus on the actual artworks and lighting. The devices were a mere aid to access a greater amount of information, to examine the artworks more closely, and to focus the mind in an environment that may otherwise be perceived as "overwhelming."

Exploring a complex and monumental artwork such as the *Crucifixion* in such detailed resolution permits a different approach to the painting. In the course of our long on-site tests, we found that the members of the archconfraternity (people who had lived and worked in the Scuola for most of their lives and who were deeply attached to, and familiar with, its artworks) were amused by these interactive high-resolution images, which allowed them to discover details, characters, and expressions that they had never seen. Simultaneously enlarging and narrowing the field of vision through the use of digital technologies revealed things that had hitherto lain hidden in plain sight.[30]

## Conclusion

The two case studies discussed in this chapter illustrate different approaches to recreating and engaging with art-historical environments through techniques of virtual and augmented reality. In the first case (the digital simulation of the Belfiore *studiolo*), the research process and curatorial perspective took prominence over technological innovation. The virtual environment served as a didactic tool, the insights from which could be accessed off-site via a dedicated web page. While offering a hypothetical simulation of the original space and its contents, the system proved effective in stimulating audience curiosity and allowed users not only to engage with the history the artworks but also to access the culture of the age.

The aim of integrating digital devices into audiences' experience of the *Crucifixion* painting in San Rocco was to augment visual engagement with the work. This opportunity to engage in detailed looking was undertaken without reconstructing the work's cultural context. Communication of the historical narrative thus required the support of a guide who accompanied the public on their journey into the background of the artwork. In contrast to the case of the Belfiore *studiolo*, emphasis was placed on devising technologies that granted access to levels of visual information that were otherwise inaccessible.

Both approaches succeeded in highlighting, both metaphorically and physically, two important examples of European art history, whether still in existence (The Pinacoteca Nazionale, the Scuola Grande di San Rocco) or lost (the Belfiore *studiolo*). In each case, digital technologies of virtual and augmented reality invited the public to explore, rediscover, and understand the story of artworks in a new "intersemiotic" space that developed from the material and cultural contexts in which those works originated.

## Notes

1. Johanna Drucker, "Is There a Digital Art History?" *Visual Resources. An International Journal on Images and Their Uses* 29 (2013): 5–13.
2. Ibid., 7.
3. Johanna Drucker, Anne Helmreich, Matthew Lincoln, and Francesca Rose, "Digital Art History: la scène américaine," 2015, http://journals.openedition.org/perspective/6150; https://doi.org/10.4000/perspective.6150.
4. George Schelbert, "Art History in the World of Digital Humanities: Aspects of a Difficult Relationship," *kunsttexte.de*, no. 4 (2017), accessed September 22, 2019, www.kunsttexte.de.
5. Claire Bishop, "Against Digital Art History," *International Journal of Digital Art History* no. 3 (2018): 124.
6. Schlebert, "Art History in the World of Digital Humanities."
7. The museum complex also comprises the Galleria Estense di Modena, the Estense lapidary, the Biblioteca Estense, and the Palazzo Ducale di Sassuolo. Accessed September 22, 2019, www.gallerie-estensi.beniculturali.it/.
8. Estense Digital Library, accessed September 22, 2019, https://progetto.esten.se/.
9. Ferrara, Pinacoteca Nazionale di Ferrara—Palazzo dei Diamanti, December 13, 2018–May 5, 2019.
10. On Leonello d'Este, see the monograph by Pardi, Leonello d'Este; further information can be found in Enea Gualandi, "Antonio Sarzanella di Manfredi, oratore estense del sec. XV. Carteggio inedito di Leonello d'Este (1441–1450)," *Atti e Memorie Dep. Ferr. St. Patria. Nuova Serie* no. 27 (1963).
11. On the Sacrati-Strozzi collection, see Giuliana Marcolini, *La collezione Sacrati Strozzi; i dipinti restituiti a Ferrara* (Ferrara: Fondazione CARIFE, 2005); Francesca Cappelletti, Cecilia Vicentini, and Barbara Ghelfi, *Una storia silenziosa* (Venezia: Marsilio, 2012).
12. On the studioli, see the seminal work by Wolfang Liebenwein, *Studiolo. Storia e tipologia di uno spazio culturale* (Modena: Panini, 1988).
13. Unless otherwise stated, all translations are by the authors.
14. Cristina De Benedictis, *Per storia del collezionismo italiano* (Firenze: Ponte alle Grazie, 1995), 37.
15. On the choice of the theme of the Muse as protectors of the arts and sciences, see Michael Baxandall, "A Dialogue on Art from the Court of Lionello d'Este," *Journal of the Warburg and Courtauld Institutes* 26, no. 3/4 (1963): 304–26.
16. Guarino da Verona, "letter to Leonello d'Este all'illustrissimo principe e eccellente signore Leonello d'Este (Ferrara 5 novembre 1447)," in *Lo studiolo di Lionello D'Este e il programma di Guarino da Verona*, ed. Eorsi ([s.l.]: [s.n.], 1975), 22.
17. The work of reference on the artists of the Ferrarese School is Roberto Longhi, *Officina ferrarese* (Firenze: Sansoni, 1956).

18. On the inlay artists employed at the Estense courts, see Graziano Manni, *Belfiore. Lo studiolo intarsiato di Leonello d'Este. 1448–1453* (Modena: Artioli, 2006).
19. On this issue, see Marco Folin, *Rinascimento estense. Politica, cultura, istituzioni di un antico stato italiano* (Roma-Bari: Laterza, 2001).
20. Coordinated by Marcello Toffanello and Alessandro Iannucci; video-narratives by Simone Zambruno and Federico Taverni; 3D reconstructions by Marco Orlandi; web design by Manuela De Vivo; texts and iconographic research by Marcello Toffanello, Raffaele Campion, Maria Giulia Rinaldi, Alessia Beraldo, and Alessandro Iannucci.
21. FrameLab, accessed September 22, 2019, https://patrimonioculturale.unibo.it/.
22. On the architecture of the Delizie, beside the conference proceedings Delizie estensi, Delizie in villa, see the exhibition catalog *Le muse e il principe. Arte di corte nel Rinascimento padano* (Modena: Panini; Milano: Museo Poldi Pezzoli, 1991); on the architecture of Ferrara, see Carla Di Francesco, Rita Fabbri, and Fabio Bevilacqua, *Atlante dell'architettura ferrarese: elementi costruttivi tradizionali* (Ferrara: Fondazione Carife-Cassa di Risparmio di Ferrara, 2006).
23. "The Belfiore Studiolo," accessed September 22, 2019, https://patrimonioculturale.unibo.it/studiolobelfiore/il-progetto/.
24. Studio Pasetti, accessed September 22, 2019, www.studiopasetti.it/.
25. Accessed September 22, 2019, www.scuolagrandesanrocco.org/home-en/tintoretto/sala-dell-albergo/.
26. See the international conference "Dal buio alla luce: scrittori al museo 1798–1898," Venice, April 27–29, 2016, accessed September 22, 2019, www.scuolagrandesanrocco.org/home-en/2016/03/30/convegnointernazionale/.
27. The main reference of the team involved are Nuovo Studio, www.nuovostudio.it; Luca Vascon, www.lucavascon.net; Chiara Masiero Sgrinzatto, www.chiaramasierosgrinzatto.com.
28. Demonstrations of the VR 360° are available at the following links: "Dynamic Light and Augmented Reality to Deepen Cultural Heritage," *Vimeo*, accessed September 22, 2019, https://vimeo.com/161486574; "Scuola Grande di S. Rocco, Sala dell'Albergo," Officine Panottiche, accessed September 22, 2019, www.officinepanottiche.com/dynamic_light_and_augmented_reality/.
29. This concerns the abstract single-image representation of a 360° space. The full space, seen from a single point, can be assimilated to a painted sphere of unlimited diameter (a "perceptual sphere" or "virtual sphere").
30. The new lighting setups were officially presented to the public in 2014 for the Sala dell'Albergo and in 2018 for the Sala Capitolare. At this stage, our system is still a working prototype, whose final contents and mode of operation remain to be refined. However, our AR project did receive an honorable mention at the Compasso d'Oro awards of the Italian Association of Industrial Design (ADI). Adi Design Index, "Dynamic Light and Augmented Reality to Deepen Cultural Heritage," accessed September 22, 2019, www.adidesignindex.com/it/design-per-la-comunicazione/2017/dynamic-light-and-augmented reality-to-deepen-cultural-heritage.

## Bibliography


Adi Design Index. "Dynamic Light and Augmented Reality to Deepen Cultural Heritage." Accessed September 22, 2019. www.adidesignindex.com/it/design-per-la-comunicazione/2017/dynamic-light-and-augmented-reality-to-deepen-cultural-heritage

Baxandall, Michael. "A Dialogue on Art from the Court of Lionello d'Este." *Journal of the Warburg and Courtauld Institutes* 26 (1963): 304–26.

Bishop, Claire. "Against Digital Art History." *International Journal of Digital Art History* no. 3 (2018): 123–32.

Cappelletti, Francesca, Barbara Ghelfi, and Cecilia Vicentini. *Una storia silenziosa. Il collezionismo privato a Ferrara nel Seicento*. Venezia: Marsilio, 2012.

Ceccarelli, Francesco, and Marco Folin (eds.). *Delizie estensi: architetture di villa nel Rinascimento italiano ed europeo*. Firenze: Olschki, 2009 (Proceedings, Ferrara 2006).

Ceccarelli, Francesco, and Gianni Venturi (eds.). *Delizie in villa. Il giardino rinascimentale e i suoi committenti*. Firenze: Olschki, 2008 (Proceedings, Ferrara 2005).

Chiara Masiero Sgrinzatto. Accessed September 22, 2019. www.chiaramasierosgrinzatto.com

De Benedictis, Cristina. *Per la storia del collezionismo italiano. Fonti e documenti*. Firenze: Ponte alle Grazie, 1991.

Di Francesco, Carla, Rita Fabbri, and Fabio Bevilacqua. *Atlante dell'architettura ferrarese, elementi costruttivi tradizionali*. Milano: Motta, 2006.

Drucker, Johanna. "Is There a *Digital Art History*?" *Visual Resources. An International Journal on Images and Their Uses* 29, no. 1–2 (2013): 5–13.

Drucker, Johanna, Anne Helmreich, Matthew Lincoln, and Francesca Rose. "*Digital Art History*: la scène américaine." *Perspective* [Online] no. 2 (2015). Accessed September 2, 2019. http://journals.openedition.org/perspective/6150; https://doi.org/10.4000/perspective.6150

Eorsi, Anna K. "Lo studiolo di Lionello d'Este e il programma si Guarino da Verona." *Acta Historiae Artium Accademiae Scientiarum Hungaricae* no. 21 (1975): 22.

Folin, Marco. *Rinascimento estense. Politica, cultura, istituzioni di un antico stato italiano*. Roma-Bari: Laterza, 2001.

Gualandi, Enea. "Antonio Sarzanella di Manfredi, oratore estense del sec. XV. Carteggio inedito di Leonello d'Este (1441–1450)." *Atti e Memorie Dep. Ferr. St. Patria. Nuova Serie* no. 27 (1963).

Liebenwein, Wolfgang. *Studiolo. Storia e tipologia di uno spazio culturale*. Modena: Panini, 1988.

Longhi, Roberto. *Officina Ferrarese*. Firenze: Sansoni, 1956.

Luca Vascon. Accessed September 22, 2019. www.lucavascon.net

Manni, Graziano. *Belfiore. Lo studiolo intarsiato di Leonello d'Este. 1448–1453*. Modena: Artioli, 2006.

Marcolini, Giuliana. *La collezione Sacrati-Strozzi. I dipinti restituiti a Ferrara*. Milano: Motta, 2005.

Mottola Molfino, Alessandra, and Mauro Natale. *Le muse e il principe. Arte di corte nel Rinascimento padano* 2 vols. Modena: Panini, 1991.

Nuovo Studio. Accessed September 22, 2019. www.nuovostudio.it

Officine Panottiche. "Scuola Grande di S. Rocco, Sala dell'Albergo." Accessed September 22, 2019. www.officinepanottiche.com/dynamic_light_and_augmented_reality/

Pardi, Giuseppe. *Leonello d'Este. Marchese di Ferrara*. Bologna: Zanichelli, 1904.

Schelbert, George. "Art History in the World of Digital Humanities. Aspects of a Difficult Relationship." *kunsttexte.de* no. 4 (2017). Accessed September 1, 2019. www.kunsttexte.de Websites

Scuola Grande di San Rocco. Accessed September 22, 2019. www.scuolagrandesanrocco.org/

Studio Pasetti. Accessed September 22, 2019. www.studiopasetti.it/

Vimeo. "Dynamic Light and Augmented Reality to Deepen Cultural Heritage." Accessed September 22, 2019. https://vimeo.com/161486574

# PART IV

# Computational Techniques for Analyzing Artworks

# 21

# CURATION, CONTENT, CREATION

## Computer Approaches to the Fine Arts

*Javier de la Rosa and Juan-Luis Suárez*

*Portrait of Edmond de Belamy*, an "algorithmically" generated painting featured at New York auction house Christie's, sold for $432,500 in October of 2018. An anonymous bidder acquired the piece over the phone for a price nearly forty-five times the highest estimate. In the process, Christie's became the "first auction house to offer a work of art created by an algorithm," for whatever that is worth.[1] The gold-framed but otherwise dull depiction of a fictional man mimicking the style of nineteenth-century European portraiture set the path for more contenders to enter the increasingly bigger artificial intelligence–fueled art market. A few months later, New York's HG Contemporary gallery in Chelsea presented *Faceless Portraits Transcending Time*, an exhibition where all paintings were created by a computer; in particular the paintings were produced by the "collaboration" between an algorithm named AICAN and its creators [2] although arguably the machine did most of the work.[3] And while some have long foreseen the apocalypse of art in these new approaches,[4] it remains to be seen for how long these attempts will survive in a market that favors freshness and originality over innovation, as John McCormack put it when referring to the "precious bubble."[5] Certainly, it has become almost impossible to escape the hype of technology in every field imaginable, and the frontiers of what separates human from artificial creation is ever blurrier. However, every technological process, no matter how far-fetched or future changing, has people involved one way or another. Algorithms and artificial intelligence build upon human knowledge, be it as the curators of the data sets used to teach the machines or the specialists who validate newly produced artifacts. To get to the current moment in the fine arts and art history, an invaluable amount of labor has been put in throughout time by many experts, curators, art historians, librarians, scholars, and students. This is not to say that the technological advances can be trivialized; rather, that for them to burst into the art scene the previous painstaking effort is often made invisible or even forgotten. We try to highlight how those endeavors are moving or might move into the digital domain, with a great deal of human ingenuity involved. In this chapter we describe three of the main aspects embroiled in the generation of such AI-crafted—allowing the craftsmanship metaphor—paintings: curation, content, and creation. We illustrate how each step is a rich research field in itself and provide details on specific projects that have been carried out and the ranging variety of tools used. The chapter is also meant to point to the variety of paths opening up for experts of the fine arts in the digital age.

## Curation

Data-related projects in fine arts usually start with the construction of a data set, which in the humanities might also be referred to as a corpus or collection, depending on the discipline. It is important to note that this first step, the construction of the data set, represents the most burdensome phase since in most cases, and certainly in cases that deal with history prior to the digital age, researchers need to digitize the materials. If, on the contrary, one works with contemporary art it is more likely that the information has already been digitized. When the primary elements of a data set are images or digitized versions of images, metadata plays a fundamental role. Quality curation of content is an intensive and time-consuming task performed manually by humans, but once a data set has been built, its many secrets can be exploited in multiple forms until exhausted. The formats vary from formal relational databases built with schemas and models of the reality in mind to somewhat chaotic and ad hoc spreadsheets or text files.[6] Regardless, all of them attempt to capture some particular nuances of the relevant subject domain: a slice of reality in computer form from a human's vantage point. The Hispanic Baroque Project is an example of such practices.[7] With the ambitious goal of characterizing the complexity of the First Atlantic Culture, the project set to trace interactions that generated the cultural complexity that was characteristic of the Hispanic Baroque from the mid-sixteenth to early nineteenth centuries, and that allowed for their reproduction in, and transfer of models to, other cultural settings even today.[8] Methodologically, in order to analyze three spheres of Baroque culture—the Baroque constitution, its religious expressions, and its urban aspects—some ideas from complexity theory such as emergence, dynamic stability, or efficiency were applied. These concepts, once arcane to humanistic endeavors, started to make sense precisely at the intersection of various disciplines and methods, and became instrumental for the project once the use of graph theory and network science was leveraged. Thus, the project embarked on the construction of several databases and tools to better achieve its goals. One of these databases still active today is BaroqueArt, a data collection of Hispanic Baroque painters, places, and paintings from 1550 to 1850.[9] Populated through fieldwork data collection and manual data extraction from existing print catalogues, the database contains close to seventeen thousand items from fourteen hundred bibliographical resources, where each item might be annotated by up to two hundred descriptors. Since the scope of the database is Hispanic Baroque art, entries are of varying geographies and artistic styles. The selection follows historical context as well as artistic and scholarly principles such as influence and knowledge transfer. Interestingly, the aforementioned descriptors were put together using a team-based, manual curation approach to create a comprehensive ontology based on rich annotations of the main object of study: the paintings.[10] These descriptors ranged from the abstract (e.g. "virtuality") to the concrete (e.g. the kind of ink used on the physical canvas) and served as a proxy to build a network of paintings.[11] After annotation, a link was established between any pair of paintings if they shared at least five or more annotations, using this cardinality as the weight of the created edge in the graph. The resulting network, divided into periods of twenty-five years, together with the geographical information that tracked the place of production and current location of the paintings, allowed for a rich analysis that proved the importance of symbols in the creation and sustainability of the First Transatlantic Culture.[12] The study introduced a new methodology that aspired to establish the foundations of a digital geography of art and culture. At the same time, it left a database of thousands of paintings with extremely detailed metadata, from religious descriptors such as "virgins" or "saints," to the use of the "civil" descriptor that signaled more secular aspects of Latin American paintings as these nations moved toward independence. In other words, it curated a vast number of artifacts for future filtering, querying, and retrieving that could be utilized to, for example, select all paintings of male portraits in a specific style.

## Content

One natural step after the analysis of metadata is to study the actual content of the digital images of paintings: that is, what it is that they depict, how this is materialized in the painting, what meanings those depictions carry with them, and what can we learn from them. In this sense, different approaches have been tested over the years. Particularly notorious and numerous are those that seek to identify—by computational means—styles in a painting, either the author's personal signature or the pictorial style within a time period.[13] Although less prolific in the literature, other avenues of research have been explored: extraction of meaning,[14] influence networks,[15] and trends over time,[16] to name a few. It is in this latter category that we can place the Faces Project, which studied how people were depicted across time and what relation those depictions had to present day evolutionary conceptions of perceived attractiveness. The main goal of the project was to assess whether human beauty had always been universally perceived in the same manner or had changed over time and across cultures.[17] This is, however, an almost unprovable issue since beauty is a changing and subjective notion and as such cannot be measured scientifically. If we add that we lack reliable photographic evidence of most periods of human history, we can agree that accessing the past of the notion of beauty is a difficult task. In addition, no representative sample of the respective populations of the past will ever be possible to obtain as we can only make inferences as to the representativeness of the human types depicted in art history across cultures. To overcome these limitations, the project considered instead a definition of perceived attractiveness valid in evolutionary psychology and neuro-aesthetics that is supposed to be universal yet comprehensible and feasible to extract numerically. It was then used as a proxy for beauty on a corpus of over 120,000 paintings from all over the world and time periods. However, for different reasons the collection ended up having a major participation of Western paintings and styles, thus limiting the scope of the results. Before the popularization of WikiArt, the current de facto paintings database,[18] collecting a data set of these characteristics was a challenge, and the project had to turn to a comprehensive but private collection of images made public on the internet.[19] Fortunately, the situation is slowly changing and we can now find cultural institutions releasing their data openly to the public and for free.[20] Paintings are possibly the only artifacts known to have reliably recorded the various aspects of human attributes before the invention of photography, and while there is no guarantee that depicted people are representative of the general population, it still is the best resource there is to track changes in the representation of the human face.[21] It is important to note that the project does not make any claims on current or past standards of beauty. Rather it applies a supposedly objective approximation of it on a faceted corpus of paintings and analyzes the results and their implications. That is to say, if we were to accept a scientific definition of perceived attractiveness, the Faces Project describes how depicted people, periods, and styles would fare against it. In assessing the perceived attractiveness of a given face, two main factors influence the outcome. First, symmetry—measured as the sum of the distances of facial attributes to the center of the face as defined by the perpendicular line that crosses it through the middle horizontal point of the nose and that divides the face in two hemi-faces. Second, averageness—a slightly more elusive concept that is defined as the difference between an individual's facial attributes and those of the average of a group. Effectively, this calculation consists in the difference between an individual's face symmetry value and that of the average composite image of all faces of a group, being a group defined by a time period or a painting style. At the technical level, all of these measurements built upon proven face recognition algorithms that provided exact facial feature coordinates within images: a couple of points for each eye, three for the mouth, and another three for the nose. Moreover, these borrowed techniques from machine learning also gave estimations of gender, age, and the head pose of the recognized faces, allowing for a demographic aggregation and rich comparison of the results.

The project showed that the representation of human faces has not remained constant and that there are substantial differences between the faces depicted between the fifteenth and eighteenth centuries when compared to those of both the thirteenth and twentieth centuries. Especially significant was the decrease in the perceived attractiveness of faces in twentieth-century paintings, as the freedom of artists and the openness of society fostered the representation of different types of human face other than those associated with classical styles.

The Faces Project also set the path for a digital demography in the fine arts as it explored demographic distributions and age pyramids for the first time. As an unexpected side effect of the project, valuable data on the demographics of people in paintings were uncovered, both by century and by painting style. Therefore, it became possible to characterize, for example, the most common types of individual depicted in a specific period of time, including the preferred age and gender in a particular painting style,[22] or the composition, poses, proportions, and spatial locations in which particular types appear.

## Creation

The final step in the pipeline is the creation process itself. We now have a sense of how important the proper curation of collections is and how it enables the selection of paintings in different painting styles. Moreover, through the analysis of their content, further filters can be applied (e.g. retaining those paintings that display only one woman in a central role). Although very different methodologically, both aspects combine to produce rich labeled samples from which, theoretically, a machine can learn. However, while learning by example is one of the ways in which art can be artificially produced, all AI-generated artworks are technically under the umbrella of what is called generative art.

Generative art, in which human participation is drastically reduced if not completely eliminated from the creative process, is by no means a novel idea.[23] Although many different methods exist, both disciplinary (mechanical, chemical, biological, mathematical, robotic, etc.) as well as conceptual (emergence, evolution, embodiment, self-organization, etc.), the creation of art by autonomous systems has been historically tied to rule-based and algorithmically determined computer processes. Since its birth in the computer graphics scene in Stuttgart in 1965 with *Generative Computergraphik*, presumably the first exhibition to show generative computer art,[24] dynamic artwork-systems have evolved in parallel with the technology that made them possible. From the mid-1960s onwards, artists played with the idea of generating art by leveraging concepts from Artificial Life (e.g., L-systems, genetic algorithms, cellular automata) and Artificial Intelligence. AARON, a piece of software built over a forty-year period by the abstract painter Harold Cohen, is perhaps one of the first attempts to use artificial intelligence to produce art.[25] Its style and aesthetic dexterity have evolved over many existing versions since its conception: from basic abstract black and white compositions to the inclusion of color and figurative elements. It even debuted in an exhibition at the Tate Gallery in London, United Kingdom in 1983, where the works are still housed after the passing in 2016 of its creator.

However, what makes AARON fundamentally different from AICAN (Artificial Intelligence Creative Adversarial Network), namely the technique used to generate the series *Faceless Portraits*

*Transcending Time*, is the school of thought from which the two approaches of artificial intelligence come. AARON uses what is called a symbolic approach, in which the expert of the domain must manually encode a number of rules in the algorithm that govern the creation process. By contrast, AICAN uses a connectionist approach, meaning that instead of hard coding the rules that guide the creative process, the algorithm learns the general ideas from previous examples until it is able to produce new and hitherto unseen artworks. In computer science literature, the latter method is referred to as an artificial neural network, since it is vaguely inspired by the biological neural networks in animal brains. A neural network is more a framework for a specific learning task than an algorithm itself, since no prior task-specific rules are programmed into them.

Typically, neural networks are internally structured in layers connected to each other in such a way that the input layer receives a numerical representation of an object to be classified and the output layer produces values that assign the input to one of several possible classes. Each of these layers have artificial neurons that perform some computation based on an activation function and some pre-defined weights. With some reservations, the process of learning or training is then reduced to processing the input iteratively and adjusting the weights until a certain loss function is minimized in the output layers. When the number of layers increases, we talk about deep neural networks or deep learning.[26]

In the case of image recognition by artificial intelligence, a common kind of neural net is the Convolutional Neural Network (CNN) that works by reducing images successively using a form of matrix multiplication named convolution—technically, a cross-correlation—until the resulting image can be assigned a class from a limited number of options.[27] For example, in a data set comprising exclusively images of paintings by Joan Miró and Van Gogh, a CNN might be able to extract features of the images at an increasing level of abstraction: beginning with the identification of pixels that form edges and borders; progressing to the identification of blobs and shapes; and, finally, distinguishing individual strokes, themes, or styles. Instead of feeding all this information independently, a CNN automatically generates identifying characteristics from the data sets it processes. This results in one of the best and worst qualities of this method: A neural network will always be as good (and as biased) as the data used to train it. As described, CNNs are very good at classifying images, but not very useful at generating them by themselves. One way to adapt them to the task of image creation is to run the classification process in reverse order: If the outermost layers of a CNN encode information from images by moving from the more abstract to the more concrete, it is possible to reverse the process just before the final layers and move from the dense codification of an image (or a random list of numbers for that matter) back to an image again.

This is indeed the idea behind Generative Adversarial Networks (GANs) the core mechanism inside AICAN, with the addition of a clever trick: every time a new image is generated from a random input vector by the generative network, another network (the discriminant) evaluates (classifies) the resulting image as valid or not depending on how real the image would look to a human. These two networks enter in a contest with each other in a zero-sum game. Every time the generator presents a new, more appealing candidate, the discriminator has also become better at the process of evaluation. For each misclassification, information about the difference between the generated image and a valid image is fed back to both networks. After many iterations of the training process, the images that pass the filter imposed by the discriminator are surprisingly natural looking, even to the point of deceiving the human eye.[28] These GANs learn approximations of the meaning of visual features in their own way. Sometimes this resembles the human way of understanding things, while on other occasions it is basically senseless.[29] AICAN is a variation of a GAN where the discriminator tries to assess whether generated images are of artistic value. Certainly, the approach seems to have some validity since both the creators of *The Portrait of Edmond de Belamy* and the series *Faceless Portraits Transcending Time* have received acknowledgment for their work either in monetary form or as public recognition,[30] either of which might meet the ambitions of the works' creators.

## Conclusion

In this chapter, we have shown how the curation of metadata is far from a burden imposed by library and catalogue practices, but rather is a process can generate fruitful and impactful research. The proper curation of data sets might eventually be leveraged to enrich the analysis of the content of catalogued images. This, in turn, could be used to build generative models that produce pieces of artistic value or, at least, to create new data and, therefore, new research questions for the digital fine arts. This process raises some interesting questions.

The first issues that arises is the question of authorship. It is not entirely clear to whom authorial credit should be attributed in the case of AI generated works. Should it be ascribed to the numerous training samples? To the designer of the GAN? To the person who simply uses the trained model to produce new artworks? To the computer artifact itself? To all of them? This latter case has important implications and might require re-examination of our theories of the self,[31] of artistic identity, and of art market practices. The digital copyright wars of the 2000s could become insignificant when compared to upcoming battles against algorithmically generated content. Although writing in different contexts, some scholars have stated that knowing the author of a work "changes its meaning by changing its context [ . . . ,] certain kinds of meaning are conferred by its membership and position in [. . .] the *oeuvre*."[32] This might have the effect of deeming computational creations as mere "computer-output" instead of paintings by virtue of the simple fact that they are computer-generated.[33] This perception often arises after discovering that the artwork in question is computationally generated, a point that affects its authenticity and hinders its aesthetic approval: The computer could generate new pieces endlessly with no human supervision or mediation.[34] Furthermore, while every generated piece is presumably unique, the ontological issue is not reasonably addressed. As David Cope has argued, "the fact that human composers die, [. . .] has consequences for aesthetic valuation: someone's *oeuvre* is valued in part because it is a unique set of works, now closed."[35] And for him this poses the question of whether we can identify the artwork, the uniqueness, behind the countless unique images that an artist's program can generate.[36] Do we have a theoretical framework to appreciate or measure these contributions? Do we need one or is it permissible to dismiss it, since humans cannot conceive of the infinite artist?

The further question arises as to the ontology of art itself. Does art need to reflect the inimitable experience of the artist? Does it need to be a manifestation of thought or emotion articulated in a particular medium? Does it need to manifest human creativity? Part of the praise for AICAN derives from the fact that it was considered, or labeled, as being more creative than regular generative adversarial networks. However, due to its unpredictable nature, the concept of creativity continues to be as hard to define as it has always been,[37] which makes it a problematic attribute to quantify and thus questionable to assign to machine outputs of any kind.[38] This chapter has sought to highlight the fact that pictorial art, either human or machine created, cannot fully escape either its predecessors (in the form of art's histories) or assessments (of aesthetic merit and ontology) agreed upon by experts in fine arts communities. The latter is of the utmost importance if the creators of AI generated works seek recognition of some sort. Nevertheless, the infinite—computer—artist has come to stay and we should be grateful if it stimulates the imagination of its creators: human artists.

Lastly, there is the persistent concern in all kinds of representational and statistical learning: intention. Computer generated art lacks a force that drives the creation of artworks. Ranging from monetary to altruistic motives, technical mastery to expressive desire, machines are not only unable to provide reasons for their decisions, but the processes that mediate creation remain opaque and deprived of interpretive or communication powers.[39] And while these issues have deep consequences in other fields (for example, if misused in policing), in the context of art it gives the impression of emptiness or purposelessness. Perhaps, a new kind of art will emerge, one that can only be appreciated or deciphered by other machines, a true machine art, made for and by machines, with no humans in the loop.

## Notes

1. Paris-based arts collective *Obvious* was the organization behind the production of the piece. Christie's, "The First Piece of AI-Generated Art to Come to Auction," last modified December 12, accessed April 1, 2019, www.christies.com/features/A-collaboration-between-two-artists-one-human-one-a-machine-9332-1.aspx.
2. AICAN stands for Artificial Intelligence Creative Adversarial Network. See Ahmed Elgammal et al., "CAN: Creative Adversarial Networks, Generating 'Art' by Learning About Styles and Deviating from Style Norms" (June 21, 2017), https://arxiv.org/abs/1706.07068.
3. "AI and Machine Learning Invade a New York Art Gallery," *The Atlantic*, last modified March 6, accessed April 1, 2019, www.theatlantic.com/technology/archive/2019/03/ai-created-art-invades-chelsea-gallery-scene/584134/.
4. See, for example, Anthony O'Hear, "Art and Technology: An Old Tension," *Royal Institute of Philosophy Supplements* 38 (March 1, 1995): 143–58, doi:10.1017/S1358246100007335; http://journals.cambridge.org/abstract_S1358246100007335.
5. Jon McCormack et al., "Ten Questions Concerning Generative Computer Art," *Leonardo* 47, no. 2 (April 1, 2014): 135–41, doi:10.1162/LEON_a_00533; www.mitpressjournals.org/doi/abs/10.1162/LEON_a_00533.
6. Stephen Ramsay, "Databases," in *A Companion to Digital Humanities* (Malden, MA and Chichester: Wiley-Blackwell, 2004).
7. "The Hispanic Baroque Project [Archived]," accessed April 1, 2019, http://projects.cultureplex.ca/www.hispanicbaroque.ca/.
8. Juan-Luis Suárez and Estefanía Olid-Peña, "Hispanic Baroque: A Model for the Study of Cultural Complexity in the Atlantic World," *South Atlantic Review* 72, no. 1 (January 1, 2007): 31–47 www.jstor.org/stable/27784678.
9. "BaroqueArt," accessed April 1, 2019, http://baroqueart.cultureplex.ca/.
10. "BaroqueArt Descriptors Ontology: An Ontology to Formalize the Way an Artwork Is Described," accessed April 1, 2019, http://ontologies.cultureplex.ca/baroqueart/spec/index.html.
11. Juan-Luis Suarez, Fernando Sancho Caparrini, and Javier de la Rosa Perez, "The Art-Space of a Global Community: The Network of Baroque Paintings in Hispanic-America," *IEEE*, October 2011.
12. Juan-Luis Suarez et al., "Towards a Digital Geography of Hispanic Baroque Art," *Literary and Linguistic Computing* 28, no. 4 (December 1, 2013): 718–35, doi:10.1093/llc/fqt050.
13. See, for example, Babak Saleh and Ahmed Elgammal, "Large-Scale Classification of Fine-Art Paintings: Learning the Right Metric on the Right Feature" (2016), doi:10.11588/dah.2016.2.23376; https://search.datacite.org/works/10.11588/dah.2016.2.23376; Higor Y.D. Sigaki, Matjaž Perc, and Haroldo V. Ribeiro, "History of Art Paintings Through the Lens of Entropy and Complexity," *Proceedings of the National Academy of Sciences of the United States of America* 115, no. 37 (September 11, 2018): E8594, doi:10.1073/pnas.1800083115, www.ncbi.nlm.nih.gov/pubmed/30150384; Daan Wynen, Cordelia Schmid, and Julien Mairal, "Unsupervised Learning of Artistic Styles With Archetypal Style Analysis" (May 28, 2018), https://arxiv.org/abs/1805.11155; Ahmed Elgammal et al., "The Shape of Art History in the Eyes of the Machine" (January 23, 2018), https://arxiv.org/abs/1801.07729; Laure Thompson and David Mimno, "Computational Cut-Ups: The Influence of Dada," *The Journal of Modern Periodical Studies* 8, no. 2 (November 1, 2018): 179–95, doi:10.5325/jmodeperistud.8.2.0179, www.jstor.org/stable/10.5325/jmodeperistud.8.2.0179; Eva Cetinic and Sonja Grgic, "Automated Painter Recognition Based on Image Feature Extraction," Croatian Society Electronics in Marine—ELMAR,

September 2013. For an introduction to the topic, see Lev Manovich, "Data Science and Digital Art History," *International Journal for Digital Art History*, no. 1 (2015).

14. Byunghwee Lee et al., "Heterogeneity in Chromatic Distance in Images and Characterization of Massive Painting Data Set," *PLoS One* 13, no. 9 (September 1, 2018): e0204430, doi:10.1371/journal.pone.0204430, www.ncbi.nlm.nih.gov/pubmed/30252919.
15. Babak Saleh et al., "Toward Automated Discovery of Artistic Influence," *Multimedia Tools and Applications* 75, no. 7 (April 2016): 3565–91, doi:10.1007/s11042-014-2193-x, https://search.proquest.com/docview/1776306844.
16. Leonardo Impett and Franco Moretti, *Totentanz: Operationalizing Aby Warburg's 'Pathosformeln,'* Stanford Literary Lab, Stanford, CA, 2017.
17. Javier De la Rosa and Juan-Luis Suárez, "A Quantitative Approach to Beauty: Perceived Attractiveness of Human Faces in World Painting" (2015), doi:10.11588/dah.2015.1.21640, https://search.datacite.org/works/10.11588/dah.2015.1.21640. The limitations of the data set skewed the analysis and results toward Western paintings and conceptions of beauty.
18. "WikiArt: Visual Art Encyclopedia," accessed April 1, 2019, www.wikiart.org/.
19. Although the original site was shut down and a new domain is now available with limited functionality "Ciudad De La Pintura (City of Paintings)," accessed April 1, 2019, www.ciudadpintura.com/.
20. See, for example, the released of The MET's own collection of paintings as free and open data sets and their joint initiative with Microsoft and the MIT to support an external API for programmatic access to their data, "Open Access at the MET," accessed April 1, 2019, www.metmuseum.org/about-the-met/policies-and-documents/open-access.
21. There is some controversy about this point. On the one hand, during certain periods of history only those in a position of power could command the creation of paintings, possibly biasing the representativeness of the depicted population. It is also known that sometimes painters exerted some creative licenses adapting the faces of their models to whatever standards of beauty were reigning at the time (see Álvaro Pascual-Chenel, "Juegos De Imagen Y Apariencia: Simulación, Disimulación Y Propaganda Política Durante El Reinado De Carlos II," *El Universo Simbólico Del Poder En El Siglo De Oro* (January 1, 2012): 4.). On the other hand, even when only random people were depicted on a figurative fashion, no claim can be made on how that would relate to the general population's beauty. The Faces Project does not try to make the claim that only beautiful people were painted nor that the study can be blindly interpolated to all of human paintings, rather it just establishes a framework to assess how those that were indeed painted for posterity would be evaluated from a biologically evolutionary definition of perceived attractiveness today. Moreover, the study never states that our current standard of beauty is better or worse in any aspect to those of the past.
22. Ironically, most modern methods to estimate age and gender from pictures are now based on neural networks.
23. Alan Dorin et al., "A Framework for Understanding Generative Art," *Digital Creativity* 23, no. 3–4 (December 2012): 239–59, doi:10.1080/14626268.2012.709940.
24. Margaret A. Boden and Ernest A. Edmonds, "What Is Generative Art?" *Digital Creativity* 20, no. 1–2 (June 1, 2009): 21–46, doi:10.1080/14626260902867915, www.tandfonline.com/doi/abs/10.1080/14626260902867915.
25. See Harold Cohen, "The Further Exploits of AARON, Painter," *Stanford Humanities Review* 4, no 2 (1995): 141–58; Harold Cohen, "A Million Millennial Medicis," in *Explorations in Art and Technology* (London: Praxis, 2002), 91–104.
26. For a good introduction see Ian Goodfellow, Yoshua Bengio, and Aaron Courville, *Deep Learning* (Cambridge, MA and London, UK: MIT Press, 2016).
27. Ibid., Ch. 20.
28. Tero Karras, Samuli Laine, and Timo Aila, "A Style-Based Generator Architecture for Generative Adversarial Networks" (December 12, 2018), https://arxiv.org/abs/1812.04948.
29. Shan Carter et al., "Exploring Neural Networks with Activation Atlases," *Distill* (March 6, 2019), doi:10.23915/distill.00015, https://distill.pub/2019/activation-atlas/.
30. "Faceless Portraits Transcending Time," HG Contemporary New York, accessed April 1, 2019, www.hgcontemporary.com/exhibitions/faceless-portraits-transcending-time.
31. To put it in perspective, the problem is the same that autonomous vehicles face if they run over a pedestrian. Who would be to blame in that case?
32. Harold Love, *Attributing Authorship: An Introduction* (Cambridge, MA: Cambridge University Press, 2002) 46.

33. David Cope, *Computer Models of Musical Creativity* (Cambridge, MA: MIT Press, 2005).
34. Boden and Edmonds, "What Is Generative Art?" 24.
35. Ibid., 42.
36. Ibid., 22.
37. See these two opposite views in the classic Margaret A. Boden, *The Creative Mind: Myths and Mechanisms*, 2nd ed. (London: Routledge, 2004), doi:10.4324/9780203508527, www.taylorfrancis.com/books/9781134379576; and the approach taken by some of the creators of AICAN Ahmed Elgammal and Babak Saleh, "Quantifying Creativity in Art Networks" (June 1, 2015), https://arxiv.org/abs/1506.00711.
38. Boden, *The Creative Mind*, Ch. 4.
39. Mike Ananny and Kate Crawford, "Seeing Without Knowing: Limitations of the Transparency Ideal and Its Application to Algorithmic Accountability," *New Media & Society* 20, no. 3 (March 2018): 973–89, doi:10.1177/1461444816676645, https://journals.sagepub.com/doi/full/10.1177/1461444816676645.

## Bibliography


Ananny, Mike, and Kate Crawford. "Seeing Without Knowing: Limitations of the Transparency Ideal and Its Application to Algorithmic Accountability." *New Media & Society* 20, no. 3 (March 2018): 973–89. doi:10.1177/1461444816676645.https://journals.sagepub.com/doi/full/10.1177/1461444816676645

Boden, Margaret A. *The Creative Mind: Myths and Mechanisms*. 2nd ed. London: Routledge, 2004. doi:10.4324/9780203508527. www.taylorfrancis.com/books/9781134379576.

Boden, Margaret A., and Ernest A. Edmonds. "What Is Generative Art?" *Digital Creativity* 20, no. 1–2 (June 1, 2009): 21–46. doi:10.1080/14626260902867915. www.tandfonline.com/doi/abs/10.1080/14626260902867915

Bogost, Ian. "AI and Machine Learning Invade a New York Art Gallery." *The Atlantic*. Accessed April 1, 2019. www.theatlantic.com/technology/archive/2019/03/ai-created-art-invades-chelsea-gallery-scene/584134/

Byunghwee Lee, Daniel Kim, Seunghye Sun, Hawoong Jeong, and Juyong Park. "Heterogeneity in Chromatic Distance in Images and Characterization of Massive Painting Data Set." *PLoS One* 13, no. 9 (September 1, 2018): e0204430. doi:10.1371/journal.pone.0204430. www.ncbi.nlm.nih.gov/pubmed/30252919

Carter, Shan, Zan Armstrong, Ludwig Schubert, Ian Johnson, and Chris Olah. "Exploring Neural Networks with Activation Atlases." *Distill* (March 6, 2019). doi:10.23915/distill.00015. https://distill.pub/2019/activation-atlas/

Cetinic, Eva, and Sonja Grgic. "Automated Painter Recognition Based on Image Feature Extraction." Croatian Society Electronics in Marine—ELMAR, September 2013.

Christie's. "The First Piece of AI-Generated Art to Come to Auction." Accessed April 1, 2019. www.christies.com/features/A-collaboration-between-two-artists-one-human-one-a-machine-9332-1.aspx

"Ciudad De La Pintura (City of Paintings)." Accessed April 1, 2019. www.ciudadpintura.com/

Cohen, Harold. "The Further Exploits of AARON, Painter." *Stanford Humanities Review* 4, no. 2 (1995): 141–58.

———. "A Million Millennial Medicis." In *Explorations in Art and Technology*, 91–104. London: Praxis, 2002.

Cope, David. *Computer Models of Musical Creativity*. Cambridge, MA: MIT Press, 2005.

The CulturePlex Lab. "BaroqueArt." Accessed April 1, 2019. http://baroqueart.cultureplex.ca/.

———. "BaroqueArt Descriptors Ontology: An Ontology to Formalize the Way an Artwork Is Described." Accessed April 1, 2019. http://ontologies.cultureplex.ca/baroqueart/spec/index.html.

De la Rosa, Javier, and Juan-Luis Suárez. "A Quantitative Approach to Beauty. Perceived Attractiveness of Human Faces in World Painting." 2015. doi:10.11588/dah.2015.1.21640. https://search.datacite.org/works/10.11588/dah.2015.1.21640

Dorin, Alan, Jonathan McCabe, Jon McCormack, Gordon Monro, and Mitchell Whitelaw. "A Framework for Understanding Generative Art." *Digital Creativity* 23, no. 3–4 (December 2012): 239–59 doi:10.1080/14626268.2012.709940

Elgammal, Ahmed, and AICAN. "Faceless Portraits Transcending Time." HG Contemporary New York. Accessed April 1, 2019. www.hgcontemporary.com/exhibitions/faceless-portraits-transcending-time

Elgammal, Ahmed, Bingchen Liu, Mohamed Elhoseiny, and Marian Mazzone. "CAN: Creative Adversarial Networks, Generating 'Art' by Learning About Styles and Deviating from Style Norms" (June 21, 2017). https://arxiv.org/abs/1706.07068

Elgammal, Ahmed, Marian Mazzone, Bingchen Liu, Diana Kim, and Mohamed Elhoseiny. "The Shape of Art History in the Eyes of the Machine" (January 23, 2018). https://arxiv.org/abs/1801.07729.

Elgammal, Ahmed, and Babak Saleh. "Quantifying Creativity in Art Networks." (June 1, 2015). https:// arxiv.org/abs/1506.00711.

The Hispanic Baroque Project. "The Hispanic Baroque Project [Archived]." Accessed April 1, 2019. http:// projects.cultureplex.ca/www.hispanicbaroque.ca/.

Impett, Leonardo, and Franco Moretti. *Totentanz: Operationalizing Aby Warburg's "Pathosformeln."* Stanford, CA: Stanford Literary Lab, 2017.

Karras, Tero, Samuli Laine, and Timo Aila. "A Style-Based Generator Architecture for Generative Adversarial Networks" (December 12, 2018). https://arxiv.org/abs/1812.04948.

Love, Harold. *Attributing Authorship: An Introduction.* Cambridge: Cambridge University Press, 2002.

Manovich, Lev. "Data Science and Digital Art History." *International Journal for Digital Art History* no. 1 (2015).

McCormack, Jon, Oliver Bown, Alan Dorin, Jonathan McCabe, Gordon Monro, and Mitchell Whitelaw. "Ten Questions Concerning Generative Computer Art." *Leonardo* 47, no. 2 (April 1, 2014): 135–41. doi:10.1162/LEON_a_00533. www.mitpressjournals.org/doi/abs/10.1162/LEON_a_00533.

O'Hear, Anthony. "Art and Technology: An Old Tension." *Royal Institute of Philosophy Supplements* 38 (March 1, 1995): 143–58. doi:10.1017/S1358246100007335. http://journals.cambridge.org/ abstract_S1358246100007335.

Ramsay, Stephen. "Databases." In *A Companion to Digital Humanities*, edited by Susan Schreibman, Ray Siemens, and John Unsworth. Malden, MA and Chichester: Wiley-Blackwell, 2004.

Saleh, Babak, Kanako Abe, Ravneet Arora, and Ahmed Elgammal. "Toward Automated Discovery of Artistic Influence." *Multimedia Tools and Applications* 75, no. 7 (April 2016): 3565–91. doi:10.1007/s11042-014-2193-x. https://search.proquest.com/docview/1776306844.

Saleh, Babak, and Ahmed Elgammal. "Large-Scale Classification of Fine-Art Paintings: Learning the Right Metric on the Right Feature." 2016. doi:10.11588/dah.2016.2.23376. https://search.datacite.org/ works/10.11588/dah.2016.2.23376.

Sigaki, Higor Y. D., Matjaž Perc, and Haroldo V. Ribeiro. "History of Art Paintings Through the Lens of Entropy and Complexity." *Proceedings of the National Academy of Sciences of the United States of America* 115, no. 37 (September 11, 2018): E8594. doi:10.1073/pnas.1800083115. www.ncbi.nlm.nih.gov/ pubmed/30150384

Suárez, Juan-Luis, and Estefanía Olid-Peña. "Hispanic Baroque: A Model for the Study of Cultural Complexity in the Atlantic World." *South Atlantic Review* 72, no. 1 (January 1, 2007): 31–47. www.jstor.org/ stable/27784678.

Suarez, Juan-Luis, Fernando Sancho-Caparrini, Elika Ortega, Javier de la Rosa, Natalia Caldas, and David Brown. "Towards a Digital Geography of Hispanic Baroque Art." *Literary and Linguistic Computing* 28, no. 4 (December 1, 2013): 718–35. doi:10.1093/llc/fqt050.

Suarez, Juan-Luis, Fernando Sancho-Caparrini, and Javier de la Rosa Perez. "The Art-Space of a Global Community: The Network of Baroque Paintings in Hispanic-America." *IEEE*, October 2011.

Thompson, Laure, and David Mimno. "Computational Cut-Ups: The Influence of Dada." *The Journal of Modern Periodical Studies* 8, no. 2 (November 1, 2018): 179–95. doi:10.5325/jmodeperistud.8.2.0179. www.jstor.org/stable/10.5325/jmodeperistud.8.2.0179.

Wynen, Daan, Cordelia Schmid, and Julien Mairal. "Unsupervised Learning of Artistic Styles with Archetypal Style Analysis" (May 28, 2018). https://arxiv.org/abs/1805.11155.

# 22
# COMPUTERIZED ANALYSIS OF PAINTINGS

*James Z. Wang, Baris Kandemir, and Jia Li*

With advancements in imaging technologies, the efforts to digitize fine art paintings have increased dramatically since the turn of the century. These efforts have made hundreds of thousands of paintings digitally available. This unprecedented access enables researchers to analyze computationally a large number of paintings concurrently and in a way that was previously impossible. The analysis tasks, such as stylometry, attribution, authentication, dating, and comparative study, which used to be done on a small number of artworks by art historians and connoisseurs, can now be conducted over a large digital collection of artworks using automated methods.

Traditionally, art historians have employed a range of tools to analyze paintings.[1] In particular, to scrutinize materials that artists used in the paintings, art historians have exploited raking light photography, ultraviolet fluorescence illumination, infrared imaging, cross-section paint and varnish analysis, microscopic analysis, chemical composition analysis, X-ray imaging, multi-spectral imaging, laser 3D scans, and synchrotron induced X-ray fluorescence mapping. Connoisseurs often have in-depth knowledge about an artist's distinctive way of painting, his or her "signature brushstroke style," and unique techniques. Art historians also comb artists' letters, diaries, notes, and other written materials in their analyses, especially for the purpose of verifying the authenticity of paintings.

The computerized analysis of paintings cannot replace conventional methods used by art historians, but it does provide three benefits. First, it is in general noninvasive. Computerized analysis is usually conducted on digital images of paintings, and thus, no additional damage happens to the painting beyond what may be caused by the imaging technique itself. Second, computerized analysis provides information not available from other techniques. With the advancements of modern computer vision and image analysis, one can analyze the artist's style used in a painting through the statistics gathered from thousands of extracted brushstrokes, lines, curves, angles, and/or color patches. Modern computer graphics methods can also provide information on the accuracy of the artist's depiction of the three-dimensional world and the lighting environment. Third, computers can analyze and discover useful findings from a virtually unlimited number of paintings. This advantage allows art historians and scientists to build models of artistic styles from collections of paintings of a particular period of an artist, the lifetime of an artist, an artist's school, an art movement, a painting genre, and so on. Since the early 2000s, we have undertaken computerized analyses of paintings from different cultures, ranging from Chinese ink paintings to Post-Impressionist oil paintings.[2] In this chapter we will share some of our experience, discuss related work by other scientists, and propose possible future directions.

Stylistic analysis requires knowledge of composition principles and techniques employed in different art movements or by artists in various time periods. The disparities and commonalities between styles or art movements are intricate, making it impractical for a single expert or a small group to master even a significant portion of the facts and relationships about all styles or movements. Furthermore, stylistic analysis demands an immense amount of time as it is necessary to go through each painting meticulously and to compare the details with other paintings in a large collection. Art historians, artists, and curators must devote many hours to this task, which can be prohibitive for often insufficiently funded artistic establishments. As a result, existing studies focusing on stylistic comparison are limited in scope. Efforts to automate this long and resource-consuming process have arisen in computer vision analysis. Computerized style analysis enables the automation of several relevant tasks, including cataloging and chronological sorting. When styles can be automatically distinguished and categorized, the once tedious work of cataloging an extensive collection of paintings becomes manageable. Matching styles with different eras or different periods in a painter's life is another important inquiry for art historians and curators that can be assisted tremendously by computerized analysis.

The authentication of artworks is another pursuit of art historians that demands expert knowledge and an enormous amount of time, but it is open to computerized analysis to a certain extent. The computational approaches, if carried out properly, can be advantageous. For instance, with the help of unlimited computing power, authentication can be determined from information and statistics based on high-confidence attributions from hundreds or even thousands of paintings, making the process evidence-based and substantially more objective. Furthermore, modern imaging modalities may reveal properties inherent to a specific painting that are invisible to the naked eye and difficult for humans to evaluate due to their high dimensionality or other properties. Computer algorithms (i.e. processes computers take in solving problems) can be developed to take advantage of the large quantity of available visual data. A new field of science—data science—is advancing rapidly to use computing and statistics for extracting useful knowledge or insight from data. Computerized comparative methods can be leveraged to compare and authenticate various paintings in a time efficient manner. Similar methods can be utilized to obtain information about unattributed paintings that were found many years after they were painted.

Data-driven methods, however, are not applicable in every situation. Because such methods often rely on high-quality manually annotated data for training (a process to "teach" computers about various concepts), application is limited by the availability of data. For example, determining whether a particular painting is a forgery through data-driven methods would require exposing the computer program to a representative collection of counterfeit paintings for the relevant artist. This requirement is often difficult to satisfy because it is impossible to procure a large and representative collection of counterfeits. While comparisons can be made directly to known genuine works of a painter to assess proximity to the painter's style, such methods are not always dependable. For instance, it is possible that the stylistic differences between the genuine works and some counterfeits are not captured in the computed features used for the comparison. This can lead to false acceptance of counterfeits as genuine works. Also, some genuine works of a painter whose styles are divergent may deviate from the set of known genuine works with which the paintings are compared with, and that can lead to false alarms.

Computerized analysis, despite the aforementioned limitation, allows for novel research on how humans interact with art. With recent technological advances in affective computing and personalization, for example, researchers have begun to develop algorithms to predict the emotions elicited by paintings and their properties such as style, color, and composition. This information can be leveraged for encouraging particular audience responses to an exhibition (whether physical or online) and personalizing such experience. Research in this area often makes use of psychological theories of emotions and human-generated emotion data, which creates certain curatorial and analytical challenges. Emotion is highly subjective, making its modeling extremely difficult even in the case of naturalistic photographic images. To model the emotions generated by paintings, particularly those that are abstract in nature, an additional challenge is the absence of high-quality, human-generated emotion data derived from responses to such works.

In the remainder of this chapter, we introduce recent computational advancements in analyzing paintings. We first provide information on data sets used in computational painting analysis studies and then explain how the tasks just mentioned benefit from computerized methods.

## Data Sets for Analyses

Computerized painting analysis relies on equipping computers with detailed information about historical artistic concepts and styles—a process that is often referred to as "training." This process demands high-quality image data sets and manually generated annotations. The selection of the paintings for a data set needs to be appropriate for the goals of the particular study. This typically requires the data set to be large enough, sufficiently representative, and of high digitization quality to cover pertinent details and nuances.

The proper digitization of color paintings involves significant technologies and skills. The lighting conditions, camera quality and settings, digitization process, and the color space (in this context, a mathematical model to describe colors in the physical world using numerical values) and the digital image format used to store the images can all affect the fidelity and usefulness of the resulting images. For example, if the color balance is not based on a standard color calibration chart, the resulting images can suffer a color shift that is impossible to eliminate completely at the stage of computational analysis. Similarly, different digitization processes can also introduce various technical artifacts (sometimes referred to as "noise") that can steer some machine learning methods to focus on the noise profiles rather than on the actual useful information from the image data. To manage issues of image quality for conventional imaging methods, we have developed shape- and texture-based methods that are less affected by the problems with color accuracy or digitization quality.[3]

Lumiere Technology, a company based in France, has been digitizing some of the world's best known paintings, including Leonardo da Vinci's *Mona Lisa*, using specialized multi-spectral imaging equipment.[4] As such high-quality image data becomes available, researchers can analyze paintings with accurate colors ranging from ultraviolet to infrared that extend well beyond ordinary human perception.

Existing computational studies utilize small to medium range data sets with varying digitization quality for method validation (a principled process to justify the performance of a proposed method on data that was kept apart during training). These can be grouped into three categories: artistic style, artist, and genre.[5]

- **Artistic Style Data Sets.** In one study, the data set comprised 513 paintings by nine different painters (Claude Monet, Jackson Pollock, Vincent van Gogh, Pierre-Auguste Renoir, Wassily Kandinsky, Mark Rothko, Salvador Dalì, Max Ernst, and Giorgio de Chirico).[6] A different study included local annotations such as poses and style labels for 988 monochromatic paintings acquired from the Artstor digital art library.[7] Khan et al. introduced a data set of 4,266 paintings from ninety-one artists that provides artist and style annotations along with eye-tracking information. Another study in style identification involved two large data sets, with one containing approximately fifty thousand images obtained from community-curated Flickr groups[8] and the other containing about one hundred thousand images procured from WikiPaintings (WikiArt). A study that investigated children's book illustration styles included 6,468 illustrations by twenty-four different illustrators.[9]

- **Artist Data Sets.** Johnson et al. worked with museums to create a data set of 101 high-resolution scans for the purpose of analyzing and dating Van Gogh's paintings.[10] Among the 101 paintings, eighty-two were consistently attributed to Van Gogh, six were identified as not being by Van Gogh, and thirteen had previously been attributed to him or were in question. Another data set was introduced by Elgammal, Kang, and Leeuw that contains 297 authentic drawings attributed to Pablo Picasso, Henri Matisse, Egon Schiele, and Amedeo Modigliani among others, as well as eighty-three forged drawings by those artists.[11] In a visual recognition challenge in 2014, a fairly large data set was created that contained 112,039 high-quality artwork images from 6,629 artists with 1,824 art types (e.g., printmaking, painting) along with material and date labels.[12] In addition, the data set provides annotations for the year of and materials used for creating the artwork.
- **Genre Data Sets.** While genre classification is, in general, not of interest to art historians, it poses a challenging problem to artificial intelligence (AI) researchers. Different from conventional photo classification problems, the expressive or abstract nature of artistic paintings makes their computerized classification more difficult. Siddiquie, Vitaladevuni, and Davis created a data set that included 498 paintings derived from six genres: Abstract Expressionism, Baroque painting, Cubism, Graffiti, Impressionism, and Renaissance art.[13] In another genre classification study, a data set comprising 353 images was produced from works associated with Abstract Expressionism, Cubism, Impressionism, Pop art, and Realism.[14] Recent studies are producing larger data sets. Agarwal et al. presented a data set containing eighteen hundred images from six genres (three hundred images for each genre).[15] Florea, Toca, and Gieseke introduced a data set of 18,040 paintings from eighteen genres, with balanced numbers of images in each genre.

The increase in data set number and size signifies the importance and interest paid to the computerized analysis of paintings in technical communities. Along the same lines, the diversity in data sets contributes to the ability of computer-based approaches to take on different tasks in this domain. Having different data sets available inspires art historians and computer and information scientists to formulate new challenges. We hope that, over time, more integrated data sets with high quality digitization methodology and comprehensive metadata descriptions of the works can be available.

## Stylistic Analysis

An interest in automating stylistic analysis has developed in the computer vision community, leading to a number of different approaches. Existing approaches fall roughly into two groups: "feature engineering-based methods" and "feature learning-based methods."

In *feature engineering*, visual features are first designed and programmed by computer scientists. The programs are applied to images of painting to extract numerical features, which are taken as input for a statistical classification algorithm. Such methods leverage the skills, experience, and intuition of experts who are required to identify salient and computable features of the works. In the early 2000s, Li and Wang pioneered this method of analysis in their study of classic Chinese ink paintings.[16] Performance of such methods depends on the relevance of the selected features to the style of the work and the effectiveness of the classification algorithms.

Painting styles pertain to identifiable statistical characteristics such as wavelet features and edge orientation.[17] Most of the features extracted across studies involve a focus on edge properties, texture, and color.[18] Other examples include active shape models for face detection and MPEG-7 description features. (MPEG-7 is a multimedia content description standard which makes the search of multimedia content easier. The standard includes encoded information about the color and texture of the content.)[19]

The work of Li and Wang models local features constructed from wavelet coefficients by spatial stochastic processes (i.e. mathematical models that capture random behavior of a system over time or space), in particular, the multiresolution 2D (i.e. spatial) hidden Markov models. The computational process essentially characterizes different types of brushstrokes in Chinese ink paintings, e.g. swift and thin strokes on relatively smooth backgrounds, flat controlled strokes, heavy and thick wash, straight and pale wash with some vertical lines, small dark strokes, sharp lines and straight washes, and pale and diluted wash. Figure 22.1 shows an example patch of each of these brushstroke types as detected by the computer program.[20]

A more recent work by Vieira et al. leveraged shape, texture complexity, and curvature features for stylometry (i.e. a set of principled approaches in art to understand and quantify the visual style of an artist). After an initial image segmentation, shape measures, e.g., perimeter (contour length of segments), area (number of pixels for each segment), convex hull area and its ratio to original segment area, and circularity (ratio of perimeter and area of each segment) are computed. To characterize texture, entropy (i.e. a mathematical measure of the amount of changes within an image region) and Haralick features (i.e. visual features computed through co-occurrence of similar tonal values within sub-regions of an image) were employed. Mean and standard deviation of edge curvatures were calculated, then high curvature points (peaks) and distance between peaks were added. Applying feature selection showed that the mean of curvature peaks and the average segment area were the most relevant for style classification. They created a "painting space" and style centroids for classification.[21]

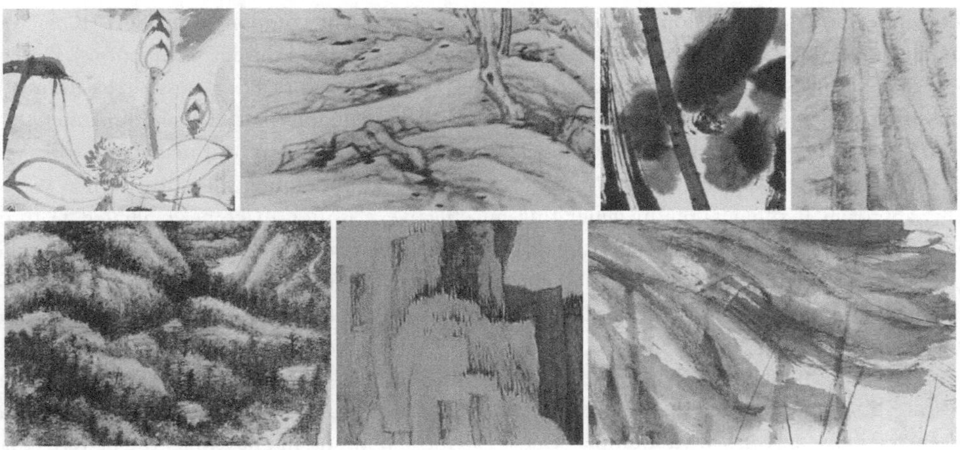

*Figure 22.1* Different types of brushstrokes from classic Chinese ink paintings extracted from the paintings and used to compare the styles of different artists.[22] The patches are from color ink paintings by Zhang Daqian (1899–1983), with color information not used in the analysis.

Liu et al. applied multi-task dictionary learning to features extracted from paintings of six different styles: Baroque, Cubism, Impressionism, Postimpressionism, Renaissance, and Modern. This method exploits color, composition, and line features. Global and local color features captured include the temperature of color, weight of color (darker/lighter shades), and expressiveness of color (contrasts in hue, saturation, and value channels). Composition quality measures were defined based on spatial saliency map distribution for the "rule of thirds," and symmetry and rectangularity in saliency for the "golden section principle." The means and standard deviations of the detected line slopes and lengths were computed. Using these features, the researchers created a dictionary to classify painting styles.[23] Another classification method uses scale-invariant feature transform (SIFT), gist features, histogram of gradients (HoG), local binary patterns (LBP), gray level co-occurrence matrix (GLCM), and Lab color distribution.[24] The extracted information is then fed into an ensemble of support vector machines (SVM) for classification.

Li, Ray, and Lindsay advanced a nonparametric statistical approach that can be used for dominant color detection.[25] This approach detects clusters by picking samples that approach the same frequent information (modes). This method can detect the dominant colors in a painting and provides color palette-like information which can be used to study style. Figure 22.2 shows the resulting dominant colors detected from paintings and the color's locations on the color wheel.

Another study benefits from discrete tonal and variational measures.[26] Tonal measure characterizes tonal variations within differently sized "visual neighborhoods" in an image. Variational measure represents the entropy within those "visual neighborhoods." The study shows that tonal distribution and variations in color and texture are important to quantify visual style. In a different study, MPEG-7 multimedia content description scheme was leveraged in art style classification.[27] The content description includes features such as scalable color, color layout, color structure, dominant color, edge histogram, and homogeneous texture. The authors experimented with a data set of six hundred paintings of eighteen artists from different movements and showed the usefulness of the feature for classification.

An interesting study of Byzantine religious iconography that does not explicitly depend on color, texture, or orientation features has made use of facial landmark features.[28] The immense amount of time that has passed since the works were made presents challenges such as loss of paint and cracks in the icons themselves. The facial features of the subjects were computed following the selection of forty-four "landmark points" on each face. In order to overcome the noise caused by the aforementioned reasons, independent component analysis (ICA) was applied to sieve out more robust image representations (second and third basis functions). Different shape models were utilized for different poses. This approach makes it possible to automate classification and analysis of the evolution of religious iconographs in a structured manner.

*Feature learning* makes use of statistical learning methods (e.g. artificial neural networks) to determine the relevant features for an analysis task instead of defining them in advance. While this approach is often faster in generating an effective classifier, machine-generated features commonly do not offer the ability to explain the reasoning behind the decisions made by the program in a way that art historians and art enthusiasts can interpret and use in their art historical analyses. Further, such methods are prone to biases introduced in the data set and/or the modeling process.

The use of neural networks for feature learning eliminates the phase of handcrafting visual features that might be relevant for computerized painting analysis.[29] A sufficiently deep neural network, i.e., a network with multiple layers of artificial neurons, might extract the patterns that are common to certain group of paintings.[30] The different layers of the network become attuned to those patterns. These learned patterns can be fed into a classical classification framework.[31] Another approach that replaces designing visual features that may distinguish paintings involves

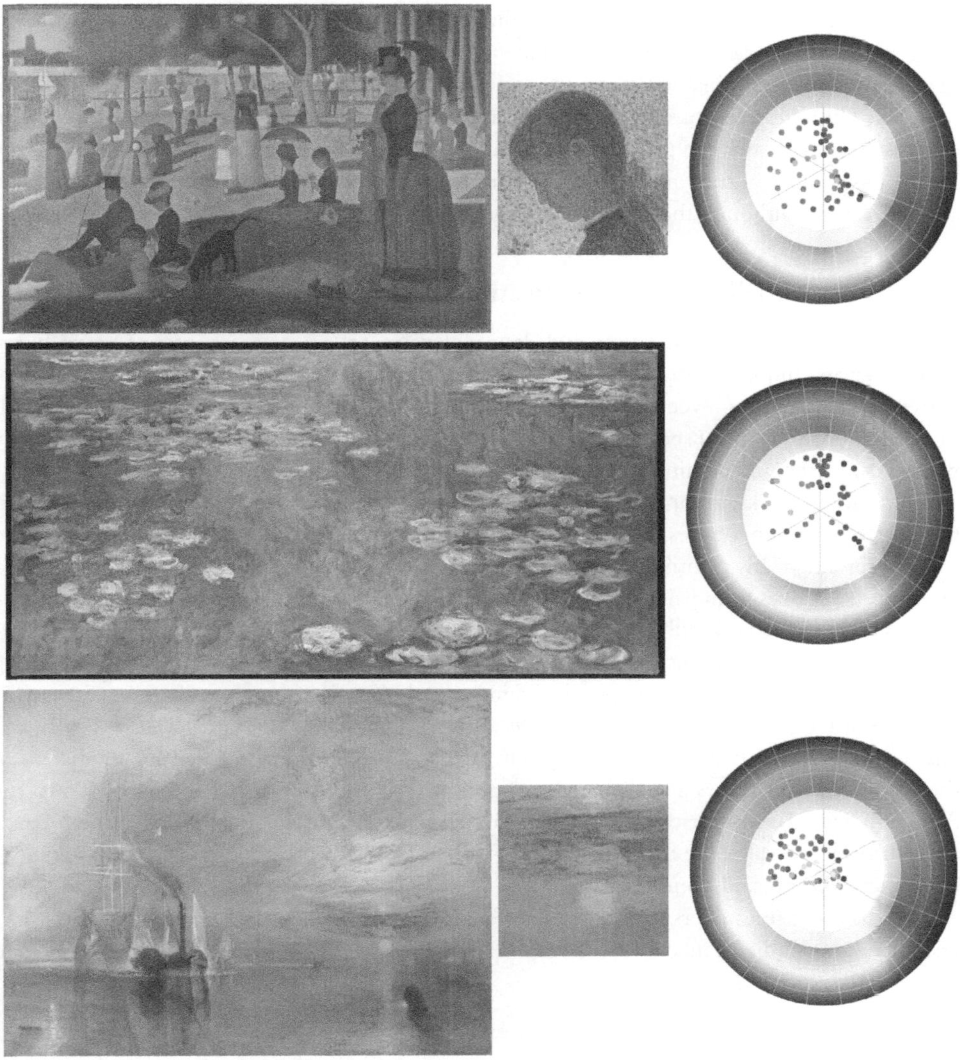

*Figure 22.2* Dominant colors used by an artist revealed through a statistical computing method:[32] *A Sunday Afternoon on the Island of La Grande Jatte* (and a portion enlarged) by Georges Seurat (1884–1886); *Water Lilies* by Claude Monet (1919); and *The Fighting Temeraire* (and a portion enlarged) by J.M.W. Turner (1838).

*Source*: Images courtesy of the Art Institute of Chicago and the Google Art Project, The Metropolitan Museum of Art (New York), and The National Gallery (London), respectively. The images showing the dominant colors courtesy of Jia Li.

a statistical approach.[33] An atomic visual library is created, which contains small image patches that frequently occur among similar paintings (called "visual words"). By learning the vocabulary, similar style paintings can be identified as they usually contain similar visual words. This approach can capture global and local properties of paintings. In a children books illustration study, Hicsonmez et al. demonstrated that performance of different deep-learning-based methods is better than traditional low-level feature-based methods in style classification.[34]

Furthermore, neural networks can be utilized in a generative way to understand the underlying structures of classes of paintings. This framework is composed of two neural networks (generative and discriminative) where the generative network tries to deceive the discriminative network. Through iterations, the former produces images close to training data samples. The analysis of this network can provide ideas about which features can be used to classify the paintings. A by-product of such methods is the automatic generation of art-like images that imitate artists' creativity although this approach is limited and in its infancy.[35]

## Attribution, Authentication, Dating, and Restoration

Artist identification, authentication, and dating of paintings are of great interest to art historians, curators, and collectors. Providing definitive answers to questions of attribution is often extremely challenging, even when using a combination of modern technologies. Different imaging modalities can inspect various aspects of paintings in more detail, while high-energy physics can detect underpaintings and the material makeup of the painting.

Our earlier work attempts to find characteristics that distinguish Van Gogh's works from those of his contemporaries, to identify works in different periods of Van Gogh's career, and to date certain of his paintings.[36] As shown in Figure 22.3, a computer program was able to extract brushstrokes from paintings automatically. On the basis of this data, we computed brushstroke statistics based on individual brushstrokes, interactions between brushstrokes, and whole-painting statistics. The method offers the ability to explain to art historians the exact reasoning behind the conclusions. For example, the team was tasked to date three paintings that are attributed to Van Gogh: *Still Life: Potatoes in a Yellow Dish* (ID# F386), *Willows at Sunset* (F572), and *Crab on Its Back* (F605). Their method produced explainable evidence, based on an analysis of thousands of brushstrokes and their interrelations, to date the paintings F386 and F605 to the Arles and Saint-Rémy period, and the painting F572 to the Paris period. Further, the method has statistically revealed the marking attributes of Van Gogh's brushstroke style: density, elongatedness, straightness, and homogeneity.

Various other researchers have devised different methods to detect or analyze specific painters. They have studied Vincent van Gogh,[37] Pieter Bruegel the Elder,[38] Jackson Pollock,[39] and

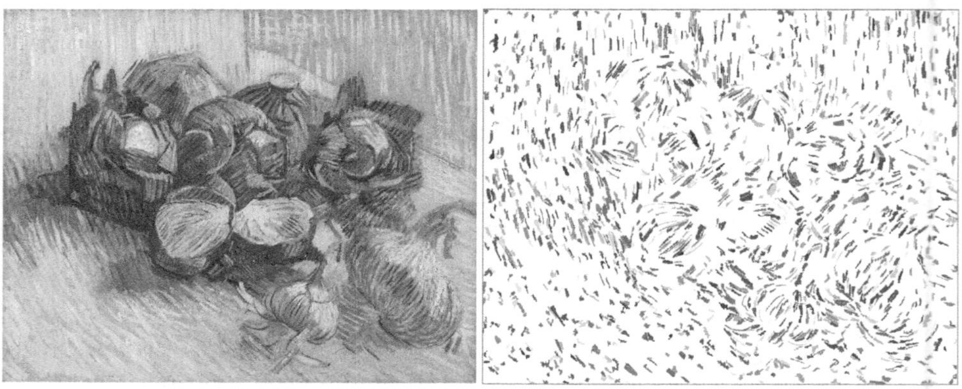

*Figure 22.3* Brushstrokes automatically extracted from *Red Cabbages and Onions* by Vincent van Gogh (1887).[40]

*Source:* The image of the painting is courtesy of the Van Gogh Museum, Amsterdam (Vincent van Gogh Foundation). The brushstroke image courtesy of the James Z. Wang Research Group (The Pennsylvania State University).

Piet Mondrian,[41] for instance. Studies have also been carried out to distinguish genuine works from imitations[42] or forgeries.[43]

Computerized analysis has been shown to be valuable to help answer anthropological and archaeological questions. Wang et al. used machine learning to study the roles of men and women in prehistoric contexts by analyzing the sexual identities of human handprints stenciled on the breathtaking wall panel of the Gua Tewet cave of eastern Borneo and around the *Leopard Spotted Horses* mural of the Pech-Merle cave in southern France.[44] The study provides quantitative evidence relevant to sexual dimorphism and the sexual division of labor in Upper Paleolithic societies.

In addition to automated direct attribution and authentication, image analysis can also assist with the physical analysis of paintings through cleaning the artifacts or restoring them for further analysis in different imaging modalities. For instance, Cornelis et al. determined how to remove canvas patterns that show up during the high resolution and X-ray imaging of paintings. The authors propose a two-stage approach. First, they decompose the image into two parts where the first part contains contrasted shapes (cartoon) and the second part consists of oscillating patterns (texture). The textural part contains the canvas patterns. Multiscale thresholding was then applied to the textural part in the frequency domain to filter out the canvas patterns.[45]

Image analysis is also employed to restore cracks or faded colors in paintings. A method for crack detection and inpainting was put forward by Cornelis et al. The method combined three approaches for crack detection, including the use of oriented-elongated filters, morphological operations, and sparse representation dictionaries. Each approach investigates a different quality of the cracks: sensitivity, width selectivity, and smoothness. The background and foreground of a detected crack were first delineated with a Markovian field segmentation. In this process, candidate patches of variable sizes were selected as targets, the cracks were filled and the image was restored.[46] Color fading due to chemical and physical changes is an unfortunate reality for paintings, and computerized methods may help with color restoration. A recent approach utilized how pixels compare to neutral gray, the reflectance, and shading values to detect cracks and they were filled in.[47]

Besides color restoration, computational image analysis has been put to work to inspect the position and direction of light source in paintings. These analyses may provide insights about a particular artist's technique. For instance, Johnson et al. studied the light source in Johannes Vermeer's *Girl With a Pearl Earring*. The linear beams passing through shadow pixels and light area pixels (cast-shadow method) was combined with an analysis of vectorial normals of contours separating light and dark regions (occluding contour analysis).[48] These analyses substantiated the belief that realist painters, including Vermeer, possessed the ability to appropriately and coherently render actual lighting information in the scene.

## Affective Analysis

Affective computing, which involves the affective analysis of digital content, is yet another relatively young research field. "Affect" is the psychological state of a person during his or her sensory interactions with the environment. Computerized analysis methods have been developed to analyze the emotions that photographs and paintings elicit from viewers. These approaches may help with classifying a large collection of paintings into categories according to their affective content, or may provide insight into different career periods of an individual painter. Specialist methodologies have been developed to investigate the affective content of abstract paintings. Sartori et al. created professional (MART data set) and amateur (deviantArt) abstract painting data sets to acquire the emotional ratings of works by human subjects. They extracted visual words from small patches in each image, which represent color and texture information. These visual words were employed to classify positive and negative emotions evoked by the paintings.[49]

Other studies considered a more complex approach to affect rather than the positive-negative separation of emotions. Lu et al. adopted a two-dimensional approach to affect in order to account for both the intensity of emotions and positivity. They leveraged adaptive learning to extend knowledge of emotional content in photographs to paintings. This approach was required because the statistical distribution of visual features was not the same for photographs as it was for paintings.[50] Inspired by the fact that artists often use triangles in their compositions to portray a dynamic, stable, and/or balanced feeling, He et al. devised a method to detect inherent triangles in portraits by analyzing line segments in pairs and measuring how close these pairs came to creating a triangle.[51] Such methods have the potential to improve our ability to understand how the composition of artworks trigger particular (often unconscious) emotional responses on the part of the viewer.

## Opportunities and Challenges for Future Innovation

While we have seen a number of exciting developments in the past two decades, the field of computerized analysis of paintings is in an early stage. We believe existing work has only scratched the surface of some deep and challenging questions. First, computerized analysis will continue to offer insights to art historians. With some examples of successful collaboration, we hope there will be more close collaborations between art historians and technology researchers. As large-scale, high-quality image data sets become increasingly available, art historians can partner with technologists to define and address new research questions. As scientists developing new technologies, we are always enthusiastic about tackling art historical questions of significance.

Second, computerized analysis may offer useful information to artists in their own practice. With millions of images of paintings at their disposal, computers hold the promise to reveal the development of paintings, to reveal networks of influence, and to offer insight into painting techniques.

Third, computerized analysis will be incorporated into painting retrieval systems, virtual museums, and designer systems so that audiences can make better use of cultural heritage. Such systems will demand technological advances in visual feature indexing, linguistic indexing, affective indexing, and explainable AI.

Finally, computer and information scientists will continue to find inspiration from working on research questions relating to painting analysis. Paintings have the ability to transcend cultural and national boundaries as well as language differences. They make people think beyond the objects or scenes depicted, elicit emotion, and engage the imagination. How can an AI understand the meaning of an artwork, appreciate its aesthetic value, interpret it, or experience the emotions it generates? Computer and information sciences will need revolutionary advances on multiple fronts, well beyond what are considered "intelligent" today, in order to confront such questions.

## Notes

1. D. Gavrilov, R.G. Maev, and D.P. Almond, "A Review of Imaging Methods in Analysis of Works of Art: Thermographic Imaging Method in Art Analysis," *Canadian Journal of Physics* 92, no. 4 (2014): 341–64.

2. Jia Li and James Z. Wang, "Studying Digital Imagery of Ancient Paintings by Mixtures of Stochastic Models," *IEEE Transactions on Image Processing* 13, no. 3 (2004): 340–53; Jia Li et al., "Rhythmic Brushstrokes Distinguish van Gogh from His Contemporaries: Findings via Automated Brushstroke Extraction," *IEEE Transactions on Pattern Analysis and Machine Intelligence* 34, no. 6 (2012): 1159–76.
3. Ibid.
4. Mady Elias and Pascal Cotte, "Multispectral Camera and Radiative Transfer Equation Used to Depict Leonardo's Sfumato in Mona Lisa," *Applied Optics* 47, no. 12 (2008): 2146–54.
5. Fahad Shahbaz Khan et al., "Painting-91: A Large Scale Database for Computational Painting Categorization," *Machine Vision and Applications* 25, no. 6 (2014): 1385–97.
6. Lior Shamir et al., "Impressionism, Expressionism, Surrealism: Automated Recognition of Painters and Schools of Art," *ACM Transactions on Applied Perception* 7, no. 2 (2010): 8–17.
7. Gustavo Carneiro et al., "Artistic Image Classification: An Analysis on the PRINTART Database," *European Conference on Computer Vision* (Springer 2012): 143–57.
8. Sergey Karayev et al., "Recognizing Image Style," in *Proceedings of the British Machine Vision Conference* (Surrey, UK: BMVA Press, 2014).
9. Samet Hicsonmez et al., "DRAW: Deep Networks for Recognizing Styles of Artists Who Illustrate Children's Books," in *Proceedings of International Conference on Multimedia Retrieval* (ACM, 2017), 338–46.
10. C. Richard Johnson et al., "Image Processing for Artist Identification," *IEEE Signal Processing Magazine* 25, no. 4 (2008): 37–48.
11. Ahmed Elgammal, Yan Kang, and Milko Den Leeuw, "Picasso, Matisse, or a Fake? Automated Analysis of Drawings at the Stroke Level for Attribution and Authentication," in *Conference on Artificial Intelligence* (AAAI, 2018), 42–50.
12. Thomas Mensink and Jan Van Gemert, "The Rijksmuseum Challenge: Museum-Centered Visual Recognition," in *Proceedings of International Conference on Multimedia Retrieval* (ACM, 2014), 451–55.
13. Behjat Siddiquie, Shiv N. Vitaladevuni, and Larry S. Davis, "Combining Multiple Kernels for Efficient Image Classification," in *Workshop on Applications of Computer Vision* (IEEE, 2009), 1–8.
14. Jana Zujovic et al., "Classifying Paintings by Artistic Genre: An Analysis of Features & Classifiers," in *International Workshop on Multimedia Signal Processing* (IEEE, 2009), 1–5.
15. Siddharth Agarwal et al., "Genre and Style Based Painting Classification," in *Winter Conference on Applications of Computer Vision* (IEEE, 2015), 588–94.
16. Li and Wang, "Studying Digital Imagery of Ancient Paintings by Mixtures of Stochastic Models."
17. Daniel J. Graham et al., "Statistics, Vision, and the Analysis of Artistic Style," *Wiley Interdisciplinary Reviews: Computational Statistics* 4, no. 2 (2012): 115–23.
18. Li and Wang, "Studying Digital Imagery of Ancient Paintings by Mixtures of Stochastic Models"; Vilson Vieira et al., "A Quantitative Approach to Painting Styles," *Physica A: Statistical Mechanics and Its Applications* 417 (2015): 110–29; Gaowen Liu et al., "Inferring Painting Style with Multi-Task Dictionary Learning," in *International Joint Conference on Artificial Intelligence* (AAAI, 2015), 2162–68; Catherine A. Buell, William P. Seeley, and Ricky J. Sethi, "A Framework for Computing Artistic Style Using Artistically Relevant Features," in *International Conference on e-Science* (IEEE, 2017), 432–33.
19. Guifang Duan et al., "Analysis of Cypriot Icon Faces Using ICA-Enhanced Active Shape Model Representation," in *Proceedings of International Conference on Multimedia* (ACM, 2011), 901–4; Krassimira Ivanova et al., "Features for Art Painting Classification Based on Vector Quantization of MPEG-7 Descriptors," in *Data Engineering and Management* (Springer, 2012), 146–53.
20. Li and Wang, "Studying Digital Imagery of Ancient Paintings by Mixtures of Stochastic Models."
21. Vieira et al., "A Quantitative Approach to Painting Styles."
22. Li and Wang, "Studying Digital Imagery of Ancient Paintings by Mixtures of Stochastic Models."
23. Liu et al., "Inferring Painting Style With Multi-Task Dictionary Learning."
24. Agarwal et al., "Genre and Style Based Painting Classification."
25. Jia Li, Surajit Ray, and Bruce G. Lindsay, "A Nonparametric Statistical Approach to Clustering Via Mode Identification," *Journal of Machine Learning Research 8* (August 2007): 1687–723.
26. Buell et al., "A Framework for Computing Artistic Style Using Artistically Relevant Features."
27. Ivanova et al., "Features for Art Painting Classification Based on Vector Quantization of MPEG-7 Descriptors."
28. Duan et al., "Analysis of Cypriot Icon Faces Using ICA-Enhanced Active Shape Model Representation."
29. Yaniv Bar, Noga Levy, and Lior Wolf, "Classification of Artistic Styles Using Binarized Features Derived From a Deep Neural Network," in *Proceedings of the Where Computer Vision Meets Art Workshop,*

*in Conjunction With the European Conference on Computer Vision* (Springer, 2014), 71–84; Karayev et al., "Recognizing Image Style"; Shin Matsuo and Keiji Yanai, "CNN-Based Style Vector for Style Image Retrieval," in *Proceedings of International Conference on Multimedia Retrieval* (ACM, 2016), 309–12; Rao Muhammad Anwer et al., "Combining Holistic and Part-Based Deep Representations for Computational Painting Categorization," in *Proceedings of International Conference on Multimedia Retrieval* (ACM, 2016), 339–42; Ahmed Elgammal et al., "CAN: Creative Adversarial Networks, Generating 'Art' by Learning About Styles and Deviating From Style Norms," *arXiv preprint:1706.07068* (2017); Hicsonmez et al., "DRAW: Deep Networks for Recognizing Styles of Artists Who Illustrate Children's Books."

30. Karayev et al., "Recognizing Image Style."
31. Bar et al., "Classification of Artistic Styles Using Binarized Features Derived From a Deep Neural Network."
32. Li, Ray, and Lindsay, "A Nonparametric Statistical Approach to Clustering Via Mode Identification."
33. Anwer et al., "Combining Holistic and Part-Based Deep Representations for Computational Painting Categorization."
34. Hicsonmez et al., "DRAW: Deep Networks for Recognizing Styles of Artists Who Illustrate Children's Books."
35. Elgammal et al., "CAN: Creative Adversarial Networks, Generating 'Art' by Learning About Styles and Deviating From Style Norms."
36. Li et al., "Rhythmic Brushstrokes Distinguish van Gogh from His Contemporaries"; Johnson et al., "Image Processing for Artist Identification."
37. Fabrizio Lamberti, Andrea Sanna, and Gianluca Paravati, "Computer-Assisted Analysis of Painting Brushstrokes: Digital Image Processing for Unsupervised Extraction of Visible Features from van Gogh's Works," *EURASIP Journal on Image and Video Processing* no. 1 (2014): 53–60.
38. James M. Hughes, Daniel J. Graham, and Daniel N. Rockmore, "Quantification of Artistic Style Through Sparse Coding Analysis in the Drawings of Pieter Bruegel the Elder," *Proceedings of the National Academy of Sciences* 107, no. 4 (2010): 1279–83.
39. Jim Coddington et al., "Multifractal Analysis and Authentication of Jackson Pollock Paintings," in *Computer Image Analysis in The Study of Art*, vol. 6810 (Bellingham: SPIE—International Society for Optics and Photonics, 2008), 68100F1–12.
40. Li et al., "Rhythmic Brushstrokes Distinguish van Gogh from His Contemporaries."
41. David Andrzejewski et al., "Inferring Compositional Style in the Neo-Plastic Paintings of Piet Mondrian by Machine Learning," in *Computer Vision and Image Analysis of Art*, vol. 7531 (Bellingham: SPIE—International Society for Optics and Photonics, 2010), 75310G1–11.
42. Siwei Lyu, Daniel Rockmore, and Hany Farid, "Wavelet Analysis for Authentication," in *Art + Math = X Conference* (Boulder: University of Colorado, 2005).
43. Paul Buchana et al., "Simultaneous Forgery Identification and Localization in Paintings Using Advanced Correlation Filters," in *International Conference on Image Processing* (IEEE, 2016), 146–50.
44. James Z. Wang et al., "Determining the Sexual Identities of Prehistoric Cave Artists Using Digitized Handprints: A Machine Learning Approach," in *Proceedings of the International Conference on Multimedia* (ACM, 2010), 1325–32.
45. Bruno Cornelis et al., "Removal of Canvas Patterns in Digital Acquisitions of Paintings," *IEEE Transactions on Image Processing* 26, no. 1 (2017): 160–71.
46. Bruno Cornelis et al., "Crack Detection and Inpainting for Virtual Restoration of Paintings: The Case of the Ghent Altarpiece," *Signal Processing* 93, no. 3 (2013): 605–19.
47. Ayman M. T. Ahmed, "Color Restoration Techniques for Faded Colors of Old Photos, Printings and Paintings," in *International Conference on Electro/Information Technology* (IEEE, 2009), 151–56.
48. Micah K. Johnson et al., "Inferring Illumination Direction Estimated From Disparate Sources in Paintings: An Investigation into Jan Vermeer's Girl With a Pearl Earring," in *Computer Image Analysis in the Study of Art*, vol. 6810 (Bellingham: SPIE—International Society for Optics and Photonics, 2008), 68100I.
49. Andreza Sartori et al., "Affective Analysis of Professional and Amateur Abstract Paintings Using Statistical Analysis and Art Theory," *ACM Transactions on Interactive Intelligent Systems* 5, no. 2 (2015): 8.
50. Xin Lu et al., "Identifying Emotions Aroused from Paintings," in *Proceedings of the Workshop on Visual Analysis of Sketches, in Conjunction with the European Conference on Computer Vision* (Springer, 2016), 48–63.
51. Siqiong He et al., "Discovering Triangles in Portraits for Supporting Photographic Creation," *IEEE Transactions on Multimedia* 20, no. 2 (2017): 496–508.

## Bibliography


Agarwal, Siddharth, Harish Karnick, Nirmal Pant, and Urvesh Patel. "Genre and Style Based Painting Classification." In *Winter Conference on Applications of Computer Vision*, 588–94. Piscataway, NJ: IEEE, 2015.

Ahmed, Ayman M. T. "Color Restoration Techniques for Faded Colors of Old Photos, Printings and Paintings." In *International Conference on Electro/Information Technology*, 151–56. Piscataway, NJ: IEEE, 2009.

Andrzejewski, David, David G. Stork, Xiaojin Zhu, and Ron Spronk. "Inferring Compositional Style in the Neo-Plastic Paintings of Piet Mondrian by Machine Learning." In *Computer Vision and Image Analysis of Art*, vol. 7531, 75310G1-11. Bellingham, Washington, DC: SPIE—International Society for Optics and Photonics, 2010.

Anwer, Rao Muhammad, Fahad Shahbaz Khan, Joost van de Weijer, and Jorma Laaksonen. "Combining Holistic and Part-Based Deep Representations for Computational Painting Categorization." In *Proceedings of International Conference on Multimedia Retrieval*, 339–42. New York: ACM, 2016.

Bar, Yaniv, Noga Levy, and Lior Wolf. "Classification of Artistic Styles Using Binarized Features Derived from a Deep Neural Network." In *Proceedings of the Where Computer Vision Meets Art Workshop, in Conjunction with the European Conference on Computer Vision*, 71–84. Berlin/Heidelberg, Germany: Springer, 2014.

Buchana, Paul, Irina Cazan, Manuel Diaz-Granados, Felix Juefei-Xu, and Marios Savvides. "Simultaneous Forgery Identification and Localization in Paintings Using Advanced Correlation Filters." In *International Conference on Image Processing*, 146–50. Piscataway, NJ: IEEE, 2016.

Buell, Catherine A., William P. Seeley, and Ricky J. Sethi. "A Framework for Computing Artistic Style Using Artistically Relevant Features." In *International Conference on e-Science*, 432–33. Piscataway, NJ: IEEE, 2017.

Carneiro, Gustavo, Nuno Pinho da Silva, Alessio Del Bue, and Joa˜o Paulo Costeira. "Artistic Image Classification: An Analysis on the Printart Database." In *European Conference on Computer Vision*, 143–57. Springer, 2012.

Coddington, Jim, John Elton, Daniel Rockmore, and Yang Wang. "Multifractal Analysis and Authentication of Jackson Pollock Paintings." In *Computer Image Analysis in The Study of Art*, vol. 6810, 68100F1–12. Bellingham: SPIE—International Society for Optics and Photonics, 2008.

Cornelis, Bruno, T. Ruzˇicˊ, Emile Gezels, Ann Dooms, A. Pizˇurica, L. Platisˇa, Jan Cornelis, Maximiliaan Martens, Marc De Mey, and Ingrid Daubechies. "Crack Detection and Inpainting for Virtual Restoration of Paintings: The Case of the Ghent Altarpiece." *Signal Processing* 93, no. 3 (2013): 605–19.

Cornelis, Bruno, Haizhao Yang, Alex Goodfriend, Noelle Ocon, Jianfeng Lu, and Ingrid Daubechies. "Removal of Canvas Patterns in Digital Acquisitions of Paintings." *IEEE Transactions on Image Processing* 26, no. 1 (2017): 160–71.

Duan, Guifang, Neela Sawant, James Z. Wang, Dean Snow, Danni Ai, and Yen-Wei Chen. "Analysis of Cypriot Icon Faces Using ICA-Enhanced Active Shape Model Representation." In *Proceedings of International Conference on Multimedia*, 901–4. ACM, 2011.

Elgammal, Ahmed, Yan Kang, and Milko Den Leeuw. "Picasso, Matisse, or a Fake? Automated Analysis of Drawings at the Stroke Level for Attribution and Authentication." In *Conference on Artificial Intelligence*, 42–50. Palo Alto, CA: AAAI, 2018.

Elgammal, Ahmed, Bingchen Liu, Mohamed Elhoseiny, and Marian Mazzone. "CAN: Creative Adversarial Networks, Generating 'Art' by Learning About Styles and Deviating from Style Norms." *arXiv preprint:1706.07068* (2017).

Elias, Mady, and Pascal Cotte. "Multispectral Camera and Radiative Transfer Equation Used to Depict Leonardo's Sfumato in Mona Lisa." *Applied Optics* 47, no. 12 (2008): 2146–54.

Florea, Corneliu, Cosmin Toca, and Fabian Gieseke. "Artistic Movement Recognition by Boosted Fusion of Color Structure and Topographic Description." In *Winter Conference on Applications of Computer Vision*, 569–77. IEEE, 2017.

Gavrilov, D., R. G. Maev, and D. P. Almond. "A Review of Imaging Methods in Analysis of Works of Art: Thermographic Imaging Method in Art Analysis." *Canadian Journal of Physics* 92, no. 4 (2014): 341–64.

Graham, Daniel J., James M. Hughes, Helmut Leder, and Daniel N. Rockmore. "Statistics, Vision, and the Analysis of Artistic Style." *Wiley Interdisciplinary Reviews: Computational Statistics* 4, no. 2 (2012): 115–23.

He, Siqiong, Zihan Zhou, Farshid Farhat, and James Z. Wang. "Discovering Triangles in Portraits for Supporting Photographic Creation." *IEEE Transactions on Multimedia* 20, no. 2 (2017): 496–508.

Hicsonmez, Samet, Nermin Samet, Fadime Sener, and Pinar Duygulu. "DRAW: Deep Networks for Recognizing Styles of Artists Who Illustrate Children's Books." In *Proceedings of International Conference on Multimedia Retrieval*, 338–46. ACM, 2017.

Hughes, James M., Daniel J. Graham, and Daniel N. Rockmore. "Quantification of Artistic Style Through Sparse Coding Analysis in the Drawings of Pieter Bruegel the Elder." *Proceedings of the National Academy of Sciences* 107, no. 4 (2010): 1279–83.

Ivanova, Krassimira, Peter Stanchev, Evgeniya Velikova, Koen Vanhoof, Benoit Depaire, Rajkumar Kannan, Iliya Mitov, and Krassimir Markov. "Features for Art Painting Classification Based on Vector Quantization of MPEG-7 Descriptors." In *Data Engineering and Management*, 146–53. Springer, 2012.

Johnson, C. Richard, Ella Hendriks, Igor J. Berezhnoy, Eugene Brevdo, Shannon M. Hughes, Ingrid Daubechies, Jia Li, Eric Postma, and James Z. Wang. "Image Processing for Artist Identification." *IEEE Signal Processing Magazine* 25, no. 4 (2008): 37–48.

Johnson, Micah K., David G. Stork, Soma Biswas, and Yasuo Furuichi. "Inferring Illumination Direction Estimated from Disparate Sources in Paintings: An Investigation into Jan Vermeer's Girl with a Pearl Earring." In *Computer Image Analysis in the Study of Art*, vol. 6810, 68100I. Bellingham: SPIE—International Society for Optics and Photonics, 2008.

Karayev, Sergey, Matthew Trentacoste, Helen Han, Aseem Agarwala, Trevor Darrell, Aaron Hertzmann, and Holger Winnemoeller. "Recognizing Image Style." In *Proceedings of the British Machine Vision Conference*. Surrey, UK: BMVA Press, 2014.

Khan, Fahad Shahbaz, Shida Beigpour, Joost Van de Weijer, and Michael Felsberg. "Painting-91: A Large Scale Database for Computational Painting Categorization." *Machine Vision and Applications* 25, no. 6 (2014): 1385–97.

Lamberti, Fabrizio, Andrea Sanna, and Gianluca Paravati. "Computer-Assisted Analysis of Painting Brushstrokes: Digital Image Processing for Unsupervised Extraction of Visible Features from van Gogh's Works." *EURASIP Journal on Image and Video Processing* 2014, no. 1 (2014): 53–60.

Li, Jia, Surajit Ray, and Bruce G. Lindsay. "A Nonparametric Statistical Approach to Clustering Via Mode Identification." *Journal of Machine Learning Research* 8 (August 2007): 1687–723.

Li, Jia, and James Z. Wang. "Studying Digital Imagery of Ancient Paintings by Mixtures of Stochastic Models." *IEEE Transactions on Image Processing* 13, no. 3 (2004): 340–53.

Li, Jia, Lei Yao, Ella Hendriks, and James Z. Wang. "Rhythmic Brushstrokes Distinguish van Gogh from His Contemporaries: Findings Via Automated Brushstroke Extraction." *IEEE Transactions on Pattern Analysis and Machine Intelligence* 34, no. 6 (2012): 1159–76.

Liu, Gaowen, Yan Yan, Elisa Ricci, Yi Yang, Yahong Han, Stefan Winkler, Nicu Sebe, et al. "Inferring Painting Style with Multi-Task Dictionary Learning." In *International Joint Conference on Artificial Intelligence*, 2162–68. AAAI, 2015.

Lu, Xin, Neela Sawant, Michelle G. Newman, Reginald B. Adams, James Z. Wang, and Jia Li. "Identifying Emotions Aroused from Paintings." In *Proceedings of the Workshop on Visual Analysis of Sketches, in Conjunction with the European Conference on Computer Vision*, 48–63. Springer, 2016.

Lyu, Siwei, Daniel Rockmore, and Hany Farid. "Wavelet Analysis for Authentication." In *Art + Math = X Conference*. Boulder: University of Colorado, 2005.

Matsuo, Shin, and Keiji Yanai. "CNN-Based Style Vector for Style Image Retrieval." In *Proceedings of International Conference on Multimedia Retrieval*, 309–12. ACM, 2016.

Mensink, Thomas, and Jan Van Gemert. "The Rijksmuseum Challenge: Museum-Centered Visual Recognition." In *Proceedings of International Conference on Multimedia Retrieval*, 451–55. ACM, 2014.

Sartori, Andreza, Victoria Yanulevskaya, Almila Akdag Salah, Jasper Uijlings, Elia Bruni, and Nicu Sebe. "Affective Analysis of Professional and Amateur Abstract Paintings Using Statistical Analysis and Art Theory." *ACM Transactions on Interactive Intelligent Systems* 5, no. 2 (2015): 8.

Shamir, Lior, Tomasz Macura, Nikita Orlov, D. Mark Eckley, and Ilya G. Goldberg. "Impressionism, Expressionism, Surrealism: Automated Recognition of Painters and Schools of Art." *ACM Transactions on Applied Perception* 7, no. 2 (2010): 8–17.

Siddiquie, Behjat, Shiv N. Vitaladevuni, and Larry S. Davis. "Combining Multiple Kernels for Efficient Image Classification." In *Workshop on Applications of Computer Vision*, 1–8. IEEE, 2009.

Vieira, Vilson, Renato Fabbri, David Sbrissa, Luciano da Fontoura Costa, and Gonzalo Travieso. "A Quantitative Approach to Painting Styles." *Physica A: Statistical Mechanics and Its Applications* 417 (2015): 110–29.

Wang, James Z., Weina Ge, Dean R. Snow, Prasenjit Mitra, and C. Lee Giles. "Determining the Sexual Identities of Prehistoric Cave Artists Using Digitized Handprints: A Machine Learning Approach." In *Proceedings of the International Conference on Multimedia*, 1325–32. ACM, 2010.

Zujovic, Jana, Lisa Gandy, Scott Friedman, Bryan Pardo, and Thrasyvoulos N. Pappas. "Classifying Paintings by Artistic Genre: An Analysis of Features & Classifiers." In *International Workshop on Multimedia Signal Processing*, 1–5. IEEE, 2009.

# 23

# DIGITAL 3D MODELING FOR THE HISTORY OF ART

*Amy Jeffs*

Reproductions are, arguably, the lifeblood of art history. The discipline may depend on images of art as much as the art itself. Yet, while reproductions affect when and where we see art, they also affect *how* we see it. A miniature plaster cast of Michelangelo's *David* may be rotated so that details of form can be observed from many angles, but the scale of the original will be lost and false information about weight and texture imposed. Likewise, a photograph of Giotto's *Lamentation* in the Arena Chapel may convey a relatively accurate impression of iconography and color, but nothing about the effect of its elevated placement in a cavernous space, nor of its relationship to other scenes of the fresco cycle. Reproductions convey some aesthetic features, while muting or drowning out others.

Digital 3D modeling is being increasingly used to reproduce works of art. Although the technology has been viable since the late 1980s, it is only now widely accessible.[1] Despite its recent availability, its conceptual roots can be found as early as the 1850s, when stereoscopes were employed to create an illusion of three-dimensional space.[2] A stereoscopic image is made by placing off-set images over the eyes. However, they still contained no more actual information than a photograph. In the same era, plaster casts of artworks were made zealously and justified as a museological imperative with the 1867 "Convention for promoting universally Reproductions of Works of Art for the Benefit of Museums of all Countries."[3] These reproductions, examples of which are displayed in the Victoria & Albert Museum's "cast court" in London, reproduce form and size.

Experimentation continued until, in the late 1800s, something more akin to the generated 3D print was created by François Willème and Willy Selke. This involved cutting out images of sculpture from large numbers of photographs to construct 3D surrogates. As photographically derived physical models, they contained the spatial information that differentiates the true 3D model. Translated into the virtual sphere, digital 3D models combine data about form, color and size. While computer tomography (CT) and light scanning can both be used to generate 3D models, the most accessible method is based on photogrammetry (measurements taken by means of photographs) and will be the form explicated in this overview. Researchers are only now realizing the true extent of 3D models' utility and have had particular successes comparing certain artworks spatially or addressing others the study of which was limited by photographic reproduction. Display via the digital platform means that models can be infinitely copied and shared. However, the essential three-dimensionality of the model (whether virtual or printed) means that it is incompatible with traditional analogue (and many digital) forms of publication. As digital publication platforms gain authority, this is bound to change. Tracking such developments is a reminder of how practical infrastructures—in this case the symbiotic relationship between artworks studied, reproduction technologies and means of publication—help shape a discipline.

This introduction to digital 3D modeling for art history has three main aims: to explain what it is and how it is done, to give examples of how it can be of practical and theoretical benefit to art historical activities and to direct readers to further resources. In the process, three projects will be presented. The Digital Pilgrim Project, hosted by the University of Cambridge (co-convened by the author) applied 3D modeling to medieval pilgrim souvenirs and secular badges in museum collections in order to promote study and appreciation of this little-known corpus of mass-produced medieval micro-sculpture. The project's method for 3D modeling will provide a "how to" for photogrammetric 3D modeling. Sofia Gans' study of the tomb of Archbishop Ernst of Saxony in Magdeburg Cathedral, a late medieval brass assemblage by the Vischer workshop of Nuremberg, will offer an example of how a scientific hypothesis was proven by taking advantage of photogrammetric models' spatial data. Finally, Robert Hawkins' application of 3D modeling to the fish-eye sculpted surfaces of medieval stone bosses will show how 3D technologies can enrich theoretical debates. This will be expanded with a closing reflection on the wider theme of the reproduction of art and its importance to art history.[4]

I have elected to forgo discussing the use of 3D modeling to reconstruct damaged and whole buildings due to the scope and proliferation of case studies. Readers are directed to the *Virtual St Stephen's* project and the reconstruction of the destroyed church of San Pier Maggiore, Florence, for an insight into this field.[5] Likewise, the study of 3D modeling as an independent art form and discussion of 3D printing—the physical extension of 3D modeling—is beyond the scope of this chapter. The collaborative work between groups such as "Think See 3D" or "Factum Arte" and cultural heritage institutions shows how weight and surface are being tailored to make the 3D print ever more convincing.[6] The virtual 3D reproduction—the realm of the present discussion—will be shown to have the potential to generate new research questions and encourage alternative ways of seeing.[7]

## What Is a 3D Model?

A 3D model is a computer graphic that represents a surface or object using specialized software. Photogrammetric 3D models are formed of color and texture imposed on a polygonal mesh. They are displayed virtually using linear perspective to create the illusion of three-dimensionality. All this information is derived from photographs.

## 3D Modeling Small Objects: A Method

At a basic level, a 3D model is constructed from photographs of an object taken from many angles.[8] These are then uploaded onto software which generates a photogrammetric model. Exactly how this is achieved varies from object to object. For instance, for the Digital Pilgrim Project, which modeled twelve pewter pilgrim souvenirs, the badges were small enough to place on a rotating plate. A digital SLR camera was positioned on a tripod near the object. Photographs were taken as the plate was turned incrementally, allowing overlap between each photograph. The object itself was repositioned after every full rotation, so that it could be captured from every angle. Each Digital Pilgrim 3D model is built from about three hundred photographs. Photogrammetric 3D models can be made with fewer images, as long as they are carefully overlapped.[9] The images were then processed within Structure-from-Motion (SfM) software. The software links points of commonality between the pictures, generating what is called a "low-density point-cloud." This model is then converted into a high-density point-cloud which is, in turn, made into a polygonal mesh by means of automated connection of all the points. This is the basic photogrammetric model, which is finally overlaid with texture and color taken from the photographs (Figure 23.1).

The brightness, contrast, and cast of the resultant model can be edited just like a 2D digital image. With good quality base photographs (ideally shot in RAW format), the model will appear very true to life. However, reproducing reflective surfaces through 3D modeling poses a technical challenge which is hard to overcome. Especially shiny surfaces such as silver can be imported separately and applied to the model, but this technique will inevitably introduce false

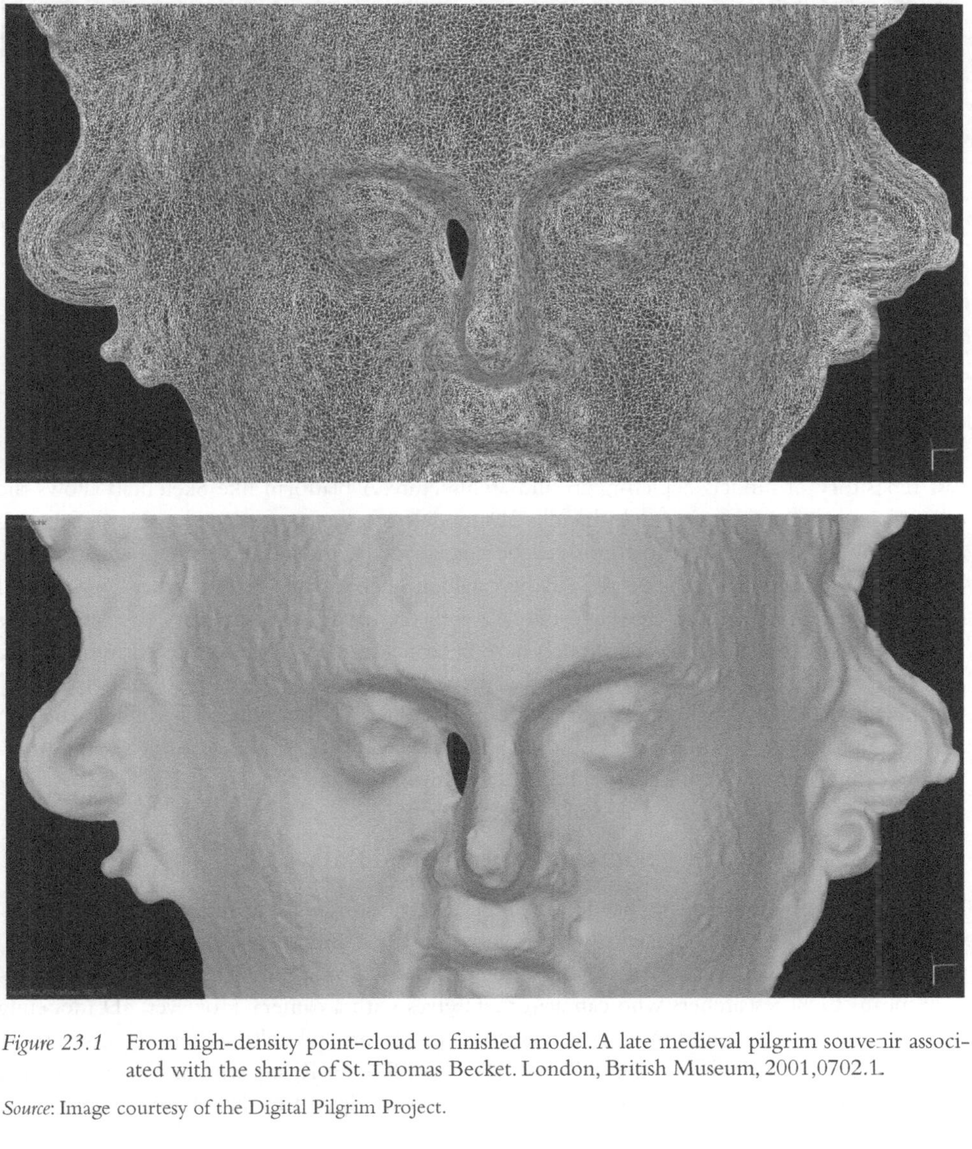

*Figure 23.1* From high-density point-cloud to finished model. A late medieval pilgrim souvenir associated with the shrine of St. Thomas Becket. London, British Museum, 2001,0702.1.

*Source*: Image courtesy of the Digital Pilgrim Project.

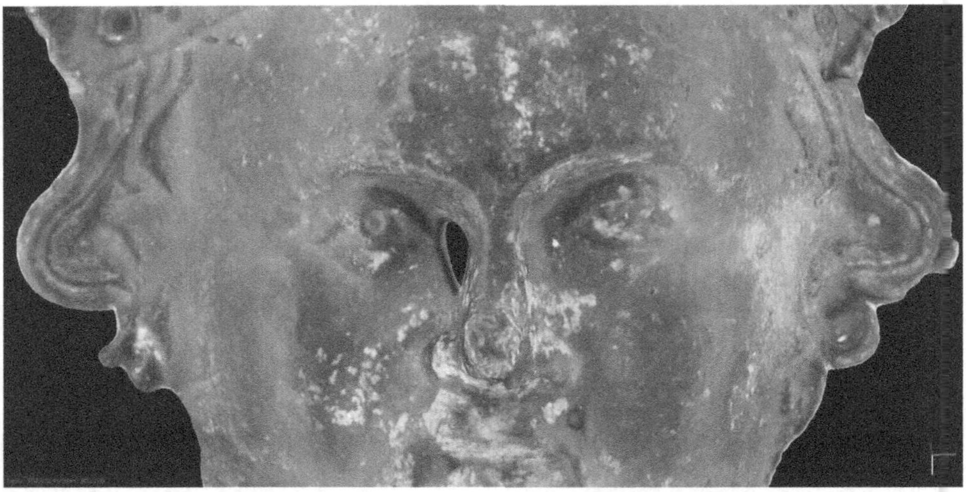

*Figure 23.1* (Continued)

information and should therefore be used with care. This brings into doubt the authenticity of the derivation. Once the model is complete, it can be uploaded to an online platform, printed, or manipulated in desktop software.

## Display Platform: Sketchfab

The Digital Pilgrim models are displayed via the British Museum's account with the 3D modeling platform Sketchfab. Anybody with access to the internet can make an account and upload models to it. One of its primary categories is "Cultural Heritage," which has rapidly become a vast repository of models depicting art and architecture. A platform like Sketchfab allows the online visitor to view and pseudo-handle 3D models of objects on their screens by rotating and zooming. Numbered annotations can be tagged to the model and there is a static space beside the model which can receive a basic catalogue entry with links to other websites. All these features encourage the viewer to interact with the model, read auxiliary text, and access further information. Once several models have been made, they can be gathered into discrete collections, emulating the organization of a gallery space. The models can be found directly by searching the platform or embedded in external websites as illustrations for digital articles.[10] Sketchfab provides a versatile means of storing and displaying collections of models and is proving increasingly popular with cultural heritage institutions.[11]

## Sourcing Expertise and Data

Engagement with 3D modeling need not compel all art historians to acquire advanced IT skills. Courses *are* available for those who wish to learn, and free and open-source software (FOSS) means it is easier than ever to self-teach.[12] The SfM method of 3D modeling is the most accessible means to all researchers who can arm themselves with a camera. However, 3D modeling expertise can now be found in many university departments and cultural heritage institutions. Digital Pilgrim benefited from the skills and insights of Robert Kaleta who had been modeling bronze axe-heads for a PhD in archaeology and had participated in the MicroPasts project at the British Museum.[13] Gans sought tuition from the staff of Cultural Heritage Imaging in San Francisco. Hawkins found instructions online. What matters is that art historians take full advantage of available tools. As more and more models are uploaded via display platforms including Sketchfab, projects (see "Scan the World") and as raw data from online repositories (see "GitHub"), so the obstacles to using digital technologies will continue to dissipate.[14]

## The Digital Pilgrim Project: Close Encounters

Between 2016 and 2017, the Digital Pilgrim Project produced 3D models of twelve medieval badges in the British Museum's 680-strong collection.[15] As everyday image-bearing objects in medieval Northwestern Europe, they are a crucial insight into the visual language of the general population.[16] By extension, they deserve more art historical attention than they have received. Not all are pilgrim souvenirs. Some display the emblem of a noble family; yet others are bawdy, depicting winged phalluses or vulvas dressed as pilgrims. They were moving images, designed to be worn, handled, recognized on approach, and viewed close up. Later, impressed-foil badges were sewn into manuscripts. For the most part, they were eventually thrown away, consigned to sewers and rubbish heaps and the river banks where they are now found.[17] Though they shone silver when freshly cast, most have dulled and degraded, their imagery obscured. The potential to handle virtually and to scrutinize these micro-sculptures as 3D models, using fingers on a touch screen or a mouse, simulates the experience of the original owners, who may also have held, observed, and rotated their badges in their hands.

From a curatorial perspective, 3D modeling medieval badges was appropriate. Whatever the collection item, it creates a data-rich archival record, and display online makes material available for study and teaching. Badges' small size, dulled appearance and hard-to-read imagery make them challenging to display in the gallery space and thus even more needful of auxiliary resources.

The Digital Pilgrim Project models have been used for museum outreach, undergraduate dissertations, seminars, lectures and online articles; they have been shared on social media, embedded in blogs and cited in print publications.[18] The twelve models, the subjects of which have had little or no contact with the public since the nineteenth century, have received nearly nine thousand views at the time of writing. The project has demonstrated how high-quality 3D models can facilitate the study and appreciation of objects that are otherwise hard to see or little known due to size, location or fragility. Furthermore, accessible reproduction of primary sources is often the first step in bringing them to the attention of scholars.

## Photogrammetry: Art in Space

However, the 3D model is more than an engaging visual record. The data behind it includes spatial information: a significant part of the reproduction's data capital. This photogrammetric data offers art historians a practical means of comparing minute differences in objects' size and shape. Such information can be helpful when it comes to, for instance, finding brass sculptures cast from the same model. It has the means of making virtual 3D reproduction a way of identifying physical 3D reproduction.

Just such a methodology was applied to late medieval brass sculpture by Sofia Gans as part of her doctoral research with Columbia University.[19] Gans sought to demonstrate that indirect bronze casting was being used in German-speaking lands as early, if not earlier, than in Italy. Indirect bronze casting allows multiple sculptures to be generated from a single model. Her research centered on Nuremberg, which was the home of the Vischer workshop, active from 1453 to the

1540s. The Vischer tomb of Archbishop Ernst of Saxony in Magdeburg Cathedral, cast c. 1495, has pairs of bronze figures differentiated by small alterations in gesture and attribute. By creating photogrammetric models alongside a scale bar with .0001 mm accuracy, Gans used Agisoft Photoscan to create scaled point clouds.[20] The casts' clouds were then superimposed onto each other using the software CloudCompare to generate a depth map.[21] Points of difference and similarity were highlighted on the map using a color spectrum. This research showed that the sculptures were identical apart from these small modifications, suggesting they were made from the same initial model, with small variations to an intermediate wax model, for example, by the addition of a staff or book. The software enabled Gans to illustrate that the sculptors employed indirect casting long before their Italian counterparts. Her contextual research showed no documented communication with Italian artisans. Together these approaches served to reveal and challenge the Italo-centric bias of the dominant consensus on the history of bronze casting.

## Simulating the Moving Viewer

Robert Hawkins, PhD candidate at the University of Cambridge, at the time of writing, is using 3D modeling to highlight the inadequacy of conventional photography as a medium for the reproduction of sculpture, and to ensure that the three-dimensionality of sculptural objects is remembered. His end goal is not to study modern perceptions of sculpture, but medieval ones.[22] The objects of his study, fifteenth-century sculpted bosses from Norwich Cathedral cloister are difficult to photograph. Busy narrative scenes appear wrapped over their convex surfaces, demanding that the viewer walk around the sculptures, reading their stories on the move. For instance, the boss depicting the martyrdom of John the Baptist at the feast of Herod and Herodias seamlessly condenses no fewer than five narrative scenes onto a hemispherical surface.[23] They are distorted such that the figures in each scene inhabit their own facet of the surface: there is no single viewing angle from which to appreciate the whole sculpture (Figure 23.2).

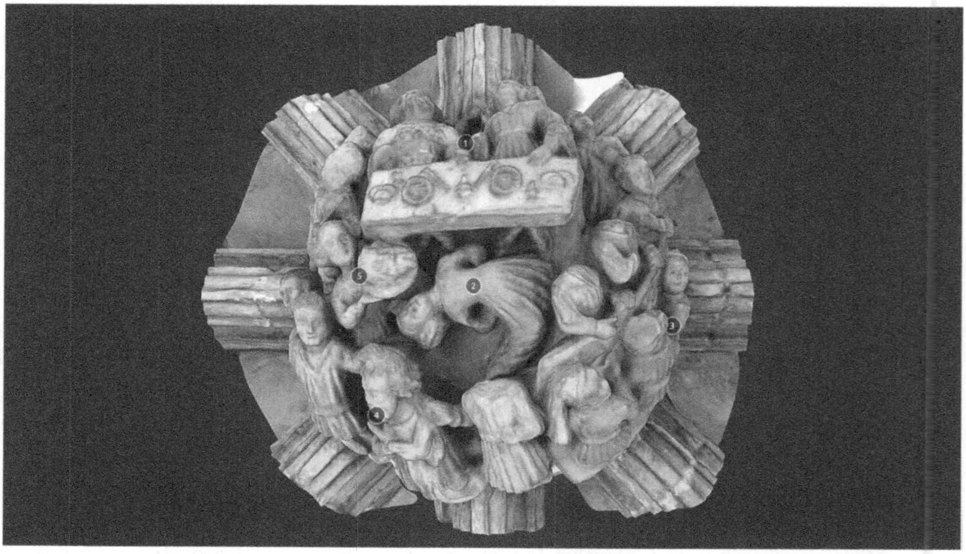

*Figure 23.2* Carving of Herod and Herodias, c. 1420–30. Digital replica of decorative element in the cloister of Norwich Cathedral.

*Source*: Model created by Robert Hawkins (2017).

Hawkins has shown that medieval contentment with the roaming viewer flies in the face of more recent ideas of what constitutes "good" sculpture.[24] In 1896–97 and 1915 Heinrich Wölfflin published articles outlining how to photograph sculpture. "Good" works, he states, lend themselves to being imaged from one or, at the most, two dominant angles.[25] Wölfflin's friend Adolf von Hildebrand similarly stipulated that sculptors ought not to impel their viewers to be "driven all around," but rather to prioritize what Hawkins terms a "planocentric" approach.[26] It is thus evident that the reproduction of sculpture—and even its aesthetic ideals—have been shaped by the limitations of photography.

In recent years, problems with the photographic reproduction of sculpture have been highlighted by Jacqueline Jung and Jules Lubbock. Both favor illustrating their publications with successions of images to convey the potential multiplicity of a work's viewing angles.[27] However, as Hawkins observes, even sequences of photographs reduce sculpture to series of planes. His 3D models of the Norwich Cloister bosses, now uploaded to Sketchfab, create the potential for fluid, analogue viewing, guided by the viewer. He seeks to restore the viewer's freedom to roam. This recalls how the Digital Pilgrim Project models encouraged pseudo-handling. 3D modeling can permit a conceptual return "to the sculptural aesthetics of the past," a compelling counter to the tempting assumption that all new technology must signify a step away from historical experience.

## Reproducing Art

Both Gans' and Hawkins' projects use 3D reproductions of artworks to tackle broad theoretical questions. A theme on which to close this overview is that of reproduction. It is appropriate that the Digital Pilgrim Project modeled pilgrim souvenirs. These too are often miniature reproductions of monumental sculpture and constitute one of the earliest forms of mass reproduction of art in Western Europe: a popular form of pewter souvenir sold at the shrine of St. Thomas Becket in Canterbury represents his ornate gold head reliquary; another, his shrine.[28] Indeed, the father of printing, Johannes Gutenberg, designed and produced pilgrim souvenirs for the town of Aachen in Germany.[29] Tokens were produced in tens of thousands via stamps and molds and sold to hordes of pilgrims who pinned them to clothes and accessories or sewed them into manuscripts. They were designed to be image-bearing, portable, and affordable.[30]

Contemporaries were not oblivious to these souvenirs' relevance to the long-standing Christian discourse on image-making. Discussion of it appears in the imagery of folio 134r of the delicate prayer book of Joanna of Castile, dated 1486–1506.[31] It contains an author portrait of St. Luke at his desk, composing the Gospel text. Above him rests an icon depicting the Virgin and Child. The Evangelist's eyes appear lifted to the image, as though he is using it to mediate his communication with God. The icon alludes to the widely held belief that Luke had painted the Virgin and Child from life. Beneath the scene is the opening of Luke's Gospel account of the Annunciation, when Mary conceived Christ (Luke 1:26), and it follows the opening passage of the Gospel of John concerning the Word made flesh. According to Augustinian theology, the Incarnation of Christ justified the making of images, because God himself had become visible.[32] The textual context of the author-portrait thus authorizes Luke's icon of the Virgin and Child. However, the portrait is part of an even more profound statement about image reproduction. It is enclosed by a green border filled with seventeen, *trompe-l'œil*-style images of pilgrim souvenirs. They have been painted to look as though they are sewn into the margins, as real tokens often were. The artist has placed one *trompe l'œil* souvenir depicting the Virgin and Child souvenir close to Luke's icon. It seems to claim its authority from the portrait itself and, by extension, from its holy subjects. As a painstakingly crafted illusion, the souvenir—a symbol of cheap multiplicity—is elevated to the status of a virtuoso work of art and juxtaposed with the image of a sacred one. The decorated page thus explores the relative status of two images of artworks depicting the same subject: one, the mass-produced copy and the other, a unique original.

Responses to the rise of printing appear grounded in the same debate. Renaissance humanist Abbot Trithemius (d. 1516) claimed that "he who ceases from zeal for writing because of printing is no true lover of scripture" and "cares not for the edification of posterity."[33] Trithemius feared that rapid reproduction was synonymous with a loss of intrinsic quality. Printing, like pilgrim souvenirs, permitted cheap proliferation and had potential for a corresponding disappearance of something more precious and less tangible.

Developments in the technologies of cheap and accessible reproduction only amplify this trend. When photography became widely available, critics quailed at its many reproductions of art and their potentially deleterious effect on the status of the original. In his renowned 1936 essay, Walter Benjamin argued that

> Reproductive technology, we might say in general terms, removes the thing reproduced from the realm of tradition. In making many copies of the reproduction, it substitutes for its unique incidence a multiplicity of incidences. And in allowing the reproduction to come closer to whatever the person apprehending it is in, it actualizes what is reproduced. These two processes usher in a mighty upheaval of what is passed on—an upheaval of tradition that is the verso of the current crisis and renewal of mankind.[34]

Whatever one makes of Benjamin's claim, viewed in the light of these other examples, we are prompted to ask how the virtual 3D reproduction is challenging deep-seated art historical questions about the original versus the copy. It is an important political issue for museums and galleries. Guidelines have been developed since the turn of the millennium for computer-based visualization of cultural heritage.[35] In 2017, representatives of relevant institutions from around the world met to discuss a convention for best practice in relation to the reproduction, storage and dissemination of works of art and cultural heritage ("ReACH": *Reproduction of Art and Cultural Heritage*).[36] In the project's introductory video, CEO of the *Peri Foundation*, Polina Filippova, observes a "general feeling in the museum communities that new technologies present more danger than opportunity."[37] Matthew Vincent of *Rekrei* likewise discusses institutions' discomfort with the reality that "once you create it [open access data], it's reproducible again, and again, and again."[38] Digital technologies, especially of reproduction, are demanding the clarification of artworks' various values and who or what can claim them. This seems to reflect the same ambivalence toward the site of authority in earlier Western art and may be discussed in the same breath.

## Conclusions

Employing 3D modeling to reproduce works of art enriches the discipline of art history in terms of both teaching and research. It is now possible to build, view, and download 3D models with basic and affordable equipment, presenting art historians with the opportunity to incorporate this long-anticipated technology into their everyday academic activities. Three projects that depended on 3D modeling are outlined previously. Digital Pilgrim and Hawkins have shown how it can transform access to artworks that resist effective display or conventional photography. The chosen subjects—medieval badges and sculpted bosses—furthermore benefit from viewers' freedom to choose a multiplicity of viewing angles, simulating the fluid viewing experience of a pre-photographic or "pre-planocentric" age. Gans' project demonstrates the scientific value of 3D models' spatial data and offers a technical methodology for its investigation that could be applied elsewhere. The 3D model can be used for engaging illustration, theoretical interrogation, and physical analysis, but there is a great deal more to discover. Reflecting on the discourse of reproduction encourages modern art historians not to view its "digital" manifestation as a discrete phenomenon but as the latest in a long history of technological changes.

3D modeling is a form of *trompe l'œil*. While not always aesthetic in purpose, it can be hyper-naturalistic and, by engaging the sense of touch, uncannily convincing.[39] We can talk about it in relation to photography, the 3D print, casts, and yet, by comparing these different kinds of reproduction, we always come back to the paradox of the original. Medieval pilgrims caught the reflection of reliquaries in mirrors.[40] We capture culture in lenses and screens. To quote David Rodowick, "the experience of the work does not lie in any one element—whether textual, acoustical, photographic, videographic, or now 3-D computer modeling—but rather hovers between in mobile acts of perception and memory."[41]

Digital 3D modeling to the contemporary art historian represents a theoretical challenge as well as a practical tool.

## Notes

1. Sorin Hermon, "Reasoning in 3D: A Critical Appraisal of the Role of 3D Modeling and Virtual Reconstructions in Archaeology," in *Beyond Illustration: 2D and 3D Technologies as Tools for Discovery in Archaeology*, BAR International Series Oxford: Archaeopress, 2008), 36–45.
2. These references are collated in: Robert Hawkins, "Modeling the Norwich Cathedral Cloister Bosses: Sculpture, Photogrammetry and the Mobile Spectator," in *Peregrinations: Journal of Medieval Art and Architecture* 6, no. 2 (June 2017): 76, accessed June 6, 2018, http://digital.kenyon.edu/perejournal/vol6/iss2/9; see Geraldine A. Johnson, "Photographing Sculpture, Sculpting Photography," in *Photography and Sculpture: The Art Object in Reproduction*, eds. Sarah Hamill and Megan R. Luke (Los Angeles: Yale University Press, 2017); and, more specifically, Robert A. Sobieszek, "Sculpture as the Sum of Its Profiles: François Willème and Photosculpture in France, 1859–1868," *The Art Bulletin* 52 (1980): 617–30; one of Roger Fenton's stereoscopic images of the British Museum is reproduced as a GIF in the British Museum blog "Photography at the Museum: A Developing Story," accessed June 6, 2018, https://blog.britishmuseum.org/photography-at-the-museum-a-developing-story/.
3. *Convention for Promoting Universally Reproductions of Works of Art for the Benefit of Museums of All Countries*, released by Henry Cole, Director of the South Kensington Museum (1867).
4. I would like to thank Gabriel Byng, Thomas Flynn, Sofia Gans, Robert Hawkins, and Dan Pett for reading drafts of and offering feedback on this chapter.
5. "Virtual St Stephen's," based at The University of York (UK), reconstructs the chapel as it may have appeared in the Middle Ages and its appearance after having been converted into a dedicated House of Commons; see "Virtual St Stephen's," accessed June 6, 2018, www.virtualststephens.org.uk/; the destroyed church of San Pier Maggiore, Florence, was reconstructed by scholars at Cambridge University as a point cloud and furnished with Botticini Palmieri's surviving *Assumption of the Virgin* altarpiece, which was originally commissioned for the church, see "Visions of Paradise," accessed June 6, 2018, www.nationalgallery.org.uk/visions-of-paradise.
6. "Think See 3D," accessed June 6, 2018, www.thinksee3d.com/; "Factum Arte," accessed June 6, 2018, www.factum-arte.com.
7. For a foundational essay confronting viewer perspectives, see John Berger, *Ways of Seeing* (London: British Broadcasting House and Penguin Books, 1972).
8. A more general guide can be found on the site for "Cultural Heritage Imaging," accessed June 6, 2018, http://culturalheritageimaging.org/Technologies/Photogrammetry/.
9. See the section entitled "How to Capture Images," accessed June 6, 2018, http://culturalheritageimaging.org/Technologies/Photogrammetry/.
10. The online journal *British Art Studies* integrated numerous 3D models of medieval works of art into Issue 6, *Invention and Imagination in British Art and Architecture, 600–1500*. They appear both as

introductory banners and as illustrations embedded into the main text. See Sandy Heslop, "An Ivory Staff Terminal from Alcester: One Object," in *British Art Studies, Issue 6, Invention and Imagination in British Art and Architecture, 600–1500* (2017), accessed June 6, 2018, www.britishartstudies.ac.uk/issues/issue-index/issue-6/alcester-crozier.

11. When the Digital Pilgrim Project uploaded its first models in April 2016, the British Museum had a total of thirty-four other models on its account. At the time of writing that number stands at 248. For the British Museum's collection of 3D models, visit "The British Museum, Sketchfab," accessed June 6, 2018, https://sketchfab.com/britishmuseum; according to figures collected by the website's cultural heritage lead, Thomas Flynn, there are now more than six hundred museums registered on Sketchfab, 907 nonprofit organizations, and around fifty thousand models in the 'Cultural Heritage and History' category (accounting for occasional miscategorisation).
12. Among the numerous programs available to students is "The Digital Humanities Venice Fall School." It is described on its website as "an opportunity for a select group of students from the fields of Humanities, Social Sciences, Computer Science and Engineering to participate in the historical, economic, artistic and geographical reconstruction of Venice over the past 1000 years. For one week each year, students follow seminars by leading academics, conduct fieldwork in Venice and present a concrete case study as a conclusion to the scientific adventure." Accessed June 6, 2018, www.unive.it/pag/10065/; tutorials in 3D modeling can be found via the Sketchfab blog, accessed June 6, 2018, https://blog.sketchfab.com/category/tutorial/; most universities will have digital humanities representatives who can match up projects with relevant expertise. At the Courtauld Institute of Art "The Digital Art History Research Group" (#DAHRG) organizes regular workshops for students.
13. The "Micropasts" project at the British Museum generates crowd-fueled and crowd-sourced archaeological data, accessed June 6, 2018, https://crowdsourced.micropasts.org/.
14. "Scan the World" describes itself as "a community built museum of the future archiving the world's sculptures, statues and artifacts using 3D scanning and printing technology. Using photogrammetry, the scans are free to download, bringing art to the world for the purposes of cultural heritage, accessibility, preservation and education. From digital archeology to downloadable monuments and buildings, you'll be able to find it with MyMiniFactory and Scan the World." www.myminifactory.com/category/scan-the-world; Computer code to build virtual 3D models can be stored in online repositories such as "GitHub," accessed June 6, 2018, https://github.com/. Dan Pett, Head of Digital and IT at the Fitzwilliam Museum and formerly at the British Museum, has made the data for his model of the British Museum's Rosetta Stone available via this site, https://github.com/portableant/rosettaStone.
15. The Digital Pilgrim Project was supported by a Digital Project Grant from the Paul Mellon Centre for Studies in British Art in the grant's inaugural year. Its 3D models were created by Robert Kaleta, who was then undertaking a PhD in Bronze Age archaeology at University College London. Access to the objects was provided by the British Museum's Ferguson curator of Medieval Europe, Lloyd de Beer.
16. According to a search of the "Portable Antiquities Scheme" database, medieval badges and pilgrim souvenirs represent 15% of all UK metalwork finds dated to between 1250 and 1350.
17. Jennifer Lee, "Medieval Pilgrim Badges in Rivers: The Curious History of a Non-Theory," in *Journal of Art Historiography* 11 (2014): 1–11.
18. The British Museum used Digital Pilgrim models to tweet about medieval pilgrim souvenirs on July 14, 2016, accessed June 6, 2018, https://twitter.com/britishmuseum/status/753636056965210112.
19. Gans outlines the project in "Disciplining the Digital: Virtual 3D Reproduction, Pilgrim Badges and the Stuff of Art History," conversation piece coordinated by Amy Jeffs, *British Art Studies* (2017), accessed June 6, 2018, https://doi.org/10.17658/issn.2058-5462/issue-06/conversation/p54.
20. Gans' collection of 3D models are displayed on her Sketchfab page, accessed June 6, 2018, https://sketchfab.com/SofiaGans/models; "Agisoft Photoscan," accessed June 6, 2018, www.agisoft.com/.
21. "CloudCompare," accessed June 6, 2018, www.danielgm.net/cc/.
22. Hawkins, "Modeling the Norwich Cathedral Cloister Bosses," 72–79; Hawkins summarizes the project in "Disciplining the Digital," *British Art Studies* (2017), accessed June 6, 2018, https://doi.org/10.17658/issn.2058-5462/issue-06/conversation/p67.
23. The boss depicting Herod's Feast can be viewed on Robert Hawkins Sketchfab page, accessed June 6, 2018, https://skfb.ly/67ZNT.
24. Hawkins, "Modeling the Norwich Cathedral Cloister Bosses," 73.
25. Heinrich Wölfflin, "How One Should Photograph Sculpture: A Translation of His Articles of 1896–7 and 1915," trans. Geraldine A. Johnson, in *Art History* 36 (2013): 52–71.

26. Adolf von Hildebrand and Max Friedrich Meyer, *The Problem of Form in Painting and Sculpture* (New York: G. E. Stechert & Co., 1907), 95.
27. Jacqueline Jung, "The Kinetics of Gothic Sculpture: Movement and Apprehension in the South Transept of Strasbourg Cathedral and the Chartreuse de Champmol in Dijon," in *Mobile Eyes: Peripatetisches Sehen in Den Bildkulturen Der Vormoderne*, edited by David Ganz and Stefan Neuner (Eikones, Munich: Wilhelm Fink, 2013), 133–73; Jules Lubbock, *Storytelling in Christian Art from Giotto to Donatello* (New Haven, CT: Yale University Press, 2006).
28. See London, British Museum, 2001,0702.1 and New York, Metropolitan Museum of Art, 2001.310.
29. Diana Childress, *Johannes Gutenberg and the Printing Press* (Minneapolis: Twenty-First Century Books, 2008), 35.
30. For an overview of the object-type, see Brian Spencer, *Pilgrim Souvenirs and Secular Badges* (London: Boydell Press, 1998).
31. London, British Library, Add. MS 18852, f. 184r (the manuscript is fully digitized on the British Library's Digitised Manuscripts platform, accessed June 6, 2018, www.bl.uk/manuscripts/FullDisplay.aspx?index=0&ref=Add_MS_18852).
32. For a full discussion of Augustine of Hippo's theology of image-making, see Gerald Boersma, *Augustine's Early Theology of an Image: A Study in the Development of Pro-Nicene Theology* (Oxford: Oxford University Press, 2016), especially 183.
33. Abbot Trithemius, *De laude scriptorium manualium* (1492), cited in Noël L. Brann, *The Abbot Trithemius (1462–1516): The Renaissance of Monastic Tradition* (Leiden: E. J. Brill, 1981), 158.
34. Walter Benjamin, *The Work of Art in the Age of Mechanical Reproduction*, trans. J. A. Underwood (London: Penguin Books, 2008).
35. "The London Charter for the Computer-Based Visualisation of Cultural Heritage" (2009), accessed June 6, 2018, www.londoncharter.org/introduction.html; see Hugh Denard, "A New Introduction to the London Charter," in *Paradata and Transparency in Virtual Heritage*, eds. Anna Bentkowska-Kafel and Hugh Denard (London and New York: Routledge, 2012), 57–71; "Principles of Seville: International Principles of Virtual Archaeology," accessed June 6, 2018, http://smartheritage.com/seville-principles/seville-principles.
36. A version of the ReACH Declaration (*Reproduction of Art and Cultural Heritage*) has been signed by participants and made available online. The project was launched at UNESCO in May 2017. ReACH (Reproduction of Art and Cultural Heritage) is a global initiative led by the V&A in partnership with the Peri Charitable Foundation. "ReACH Declaration": the V&A website features an explanatory video and version signed on December 8, 2017, at the V&A; accessed June 6, 2018, www.vam.ac.uk/research/projects/reach-reproduction-of-art-and-cultural-heritage.
37. "ReACH: Towards a New Convention #ReACHDialogue," Polina Filippova: 5:00 Minutes, accessed June 6, 2018, https://youtu.be/6Lwpjst6C5E. The Peri Foundation is a charity that supports education through the use and accessibility of new technologies.
38. "Matthew Vincent, 4:45 Mins," accessed June 6, 2018, https://youtu.be/6Lwpjst6C5E. "Rekrei" seeks to restore lost cultural heritage through crowd-sourced photogrammetric reconstructions; accessed June 6, 2018, https://projectmosul.org/.
39. See general discussion of illusion in Ernst Gombrich, *Art and Illusion: A Study in the Psychology of Pictorial Representation* (London: Phaidon, 1960).
40. Brian Spencer, *Medieval Pilgrim Souvenirs and Secular Badges* (London: Boydell Press, 1998), 17–18.
41. David Rodowick, "The Virtual Presence in Space," in *Photography and Sculpture—The Art Object in Reproduction,* eds. Sarah Hamill and Megan R. Luke (Los Angeles: Yale University Press, 2017), 276–91.

## Bibliography

### *Websites*

"Agisoft Photoscan." Accessed June 6, 2018. www.agisoft.com/
British Library. "Digitised Manuscripts." Accessed June 6, 2018. www.bl.uk/manuscripts/Default aspx
"CloudCompare." Accessed June 6, 2018. www.danielgm.net/cc/
"Cultural Heritage Imaging." Accessed June 6, 2018. http://culturalheritageimaging.org/Technologies/Photogrammetry/

"The Digital Humanities Venice Fall School." Accessed June 6, 2018. www.unive.it/pag/10065/
"Factum Arte." Accessed June 6, 2018. www.factum-arte.com
"GitHub." Accessed June 6, 2018. https://github.com/
"The London Charter for the Computer-based Visualisation of Cultural Heritage." 2009. Accessed June 6, 2018. www.londoncharter.org/introduction.html
"Micropasts." Accessed June 6, 2018. https://crowdsourced.micropasts.org/
The National Gallery in collaboration with the University of Cambridge. "Visions of Paradise." Accessed June 6, 2018. www.nationalgallery.org.uk/visions-of-paradise
"Principles of Seville: International Principles of Virtual Archaeology." Accessed June 6, 2018. http://smart heritage.com/seville-principles/seville-principles.
"ReACH Declaration." Accessed June 6, 2018. www.vam.ac.uk/research/projects/reach-reproduction-of-art-and-cultural-heritage
"Rekrei." Accessed June 6, 2018. https://projectmosul.org/
"Sketchfab." Accessed June 6, 2018. https://sketchfab.com/
"Think See 3D." Accessed June 6, 2018. www.thinksee3d.com/
University of York. "Virtual St Stephen's." Accessed June 6, 2018. www.virtualststephens.org.uk/

## Books and Periodicals

Benjamin, Walter. *The Work of Art in the Age of Mechanical Reproduction*, translated by J. A. Underwood. London: Penguin Books, 2008.
Bentkowska-Kafel, Anna, and Hugh Denard (eds.). *Paradata and Transparency in Virtual Heritage*. London and New York: Routledge, 2012.
Berenbeim, Jessica, and Sandy Heslop. *British Art Studies, Issue 6, Invention and Imagination in British Art and Architecture, 600–1500*, 2017. Accessed June 6, 2018. www.britishartstudies.ac.uk/issues/issue-index/issue-6/
Berger, John. *Ways of Seeing*. London: Penguin, 1972.
Bilbey, Diane, and Trusted, Marjorie. "'The Question of Casts'—Collecting and Later Reassessment of the Cast Collections at South Kensington." In *Plaster Casts: Making, Collecting, and Displaying from Classical Antiquity to the Present*. New York: De Gruyter, 2010.
Boersma, Gerald. *Augustine's Early Theology of an Image: A Study in the Development of Pro-Nicene Theology*. Oxford: Oxford University Press, 2016.
Brann, Noël L. *The Abbot Trithemius (1462–1516): The Renaissance of Monastic Tradition*. Leiden: E. J. Brill, 1981.
Childress, Diana. *Johannes Gutenberg and the Printing Press*. Minneapolis: Twenty-First Century Books, 2008.
Gans, Sofia. "'An Entire Chapel Cast and Engraved with Images': New Perspectives on the Tomb of St. Sebald in Nuremberg." PhD Diss., Columbia University, 2018.
———. "Wood and Wax, Models and Molds: The Vischer Workshop of Nuremberg and Late Medieval German Casting Models." In *Les modèles dans l'art du Moyen Age (XIIe-XVe siècles)/Models in the Art of the Middle Ages (12th–15th Centuries)*, edited by Denise Borlée and Laurence Terrier Aliferis, 223–31. Turnhout: Brepols, Les Etudes du Rilma, 2018.
Gombrich, Ernst. *Art and Illusion: a Study in the Psychology of Pictorial Representation*. London: Phaidon, 1960.
Hamill, Sarah, and Megan R. Luke, eds. *Photography and Sculpture—The Art Object in Reproduction*. Los Angeles: Yale University Press, 2017.
Hawkins, Robert. "Modeling the Norwich Cathedral Cloister Bosses: Sculpture, Photogrammetry and the Mobile Spectator." *Peregrinations: Journal of Medieval Art and Architecture* 6, no. 2 (June 2017).
Hermon, Sorin. "Reasoning in 3D: A Critical Appraisal of the Role of 3D Modeling and Virtual Reconstructions in Archaeology." In *Beyond Illustration: 2D and 3D Technologies as Tools for Discovery in Archaeology*, BAR International Series. Oxford: Archaeopress, 2008.
Jeffs, Amy. "Disciplining the Digital: Virtual 3D Reproduction, Pilgrim Badges and the Stuff of Art History." Conversation piece coordinated by Amy Jeffs, *British Art Studies*, 2017. Accessed June 6, 2018. www.britishartstudies.ac.uk/issues/issue-index/issue-6/virtual-reproduction
Jessop, M. "Digital Visualization as a Scholarly Activity." *Literary and Linguistic Computing* 23, no. 3 (2008): 281–93.
Jung, Jacqueline. "The Kinetics of Gothic Sculpture: Movement and Apprehension in the South Transept of Strasbourg Cathedral and the Chartreuse de Champmol in Dijon." In *Mobile Eyes: Peripatetisches Sehen*

*in Den Bildkulturen Der Vormoderne*, edited by David Ganz and Stefan Neuner, 133–73. Eikones, Munich: Wilhelm Fink, 2013.
Lee, Jennifer. "Medieval Pilgrim Badges in Rivers: The Curious History of a Non-Theory." *Journal of Art Historiography* 11 (2014): 1–11.
Lubbock, Jules. *Storytelling in Christian Art from Giotto to Donatello*. New Haven, CT: Yale University Press, 2006.
Rodowick, David. "The Virtual Presence in Space." In *Photography and Sculpture—The Art Object in Reproduction*, edited by Sarah Hamill and Megan R. Luke, 276–91. Los Angeles: Yale University Press, 2017.
Sobieszek, Robert A. "Sculpture as the Sum of Its Profiles: François Willème and Photosculpture in France, 1859–1868." *The Art Bulletin* 62 (1980): 617–30.
Spencer, Brian. *Pilgrim Souvenirs and Secular Badges*. London: Boydell Press, 1998.
von Hildebrand, Adolf, and Max Friedrich Meyer. *The Problem of Form in Painting and Sculpture*. New York: G. E. Stechert & Co., 1907.
Wölfflin, Heinrich. "How One Should Photograph Sculpture: A Translation of His Articles of 1896–7 and 1915.", translated by Geraldine A. Johnson. *Art History* 36 (2013): 52–71.

# 24

# METADATA, MATERIAL CULTURE, AND GLOBAL ART HISTORY

*Robert Wellington*

The "computational turn" in the humanities has come at the time of another radical shift, the "global turn." Global art history, like the evolution of the personal computer and hand-held devices, has been more than forty years in the making.[1] Changes to art-historical practice have increased exponentially in the last twenty years in response to the web. The digital revolution in research has collapsed spatial boundaries for those of us who do not have access to all of the sites, objects, and texts that we study. Where would we be today without the powerful search engines that allow us to access digitized archives and publications, not to mention high-resolution reproductions of the works of art, architecture, and design that form the basis of our research? Now that we can make virtual field trips to museums, archives, and libraries across the world at the stroke of a few keys, it seems as if the whole world (or at least its digital counterpart) is within our purview.

As the digitization of public, and sometimes private, collections decreases the spatial and geographical limitations of research, it becomes ever more feasible to expand studies to include objects that have been dispersed across the globe throughout history. Investigation of the "lives" of those traveling objects has become a particularly rich field in the last two decades and continues to gain momentum.[2] Studies have generally focused on the movement of objects to Europe from outside, with the fanciful recreation of other world cultures in the salons and palaces of wealthy Europeans.[3] This is not surprising, given the Eurocentric biases of art history and postcolonial studies that, until recently, have failed to acknowledge the autonomy of people and states outside Europe. The problems of a Western-focused art history are not only perpetuated by academic texts published in the West, but are also encoded within the very fabric of valuable digital resources that are published online with the aim of making the world's cultural heritage available to all.

In this chapter I address the digitization of objects as an art-historical practice. In doing so, I trouble the distinction between the "digital" and the "digitized" proposed by Johanna Drucker in her field-defining article, "Is There a Digital Art History?"[4] Drucker reminds us that the digitization of the objects we work upon continues long-established practices of cataloguing and record keeping. She suggests that object digitization is distinct from digital art history, and that the latter is premised on computational processes that enable a different kind of research—one that can collect, aggregate, and analyze large sets of data. I argue that creating metadata for digital objects following the principles of Linked Open Data not only lays the groundwork for digital projects, but also constitutes a form of art-historical writing.

This chapter also aims to respond to Avinoam Shalem's call for histories of art that can account for complicated histories of belonging.[5] As Shalem points out, art historians tend to take a positivist approach to traveling objects that focuses on the latter's physical and material transformations. But how do we account for changes that happen on the level of an object's "anima" to use Shalem's term? Or as he puts it "the thoughts that objects carry with them."[6] Shalem proposes a radical revision of writing art histories to reflect the ways that objects can change conceptually in different contexts irrespective of material transformation. When metadata is created according to the principles of Linked Open Data for the digital surrogates we make, our objects of study become part of a flexible information network better suited to documenting traveling objects that do not fit neatly into a single cultural narrative.

The case study I present here is drawn from a project that investigates questions about cross-cultural exchange that are raised when copies of multiples—prints or medals—are found in many lands across the globe at the same time. I focus on a portrait medal first struck in 1693 to commemorate Louis XIV (r.1643–1715) and the Bourbon dynasty (Figures 24.1 and 24.2). Medals such as this did not have just one but many lives that unfolded through the various journeys that each different copy made around the world. Extant copies of that medal rarely underwent drastic physical change. But when such objects travel, as Shalem observed, they undergo a metaphysical transformation and accrue new meanings as they pass from one culture to another.

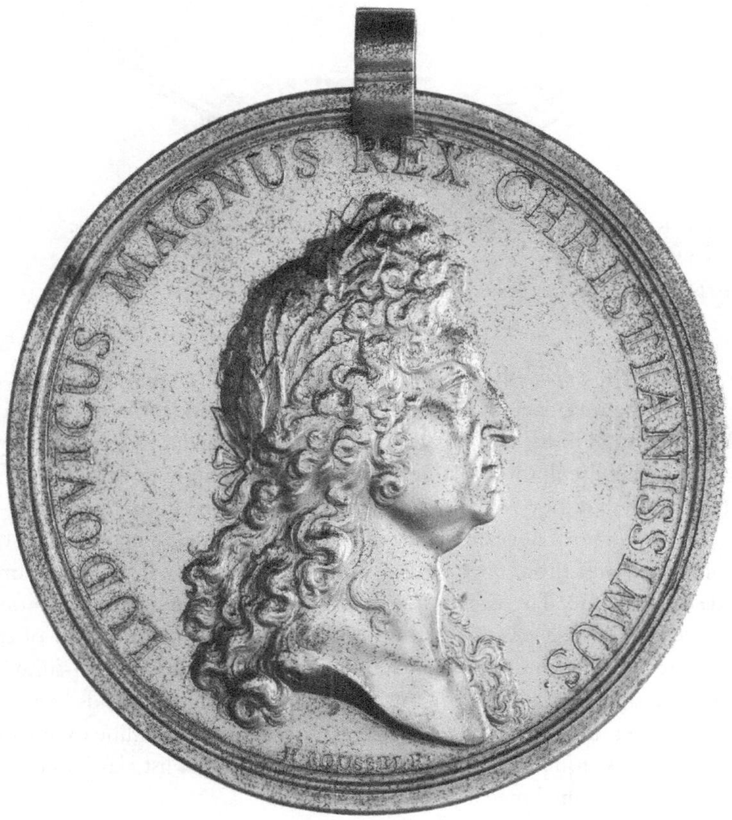


*Figure 24.1* *Felicitas Domus Augustae* [The Joy of the Royal House], c. 1700, silver medal, 75 mm (diameter).
*Source*: American Numismatic Society. See http://numismatics.org/collection/1908.277.1.

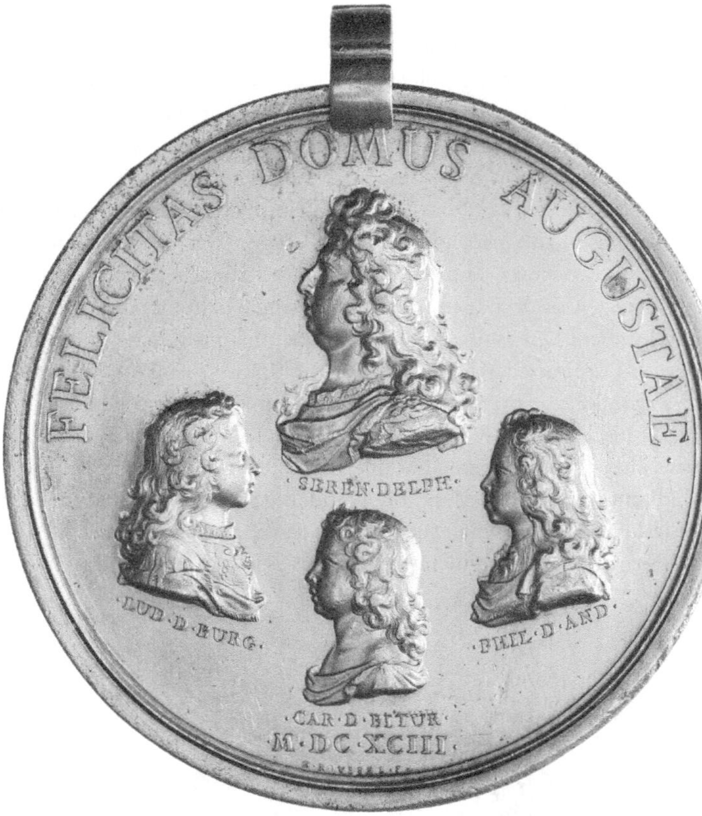


*Figure 24.2* *Felicitas Domus Augustae* [The Joy of the Royal House], c. 1700, silver medal, reverse side, 75 mm (diameter).

*Source*: American Numismatic Society. See http://numismatics.org/collection/1908.277.1.

With the example of the *Famille Royale* medal I aim to show that the vocabularies and ontologies that we use for the metadata of digitized objects lay the foundations for collaborative, multivalent, and multicultural histories of art that challenge the hegemony of our discipline.

Medals are hand-held sculptures that belong to the same family of objects as those awarded for excellence or valor, but they were not always made to be used in that way. Coin-like but not currency, they include a portrait of an illustrious figure on one side, and an image on the other, with inscriptions that link those portrayed to events, extols their virtues, or records the plans that they made in perpetuity. The *Famille Royale* medal carries a Latin inscription on the reverse, "*felicitas domus augustae*" ("the joy of the royal house"), referring to the birth of the grandson that promised to secure the Bourbon dynasty. Inscriptions make medals well-suited to keyword searches online and a Google search for the medal under discussion finds copies in different materials (bronze, silver, and gold), and in various sizes, with links to online catalogues for museums and auction houses around the world. The first record in that list classifies this very French object as an American colonial medal.[7]

Searching the online catalogue (MANTIS) of the American Numismatic Society (ANS) reveals a similar problem, with different copies of the same medal designated as either French or Canadian.[8] This confusion arises from the practice of French colonists gifting the *Famille*

*Royale* medal to First-Nations allies to bind them to their interests in the late seventeenth and early eighteenth centuries. Those warriors proudly wore their French medals about their necks as a sign of martial valor. But what constitutes a true First-Nations medal? Is it a medal with a proven history of First-Nations ownership, or a medal of the same design as that presented to First Peoples? Does a French medal cease to be French and become American or Canadian once a history of First-Nations ownership has been established? It seems reasonable to suggest that the *Famille Royale* medal could be both French *and* Canadian/American. However, our cataloguing protocols often force us to choose a culture to which an object belongs.

It might come as a surprise to learn that these arcane objects are ideally suited to discuss the potential of the Semantic Web. Indeed, the particular problems posed by numismatic study that needs to account for thousands of objects dispersed over many collections have inspired some of the most advanced and successful experiments with Linked Open Data. The American Numismatic Society (ANS) hosts a number of innovative online resources for the study of coins and medals, including *Online Coins of the Roman Empire* (OCRE), and *Online Greek Coinage* (*OGC*) for ancient coins, and *Art of Devastation: Medallic Art of the Great War* for medals of the first World War.[9] Linked Open Data projects such as these are built from the ground up from high quality, standardized data—a mode of history making founded on a systematic approach to the digitization of cultural objects.

When a digital record is made for a work of art or an artifact of material culture, a new informational surrogate is created for the real-world object. Anne Gilliland usefully defines these surrogates as "information objects."[10] All information objects, regardless of their material or immaterial counterparts, comprise data and metadata. The distinction between those two terms is somewhat fluid. However, we might define "data" as information for the general human user often expressed as figures or text or attached files such as images. "Metadata" is data about that data, which might appear as keywords; the titles, dates, and sizes of files; or phrases written in a programming language (code) that a computer can read more easily.[11] The purpose of metadata is to link the digital information objects that we create to broader information networks so that they are easier for others to find and to use. All of the data recorded for an information object can be mined by search engines when it is made available online.

"Linked Open Data" is the term used for "a set of techniques to represent and connect structured data on the Web."[12] The ultimate aim is to "make the World Wide Web into a global database."[13] The guiding principle is to use the Five Star criteria of Linked Open Data to make information openly available online.[14] The Five Star criteria call for the use standardized metadata vocabularies and unique identifiers for individual referents called Uniform Resource Identifiers (or URIs) to automatically link the information an individual creates to a pre-existing and ever-expanding network. These URIs are often expressed as a stable web address (URL) at which detailed information can be recorded about the concept, property, or object in question. URLs provide a stable point of connection that can be used in other databases to ensure that there is no ambiguity about which particular person, thing, subject, or concept to which a digital record refers.

Resources have been developed to create stable URIs for general, non-discipline specific concepts such as people (viaf.org) and places (geonames.org). The Getty Vocabularies are the gold standard for discipline-specific terms within art history.[15] It is considered best practice to reference recognized standard vocabularies and to ensure that concepts are linked to a broad, multidirectional information network. The URI provided by the Getty *Union List of Artist Names Online* for noted patron of the arts, Louis XIV, in turn points to VIAF.[16] Similarly, a standard vocabulary for numismatic concepts has been developed collaboratively by experts and with six thousand field-specific terms published by *Nomisma*.[17]

Most Linked Open Data projects begin with a column-oriented database or spreadsheet with a set of standard field names to record the material and abstract properties of objects.[18] The protocols for developing a digital numismatic catalogue have been established by a panel of leading experts as the *Numismatic Description Standard* (NUDS).[19]

*Online Coins of the Roman Empire* (OCRE) uses Linked Open Data to build a sophisticated online corpus of Roman Imperial coinage.[20] The project draws upon data sets of twenty American and European collections that have been formatted according to the standardized categories and vocabularies developed by NUDS and *Nomisma*. The standardization of these data sets allows OCRE users to find and compare similar coins from among many thousands that have been catalogued in a matter of moments. One of the real benefits of the standardization of metadata in this way is that the reach of the project will grow when more digital collection records are reconfigured to conform to the same digitization standards. This project is an excellent example of how metadata modeled along Linked Open Data principles can aggregate digital surrogates to create virtual super collections freely available to users around the globe.

ANS has created URIs for objects listed in their online catalogue, *MANTIS*, including three copies of the *Famille Royale* medal. While these objects all share the same design, they are different sizes, struck from different metals, and perhaps most confusingly catalogued as belonging to different geographic regions: 'France' for the silver copy, and 'Canada' for the two bronze copies. This is not so strange if we recall that this particular medal was a popular and highly coveted reward for the First-Nations People who allied themselves with the French settlers in Canada. But the *Famille Royale* medal was generic enough to be suitable for various occasions. Copies were also gifted to an African Prince, Aniaba of Assinie, and to Shah Soltan Hossayn of Persia.[21] How should we decide, then, which geographic region these medals belong to? If there is evidence that a particular copy traveled to Canada, should we list its origin, or its destination as the geographic region? The benefit of documenting an object following the principles of Linked Open Data is that it does not require us to choose only one geographic location. Indeed, there is no limit to the number of places that can be linked to a digital information object using Resource Description Framework (RDF) triples.

Anyone can make their research Linked-Open-Data ready by using standard vocabularies and URIs in research databases. However, creating truly linked data for digital projects requires the assistance of a programmer or someone well-versed in the computer programming languages used to link URIs together to make statements that are more meaningful to computers. While it is beyond the parameters of this chapter to describe RDF data models in detail, it does help to understand the basic principle of the RDF triple as it is the standard way to model Linked Data "behind the scenes" of the user-friendly online platforms that are designed for users to navigate.

RDF is based on simple phrases that express a particular property or quality of the subject of the phrase. The statement "this medal was minted in Paris, France" would be expressed in RDF as follows: This medal (subject)—was minted in (predicate)—Paris, France (object). For Linked Data, the subject, predicate, and object of the phrase must be expressed as URIs. Using the silver *Famille Royale* medal in the ANS collection as an example, the elements of the phrase expressed in URIs would be:

http://numismatics.org/collection/1908.277.1 (subject)
http://nomisma/ontology/hasMint (predicate)
www.geonames.org/2988507/paris.html (object)[22]

Expressing this phrase in URIs not only implies meanings behind words that rest somewhere between common knowledge and rarefied expertise, it links these concepts to stable expert definitions that can be retrieved at the URLs provided.

There is no limit to the number of RDF triples that can be added to the metadata that we create for digital object surrogates, allowing researchers to record the various cultures that have a stake in certain traveling objects. If we can prove that the silver copy of the *Famille Royale* medal held by the ANS was once owned by a First-Nations family (doubtful), that might be expressed using the predicate concept "provenance" defined by Dublin Core, and by the Getty Art and Architecture Thesaurus online. Should we have evidence of this particular medal passing through other hands, or being in other places, we can create more links as necessary.

Extant copies of the *Famille Royale* medal are often made to carry the burden of the lives of all the medals of that design. This issue was bought sharply into focus when a gold copy of the *Famille Royale* medal from the collection of the Bibliothèque nationale de France was placed on display at an exhibition in 2018 at the Palace of Versailles and in the Metropolitan Museum of Art in New York to represent all of the medals gifted to international allies during the Sun King's reign. In this case, there has been a category shift from the particular example of the medal to the design type. Likewise, it is misleading to catalogue the bronze strikes of that medal held by the ANS as Canadian medals, as no bronze medals were sent to Canada to be given to First-Nations allies. Only three to four gold medals were awarded to Abenaki chiefs, and the rest (one hundred or more) were silver. Whether or not those bronze strikes of the *Famille Royale* medal once belonged to First-Nations People, we still want to use them to tell the story of French colonial relations with the First People of Canada. As historians, curators and collectors, we want to connect these bronze strikes to the fascinating multiple lives of medals of the same design in a meaningful way, without giving a false impression of their provenance.

One way to address this problem would be to create a new digital record that aggregates all copies of the *Famille Royale* medal as a set (or type), with a URI that could be assigned to all of the medals that carry the same design. The URIs for object types like this are typically defined at the project level. OCRE uses the existing ten-volume "type catalogue," *Roman Imperial Coinage*, as a standard reference work to establish permanent identifiers through the "type numbers" recorded in that catalogue. A silver denarius of Augustus catalogued as 2a in the second edition of the first volume of *Roman Imperial Coinage* has been given the URI: http://numismatics.org/ocre/id/ric.1(2).aug.2A. Every example of that coin that has been found in the data sets of contributing organizations can be linked to this URI and displayed on a single page on the *Numishare* platform.[23]

There is no standard published complete catalogue of Louis XIV medals, which explains why the *Famille Royale* medal has been miscatalogued in American and Canadian collections. Instead, American collections and auction houses have used another standard reference: C. Wyllys Betts, *American Colonial History illustrated by Contemporary Medals* (1894).[24] The Betts catalogue fails to recognize multiples uses of the *Famille Royale* medal outside the American and Canadian context and privileges an outdated conception of the role that design played in American colonial history. The first step to resolving this problem and opening this medal to multiple potential cultural perspectives is to create a digital record that defines it as a design type with a stable URI that can then be referred to using the Dublin Core predicate dc:hasVersion to establish that this is an edition of a multiple. This could be applied to records for all of the known examples of this medal recorded in collections, or in historical inventories, regardless of whether they remain extant.

Implementing design types for Louis XIV medals as a recognized Linked Data standard requires collaboration with institutions who hold examples of them. Each institution would need to re-model the metadata for its medals to link to the new type records. Modeling digital records along Linked Open Data principles does not automatically connect a project to all online digital surrogates of the objects studied, but it does provide a framework for collaboration with institutions. Ensuring that data is modeled using recognized vocabularies for names, concepts and places would help programmers to query other data sets published in the Linked Open Data format and to make meaningful connections for research.

For RDF phrasing to work in a way that will facilitate the querying of data and to find meaningful relationships between digital surrogates, the relationships between metadata concepts that are referenced must be structured as an ontology. For Linked Open Data, the term ontology is used to refer to the categories of data ("classes") and the structural relationships between them ("properties"). If one imagines an ontology as an information network, "classes" are the nodes (the categories of "subjects" and "objects" of an RDF triple), and "properties" are the vectors (RDF "predicates"). Ontologies classify things, properties of things, and the abstract ideas related to them according to a particular viewpoint or field of expertise. There are many existing ontologies that are used for documenting cultural objects, and like the standard vocabularies just noted, these range from the general to the particular.[25] Many consider it best practice for Linked Open Data projects to use pre-existing terminology described in these existing ontologies to ensure that data will have the broadest reach and efficacy. The FOAF ("friend of a friend") ontology is commonly used to describe people, their personal details and their relationships to other people, and Dublin Core to describe things. Ontologies are by no means mutually exclusive and new ontologies should only be developed where there is no pre-existing class-property relationship modeled elsewhere. These new ontologies should build upon pre-existing ones to expand the potential network of ideas. The Nomisma ontology was developed by numismatists in an attempt to map out all of the ideas related to coins and medals that were not found in other general ontologies.

It might seem that this strict need for standardization in the modeling for Linked Open Data leads to the kind of cultural homogeneity that privileges the English language and Western structures of thought that we are trying to avoid. But on the contrary, the intrinsically collaborative way that ontologies are developed for Linked Open Data provides an exciting opportunity for multivalence, nuance, and ambiguity that is needed for situating objects in a global context.

Ontologies might be described as representing a particular worldview. The Nomisma ontology understands numismatic objects through the lens of the principles of an area of specialist study. It maps out a series of concepts that are of particular interest to numismatists, such as "coin wear" (the wear on an item as a result of its use) or "die wear" (the evidence of wear on the die that struck the coin as a result of its use), that might not occur to those approaching coins and medals from outside the discipline. These are the particular concepts that us help to understand numismatic objects that have been developed within the discipline over the last four centuries. The Nomisma ontology is, thus, a cultural expression that constructs a way of thinking about coins and medals from the perspective of the field of numismatics developed in the West since the sixteenth century.

As a thought experiment, let us imagine an ontology developed for the study of coins and medals that classifies these objects from the perspective of First Nations People whose ancestral lands were once occupied by French colonists. What concepts and properties would be necessary to classify a silver strike of the *Famille Royale* medal awarded to a Wendat chief in the early eighteenth century? As a scholar born in England in the twentieth century with no Wendat heritage, and very little firsthand experience of their language and culture, it would not only be extremely difficult for me to reconstruct such an ontology, it would also be unethical. The challenge of reconstructing historical and cultural worldviews from the outside is a critique levelled at Erwin Panofsky's influential theories about the study of art.

Panofsky's method of iconology, that measures formal analysis with deep historical and contextual research in order to learn about cultural meanings that images convey, has quite rightly been described as the foundation of our discipline.[26] His method requires an extraordinary depth of archival research, the mastery of languages, and a level of erudition that might preclude many from practicing his techniques as well as he did. Panofsky's ideal art historian is a lone agent, an erudite scholar who amasses a vast body of cultural knowledge from immersion in the artifacts of that culture for the purpose of analyzing not only the appearance of objects, but also the cultural and intellectual network into which they can be placed. The global turn in our discipline shines a light on the shortcomings of this methodology. Panofsky's call for scholars to reconstruct the *Weltanschauung* (worldview) of the culture that produced an object of study attempts the impossible, as we cannot assume to inhabit the worldview of another. Moreover, the notion of a single homogeneous worldview fails to capture the true nature of human cultures which are complex, multivalent, and networked. Linked Open Data can provide a necessary corrective to Panofsky's method.

We will need to work collaboratively to develop of new ontologies for Linked Open Data with those who hold a cultural stake in the artifacts we study. An ontology that maps the concepts and properties of an object from a Wendat perspective requires direct engagement with that First-Nations community, and with scholars who have made it their life's work to study the Algonquin language. The Wendat ontology would comprise "classes" and "properties" based on Algonquin linguistic terms and described in relation to local cultural ideas. What I am proposing is a radical expansion of standard vocabularies to incorporate non-English language terms and concepts not as variants of English words, but as separate conceptual nodes in our information networks.

The idea of a "multilingual Semantic Web" has become an important topic of discussion in the Semantic Web community.[27] One of the greatest challenges facing those who want to facilitate the querying of Linked Open Data across languages will be the trap of false equivalence and untranslatability. On the contrary, it will be essential to preserve cultural concepts in local languages within our vocabularies and ontologies to affirm the cultural sovereignty of the people who hold an historical stake in the shared artifacts of material culture. These concepts can be linked and cross-referenced by specialists who are more familiar with the ways that cultural ideas relate to objects. Indeed, that practice of inscribing metadata into the digital surrogates surely counts as a nuanced form of history writing well-suited to addressing the problems raised by global histories of art.

Those working on traveling objects with complicated histories of belonging must advocate for the development of distinct but interrelated vocabularies and ontologies authored collaboratively with a range of cultural interest groups that record specific cultural ideas, and conceptual taxonomies using local language terms. For my study of diplomatic gifts presented on behalf of Louis XIV to visitors, collaborators, and allies outside Europe, I see the potential to develop vocabularies and ontologies with colleagues in Canada, North America, China, Persia, Turkey, Thailand and North Africa that will allow the medals that I study to be viewed from many cultural perspectives. Working collaboratively, we can incorporate multivalent readings of objects of study into the metadata of the digital surrogates that we will publish online. These digital records should be created following the principles of Linked Open Data, so that they can be accessed freely and assessed from a variety of cultural perspectives.

A collaborative, multi-cultural approach to documenting the things we research can help us to decolonize the archive and to make cultural treasures available to all communities who have a vested interest in them. As William Hagan has put it in relation to the crisis of First-Nations historical identity in North America, "to be an Indian is having non-Indians control the documents from which other non-Indians write their version of your history."[28] The development of Linked Open Data vocabularies and ontologies cannot fix the problem of First-Nations

Peoples' access to their cultural materials that are held in collections outside their communities, but it may go some way to ameliorating the problem. By attributing stable definitions to cultural ideas and placing these terms within the very fabric of the digital surrogates that we create for objects, we would be acknowledging the multiple lives of those objects and paying respect to the people who are connected to them. Linked Open Data provides us with an exciting opportunity to develop our research with the participation of previously marginalized sectors of our community.[29]

While direct engagement between researchers and community groups would be ideal, providing a tool for users to add their own metadata tags on public platforms of the digital projects that we publish online will also help to expand the vocabularies and ontologies that we develop for cultural objects. "Folksonomies"—the term given to these user-generated descriptors—are an important aspect of community engagement in the cultural sector. Online resources such as *Trove* published by the National Library of Australia allows registered users to generate their own keyword tags for objects that they find online.[30] User-generated indexing systems such as this have the potential to expand community engagement with our research that could function effectively as a feedback process overtime. It is quite feasible that folksonomies developed for our objects online will broaden the horizons of our research and provide us with a greater insight into the kinds of questions that we need to address.

We are often faced with the challenge of writing histories of traveling objects such as these without the objects themselves as they are so often lost, destroyed, or radically changed from phases of reuse over time. The multiple copies of portrait medals that I work on has ensured their survival, but has presented other interesting conundrums. This chapter has focused on the challenges of documenting multiples, specifically Louis XIV medals, as objects with many lives. I have argued that Linked Open Data provides a framework for recording information about these objects that allows for many layers of interpretation. I would go so far as to say that documenting objects with existing stable vocabularies and ontologies is a complex collaborative form of history writing, and one ideally suited to our current methodological predicament. The standardization protocols required of Linked Open Data might threaten to homogenize our data to conform to a single cultural narrative. But the potential to develop new vocabularies and ontologies that incorporate non-English language terms, concepts, and conceptual taxonomies that build upon this system offers an exciting corrective to the Western and anglophone bias of our discipline.

The metadata that we create with URIs and RDF triples "behind the scenes" of the digital projects published online can link these objects in the complex and multidirectional ways that are required for placing these objects within a global context. However, the challenge remains as to how to present these objects on a user-friendly platform that allows the viewer to understand the layers of cultural meaning with which such objects are imbued. The Numishare platform developed at the ANS for OCRE and other numismatic projects offers an excellent model to inspire more creative ways to publish our research online.

Objects with multivalent histories are not well suited to traditional research outputs presented as arguments in conference papers, written articles, or books. The need to present simultaneous histories of traveling objects could easily appear to be a confusing mix of equivocation in those formats. I would like to propose that a screen-based interface that draws upon Linked Open Data provides a better alternative. An interactive interface that incorporates maps and multiple tabs to allow users to navigate the cultural trajectories of these objects might be one way to approach this. The interface should encourage user-generated content to incorporate a participatory approach to documenting cultural objects. By making the ontology of concepts and properties for each of the objects documented explicit in the publication of our research, we can explore our cultural biases and reveal the particular worldview that we bring to our studies of the many lives of traveling objects.

## Acknowledgment

My thanks to the editors and to Terhi Nurmiko-Fuller for her expert advice on the topic of Linked Open Data.

## Notes

1. 2018 marks the fortieth anniversary of the publication of Edward Said's landmark study *Orientalism,* which helped to expose the Western bias of our discipline, and forty-two years since the release of the first Apple computer. Edward W. Said, *Orientalism* (New York: Vintage, 1978).
2. Arjun Appadurai, ed., *The Social Lives of Things Commodities in Cultural Perspective* (Cambridge: Cambridge University Press, 1988); Bill Brown, "Thing Theory," *Critical Inquiry* 28, no. 1 (2001): 1–22; Barry Flood, *Objects of Translation: Material Culture and Medieval 'Hindu-Muslim' Encounter* (Princeton, NJ: Princeton University Press, 2009); Thomas DaCosta Kaufmann, Catherine Dossin, and Béatrix Joyeaux-Prunel, *Circulations in the Global History of Art* (Farnham and Burlington: Ashgate, 2015); Daniela Bleichmar, and Meredith Martin, "Introduction: Objects in Motion in the Early Modern World," *Art History* 38, no. 4 (2015): 604–19.
3. Said, *Orientalism*; Linda Nochlin, "The Imaginary Orient," *Art in America* 71, no. 5 (1983): 118–31, 187–91; Bleichmar and Martin, "Introduction."
4. Johanna Drucker, "Is There a 'Digital' Art History?" *Visual Resources* 29, no. 1–2 (2013): 5–13.
5. Avinoam Shalem, "Histories of Belonging and George Kubler's Prime Object," *Getty Research Journal* 3 (2011): 1–14.
6. Ibid., 2.
7. NGC Coin Collectors Society, accessed August 18, 2018, https://coins.www.collectors-society.com/wcm/coinview.aspx?sc=7923.
8. American Numismatic Society, MANTIS, accessed August 18, 2018, http://numismatics.org/search/results?q=felicitas+domus+augustae+AND+department_facet%3A%22Medal%22&lang=en.
9. Each of these projects uses the *Numishare* platform developed by Ethan Gruber. See American Numismatic Society, accessed August 18, 2018, http://numismatics.org/resources/.
10. Anne J. Gilliland, "Setting the Stage," in *Introduction to Metadata*, ed. Murtha Baca, 3rd ed. (Los Angeles: Getty Publications, 2016), accessed August 18, 2018, www.getty.edu/publications/intrometadata/setting-the-stage/.
11. See ibid.
12. David Wood, Marsha Zaidman, Luke Ruth, Michael Hausenblas, and Tim Berners-Lee, *Linked Data: Structured Data on the Web* (Shelter Island, NY: Manning, 2014), xix; see also Tim Berners-Lee, "Linked Data," World Wide Web Consortium, 2006, accessed August 18, 2018, www.w3.org/DesignIssues/LinkedData.html.
13. Wood et al., *Linked Data*, xix.
14. For the Five Star criteria of Linked Open Data, see Terhi Nurmikko-Fuller, "Publishing Sumerian Literature on the Semantic Web," in *CyberResearch on the Ancient Near East and Neighboring Region: Case Studies on Archaeological Data, Objects, Texts, and Digital Archiving*, eds. Vanessa Bigot Juloux, Amy Rebecca Gansell, and Alessandro Di Ludovico (Leiden: Brill, 2018), 336–63.
15. Getty Research Institute, *Getty Vocabularies,* accessed August 18, 2018, www.getty.edu/research/tools/vocabularies/.
16. Getty Research Institute, "Louis XIV," *Union List of Artists Online*, accessed August 18, 2018, http://vocab.getty.edu/page/ulan/500122256; "Louis XIV," Virtual International Authority File, accessed August 18, 2018, http://viaf.org/viaf/268675767.
17. Nomisma, accessed August 19, 2018, http://nomisma.org/.
18. The *Online Greek Coinage* project has provided an excellent model of a column-oriented spreadsheet for ancient coins that can easily be adapted for other numismatic objects: accessed August 18, 2018, www.greekcoinage.org/handbook-for-authors.html.
19. Numismatic Description Standards (NUDS), accessed August 18, 2018, http://nomisma.org/nuds.
20. Online Coins of the Roman Empire (OCRE), accessed August 18, 2018, http://numismatics.org/ocre/.

21. Robert Wellington, "Médailles en mouvement: la réception des médailles de Louis XIV à la croisée des cultures," in *Le Médailles de Louis XIV et Leur Livre*, dir. Yvan Loskutoff, trans. Y. Loskutoff (Mont-Saint-Aignan: PURH, 2016).
22. For a more detailed explanation of the way in which RDF is expressed as code, see Wood et al., *Linked Data*. For the RDF querying language SPARQL, see Bob DuCharme, *Learning SPARQL Querying and Updating with SPARQL 1.1*, 2nd ed. (Sebastopol, CA: O'Reilly, 2013).
23. See DuCharme, *Learning SPARQL Querying and Updating with SPARQL 1.1*. For Numishare, see Ethan Gruber, *Numishare Blogspot*, accessed August 18, 2018, http://numishare.blogspot.com/p/about-numishare.html.
24. Charles Wyllys Betts, *American Colonial History Illustrated by Contemporary Medals* (New York: Scott Stamp and Coin Company, 1894).
25. See the excellent glossary of metadata standards and accompanying chart published online by Jenn Riley: Jenn Riley, *Seeing Standards: A Visualisation of the Meta Universe,* accessed August 18, 2018, http://jennriley.com/metadatamap/.
26. Michael Ann Holly, *Panofsky and the Foundations of Art History*, 7th ed. (Ithaca, NY: Cornell University Press, 2006).
27. Paul Buitelaar and Philipp Cimiano, eds., *Towards the Multilingual Semantic Web Principles, Methods and Applications* (Berlin: Springer, 2016).
28. William Hagan, "Archival Captive—The American Indian," *The American Archivist* 41, no. 2 (April 1978): 135–42.
29. Katie Shilton and Ramesh Srinivasan, "Participatory Appraisal and Arrangement for Multicultural Archival Collections," *Archivaria* 63 (2007): 87–101.
30. National Library of Australia, Trove, accessed August 18, 2018, Trove.nla.gov.au; for folksonomies, see G.G. Chowdhury and Schubert Foo, eds., *Digital Libraries and Information Access: Research Perspectives* (London: Facet Publishing, 2013), 32–33.

## Bibliography


American Numismatic Society. Accessed August 18, 2018. http://numismatics.org/resources/.

Arjun Appadurai, ed. *The Social Lives of Things Commodities in Cultural Perspective*. Cambridge: Cambridge University Press, 1988.

Berners-Lee, T. "Linked Data." World Wide Web Consortium, 2006. Accessed August 18, 2018. www.w3.org/DesignIssues/LinkedData.html.

Betts, C. W. *American Colonial History Illustrated by Contemporary Medals*. New York: Scott Stamp and Coin Company, 1894.

Bleichmar, D., and M. Martin. "Introduction: Objects in Motion in the Early Modern World." *Art History* 38, no. 4 (2015): 604–19.

Brown, B. "Thing Theory." *Critical Inquiry* 28, no. 1 (2001): 1–22.

Buitelaar, P., and P. Cimiano, eds. *Towards the Multilingual Semantic Web Principles, Methods and Applications*. Berlin: Springer, 2016.

Chowdhury, G. G., and S. Foo, eds. *Digital Libraries and Information Access: Research Perspectives*. London: Facet Publishing, 2013.

DaCosta Kaufmann, T., C. Dossin, and B. Joyeaux-Prunel. *Circulations in the Global History of Art*. Farnham and Burlington: Ashgate, 2015.

Drucker, J. "Is There a 'Digital' Art History?" *Visual Resources* 29, no. 1–2 (2013): 5–13.

DuCharme, B. *Learning SPARQL Querying and Updating with SPARQL 1.1*. 2nd ed. Sebastopol, CA: O'Reilly, 2013.

Flood, B. *Objects of Translation: Material Culture and Medieval "Hindu-Muslim" Encounter*. Princeton: Princeton University Press, 2009.

Getty Research Institute. *Getty Vocabularies*. Accessed August 18, 2018, www.getty.edu/research/tools/vocabularies/.

Gilliland, A. J. "Setting the Stage." In *Introduction to Metadata*. Edited by Murtha Baca. 3rd edition (Los Angeles: Getty Publications, 2016).

Gruber, E. Numishare Blogspot. Accessed August 18, 2018. http://numishare.blogspot.com/p/about-numishare.html.

Hagan, W. "Archival Captive—The American Indian." *The American Archivist* 41, no. 2 (April 1978): 135–42.

Holly, M. A. *Panofsky and the foundations of art history*, 7th ed. Ithaca, NY: Cornell University Press, 2006.

National Library of Australia. Trove: Trove.nla.gov.au. Accessed August 18, 2018.

Nochlin, L. "The Imaginary Orient." *Art in America*, 71, no. 5 (1983): 118–31, 187–91.

Nomisma. Accessed August 18, 2018. http://nomisma.org/.

Numismatic Description Standards (NUDS). Accessed August 18, 2018. http://nomisma.org/nuds.

Nurmikko-Fuller, T. "Publishing Sumerian Literature on the Semantic Web." In *Cyberresearch on the Ancient Near East and Neighboring Region: Case Studies on Archaeological Data, Objects, Texts, and Digital Archiving*, edited by Vanessa Bigot Juloux, Amy Rebecca Gansell and Alessandro Di Ludovico, 336–63. Leiden: Brill, 2018.

*Online Coins of the Roman Empire* (OCRE). Accessed August 18, 2018. http://numismatics.org/ocre/.

*Online Greek Coinage*. Accessed August 18, 2018. www.greekcoinage.org.

Riley, J. *Seeing Standards: A Visualisation of the Meta Universe*. Accessed August 18, 2018. http://jennriley.com/metadatamap/.

Said, E. W. *Orientalism*. New York: Vintage, 1978.

Shalem, A. "Histories of Belonging and George Kubler's Prime Object." *Getty Research Journal* 3 (2011): 1–14.

Shilton, K., and R. Srinivasan. "Participatory Appraisal and Arrangement for Multicultural Archival Collections." *Archivaria* 63 (2007), 87–101.

Virtual International Authority File (VIAF). Accessed August 18, 2018. http://viaf.org/viaf/268675767.

Wellington, R. "Médailles en mouvement: la réception des médailles de Louis XIV à la croisée des cultures." In *Le Médailles de Louis XIV et Leur Livre*, dir. Yvan Loskutoff, trans. Y. Loskutoff. Mont-Saint-Aignan: PURH, 2016.

Wood, D., M. Zaidman, L. Ruth, M. Hausenblas, and Tim Berners-Lee. *Linked Data: Structured Data on the Web*. Shelter Island, NY: Manning, 2014.

# 25

# IMAGE PROCESSING AND COMPUTER VISION IN THE FIELD OF ART HISTORY

*Nuria Rodríguez-Ortega*

Art history is, to a large extent, the history of the forms and systems of production and circulation of images of cultural artifacts. The crucial connection between the founding period of art history in the nineteenth century and the invention of photography has been highlighted within the discipline. However, in this timeline, we must also include: the circulation of prints and engravings, which, for many years, were the primary means of knowing, ordering, and analyzing artistic-cultural production; and language itself, which, through the descriptions associated with the *ekphrasis* genre, provided some of the earliest images—mental imagery in this case—of the artifacts described.

If we also consider that one of the central discourses of art history has made visual matter a primary subject of study, and, consequently, that vision has become one of the main cognitive mechanisms of art historians, it is easy to understand why one of the hopes for the field resides in image processing and computer vision technologies. Until recently, these technologies have had limited applications in art history, but developments in the ability of computer algorithms to process images (especially in the field of computer vision), deep learning techniques (a branch of the artificial intelligence revolution), increases in hardware processing capacity, and an ever-growing amount of visual data open up new paths of exploration. We are witnessing a turning point in digital art history to the extent that we are now able to directly process visual information rather than metadata, which has been the fundamental focus to date.

The field is still emerging, with studies that are more experimental than conclusive in their results. Yet, this new scenario deserves special attention for two reasons: (1) it opens up a rich field of research possibilities, locating the history of the culture of images that we have called "art history" in a new order of scale and complexity; and (2) it entails important intellectual challenges that impel us critically to reconsider our object of study, the methodological principles on which research about art images has rested thus far, and the visual-formal problems that have concerned us for centuries. Without delving into technical details, the purpose of this paper is to provide insight into this field, considering both perspectives from an art historian's point of view and debating some key issues that might shape art historians' agenda in coming years.[1]

## Overview of Current Applications in the Field of Art Images

A short overview of the possibilities of visual-formal analysis provided by image processing technologies outlines the promising future of artistic-visual studies.[2] These technologies

(Convolutional Neural Networks (CNN), computational pattern recognition, visual instance retrieval, etc.) are able to automatically recognize specific motifs, objects, figures, details, or particular image regions in large iconographic collections, and to select and group images accordingly;[3] to perform semantic-level predictions, that is, to recognize object categories, human body postures, and activities in a scene;[4] to detect visual-formal similarities and differences in large sets of images;[5] to quantify and measure the degree of similarity and difference between images;[6] to find visual-formal patterns in large image corpora;[7] to calculate and rank visual complexity grades:[8] to group images according to visual family resemblance;[9] to measure and rank low-level (e.g. color, texture, brightness, shadow) and high-level (e.g. movement, facial expression, interactions) visual features; and many others.

Many of these technologies have found applications in the optimization of processes of automatic classification or pre-classification of large sets of images;[10] the detection and categorization of pictorial styles;[11] the detection of copies, duplicates, and derived images in repositories and collections;[12] and the detection of painting's date of production. Likewise, they are being used for authentication and attribution, applying methodologies that closely follow the stylometric techniques used in the fields of linguistics and literature studies for authorial attribution.[13] In all these cases, the final purpose is the implementation of computational tools not only intended to support art historians' activities, but also to provide additional objectivity derived from quantitative and computational processes.

Beyond these computer-aided practices, the introduction of image processing technologies in art history also enables us to address issues that are part of the intellectual and critical concerns of the discipline and that are not alien to the methodologies that have guided the analysis of images since the early nineteenth century. For example, these technologies enable the investigation of the combinatorial mechanism that underlies image-building practices during specific time periods. Elizabeth Honig and her team, as part of their ongoing Brueghel Catalogue Raisonné Project,[14] are using these techniques to analyze the intricate web that comprises the thousands of paintings, prints, and drawings produced in the Brueghel family workshop, where copying, variations in the same formal schemes, and the production of compositional patterns using individual motifs was a systematic practice (see Figure 25.1).[15] To the extent that the methods employed in this project can be used to analyze other artists and periods, the results will help

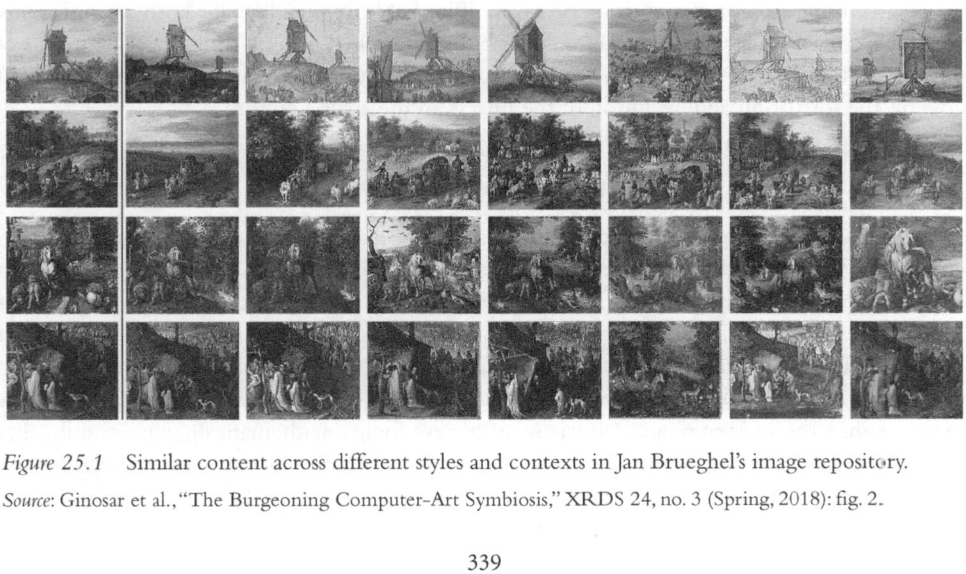

*Figure 25.1* Similar content across different styles and contexts in Jan Brueghel's image repository.

*Source*: Ginosar et al., "The Burgeoning Computer-Art Symbiosis," XRDS 24, no. 3 (Spring, 2018): fig. 2.

develop a new perspective on ideas regarding originality, creativity, and invention as triggering mechanisms of the image-production process.

The possibility of detecting the reuse of similar elements in diverse images that range over time and space will allow us to place artworks in a much broader framework of comparison; delve into the visual genealogy of paintings; explore the mobility of visual elements; track the circulation of patterns and motifs; analyze processes of cultural re-appropriation of forms, figures, and patterns; examine mechanisms through which the same visual elements produce different meanings when they are placed in different context;[16] retrace the evolution of a specific pictorial motif and its variants; reconstruct connections between workshops and artists; unveil image transmission networks;[17] and explore the material conditions that make possible such transmission (e.g. when image processing techniques are able to discriminate between similar prints produced by different woodblocks).[18]

The possibility of tracking similarities and changes in motifs, visual structures, and compositions over time and unveiling the patterns that have shaped our visual culture[19] allow us to address issues about the evolution, transformation, or persistence of taste and the perception of beauty; and bring to an unprecedented scale Warburg's investigations of the persistence of the images or Kubler's investigations about the serialization of images.[20] It also assists in examining discuss processes of canonicity or mainstreaming according to the greater or lesser concentration of similar images in collections.[21]

The ability to discover the essential forms and compositions that underlie the variety of images that constitute visual culture through processes of mathematical abstraction allows us to explore fundamental concepts that have shaped the intellectual tradition of art history. Thus, for example, the project completed by the Uruguayan visual artist Vladimir Muhvich, *Engrama*, recovers the Warburgian notion of "cultural engram"[22] to analyze the latent visual-formal schemes in certain collections of images.[23] To do this, Muhvich generated models of morphological and evolutionary visualization of the collections on the basis of clustering information under mathematical models which are displayed in the topography of a graph (Figure 25.2).

Within this framework, *The Origin of Forms in Art* (1965), where Read affirmed that artistic forms can be formalized and reduced to certain shapes, also comes to mind. Even more, we might explore the idea of visual universals, namely the visual-formal units that are the basis of the configuration of artistic images and perhaps of our cognitive structures—those through which we understand the world. Such explorations echo Riegl's general laws[24] and the neo-Kantian stylistic categories systematized by Wölfflin.[25] Not coincidentally, both art historians' works have been used as theoretical frameworks by researchers aiming to discover by means of physico-mathematical principles, to which I will return in the following sections, the logic that governs the formation and evolution of the images of the artistic culture.[26]

## Critical and Intellectual Debates

Along with new research opportunities, the introduction of image processing algorithms and computer vision techniques entails significant intellectual challenges for art historians. Such technologies necessitate epistemological and methodological redefinitions of the way images are understood and analyzed, and this demands critical inquiry. This task is not new because art history has frequently had to construct methodologies for visual-formal analysis and to develop theories about the nature of cultural images and their functioning—a task that we must now locate within the epistemological horizon of a new logic (mathematical), a new rationality (algorithms), and a new scale. I will briefly examine the issues that I consider most relevant and that will require attention in the coming years.

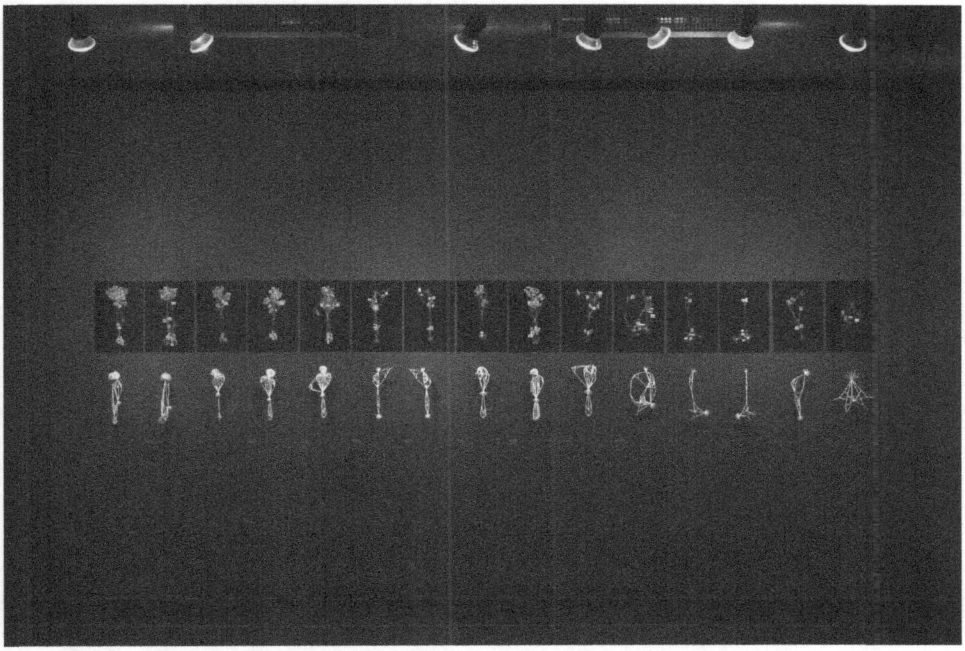

*Figure 25.2* Vladimir Muhvich. Proyecto Engrama Oficial del Campo del Arte Uruguayo II, Montevideo, Uruguay 2015.

*Source*: © Photograph: Martin De Rossa.

## The Matter of Quantification

The theoretical-scientific approaches that conceptualize the act of seeing as a series of information processing tasks[27] and the ontological shift implied in the nature of the digital image (our new object of analysis) have profound effects. Although the reconstitution of the image on a screen can obscure this, digital images are simply a mass of information in the form of bytes and pixels, a binary code of numbers. The visual features of cultural artifacts, when digitized, are transformed into visual data, which are numerical values that can be algorithmically computed and segmented into discrete information units. This ontological shift entails a dramatic change in the way we understand images considering that, until now, images have been presented to our consciousness as visual entities unto themselves.[28]

It is important to be aware of this transformation because sometimes the words we use to name phenomena and the rhetoric we employ to explain them can be confusing or misleading. As Harald Klinke notes, "the computer knows no image, only numbers. It does not 'see'—it only calculates."[29] Or perhaps we could better say that the way computers see is by calculating. It is therefore crucial to consider that image processing algorithms are mathematical equations and that computer vision, based on mathematical models of human visual perception, is designed to extract data from the real world and to transform it into numerical or symbolic information.[30]

This ontological change implies that the image becomes a mathematical problem. So, one of the key questions that we have to face is how to adequately describe an image in mathematical terms. Correspondingly, formal-visual analysis becomes a problem of quantification, mathematical calculation, and measurement. This is why the style of an artist can now be defined as a statistical model of visual characteristics and the image as a statistical set of visual features. This quantitative perspective also means that investigations based on image processing focus on visual features that are easily quantifiable (such as color saturation, brightness, brushstrokes, and texture) and that physical–mathematical concepts (such as fractal dimension, entropy, and roughness exponent) are increasingly used to describe the structures, visual configuration of images, and their historical evolution.[31]

Consequently, the aspects of visual-formal analysis of images that formerly concerned us are now dissected according to mathematical logic. For example, in the research by Lee et al.,[32] the question posed by the authors was: How do color contrast relations evolve in Western pictorial production over a long period of time (from the fourteenth century to the present)? This question is not completely new in the field of art history, but the approach was. To answer this question, the authors designed an algorithm to compute the inter-pixel color distances' differences. This resulted in a quantity called "seamlessness (S)," which measures the color contrast and becomes a useful indicator to track the stylistic evolution of Western painting (see Figure 25.3).[33]

This physical-mathematical translation implies a new formulation in quantitative terms of concepts that are part of the epistemic tradition of art history (see, for instance, the mathematical models developed in relation to the concepts of influence,[34] artistic creativity,[35] style,[36] beauty,[37] and so on). Simultaneously, it is producing an epistemological expansion to the extent that new categories are being built to explain phenomena observed through the algorithmic computation of images. In consequence, we are witnessing the emergence of a new categorical system of a mathematical and physical nature. Consider, for example, the concept of "metamorphosality" resulting from the application of the S measurement. "Metamorphosality" (a quantity that measures the degree of transformation of chromatic contrasts throughout an artist's career whether in positive terms (more color contrasts) or in negative terms (less color contrast)) enables comparisons to be made among artists according to this parameter. This formula is nothing less than a new category for interpreting artistic practice and creative processes and the evolution of visual culture. Likewise, new categories are emerging to order and classify visual-formal artifacts, such as those associated to fractality values and complexity measures.[38] I will return to this point in the next section.

This formulation of new categories for visual-formal analysis has raised controversies and critical discussions.[39] Consider the mathematical formalization of creativity proposed by Elgammal and Saleh in 2015:[40] If one of the two variables of the mathematical model proposed by the authors to measure the degree of creativity of image production is the capacity of an image to resonate in images produced later, is the idea of creativity being modeled or is this closer to

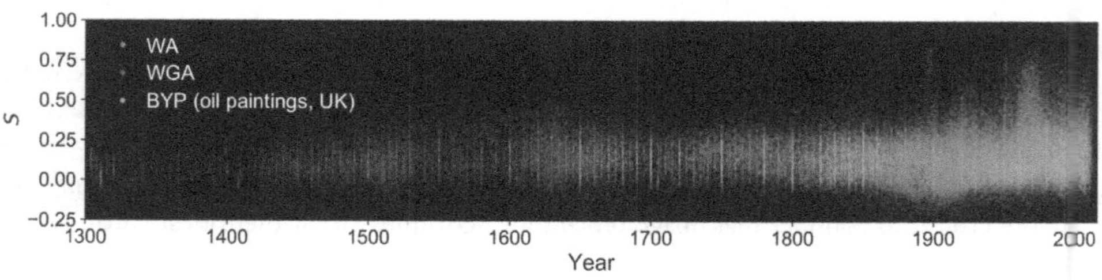


*Figure 25.3* Scatter plot of S from 1300 CE to 2400 CE. An increase in the average and the variance of S is observed.

*Source*: Lee, B., D. Kim, S. Sun, H. Jeong, and J. Park. "Heterogeneity in Chromatic Distance in Images and Characterization of Massive Painting Data Set." *PLoS One* 13, No. 9 (2018), e0204430. https://doi.org/10.1371/journal.pone.0204430, fig. 4b.

the notion of impact? Is the ability to influence others a *sine qua non* variable of creativity? We do not know whether this resonance derives from causal lines of real influences because this information is not provided by algorithmic processing; these might be autonomous, parallel occurrences without connection to each other, as sometimes occurs in complex systems. How many assumptions are being applied, then, in the interpretation of the results and in the building of the model itself? Are we simultaneously validating a paradigm of chronological sequence as an interpretation of the visual-formal dynamics of artistic imagery when using this paradigm as the basis of a mathematical model?

Similar arguments could be made regarding the research conducted by Kim et al.[41] In this study, different image processing techniques were used to quantify changes in the variety of painted colors and their spatial structures over time, producing remarkable conclusions about the historical development of colors. However, the *a priori* use of ten historical periods of Western paintings to demarcate the evolution of color (taking as a base the "traditional stylistic classification of Art History") involves projecting a certain schema that determines the research and its interpretation. Meanwhile, key concepts, such as the concept of style itself and its ability to describe and or explain the visual-formal evolution of artistic images,[42] remained uninterrogated.

As algorithms, mathematical models, and metrics have become a fundamental part of interpreting a world driven by the continuous flow of data, it is vital that art historians be involved in the development of a new understanding of images based on statistical methods, mathematical models, algorithmic indexes, and metrics. This allows us to quantitatively and qualitatively characterize visual structures and features that expand our comprehension of cultural imagery. The exploration of the appropriate measures and formal models to characterize visual structures and their features should be one of the main tasks of the art historian's future agenda. Such work needs to be undertaken in close collaboration with mathematicians, computer scientists, physics, and experts in computer vision and data science.

Maintaining this critical discussion and interdisciplinary exchange is fundamental because the analysis derived from the application of algorithms, metrics, and mathematical formulas is not only quantitative, but also qualitative. Every mathematical formalization implies a conceptual model—that is, an intellectual construction through which the domain of reality that is being modeled (its entities, variables, functions, parameters, and relationships) is represented. If we are talking about formal–visual analysis within the framework of art history, what is implicit in these analyses is a certain theory about the image, the evolution of imagery, and modes of vision. This is why analysis based on the computational processing of images should be considered not only as the application of mathematical, physical, and/or statistical formulas, but as a theoretical construction of what could, and perhaps should, emerge as a new image and visuality theory. It also demands awareness of the epistemological and ideological determinations that are embedded in the analysis strategies we are using.

Complementarily, a new vocabulary needs to be created to name the new phenomena that emerge from image processing. It is important to elucidate new concepts in connection to existing art history epistemology, and one way to do so is to develop a vocabulary that allows us to name the phenomena that become relevant for the visual–formal analysis. Consequently, elucidation, disambiguation, and terminological clarity are also crucial tasks for art historians in the coming years.

Finally, this mathematical translation requires further reflection on how the way in which we look at images is affected. Art historians also need to adopt a critical position to think about what remains irreducible to quantification and computation[43] and what cannot be explained in quantitative terms.

## *Scale and Complexity*

The change of scale associated with the analysis of large sets of images that expand over time and space is also revolutionizing our understanding of image analysis. In this new scenario, several questions need to be considered. First, some problems concerning large-scale databases or repositories that are used as the basis of analysis must be addressed.[44] This concerns, for example, whether available data sets are sufficiently diverse from a cultural point of view to allow us to perform analyses on a truly global scale and not exclusively at the Western level. Consideration needs to be given to differences in access to image databases according to countries and regions; copyright issues; the heterogeneity of image quality grades; differences in accuracy labels; and the limited nature of many collections that are composed exclusively of images from a particular art "tradition."

Second, large-scale databases and repositories of images confront us with new possibilities of exploration that allow us to map culture on a global scale: diversity, structures (networks, clusters, relationships, etc.); dynamics (temporal changes); and variability.[45] This is what we essentially seek to uncover when we analyze large-scale image collections. Consequently, the fundamental questions of art history in relation to images and visuality must be reformulated within this broader paradigm of cultural interpretation.

In the context of visual studies, the bibliography on the new ecology of images that emerged from the explosion of visual media and the internet is vast. However, the possibility of materializing and quantifying visual connections between these images, forms, compositional structures, and motifs allows us to approach the ecology of images from the perspective of complex systems. This includes establishing degrees of proximity and similarity, neighborhoods, lines of contagion; and unveiling structures, dynamics, interactions, and logic of behavior over time through the use of mathematical models, advanced computing, simulations, and physics-inspired approaches. Thinking about visual imagery in terms of complex systems involves becoming aware that we can confront systems that are n-dimensional, nonlinear, self-organized, open, interdependent on other systems (adjacent or not), dynamic, and of increasing complexity.[46]

It is important to keep in mind that complexity is not an attribute belonging to the ontological nature of a certain reality. Complexity is a behavior that can be observed in the visual-formal configuration of a single image, in a set of images,[47] or at a large scale.[48] The approach to images and artistic forms from the perspective of complexity has been the subject of much scientific literature, most of which has been developed in Departments of Physics, Mathematics, Computer Science and Psychology. "When regarding an artistic form, the challenge to the complexity scientist is to address two basic questions: How do we define and characterize the system-theoretic fingerprints of an artistic form and how can we actually measure them?" argue physicists Boon, Casti, and Taylor.[49] However, from the point of view of art history, the question is not only a matter of quantity or measurement. The fundamental question is how complexity can provide us with renewed epistemic and methodological tools to address the intellectual problems that have been part of the tradition of art history, while also enabling us to expand our interpretative horizon and to explore new narratives.

Complex systems allow us to expand the notions of temporality that we have used to explain the evolution of images, their formal qualities, and the links between them. In an effort to build a narrative of the history of images and their features, art history has formulated operating principles, established explanatory cultural categories, and explored the causes of formal transformation. The approach of complex systems encourages the exploration of such processes, taking the evolutionary dynamics of increasing complexity and order-disorder transitions as a basis. This leads us to question whether the imagery produced by a particular artist or in a particular cultural context or temporal range evolves toward increasing complexity, insofar as the combination of elements becomes more unpredictable and random or more ordered and regular. What kind of complexity characterizes the evolution of artistic images and forms over time? What are the best measures for accounting for such complexity? What are the moments of rupture and disorder that give rise to new creation and, therefore, enable evolution and how are they produced?

In this context, the research conducted by Sigaki, Perc, and Ribeiro[50] is of interest. Applying two measures of complexity associated with the local order of the pixel arrangement in almost 140,000 visual artworks (the normalized permutation entropy and the statistical complexity), the authors built a complexity–entropy plane. This is a quantitative and qualitative space that can be understood as an order–disorder plane, where a set of artworks is located according to the average values of such measures. Figure 25.4 shows the artistic styles displayed on this plane, demonstrating a distribution that breaks the traditional narrative of stylistic sequencing and giving rise to new forms of organization.

Networked systems that emerge from algorithmically computed visual-formal connections generate a framework of spatial and morphological analysis that is not historical in the chronological sense. The questioning of time as a sequential structure is by no means new in the field of art history. Examples include Warburg's transchronology positioning,[51] Didi-Huberman's critical revision,[52] and Moxey's notion of heterochronies.[53] In addition, numerous artistic facts challenge the narrative of time as a succession.[54] The acknowledgment of the existence of formal breaks

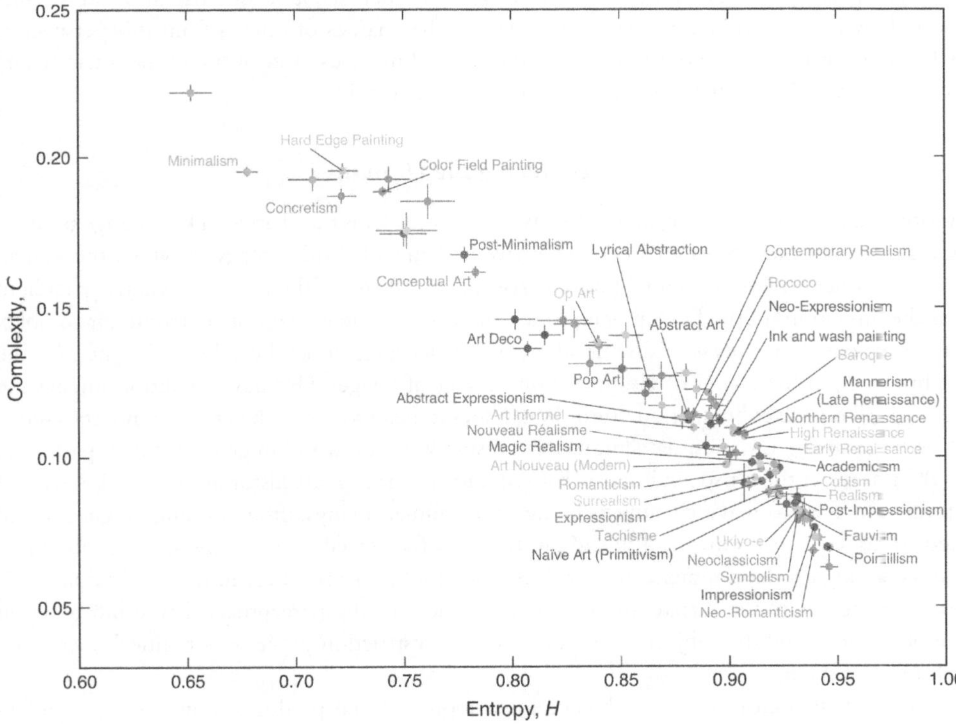


*Figure 25.4* Distinguishing among different artistic styles with the complexity–entropy plane.

*Source*: Sigaki, Higor Y.D., Matjaz Perc, and Haroldo V. Ribeiro. "History of Art Paintings Through the Lens of Entropy and Complexity." *PNAS* 115, no. 37 (July 19, 2018): fig. 2.

and discontinuities call into question the paradigms of chronological sequencing and causality, chains of influence, the resolution of formal problems, and genetic succession or formal genealogies. What the science of complexity and its related theories offer us are methodological and epistemological tools to interpret these qualitative leaps, such as the notion of "emergence," already applied to explain social phenomena.[55]

As noted earlier, the interpretation of the networked systems built from visual connections between images is based on interpreting the clustering set's distribution or the graph's morphology. In a graph or set of clusters, similarities or differences between images are based on values of distance calculated mathematically in a metric space. There are, however, also related to the position of the elements and their established spatial relationships. The geographical and geopolitical space in which images and forms circulate becomes, therefore, a qualitative and symbolic space that is constructed by the images themselves in their continuous process of interaction.[56] Thus, interest shifts from the characteristics or attributes that define the images as entities in themselves to the functional dimensions and interactions through which the space of image is configured and reconfigured.

Complexity science and its related theories[57] open up a wide range of research lines, offering models and theories to analyze not only the transformation of simple forms into qualitatively more complex forms, but also the discontinuities, bifurcations, leaps, and occurrences that cannot be explained from the point in view of classical logic. However, it is the responsibility of art historians to determine the limits of these models and theories. Some analyses based on fractal geometry (which explains natural phenomena very well) do not serve to explain cultural, social, or visual behavior.[58] Yet, if formal and mathematical models account for structures and dynamics underlying the world we inhabit, approaching the analysis of images from this perspective will help us to understand our universe better and will make us more aware of the intricate and evolving network of structures and connections that comprise it.

## Decentering the Human

Another fundamental transformation that we must consider is the change in knowledge production systems. In our post-digital era, these have become a hybrid ecology in which the human being no longer holds the central position. Assuming the end of the encephalocentric paradigm (i.e. the limitations of the human brain to see, understand, and explain the dynamics of complex processes) entails a process of disembodiment and decentering of the subject (in our case, the art historian) as the center of vision and interpreter of images. This new condition implies the need to ask ourselves broader questions: What does it mean to see in the era of computer vision? Where is human vision resituated in its relationship with the world in general and, in particular, to the images of the artistic culture? What will our new role as art historians be in a knowledge production system in which human beings, non-human beings, programming languages, and algorithms are equally involved in the production of knowledge about visual materials? Thus, the technological developments of our time place the problems of art history and visual studies at the center of the debate: the problem of vision, of the perceptual relationship between the object seen and the subject who sees, and the construction processes—political, social, and cultural—of the gaze.

Since technological devices influence ideas about cultural production and generate different visual paradigms,[59] the mediation of artificial devices creates new spaces for critical discourse. Although some theoretical approaches posit that the way machines see is objective, computer vision is not neutral. It, too, is constructed vision. The artificial gaze is not subject to the conditions of human perception or its subjectivities, but other mechanisms come into play:

Algorithms that follow certain criteria or the set of images used for deep learning techniques are just two examples.

I previously referred to the selection mechanisms used by Google Images as a factor to be considered in the process of building visual imagery in the twenty-first century.[60] The situation has become more complicated given the ubiquity and opacity of artificial devices that process millions of images on the internet. This gives rise to new responsibilities. For example, photography platforms are programmed to select images from the millions that are shared daily by users according to automated evaluation technologies based on artificial intelligence. These technologies aim to estimate the aesthetic quality of the image without any user involvement (Automatic Aesthetic Quality Estimation). This task of evaluation, through which a certain average aesthetic rating is assigned to a photo, implies the definition of a good photograph and the qualities that make it so.[61] Part of image processing is based on millions of data points contributed by users according to elements that they find attractive or aesthetically rewarding. The final result depends, however, on a non-transparent algorithm that determines certain aesthetic evaluation criteria as valid. Consequently, we are not only witnessing the construction of a system of aesthetic values and taste based on the logic of algorithms, but also a scenario that compels us to think of these new aesthetic forms as a new cultural hegemony that is transferred through artificial intelligence systems. It is necessary to explore the channels (institutional, formal, informal, etc.) through which they circulate, how this hegemonic aesthetic system is reinforced as artificial devices continue learning from the new inputs contributed by users, and how this new scenario will affect the concept of aesthetics and its perception.

Given the constructed nature of artificial vision, the processed images returned to us by neural networks or computer vision algorithms constitute a determined interpretation of the processed visual materials that are subjected, in turn, to numerical transformation in the course of digitalization. Art historians will later focus on this visual material that has already been "interpreted." What then emerges is an interpretative-hermeneutic dynamic that becomes more complex because humans and artificial devices are involved in its articulation. Some may argue that the photographic images on which the work of art historians was based during the nineteenth century and a good part of the twentieth century are also interpretations of the cultural artifacts they represent. This is so, but it is important to remember that it is the human eye and brain that operate behind a camera which has no capacity for autonomous choice.

Mediation by artificial vision devices requires us to understand how artificial intelligence and computer algorithms work. It forces us to ask ourselves how the intellectual mechanisms that we have traditionally used to analyze, categorize, classify, and interpret art-historical images change when they are conducted by algorithmic calculations and neural networks without direct human interaction. The good news is that understanding how artificial intelligence works and how algorithms and neural networks develop their understanding of images may be fruitful for the field of art history and for enhancing our comprehension of the behavioral logic of artistic visual culture.

First, computer vision confronts us with what occurs in the precognitive stage of vision—what happens before culturally weighted cognition affects visual perception. In the pre-cognitive stage, shadows, surfaces, areas, shape limits, etc. are recognized. These visual characteristics are essential to distinguishing a human form from an object, as we can now see through the functioning of neural networks. The systems of image analysis developed in the context of the Western theory of art history had considered visual-cognitive perception, so should we now also incorporate this other pre-cognitive dimension? In this sense, Harald Klinke[62] has proposed expanding the layers of analysis on Panofsky's triadic scheme. Yet this question requires further reflection.

Second, these technologies also compel us to rethink crucial concepts in visual analysis. I am not only referring to art-historical concepts (e.g. the notion of style transformed into a statistical model of visual features as mentioned earlier), but more essential concepts such as similarity or analogy that are key components of the logic that underlies computer vision analysis. This is not a trivial question if we consider that the task of finding similarities and differences among images is the basic intellectual activity upon which art history is built. The capacity of algorithms and computer techniques to analyze complex information allows us to consider many more visual features than our human brain can process. Consequently, art historians now have the opportunity to explore more deeply variations of "similarity." However, as Mathew Lincoln has stated,[63] we first need to understand what similarity means in computational terms. We need to understand the notions of similarity, difference, proximity, and resemblance as seen through neural networks and algorithms.

Third, insofar as technologies advance without human supervision, we also need to reflect on how the artistic-visual universe will change once concepts traditionally used for image classification or description are replaced by computational processes. For instance, how do we confront the units, patterns, correlations, and visual regions generated by computer vision algorithms that exceed the traditional notions of forms, motifs, and topoi that have formed the basis of our image analysis to date?

Despite a possible destabilization of our traditional visual regimes, these new ways of seeing have a heuristic value of which we should take advantage. The ways in which algorithms see, interpret, and classify images draws attention to visual-formal aspects that have hitherto gone unnoticed. In turn, these visual units, observed as a whole and grouped according to their degree of similarity, acquire new meaning. As Pilar Rosado[64] has demonstrated through her research on Miquel Planas's work, these units configure the creator's visual vocabulary, and their combinatorial patterns help us to understand his creative process (see Figure 25.5). Thus, computer vision algorithms entail the emergence of a new formal vocabulary and a new method of cataloging, recording, or ordering. These tasks can, however, only be completed in collaboration with artificial devices that will generate the visual units on which we will work in the coming years

Examining how algorithms or neural networks see leads us to rethink our own observation processes. In this way, the hermeneutic-critical system to which I referred previously becomes an iterative cycle: The observation of images as they are seen by artificial intelligence modifies our own way of observing and transforms our visual understanding. One of the aims of the Cátedra Picasso Fundación Málaga of the University of Málaga, is to use computer vision techniques for the purpose of analyzing developments in Pablo Picasso's drawings that comprise his *Album* 7.[65] The key question that triggered the research arose when we saw the first output delivered by the neural network. We asked ourselves what changes in our modes of perception and visual comprehension occur when the morphology of Picasso's drawing is analytically segmented into its formative attributes (see Figure 25.6). The result was a new observational process based on the analysis and categorization of graphic and formal units within Picasso's sign vocabulary and the exploration of its combinatorial logic and transitions to more complex forms. The comparison between the result of human observation and that of artificial observation will be the first research output of the project and the basis of the methodological process.

The comparison between how human cognition is configured and how computational devices produce knowledge provides an unprecedented opportunity to deepen the mechanisms of vision. It also enables us to unravel different cultural and epistemological layers that intersect in human seeing. For example, grouping images into dendrograms not only enables a sort of visual phylogenetic reconstruction of objects, but also challenges the criteria used by the algorithm to elucidate the patterns and/or relationships that go unnoticed by the human eye.

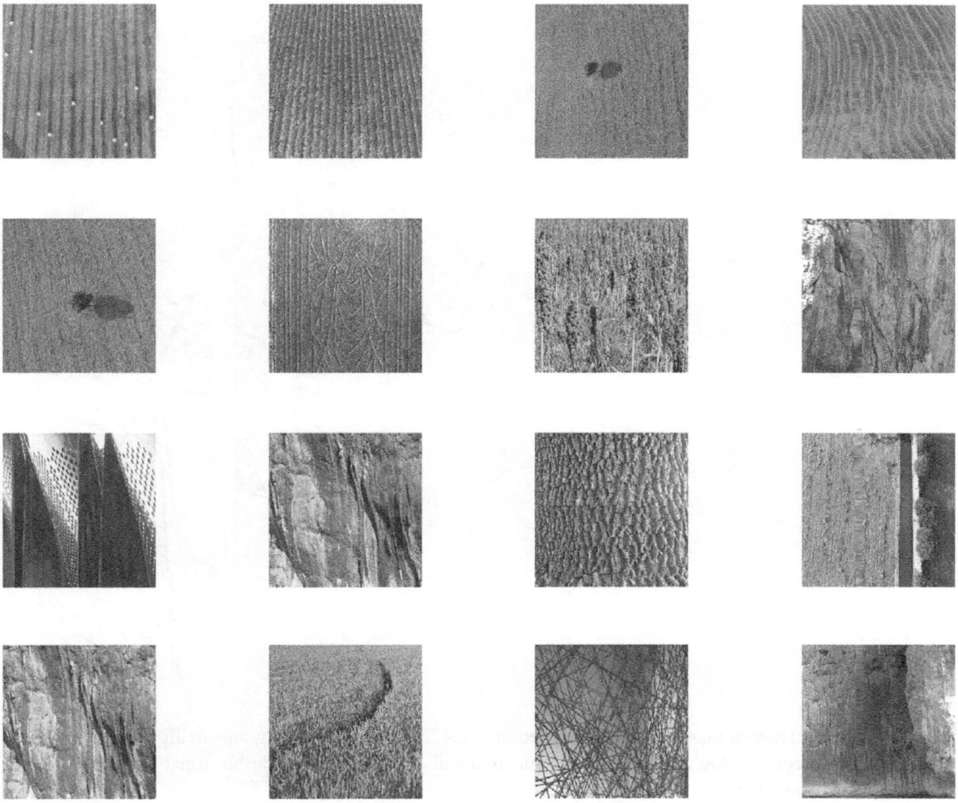

*Figure 25.5* Set of sixteen images grouped by the visual appearance "Vertical irregular textured" in Miquel Planas's photograph collection.

*Source*: Rosado Rodrigo, Pilar. "Formas latentes: protocolos de visión artificial para la detección de analogías aplicados a la catalogación y creación artística." PhD dissertation, Universidad de Barcelona, 2015: fig. 3.31.

And fourth, collaborating with experts in computer vision within the framework of deep learning interpretability (the research field devoted to unraveling neural networks and algorithms) may be of interest for art historians who wish to understand the features that shape artistic imagery and provoke its changes over time. In so doing, researchers participate in the building of a future "explainable artificial intelligence" (XAI).[66] Researchers may also create their own models of computer vision based on theories of vision that facilitate the exploration of ways of seeing in other historical-cultural periods. An example is the recent prototype developed by Leonardo Impett based on seventeenth-century theories of vision.[67]

On the other hand, the logic underlying image processing and computer vision techniques based on strictly visual and morphological criteria is producing a sort of neoformalism or neovisualism in the field of art history. This includes the recovery of formalist theories embedded in the foundations of the discipline and that have been widely discussed and revised, such as those of Wölfflin or Riegl. We have the opportunity to write histories of visual morphologies independently of social, cultural, and historical contexts, and independently of the semantic determinations attached to language that have traditionally accompanied the images. However, we have critically to consider the consequences of these trends. We know that ways of seeing, morphologies, and notions of similarities and differences are imbricated in a complex network

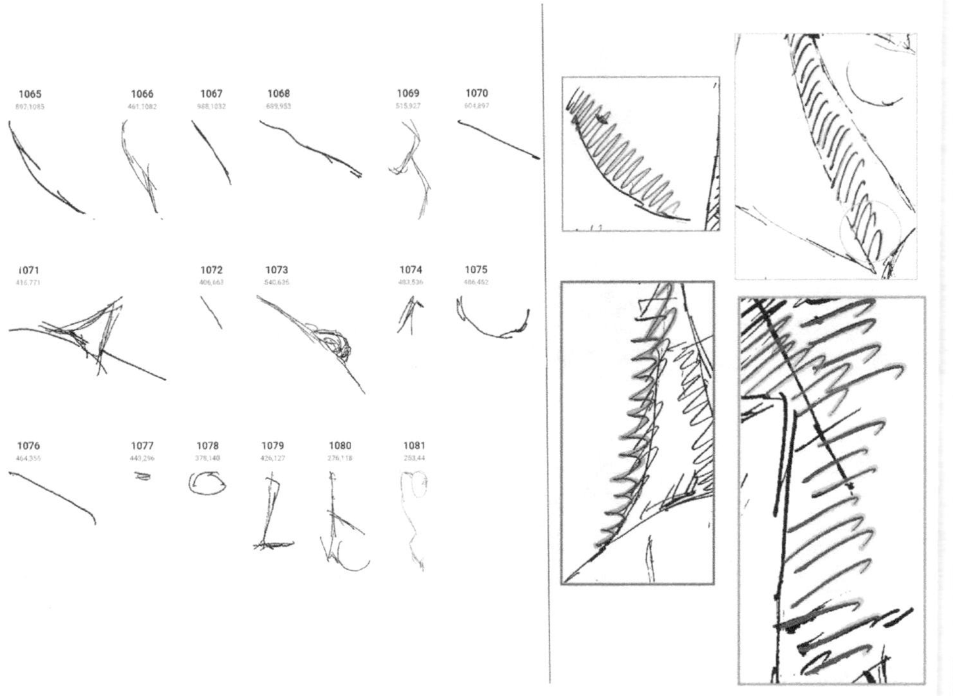


*Figure 25.6* Left: Segmentation of Picasso's drawing L47R (Album 7) using an intelligent system of edge detection. Right: eye-detected and manually colored basic graphic units in Picasso's Album 7 drawings.

*Source*: © Cátedra Picasso Fundación Málaga.

of meanings that exceed the merely visual. Therefore, we must also foster a critical discussion about the orientation of art history in the immediate future: whether toward a lost culture (due to the way machines now work), or, conversely, whether human beings should operate as a bridge that links visual-contextual knowledge to purely quantitative-algorithmic knowledge. Perhaps a conciliation between the computational rationale and the human hermeneutic perspective is the key. In reality, this conciliation will anchor art historians in their role of unveiling cultural factors that underlie visual structures currently generated by algorithms.

The emergence of neoformal approaches have to be included in a broader redefinition of the epistemology of art history which is moving toward a formal-visual, topological epistemology based on the heuristics of generative images' morphology.[68] The processing of millions of informational units, variables, and parameters requires readable, intelligible interfaces for human beings. Diagrams, charts, and data visualizations of all kinds are becoming the common language of art-historical research when approached from a computational perspective, and they are fundamental material for interpretative–hermeneutic work.

If computer systems are capable of analyzing the multiple variables inscribed in images in ways that the human brain cannot, and if image ecosystems can be projected in multiple directions and in an infinite number of dimensions from the perspective of complex systems, it is necessary to think in terms of a new n-dimensional space (or high-feature space, in Lev Manovich's words).[69] Such a space surpasses the three-dimensional Euclidean space in which we are used to considering art images and other cultural artifacts. This compels us to address the problem of how to visualize multidimensionality without resorting to a dimension reduction, as usually currently occurs. Dimension reduction implies selecting which variables or dimensions are projected, and this confronts us with traditional problems of cultural criticism and the politics of representation. However, we must also be mindful of the impossibility of representing the totality. The question arises, therefore, as to how to achieve an equilibrium in the context of these new representational practices.

Some visualizations or meta-images (as Klinke[70] calls them, following the terminology proposed by W.J.T. Mitchell) that are being produced also raise an interpretative problem. Many of them are still just visual artifacts to play with or upon which to speculate. We still have much work to do to explore their epistemic potential and their capacity to express a theory or new construction of the visual. In this sense, we might try setting these new images in the tradition of visual epistemology that is already present in the discipline. Warburg is the first example that comes to mind, but a systematic investigation of theoretical-epistemic constructions based on visual practices could help us to discover other examples and to outline a new historiographical narrative to explain the construction of discourses about images and modes of visuality over the last two centuries.

## Conclusion

In conclusion, I suggest that four questions need to be considered: (1) how images of cultural artifacts are transformed into units of computable information; (2) how the visual material that constitutes those cultural artifacts are represented in quantifiable binary code (visual data); (3) how these transformed images and visual materials coexist in an expanded field with thousands of other transformed images; and (4) how human vision is subjected to a process of decentering and disembodiment.

Within this new research scenario, computational image processing techniques provide us with an opportunity to reconnect with concepts and approaches that have been key components of nineteenth- and twentieth-century art history. Thus, art historians now have an invaluable toolkit at their disposal to explore the intellectual dialectics (transformation–persistence, sequence–simultaneity, variation–unity, diachrony–structure, and discontinuity–continuity) of visual forms, matters that have long been preoccupations of art history. These techniques also lead to broader questions about how we know, see, understand, and relate to the world. Perhaps we are now in a position to respond to the question of whether the visual-formal traits through which we identify an object are universal and objective or depend on systems of cultural representation.

Simultaneously, experimentation in close collaboration with mathematicians, experts in computer vision, and computer scientists promises fruitful avenues to redefine our understanding of images and visual culture. It also generates the possibility of a hybrid knowledge field intermediated by heterogeneous, but complementary disciplines.

The techniques and methodologies discussed in this chapter also impel us to take a critical position that involves investigating new art-historical epistemology and intellectual inquiries. Computational image processing techniques must serve as critical tools to reassess the practices, concepts, and assumptions that we have used to date in the analysis of artistic images instead of becoming a means by which perpetuate them in an uncritical way. The fundamental question to be considered is how art historians can become involved in the conversation, contributing their theoretical knowledge and points of view. A review of image processing and computer vision techniques applied to art images reveals the absence of art historians in most of the research groups.

Much of the research conducted in the field of computational image processing is guided by the ideal of transforming the exploration of images and visuality in a quantitative, scientific objective field. This involves looking for an unbiased measure of complexity in artworks as an alternative to human judgments or envisioning art history as a predictive science. These approaches are part of a trend in the field of knowledge that exceeds the limits of digital art history itself: the search for a science of culture and images based on the empirical principles of the natural, physical, and biological sciences. This approach opens up interesting lines of exploration. It is, however, also necessary to delve into the specificities of cultural, formal, and visual complexities of art image production and evolution to understand what might be the limits of these models and theories in order to explain them. Intellectual collaboration, then, becomes more necessary than ever.

Ultimately, the questions raised in this chapter draw attention to how technological materialities act as agents in the production of visual knowledge and how we need to reconcile computer reasoning and human cognition, artificial devices, and human beings. In my view, establishing spaces of convergence and collaboration is a better strategy than developing a confrontational rhetoric of human beings vs. machines. Establishing a space in which mutual feedback helps us to move toward a better understanding of ourselves as a species, of the world we inhabit, and of the culture we produce should be the main purpose of the humanist's agenda in years to come.

## Notes

1. For reasons of space, I will not address the issues related to the production of post-human images by artificial devices neither the issues related to computer creativity. Nor will I address the issues concerning the subject's aesthetic response to such images or the ability of artificial intelligence to generate images that consciously appeal to the emotionality of the viewers.
2. For a general overview of the history of the field and early applications, see David G. Stork, "Computer Vision and Computer Graphics Analysis of Paintings and Drawings: An Introduction to the Literature," in *CAIP* 2009, eds. X. Jiang and N. Petkov, LNCS 5702 (Heidelberg: Springer, 2009), 9–24; David G. Stork, Jim Coddington, and Anna Bentkowska-Kafel, eds., "Computer Image Analysis in the Study of Art," *Proceedings of SPIE*, vol. 6810 (Bellingham: International Society for Optics Photonics, 2008); David G. Stork, Jim Coddington, and Anna Bentkowska-Kafel, "Computer Vision and Image Analysis of Art," in *Proceedings of SPIE*, vol. 7531 (Bellingham: International Society for Optics Photonics, 2010); David G. Stork, Jim Coddington, and Anna Bentkowska-Kafel, "Computer Vision and Image Analysis of Art II," in *Proceedings of SPIE,* vol. 7869 (Bellingham: International Society for Optics Photonics, 2011); Benjamin Zweig, "Forgotten Genealogies: Brief Reflections on the History of Digital Art History," *Digital Art History International Journal* no. 1 (2015): 39–49.
3. Elliot J. Crowley and Andrew Zisserman, "In Search of Art," in *ECCV 2014 Workshops, Part I,* eds. L. Agapito et al., LNCS 8925 (Heidelberg: Springer, 2015), 54–74, https://doi.org//10.1007/978-3-319-16178-5_4; Ginosar et al., "The Burgeoning Computer-Art Symbiosis," *XRDS Crossroads: The ACM Magazine for Students* 24, no. 3 (Spring 2018): 30–33.
4. Joseph Schlecht, Bernd Carqué, and Bjönr Ommer, "Detecting Gestures in Medieval Images," *2011 IEEE International Conference on Image Processing, ICIP* (September 11–14, 2011): 1285–88, doi:10.1109/ICIP.2011.6115669.
5. Joon Son Chung et al., "Re-presentations of Art Collections," in *ECCV 2014 Workshops, Part I,* ed. L. Agapito et al., LNCS 8925 (Springer, 2015), 85–100, https://doi.org//10.1007/978-3-319-16178-5_6; Babak Saleh, Kanako Abe, Ravneet Sing Arora, and Ahmed Elgammal, "Toward Automated Discovery of Artistic Influence," *Multimedia Tools and Applications* 75, no. 7 (April 2016): 3565–91.
6. Stefka Hristova, "Images as Data: Cultural Analytics and Aby Warburg's Mnemosyne," *Digital Art History: International Journal* 2 (2017): 116–31.
7. Xi Shen, Alexei A. Efros, and Mathieu Aubry, "Discovering Visual Patterns in Art Collections with Spatially-Consistent Feature Learning," *arXiv:1903.02678v2* (March 8, 2019).
8. Alex Forsythe et al., "Predicting Beauty: Fractal Dimension and Visual Complexity in Art," *British Journal of Psychology* 102 (2011): 49–70, https://doi.org/10.1348/000710X498958; Daniel Kim,

Seung-Woo Son, and Hawoong Jeong, "Large-Scale Quantitative Analysis of Painting Arts," *Scientific Reports* 4, no. 7370 (December 2014): 1–7, https: //doi.org/10.1038/srep07370; Higor Y. D. Sigaki, Matjaz Perc, and Haroldo V. Ribeiro, "History of Art Paintings Through the Lens of Entropy and Complexity," *PNAS* 115, no. 37 (July 19, 2018): 8585–94.

9. Loan Tran, Poshen Lee, Jevin West, and Maximilian Schich, "Chromatic Structure and Family Resemblance in Large Art Collections," in *Digital Humanities 2018*, accessed July 10, 2019, https://dh2018.adho.org/chromatic-structure-and-family-resemblance-in-large-art-collections-exemplary-quantification-and-visualizations/.
10. Sean Yang et al., "Classifying Digitized Art Type and Time Period," in *Proceedings of International Journal for Digital Art History* (London, UK, August 2018), https://doi.org/10.1145/nnnnnnn.nnnnnnn.
11. Lior Shamir et al., "Impressionism, Expressionism, Surrealism: Automated Recognition of Painters and Schools of Art," *ACM Transactions on Applied Perception* 7, no. 2 (2010); Sergey Karayev et al., "Recognizing Image Style," *arXiv:1311.3715* (2013); Ahmed Elgammal et al., "The Shape of Art History in the Eyes of the Machine," *arXiv:1801.07729v2* (February 12, 2018).
12. John Resig, "Using Computer Vision to Increase the Research Potential of Photo Archives," *Journal of Digital Humanities* 3, no. 2 (Summer 2014), accessed July 1, 2019, http://journalofdigitalhumanities.org/3-2/using-computer-vision-to-increase-the-research-potential-of-photo-archives-by-john-resig/.
13. Patrice Abry, Herwig Wendt, and Stéphane Jaffard, "When Van Gogh Meets Mandelbrot: Multifractal Classification of Painting's Texture," *Signal Processing* 93, no. 3 (April 2013): 554–72.
14. "Brueghel Family: Jan Brueghel the Elder, The Brueghel Family Database," University of California, Berkeley, accessed July 10, 2019, http://janbrueghel.net.
15. Ginosar et al., "The Burgeoning Computer-Art Symbiosis"; Shen et al., "Discovering Visual Patterns."
16. Schlecht et al., "Detecting Gestures."
17. Benoit Seguin, Isabella di Leonardo, and Fréderic Kaplan, "Tracking Transmission of Details Paintings," in *Digital Humanities DH2017* (2017), accessed July 1, 2019, https://dh2017.adho.org/abstracts/562/562.pdf
18. Chung, "Re-presentations."
19. Byunghwee Lee et al., "Heterogeneity in Chromatic Distance in Images and Characterization of Massive Painting Data Set," *PLoS One* 13, no. 9 (2018): e0204430, https://doi.org/10.1371/journal.pone.0204430; Javier de la Rosa and Juan-Luis Suárez, "A Quantitative Approach to Beauty, Perceived Attractiveness of Human Faces in World Painting," *Digital Art History: International Journal* 1 (2016): 112–29; Kim et al., "Large-Scale"; Sigaki et al., "History of Art."
20. George Kubler, *The Shape of Time: Remarks on the History of Things* (New Haven: Yale University Press, 1962).
21. Tran et al., "Chromatic Structure."
22. 'Engram': Neurophysiological footprint in the brain that is the basis of a memory. 'Cultural engram': traces or visual symbols that are recorded in the archives of the memory of the culture.
23. "Engrama Oficial del Campo del Arte Uruguayo," accessed July 10, 2019, www.vladimirmuhvich.com/#text_block_8.
24. Alöis Riegl, *Stilfragen. Grundlegungen zu einer Geschicte der Ornamentik* (1893). Spanish translation: *Problemas de estilo. Fundamentos para una historia de la ornamentación* (Barcelona: Gustavo Gili, 1980).
25. Heinrich Wölfflin, *Kunstgeschichtliche Grundbegriffe* (1915). Spanish translation: *Conceptos fundamentales de la Historia del Arte* (Madrid: Espasa Calpe, 2007).
26. Elgammal et al., "The Shape of Art History"; Kim et al., "Large-Scale"; Sigaki et al., "History of Art."
27. Edmund T. Rolls and Gustavo Deco, *The Computational Neuroscience of Vision* (Oxford: Oxford University Press, 2002).
28. It is true that the analysis of the components—whether formal or content—that constitute an image has been part of different methodological traditions of art history, but these components were always interpreted in relation to that image as an iconic unit.
29. Harald Klinke, "Big Image Data Within the Big Picture of Art History," *Digital Art History International Journal* no. 2 (2016): 21.
30. Richard Szeliski, *Computer Vision: Algorithms and Applications* (London: Springer-Verlag, 2010).
31. Richard P. Taylor, Adam P. Micolich, and David Jonas, "Fractal Analysis of Pollock's Drip Paintings," *Nature* 399 (June 3, 1999): 422; Katherine Jones-Smith, Harsh Marthur, and Lawrence Krauss, "Drip Paintings and Fractal Analysis," *arXiv: 0710.4917v2* (October 25, 2007); Katherine Jones-Smith and Harsh Marthur, "Fractal Analysis: Revisiting Pollock's Drip Paintings," *Nature* 444 (2006): E9–E10; E. M. de la Calleja, F. Cervantes, and J. de la Calleja, "Order-Fractal Transition in Abstract Paintings,"

*arXiv: 1510.06767v3* (April 12, 2019); Jean Pierre Boon, John Casti, and Richard P. Taylor, "Artistic Forms and Complexity," *Nonlinear Dynamics Psychology and Life Sciences* 15 (April 2011): 265. See also references in note 8.

32. Lee et al., "Heterogeneity."
33. Actually, this quantity called [S] is no more than a digital extrapolation of how the artist places the color pigments spatially on the canvas.
34. Saleh et al., "Toward Automated Discovery."
35. Ahmed Elgammal and Babak Saleh, "Quantifying Creativity in Art Networks," *arXiv:1506.00711v1* (June 2, 2015).
36. Elgammal et al., "The Shape of Art History."
37. De la Rosa and Suárez, "A Quantitative Approach."
38. See references in note 8.
39. Claire Bishop, "Against Digital Art History," *Digital Art History: International Journal* no. 3 (2016): 123–31.
40. Elgammal and Saleh, "Quantifying Creativity."
41. Kim et al., "Large-Scale," 1–7.
42. The same could be said about the concepts of "creativity," "influence," "beauty," etc.
43. Nuria Rodríguez-Ortega, "Digital Art History: The Questions That Need to Be Asked," *Visual Resources* 35, no. 1–2 (March–June 2019): 6–20.
44. Together the image data sets made available by museums, large-scale image database frequently used are Web Art Gallery, Wikimedia, ImageNet, Google Art Project, WikiArt, Artsy.
45. Lev Manovich, "Can We Think Without Categories?" *Digital Culture & Society* 4, no. 1 (2018): 17–28, https://doi.org/10.14361/dcs-2018.0103.
46. Carlos Eduardo Maldonado, "¿Qué es un sistema complejo?" *Revista Colombiana de Filosofía de la Ciencia* 14, no. 29 (2014): 71–93.
47. See, for example, the application of complexity measures based on fractal dimensions to the Pollock's work or abstract paintings in general. In the case of Pollock's work, researcher observed a systematic behavior since the fractal dimension increased as a function of the year in which the paintings were painted. See references in note 34.
48. Lee et al., "Heterogeneity"; Kim et al., "Large-Scale"; Sigaki et al., "History of Art."
49. Boon et al., "Artistic Forms."
50. Sigaki et al., "History of Art."
51. Aby Warburg, *Der Bilderaltas Mnemosyne,* ed. Martin Wranke and Claudia Brink (Berlin: Akademie Verlag, 2000). Spanish translation (Madrid: Akal, 2010).
52. Georges Didi-Huberman, *Ante la imagen* (Murcia: Cendeac, 2010), first published in 1999.
53. Keith Moxey, *El tiempo de lo visual. La imagen en la historia* (Vitoria Gasteiz: Sans Soleil, 2015).
54. Among others, Audrey Rieber mentions the survivals, the anachronisms, the pseudomorfosis and the recreations. Audrey Rieber, "El arte como forma de tiempo. Algunas observaciones sobre la obra de arte y la historia basadas en relfexiones de y sobre Erwin Panofsky," in *Síntomas culturales. El legado de Erwin Panosky*, ed. Luis Vives-Ferrándiz Sánchez (Vitoria-Gasteiz: Sans Soleil, 2018), 77.
55. R. Keith Sawyer, *Social Emergence: Societies as Complex Systems* (Cambridge: Cambridge University Press, 2005).
56. See, for example, the *Gesture Atlas* developed by Leonardo Impett, Biblioteca Hertziana Digital Humanities Lab, 2019, accessed July 10, 2019, https://biblhertz.github.io/atlas/.
57. Carlos Maldonado, *Complejidad de las ciencias sociales. Y de otras ciencias y disciplinas* (Bogotá: Ediciones desde Abajo, 2016).
58. Boon et al., "Artistic Forms."
59. John Berger, *Ways of Seeing,* BBC Two (London: Penguin, 1972). Spanish translation: *Modos de ver* (Barcelona: Gustavo Gili, 1972).
60. Nuria Rodríguez-Ortega, "Mediación digital en los procesos de recepción, construcción e interpretación de la herencia cultural," in *Memoria y significado,* ed. Luis Arciniega (Valencia: Universitat de Valencia, 2013), 443–61.
61. Juan Martín Prada, *El ver y las imágenes en el tiempo de Internet* (Madrid: Akal, 2018), 125–34.
62. Klinke, "Big Image," 25.
63. Matthew Lincoln, "Holding Out for a CV Hero: The Frick Computer Vision Symposium," *Matthew Lincoln, PhD* (blog), April 18, 2018, accessed July 5, 2019, https://matthewlincoln.net/2018/04/16/holding-out-for-a-cv-hero-the-frick-computer-vision-symposium.html.

64. Pilar Rosado Rodrigo, "Formas latentes: protocolos de visión artificial para la detección de analogías aplicados a la catalogación y creación artística" (PhD diss., Universidad de Barcelona, 2015).
65. Pablo Picasso, *Album* 7 (c. May–June 1907). The set of drawings are considered to be related with the work for *Les demoiselles d'Avignon* (1907). The Album belongs to Fundación Picasso Museo Casa Natal (Málaga, Spain). Eugenio Carmona, *Picasso y la escultura Africana. Los orígenes de las Señoritas de Avignon* (Tenerife: TEA, 2010).
66. Quanshi Zhang and Song-Chun Zhu, "Visual Interpretability for Deep Learning: A Survey," *arXiv:1802.00614v2* (February 7, 2018); Leilani H. Gilpin et al., "Explaining Explanations: An Overview of Interpretability of Machine Learning," *arXiv:1806.00069v3* (February 3, 2019).
67. Leonardo Impett, "Early Modern Computer Vision," in *Digital Humanities 2019*, accessed July 1, 2019, https://dev.clariah.nl/files/dh2019/boa/0820.html.
68. Johann Drucker, *Graphesis: Visual Forms of Knowledge Production* (Boston: Harvard University Press, 2014).
69. Lev Manovich, "Data Science and Digital Art History," *Digital Art History: International Journal* no. 1 (2014): 13–35.
70. Klinke, "Big Image," 25.

## Bibliography


Abry, Patrice, Herwig Wendt, and Stéphane Jaffard. "When Van Gogh Meets Mandelbrot: Multifractal Classification of Painting's Texture." *Signal Processing* 93, no. 3 (April 2013): 554–72.

Berger, John. *Ways of Seeing*. BBC Two. London: Penguin, 1972. Spanish translation: *Modos de ver* Barcelona: Gustavo Gili, 1972.

Bishop, Claire. "Against Digital Art History." *Digital Art History. International Journal*, no. 3 (2016): 123–31.

Boon, Jean Pierre, John Casti, and Richard P. Taylor. "Artistic Forms and Complexity." *Nonlinear Dynamics Psychology and Life Sciences* 15 (April 2011): 265–83.

Chung, Joon Son, Relja Arandjelović, Giles Bergel, Alexandra Franklin, and Andrew Zisserman. "Re-presentations of Art Collections." In *ECCV 2014 Workshops*, Part I, LNCS 8925, edited by L. Agapito et al., 85–100. Springer, 2015. https://doi.org//10.1007/978-3-319-16178-5_6.

Crowley, Elliot J., and Andrew Zisserman. "In Search of Art." In *ECCV 2014 Workshops*, Part I, LNCS 8925, edited by L. Agapito et al., 54–74. Heidelberg: Springer, 2015. https://doi.org//10.1007/978-3-319-16178-5_4.

Daniel Kim, Seung-Woo Son, and Hawoong Jeong. "Large-Scale Quantitative Analysis of Painting Arts." *Scientific Reports* 4, no. 7370 (December 2014): 1–7. https: //doi.org/10.1038/srep07370.

De la Calleja, E. M., F. Cervantes, and J. de la Calleja. "Order-Fractal Transition in Abstract Paintings." *arXiv: 1510.06767v3* (April 12, 2019).

De la Rosa, Javier, and Juan-Luis Suárez. "A Quantitative Approach to Beauty, Perceived Attractiveness of Human Faces in World Painting." *Digital Art History. International Journal* 1 (2016): 112–29.

Didi-Huberman, Georges. *Ante la imagen*. Murcia: Cendeac, 2010. (First published in 1999.)

Drucker, Johanna. *Graphesis. Visual Forms of Knowledge Production*. Boston: Harvard University Press, 2014.

Elgammal, Ahmed, Marian Mazzone, Bingchen Liu, Diana Kim, and Mohamed Elhoseiny. "The Shape of Art History in the Eyes of the Machine." *arXiv:1801.07729v2* (February 12, 2018.)

Elgammal, Ahmed, and Babak Saleh. "Quantifying Creativity in Art Networks." *arXiv:1506.00711v1* (June 2, 2015).

Forsythe, Alex, Marcos Nadal, Noel Sheehy, Camilo José Cela-Conde, and Martin Sawey. "Predicting Beauty: Fractal dimension and Visual Complexity in Art." *British Journal of Psychology* 102 (2011): 49–70. https://doi.org/10.1348/000710X498958.

Gilpin, Leilani H., David Bau, Ben Z. Yuan, Ayesha Bajwa, Michael Specter, and Lalana Kagal. "Explaining Explanations: An Overview of Interpretability of Machine Learning." *arXiv:1806.00069v3* (February 3, 2019.)

Ginosar, Shiri, Xi Shen, Karan Dwivedi, Elizabet Honig, and Mathieu Aubry. "The Burgeoning Computer-Art Symbiosis." *XRDS Crossroads. The ACM Magazine for Students* 24, no. 3 (Spring 2018): 30–33.

Hristova, Stefka. "Images as Data: Cultural Analytics and Aby Warburg's Mnemosyne." *Digital Art History. International Journal* 2 (2017): 116–31.

Impett, Leonardo. "Early Modern Computer Vision." In *Digital Humanities 2019*. Accessed July 1, 2019. https://dev.clariah.nl/files/dh2019/boa/0820.html.

Impett, Leonardo, and Franco Moretti. "Totentanz: Operationalizing Aby Warburg's *Pathosforlmen*." In *Pamphlets of the Stanford Literary Lab* 16 (November 2017): 1–10.

Jones-Smith, Katherine, and Harsh Marthur. "Fractal Analysis: Revisiting Pollock's Drip Paintings." *Nature* 444 (2006): E9–E10.

Jones-Smith, Katherine, Harsh Marthur, and Lawrence Krauss. "Drip Paintings and Fractal Analysis." *arXiv: 0710.4917v2* (October 25, 2007).

Karayev, Sergey, Matthew Trentacoste, Helen Han, Aseem Agarwala, Trevor Darrell, Aaron Hertzmann, and Holger Winnemoeller. "Recognizing Image Style." *ArXiv:1311.3715* (July 23, 2014).

Klinke, Harald. "Big Image Data within the Big Picture of Art History." *Digital Art History. International Journal*, no. 2 (2016): 14–36.

Kubler, George. *The Shape of Time: Remarks on the History of Things*. New Haven: Yale University Press, 1962.

Lee, B., D. Kim, S. Sun, H. Jeong, and J. Park. "Heterogeneity in Chromatic Distance in Images and Characterization of Massive Painting Data Set." *PLoS One* 13, no. 9 (2018): e0204430. Accessed July 5, 2019. https://doi.org/10.1371/journal.pone.0204430.

Lincoln, Matthew. "Holding Out for a CV Hero: The Frick Computer Vision Symposium." *Matthew Lincoln, PhD* (blog), April 18, 2018. Accessed July 5, 2019. https://matthewlincoln.net/2018/04/16/holding-out-for-a-cv-hero-the-frick-computer-vision-symposium.html

Maldonado, Carlos Eduardo. *Complejidad de las ciencias sociales. Y de otras ciencias y disciplinas*. Bogotá: Ediciones desde Abajo, 2016.

———. "Qué es un sistema complejo?" *Revista Colombiana de Filosofía de la Ciencia* 14, no. 29 (2014): 71–93.

Manovich, Lev. "Can We Think Without Categories?" *Digital Culture & Society* 4, no. 1 (2018): 17–28. https://doi.org/10.14361/dcs-2018.0103.

———. "Data Science and Digital Art History." *Digital Art History. International Journal* no. 1 (2014): 13–35.

Martín Prada, Juan. *El ver y las imágenes en el tiempo de Internet*. Madrid: Akal, 2018

Moxey, Keith. *El tiempo de lo visual. La imagen en la historia*. Vitoria Gasteiz: Sans Soleil, 2015.

Resig, John. "Using Computer Vision to Increase the Research Potential of Photo Archives." *Journal of Digital Humanities* 3, no. 2 (Summer 2014). Accessed July 1, 2019. http://journalofdigitalhumanities.org/3-2/using-computer-vision-to-increase-the-research-potential-of-photo-archives-by-john-resig/.

Rieber, Audrey. "El arte como forma de tiempo. Algunas observaciones sobre la obra de arte y la historia basadas en relfexiones de y sobre Erwin Panofsky." In *Síntomas culturales. El legado de Erwin Panofsky*, edited by Luis Vives-Ferrándiz Sánchez, 69–88. Vitoria-Gasteiz: Sans Soleil, 2018.

Riegl, Alöis. *Stilfragen. Grundlegungen zu einer Geschicte der Ornamentik* (1893). Spanish translation: *Problemas de estilo. Fundamentos para una historia de la ornamentación*. Barcelona: Gustavo Gili, 1980.

Rodríguez-Ortega, Nuria. "Digital Art History: The Questions that Need to Be Asked." *Visual Resources* 35, no. 1–2 (March–June 2019): 6–20.

———. "Mediación digital en los procesos de recepción, construcción e interpretación de la herencia cultural." In *Memoria y significado*, edited by Luis Arciniega, 443–61. Valencia: Universitat de Valencia, 2013.

Rolls, Edmund T., and Gustavo Deco. *The Computational Neuroscience of Vision*. Oxford: Oxford University Press, 2002.

Rosado Rodrigo, Pilar. "Formas latentes: protocolos de visión artificial para la detección de analogías aplicados a la catalogación y creación artística." PhD diss., Universidad de Barcelona, 2015.

Saleh, Babak, Kanako Abe, Ravneet Sing Arora, and Ahmed Elgammal. "Toward Automated Discovery of Artistic Influence." *Multimedia Tools and Applications* 75, no. 7 (April 2016): 3565–91.

Sawyer, R. Keith. *Social Emergence: Societies as Complex Systems*. Cambridge: Cambridge University Press, 2005.

Schlecht, Joseph, Bernd Carqué, and Bjönr Ommer. "Detecting Gestures in Medieval Images." *2011 IEEE International Conference on Image Processing, ICIP* (September 11–14, 2011): 1285–88. doi:10.1109/ICIP.2011.6115669.

Seguin, Benoit, Isabella di Leonardo, and Fréderic Kaplan. "Tracking transmission of details paintings." In *Digital Humanities DH2017* (2017). Accessed July 1, 2019. https://dh2017.adho.org/abstracts/562/562.pdf

Sigaki, Higor Y. D., Matjaz Perc, and Haroldo V. Ribeiro. "History of Art Paintings Through the Lens of Entropy and Complexity." *PNAS* 115, no. 37 (July 19, 2018): 8585–94.

Shamir, Lior, Tomasz Macura, Nikita Orlov, D. Mark Eckley, and Ilya G. Goldberg. "Impressionism, Expressionism, Surrealism: Automated Recognition of Painters and Schools of Art." *ACM Transactions on Applied Perception* 7, no. 2 (2010): 1–17. http://dx.doi.org/10.1145/1670671.1670672.

Shen, Xi, Alexei A. Efros, and Mathieu Aubry. "Discovering Visual Patterns in Art Collections with Spatially-Consistent Feature Learning." *arXiv:1903.02678v2* (March 8, 2019.)

Stork, David G. "Computer Vision and Computer Graphics Analysis of Paintings and Drawings: An Introduction to the Literature." In *CAIP* 2009, edited by X. Jiang, and N. Petkov, 9–24. *LNCS* 5702. Heidelberg: Springer, 2009.

Stork, David G., Jim Coddington, and Anna Bentkowska-Kafel, eds. "Computer Image Analysis in the Study of Art." In *Proceedings of SPIE*, vol. 6810. Bellingham: International Society for Optics Photonics, 2008.

———, eds. "Computer Vision and Image Analysis of Art." In *Proceedings of SPIE* 7531. Bellingham: International Society for Optics Photonics, 2010.

———, eds. "Computer Vision and Image Analysis of Art II." In *Proceedings of SPIE* 7869. Bellingham: International Society for Optics Photonics, 2011.

Szeliski, Richard. *Computer Vision: Algorithms and Applications*. London: Springer-Verlag, 2010.

Taylor, Richard P., Adam P. Micolich, and David Jonas. "Fractal analysis of Pollock's drip paintings." *Nature* 399 (June 3, 1999): 422.

Tran, Loan, Poshen Lee, Jevin West, and Maximilian Schich. "Chromatic Structure and Family Resemblance in Large Art Collections." In *Digital Humanities 2018*. Accessed July 10, 2019. https://dh2018.adho.org/chromatic-structure-and-family-resemblance-in-large-art-collections-exemplary-quantification-and-visualizations/.

Warburg, Aby. *Der Bilderaltas Mnemosyne*. Edited by Martin Wranke and Claudia Brink. Berlin: Akademie Verlag, 2000. Spanish translation: Madrid: Akal, 2010.

Wölfflin, Heinrich. *Kunstgeschichtliche Grundbegriffe* (1915). Spanish translation: *Conceptos fundamentales de la Historia del Arte*. Madrid: Espasa Calpe, 2007.

Yang, Sean, Bum Mook Oh, Daniel Merchant, Bill Howe, and Jevin West. "Classifying Digitized Art Type and Time Period." In *Proceedings of International Journal for Digital Art History*. London, August 2018. https://doi.org/10.1145/nnnnnnn.nnnnnnn

Zhang, Quanshi, and Song-Chun Zhu. "Visual Interpretability for Deep Learning: A Survey." *arXiv:1802.00614v2* (February 7, 2018).

Zweig, Benjamin. "Forgotten Genealogies: Brief Reflections on the History of Digital Art History." *Digital Art History. International Journal* no. 1 (2015): 39–49.

# 26

# POINTERS AND PROXIES

## Thoughts on the Computational Modeling of the Phenomenal World

*Alison Langmead and David Newbury*

In his 1966 article presenting the results of applying computational methods to the study of the career of John Singleton Copley, Jules David Prown (Yale professor of art history), walked a careful line between expressing his enthusiasm for the research that digital machinery had made possible and acknowledging the skepticism he presumed he would face in applying such methods to his topic. He noted:

> At first consideration the art historian and the computer would seem to be eccentric companions. Art historians are concerned with qualitative discriminations that reveal themselves slowly, and at an unpredictable tempo, to the investigations of a trained mind and sensitive eye. The computer, on the other hand, deals with quantitative computations at an unvarying pace with incredible speed. Its monotonous, inflexible, unthinking efficiency sends a shudder down the spine of any self-respecting art historian.[1]

This vivid tension between the sensitive, human-oriented approach of the humanist and the aloof, numbers-oriented techniques of the technologist has long been a topos of the digital humanities, and more specifically, of digital art history. Even so, art historians have participated in the conversations surrounding the application of digital computing to the humanities almost since its inception. Indeed, this is true in spite of the fact that the earliest machines could only present numbers and uppercase Roman, alphabetic characters, thereby restricting art history's engagement to texts and catalog entries describing their image-based objects of inquiry.[2] As Prown himself asserted, "The obvious, primary application of the computer to the history of art will be in automated retrieval systems for art libraries and photographic archives."[3]

Owing to the narrow, text-focused field of entry offered by early computers, most of the work done at the intersection of digital computing and art history in the mid- to late twentieth century did indeed center on the design and application of such "image databases," those technologies that store, organize, and disseminate character-based information in order to describe and *point to* objects outside the machine.[4] This use of computers as information managers, as database-driven analogues to the librarians who maintain catalogs about art history's objects of study, has long offered a fundamental contribution to the field. Scholarly resources such as the *Index of Medieval Art*, the *Art & Architecture Thesaurus*, and *Europeana*, just to name a few, were born from such efforts, as were other general-use tools such as Wikipedia and Google Images.[5]

And yet, despite his own claims that the primary strength of digital computing lay in "automated retrieval systems," Prown and his team did not focus on such techniques in their digital research. Instead, they partook of another method, that of computing over *proxies for* historical phenomena in order to reveal statistical patterns, in this case, the pattern of patronage associated with 240 of Copley's sitters. This form of computational analysis relied on these researchers' ability to identify appropriate information about the complex human behavior known as "patronage" that could be successfully encoded and numerically manipulated to use the power of statistics to provide predictive insight into historical events—a fundamentally different way to approach digital art history than the production of representations that serve to point and describe, but not manipulate analytically.

The proxies identified and encoded onto punch cards for Prown's study included the following information on the sitters:

> birth and death dates, place of residence, occupation, college education, church affiliation, political allegiance, marital status, an estimate of income, public offices held (highest office at time of portrait), age of the sitter, the date of the portrait, its size, the medium used, whether the painting was paired with another, and other associated information.[6]

This list of features describes a particular, and indeed, common way to look at patronage: one that relies on the social standing of the sitters to stand in as a proxy for the patterns of behavior that occurred between them and their portrait artists. Computing over these proxies is an act of interpretive argumentation which asserts that "analyzing," "summarizing," and "cross-referencing" these historical qualities will reveal information about the human relationship that art historians call "patronage."[7] Prown and his team ran a number of statistical tests over this information, looking for patterns in the data that were unexpected and that could, therefore, offer new insight into the patterns of Copley's patronage. They found, for example, that Copley painted a higher number of Tories than might be statistically expected and that the percentage of sitters who were women doubled unexpectedly between 1762 and 1764. Once revealed, Prown's team could get to work interpreting these patterns and situating them within their historical context.

Both of these computational approaches to humanities research, that is, using *pointers to* and *proxies for* events and objects in the phenomenal world (acts described by contemporary technologist Jer Thorp as the process of "collection, computation, and representation"), are heavily informed by the capabilities of our technologies.[8] They are not, however, entirely mechanistic. Indeed, they are fundamentally interpretive. Understanding what aspects of the phenomenal world are essential for the task at hand, how those aspects can be appropriately structured within the rigid confines of a data model, how that data will be operated on by the underlying computational machinery, and how the results of that machinery will be best represented to and by human beings, requires deep domain knowledge across the disciplines of both the humanities and computing. It also involves expert interpretation at every step. Taken all together, this workflow produces a *data system*, and the work required to create an effective data system necessarily crosses disciplinary boundaries and often entails collaborative effort.[9] Data systems vary in complexity—from simple lists to complex information networks—but each is a self-contained encapsulation of a particular viewpoint on the phenomenal world and embodies an intricate set of implicit, interpretive decisions.

To maximize the benefits of digital computing within the field of art history, it is not only critical to understand the differences between, and implications of, these different types of data system, but also the scope of their effectiveness. Indeed, two of the most fundamental approaches to producing a data system are the two just mentioned—the pointer-based relationship to the phenomenal world and the proxy-based relationship—and this chapter will focus on explaining their features and gesturing toward their broader disciplinary and societal utility.

## Pointers, Proxies, and Data Systems

When using computers to store, organize, and retrieve pointers to the objects, events, and ideas that pervade the phenomenal world, we essentially use them to enhance human memory and recall, augmenting these faculties by means of external technologies such as databases and search engines. Such data systems function as a representational map or index, with each pointer identifying a distinct location within a space of inquiry. Using input from a human, these systems retrieve and display search results, each one of which stands in as a reference, a pointer, for a potential object of interest in this space.

Pointer-based data systems are not designed to facilitate a direct analysis of the information contained within them. Instead, the computational processes that are executed against these pointers enable the user selectively to reduce vast stores of information to something manageable by the human mind in order to facilitate the identification and retrieval of specific resources. Their effectiveness is assessed on whether or not the information used to represent a chosen part of world (say, a painting in the collection of the Metropolitan Museum of Art) epitomizes its most-commonly recognized features well enough to demonstrate that a given object, once recalled by means of the terms selected by a human, is in fact the object that was sought.

This process, known as information retrieval in the computer and information sciences, has become one of the fundamental drivers of the digital age. Such systems have been designed to respond to common human patterns of inquiry and to facilitate particular user tasks, and in turn, humans have come to expect certain qualities of interactivity with these data systems, especially search engines and catalogs. This suite of common information retrieval behaviors, known within the information sciences as "Find, Identify, Select, and Obtain," shaped and informed traditional, paper-based cataloging practices and continues to serve as a set of fundamental concepts for digital information retrieval practice.[10]

Within the particular context of the humanities, information retrieval is a well-understood, and even well-loved, technique that holds a strong historical connection to the field, as it performs similar tasks to the librarian or archivist. Humanists have long been trained to work with, and rely upon, such information professionals. In turn, they have also become increasingly reliant upon the computerized tools that perform similar work, such as library catalogs and image databases. Representing objects and ideas within the computer in ways that allow scholars to store and retrieve accurate information about those objects has had a transformative impact on the field, especially as the sheer quantity of information available has grown.

This explosion of digital information has also encouraged art historians to use computers not only as a tool to enable information retrieval, but also as a tool for statistical analysis. To accomplish this latter task, however, scholars and technologists must produce *proxies of*, as distinct from *pointers to*, the phenomenal world. This shift from pointer to proxy is not one to be made lightly. It is a fundamental reconsideration of the way in which information functions within the computer as well as within the work of humanistic analysis. When a proxy-based data system is executed, it does not search for and retrieve previously catalogued information. Instead, it manipulates and analyzes its data with an eye toward revealing potential statistical patterns in the information that might, when interpreted by the user, offer new understandings of the phenomenal world. Proxy-based systems are not designed to work as an augmentation of human memory, serving as a map to help humans find their way in a representational space. Rather, they comprise a method of data analysis.

The information thus stored in, and manipulated by, the computer in a proxy-based data system is a carefully crafted collection of data points that serves not to index, but in fact to *characterize* some chosen part of the world (say, the patronage patterns of John Singleton Copley). To function successfully, this process must isolate a meaningful phenomenon from its context and simplify it by means of a series of proxies to fit within a schema that has been designed by the researchers to serve as the basis for a fruitful computational analysis. These proxies, such as those used by Prown, may include whatever properties seem appropriate to the question at hand, but must also be amenable to codifications necessary for effective computation. This violent reduction of reality produces something that is almost entirely, but not completely, unlike the phenomenal world. It is a human-constructed data system that *stands in* for that world—a functionally equivalent representation, created with the purpose of being manipulated symbolically in order to allow researchers to ask specific questions and to allow for particular types of interpretation.

A critical insight to be emphasized here is that the analyses produced by proxy-based data systems cannot, and do not, reflect or explain the bona fide human experience of the phenomenal world. They can instead only describe the patterns found within the closed world of the data system itself. The wider applicability of any results depends entirely on how effectively the researchers have captured the salient aspects of the part of the phenomenal world under consideration, and the skill with which the results are interpreted and re-contextualized by human beings.

## Pointers and Proxies in a Disciplinary Context

Producing pointers and proxies in the service of research and then thinking about the ways that such representations might help scholars learn more about the lived, human experience is not a pattern of scholarly behavior that was invented alongside digital computing. Indeed, such techniques and rhetorical gestures are a part of the toolkit that humanists have always used when weaving together arguments and narratives out of examples.[11] One might even stipulate that the production and contemplation of art objects serves some of these same societal functions. However, creating computer-readable pointers and proxies and using computational devices to perform operations over them (especially in those proxy-based systems that produce summarized, simplified, statistical results) is definitively a product of the twentieth century. These mechanized data systems have particular properties that contemporary art historians should keep at the forefront of their minds as they take advantage of their powerful affordances.

Within the field of art history, pointer-based data systems, such as ArtStor, Europeana, and TMS (The Museum System), have been prominent since the late 1960s, but research projects that focus on proxy-based data systems, such as Prown's pioneering work, have seen a sharp rise in recent years.[12] This increase can be attributed in part to the explosion of available digital and digitized information, but also to the fact that computers can now store, describe, and compute over encoded image data. Indeed, it was only in the late 1980s that the first art-historical applications designed to manipulate and investigate image-based digital representations began to take shape.[13] This approach must, by definition, use digital images as proxies for art objects, as scholars who walk this path investigate what, if anything, the information contained by the digitized images (not the descriptive metadata, but the pixel information itself) might be able to convey about the objects depicted in those digitizations.

More recently, however, this increased interest in utilizing proxy-based data systems to forward the aims of art history can be associated with the rise of a series of popular computational techniques, often described as "machine learning" and/or "deep neural nets."[14] From image recognition (including facial recognition) to recommendation engines, from machine-based language translation to the distribution of targeted online advertisements, the computing machinery of the twenty-first century has been built on technologies of machine learning and automated classification. Indeed, in the past decade, computer science as a discipline has reoriented a large part of its collective research agenda around these approaches, especially in the subfield of artificial intelligence.

Machine learning, by and large, plays off of the human desire and ability to create simplified, abstract models of the world for the purpose of predicting future outcomes. This particular form of predictive modeling operates by describing a desired outcome and then using data to generate a set of algorithmic, symbolic manipulations that then appear to produce that outcome. In this approach, the data itself is not the object of inquiry, but is instead used as an encapsulation of the past to allow for an investigation of speculative pasts, presents, and futures.[15] Machine learning, then, can be described as a technique for automatically generating an effective proxy. The effectiveness of this proxy, though, is judged not by how clearly its workings parallel the phenomenal world, but rather by how accurately its outcomes match our expectations. According to the statistician Galit Shmueli, predictive models "seek to minimize the combination of bias and estimation variance, occasionally sacrificing theoretical accuracy for improved empirical precision."[16] That is, predictive models can, and will, be tweaked until their output matches what we perceive in the world, even if it means that the model itself departs from being a valid description of the way the world actually appears to function. What matters are the results.

## Data Systems as Types of Models

When framed as "computer-manipulable models of the world," both pointer- and proxy-based data systems can be fruitfully brought into direct conversation with broader discourses in the digital humanities itself, especially those centered on the ways that humanists can effectively take up and use modeling in their research. Willard McCarty has provided a helpful scaffold for understanding the basic outline of this disciplinary discussion. Applying terms originally proposed by Clifford Geertz, McCarty provides a top-level distinction between producing "models for" a given purpose and producing "models of" a phenomenon: "A model *of* something is an exploratory device, a more or less 'poor substitute' for the real thing. [. . .] In contrast, a model *for* something is a design, exemplary ideal, archetype or other guiding preconception."[17] Both pointer- and proxy-based data systems serve, in their own ways, as models *of* and models *for*, and it is important to understand how they reify these distinctions in order to use them most appropriately within the context of digital art history.

Both types of data system contain "models of" whatever phenomenon is currently under consideration, whether that be the patronage of John Singleton Copley or a descriptive representation of the *Mona Lisa*. In both cases, scholars extract salient characteristics from the world as it appears to them, codify them in a series of fixed data categories, and assert some form of relationship between those categories and the objects or events under consideration. But complete data systems are also "models for" a particular task, and the "models of" the world created for these systems are necessarily produced with an eye toward this eventual use. The work of applying any data system within a disciplinary context must emphasize the proper alignment between the data, the computation, and the precise interpretive task at hand.

For pointer-based data systems to be effective, the chosen "model of" the part of the world under consideration must stand in concrete relation to human understandings of that world. This is, in no small part, because pointer-based data systems are "models for" information retrieval. For example, the metadata standard, Categories for the Description of Works of Art (CDWA), is a descriptive "model of" the way that a large community of art historians and scholars talk about works of art.[18] When this standard is embedded within an information retrieval system, if it did not accurately reflect the way that artworks were commonly identified and described by this community, scholars would not be able to connect their understanding of artistic production to its representation within the computer. They would have no way to guess appropriate search terms and could not be offered intuitive ways to filter categories in order to locate the information that they sought. The selection of properties within a pointer-based data system is informed and, in fact, driven by a need to reflect the ways that scholarly discourse operates.

Numerous contemporary digital art history projects such as *Mapping Titian*, *Art Tracks*, and *Mapping Gothic France* take up pointer-based representations of historical objects, spaces, and time as their foundational digital turn.[19] They model salient historical objects and events using terms and descriptors that scholars recognize and use as the basis for demonstrating larger geospatial and art-historical patterns. These projects are wholly interpretive, down to the very detailed construction of their underlying digital models. But these models of the world are designed as a description of the past rather than as the prediction of alternate pasts, presents, futures.

Proxy-based data systems, by contrast, are "models for" prediction, not information retrieval, and they therefore embody different "models of" the part of the world under consideration. Unlike in a pointer-based system, proxy-based "models of" need not stand in direct and concrete relation to the phenomenal world. This is because the believability and effectiveness of the results have been prioritized over ensuring that the model provides an accurate representation of the world. For example, the work done by scholars C. Richard Johnson Jr. and William A. Sethares using digitally identified canvas thread counts to serve as a proxy for identifying similar bolts of cloth used in paintings by Vermeer does not attempt accurately to characterize the paintings or even the particular threads used in their canvases. Instead, this research uses the strength of a signal seen in a digital radiograph as a proxy for the density of threads, and that density as a proxy for identity of the canvas, and that identity as a proxy for co-creation of works of art. This chain of proxies can only help to produce new interpretive knowledge if the data extracted from the canvases is prepared, a priori, with an eye toward the types of manipulation it will need to undergo to achieve an expected outcome.[20] Another example of proxy-based art-historical research is Sandra van Ginhoven and Matthew Lincoln's analysis of the profitability of the art dealer, Knoedler and Co. The information in the dealer stockbooks, proxied via the Getty Provenance index and then further summarized and reduced in scope specifically for this project by the researchers, is used to estimate the sale prices of paintings. This data is, in turn, used as a proxy for the profitability of a gallery.[21] The data extracted from the phenomenal world for the purposes of a proxy-based data system is thus less appropriately termed "descriptive" as it is "characteristic for a given purpose." Properties are selected entirely for their ability to improve the analytic power of the data system itself and often bear little resemblance to the way in which the field would typically describe or represent the same phenomenon in normal discourse.

Neither the proxy- nor the pointer-based approach is more "accurate" or more "useful" than the other. Indeed, all models produced by humanists, whether digitally embodied or not, are imagined realities that perform different interpretive functions and may be appropriate for different purposes. Computer-based models, like all models, can only provide a connection between the phenomenal world as it is experienced, and human mental preconceptions, theories, and dreams of how it might operate, either now or in the past. As McCarty quipped,

"Models *realize*."[22] What they realize, however, is up to the designer of the data system itself, from the production of the "model of" to the implementation of the "model for."

## Tacit and Explicit Human-Computer Decision Making

Both pointer- and proxy-based systems thus provide effective ways to understand and compute the phenomenal world while, at the same time, reducing that world for different purposes and with different limitations. Some of the most salient limitations to be identified in these data systems prior to selecting one of them are the ways in which they do, and do not, clearly expose the human decisions made in their construction and use.

Pointer-based systems are frequently understood as convenient and highly simplified representations of the world that are produced to support various human research purposes (e.g. locating digital images or learning where an historical event took place). By their nature, they not only make it clear, but make it necessary, for the lion's share of the interpretive work to lie in the hands of scholars. However, this is not to say that pointer-based data systems do not incorporate human bias or interpretations. The construction of the "model of" component of these systems embodies thousands of individual decisions and can be deeply embedded in value systems that cannot be generalized.[23] The "model for" component of a pointer-based data system also assumes a particular type of user—one who wishes to store or retrieve data based on the patterns and assumptions of their lived experience and disciplinary training. In these ways, pointer-based systems tacitly and explicitly embody the assumptions of their creators. Openly considering the constructed-nature of such data systems is not common outside the digital humanities and library and information sciences, and this, coupled with the apparent simplicity of the information retrieval process, can lead to the assumption that such systems are somehow more passive, more transparent, even more "objective," than other types of data system. They are, however, complex mechanisms with many different human assumptions distributed across their breadth.[24]

Proxy-based data systems reveal their complexity more plainly, and seem much less transparent and passive by their very nature. As noted previously, the simplification process required to produce the "model of" required by such systems translates the real world into a representation that is almost entirely divorced from the human mind and lived experience. It therefore becomes a strong, interpretation-heavy reduction of that experience. Moreover, the efficiency of computation within the "model for" this system depends on including only relevant features, increasing the pressure on creating as efficient a simplification as possible. This selection process is necessarily reductionist, particularly so when applied to the fields of the humanities. Human behavior is exquisitely complicated. No system can fully capture this complexity, and so the process of selection and reduction is informed by the computational intent of the system as a whole.

Effective proxies also capture a specific subset of information in their "model for" computation that isolates entities from causal dependencies that are irrelevant to the question at hand, an approach that facilitates the meaningful re-application of the results of the computation to the phenomenal world. However, as noted previously, this process often simplifies the internal representation of these entities to the extent that they no longer resemble the object in a way that is meaningful outside the data system. Because the outputs of proxy-based systems tend to spark effective action in the world so long as they appear to be valid or even reasonable, the intense amount of interpretive work that is needed to create appropriate proxies in the disciplines of the humanities—or in any effective societal setting—cannot be overstated.

It is also worth noting that proxy-based data systems can hide, or misdirect attention from, the locus of effective action within the research process. When working with proxies, the computer can appear to become an active participant in the interpretive work of humanities scholarship because the results of their symbolic manipulations closely mirror humanist practices: that is, the *computer* itself appears to assess and summarize the data in order to reveal previously unnoticed connections. But such cannot be the case. The ability to reduce reality into a functioning, computational model is a core skill of the human technologist and can only be accomplished with a keen understanding of the data and the manipulations that are possible within a computer. The technologist is the true agent of assessment and summarization whose work appears to parallel the work of the humanist in this context; the computer only does the human's her bidding.[25]

Whereas proxy-based data systems more obviously tend to hide the role of human interpretation both in the creation of data sets ("models of") and in the design of the symbolic manipulations that analyses them ("models for"), the apparent transparency of pointer-based systems does its own form of concealing the importance of human interpretation in its production and use. The pervasive role of human-computer decision making throughout any data system should be made apparent at every possible opportunity in order for these tools to be used effectively in the context of the humanities, or, indeed, in any human context.

## The Limits of Data Reuse

Scholarship builds upon prior work. Data systems, as works of research and scholarship, are therefore also implicated in this tradition. In the digital age, however, works of digital scholarship must be understood to comprise the *complete* system, including the design of the computation, not just the data contained within. Data generated for use within a system has built into it implicit "fitness for purpose": it is only a sufficient as a "model of" within the particular intellectual framework of the "model for" for which it was produced. Reuse of information captured in one type of data system within the context of another, without fully re-interpreting that data in within the context of the new system, is problematic. This does not mean that data cannot be reused, only that reuse requires an understanding of the system in which it was created and a reinterpretation of that data within its new context.

This is to say, the act of creating any data system effectively decides in advance the type of questions that can be meaningfully asked. Pointer-based systems, as models for information retrieval, rely on the assumption that much of the meaning will be contained within the object retrieved rather than in its descriptors. They therefore often exclude essential details that would be needed for predictive, proxy-based modeling. As an example, a museum catalog rarely describes the colors of paintings, and a library catalog rarely contains the text of the books. This is not a failure of such data systems; the system simply assumes specific patterns of analysis and is optimized for that purpose. When producing a computable simulation over a set of proxies, on the other hand, technologists must craft a mechanical model of the way the world works that functions within this different set of constraints. The proxies are themselves a selective, interpretive, data-centric model of the way the world appears, and to be effective the "model for" must respond precisely to these contours. When analyzing the weave of canvas, for example, the model does not need to know what paint may exist on that canvas, or even that it is a work of art. The determination of weave similarity depends only on the relevant features, and it would be both technically and professionally problematic to provide the model with information that might unintentionally skew the results. These two computational approaches, while not mutually exclusive, are clearly quite distinct. Using one often forestalls the use of the other with the same data, since both rely on different reductions of the phenomenal world to produce an effective model. One must proceed carefully and with great intention.

## The Model of the World Is Not the World

Digital art historians, and humanists in general, seem among the most likely of communities to recognize and avoid the possible intellectual and social pitfalls inherent to the decontextualized application of models and complex data systems within their disciplines. However, it is certainly worthy of deep consideration that the anthropologist Daniel Miller and the sociologist James Carrier consider a pervasive intellectual preference for the clarity of abstract models over the mess of the world to be one of the most distinctive patterns of social behavior in the twenty-first-century industrialized West. Miller and Carrier argue that it has become increasingly common in this context for "virtual reality"—or the fictions and models that humans produce about and around themselves—to be prioritized over the actual, lived, human experience of reality. They call this slippery cultural structure "virtualism," stating: "Perceiving a virtual reality becomes virtualism when people take this virtual reality to be not just a parsimonious description of what is really happening, but prescriptive of what the world ought to be; when, that is, they seek to make the world conform to their virtual vision."[26]

Miller and Carrier argue that when the phenomenal world no longer matches the model (the "virtual reality"), pressure arises to make the real conform to the virtual, rather than the other way around. Rationalized, statistically based models of the world, such as the ones that economists produce, can come to stand "in the stead" of the phenomena they previously purported merely to represent. In many cases the model (and, more importantly, the people who control the model) is able to co-opt the power of the original agent.[27] If Miller and Carrier are correct, then the true power of our "virtual moment" lies in the hands of people who control the most persuasive *models* of the world, not the resources of the world itself.

This dangerous ability, and perhaps even desire, to prioritize the power of an effective model over our lived experience has proven to be one of the quintessential moves of digital computing in the early twenty-first century. Machine learning is a powerful technique for creating just these types of convincing models of the world, and their effectiveness lies in no small part in the fact that they are designed to offer convincing outputs—that is to *appear* correct. As scholars M. C. Elish and danah boyd have noted, in machine learning,

> knowledge is derived by crunching vast amounts of data, detecting patterns, and producing probabilistic results. In these equations, "meaning" is beside the point; the algorithm "knows" in the sense that it can correlate certain relevant variables accurately. *It does not matter if a system thinks like a human—as long as it appears to be as knowledgeable as a human.*[28]

By their very principles of construction, the mechanisms and symbolic manipulations (the "models for") that machine learning systems use to arrive at their outcomes have no direct relation to the workings of the phenomenal world, and yet they are deemed effective when their results *seem* reasonable on human terms. The necessary and appropriate disconnect between a model and the world is certainly clear, but the powerful role of those human beings who willingly accept, and even possibly prioritize, results that merely *seem* plausible is equally important to recognize.

Offering true and effective power to such systems is, at the very least, at odds with the way the humanities have traditionally been performed. It may be, at its most extreme, also a threat to the humanities itself. If the pressure of virtualism is indeed so pervasive, there is a real risk in any context, including the humanities, of having the model become the leader, and the world, its follower. But humanists are well-versed in the fundamental workings of this system and can easily avoid one of its most prominent pitfalls by maintaining a connection to their disciplinary training: it is *abstraction and representation themselves* that serve as the foundation for both model creation and, by extension, virtualism. But, as Miller notes, it is not the mere act of abstraction that is the danger: "All new forms of abstraction are to be welcomed if they can be recognized as human constructions and can be re-appropriated as part of the enhancement of human self-understanding and cultural development."

Indeed, the use of abstraction and representation, or the process of producing meaning and the constant re-interpretation of those meanings, is fundamental to humanist practice. We are expert manipulators of these rhetorical tools, and ought not be misled by them in the context of computation. Both written essays and data systems are means to represent reality and to provide a structured understanding of that reality within a particular bounded context. As the George Mason Digital History Working Group recently asserted: "A historical narrative, after all, is a deliberately simplified account of the past which is illuminating because of, not despite, its simplifications. For all the surface dissimilarities of a statistical model and a historical narrative, they share a fundamental similarity as representational models."[29] Thus, both essay-based and data-based methods of analysis simplify in order to help interpret the world, and they both re-present that interpretation for use in further scholarship. The unreasonable effectiveness of the data-driven methods, however, have pervasive effects beyond the academy that deserve proactive attention above and beyond any parallels they may have to traditional humanistic approaches.

Ensuring that all acts of abstraction and modeling into deeply embedded into meaningful, socially situated contexts is the beating heart of the humanities. Being able to understand and explain how and why these abstract models work, as well as clearly elucidating their boundaries and their limitations, is a culture-critical knowledge for the twenty-first century. It is one that humanists train their whole lives to practice and one that they have a responsibility to display and disseminate in the context of their digital methods.

## Conclusion

In his discussion of his team's computer-assisted findings, Prown noted: "The computer, while it had not done our thinking for us, had arranged and clarified the material, pointing us in a fruitful direction and permitting more concrete and comprehensive conclusions to be drawn."[30] This clear understanding of the relationship between the scholar and the computer is one that twenty-first-century art historians would do well to keep present in their minds as the work of the machines becomes increasingly a reflection of—even at times a mistaken replacement for—human lived experience of the phenomenal world.

Digital art historians can and should take advantage of the power of pointer- and proxy-based data systems in their research. Indeed, they have been doing so since at least the 1960s. But all digital humanists should use such technologies mindfully and with an eye toward making their implicit dangers clear to their audiences. None of the tools that humanists use to perform their work are value-neutral, and digital techniques are equally implicated. Data systems have tacit and explicit contexts, and these cannot be moved to other contexts without damage to their intellectual coherence and subsequent impact. Using these tools involves making choices about relative importance and value, and the professional ethics of our discipline holds us to certain standards in this area. The machines only compute what they are told to compute, and the use of increasingly sophisticated techniques does not change this fundamental principle.

The humanities address unbounded scenarios, unbounded questions. Many of these are fundamentally unanswerable and are "problems" for which no amount of data and no amount of number-crunching can lead to an operational "solution." But while the socio-cultural environments that humanists investigate are inherently imbued with gaps and imprecision, effective computation is predicated on logic and precision. Indeed, if humanists can be said to address "problems" at all, they are problems in the sense of a "mental representation of a task," rather than as a "a difficulty or a deficiency" in the way the world works.[31] As Michael Witmore once noted: "The humanities—and literary criticism, at least—is a sustained conversation about things we cannot really fully say."[32] Humanists thus have every right to be skeptical of the use of the digital computer, with its need for bounded problems, in such a conversation.

This places the digital humanities in a bind, although not one that is inescapable. To produce models of the messiness of the real world in the context of the rigor of the mathematized world of the computer requires compromise and skill. It is critical to admit that, for digital humanists to take advantage of the affordances offered by computers, they *must* transform unbounded experience into bounded problems. This is not problematic if the very acts of translation, transformation, and simplification for a particular purpose are emphasized as critical to our scholarship and kept at the forefront of our research. The work of producing our computational data systems is the interpretive work of the humanities itself. Reducing the unbounded experience of the phenomenal world into a "model of" and a "model for" can be ethically problematic only if this responsibility is taken up by those who think that unbounded experience truly can be reduced to a series of bounded problems and does not instead serve a particular purpose, at a particular time, for a particular group of people.

The value of the process of using computers to advance humanistic inquiry is not found simply within the act of computation, but in the process of interaction that happens between the humans manipulating the models of the world and designing the computation that works over those models. As Brian Cantwell Smith notes: "Computation in the wild," that is, computation as it is fully experienced, is a *practice*.[33] Without the process of computation eventually terminating and displaying some result to a human, and without that human taking that information and incorporating it into the social world, all that the computer does is generate heat. We build models, populate those models with information, and define manipulations in order to generate an output that we can then use in the real world to help us as humans understand lived reality. They are not designed to replace humanity. Humanists would do well to shout this to the rafters.

## Notes

1. Jules David Prown, "The Art Historian and the Computer: An Analysis of Copley's Patronage, 1753–1774," *Smithsonian Journal of History* 1 (1966–1967): 17.
2. See, for example, Kenneth C. Lindsay, "Art, Art History, and the Computer," *Computers and the Humanities* 1, no. 2 (November 1966): 27–30; Michael Greenhalgh, "Databases for Art Historians: Problems and Possibilities," in *History and Computing*, ed. Peter Denley and Deian Hopkin (Manchester: Manchester University Press, 1987), 156–67; Sally M. Promey and Miriam Stewart, "Digital Art History: A New Field for Collaboration," *American Art* 11, no. 2 (Summer 1997): 36–41.
3. Prown, "The Art Historian and the Computer," 18.
4. It is also worth noting that, to art historians, these digital pointers point at things (digital or photographic images) that are themselves pointers to the actual objects of visual culture under scrutiny. For more on this see, Alison Langmead, "Art and Architectural History and the Performative, Mindful Practice of the Digital Humanities," *The Journal of Interactive Technology & Pedagogy* 12 (February 12, 2018), https://jitp.commons.gc.cuny.edu/art-and-architectural-history-and-the-performative-mindful-practice-of-the-digital-humanities/.
5. The Index of Medieval Art can be found at https://ima.princeton.edu/, the Art and Architecture Thesaurus can be found at www.getty.edu/research/tools/vocabularies/aat/, and Europeana can be found at www.europeana.eu/portal/en.
6. Prown, "The Art Historian and the Computer," 20.

7. Prown and his research assistant, G.B. Warden commonly used three words to describe the computing that they did over these features, "data analysis," "summarizing," and "cross-referencing." For their full analysis of this data see, Jules David Prown, "Analysis of Data," in *John Singleton Copley*, vol. 1 (Cambridge, MA: Harvard University Press, 1966), 128–37.
8. Jer Thorp, "You Say Data, I Say System," *Hackernoon* (July 13, 2007), accessed February 22, 2019, https://hackernoon.com/you-say-data-i-say-system-54e84aa7a421.
9. For more on effective multi-party collaboration in digital art history, see Tracey Berg-Fulton, et al., "A Role-Based Model for Successful Collaboration in Digital Art History," *International Journal for Digital Art History* 3 (2018): 152–80.
10. See, for example, one of the foundational texts of library classification, Charles A. Cutter, *Rules for a Printed Dictionary Catalogue* (Washington, DC: Government Printing Office, 1876), 10. For a more recent reference, see Barbara Tillett, "What Is FRBR? A Conceptual Model for the Bibliographic Universe," *The Australian Library Journal* 54, no. 1 (2005): 24–30.
11. Michael Witmore has some excellent thoughts on the ways that humanists use examples, and even confirmation bias, to effective ends in their scholarship. See, for example, Michael Witmore, "Latour, the Digital Humanities, and the Divided Kingdom of Knowledge," *New Literary History* 47, no. 2–3 (Spring–Summer 2016): 353–75; Michael Witmore, "Shakespeare from the Waist Down," Filmed February 21, 2012, at the Maryland Institute for Technology in the Humanities Digital Dialogues Series, College Park, Maryland, Video, 43:33, accessed March 11, 2019, https://mith.umd.edu/dialogues/shakespeare-from-the-waist-down/; Michael Witmore, "What Should Humanists Think About in the Age of the Algorithm," Filmed June 16, 2018 at the 2018 Annual Meeting of the Consortium of Humanities Centers and Institutes, Charlottesville, VA, Video, 1:22:32, accessed February 22, 2019, http://ihgc.as.virginia.edu/chci-2018-humanities-informatics.
12. For example, see the work of John A. Bateman et al., "An Open Multilevel Classification Scheme for the Visual Layout of Comics and Graphic Novels: Motivation and Design," *Digital Scholarship in the Humanities* 32, no. 3 (2017): 476–510; Leonardo Impett and Franco Moretti, "Totentanz: Operationalizing Aby Warburg's *Pathosformeln*," *New Left Review* 107 (September–October 2017): 68–97; Lev Manovich, "Data Science and Digital Art History," *International Journal for Digital Art History* no. 1 (June 2015): 13–35. Many of these sorts of proxy-driven research projects use the features of *digital* images to stand in as proxies for features of the physical object that the images represent.
13. See here, for example, William Vaughan, "The Automated Connoisseur: Image Analysis and Art History," in *History and Computing*, ed. Peter Denley and Deian Hopkin (Manchester: Manchester University Press, 1987), 215–21; William Vaughan, "Automated Picture Referencing: A Further Look at 'Morelli,'" *Computers and the History of Art* 2, no. 1 (1992): 7–18.
14. On machine learning, see the popular article by the three Google engineers, Alon Halevy, Peter Norvig, and Fernando Pereira, "The Unreasonable Effectiveness of Data," *IEEE Intelligent Systems* (March/April 2009): 8–12. For a basic technical overview on deep learning and neural networks, see Jürgen Schmidhuber, "Deep Learning in Neural Networks: An Overview," *Neural Networks* 61 (January 2015): 85–117.
15. This is in contrast to explanatory modeling, more commonly used in the sciences, which first attempts to understand or theorize an understanding the world and then encodes that understanding as a computational model, using data to validate that understanding. For more on this distinction, see Galit Shmueli, "To Explain or to Predict?" *Statistical Science* 25, no. 3 (2010): 289–310.
16. Shmueli, "To Explain or to Predict?" 293.
17. Willard McCarty, "21. Knowing. . .: Modeling in Literary Studies," in *A Companion to Digital Literary Studies*, eds. Susan Schreibman and Ray Siemens (Oxford: Blackwell, 2008), n.p., accessed February 22, 2019, https://onlinelibrary.wiley.com/doi/10.1002/9781405177504.ch21, emphases his. For McCarty's take on modeling, see also "19. Modeling: A Study in Words and Meanings," in *A Companion to Digital Humanities*, ed. Susan Schreibman, Ray Siemens and John Unsworth (Oxford: Blackwell Publishing, 2004), n.p., accessed February 22, 2019, https://doi.org/10.1002/9780470999875.ch19; Meurig Beynon, Steve Russ, and Willard McCarty, "Human Computing—Modelling with Meaning," *Literary and Linguistic Computing* 21, no. 2 (2006): 141–57. Further discussions on modeling within the digital humanities can be found in Edward Vanhoutte, "The Gates of Hell: History and Definition of Digital | Humanities | Computing," in *Digital Research in the Arts and Humanities: Defining Digital Humanities: A Reader*, ed. Melissa Terras, Julianne Nyhan, and Edward Vanhoutte (Farnham: Routledge, 2013), 119–45.

18. The CDWA standard can be found here: accessed February 22, 2019, www.getty.edu/research/publications/electronic_publications/cdwa/.
19. For more on *Mapping Titian*, see accessed February 22, 2019, www.mappingtitian.org/. For more on Art Tracks, see accessed February 22, 2019, www.museumprovenance.org/. For more on Mapping Gothic France, see accessed February 22, 2019, http://mappinggothic.org/.
20. For such an approach, see C. Richard Johnson Jr. and W.A. Sethares, "Canvas Weave Match Supports Designation of Vermeer's *Geographer and Astronomer* as a Pendant Pair," *Journal of Historians of Netherlandish Art* 9, no. 1 (Winter 2017), accessed February 22, 2019, http://doi.org/10.5092/jhna.2017.9.1.17.
21. For more information, see Matthew Lincoln and Sandra van Ginhoven, "Modeling the Fragmented Archive: A Missing Data Case Study From Provenance Research," Paper given at Digital Humanities 2018, DH 2018, El Colegio de México, UNAM, and RedHD, Mexico City, Mexico, June 26–29, 2018, accessed February 22, 2019, https://dh2018.adho.org/en/modeling-the-fragmented-archive-a-missing-data-case-study-from-provenance-research/.
22. McCarty, "19. Modeling," n.p.
23. For more on this, see Miriam Posner, "Humanities Data: A Necessary Contradiction," *Miriam Posner's Blog*, June 25, 2015, accessed February 22, 2019, http://miriamposner.com/blog/humanities-data-a-necessary-contradiction/ (originally a presentation to the Harvard Purdue Data Management Symposium made on June 17, 2015); Katie Rawson and Trevor Muñoz, "Against Cleaning," in *Debates in the Digital Humanities 2019*, eds. Lauren F. Klein and Matthew Gold (Minneapolis: University of Minnesota Press, 2019), https://dhdebates.gc.cuny.edu/read/untitled-f2acf72c-a469-49d8-be35-67f9ac1e3a60/section/07154de9-4903-428e-9c61-7a92a6f22e51#ch23. Work originally published as, "Against Cleaning," *Curating Menus*, website produced by Katie Rawson and Trevor Muñoz, July 6, 2016, accessed March 11, 2019, http://curatingmenus.org/articles/against-cleaning/.
24. The works of Bruno Latour, Annemarie Mol, and John Law are, methodologically speaking, particularly salient to mention here, as their writings, along with other theorists working along Actor-Network Theory lines, have shown the manifold ways that rich descriptions and deep investigation of the tools and practices surrounding highly professionalized activities can reveal the complex interplay between deeply held human assumptions and the embedded affordances of the technologies they use. See, as foundational examples, John Law, "Making a Mess with Method," in *The Sage Handbook of Social Science Methodology*, ed. William Outhwaite and Stephen P. Turner (London: Sage Publications, 2007), 595–606; Annemarie Mol and John Law, "Complexities: An Introduction," in *Complexities: Social Studies of Knowledge Practices*, ed. John Law and Annemarie Mol (Durham and London: Duke University Press, 2002), 1–22; Bruno Latour, "Technology Is Society Made Durable," *Sociological Review* 38 (May 1990): 103–31. Latour has also done some work with Adam Lowe that involves the latter professional's art reproduction/restoration firm, Factum Arte, that may be of interest to this audience: Bruno Latour and Adam Lowe, "The Migration of the Aura, or How to Explore the Original Through Its Facsimiles," in *Switching Codes: Thinking Through Digital Technology in the Humanities and the Arts*, ed. Thomas Bartscherer and Roderick Coover (Chicago: University of Chicago Press, 2011), 275–97.
25. For more on computers serving as servants or partners, see Beynon et al., "Human Computing—Modelling with Meaning."
26. James Carrier, "Introduction," in *Virtualism: A New Political Economy*, ed. James G. Carrier and Daniel Miller (Oxford: Berg, 1998), 2.
27. "Neo-classical economics has claimed authority to determine the direction of most governments and international bodies by claiming that its model of the market will be to the ultimate benefit of consumers, but in reality taking this authority and giving it to economists." Daniel Miller, "The Virtual Moment," *Journal of the Royal Anthropological Institute* 9 (2003): 73.
28. M.C. Elish and danah boyd, "Situating Methods in the Magic of Big Data and AI," *Communication Monographs* 85, no. 1 (2018): 62, emphasis ours.
29. Arguing with Digital History Working Group, "Digital History and Argument," eds. Stephen Robertson and Lincoln Mullen, White Paper, Roy Rosenzweig Center for History and New Media (November 13, 2017), accessed February 22, 2019, https://rrchnm.org/argument-white-paper/.
30. Prown, "The Art Historian and the Computer," 26.
31. Willemien Visser, "Designing as Construction of Representations: A Dynamic Viewpoint in Cognitive Design Research," *Human—Computer Interaction* (Special Issue: 'Foundations of Design in HCI') 21, no. 1 (2006): 106.

32. Witmore, "What Should Humanists Think About in the Age of the Algorithm," video, timestamp 51:42.
33. Brian Cantwell Smith, "Section 6: Age of Significance," *Age of Significance*, website last modified May 1, 2017, content retrieved from the Internet Archive, accessed March 11, 2019, https://web.archive.org/web/20170501022356/; http://ageofsignificance.org/aos/en/aos-v1c0.html. For more on Cantwell Smith's philosophical position, please also see, "The Philosophy of Computation: Meaning, Mechanism, and Mystery," *YouTube*, posted by André Souza Lemos, July 10, 2013, accessed February 22, 2019, https://youtu.be/USF1H70bRl0; and "The Couch or the Bottle: Levels of Abstraction and the Anxious Mind," *YouTube*, video posted by BrainMindConsci (The Brain, Mind, and Consciousness Society at the University of California, Santa Cruz), November 11, 2015, accessed February 22, 2019, https://youtu.be/C0g4OwtkoCQ.

## Bibliography


Arguing with Digital History Working Group. "Digital History and Argument." White paper edited by Stephen Robertson and Lincoln Mullen, Roy Rosenzweig Center for History and New Media (November 13, 2017). Accessed February 22, 2019. https://rrchnm.org/argument—white—paper/.

Balci, Osman, and William F. Ormsby. "Conceptual Modelling for Designing Large—Scale Simulations." *Journal of Simulation* 1, no. 3 (August 2007): 175–86.

Bateman, John A. et al. "An Open Multilevel Classification Scheme for the Visual Layout of Comics and Graphic Novels: Motivation and Design." *Digital Scholarship in the Humanities* 32, no. 3 (2017): 476–510.

Berg—Fulton, Tracey, Alison Langmead, Thomas Lombardi, David Newbury, and Christopher Nygren. "A Role—Based Model for Successful Collaboration in Digital Art History." *International Journal for Digital Art History* 3 (2018): 152–80.

Beynon, Meurig, Steve Russ, and Willard McCarty. "Human Computing—Modelling with Meaning." *Literary and Linguistic Computing* 21, no. 2 (2006): 141–57.

Borgman, Christine L. *Big Data, Little Data, No Data: Scholarship in the Networked World*. Cambridge, MA: MIT Press, 2015.

Bradley, John. "No Job for Techies: Technical Contributions to Research in the Digital Humanities." In *Collaborative Research in the Digital Humanities*, edited by Marilyn Deegan and Willard McCarty, 11–25. Farnham, Surrey: Ashgate, 2012.

Carrier, James. "Introduction." In *Virtualism: A New Political Economy*, edited by James G. Carrier and Daniel Miller, 1–24. Oxford: Berg, 1998.

Coeckelbergh, Mark. "Virtual Moral Agency, Virtual Moral Responsibility: On the Moral Significance of the Appearance, Perception, and Performance of Artificial Agents." *AI & Society* 24, no. 2 (2009): 181–89.

Cutter, Charles A. *Rules for a Printed Dictionary Catalogue*. Washington, DC: Government Printing Office, 1876.

Daston, Lorraine. "On Scientific Observation." *Isis* 99 (2008): 97–110.

Dourish, Paul. *The Stuff of Bits: An Essay on the Materialities of Information*. Cambridge, MA: MIT Press, 2017.

Drucker, Johanna. "Is There a 'Digital' Art History?" *Visual Resources* 29, no. 1–2 (June 2013): 5–13.

Elish, M. C., and danah boyd. "Situating Methods in the Magic of Big Data and AI." *Communication Monographs* 85, no. 1 (2018): 57–80.

Flanders, Julia. "The Productive Unease of 21st–Century Digital Scholarship." *DHQ: Digital Humanities Quarterly* 3, no. 3 (2009). Accessed February 22, 2019. http://digitalhumanities.org/dhq/vol/3/3/000055/000055.html.

Fletcher, Pamela. "Pamela Fletcher. Essay on 'Reflections on Digital Art History.'" *caa.reviews*, June 2015. Accessed February 22, 2019. http://dx.doi.org/10.3202/caa.reviews.2015.73.

Gebru, Timnit et al. "Datasheets for Datasets." *ArXiv:1803.09010 [Cs], arXiv.org*, March 2018. Accessed February 22, 2019. http://arxiv.org/abs/1803.09010.

Gigerenzer, Gerd. "Towards a Rational Theory of Heuristics." In *Minds, Models, and Milieux*, edited by Roger Frantz and Leslie Marsh, 34–59. London: Palgrave Macmillan, 2016.

Greenhalgh, Michael. "Databases for Art Historians: Problems and Possibilities." In *History and Computing*, edited by Peter Denley and Deian Hopkin, 156–67. Manchester: Manchester University Press, 1987.

Halevy, Alon, Peter Norvig, and Fernando Pereira. "The Unreasonable Effectiveness of Data." *IEEE Intelligent Systems* (March–April 2009): 8–12.

Harris, Jacob. "Consider the Boolean." *Source*, February 18, 2015. Accessed March 11, 2019. https://source.opennews.org/articles/consider—boolean/.

Hew, Patrick Chisan. "Artificial Moral Agents Are Infeasible with Foreseeable Technologies." *Ethics and Information Technology* 16 (2014): 197–206.

Impett, Leonardo, and Franco Moretti. "Totentanz: Operationalizing Aby Warburg's *Pathosformeln*." *New Left Review* 107 (September–October 2017): 68–97.

Johnson Jr., C. Richard, and W. A. Sethares. "Canvas Weave Match Supports Designation of Vermeer's *Geographer and Astronomer* as a Pendant Pair." *Journal of Historians of Netherlandish Art* 9, no. 1 (Winter 2017). Accessed February 22, 2019. http://doi.org/10.5092/jhna.2017.9.1.17.

Langmead, Alison. "Art and Architectural History and the Performative, Mindful Practice of the Digital Humanities." *The Journal of Interactive Technology & Pedagogy* 12 (February 12, 2018). https://jitp.commons.gc.cuny.edu/art—and—architectural—history—and—the—performative—mindful—practice—of—the—digital—humanities/.

Latour, Bruno. "Technology Is Society Made Durable." *Sociological Review* 38 (May 1990): 103–31.

Latour, Bruno, and Adam Lowe. "The Migration of the Aura, or How to Explore the Original through its Facsimiles." In *Switching Codes: Thinking Through Digital Technology in the Humanities and the Arts*, edited by Thomas Bartscherer and Roderick Coover, 275–97. Chicago: University of Chicago Press, 2011.

Law, John. "Making a Mess with Method." In *The Sage Handbook of Social Science Methodology*, edited by William Outhwaite and Stephen P. Turner, 595–606. London: Sage Publications, 2007.

Lincoln, Matthew, and Sandra van Ginhoven. "Modeling The Fragmented Archive: A Missing Data Case Study From Provenance Research." Paper given at Digital Humanities 2018, DH 2018, El Colegio de México, UNAM, and RedHD, Mexico City, Mexico, June 26–29, 2018. Accessed February 22, 2019. https://dh2018.adho.org/en/modeling—the—fragmented—archive—a—missing—data—case—study—from—provenance—research/.

Lindsay, Kenneth C. "Art, Art History, and the Computer." *Computers and the Humanities* 1, no. 2 (November 1966): 27–30.

Manovich, Lev. "Data Science and Digital Art History." *International Journal for Digital Art History* no. 1 (June 2015): 13–35.

Mansfield, Elizabeth C., ed. *Art History and Its Institutions: Foundations of a Discipline*. London: Routledge, 2002.

Matejka, Justin, and George Fitzmaurice. "Same Stats, Different Graphs: Generating Datasets with Varied Appearance and Identical Statistics through Simulated Annealing." In *Proceedings of the 2017 CHI Conference on Human Factors in Computing Systems*, 1290–94. Denver, CO, May 6–11, 2017. Accessed March 11, 2019. https://doi.org/10.1145/3025453.3025912

McCarty, Willard. "19: Modeling: A Study in Words and Meanings." In *A Companion to Digital Humanities*, edited by Susan Schreibman, Ray Siemens and John Unsworth, n.p. Oxford: Blackwell Publishing, 2004. Accessed March 11, 2019. www.digitalhumanities.org/companion/view?docId=blackwell/9781405103213/9781405103213.xml&chunk.id=ss1–3–7&toc.depth=1&toc.id=ss1–3–7&brand=default.

———. "21: Knowing . . . Modeling in Literary Studies." In *A Companion to Digital Literary Studies*, edited by Susan Schreibman and Ray Siemens, n.p. Oxford: Blackwell, 2008. Accessed February 22, 2019. https://onlinelibrary.wiley.com/doi/10.1002/9781405177504.ch21.

Miller, Daniel. "Conclusion: A Theory of Virtualism." In *Virtualism: A New Political Economy*, edited by James G. Carrier and Daniel Miller, 187–215. Oxford: Berg, 1998.

———. "The Virtual Moment." *Journal of the Royal Anthropological Institute* 9 (2003): 57–75.

Mol, Annemarie, and John Law. "Complexities: An Introduction." In *Complexities: Social Studies of Knowledge Practices*, edited by John Law and Annemarie Mol, 1–22. Durham and London: Duke University Press, 2002.

Parsons, Mark A., and Peter A. Fox. "Is Data Publication the Right Metaphor?" *Data Science Journal* 12 (February 10, 2013): WDS32–WDS46.

Posner, Miriam. "Humanities Data: A Necessary Contradiction." *Miriam Posner's Blog*, June 25, 2015. Accessed February 22, 2019. http://miriamposner.com/blog/humanities—data—a—necessary—contradiction/.

Promey, Sally M., and Miriam Stewart. "Digital Art History: A New Field for Collaboration." *American Art* 11, no. 2 (Summer 1997): 36–41.

Prown, Jules David. "Analysis of Data." In *John Singleton Copley*, vol. 1, 128–37. Cambridge, MA: Harvard University Press, 1966.

———. "The Art Historian and the Computer: An Analysis of Copley's Patronage, 1753–1774." *Smithsonian Journal of History* 1 (1966–1967): 17–30.

Rawson, Katie, and Trevor Muñoz. "Against Cleaning." In *Debates in the Digital Humanities 2019*, edited by Lauren F. Klein and Matthew Gold, n.p. Minneapolis: University of Minnesota Press, 2019. Work originally published as, "Against Cleaning." *Curating Menus*. Website produced by Katie Rawson and Trevor Muñoz, July 6, 2016. Accessed March 11, 2019. http://curatingmenus.org/articles/against—cleaning/.

Rittel, Horst W.J., and Melvin M. Webber. "Dilemmas in a General Theory of Planning." *Policy Sciences* 4 (1973): 155–69.

Schmidhuber, Jürgen. "Deep Learning in Neural Networks: An Overview." *Neural Networks* 61 (January 2015): 85–117.

Seaver, Nick. "Algorithms as Culture." *Big Data & Society* (July–September 2017): 1–12.

Shmueli, Galit. "To Explain or to Predict?" *Statistical Science* 25, no. 3 (2010): 289–310.

Simon, Herbert. "A Behavioral Model of Rational Choice." *The Quarterly Journal of Economics* 69, no. 1 (February 1955): 99–118.

Smith, Brian Cantwell. "The Couch or the Bottle: Levels of Abstraction and the Anxious Mind." *YouTube*, video posted by BrainMindConsci (The Brain, Mind, and Consciousness Society at the University of California, Santa Cruz), November 11, 2015. Accessed February 22, 2019. https://youtu.be/C0g4OwtkoCQ.

———. "The Philosophy of Computation: Meaning, Mechanism, and Mystery." *YouTube*, posted by André Souza Lemos, July 10, 2013. Accessed February 22, 2019. https://youtu.be/USF1H70bRl0.

———. "Section 6: Age of Significance." *Age of Significance*. Last modified May 1, 2017. Retrieved from the Internet Archive. Accessed March 11, 2019. https://web.archive.org/web/20170501022356/http://ageofsignificance.org/aos/en/aos—v1c0.html.

Thorp, Jer. "You Say Data, I Say System." *Hackernoon*, July 13, 2007. Accessed February 22, 2019. https://hackernoon.com/you—say—data—i—say—system—54e84aa7a421.

Tillett, Barbara. "What Is FRBR? A Conceptual Model for the Bibliographic Universe." *The Australian Library Journal* 54, no. 1 (2005): 24–30.

Tolk, Andreas et al. "Epistemology of Modeling and Simulation." *Proceedings of the IEEE 2013 Winter Simulations Conference*, 1152–66. December 8–11, 2013. Accessed March 11, 2019. https://doi.org/10.1109/WSC.2013.6721504.

Vanhoutte, Edward. "The Gates of Hell: History and Definition of Digital | Humanities | Computing." In *Digital Research in the Arts and Humanities: Defining Digital Humanities: A Reader*, edited by Melissa Terras, Julianne Nyhan, and Edward Vanhoutte, 119–45. Farnham: Routledge, 2013.

Vaughan, William. "The Automated Connoisseur: Image Analysis and Art History." In *History and Computing*, edited by Peter Denley and Deian Hopkin, 215–21. Manchester: Manchester University Press, 1987.

———. "Automated Picture Referencing: A Further Look at 'Morelli.'" *Computers and the History of Art* 2, no. 1 (1992): 7–18.

Visser, Willemien. "Designing as Construction of Representations: A Dynamic Viewpoint in Cognitive Design Research." *Human—Computer Interaction* (Special Issue: "Foundations of Design in HCI") 21, no. 1 (2006): 103–52.

Witmore, Michael. "Latour, the Digital Humanities, and the Divided Kingdom of Knowledge." *New Literary History* 47, no. 2–3 (Spring–Summer 2016): 353–75.

———. "Shakespeare from the Waist Down." Filmed February 21, 2012 at the Maryland Institute for Technology in the Humanities Digital Dialogues Series, College Park, MD. Video, 43:33. Accessed March 11, 2019. https://mith.umd.edu/dialogues/shakespeare—from—the—waist—down/.

———. "What Should Humanists Think about in the Age of the Algorithm." Filmed June 16, 2018 at the 2018 Annual Meeting of the Consortium of Humanities Centers and Institutes, Charlottesville, VA. Video, 1:22:32. Accessed March 11, 2019. http://ihgc.as.virginia.edu/chci—2018—humanities—informatics.

# 27

# APPROACHING ABY WARBURG AND DIGITAL ART HISTORY

## Thinking Through Images

*Amanda Du Preez*

What does Aby Warburg (1866–1929) offer digital humanities and digital art history? In what follows, I aim to plot selected methods and strategies utilized by Warburg onto digital humanities. My underlying assumption is that Warburg's *Bilderatlas Mnemosyne* (1924–1929) allows for thinking though images using digital humanities (DH) methods. The *Bilderatlas* in its final constellation (1929) consisted of sixty-three portables frames (panels) stretched with black cloth onto which black and white photographs (971) of paintings, sculptures, coins, stamps, popular images and tarot cards, were pinned. It would not be too optimistic to state that Warburg's *Bilderatlas* anticipated DH strategies. Griselda Pollock identifies Warburg's contribution "not as an archive but, instead, [as a] psychologically aware historical study of the image, as a *thinking machine* for confronting contemporary Art History."[1] I would add: Warburg initiated a thinking machine for DH and stratagems for thinking through images.

The techniques or ideas that are highlighted in this chapter are the principle of the good neighbor through searching as researching; images as migrating units of meaning; framing as both a conceptual and structural strategy; the networked atlas; and moving between close and distant reading. As will become apparent, it is the role of the "sensitive seismograph"[2] and keen observer of culture, as Warburg describes these qualities, that is highlighted rather than a uniform methodology. Warburg cultivated principles of thinking that made use of technologies and techniques, but were not predetermined by them. This is akin to what Johanna Drucker distinguishes as "digital art history" and not merely "digitized art history."[3] In short, Warburg's *Bilderatlas* works on the principles of what I understand as critical digital humanities.[4]

### Finding the Good Neighbor: Searching as Researching

One of my favorite activities as a graduate student in art history was to visit the university library and peruse journals and books while browsing relevant shelves. It was in the pre-digital era when one still had to go to the library physically to gain access to resources. The fascinating thing was always finding other things than initially intended. Often this habit allowed me to make unexpected discoveries and links not anticipated. This was also a time when things were slower and the number of sources more containable. I have adapted that style of what I can only term "searching as researching" into my current research projects that are now mostly done online. Naturally, my current online browsing and searching are structured by algorithms and filter bubbles that I am not necessarily aware of or that I cannot control.

My experience of stumbling across sources and material was echoed by Joseph Leo Koerner's reflection of doing research in the Warburg Institute Library in London: "For as any serious visitor to the Library will attest, it is by wandering through those open stacks, sometimes with a book already targeted for retrieval, sometimes just browsing books by subject, that some of one's most robust thought trajectories get made."[5] I could relate to this statement as the act of browsing, led by curiosity and openness to what I may find, inspired much of my research. In hindsight, the searching as researching activity can be compared to the principle of the "good neighbor" ("*Gesetz der guten Nachbarschaft*") as not only proposed by Warburg, but which is embodied in the topography of the *Kulturwissenschaftliche Bibliothek Warburg* (K.B.W., Warburg Library of Cultural Studies) in Hamburg and later in the Warburg Library that relocated to London in 1933. In the words of Fritz Saxl, assistant of Warburg and later successor, it is through browsing that scholarly familiarity is gained:

> The book of which one knew was in most cases not the book which one needed. The unknown neighbour on the shelf contained the vital information, although from its title one might not have guessed this. The overriding idea was that the books together—each containing its larger or smaller bit of information and being supplemented by its neighbours—should by their titles guide the student to perceive the essential forces of the human mind and its history.[6]

According to the principle of the good neighbor, books and images dealing with modern sciences can be found next to those dealing with alchemy, astrology and magic, for instance. What the principle calls forward is the relationship and hermeneutic conversation made possible through the proximity and (coincidental) locations of books, as well as boxes with photographs and relevant corpora. As Michael Steinberg notes about the Warburg Library in London:

> Each book, and each newly acquired book, should stage a conversation with its neighbor: ask a question, provide an answer. The result is a conversation both infinite and coherent: the envy, perhaps, of today's digitized world and its infinite capacity for information but not for coherence.[7]

Steinberg alerts us here to the discrepancies between being an embodied Warburg Library user in real time and space, as opposed to sifting through the information avalanche online. In order to experience the principle of the good neighbor, the researcher needs to be physically present in the library to peruse items and not rely on predetermined algorithms or search parameters to provide the best results.[8] Ernst Cassirer famously described the unique and even "peculiar" arrangement of the Warburg Library as "dangerous."[9] The danger expressed by Cassirer should be interpreted more as astonishment, not only in terms of the overwhelming collection of materials available, but also because of the temptation of getting lost (to be imprisoned) in the Library. The Warburg Library thus yields a maze-like character (Koerner refers to the structure as "mazy passages between the self and the other,"[10] while Cassirer did indeed use the term "labyrinth"[11] to describe the Library), which can only be navigated by surrendering to its invisible and even magical organizing principles. As Wood notes: "The Library is interactive but, as an intelligent organism, it is not so easily instrumentalized. You succumb to its rhythms."[12] What one may find is in no terms certain and cannot be accurately predicted as one follows a "slithering" and serpent-like path, typical of the Warburgian method, through the material.[13]

The problem is naturally that not all interested researchers can visit the Warburg Library in person as time, funding, and access do not enable such visits. They have to make do with the Warburg Institute's online resources[14] which can in no way replicate the physical experience of browsing or "searching as researching." Analogue searching is not necessarily superior to digital searches, but one differs from the other, and they are at best complementary.[15] The question is whether the principle of the good neighbor can be experienced or recreated online? Or should one acknowledge, as Barbara Stafford so movingly argues, that the Warburg Library cannot be remade or reinvented online, but is an immersed experience that one has to live through. Thus, the intuitive connections can best be experienced when physically walking through the Library.[16]

Perhaps the best digital art history can do when engaging the Warburg experience is to take the pointers of Warburg's method seriously and determine how they can be "remediated" and "remapped" into the digital.[17] In other words, to ask: What aspect of the Warburg method is already dispersed, linked and networked? Replicating the Warburg Library online has partly been done by the digitization of its contents, but the searching as researching component may still elude the user. The Warburg Library consists of dual but complimentary entities—an image collection (The Photographic Collection) as well as a book collection. Searching the Photographic Collection, which is organized iconographically, Nina Vestberg reveals "contrary to what one would expect of a digital resource; it appeared to require more in-depth knowledge of iconography to use the database than the physical archive."[18] If you do not search with established iconographic labels, chances are you will probably not find what you are looking for.[19] Furthermore, the search will only be as effective as "the quality of the meta-data"[20] associated with the object or image. Here the implementation of online semantic searches, as in *Iconclass* for instance,[21] may aid in mediating the contextually rich Library experience, by providing more iconographical context (neighborly closeness) to online searches.

An additional complexity is that the Warburg Library embodies the relationship between image and text, and the Library user is first confronted with the image that then leads to the word, and not the other way around. The book section of the Library is arranged under the four concepts or strata: Image, Word, Orientation, and Action that are spread over the four floors, while the Photographic Collection (the initial *Bildersammlung*) is organized in four slightly differently named sections: Image—Word and Image—Orientation and Image—Action and Image.[22] The "Linking Venus" project shows the possibilities of searching the four strata separately for "relevant data on the figure of Venus" in both the Library and the Photographic Collection and how these connections can be visually mapped.[23]

Emulating an image-lead search online is tricky, however, because image recognition software is mostly under-developed, and images need to be "read" as a whole before fragments can be identified. Here the latest developments in artificial intelligence techniques, such as Deep Learning and Convolutional Neural Networks, may assist in recognizing the repetition of visual motifs, shapes and styles.[24] Although the physical searching as researching activity cannot simply be replicated online, there are aspects unique to the online search and digital environment that build on Warburg's methods.[25]

## Images as Migrating Units of Meaning

The aim of this chapter is not to renegotiate Aby Warburg's reputation as an art historian, but rather to provide a brief contextualizing of his method within the broader framework of "the histories of art."[26] It is accepted that Warburg took up a contrary position to specific traditional art historical methods of his time, most notably to the over aestheticization of art. The fact that Warburg was not interested in a narrow iconology aimed at establishing the meaning of an artwork as a closed-off unit is well-documented. Warburg refers to his project as "art-historical culture studies" (*kunstgeschichtliches Kulturwissenschaft*),[27] or a "science of culture" (*Kulturwissenschaft*) and even declares himself an "image historian" (*Bildhistoriker*).[28] His interest was in following "the meaning of the economy between a representation's (the image's) lived past and its continued sign function."[29] This means Warburg's project cannot be neatly defined. In fact, Giorgio Agamben famously refers to his project as the "nameless science,"[30] precisely because Warburg acts as both historian and sociologist/anthropologist of images' past and present existence.

Interestingly, the unit in which this "nameless science" trades most comfortably is the image (*Bild*). Warburg's *Bilderatlas*, therefore, includes images in the broadest sense, e.g. stamps, maps, coins, magazines, popular photographs, and astrology charts. Horst Bredekamp assists in contextualizing the concept *Bild* in German, which has no direct or easy translation in English. It is neither simply an image, picture, artwork, figure, or illustration.[31] *Bild*, and subsequently *Bildwissenschaft*, have a more extensive meaning and encompass a broader field of study.

Importantly, Warburg did not perceive images as "mere lifeless illustrations"[32] of a researcher's or art historian's findings. He instead perceived images as living entities. Hence his interest in all images, those created in everyday life as well as art. Warburg focused his attention on what Agamben refers to as "the force of images,"[33] rather than on their formalistic and aesthetic qualities, as art history did at the time. It is not that Warburg was not interested in formal qualities. Rather, he considered the distinction between form and content to be impossible, just as the forced difference between the history of styles and the history of culture was implausible. In Warburg's own words: "I was less interested in neat solutions than in formulating a new problem."[34] Warburg is not so much interested in solving an artistic question (formal or aesthetic), but rather a broader visual problem, namely the tension between human emotion and intellect manifested in the *Pathosformel* (an emotionally charged visual trope). The question that he identified can broadly be described as aiming to make a diagnosis of Western civilization's "soul," not merely by describing the symptoms of fluctuating between a restraining Apollonian depression and an enhancing Dionysian ecstasy, but by prescribing an (image) antidote from the past.

The inherent mobility and reproducibility of images—described by Warburg as *Bilderfahrzeug* or *Bildvehikel* (image vehicle)—become especially productive for digital art history. Images, as opposed to pictures or artworks, travel across time and space. W.J.T. Mitchell explains the difference between a picture and an image as follows: "The picture is a material object, a thing you can burn or break or tear. An image is what appears in a picture, and what survives its destruction—in memory, in narrative, in copies and traces in other media."[35] He continues: "The image never appears except in some medium or other, but it is also what transcends media, what can be transferred from one medium to another."[36] This is corroborated by Johannes von Müller:

> Warburg did not deal with frescos, paintings, sculptures and other material products of the many branches of the visual arts. They were not the matter of his primary interest. He dealt with the pictorial data carried by these works of art and other kinds of media. He may have seen and studied real frescos, paintings, etc., but he perceived images. He did not interact with works of art, but with images.[37]

The pictorial data or image migrate (*Bilderwanderung*) and journey (*Bilderfahrung*) through cultural history via "pathways." The motion and path become visible through the pictorial data transferred from one medium to another and specifically through sarcophagi, tapestries, and prints in Warburg's case.[38]

Currently, images travel effortlessly through different media and platforms, from website to smartphone, to billboard, and canvas. In essence the image is the immaterial content that is transferrable. Although Mitchell denies the mechanism of a metaphysical realm behind images' ability to travel, he does use terms such as "ghostly" and "phantasmatic appearance"[39] to describe this movement. Similarly, Georges Didi-Huberman describes Warburg's documentation of the resurrection of images as "survivals" (*Nachleben der Antike*) from ancient times, almost akin to the voices of ghosts.[40] Didi-Huberman adds: "Whereas art has a history, images have survivals."[41] Interestingly, images, and in particular the *Pathosformeln* (although fragmentary and quotidian), are survivals and not simply revivals.[42]

The survival of images becomes one of the outstanding characteristics of Warburg's *Bilderatlas*. Warburg utilized black and white albumen photographs ("surrogates"[43] as he referred to them) of selected images that could easily be mounted, replicated, swapped and that could travel from one venue to another. At the time "photography emerges as a central element [. . .] thanks to its faster reproducibility and to the innumerable possibilities for comparisons of works of art, which until then had been unimaginable."[44] Warburg's first use of documentary photography can be dated back to 1888 during his first visit to Florence.[45] As Katia Mazzucco explains:

> But image, in art historical research praxis, has a material aspect: that is, its reproduction, the photograph (or, in the past, the drawing or print) of the given image; in this sense, the visual evidence, in turn, depends on the summoning of a photograph of an original image (which may itself may be a photograph, drawing or print) that may then be used in evidence.[46]

The photo as a medium of recording becomes part of the hermeneutic process by selecting or framing the image. Warburg relied on both books (text) and photographs (image) as aids (*Hilfsmittel*) in making his visual arguments. He expressly states that he required access (to be close at hand) to both image and word as part of his "Wort-Bild heuristic binomial"[47] inquiry. The *Mnemosyne Atlas* was after all a provisional photographic exhibition before any published text version appeared. Images migrated via surrogates that became dynamic units of meaning and allowed for the discernment of "patterns of transmission."[48] The "art-documentary photographs" as used by Warburg contain both data and meta-data; an image on the recto (front) and layered hand written notes on the verso (back).[49]

The image as carrier of meaning is, however, open to other prospects and avenues of interpretation when introduced to cultural analytics[50] and data visualization. Stefka Hristova takes this route by analyzing the relationship between color and violence through the color-data of Warburg's Panel 54 from 1924. Images become "objects with features, and more specifically as image-data in and of themselves."[51] Hristova shows that there is a correlation between the colors used and themes in Panel 54 where the highest and brightest saturation is observable in images of violence. She does, however, conclude that as nodes of knowledge, images cannot merely be interpreted in terms of data (form) since the meta-data (context and content) remains similarly important. It is in the movement between data and meta-data that "critical interpretations of visual culture" are fostered.[52] Warburg allowed images to act as agents of data, but data that was always enriched by meta-data in the form of panels, overarching panel themes, and other images selected to appear in proximity. The meta-data thus continuously accompanied the data in the form of the frame, which is the next technique under discussion.

## Framing as Cognitive and Structural Strategy

The framing device is one of the most striking methods used in Warburg's *Mnemosyne Atlas* to orientate the viewer both cognitively and structurally. Art historians have used the framing device over time as heuristic tool to juxtapose their instruments and the act of interpretation.[53] From the first art historian, Giorgio Vasari who used framing as "visual rhetoric," to Warburg's incorporation of framing "not only in the already established form of the surrogate image," but also by recording the "plates/montages [as] the stages of his argument."[54]

Warburg's black panels are frames that allowed for comparison and (hermeneutic) dialog. He referred to this dialogical frame as a *Denkraum*, (or *Andachtsraum*)—a frame that allows for thinking and pondering over images. Warburg also constantly re-arranged the order and format of the images to generate different conversations and conclusions, thus proliferating frames. He would photograph panels (which is a framing technique in itself) in the process of offering a possible visual argument, but the *Bilderatlas* always remained an unfinished or incomplete project. Warburg did not provide the final frame.

Another important aspect that allowed for the construction of meaning in Warburg's *Bilderatlas* is the deliberate spaces or intervals between images. The images were not placed in the same proximity, and the areas between them differ considerably. The scale and size of the images also differed. While some were close-up details, others contained the whole image. By using this technique of montage, images are simultaneously connected and disconnected through the black intervals between them. The aim was not to unite all the images into one final, conclusive response or interpretive meaning. Rather "when the Bilderatlas unfolds, it discloses a significant multiplicity of singularities that cannot be boiled down to any unity."[55] For Warburg, it was not useful to be immersed within the "pure sensory space" (imagination), nor to identify completely with the formulaic abstraction of "the space of pure knowledge" (reason).[56] Instead the aims is to find an in-between space (*Zwischenraum*). The in-between space constitutes the "iconography of intervals"[57] and acts as a distancing strategy to create detachment so that the viewer can engage meaningfully with the frames. Warburg's panels are an attempt to open up reflective spaces, separated and bracketed off from the flow and demands of ordinary life.

The framing device converts well into the digital interface because online it becomes a nodal element.[58] The obvious comparison between the screen and the light-table shows how the framing technique is common to both analogue and digital art history. The screen as panel frames a selection of images (although the selection can be changed instantaneously with a click) and allows for the comparative consideration of the chosen images within proximity. In this digital *Denkraum* the hermeneutic dialog can take place. The framing device thus allows for linking. This was the case in the *Bilderatlas* and is also evident for instance in the *Mnemosyne. Meanderings through Aby Warburg's Atlas*[59] collaborative online project between the Cornell University Library and the Warburg Library. Warburg's use of framing to create a space for the comparison and linking of images and ideas reveals a networked character and can also be viewed as a forerunner of hypertext.[60]

## A Networked Atlas

What is an atlas? First, an atlas does not follow the linear logic of a book; in other words, we cannot "read" an atlas in the usual fashion.[61] The atlas uses tables, plates, and primarily visual forms of knowledge making (visualization) to communicate. As Didi-Huberman explains "we use an atlas in a way that combines those two dissimilar gestures: We open it, first, to look for precise information. But once we find that information, we do not necessarily put the atlas down; rather, we follow different pathways this way and that."[62] Thus, we are reminded that an atlas of images, as in the case of the *Bilderatlas*, never merely illustrates knowledge; it constructs knowledge and even, sometimes, manages to deconstruct it.[63] The atlas acts as a tool that is driven by the imagination (between magic and reason), which allows for making correspondences and analogies not discernable at first sight or direct observation.[64]

Warburg's *Atlas* forms a "multi-dimensional network"[65] of ideas, images and texts that can be linked in unforeseeable ways. The *Bilderatlas* is not an archive in the traditional sense, but operates more like a rhizome.[66] Analogous to the rhizome, which "grows horizontally, connecting and disconnecting diverse points,"[67] Warburg's atlas does not function according to pre-defined order or structure, but stages "intensive maps resulting from the connection and rupture of different plateaus."[68] Thus, mobilized as an anti-archive, the *Bilderatlas* "builds a new machinery for the production of what will be called knowledge."[69] This new knowledge undoubtedly belongs to a "science without a name" or perhaps to a digital art history as Drucker proposes.

The rhizome's operations have also been linked to the internet,[70] which indicates that the *Bilderatlas* anticipates the Web's workings in terms of open structure and connectivity. Building on Warburg's web based *Atlas* is the *Meta-Image* project, which aims to provide a network-based research environment for art history and other sciences concerning visual culture.[71] It consists of the two components: *prometheus*[72] which provides access to more than seven hundred thousand images in nearly sixty connected image databases; and *HyperImage*, a tool for image annotation.[73] According to Warnke and Dieckmann, *Meta-Image* "can be seen as an ideal [digital] platform for image discourse in art history and visual culture studies"[74] precisely because it expands on the groundwork done in the *Bilderatlas*.

## Between Close Reading and Distant Reading

How to find a synthesis between close reading (qualitative research, interpretation) and distant reading (quantitative research, formalist analysis) is one of the critical questions in digital humanities.[75] The *Mnemosyne. Meanderings Through Aby Warburg's Atlas* online project mentioned previously permits viewers to zoom in and out from selected panels. By selecting an individual panel, images can also be enlarged, with identifying information supplied when clicked upon. By allowing viewers to do this, Warburg's method of combining immersions and distancing ("iconography of the interval") can be experienced. The act of zooming in and out recollects the different motions of close reading and distant reading, enabling the extraction of patterns between form and interpretation.

In a similar manner, Christopher D. Johnson draws an analogy between the hieroglyph (image) in Warburg's *Atlas* and close reading, while identifying the use of diagrams (frames) with distant reading.[76] He describes the hieroglyph as a symbolic form that condenses meanings, whereas the diagram operates heuristically to dilate meaning. The hieroglyph and the diagram make different cognitive demands and offer different epistemological rewards, Johnson adds. The diagram—or what W.J.T. Mitchell terms diagrammatology—can be defined as "a sensible or spatial construct of interpretations of formal characteristics" and "a systematic study of the way that relationships among elements are represented and interpreted by graphic constructions."[77] Diagrammatology distils spatiotemporal, rhetorical, and thematic organization visually. In Warburg's dialectical move between imagination and rationality, the "Diagram becomes discovery."[78] In response to Johanna Drucker's question of what constitutes "ways of thinking about works of art that arise from digital methods" and how do these "reconfigure our fundamental understanding of what constitutes a work of art?,"[79] it appears that Warburg's movement between hieroglyph and diagram, distillation and dilation[80] offers a model for digital analysis.

Alternating between close and distant reading also allows for selecting patterns that is repeated, such as the *Pathosformeln*. Recently Leonardo Impett and Franco Moretti have capitalized on the diagrammatical exposition of Warburg's *Pathosformeln* by "operationalizing"[81] the formula. They have translated the formula into a "sequence of quantitative operations, some of the details of which will be discussed in the next chapter."[82] To be more precise the *Pathosformeln* is turned into an algorithm precisely because it is a repeatable visual paradigm.[83] The term *Pathosformel* already signals a formula that is repeated and therefore a pattern is detectable: "The term 'formula' usefully includes the idea of form, which reminds us that pathos is a formal operation, not a content that can be detached from its formulation."[84]

The *Pathosformel* focuses on the human body and its movements. Impett and Moretti operationalize the formula by annotating each figure identified in an image. As Impett and Süsstrunk conclude: "Our morphological model for *Pathosformeln* is statistically strong: but what are the art-historical implications?"[85] I concur that this type of operationalization and quantifying project still has to show its relevance for answering specific research questions. Can it be used to predict the pathos formula in images, for instance? Can it recognize Warburg's pathos formula in other images? Probably not at this stage, but it is Warburg's open-ended oscillation between close and distant reading that made it possible for these researchers to venture into digital art history.

## Notes

1. Griselda Pollock, "Whither Art History?" *The Art Bulletin* 96, no. 1 (2014): 11.
2. Christopher D. Johnson, *Memory, Metaphor, and Aby Warburg's Atlas of Images* (Ithaca, NY: Cornell University Press and Cornell University Library, 2012), 169.
3. Joanna Drucker, "Is There a 'Digital' Art History?" *Visual Resources* 29, no. 1–2 (2013): 7.
4. David Berry and Anders Fagerjord in *Digital Humanities: Knowledge and Critique in a Digital Age* (2017) identify critical digital humanities as moving beyond the novelty value of digital technologies. By not treating the computer as a "truth machine" and instead turning "our hermeneutic skills on the very software and algorithms that make up [DH] systems," the foundation for a "critical digital humanities" is laid.
5. Joseph L. Koerner, "Writing Rituals: The Case of Aby Warburg," *Common Knowledge* 18, no. 1 (2012): 89.
6. Fritz Saxl, "The History of Warburg's Library (1886–1944)," in *Aby Warburg: An Intellectual Biography*, appendix to E. H. Gombrich (Oxford: Phaidon Press, 1986), 325–38.
7. Michael P. Steinberg, "The Law of the Good Neighbor," *Common Knowledge* 18, no. 1 (2012): 128.
8. Nina Lager Vestberg, "Ordering, Searching, Finding," *Journal of Visual Culture* 12, no. 3 (2013): 474.
9. Carlo Ginzburg, "Une Machine a Penser," *Common Knowledge* 18, no. 1 (2012): 82.
10. Koerner, "Writing Rituals," 105.
11. Alberto Manguel, *The Library at Night* (New Haven: Yale University Press, 2008), 198.
12. Christopher S. Wood, "Dromenon," *Common Knowledge* 18, no. 1 (2012): 106–16.
13. Steinberg, "The Law of the Good Neighbor," 132.
14. Available: https://warburg.sas.ac.uk.
15. Vestberg, "Ordering, Searching, Finding," 472–89.
16. Barbara Maria Stafford, "Reconceiving the Warburg Library as a Working Museum of the Mind," *Common Knowledge* 18, no. 1 (2012): 180.
17. Emanuela Patti and François Quiviger, "'Linking Venus' New Technologies of Memory and Reconfiguration of Space at the Warburg Library," *Between* IV, no. 8 (2014): 2.
18. Vestberg, "Ordering, Searching, Finding," 478.
19. Hans Brandhorst, "Aby Warburg's Wildest Dreams Come True?" *Visual Resources* 29, no. 1–2 (2013): 75.
20. Ibid., 83.
21. *Iconclass* (www.iconclass.org) is "a classification system designed for art and iconography. It is the most widely accepted scientific tool for the description and retrieval of subjects represented in images (works of art, book illustrations, reproductions, photographs, etc.) and is used by museums and art institutions around the world."
22. Katia Mazzucco, "Images on the Move: Some Notes on the Bibliothek Warburg Bildersammlung (Hamburg) and the Warburg Institute Photographic Collection (London)," *Art Libraries Journal* 38, no. 4 (2013): 18.
23. Patti and Quiviger, "Linking Venus," 13.
24. For examples of projects implementing artificial intelligence, see the *Replica* project led by the Fondazione Giorgio Cini and the École polytechnique fédérale, Lausanne, that aims to build the first search engine based on iconographic search keys dedicated to pictorial and architectural artifacts.

Another example is *ArtMiner* that allows for the recognition of visual copies or duplicate patterns. *ArtMiner* is available at: https://enherit.enpc.fr/artminer.

25. This is not to imply that online searches are not also "physical" or embodied activities, naturally the user is a situated and embodied being while searching online.
26. See Griselda Pollock's utilization of a more inclusive and challenging concept of art history in *Vision and Difference: Feminism, Femininity and the Histories of Art* (London: Routledge, 1988).
27. Warburg Institute Archive WIA III.113.6, working papers for a seminar, November 1927–February 1928, 118: "Über die Methode einer kunstgeschichtlichen Kulturwissenschaft."
28. Aby Warburg, Christopher D. Johnson, and Claudia Wedepohl, "From the Arsenal to the Laboratory," *West 86th: A Journal of Decorative Arts, Design History, and Material Culture* 19, no. 1 (2012): 107.
29. Richard Woodfield, *Art History as Cultural History: Warburg's Projects* (London: Taylor and Francis, 2014), 2.
30. See Giorgio Agamben, "Aby Warburg and the Nameless Science," in *Potentialities: Collected Essays in Philosophy* (Stanford, CA: Stanford University Press, 1999), 89–103.
31. Horst Bredekamp, "A Neglected Tradition? Art History as Bildwissenschaft," *Critical Inquiry* 29, no. 3 (2003): 418.
32. Woodfield, *Art History as Cultural History*, 3.
33. Agamben, "Aby Warburg and the Nameless Science," 90.
34. Aby Warburg, "Italian Art and International Astrology in the Palazzo Schifanoia in Ferrara," in *German Essays on Art History*, ed. Gert Schiff (New York: Continuum, 1988), 252–53.
35. W.J.T. Mitchell, *Image Science: Iconology, Visual Culture, and Media Aesthetics* (Chicago: University of Chicago Press, 2015), 30.
36. Ibid., 30–32.
37. Johannes von Müller, "Metadata: New Perspectives on Aby Warburg's 'Critical Iconology,'" *Philosophy of Photography* 8, no. 1 (2017): 178.
38. Ibid.
39. Mitchell, *Image Science*, 32.
40. Georges Didi-Huberman, "Artistic Survival: Panofsky vs. Warburg and the Exorcism of Impure Time," *Common Knowledge* 9, no. 2 (2003): 273–85.
41. Ibid., 275.
42. Ibid., 277.
43. Aby Warburg, "Die Bilderausstellungen des Volksheims," in *Das Volksheim in Hamburg, Bericht über das sechste Geschäftsjahr 1906–1907* (Berlin: Akademie Verlag, 1907), 53–55.
44. Elisabetta Cunsolo, "Photo Archives and the Photographic Memory of Art History," *Visual Resources* 26, no. 4 (2010): 392.
45. Katia Mazzucco, "On the Reverse Some Notes on Photographic Images From the Warburg Institute Photographic Collection," *Aisthesis* v, no. 2 (2012): 219.
46. Mazzucco, "Images on the Move," 17.
47. Mazzucco, "On the Reverse," 221.
48. Mazzucco, "Images on the Move," 17.
49. Mazzucco, "On the Reverse," 219–20.
50. See Lev Manovich, "How to Follow Global Digital Cultures, or Cultural Analytics for Beginners" (2009) in which he proposes how to research cultural artifacts by "employ[ing] statistical data analysis, data mining, information visualization, scientific visualization, visual analytics, simulation and other computer-based techniques." Available: www.manovich.net/cultural_analytics.pdf
51. Stefka Hristova, "Images as Data: Cultural Analytics and Aby Warburg's Mnemosyne," *International Journal for Digital Art History* no. 2 (2016): 117.
52. Ibid., 129.
53. Elli Doulkaridou-Ramantani, "Reframing Art History," *International Journal for Digital Art History* 1, no. 1 (2015): 68.
54. Ibid., 70.
55. Daniela Sacco, "Composing the Symbolic: The Denkraum between Warburg and Eisenstein," *Aisthesis* VIII, no. 2 (2015): 59––75.
56. Victoria Cirlot, "Zwischenraum/Denkraum Terminological Oscillations in the Introductions to the Atlas by Aby Warburg (1929) and Ernst Gombrich (1937)," *Engramma—La Tradizione Classica Nella Memoria Occidentale* 153 (2018).
57. Ibid.
58. Doulkaridou-Ramantani, "Reframing Art History," 69.

59. Available: https://warburg.library.cornell.edu.
60. Matthew Rampley, Thierry Lenain, and Hubert Locher, *Art History and Visual Studies in Europe: Transnational Discourses and National Frameworks* (Leiden: Brill, 2012), 149.
61. Georges Didi-Huberman, *Atlas, or the Anxious Gay Science,* trans. Shane Lillis (Chicago and London: The University of Chicago Press, 2018), 17.
62. Ibid., 15.
63. Ibid., 286.
64. Ibid., 18.
65. Sara Angel, "The Mnemosyne Atlas and the Meaning of Panel 79 in Aby Warburg's Oeuvre as a Distributed Object," *Leonardo* 44, no. 3 (2011): 267.
66. Gilles Deleuze and Félix Guattari's rhizomatic concept operates through the lateral proliferation of links and connections, rather than vertical ordering.
67. María del Carmen Molina Barea, "Rhizomatic Mnemosyne: Warburg, Serres, and the Atlas of Hermes," *Contemporary Aesthetics* 16, no. 1 (2018).
68. Ibid.
69. Ibid.
70. Philip Goodchild, *Gilles Deleuze and the Question of Philosophy* (London: Associated University Presses, 1996).
71. The project is available at: www.meta-image.de. See Martin Warnke and Lisa Dieckmann, "Prometheus Meets Meta-Image: Implementations of Aby Warburg's Methodical Approach in the Digital Era," *Visual Studies* 31, no. 2 (2016) for an in-depth discussion of the research environment.
72. Available at: www.prometheus-bildarchiv.de.
73. Available at: www.hyperimage.eu.
74. Warnke and Dieckmann, "Prometheus Meets Meta-Image," 119.
75. N. Katherine Hayles, *How We Think: Digital Media and Contemporary Technogenesis* (Chicago: University of Chicago Press, 2012), 75.
76. Christopher D. Johnson, "Warburg's 'Zwischenraum': Between Hieroglyph and Diagram," Aby Warburg 150. Work. Legacy. Promise, The Warburg Institute, School for Advanced Studies, University of London, November 2016.
77. W.J.T. Michell, "Diagrammotology," *Critical Inquiry* 7, no. 3 (1981): 622–33.
78. Johnson, "Warburg's 'Zwischenraum.'"
79. Drucker, "Is There a 'Digital' Art History?" 6.
80. Johnson, "Warburg's 'Zwischenraum.'"
81. Franco Moretti, "Operationalizing"; or, The Function of Measurement in Modern Literary Stanford Literary Lab Pamphlet Series (2013), litlab.stanford.edu/LiteraryLabPamphlet6.
82. Leonardo Laurence Impett and Sabine Süsstrunk, "From Mnemosyne to Terpsichore—The Bilderatlas After the Image," Premiere Annual Conference of the International Alliance of Digital Humanities Organizations (DH 2017), Montreal, Canada, August 8–11, 2017.
83. Ibid.
84. Pollock, "Whither Art History?" 11.
85. Impett, and Süsstrunk, "From Mnemosyne to Terpsichore."

## Bibliography

Agamben, Giorgio. "Aby Warburg and the Nameless Science." In *Potentialities. Collected Essays in Philosophy*, 89–103. Stanford, California: Stanford University Press, 1999.

Angel, Sara. "The Mnemosyne Atlas and the Meaning of Panel 79 in Aby Warburg's Oeuvre as a Distributed Object." *Leonardo* 44, no. 3 (2011): 266–67.

Barea, María del Carmen Molina. "Rhizomatic Mnemosyne: Warburg, Serres, and the Atlas of Hermes." *Contemporary Aesthetics* 16, no. 1 (2018). https://contempaesthetics.org/newvolume/pages/article.php?articleID=812

Berry, David M., and Anders Fagerjord. *Digital Humanities: Knowledge and Critique in a Digital Age*. Cambridge: Polity Press, 2017.

Brandhorst, Hans. "Aby Warburg's Wildest Dreams Come True?", *Visual Resources* 29, no. 1–2 (2013): 72–88.

Bredekamp, Horst. "A Neglected Tradition? Art History as Bildwissenschaft." *Critical Inquiry* 29, no. 3 (2003): 418–28.

Cirlot, Victoria. "Zwischenraum/Denkraum Terminological Oscillations in the Introductions to the Atlas by Aby Warburg (1929) and Ernst Gombrich (1937)." *Engramma—La Tradizione Classica Nella Memoria Occidentale* 153 (2018). www.engramma.it/eOS/index.php?id_articolo=3343
Cunsolo, Elisabetta. "Photo Archives and the Photographic Memory of Art History." *Visual Resources* 26, no. 4 (2010): 391–401.
Doulkaridou-Ramantani, Eli. "Reframing Art History." *International Journal for Digital Art History* 1, no. 1 (2015): 66–83.
Didi-Huberman, Georges. "Artistic Survival. Panofsky Vs. Warburg and the Exorcism of Impure Time." *Common Knowledge* 9, no. 2 (2003): 273–85.
———. *Atlas, or the Anxious Gay Science.* Translated Shane Lillis. Chicago and London: The University of Chicago Press, 2018.
———. *The Surviving Image. Phantoms of Time and Time of Phantoms. Aby Warburg's History of Art.* Translated Harvey Mendelsohn. University Park, Pennsylvania: The Pennsylvania State University Press, 2017
Drucker, Johanna. "Is There a 'Digital' Art History?" *Visual Resources* 29, no. 1–2 (2013): 5–13.
Ginzburg, Carlo. "Une Machine a Penser." *Common Knowledge* 18, no. 1 (2012): 79–85.
Hayles, N. Katherine. *How We Think: Digital Media and Contemporary Technogenesis.* Chicago: University of Chicago Press, 2012.
Hristova, Stefka. "Images as Data: Cultural Analytics and Aby Warburg's Mnemosyne." *International Journal for Digital Art History*, no. 2 (2016): 117–32.
Impett, Leonardo Laurence, and Sabine Süsstrunk. "From Mnemosyne to Terpsichore—the Bilderatlas after the Image." In Premiere Annual Conference of the International Alliance of Digital Humanities Organizations (DH 2017), Montreal, Canada, August 8–11, 2017.
Johnson, Christopher D. *Memory, Metaphor, and Aby Warburg's Atlas of Images.* Ithaca, NY: Cornell University Press and Cornell University Library, 2012.
———. "Warburg's 'Zwischenraum': Between Hieroglyph and Diagram." *Aby Warburg 150. Work. Legacy. Promise*, The Warburg Institute, School for Advanced Studies, University of London, November 2016.
Koerner, Joseph L. "Writing Rituals: The Case of Aby Warburg." *Common Knowledge* 18, no. 1 (2012): 86–105.
Manguel, Alberto. *The Library at Night.* New Haven: Yale University Press, 2008.
Manovich, Lev. "How to Follow Global Digital Cultures, or Cultural Analytics for Beginners" (2009). www.manovich.net/cultural_analytics. pdf
Mazzucco, Katia. "Images on the Move. Some Notes on the Bibliothek Warburg Bildersammlung (Hamburg) and the Warburg Institute Photographic Collection (London)." *Art Libraries Journal* 38, no. 4 (2013): 16–24.
———. "On the Reverse Some Notes on Photographic Images from the Warburg Institute Photographic Collection." *Aisthesis* V, no. 2 (2012). www.fupress.com/aisthesis
Michaud, Philippe-Alain. *Aby Warburg and the Image in Motion.* New York: Zone Books, 2007.
Mitchell, W.J.T. "Diagrammotology." *Critical Inquiry* 7, no. 3 (1981): 622–33.
———. *Image Science. Iconology, Visual Culture, and Media Aesthetics.* Chicago: University of Chicago Press, 2015.
Moretti, Franco. "Operationalizing"; or, The Function of Measurement in Modern Literary. Stanford Literary Lab Pamphlet Series (2013). litlab.stanford. edu/LiteraryLabPamphlet6
Patti, Emanuela, and François Quiviger. "'Linking Venus' New Technologies of Memory and Reconfiguration of Space at the Warburg Library." *Between* IV, no. 8 (2014). www.betweenjournal.it.
Pollock, Griselda. *Vision and Difference: Feminism, Femininity and the Histories of Art.* London: Routledge, 1988.
———. "Whither Art History?" *The Art Bulletin* 96, no. 1 (2014): 9–23.
Rampley, Matthew, Thierry Lenain, and Hubert Locher. *Art History and Visual Studies in Europe: Transnational Discourses and National Frameworks.* Leiden: Brill, 2012.
Sacco, Daniela. "Composing the Symbolic. The Denkraum between Warburg and Eisenstein." *Aisthesis* VIII, no. 2 (2015): 59–75.
Saxl, Fritz. "The History of Warburg's Library (1886–1944)." In *Aby Warburg: An Intellectual Biography*, appendix to E. H. Gombrich, 325–38. Oxford: Phaidon Press, 1986.
Stafford, Barbara Maria. "Reconceiving the Warburg Library as a Working Museum of the Mind." *Common Knowledge* 18, no. 1 (2012): 180–87.
Steinberg, Michael P. "The Law of the Good Neighbor." *Common Knowledge* 18, no. 1 (2012): 128–33.
Vestberg, Nina Lager. "Ordering, Searching, Finding." *Journal of Visual Culture* 12, no. 3 (2013): 472–89.

Von Müller, Johannes. "Metadata: New Perspectives on Aby Warburg's 'Critical Iconology.'" *Philosophy of Photography* 8, no. 1 (2017): 171–82.

Warburg, Aby. "Italian Art and International Astrology in the Palazzo Schifanoia in Ferrara." In *German Essays on Art History*, edited by Gert Schiff, 252–53. New York: Continuum, 1988.

Warburg, Aby, Christopher D. Johnson, and Claudia Wedepohl. "From the Arsenal to the Laboratory." *West 86th: A Journal of Decorative Arts, Design History, and Material Culture* 19, no. 1 (2012): 106–24.

Warburg Institute Archive WIA III.113.6, working papers for a seminar, November 1927—February 1928, 118: "Über die Methode einer kunstgeschichtlichen Kulturwissenschaft."

Warnke, Martin. "Der Leidschatz wird Humaner Besitz." In *Die Menschenrechte des Auges: Über Aby Warburg*, edited by Werner Hofmann, George Syamken and Martin Warnke, 113–86. Frankfurt am Main: Europäische Verlagsanstalt, 1980.

Warnke, Martin, and Lisa Dieckmann. "Prometheus Meets Meta-Image: Implementations of Aby Warburg's Methodical Approach in the Digital Era." *Visual Studies* 31, no. 2 (2016): 109–20.

Wood, Christopher S. "Dromenon." *Common Knowledge* 18, no. 1 (2012): 106–16.

Woodfield, Richard. *Art History as Cultural History: Warburg's Projects*. London: Taylor & Francis, 2014.

# 28

# ANALYZING GESTURE IN DIGITAL ART HISTORY

*Leonardo Impett*

The basic tenet of this chapter is that gesture—the relative positions and articulation of the human body's limbs—is an unusually quantifiable parameter of visual studies, and therefore an extremely useful basis for Digital Art History. Gesture Studies, as it has become known, is already a strongly interdisciplinary field, containing art history, historical anthropology, psychology, semiotics and linguistics; this perhaps makes the intrusion of the computational less controversial.

In the spirit of a handbook, this chapter aims to provide a methodological guide for digital humanities projects that measure, compare, or analyze gesture over large sets of images. I will refer to two experiments to which I have contributed, but will use these solely as examples or methodological reference points on the grounds that the detailed research relating to the projects has already been published.[1]

The term "gesture" is used in this chapter quite loosely. We will chiefly address depictions of gestures made by the whole body (sometimes called "pose"), as well as those made by just the arms. These might be a mixture of movement, action, or body language; though the relationship between these factors and the articulation of the body is often indirect and ambiguous. Psycholinguistic distinctions between subconsciously produced gesture and "manifest deliberate expressiveness"[2] collapse in the case of carefully choreographed artworks, which we might term *externally deliberate*, or—in contrast to the dynamic and subconscious movements normally referred to by Gesture Studies—as *Static-Depicted Gestures*.[3] I shall return to hand gestures made with individual fingers (a thumbs-up, a raised middle finger) at the end of the chapter, but in general these are technically more difficult to capture and process.

## Art Histories of Gesture

Before considering how gesture might be a useful medium for digital art history, we should first ask where (and how) conventional art history has used gesture as a principal parameter of research. Many studies use gesture as an accessory, a fingerprint of some other historical phenomenon such as the history of style (Smyth's "poses and gestures characteristic of maniera"[4]), or the tracing of iconography (in Panofsky and Saxl's figure of Hercules).[5] A few encyclopedias of gesture in art also exist,[6] listing a wide selection of physically specific gestures, along with their possible meanings and instances. Some early work in digital art history had also used gesture as a fingerprint: a low-dimensional indicator of similarity, allowing for instance the grouping of similar religious scenes in *azulejo* tiles.[7]

Critical and historical discussions of gesture itself are rarer, and are usually consigned to historical anthropology.[8] An excellent exception is Joaneth Spicer's "The Renaissance Elbow": through the sixteenth and seventeenth centuries in Europe (Germany and Italy, but especially Holland), Spicer traces the "hand on hip" gesture of the elbow from its *sprezzatura* beginnings to the "expressive, frequently bolder, body language especially in male portraiture of the more powerful segments of society."[9] She combines literary references with gender criticism, noting that the elbow akimbo—with its militaristic connotations—is far less frequent in female portraits of the time.

Spicer's discussion contains a relatively large number of examples (more than twenty), yet her potential object of study, European or Dutch portraiture of the sixteenth and seventeenth centuries, could reasonably amount to tens or hundreds of thousands of images, containing an even greater number of elbows. The chapter's case studies, no matter how well-chosen or representative, cannot consist of more than a fraction of 1% of the elbows of the period; no matter how thorough or scholarly the preparatory work, we can assume that at least some important examples must have been overlooked.

Given that Spicer's article was published in 1991, how might we think of conducting analogous computational research today? A timely combination of two factors, both in the last half-decade, opens new possibilities:

1. The wide-scale digitization of art historical photo archives. Substantial digital archives of art already exist (e.g. from Bildlindex, Prometheus, the Fototeca Zeri); the Bibliotheca Hertziana plans to scan and publish three-quarters of a million images by 2021. This trend is accelerating: The Pharos consortium of photo-archives aims to publish twenty-five million images in the next few years. Data for film studies and advertising history have already been digitized in significant amounts.
2. The massive increase in the accuracy and recall of automatic pose and gesture detection methods from Computer Vision, particularly those based on Convolutional Neural Networks. The accuracy of gesture detection (a.k.a. *pose recognition*) in photographs on the MPII Human Pose Data set, for instance, has risen from 83% in 2016[10] to 93% in 2019.[1]

Combining these two phenomena, we could easily imagine a large-scale gestural search engine that could automatically look for particular gestures (for instance, Spicer's elbow akimbo) in a great quantity of Dutch portraits over two centuries—or indeed search for morphological analogies in Roman sarcophagi, Byzantine icons, and so on.

Such a computational reading not only changes the quantity of material being studied. It also has implications for the nature of the material itself. It is no criticism of Spicer to say that many examples in her work are from painters in the European canon: Rembrandt, Pontormo, Dürer. Aside from the obvious commercial-institutional bias in which kinds of artworks are photographed or digitized, computational analysis has no such preference, and may well bring to light a less canonical history and historical anthropology of art.

## Aby Warburg's "Pathosformel"

Although I shall return to the question of a genuinely large-scale computational history of gesture, I first want to discuss a project that began in 2015 with Franco Moretti and Sabine Süsstrunk at the EPFL (Ecole polytechnique fédérale de Lausanne). This project did not have access to a large amount of digitized material, and started too early to benefit from accurate automatic pose recognition. It did, however, form the basis for most of the methods for the computational analysis and comparison of gesture contained in this chapter.

The most famous theory of gesture in the history of art (indeed, perhaps the only history of gesture in art which can be called a generalizable "theory") is the "Pathosformel," formula for the expression of pathos, described by Aby Warburg.[12] One of the fundamental methods of Moretti's approach to the digital humanities, often known as Distant Reading, is the idea of "operationalization":[13] namely, the process of taking a concept from history, literary theory, etc. and turning it into a sequence of quantitative operations. Without this transformation, it is argued, computational analysis in the humanities would have to start from scratch; to ignore (or do without) the last four thousand years or so of cultural understanding and scholarship. But operationalizing has another motivation, as a kind of historiographical method. By converting a concept into an algorithm, one is forced to come up with a computationally explicit reading of that concept, deconstructing it into its constituent components. Our aim, therefore, was to operationalize the theory of the Pathosformeln.

Figure 28.1 is a diagrammatic representations of the five main case studies used by Warburg in the introduction to his 1905 paper, *Dürer and Italian Antiquity*, in which he attempted to introduce the concept of *Pathosformel*, the pictorial formula for the expression of extreme emotions (1905). It was this concept, more than any other, that was to structure Warburg's *Bilderatlas* twenty years later; and this was the concept at the core of our own analysis.

Consider the five images to which Warburg makes reference: (A) Dürer's woodcut; (B) an anonymous engraving from the same time from Mantegna's circle; (C) a fifth-century BC vase from Nola, now in the Louvre; (D) a fourth-century BC vase from Chiusi; (E) a late fifteenth-century Venetian book illustration. Each one depicts the death of Orpheus. For Warburg, this set is a prime example of the "Nachleben" (afterlife) of antique forms in the Italian and European Renaissance.

Looking at the five examples, it becomes clear what is consistent across a *Pathosformel*: not the lyre, nor the clothing, nor the facial expressions, nor the scenery. Even the gestural interaction with the other characters in the scene (two, three, or eight angry Thracian maenads) is not constant—the two maenads of Dürer are also found in (B) and (E), but not in the antique examples. All images have two things in common: the story (Orpheus's death, from Ovid's *Metamorphoses*), and the single gesture of Orpheus, which is consistent, but can be reflected or rotated. Warburg's later examples of *Pathosformeln* do away with the first requirement.

Our algorithmic *Pathosformel* was therefore just that: the gesture of the individual body. The unit of analysis was no longer the single artwork (or digital photograph), but the individual skeleton. One can easily draw a stick figure around a human body, which itself can be characterized by a relatively small number of variables: e.g. the x-y coordinates of each limb. But how, precisely, ought one to measure the pose of a human body in a way that permits a comparison between poses that is both general and meaningful?

Simply comparing the absolute coordinates of labeled points is insufficient. Even correcting for the dimensions of the image, or indeed of the individual human body, two-dimensional coordinates are affected by the proportion of the limbs. What of the angles of the body? This seems like a more sensible suggestion, but leads to a number of design choices to which there are no easy solutions. For instance: should the angles of the limbs be measured extrinsically (that is to say, relative to the horizon) or intrinsically (relative to each other)? This has an implication for the poses that are considered similar to each other. In Figure 28.2, [a-b] and [b-c] are similar distances in intrinsic coordinates, with the angles of the elbow and shoulder changing in both

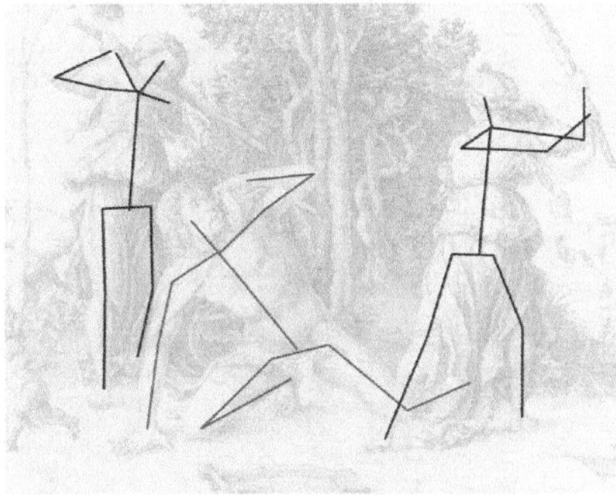

A. Dürer, 1494, Hamburger Kunsthalle

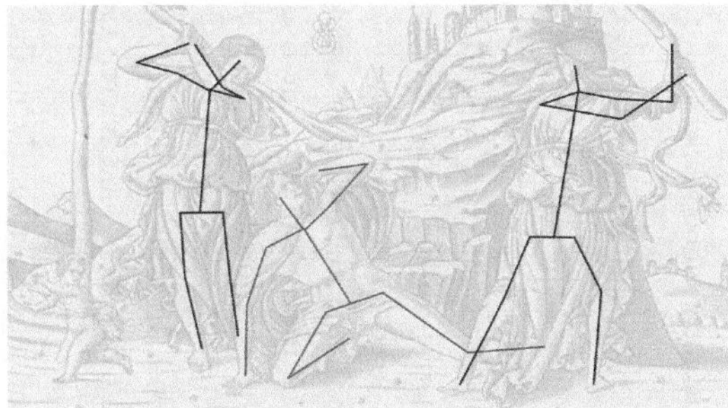

B. Master of the E-series Tarocchi, c. 1470, Hamburger Kunsthalle

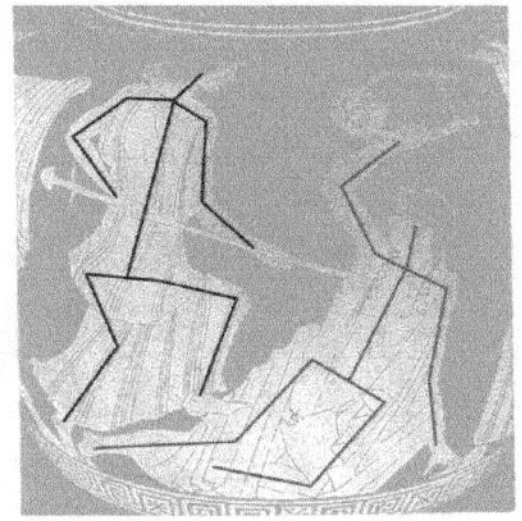

C. Vase from Nola, now in the Louvre

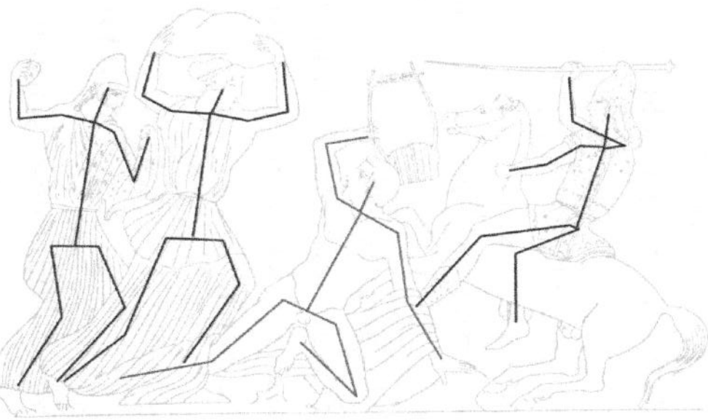

D. After vase from Chiusi

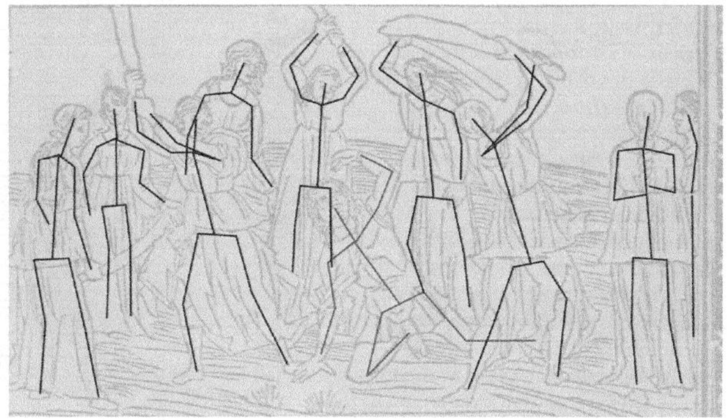

E. Woodcut from Ovid, *Metamorphoses* (Venice, 1497)

*Figure 28.1* Warburg's (1905) five initial case studies for the *Pathosformel* of Orpheus.

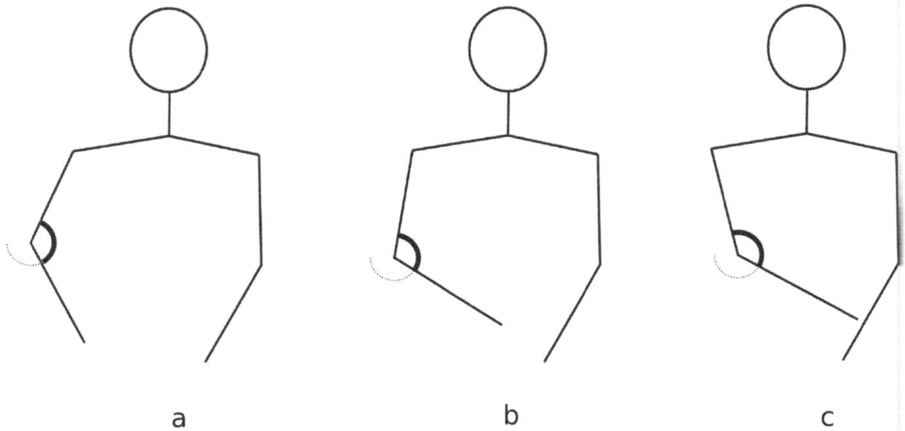


*Figure 28.2* Extrinsic (dotted line) and intrinsic (solid line) measurements of body angles.

cases. In extrinsic coordinates, [b-c] is a much smaller distance than [a-b], since the absolute angle of the forearm remains the same.

Our operationalization of the Pathosformel, therefore, is essentially an egocentric and embodied measurement. Rather than describing the geometries of the bodies on the page, it describes the angles of the limbs that a physical body might make in such a pose.

Reducing an articulated human body to a stick figure (or better, the angles of a stick figure) is a violent, even iconoclastic, act. But rather than a totalizing measurement of the body (or of the image), a more useful conceptual metaphor is that of the notational system, as it is used in music or dance. This is an explicitly incomplete representation of the images themselves, but one that affords new kinds of analysis. Indeed, these stick figures share some similarities twentieth-century choreographical notation, such as Rudolph Laban's *Schrifttanz* and Merce Cunningham's digital *LifeForms*.

Similar stick figures are also used in psychology and biology, particularly in the field of biological motion. Swedish perceptual psychologist Gunnar Johansson (1973) noticed that simple visual stimuli (white dots) would be naturally interpreted as human figures if they moved appropriately. More recently, such stimuli have been used in the field of emotional psychology. The results tell us precisely what we lose, in a psychological sense, in going from the movements of a "live" person to a stick figure. In fact, it emerges that moving stick figures are remarkably expressive, visually transmitting specific emotions[14] and even the gender[15] of the subject. More problematic for our case are static images: Atkinson[16] found that just as static images of human actors convey categorical emotions far less precisely than short videos, so too individual stick figures are significantly less communicative than videos of moving stick figures. We might well ask: Don't individual poses often themselves embody movement? We shall return to this question later in the chapter.

## From Gesture to Cluster

Two decades after his Dürer essay, Warburg set about assembling his *Atlas Mnemosyne*, an unfinished project of extreme proportions. Several recorded versions of the Atlas exist, but the last (from 1929) consists of about a thousand images of paintings, sculptures, advertisements, newspaper cuttings, etc. assembled over sixty-three black panels. If there is a thread through the many associations of the Atlas, it is the afterlife of Antique forms, most often through the vessel of Pathosformeln.

Warburg's Atlas was our test case for our operationalization of Warburg's theory of Pathosformeln. However, in the time between the Dürer essay and the *Bilderatlas*, Warburg's conceptual framework became more ambitious. Rather than following iconographic descriptions with a single reference (such as the death of Orpheus), Warburg's formulae jumped between analogous figures: pagan and Christian, male and female. This is particularly true in the case of the Nymph, a character which particularly fascinated Warburg and his friend André Jolles. The latter wrote to Warburg on 23rd December 1900:

> Now she is Salome, dancing with her lethal charm. . . . Now Judith, proud in her triumph. . . . Now she seems to hide in the budding grace of little Tobias, striding bravely and happily. . . . At times I see her in a seraphim . . . or in Gabriel, bringing the joyful message . . . in a maid at the Wedding, or in a terrified mother fleeing from the Slaughter of the Innocents. I have tried to see her again as I first had . . . but in the meantime, she has multiplied herself.[17]

Salome, Judith, Tobias, the Seraphim and Gabriel all share roughly the same gesture, as panels 46–48 of the Atlas show. This highlights one of the key elements of computer gestural analysis: unlike human observers, and unlike other forms of computational analysis based on "image similarity," a computation based on gesture ignores all other iconographic, gender, physiological, and stylistic differences. Comparisons and analogies are made not only between images from a shared historical context, but—in the tradition of *Bildwissenschaft*—between wildly disparate sources.

A preliminary experiment on Panel 46 had shown us that our stick figures could easily differentiate the protagonist of that panel, the Nymph, from other figures (Figure 28.3). But our operationalization would only prove useful if it told us something about the *Atlas*, and about the place of Pathosformeln within it. To this end, we annotated each human pose across a large cross-section of the Atlas (21 of the 63 panels). With this large number of skeletons—more than sixteen hundred bodies, each of which was manually annotated at least three times—we sought to find some kind of "clusters" of Pathosformeln within the *Atlas's* bodies. Our contention was that each type of "Pathos" should be associated with some kind of "Formel"— "to each pathos its schema," in the words of Salvatore Settis[18]—and that such Formeln ought to be discoverable through a statistical clustering of gestures.

## Clustering—Distance Metrics

Simple clustering techniques, however, cannot be used directly on this kind of gestural data. In comparing poses by angles, rather than by coordinates, we cannot properly use conventional statistics which do not take account of the wraparound property (that is, that an angle of -179 degrees is closer to +180 degrees than it is to zero). Many commonly used statistical probability functions, such as the Gaussian, have no exact analogue in directional statistics; making a direct conversion of many algorithms impossible. Directional statistics are not inherently more difficult than the regular kind, and alternatives—like the multivariate von Mises-Fisher—largely exist in theory,[19] but they must often be re-implemented in common programming environments.

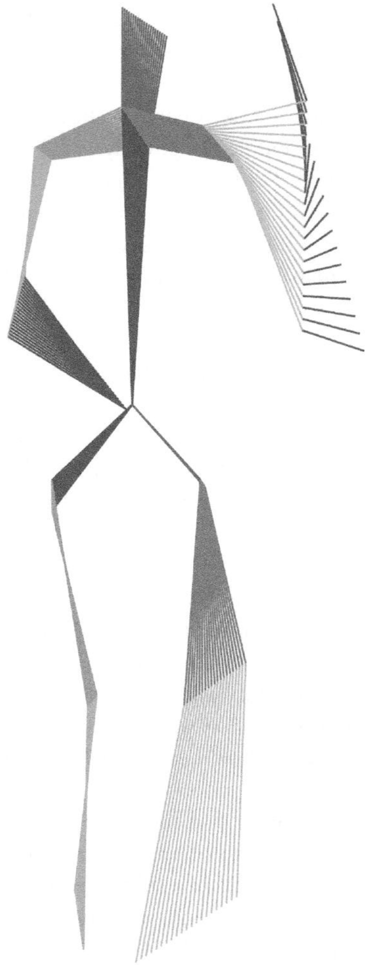

*Figure 28.3* Principal component analysis on the poses of the Atlas' panel 46, capturing strongest morphological feature of the panel: the Nymph.

Re-implementing the 2-norm—a standard measure of the distance between vectors—is quite simple. By concatenating the *N* angles of each body (*a*) into a vector ($P_a$), we can formalize the distance *d* between poses (*a* and *b*) thus:

$$d_{a,b} = \sqrt{\sum_{i=0}^{N} angdif(p_{a,i}, p_{b,i})^2}$$

Where the function *angdif* calculates the smallest difference between two angles in the range $-\varpi$ to $\varpi$).

This is a perfectly reliable and unfussy quantification of the difference between gestures, and indeed was the measure we settled upon for the Pathosformel. Yet it does have the tendency to be dominated by the movements of the upper half of the body. This is for simple anatomical reasons: As shown in the plot in Figure 28.4, the average variances in the shoulders and elbows (which can potentially reach through a full circle) is much greater than those of the ankles or knees (which have the physical capacity to travel perhaps 90 degrees).

This can be corrected by multiplying the variation of the lower body, adding a weight term to the per-angle sum:

$$d_{a,b} = \sqrt{\sum_{i=0}^{N} w_i angdif(p_{a,i}, p_{b,i})^2}$$

In the case of lower-body compensation, $w_i$ would be greater for the lower-body angles than for the upper-body angles (say, $w_{lower}=4$ and $w_{upper}=1$). A more sophisticated approach for normalizing each angle is to make the variances constant (which does involve some directional statistics, beyond the scope of this chapter), so that the weights are effectively defined as inversely proportional to the variance of the angle *i* across all poses: i.e. $w_i = 1/V_i$.

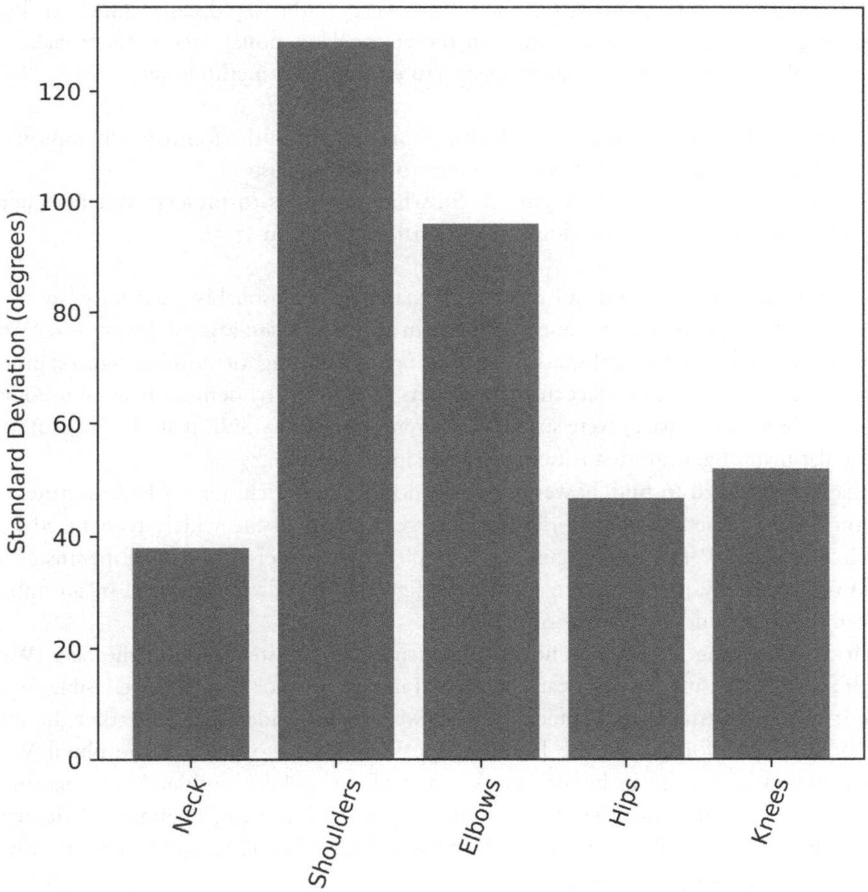


*Figure 28.4* Variances in the joint angles on the Atlas data set. Note that the standard deviation of the upper body is about twice that of the lower body.

Such complex corrections might themselves introduce undesirable effects. It could be argued that lower body indeed matters less in gesture, partly because its geometrical range is physically limited. A final complication is that for some bodies (e.g. an upper-body portrait) some angles might not be known. Bruno Wicht has proposed a solution that is effectively a Monte Carlo randomized estimate of the average distance between bodies for that particular angle.[20] In the case where angle $P_{b,i}$ is unknown:

$$angdif(P_{a,i}, P_{b,i}) = \frac{1}{N}\sum_{i=0}^{N} angdif(p_{x,i}, p_{y,i})$$

Where $x$, $y$ are distinct N-dimensional random samples from the data set of available poses (with known angle $i$).

What these considerations make clear is that only local similarity is genuinely meaningful in the comparison of human poses. It is meaningless to say that a kneeling figure is "closer" to a standing figure than to one lying down. By contrast, comparisons between relatively consistent figures, such as those in Figure 28.2, are practically useful for comparing, clustering, or searching gestures.

Now that we have a definition for the distance between two poses, a great number of dimensionality reduction and clustering techniques that accept arbitrary distance functions become usable for gesture data. Visualizing fourteen-dimensional rotational data is not trivial, and for greater insight, I have set out the resulting structure using both methods here:

- A rotational K-means clustering, which is more faithful to the fourteen-dimensional data, but does not differentiate between members of a single cluster;
- A two-dimensional t-SNE (Figure 28.5), which attempts to preserve distances between high-dimensional points in a low-dimensional visualization.

Both rotational clusters and our 2D t-SNE map gave a reasonably clear impression of the different kinds of poses and gestures common in the *Bilderatlas*: a great many unremarkable, symmetrical standing figures; clusters of embracing, of kneeling, of running figures; groups of dancing or falling figures. The fact that the clusters (which are, by definition, close in fourteen-dimensional rotational space) were spatially coherent in the 2D t-SNE map is a good indication that the flat map of gestures is a reasonably good approximation.

What we expected to find, however—a half-dozen distinct clusters of Pathosformeln, each with their own pathetic content—did not emerge. Instead, all the widely recognized Pathosformeln (Orpheus, Pentheus, Perseus, the Nymph) were clustered in a small peninsula at the top. Morphologically, it appeared to us that the figures were all characterized by an imbalance between the upper and lower parts of the bodies.

What is surprising, however, is not so much that these clusters exist in the data (Warburg himself assembled it, and he was clearly interested in gesture), nor that they are visible so clearly in the gesture-map (since this is precisely what we set out to identify), but rather the internal unity of the Pathosformel. All the literature speaks of Pathosformel<u>n</u> in the plural. Warburg himself drafted on a page in his notebook a sort of spreadsheet, entitled "Schematismus der Pathosformeln," divided into rows for "running," "dancing," "pursuit," "triumph," "victory," and so on. Instead, the Nymph and Laocoön, Fortuna and Orpheus all fit statistically into the same small peninsula of our gesture map.

It is beyond the scope of this chapter to expand on the implications of this surprising conclusion, but the important methodological point is that such internal unity—that all species of

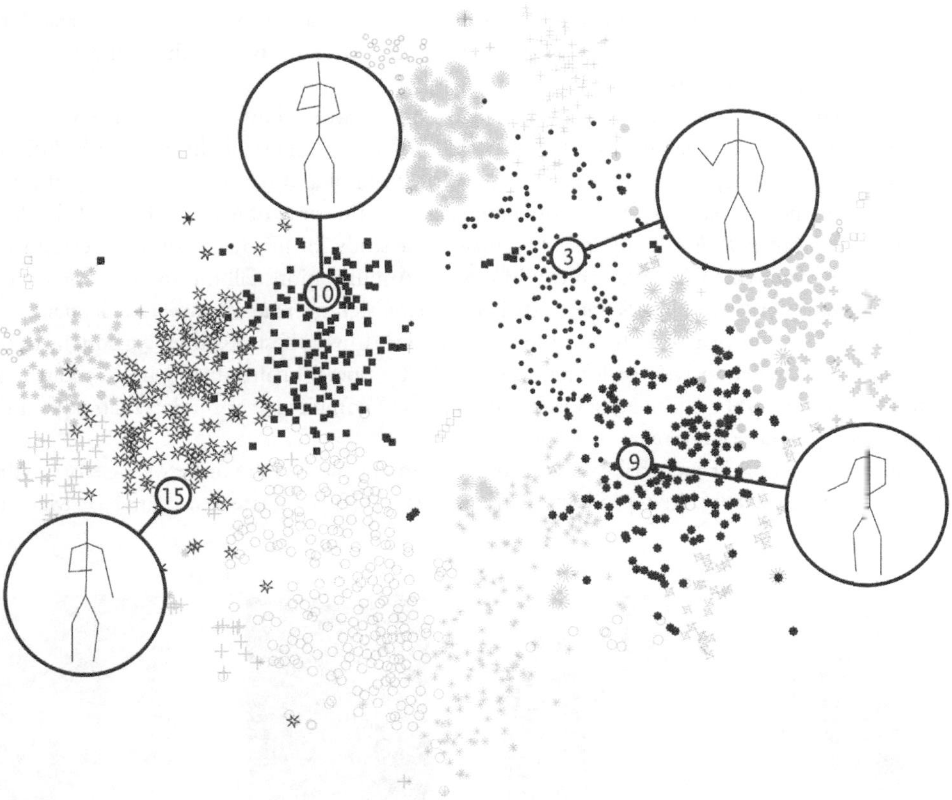


*Figure 28.5* Four of the sixteen gestural clusters, plotted on the Bilderatlas map.
*Source*: Reproduced from Impett & Moretti.

Pathosformeln were members of a joint genus—could only have been visible computationally. This is not because computational techniques could see more than a human observer (as in super-resolution or multispectral imaging), but precisely because they can see less: Because associations were not made based on historical date, iconography, style, or position in the *Atlas*, but only on the fourteen angles of the body.

## Annunciations Project—Gesture in Temporality

I mentioned at the start of this chapter that developments in automatic pose recognition and large quantities of online digitized artworks have opened new possibilities in the digital analysis of gesture. The images and poses in the *Bilderatlas* were extracted manually, but a second experiment, in collaboration with Peter Bell (University of Erlangen—Nuremberg), took advantage of both developments.[21]

Whereas gesture had proved a useful metric on the *Bilderatlas* because of its ability to ignore the character to which it related, this second project focused on the gestures of specific religious characters. The main subjects of Christian iconography (crucifixions, baptisms, annunciations) are excellent objects of study for large-scale digital approaches, precisely because they retell the same content (stories, characters, compositions, objects) in many thousands of iterations. An analogous situation in computational literary studies would be a gift to comparative narratology: ten thousand re-writings of the same short scene, over a large portion of the globe and across more than a thousand years.

In particular, we were interested in the relationship between temporality and gospel stories: how they become re-ordered in cycles, how they follow or represent the text with differing rhythms, how they depict complex sequences of theological and narrative structure within an image. Again, the approach was one of operationalization, this time of Michael Baxandall's *Painting and Experience in 15th-Century Italy*. In a major case study for his theory of the "Period Eye," Baxandall explains that fifteenth-century Florentine Annunciations fall mostly into one of four categories, as described by Fra Roberto da Lecce: *conturbatio, cogitatio, interrogatio, humilitatio*.[20]

Our aim was not primarily to test the veracity of this hypothesis. Rather, we sought to ask whether this parallel analysis of four images could be operationalized; and if so, could it be extended in the number of images, historical scope, and complexity of models that explain the internal temporality of the relevant scene?

Baxandall gives four pictorial examples of his claim, printed in the order of the story, rather than chronologically by their production (Figure 28.6). If we isolate the figures of Mary (as

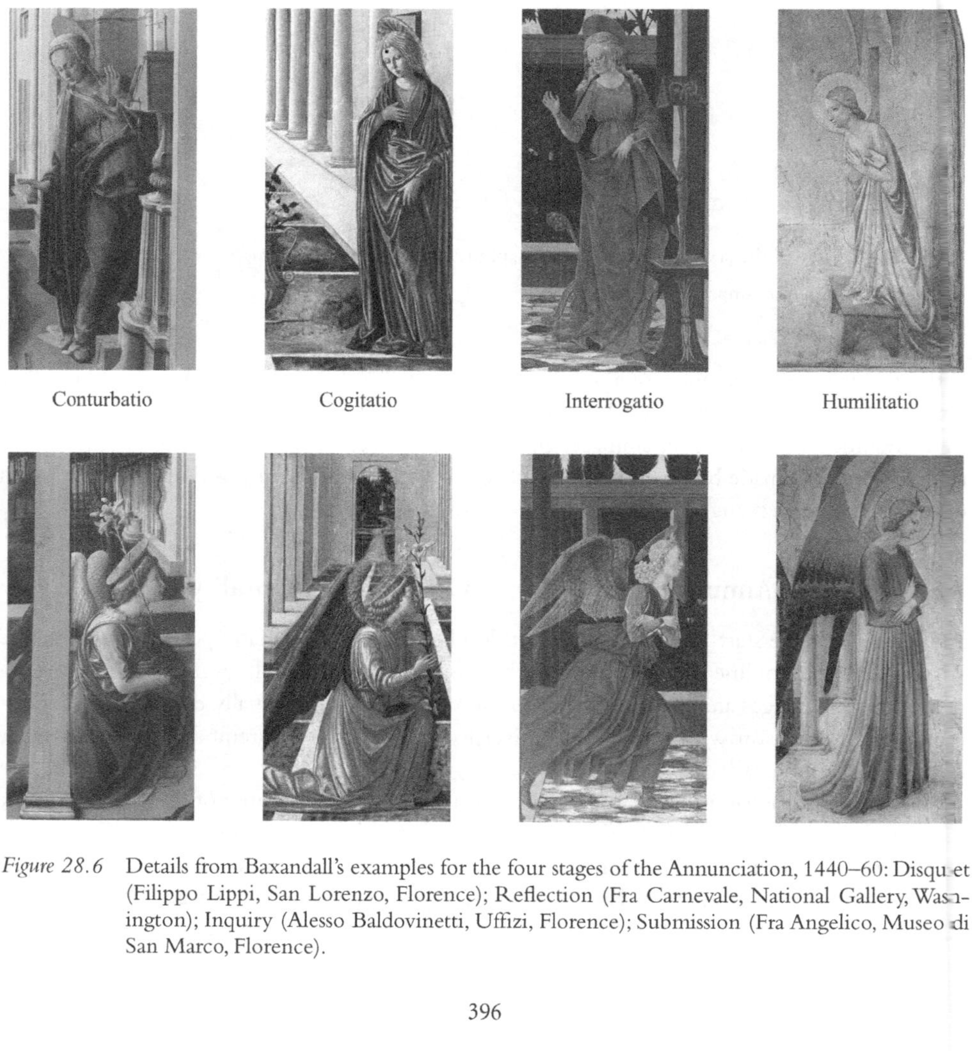


*Figure 28.6* Details from Baxandall's examples for the four stages of the Annunciation, 1440–60: Disquiet (Filippo Lippi, San Lorenzo, Florence); Reflection (Fra Carnevale, National Gallery, Washington); Inquiry (Alesso Baldovinetti, Uffizi, Florence); Submission (Fra Angelico, Museo di San Marco, Florence).

Warburg had done in Panel 46 of his *Bilderatlas*), we form a kind of flip-book of the Annunciation (inheriting, perhaps, the kinds of temporal scaffolds we're used to associating with photography). In contrast to Warburg's Pathosformeln, here a gesture moves not in space and distant historical time (across centuries), but in immediate narrative time (across seconds).

*The Annunciation*, however, clearly includes two protagonists. This begs the question that Meredith Gill had asked[23] (but not answered): namely, what are the stages of Gabriel's actions? If we line up the analogous Gabriels from the preceding example in the same order, there is not a fluid movement, but rather a range of different possibilities for Gabriel's actions, all mutually contradictory (kneeling, running, standing).

Exploiting the recent opportunities of automatic person detection and pose recognition and the large quantity of digitized Annunciation images available on the web, we sought to extend these micro-chronological scheme to a much larger range of images. We gathered more than sixty-five hundred images of the Annunciation from different periods, and having detected the bodies, annotated them manually by the identity of the character (Gabriel, Mary, the Father, other angels). In the case of Mary, we also annotated the stage, according to Fra Roberto's categories listed previously.

Thinking that one or the other character might cluster in a particular corner of the map (as the Pathosformeln had done), we plotted our poses with a two-dimensional t-SNE reduction, the same method used in the Warburg project. Those poses are shown in Figure 28.7: Neither Mary nor Gabriel seem to have a particular cluster of their own. Baxandall and Fra Roberto were describing Mary's movements of the soul and body, and we might have expected Mary's gestures to show more variation. To our surprise, however, Gabriel's gestures show the greater morphological richness.

This richness merited further exploration, not only of Gabriel's gestures, but of the images themselves. One way to do this is by a "direct visualization" of the gestures, sometimes known as a "meta-image." This is an evolution of the t-SNE map where instead of showing dots, details from images themselves are rendered at each point (Figure 28.8). Note that although

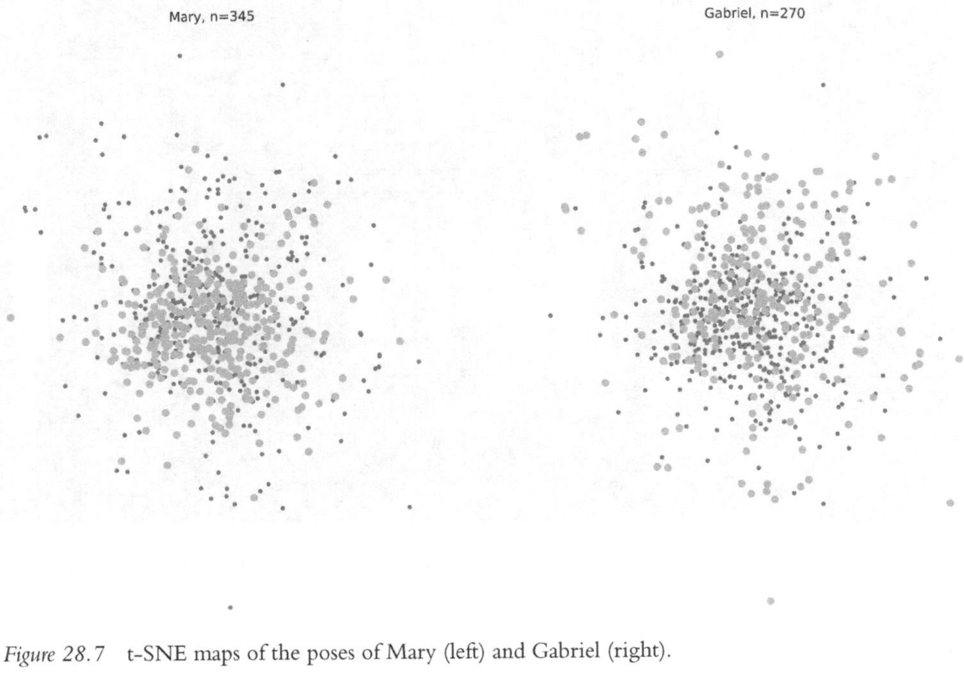


*Figure 28.7* t-SNE maps of the poses of Mary (left) and Gabriel (right).

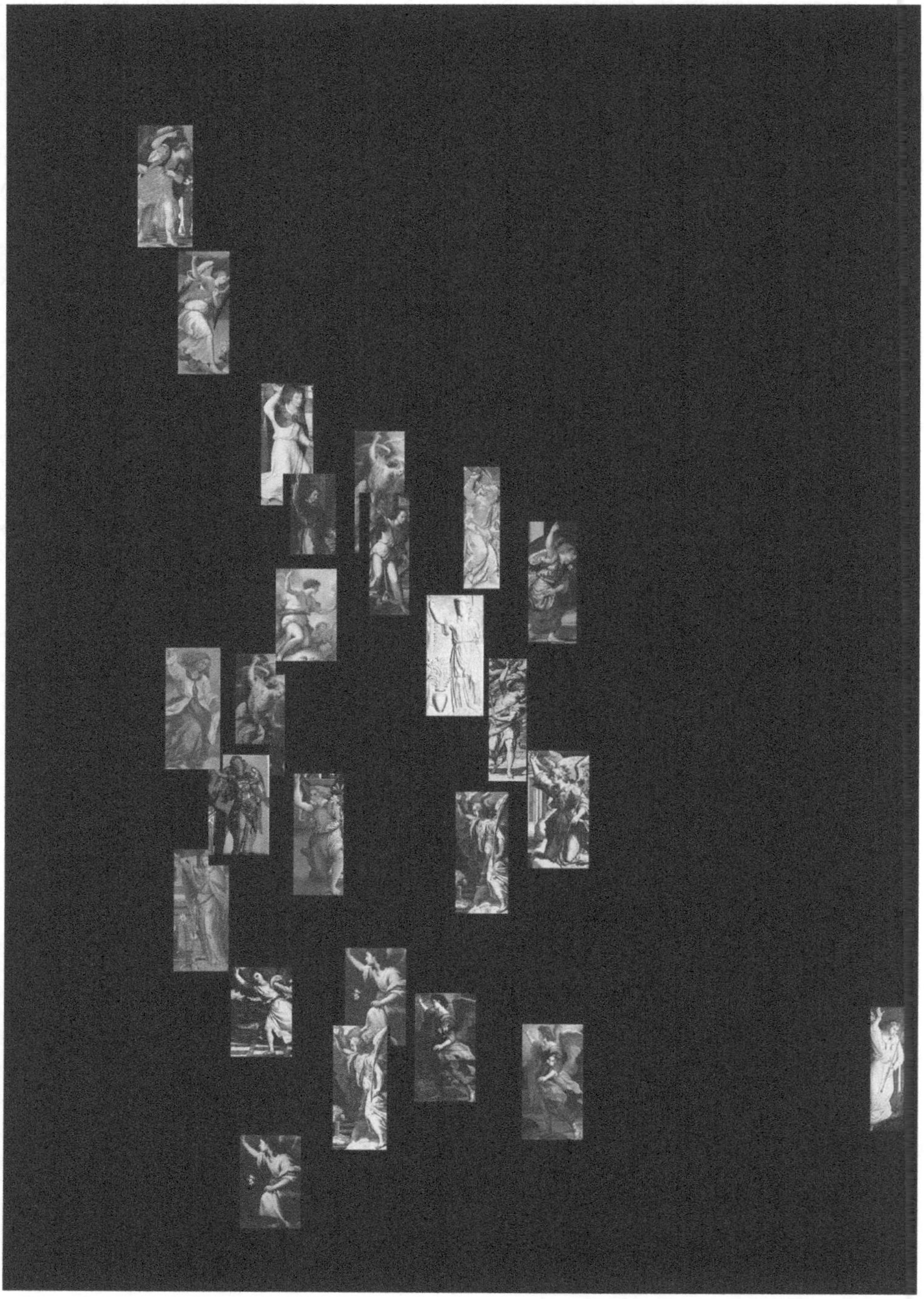

*Figure 28.8* Detail of a "direct visualization" of our t-SNE gesture-map, showing a detail of arm-raised Gabriels.

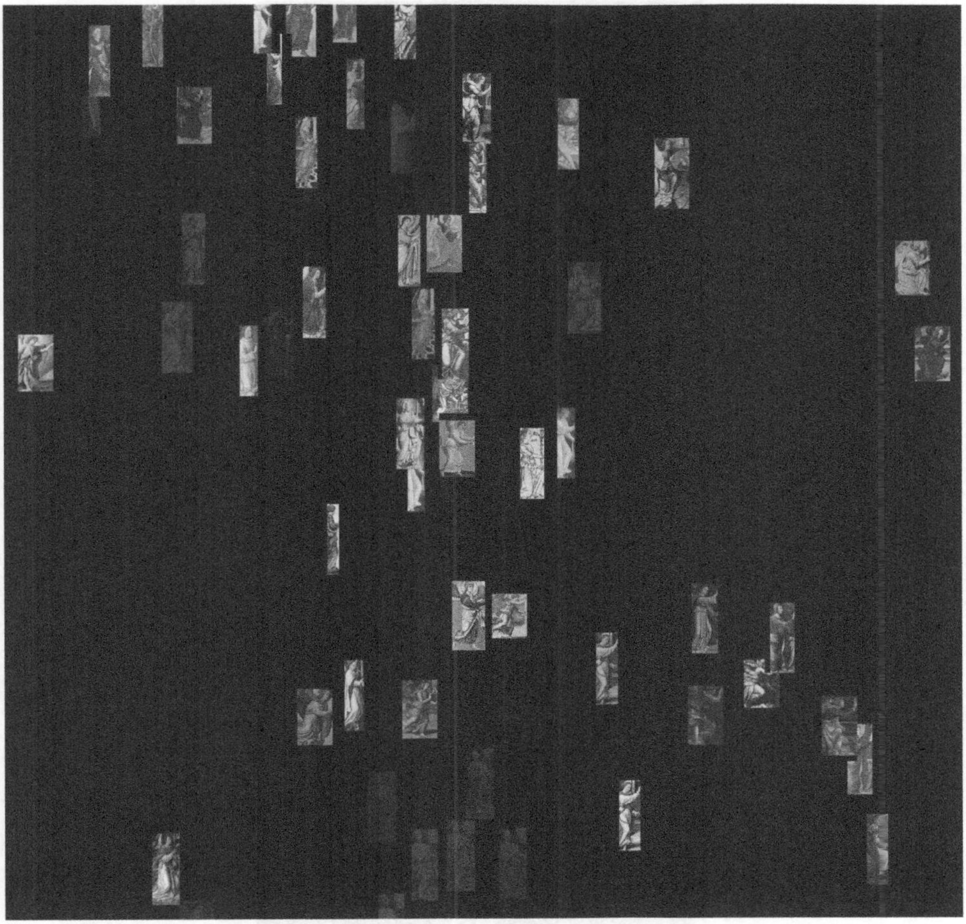

*Figure 28.9* Different figures are shown on the same map by altering transparency. Above we see opaque Gabriels and semi-transparent Marys.

the visualization now includes the entire image, plots are still produced only by comparing the angles of the body, rather than any Computer Vision metrics of image similarity.

This kind of direct visualization can be rendered directly as an image file (Figure 28.9 and Figure 28.10), in a language suitable for data manipulation and image processing (such as Python). This is the approach taken by Lev Manovich's *ImagePlot* software.[24] A medium-sized plot, however, can quickly add up to hundreds of megapixels: a more sustainable approach is to use a browser-based viewer, such as the Yale DH Lab's WebGL-based *PixPlot*.

## Movement

Coincidentally or not, the direct visualizations of gesture in a t-SNE map (or through any other dimensionality-reduction) bear some superficial resemblance to the panels of Warburg's *Bilderatlas*: with individual human figures cropped from their pictorial context, arranged into groups of similar gestures. They bear very little resemblance, however, to Baxandall's flip-book and do not naturally engender the same sorts of questions about the internal chronology of the scene.

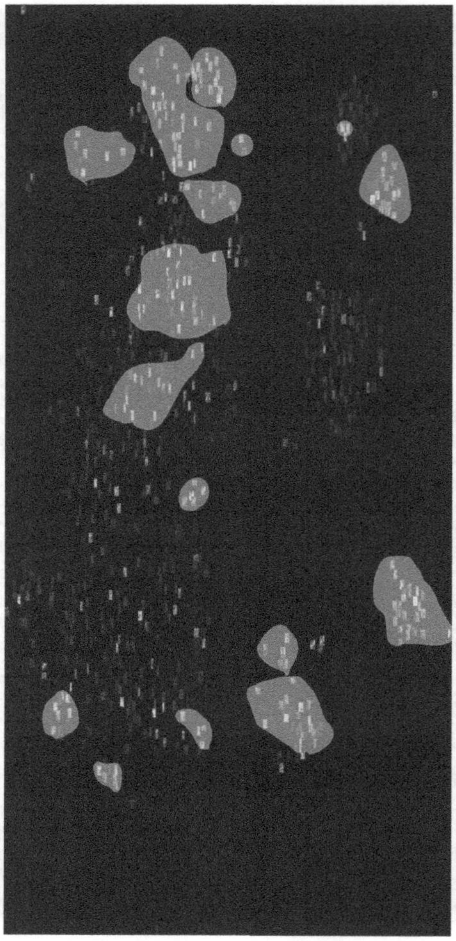

*Figure 28.10* Individual clusters of gestures annotated by hand.

How can we move from the computation of clusters (unsupervised classification) or maps (dimensionality reduction), to analyzing gestural movement or image-flows? One solution is to build a temporal network of gesture from the identified poses, using the same definition of "distance" between poses as discussed previously. Formally, we set up a weighted graph $G$ of $N$ nodes, where each node is a pose, and each weighted edge $e$ is defined by the distance between poses:

$$e_{i,j} = \frac{1}{\sum e_{i,k}^{\forall k}} \cdot (d_{i,j}^2)$$

Or, for a more sophisticated approach, we can synthesize a Markov model (Figure 28.11), where each weighted edge $e$ is the bidirectional probability of moving between two poses To save on computation, the edges can be thresholded, with edges only drawn across small distances. With this chronological network, a shortest path can be calculated between a start and end pose. The nonlinearity in the edge weights will prioritize smaller jumps.

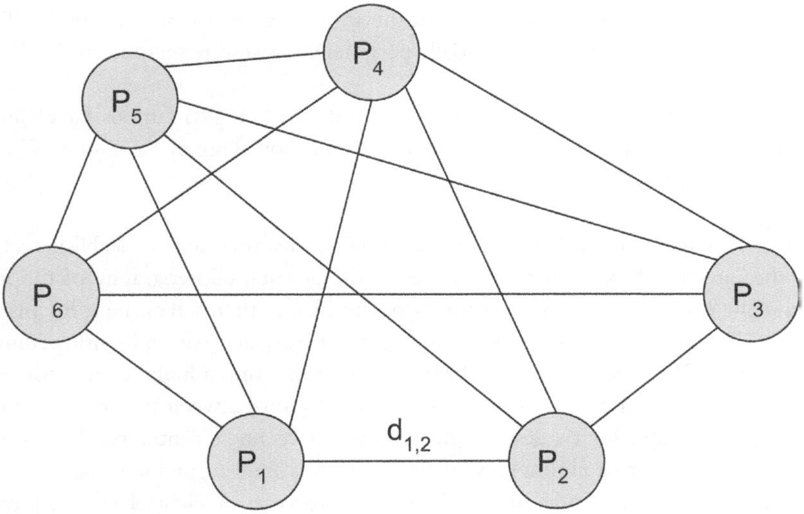


*Figure 28.11* The Markov-like gesture network made up of nodes (representing individual poses) and weighted edges (whose weight represents the distance between poses). Here six poses are shown. Many applications will have thousands of poses.

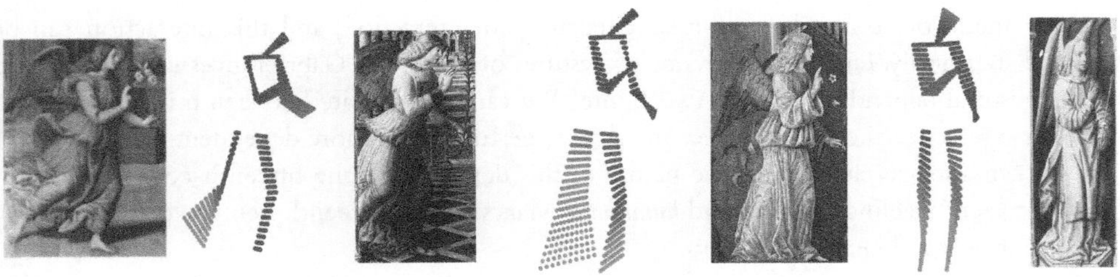

*Figure 28.12* An example route through the temporal pose-network, showing optical flow between two randomly selected poses (the start and end node).

It is possible to construct such a graph from a data set of gestures of a single character in a single scene—in our case, Gabriel and the Annunciation. We can then quickly generate many thousands of these paths, demarcating different collective imaginaries of the movement of a figure in the scene and probing which types of movement might be historically, stylistically, or theologically specific.

To see the particular movements in the space between figures, we can also calculate the optical flow of the skeleton: how far each point on each limb travels between two poses. An example of this is shown in Figure 28.12, with the "velocity" of each point rendered as color (red is greater). This shows how the gestural flow moves from the upper body (retracting arms) down to the lower (bending of knees).

We can also easily calculate simple graph properties for each gesture, which tell us something about their point in gestural-temporal space:

- *Betweenness centrality*. How many shortest paths pass through a certain pose? The lower the "betweenness" centrality, the more chronologically peripheral the gesture (appearing at the start or the end);

- *Closeness centrality*. The reciprocal sum of the shortest paths to all other nodes. The lower the closeness centrality, the more spatially peripheral the gesture (geometrically distant from most others);
- *Eigenvector centrality*. A measure of influence similar to Google's famous PageRank, where connections to other high-scoring nodes counts for more. Largely a measure of how archetypal the gesture is.

These graph-based sequences and network centrality measures help to establish a relationship between the internal chronography of the scene, the gestural choreography of the individual figures, and the historic and stylistic contexts of the images themselves. Take, for instance, the "Gabriels with a raised arm" motif shown in Figure 28.8, which we find, unsurprisingly, to be almost exclusively Baroque. It's a reasonably common trope (thus a high eigenvector centrality), but sits at an extreme limit of movement: the shortest path between two random Gabriels is unlikely to pass through such a gesture (thus a low betweenness centrality). It also has a particular point in the internal chronology of the scene: as a kind of prelude, Gabriel having not yet arrived, it stretches the limits of Fra Roberto's categories. A Gabriel who is physically in the process of kneeling (but isn't quite there yet) displays opposite characteristics; a reasonably uncommon gesture in the data set (a low eigenvector centrality), yet one which many possible movements presumably pass through—indeed, every movement which ends in kneeling—thus a high betweenness centrality. Neither of these phenomena would have been visible on a simple t-SNE plot. In the graph, however, they are both self-evident.

Movement, of course, has a fundamental role in interaction; and this interaction can be mapped statistically. The co-occurrence of gestures of Mary and Gabriel gives us an indication of the gestural dependency of the two figures. We can differentiate between milieus of greater or lesser interactional canonicity (i.e. one figure's gesture being more dependent on the other's); but we can also see clues about the nature of this dependency: the fifteenth-century dependency between kneeling Gabriels and *humilitatio* Marys, or the sixteenth-century combination of flying Gabriels and *conturbatio* Marys.

Large-scale gestural computing cannot confirm or disprove Baxandall's chronology of the Annunciation, but it can help us understand, dissect, model, and historicize the asynchronous temporal landscape of common iconography.

## Current Directions

A suite of methods for the computational analysis of gesture could not be complete without including the gestures of the hand, a topic of great interest to psycholinguistics. This presents a number of technical difficulties: the smaller size of the hand decreases the effective image resolution of the relevant parts, and their far more complex geometry makes both capturing and organizing hand gestures less straightforward.

Previously, a team at the Heidelberg Image Collaboratory, including Peter Bell, attempted to use computer vision to detect hand gestures in a medieval manuscript (the Mirror of the Saxons) with some success.[25] However, their image-based method relied on a number of fixed categories of hand-gesture, rather than a continuous geometrical description, as we have explored with whole-body gesture.

The full geometric detection of hand key points in still images has recently become more feasible,[26] particularly with integrated body-pose and hand recognition systems (such as *OpenPose*);[27] an example detection is shown in Figure 28.13. Yet even with reliable hand key point detection, calculating the distance between two hands is not trivial; if indeed the individual

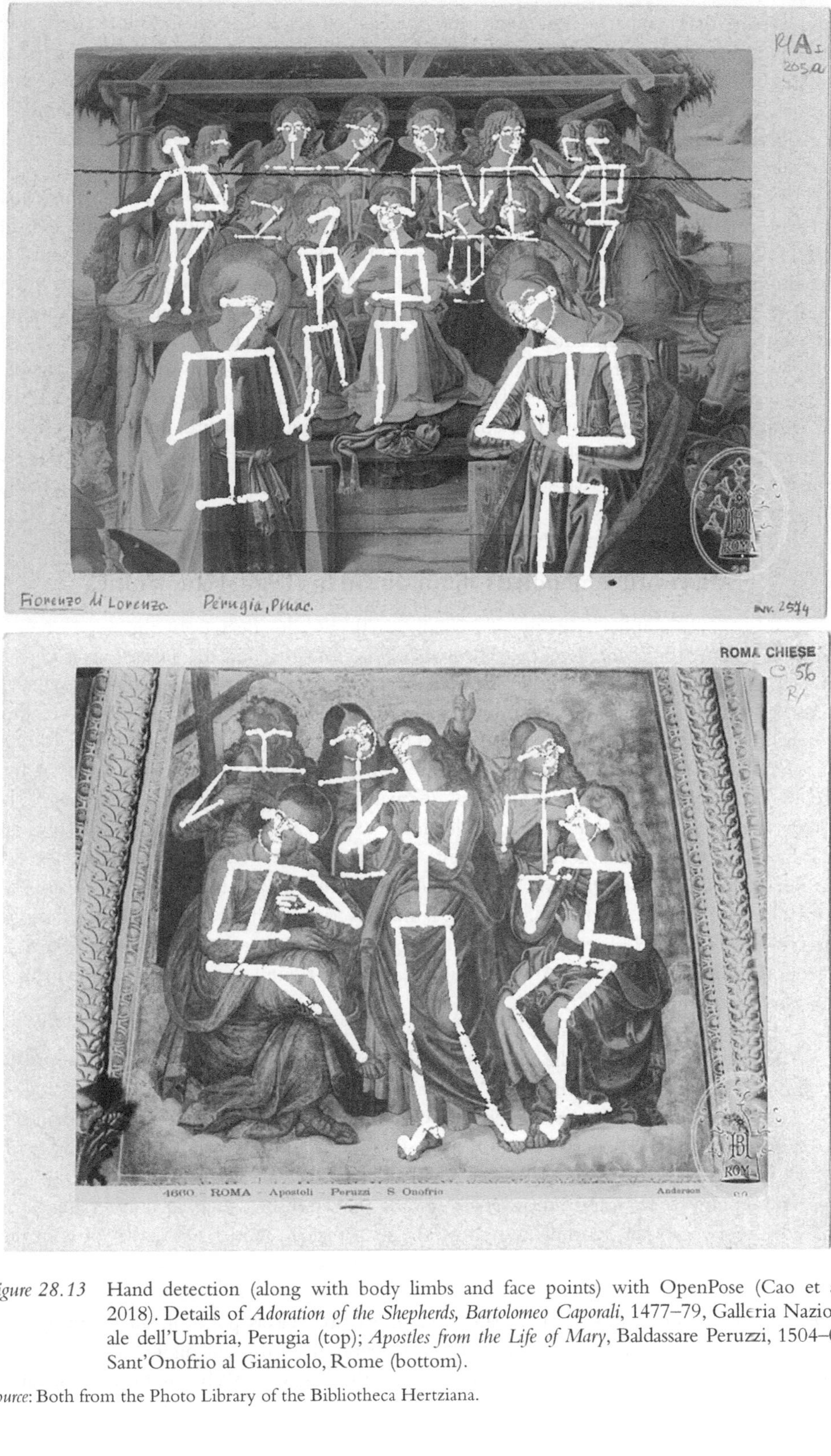


*Figure 28.13* Hand detection (along with body limbs and face points) with OpenPose (Cao et al., 2018). Details of *Adoration of the Shepherds, Bartolomeo Caporali*, 1477–79, Galleria Nazionale dell'Umbria, Perugia (top); *Apostles from the Life of Mary*, Baldassare Peruzzi, 1504–06, Sant'Onofrio al Gianicolo, Rome (bottom).

*Source*: Both from the Photo Library of the Bibliotheca Hertziana.

hand—rather than the pair—is to be the unit of analysis. Each hand contains more rigid "limbs" (nineteen) than there are in our model of the entire skeleton (fourteen). While the angle-space can still be calculated, it is less immediately useful than for whole body poses. More complex alternatives do exist, chiefly from the human-computer interaction community: methods such as manifold learning and locally linear embedding have proved popular in the comparison and recognition of hand gestures.[28]

The experimental techniques outlined in this chapter are fairly computationally inexpensive and require little manual input. It is hoped that other digital humanities teams will find them useful not only for traditional art history, but for film studies, advertising history, and visual culture more broadly conceived. Open-source versions of the code for many of these techniques are already available online.[29] For many humanities scholars, however, installing or running a pre-existing pose detection algorithm may be prohibitively complicated.

A key next step in broadening the appeal of computational gesture studies will, therefore, be to create an open and user-friendly digital platform for such research to take place. Beyond the requirement to implement the methods described earlier (uploading images, detecting and arranging gestures automatically), such a "web atlas of gesture" could enable scholars to associate primary and secondary textual sources associated with groups of gestures, particular iconographies, or historical linguistics.

## Afterword: Embodied Computing in the Digital Humanities

Gestural computing inherits many of its basic methods and ideas from the experiments of researchers in Artificial Intelligence (AI) in *embodied intelligence* and the *situated approach* to AI: interacting with the physical world. There are, it seems to me, a few critical themes which are common to both skepticism of computational methods from art historians, and the technical criticism of Symbolic AI which led researchers toward exploring embodiment in the 1990s.

Symbolic AI systems, now known as GOFAI (for "Good Old-Fashioned Artificial Intelligence"), largely used explicit, categorical, textual models of the world around them. These systems are good at codifying the knowledge of experts for high-level tasks (playing chess, or calculating appropriate mortgage interest), known as Expert Systems, but rather less good at interacting or learning from their surroundings in the way a simple organism can. Rodney Brooks, an important critic of GOFAI, famously claimed that while "elephants don't play chess,"[30] they nonetheless exhibited a number of complex behaviors far beyond the reach of current AI. Computer scientist Alison Adam's feminist critique[31] of GOFAI extended this line of reasoning toward:

1. The role of the body in the production of knowledge, ignored by GOFAI systems as the knowledge must be "disembodied" to a machine.
2. The types of knowledge privileged by GOFAI—propositional/symbolic rather than skills-based/embodied. "Experts" in GOFAI systems were lawyers or economists, rather than carpenters or potters.
3. The desubjectivization of knowledge—a false universalism which, in transferring knowledge to a computer, attempts to remove the social/racial/gender *situatedness* of knowledge (that is to say: *whose* expert knowledge is being encoded).

These legitimate criticisms (which lead to technical, as well as political, shortcomings) find strong resonances in, for instance, Claire Bishop's criticism of current digital art history.[32] It is important to note that, on a purely technical level, the Semantic Web systems and universalist symbolic "ontologies" so popular with galleries, libraries, museums and archives (most notably CIDOC-CRM from the International Committee for Museology) are precisely GOFAI Expert Systems—any Digital Humanities systems based on GOFAI suffer from the same fundamental contradictions.

Embodied and situated AI—along with other forms of *Nouvelle AI*—have not solved the problems highlighted by Adam, Brooks and others, but they have been designed with this critique in mind. Gestural computing is, in this sense, not a symbolic expert system—gestures do not have to be described according to a fixed taxonomy, or understood as part of a codified ontology. And although gestural computing clearly prioritizes the role of the body in the production of knowledge (rather than the knowledge of experts), there is much more scope for a genuinely embodied and situated Digital Humanities: one which would start from social and physical interaction with the world, rather than from symbolically encoding the propositional knowledge of generic *humanities experts*.

## Notes

1. Namely: Leonardo Impett and Franco Moretti, "Totentanz: Operationalizing Aby Warburg's Pathosformeln," *New Left Review* 107 (2017): 68–97; Peter Bell and Leonardo Impett, "Ikonographie und Interaktion. Computergestützte Analyse von Posen in Bildern der Heilsgeschichte," *Das Mittelalter. Perspektiven mediävistischer Forschung* 24, no. 1 (2019): 31–53.
2. Adam Kendon, *Gesture: Visible action as utterance* (Cambridge: Cambridge University Press, 2004), 15.
3. This distinction was made through fruitful conversation with the Egyptologist Alexandre Loktionov, and brings fruitful parallels with the semiotic study of hieroglyphs; e.g. between written gestural determinatives/semagrams and speech-accompanying disambiguative gestures.
4. Craig Hugh Smyth, *Mannerism and maniera* (Gluckstadt: JJ Augustin, 1963), 97.
5. Erwin Panofsky and Fritz Saxl, "Classical Mythology in Mediaeval Art," *Metropolitan Museum Studies* 4, no. 2 (1933): 239–49.
6. E.g. François Garnier, *Le langage de l'image au Moyen Age II: grammaire des gestes* (Paris: Le Léopard d'or, 1989), and—more recently—Floren Deuchler, *Strukturen und Schauplätze der Gestik: Gebärden und ihre Handlungsorte in der Malerei des ausgehenden Mittelalters* (Berlin: Walter de Gruyter, 2014).
7. Gustavo Carneiro, Nuno Pinho da Silva, Alessio Del Bue, and João Paulo Costeira, "Artistic image classification: An analysis on the Printart database," *European Conference on Computer Vision* (2012): 143–57.
8. Most notably, in Jean-Claude Schmitt, *La raison des gestes dans l'Occident médiéval* (Paris: Gallimard, 1990); and in Peter Burke, *The Historical Anthropology of Early Modern Italy: Essays on Perception and Communication* (Cambridge: Cambridge University Press, 2005).
9. Joaneath Spicer, "The Renaissance Elbow," in *A Cultural History of Gesture*, ed. Jan Bremmer and Herman Roodenburg (Cambridge: Polity Press, 1991), 93.
10. Leonid Pishchulin et al., "Deepcut: Joint Subset Partition and Labeling for Multi Person Pose Estimation," *Proceedings of the IEEE Conference on Computer Vision and Pattern Recognition* (2016): 4929–37.
11. Ke Sun, Bin Xiao, Dong Liu, and Jingdong Wang, "Deep High-Resolution Representation Learning for Human Pose Estimation," *Proceedings of the IEEE Conference on Computer Vision and Pattern Recognition* (2019): 5693–703.
12. Aby Warburg, "Dürer and Italian Antiquity (1905)," in *The Renewal of Pagan Antiquity: Contributions to the Cultural History of the European Renaissance*, trans. David Britt (Los Angeles: Getty Research Institute, 1999), 729–30.
13. Franco Moretti, "Operationalizing," *New Left Review* 84 (2013): 103–19.
14. Anthony Atkinson et al., "Emotion Perception from Dynamic and Static Body Expressions in Point-Light and Full-Light Displays," *Perception* 33, no. 6 (2004): 717–46.
15. Frank E. Pollick et al., "Gender Recognition from Point-Light Walkers," *Journal of Experimental Psychology: Human Perception and Performance* 31 no. 6 (2005): 1247–65.
16. Atkinson, "Emotion Perception from Dynamic."
17. Translation by Franco Moretti in Impett and Moretti, "Totentanz." The original text is in Warburg Institute Archive: WIA III, 118; an Italian translation is published in Andre Jolles, "La ninfa: uno scambio di lettere tra A. Jolles e A. Warburg," in *A. Warburg, Opere,* ed. Maurizio Ghelardi, vol. I (Turin: Aragno,

2004), 243–55; see also Daniela Sacco, "Ninfa e Gradiva: dalla percezione individuale alla memoria storica sovrapersonale," *Cahiers d'études italiennes* 23 (2016): 45–60.
18. Salvatore Settis, "Pathos ed Ethos, morfologia e funzione," *Moderna: semestrale di teoria e critica della letteratura* 6, no. 2 (2004): 29.
19. See, for example, Nicholas I. Fisher, *Statistical Analysis of Circular Data* (Cambridge: Cambridge University Press, 1995).
20. Bruno Wicht, "2D Pose Searching and Analysis in Art" (Semester diss., Ecole polytechnique fédérale de Lausanne, Spring 2017).
21. Preliminary results from this research are published (in German) in Bell and Impett, "Ikonographie und Interaktion."
22. Michael Baxandall, *Painting and Experience in Fifteenth-Century Italy: A Primer in the Social History of Pictorial Style* (Oxford: Oxford University Press, 1988), 51.
23. Meredith Gill, *Angels and the Order of Heaven in Medieval and Renaissance Italy* (Cambridge: Cambridge University Press, 2014), 104.
24. Accessed August 8, 2019, http://lab.softwarestudies.com/p/imageplot.html.
25. Peter Bell, Joseph Schlecht, and Björn Ommer, "Nonverbal Communication in Medieval Illustrations Revisited by Computer Vision and Art History," *Visual Resources* 29, no. 1 (2013): 26–37.
26. Tomas Simon, Hanbyul Joo, Iain Matthews, and Yaser Sheikh, "Hand Keypoint Detection in Single Images Using Multiview Bootstrapping," *Proceedings of the IEEE Conference on Computer Vision and Pattern Recognition* (2017): 1145–53.
27. Zhe Cao, Tomas Simon, Shih-En Wei, and Yaser Sheikh, "Realtime Multi-Person 2D Pose Estimation Using Part Affinity Fields," *Proceedings of the IEEE Conference on Computer Vision and Pattern Recognition* (2017): 7291–99.
28. Shuzhi Sam Ge, Y. Yang, and Tong Heng Lee, "Hand Gesture Recognition and Tracking Based on Distributed Locally Linear Embedding," *Image and Vision Computing* 26, no. 12 (2008): 1607–20.
29. Available at https://biblhertz.github.io/atlas/ (gesture atlas, by the author) and https://github.com/leoimpett/3dBodies/ (gesture search engine, by Bruno Wicht) (Both accessed August 8, 2019).
30. Rodney A. Brooks, "Elephants Don't Play Chess," *Robotics and Autonomous Systems* 6, no. 1–2 (1990): 3–15.
31. Alison Adam, *Artificial Knowing: Gender and the Thinking Machine* (Abington: Routledge, 1998); although she later expanded her critique to include ALife approaches, machine learning, and so forth, her treatment of Symbolic AI is the most relevant in the context of the Digital Humanities—especially in its conservative and historicist incarnations in Art History.
32. Claire Bishop, "Against Digital Art History," *International Journal for Digital Art History* 3 (2018), originally published on the website of the Franklin Humanities Institute at Duke University.

## Bibliography

Adam, Alison. *Artificial Knowing: Gender and the Thinking Machine*. Abington: Routledge, 1998.

Atkinson, Anthony P., Winand H. Dittrich, Andrew J. Gemmell, and Andrew W. Young. "Emotion Perception from Dynamic and Static Body Expressions in Point-Light and Full-Light Displays." *Perception* 33, no. 6 (2004): 717–46.

Baxandall, Michael. *Painting and Experience in Fifteenth-Century Italy: A Primer in the Social History of Pictorial Style*. Oxford: Oxford University Press, 1972, 1988.

Bell, Peter, and Leonardo Impett. "Ikonographie und Interaktion. Computergestützte Analyse von Posen in Bildern der Heilsgeschichte." *Das Mittelalter. Perspektiven mediävistischer Forschung* 24, no. 1 (2019): 31–53.

Bell, Peter, Joseph Schlecht, and Björn Ommer. "Nonverbal Communication in Medieval Illustrations Revisited by Computer Vision and Art History." *Visual Resources* 29, no. 1 (2013): 26–37.

Bishop, Claire. "Against Digital Art History." *International Journal for Digital Art History* 3 (2018).

Brooks, Rodney A. "Elephants Don't Play Chess." *Robotics and Autonomous Systems* 6, no. 1–2 (1990): 3–15.

Burke, Peter. *The Historical Anthropology of Early Modern Italy: Essays on Perception and Communication*. Cambridge: Cambridge University Press, 2005.

Cao, Zhe, Tomas Simon, Shih-En Wei, and Yaser Sheikh. "Realtime Multi-person 2D Pose Estimation using Part Affinity Fields." *Proceedings of the IEEE Conference on Computer Vision and Pattern Recognition* (2017): 7291–99.

Carneiro, Gustavo, Nuno Pinho da Silva, Alessio Del Bue, and João Paulo Costeira. "Artistic image classification: An analysis on the Printart database." *European Conference on Computer Vision* (2012): 143–57.

Deuchler, Florens. *Strukturen und Schauplätze der Gestik: Gebärden und ihre Handlungsorte in der Malerei des ausgehenden Mittelalters*. Berlin: Walter de Gruyter, 2014.
Fisher, Nicholas I. *Statistical Analysis of Circular Data*. Cambridge: Cambridge University Press, 1995.
Garnier, François. *Le langage de l'image au Moyen Age II: grammaire des gestes*. Paris: Le Léopard d'or, 1989.
Ge, Shuzhi Sam, Y. Yang, and Tong Heng Lee. "Hand Gesture Recognition and Tracking Based on Distributed Locally Linear Embedding." *Image and Vision Computing* 26, no. 12 (2008): 1607–20.
Gill, Meredith. *Angels and the Order of Heaven in Medieval and Renaissance Italy*. Cambridge: Cambridge University Press, 2014.
Impett, Leonardo, and Franco Moretti. "Totentanz: Operationalizing Aby Warburg's Pathosformeln." *New Left Review* 107 (2017): 68–97.
Johansson, Gunnar. "Visual Perception of Biological Motion and a Model for Its Analysis." *Perception & Psychophysics* 14, no. 2 (1973): 201–11.
Jolles, Andre. "La ninfa: uno scambio di lettere tra A. Jolles e A. Warburg." In *A. Warburg, Opere*, edited by Maurizio Ghelardi, vol. I, 243–55. Turin: Aragno, 2004.
Kendon, Adam. *Gesture: Visible Action as Utterance*. Cambridge: Cambridge University Press, 2004.
Moretti, Franco. "Operationalizing." *New Left Review* 84 (2013): 103–19.
Panofsky, Erwin, and Fritz Saxl. "Classical Mythology in Mediaeval Art." *Metropolitan Museum Studies* 4, no. 2 (1933): 228–80.
Pishchulin, Leonid, Eldar Insafutdinov, Siyu Tang, Bjoern Andres, Mykhaylo Andriluka, Peter V. Gehler, and Bernt Schiele. "Deepcut: Joint Subset Partition and Labeling for Multi Person Pose Estimation." *Proceedings of the IEEE Conference on Computer Vision and Pattern Recognition* (2016): 4929–37.
Pollick, Frank E., Jim W. Kay, Katrin Heim, and Rebecca Stringer. "Gender Recognition from Point-Light Walkers." *Journal of Experimental Psychology: Human Perception and Performance* 31 no. 6 (2005): 1247–65.
Sacco, Daniela. "Ninfa e Gradiva: Dalla Percezione Individuale Alla Memoria Storica Sovrapersonale." *Cahiers d'études italiennes* 23 (2016): 45–60.
Schmitt, Jean-Claude. *La raison des gestes dans l'Occident médiéval*. Paris: Gallimard, 1990.
Settis, Salvatore. "Pathos ed Ethos, morfologia e funzione." *Moderna: semestrale di teoria e critica della letteratura* 6, no. 2 (2004): 23–34.
Simon, Tomas, Hanbyul Joo, Iain Matthews, and Yaser Sheikh. "Hand Keypoint Detection in Single Images Using Multiview Bootstrapping." *Proceedings of the IEEE Conference on Computer Vision and Pattern Recognition* (2017): 1145–53.
Smyth, Craig Hugh. *Mannerism and maniera*. Gluckstadt: JJ Augustin, 1963.
Spicer, Joaneath. "The Renaissance Elbow." In *A Cultural History of Gesture*, edited by Jan Bremmer and Herman Roodenburg, 84–128. Cambridge: Polity Press, 1991.
Sun, Ke, Bin Xiao, Dong Liu, and Jingdong Wang. "Deep High-Resolution Representation Learning for Human Pose Estimation." *Proceedings of the IEEE Conference on Computer Vision and Pattern Recognition* (2019): 5693–703.
Warburg, Aby. "Dürer and Italian Antiquity (1905)." In *The Renewal of Pagan Antiquity: Contributions to the Cultural History of the European Renaissance*, translated by David Britt, 729–30. Los Angeles: Getty Research Institute, 1999.
Wicht, Bruno. "2D Pose Searching and Analysis in Art." Semester diss., Ecole polytechnique fédérale de Lausanne, Spring 2017.

# 29

# DIGITAL TECHNIQUES FOR THE STUDY OF PORTUGUESE *AZULEJOS* (GLAZED TILES)

## Between Alice's White Rabbit and the Mad Tea Party

*Rosário Salema de Carvalho, Rafaela Xavier, and Inês Leitão*

In Lewis Carroll's *Alice's Adventures in Wonderland* published in 1865, the White Rabbit is an iconic figure, present throughout the story. Always in a hurry, mumbling "Oh dear! Oh dear! I shall be too late!"; he is constantly looking at his clock and running from one place to the next. By contrast, the Mad Hatter, the March Hare, and the Dormouse, for whom time has stopped, are trapped in an eternal six o'clock tea.

This chapter, focused on the study of Portuguese tile decorations aided by digital technologies and more generally on the field of digital art history, will refer to these two temporal dimensions—the speed that characterizes the contemporary technological world and the stillness required to reflect and carry out certain tasks. The *Az Infinitum—Azulejo Indexation and Referencing System*,[1] the research-oriented documentation project we will discuss, was conceived as a digital tool, but its progress is still limited as regards the development of digital analytical techniques such as statistical and spatio-geographical readings, network analyses, or simply data visualization. The research team in charge of the project is aware of its potential, but also of the time needed to reap the fruits of such meticulous and arduous work. Some preliminary considerations are in order to understand the importance of tile decorations in Portugal, the current state of research in this field, its relationship to Portuguese art history, the reasons for the emergence of this kind of study, and the research questions it is based on.

The idea that Portugal is the land of *azulejos* is confirmed by the country's tile decorations, a constant and distinctive presence in the landscape from the late fifteenth century to the present day (Figure 29.1). Aside from its continuous and widespread use throughout the centuries, the *azulejo* stands out for its ability to reinvent itself and adapt to different contexts. As Vitor Serrão notes:

> Its remarkable originality is due to its scenographic articulation with the architecture and with the so-called "spirit of place" of different urban configurations. Tiled façades with patterned or figurative *azulejos*, private residential interiors, stairways, palace chambers and gardens, chapels and private oratories, church naves, ceilings and archways, along with other religious, social and political settings, bear testimony to the vitality of a continual and inexhaustible dialogue between architectural and ceramic shapes.[2]

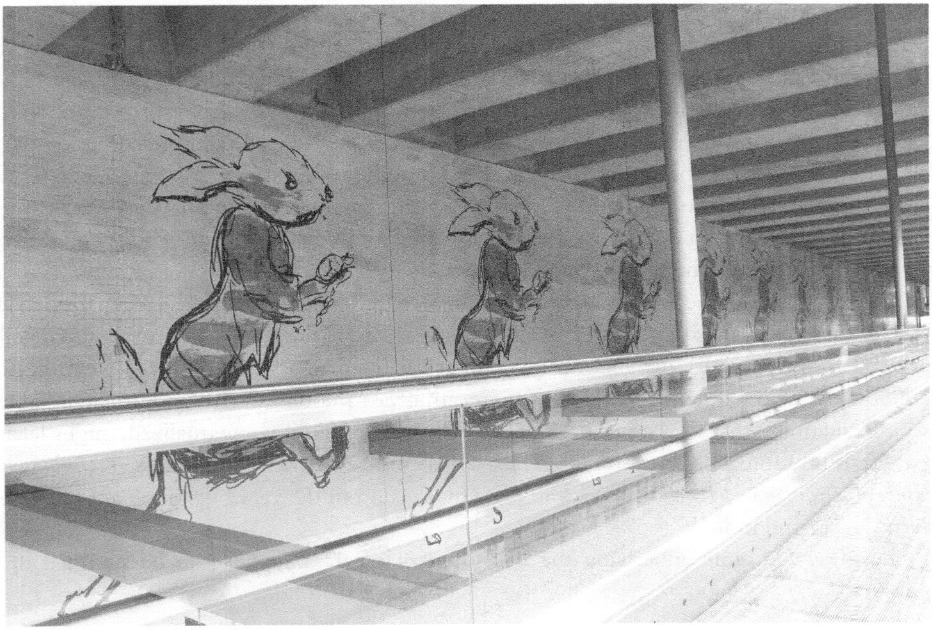

*Figure 29.1* Lisbon Underground, Cais do Sodré station.

*Source:* António Dacosta, Pedro Morais, 1998 © Arquivo Fotográfico do Metropolitano de Lisboa.

Accordingly, the study of tile decorations is not a simple matter. It spans a wide range of scientific fields, as shown by the research conducted since the second half of the nineteenth century and, in particular, over the last few decades, after the *azulejo* was elevated by João Miguel dos Santos Simões (1907–72) to an autonomous category within the realm of decorative ceramics. Existing publications offer analytical perspectives focusing mainly on iconography, decorative programs, authors and other agents, oscillating between monographic and more general approaches centered on a specific period or decorative type. Equally important is the creation of inventories, a practice which also dates back to the nineteenth century, focusing either on specific themes and types or in a specific territory. Overall, the field has come a long way from the initial surveys, reports, and manually structured files organized according to specific rules. Yet this enormous effort has not yet yielded a complete record of the country's tile heritage, but only partial records, promoted by different institutions lacking a global, integrated vision.

These issues are part of the challenges faced by art history in a country such as Portugal, where archives are still an abundant source of information, where heritage inventories are fragmented, and where new heritage is still being uncovered. In 2012, for example, researchers identified no less than four signatures on tile panels which had hitherto lain in plain sight.

## A System to Document Tile Decorations

Given such a wide and complex research field, the idea of creating a space in which to gather a maximum of information about *azulejos* became very appealing. It began to take shape with the experiments of Santos Simões, published since the 1960s, with more recent thematic inventories[3] and with the cataloguing of the Azulejo National Museum's tile collection. The experience of the first author of the present chapter in setting up a database on Filemaker, designed to structure information about the Baroque *azulejos* painters,[4] revealed both the advantages of this kind of tool and the limitations entailed by the "creation" of data models based on the requirements of a specific research task. In fact, the systematization of information has proven essential, allowing to quantify decorations signed by individual painters, for example, and to correlate that information with other chronological data. Moreover, it led to the certainty that all newly found data could be easily "filed" in the appropriate place. With this experience (as well as the previous inventories) in mind, researchers sought to extent this idea to the entire country through the creation of a collaborative sharing platform to which different scholars might contribute whenever they found new information related to *azulejos*—even if, as is often the case, they happened to be researching something completely different. The publication, in the right place, of these pieces of information, would then give rise to an increasingly wide and detailed scientific corpus. In short, the goal was to counter the fragmentary nature of *azulejo* studies and to endow the field with a tool capable of aggregating vast amounts of data and providing objective information—that is, a series of arguments that, when duly contextualized, might lead to new scientific approaches. Accordingly, what has become known, since 2012, as *Az Infinitum—Azulejo Indexation and Referencing System*, was conceived from the very beginning as a work tool, and not as an end in itself.

The ideas and aims underlying the development of *Az Infinitum* can be summed up as follows:

- To set up a database containing information about tile coverings found *in situ*, i.e. in the places for which they were originally designed, since this is one of the main features of this art form.
- To organize data in such a way as to allow for the quantification and analysis of the decorations' authorship, chronology, place of application, production and application type (patterned, figurative or ornamental), iconography, techniques, materials, etc.
- To create an open system, which can easily incorporate new data or contributions from other projects/institutions. In other words, an aggregating system.

Besides the research questions we will mention in this chapter, drawn from our own work, other important queries to be answered by the system include:

- Which decorative themes have been favored throughout the centuries? Where and when have sacred themes, for example, prevailed over mythological themes, and vice versa? Is there a correspondence between decorative themes and architectural spaces? Do the same themes appear in the same places and in similar spaces? How does the observer's reaction to the tile decorations influence experience of the different spaces?
- In the case of patterned decorations, is it possible to determine where and for how long a given pattern has been used? Which models were later reused on building façades? Does the scale of a pattern condition its spatial position? Is it possible to associate specific patterns to specific frames? And how does this association impact the museography of patterned tiles?
- Considering tile coverings as a whole, which geographic patterns can be identified? Do specific themes appear more in the North than in the South, and vice versa? What is the territorial penetration of nineteenth-century tile factories producing façade decorations? Is there a larger productive output in the south throughout the various centuries, or was this tendency reversed in the nineteenth and twentieth centuries?
- A tile decoration involves different people, be it individual actors—painters, tilers, potters—or collective ones—potteries and factories. Which professional ties did they forge and how

did they interact with other actors and professional fields? How did they pass on their knowledge? Where in the cities did they live and work? These are some of the issues raised by an extra-artistic analysis.

The research questions with which we began were later expanded as new data was introduced. With regard to research, *Az Infinitum* has therefore a double nature: (1) it was born out of specific research questions and structured accordingly; (2) it follows an open-ended approach, which consists in inserting new data and seeing how that data determines new research trajectories.

The name *Az Infinitum* speaks to this double nature: although setting up a tool of this kind is a relatively simple task, completing it would be an almost impossible, or even *infinite* task given the number of decorations found throughout the country. In light of the need to operationalize the system, it might be said that the latter amounts to a kind of utopia, to be approached step by step, but never finally attained.

What differentiates the system from other digital art history projects is the fact that, in this case, the data structure is based on a concept of inventory and cataloguing usually applied to immovable heritage and museums, following a research-oriented perspective. What is at stake is not a digitized heritage, but the gathering and processing of data enabling the creation of a digital tool, to borrow the distinction introduced by Johanna Drucker.[5]

The data categories used in the relational database *In patrimonium premium*, marketed by the company *Sistemas do Futuro*—whose research department has contributed to the development of *Az Infinitum*—can be mapped with the main international references used in the field, such as the *Core Data Index to Historic Buildings and Monuments of the Architectural Heritage* and the *Core Data Standard for Archaeological Sites and Monuments*, the *International Guidelines for Museum Object Information: the CIDOC Information Categories*, the *Categories for the Description of Works of Art* (CDWA) and *Cataloging Cultural Objects: A Guide to Describing Cultural Works and Their Images* (CCO).

Following the same documentation logic, *Az Infinitum* combines textual records, stemming both from bibliographic and documental sources and from the direct observation of tile decorations, with visual records obtained by photographing the decorations, tracking down old photographs, and identifying the decorations' original sources of inspiration (engravings, postcards, photographs, architectural treatises, etc.). While the aforementioned standards determine the system's data model, the option for collecting data (with a special emphasis on photographic records) and filling in the different information categories are determined by an internal procedural manual, published in open access in 2014 as part of the aggregation strategy of other projects.[6] Assuming that they have all followed the same logic, the interoperability of the different systems is (at least theoretically) guaranteed. The relational nature of the database allows for various forms of cross-checking, rendering the users' searches much richer than the ones made available to the public. These are currently divided into five main areas: (1) *in situ*; (2) iconography; (3) patterns and frames; (4) authorships; (5) bibliography. Generally speaking, *Az Infinitum* can be pictured as a staircase where each step corresponds to a specific level of information and knowledge, and where the available data lead the way—upwards, downwards, or toward a landing giving access to a new staircase.

Given the *azulejo*'s integrated nature, the top of the staircase refers to the buildings with tile decorations. The latter can be applied on the façades or the interior, which implies moving down one step and focusing on the architectural context, also conditioned by the other art forms present in the same space. Further down, the next step refers to the coverings themselves. They can be figurative (or ornamental) or patterned, which determines their indexation. The iconography, indexed using Iconclass, opens up a vast array of research possibilities and integrated readings—different objects, figures, themes, cycles, etc.—extended to other coverings with the same motifs. Moreover, the scope of the analysis is further widened by the indexation of the authors' sources of inspiration, also included in this web of formal and iconographic relations. What thus takes shape is a visual network extending beyond the Portuguese borders, toward other European countries—in the case of engravings—and to other continents—if one considers, for example, the decorative motifs found in Indian textiles and adapted to altarpieces. The patterns, on the other hand, are referenced with the aid of an indexation tool developed by the same team, which will be discussed later.

The authors, in turn, can be found in one of the landings leading to other staircases, giving access to the complete record of a given actor, be it a painter, a tiler or a factory, for example. This area also displays a record of the authors' works, of those that are ascribed to them, of the actors with whom they had professional or family ties. This creates a complex web combining two analytical levels: the spheres of work and personal relations (family ties, social and political connections). These, in turn, can be interpreted with the aid of network analysis or even translated into geographic and cartographic representations (for example, mapping the addresses of painters, tilers and potteries in Lisbon) thereby drawing new conclusions or corroborating what the family ties had already suggested with regard to professional collaborations.

Since many tile decorations remain anonymous, a record of who they were ascribed to over the years is another important research element that is made available by the system and explored by the authors as the data was being inserted. Given that the same work can be ascribed to different artists until a new document or signature comes to light, the evolution of ascriptions also reflects the evolution of knowledge in the field.

While uploading textual information is hardly a technological challenge—except for the aim of making the information available in Linked Open Data (LOD) and using an increasing number of standards, to guarantee the interoperability and sustainability of the system (as in the case of CIDOC-CRM)—the preparation and documentation of visual data are much more complex and challenging tasks, as we will see later.

## Reflected Images

To begin with, we must distinguish between two kinds of images used in *Az Infinitum*. The first includes photographs of coverings, mostly of a documentary nature, and digitized drawings, engravings, or book pages provided by other institutions, with their own recording procedures. Although the photographs, especially when undertaken by the professional photographers with whom we work, can bring together distant places and realities, thereby contributing to the identification of hidden aspects such as the artists' signatures (as mentioned earlier), their main role in *Az Infinitum* is to document tile decorations.

The second kind of images is obtained through digital manipulation. Used mostly in the cataloguing of patterns, these photographs acquire a new dimension—they become a surrogate of the pattern, which is both a result of the existing knowledge and a means to gain new knowledge. These photographs (or rather, the images arising from the digital manipulation of detailed photographs) replace the watercolor drawings available in non-computerized pattern catalogues.[7] This allows for a more accurate reconstruction of the decorative motifs and for the simulation of large-scale applications. Moreover, these photographs become ready-made *samples*, to be used later in the fields of computer vision or artificial intelligence, for example, in automatic image comparison.

In the following paragraphs we will discuss the preparation and the advantages of these images. We will show that this kind of work, with its unique and precise methodology, has profound research implications—not least that of calling into question the very definition of pattern: What exactly is a pattern? Or, to be more precise, what is a tile pattern?

## *How to Define a Tile Pattern*

As mentioned earlier, patterned *azulejos* are one of the leading forms of Portuguese tile decorations. They can be divided into different periods, each with its own characteristics, distinguished not only by obvious changes in the decorative motifs and compositions, but also, more discreetly, by changes in scale, lighting effects, and interaction with architecture, etc. These decorations are indeed one of the country's richest artistic expressions. They are often linked with other art forms, such as mural painting and sculpture, but this connection has yet to be properly researched. As regards their application, they can occupy small areas or cover entire walls, both interior and exterior (depending on the period), almost always enclosed by frames. The latter, in turn, can also be divided into different types, depending on the number of tiles.[8]

When applied to tile decorations, the definition of pattern is clear and depends, to some extent, on the *azulejos*' shape. However, time has shown that this is not always the case. The definition of pattern can and should be external to the *azulejos*' shape, even though we are dealing with an art form that is usually based on regular geometric shapes—squares or rectangles (the later mostly in the frames).

According to Santos Simões, the pattern is "the *unity of repetition*, that is: [it] comprises the lowest number of elements (the *azulejos* taken individually) that define the repetition.'[9] Therefore, the elements are part of a module which can then be repeated indefinitely. The pattern is defined by the module and the number of elements it comprises: there are modules made up of a single tile (1 × 1/1, where the module and the element coincide), modules made up of four tiles based on the same element (2 × 2/1), and so on until the largest known pattern, formed by 144 *azulejos* (12 × 12). This definition, specifically linked to tile decorations and to the application of the same set of tiles, has been explored, by the artist Eduardo Nery. He claims that "it is desirable for the creators of tile patterns to rely mainly on the geometry of the square" and criticizes those who ignore this rule and the *azulejo*'s modular nature. As he puts it, their work amounts merely to "artistic tile painting."[10]

Nonetheless, from a mathematical point of view, "a pattern is a bidimensional drawing based on a motif that is repeated periodically and indefinitely in two different directions, while a frieze is based on a motif repeated in only one direction. The motif is generated by one or more geometric transformations (bijective applications of the drawing within itself) based on a minimal motif."[11] According to the latter definition, the minimal motif on which a pattern is based does not depend on the physical medium. In *azulejo* coverings, a square can contain more than one minimal motif, but the motif can also arise through the combination of different squares. It all depends on the pattern's scale. Despite the seventeen pattern types and the seven frame types (or frieze types) on record, determined by their geometric transformations—translations, rotations, reflections and sliding reflections—Portuguese tile patterns are not as varied, since only tiles with other shapes could exhaust all of the aforementioned possibilities.[12] Consequently, the choice of favoring the visual effect over the *azulejo*'s specific nature (albeit taking into account its main features), combined with a long tradition of researching patterns from different centuries, have led us to base our analysis on a more geometric, and less "*azulejo*-oriented" perspective.

Furthermore, although these definitions are not incompatible when applied to patterns with regular formats, from the late fifteenth century to the present day, the same cannot be said of fifteenth-century *alicatado* compositions, checkered compositions from the late sixteenth century and the early seventeenth century, or the repeating compositions dating from the second half of the twentieth century, which in many cases cannot even be considered patterns.[13]

According to the Art and Architecture Thesaurus (AAT), the term *alicatado*—which in Spanish means "cut work"—refers to "decorations composed of mosaics formed of polygonal, colored glazed tiles in designs of geometric patterns."[14] Being composed of pieces with different formats does not prevent them from forming a pattern when applied to a given space. On the contrary, if the pieces have a regular shape, reappearing at regular intervals, the resulting design may generate a pattern, achieved not through the painting, but through the use of monochrome elements. In this case, as in that of checkered decorations, what is at stake is the mode of application. These examples can thus be considered "patterns by application," a term used for the first time on *Az Infinitum* in connection with the *alicatado* tiles of the National Palace of Sintra.

## *Digital Simulations of Patterns*

The visual cataloguing of tile patterns from different centuries entails the digital manipulation of detailed photographs. This procedure enables the interpretation of different patterns, or even, when the coverings are very degraded, a reconstitution of decorative compositions. The aim is to obtain a standard image of each pattern. The analysis and comparison of similar tiles found in different parts of the country, with a clear identification of their similarities and differences, enable a much better knowledge of each composition and allow us to simulate its application.

This work was initiated by João Miguel dos Santos Simões, in a more systematic way for the tile production from the seventeenth century, and more empirically for the fifteenth and sixteenth centuries, based on drawings and watercolors favoring the perspective of the tiler over that of the observer. That is why the very notion of pattern, as discussed previously, was determined by the *azulejos'* physical shape and not by their visual effect.

On *Az Infinitum*, when preparing these images, we also started with the seventeenth century, using digital cleaning criteria to eliminate crackles and stains that might hinder the identification of the pattern, but preserving the tiles' original plasticity. The same method was also applied to the following centuries, except for the patterns involving embossed elements, the effects of which are much harder to reproduce and that pose other challenges to the teams of photographers and designers with whom we work.

In the last six months, as part of the research of the second author of this chapter, we have started cataloguing so-called Mudejar tile patterns, the slightly embossed surface of which is typical of the *cuerda seca* and *arista* techniques. This effect is harder to recreate digitally, as are the numerous chromatic variations, sometimes in the same tile.

To catalogue is to choose, and the images compiled in the system reflect the interpretation of the multidisciplinary team responsible for this work. Researchers have opted to vectorize the photographs and then simulate the incidence of light, always from left to right, recreating both light and color effects on the embossed surfaces and color effects on the flat surfaces. Despite the need for future corrections, a work of this nature applied to the *azulejos* preserved in the National Palace of Sintra (Figure 29.2) led to the identification of seventy-eight patterns, forty-four two-*azulejo* frames, nine one-*azulejo* frames, four half-*azulejo* frames, eleven patterns by application, two two-*azulejo* frames by application, four one-*azulejo* frame by application and two half-*azulejo* frames out of a total of 135 catalogued items, excluding the *azulejos* that were stored (of which no visible applications remain) and others that went missing. This number is considerably higher than the one recorded by authors such as the Count of Sabugosa in 1903,[15] Santos Simões in 1969,[16] or Rui Trindade in 2007 (Figure 29.3).[17]

The differences between the watercolors published by the first two authors and the images obtained through digital manipulation (Figure 29.3) are a clear indication of how far we have come, and a proof of the increasing accuracy enabled by the use of photographs. This contribution is especially evident in the case of seventeenth-century *azulejos*: the comparison between

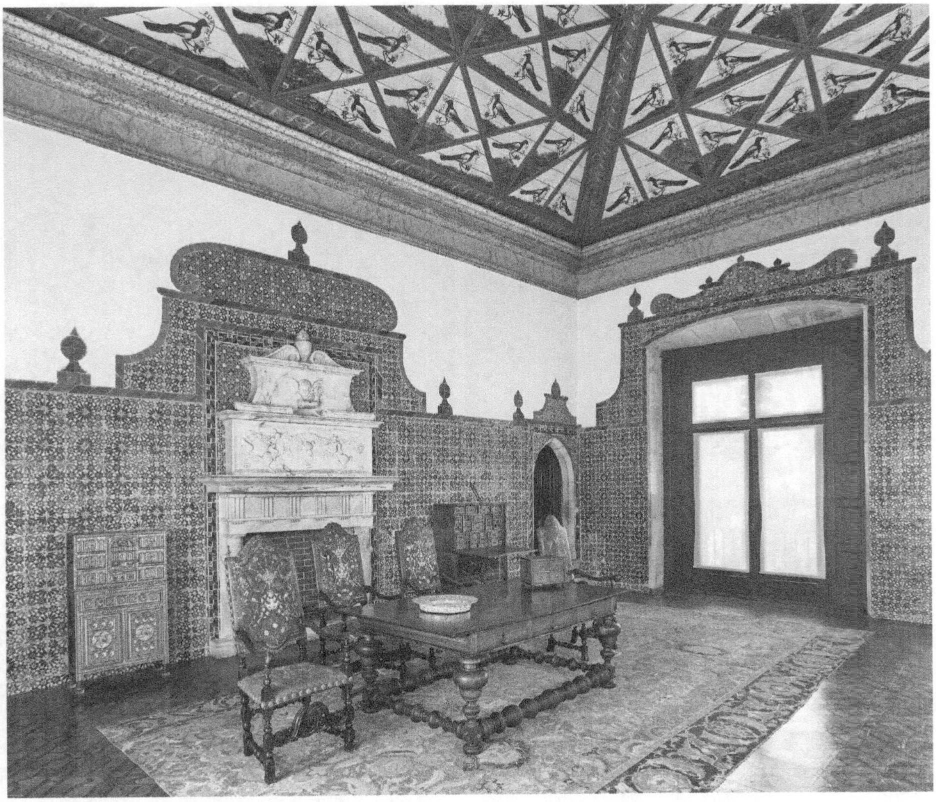

*Figure 29.2* Sintra National Palace, Magpies' Room.

*Source*: © PSML | Ângelo Hornak, 2014.

the drawings and the real items (later reduced to the manipulated images of each pattern, which are the fruit of a meticulous analysis of each decorative motif), determines the appearance of "new" patterns differing in certain details from the ones previously grouped under the same type. A pattern found in Marvila Church (Santarém) is so far the most eloquent example of this situation, with many variants labeled by Santos Simões simply as P-17–00999.

Although our initial aim of offering a global, up-to-date overview of Portuguese patterned *azulejos* is still out of reach—an indefinite number of items have yet to be catalogued, which implies future field work and appropriate photographic records—this methodology has already led to two important conclusions. First, the digital manipulation of tile patterns allows us to "read" their history in a new way. It is different from more traditional approaches in that it reveals, compares and interrelate the physical characteristics typical of each century. Second, the advantages of this procedure are made particularly clear by the use of image recognition and artificial intelligence/machine learning to automatically link up both photographs of various origins with a database such as *Az Infinitum* and the images stored in the system itself. These possibilities are being tested in an ongoing project entitled ZULEJO, developed by Catarina Pinheiro, Mathilda Larsson and David Ortega.

Even though the project PrintArt[18]—aimed at the automatic comparison between figurative tile compositions and the engravings on which they were based—was instrumental in

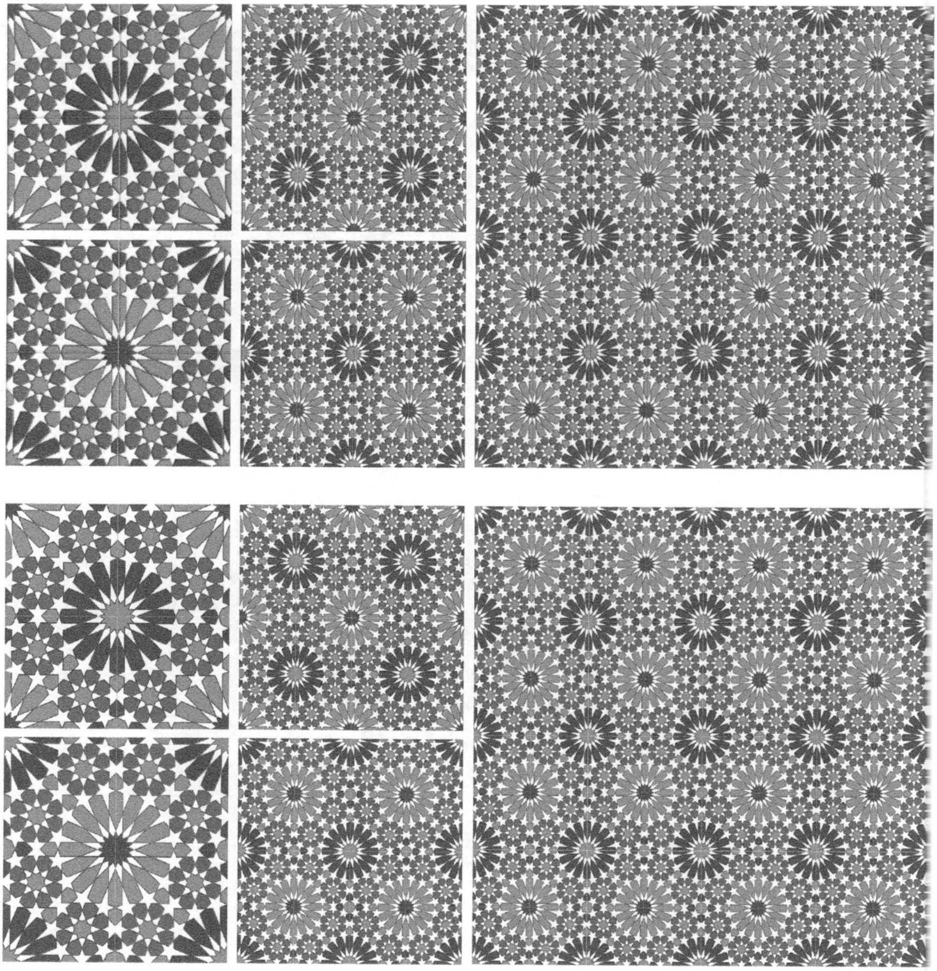

*Figure 29.3* Digital surrogates (simulating the cuerda seca technique and flat) of the Mudejar tile pattern n. P-15-16-00033, with two centers and its multiplications.

*Source:* © Az Infinitum (ARTIS-IHA/FLUL), 2019.

strengthening the link between art (or tile decorations) and computer vision, the latest technological developments will hopefully solve this problem in the near future through an application that is both easy to use and useful to historians.

## Rabbits, Hares, and Hatters: The Haste to Move Forward and the Importance of Data Preparation

In the context of digital art history and the various initiatives taking place that aim to strengthen ties between art history and technology, the imbalance between the desirable and the possible is an ever-present threat, hovering over these two different worlds. On the one hand, a good project is born of specific research questions. It is the responsibility of art historians to formulate such questions and to engage with existing technology, with the help of their fellow technologist researchers, in order to determine the best possible solution at a given moment. On the other hand, although it is desirable for historians to fantasize an ideal world, and thereby achieve scientific breakthroughs, it is equally essential to set attainable targets.

In short, and returning to the topic of tile decorations, Portugal is home to an extremely vast heritage, with various shapes and chronologies scattered across the country and owned by a variety of institutions and collectors. Although this heritage is the topic of a relatively wide historiographical output, much remains to be studied. The idea that this research is particularly fitted for the digital tools available today in the field of art history appears obvious, as does the assumption that these tools can help organize and interrelate a massive amount of information. Yet this idea can only be put to use if researchers have access to clean and curated data. After seven years of work and more than five thousand records uploaded into the system's different areas, the global, updated vision we strive for is still far from complete. As regards data insertion, we are slowly fulfilling our goals, focusing on the creation of research sub-questions that are easier to handle. However, we are still behind on data visualization techniques, and still in need of new tools that might push our work forward. Despite *Az Infinitum*'s utopian dimension, patent in its double role of inventory/cataloguing platform and aggregating system operating in a highly fragmented research universe, the project was designed to deal with such issues and to incorporate new research questions. Moreover, the attainment of partial results is a slow but sure way of moving forward, disproving the idea that the system is like a monster that cannot be controlled. Although at first sight we remain bound to the fragmented universe from which we started, the relational structure we have set up prevents us from working in a closed and isolated way. Rather, it brings different data together and promotes collaboration between different researchers.

Nonetheless, the certainty of being on the right track in what regards the documentation and study of Portuguese tile decorations found *in situ* does not prevent figures like the White Rabbit, the Mad Hatter, the March Hare and the Dormouse from haunting us. They urge us to pursue well-delimited projects, feasible within a limited time frame and with the available resources, and remind us that *Az Infinitum* is simultaneously a tool and a source of data that must be carefully prepared, even if that implies a much longer development period. Accordingly, *Az Infinitum* can also be associated with so-called slow digital art history—a term introduced by the project *Cornelia*,[19] but which also applies to our own work.

Only with quality information is it possible to move forward, as shown by some of the ongoing projects linked to *Az Infinitum*, with diverse features and timelines. Starting with the cataloguing of Mudejar patterns found in a specific location, namely the National Palace of Sintra, it is now possible to widen the spectrum and include other locations and patterns. Furthermore, this restricted universe can be extended to the entire Iberian Peninsula, in search of an integrated vision of what was once an Iberian cultural phenomenon. The cataloguing of Baroque frames, which has proven much more time-consuming, especially as regards the digital manipulation of images and all the information this provides, has helped shed light on the technique and know-how of tile painters, tilers and potters from this period.[20] Finally, the identification of more than 150 examples of contemporary tile decorations in public spaces is enabling a theoretical reassessment of the *azulejos* produced since the 1950s, proving that this art form has also benefited from an "expanded field" in its conception and application.

Alice's stories are the compromise we strive for on *Az Infinitum*—work confidently but slow, inserting data but confirming it and exploring the archives as well as the new ways of achieving data such as image analysis—mindful both of traditional issues and recent innovations (everyday new possibilities are revealed), and trying to guarantee the system's technological sustainability.

## Notes

1. *Az Infinitum* is a project developed by the group Az—Azulejo Research Network, part of ARTIS—Art History Institute of the School of Arts and Humanities of the University of Lisbon, in collaboration with the Azulejo National Museum and the company *Sistemas do Futuro*. It is coordinated by Rosário Salema de Carvalho and Alexandre Nobre Pais. See http://redeazulejo.letras.ulisboa.pt/pesquisa-az, accessed August 1, 2019.
2. Vitor Serrão, "Prefácio/Preface," in *Azulejo em/in Braga—O Largo Tempo do Barroco/The Baroque Period*, ed. Rosário Salema de Carvalho and Libório Manuel Silva (Vila Nova de Famalicão: Centro Atlântico, 2016), 11.
3. The most relevant example being the revision of Santos Simões' inventory of eighteenth-century tile decorations, promoted by the project *18th Century Tile Heritage in Portugal. Constitution and organization of an Iconography Repertory*. The project was funded by the Foundation for Science and Technology between 2004 and 2007, and coordinated by Maria Alexandra Trindade Gago da Câmara.
4. Rosário Salema de Carvalho, "A pintura do azulejo em Portugal [1675–725]: autorias e biografias—um novo paradigma" (PhD diss., Universidade de Lisboa, 2012), accessed August 15, 2019, http://hdl.handle.net/10451/6527
5. Johanna Drucker, "Is There a 'Digital' Art History?" *Visual Resources* 29, no. 1–2 (2013): 5–13.
6. Rosário Salema de Carvalho, Alexandre Pais, and Ana Paula Figueiredo, coord., *Guia de Inventário de Azulejo in situ* (Lisboa: Rede de Investigação em Azulejo—ARTIS/IHA-FLUL, 2014), https://azinfinitum.wixsite.com/guiainv, accessed August 21, 2019.
7. João Miguel dos Santos Simões, *Azulejaria em Portugal no século XVII* (Lisboa: Fundação Calouste Gulbenkian, 1997 [1971]).
8. Rosário Salema de Carvalho, "Cataloguing Baroque azulejo Frames: A Project in Progress," *ARTis ON* no. 2 (2016): 33–41.
9. Simões, *Azulejaria em Portugal no século XVII*, 20. Translation provided by the authors.
10. Eduardo Nery, *Apreciação Estética do Azulejo* (Lisboa: Edições Inapa, 2007), 86.
11. Fátima Rodrigues et al., *MATER, Matemática do Planeta Terra, Retrospectiva de uma Exposição* (Caparica: FCT/Universidade Nova de Lisboa, 2015).
12. Fátima Rodrigues and Pedro Freitas, "Tiles and Identity by Pattern Classification," *ARTis ON* no. 8 (2018): 8, http://artison.letras.ulisboa.pt/index.php/ao/article/view/218/186.
13. Many compositions suggest the idea of pattern but cannot be considered as such, since they are not repeated at regular intervals.
14. "alicatados," Art and Architecture Thesaurus, accessed August 2, 2019, http://vocab.getty.edu/page/aat/300265244, accessed August 2, 2019.
15. Conde de Sabugosa, *O Paço de Sintra* (Sintra: Câmara Municipal de Sintra, 1990).
16. João Miguel dos Santos Simões, *Azulejaria em Portugal nos séculos XV e XVI* (Lisboa: Fundação Calouste Gulbenkian, 1990 [1969]), 57.
17. Rui Trindade, *Revestimentos Cerâmicos Portugueses* (Lisboa: Edições Colibri, 2007).
18. On this project see http://printart.isr.ist.utl.pt/index.html, accessed August 1, 2019.
19. Koenraad Brosens et al., "Slow Digital Art History in Action: Project Cornelia's Computational Approach to Seventeenth-Century Flemish Creative Communities," *Visual Resources* 35, no. 1–2 (2019): 105–24.
20. See Rosário Salema de Carvalho, "Baroque Azulejo's Frames," in *Framings*, ed. Slavko Kacunko, Ellen Harlizius-Klück, and Hans Körner (Berlin: Logos Verlag Berlin GmbH, 2015), 193–210; Rosário Salema de Carvalho, "Les cadres des azulejos baroques portugais," in *Jeux et enjeux du cadre dans les systèmes décoratifs de la première modernité*, ed. Nicolas Cordon, Édouard Degans, Elli Doulkaridou-Ramantani, and Caroline Heering (Rennes: Presses Universitaires de Rennes, 2019), 59–72.

## Bibliography

Art and Architecture Thesaurus. "alicatados." Accessed August 2, 2019. http://vocab.getty.edu/page/aat/300265244.

Brosens, Koenraad, Jan Aerts, Klara Alen, Rudy Jos Beerens, Bruno Cardoso, Inez De Prekel, Anna Ivanova, Houda Lamqaddam, Geert Molenberghs, Astrid Slegten, Fred Truyen, Katlijne Van der Stighelen, and Katrien Verbert. "Slow Digital Art History in Action: Project's Cornelia's Computational Approach to

Seventeenth-Century Flemish Creative Communities." *Visual Resources* 35, no. 1–2 (2019) 105–24. doi:10.1080/01973762.2019.1553444

Carvalho, Rosário Salema de. Alexandre Pais and Ana Paula Figueiredo, coord. *Guia de Inventário de Azulejo in situ*. Lisboa: Rede de Investigação em Azulejo—ARTIS/IHA-FLUL, 2014. https://azinfinitum.wixsite.com/guiainv.

———. "Baroque Azulejo's Frames." In *Framings*, edited by Slavko Kacunko, Ellen Harlizius-Klück and Hans Körner, 193–210. Berlin: Logos Verlag Berlin GmbH, 2015.

———. "Cataloguing Baroque azulejo Frames. A Project in Progress." *ARTis ON* Special Issue—Proceedings of AzLab#14 Azulejos and Frames, no. 2 (2016): 33–41. http://artison.letras.ulisboa.pt/index.php/ao/article/view/41.

———. "Les cadres des azulejos baroques portugais." In *Jeux et enjeux du cadre dans les systèmes décoratifs de la première modernité*, edited by Nicolas Cordon, Édouard Degans, Elli Doulkaridou-Ramantani, and Caroline Heering, 59–72. Rennes: Presses Universitaires de Rennes, 2019.

———. "A pintura do azulejo em Portugal [1675–1725]: autorias e biografias—um novo paradigma." PhD diss., Universidade de Lisboa, 2012. http://hdl.handle.net/10451/6527.

Drucker, Johanna. "Is There a 'Digital' Art History?" *Visual Resources* 29, no. 1–2 (2013): 5–13. https://doi.org/10.1080/01973762.2013.761106.

Nery, Eduardo. *Apreciação Estética do Azulejo*. Lisboa: Edições Inapa, 2007.

Rodrigues, Fátima, and Pedro Freitas. "Tiles and Identity by Pattern Classification." *ARTis ON* Special Issue—Proceedings of AzLab#42 Identity(ies) of the Azulejo in Portugal, no. 8 (2018): 69–80. http://artison.letras.ulisboa.pt/index.php/ao/article/view/218/186

Rodrigues, Fátima et al. *MATER, Matemática do Planeta Terra, Retrospectiva de uma Exposição*. Caparica: FCT/Universidade Nova de Lisboa, 2015.Sabugosa, Conde de. *O Paço de Sintra*. Sintra: Câmara Municipal de Sintra/Gabinete de Estudos Históricos e Documentais, 1990.

Serrão, Vitor. "Prefácio/Preface." In *Azulejos—Maravilhas de Portugal/Wonders of Portugal*, edited by Rosário Salema de Carvalho, 11. Vila Nova de Famalicão: Centro Atlântico, 2017.

Simões, João Miguel dos Santos. *Azulejaria em Portugal no século XVII*. Lisboa: Fundação Calouste Gulbenkian, 1997 [1971].

———. *Azulejaria em Portugal nos séculos XV e XVI*. Lisboa: Fundação Calouste Gulbenkian, 1990 [1969].

Trindade, Rui. *Revestimentos Cerâmicos Portugueses*. Lisboa: Edições Colibri, 2007.

# PART V

# Digital Resources, Publication, and Education

# 30

# THE DATABASE OF MODERN EXHIBITIONS (DoME)

## European Paintings and Drawings 1905–1915

*Christina Bartosch, Nirmalie Mulloli, Daniel Burckhardt, Marei Döhring, Walid Ahmad, and Raphael Rosenberg*

In Europe, until well into the eighteenth century, painters undertook their work primarily through commissions. By contrast, in the nineteenth century, art exhibitions became the primary site through which artists could reach publics, critics, and buyers. Around 1900 exhibitions became the essential battle ground for numerous avant-garde movements—the privileged place for artists to demonstrate their modernist credentials. However, whereas research on early twentieth-century avant-garde art is extensive, we know little about the crucial history of its exhibitions. Art-historical studies have focused on a handful of events, especially those which catalyzed new art movements such as the *Salon d'Automne* of 1905 in Paris (as the starting point of *Fauvism*), the first *Blaue Reiter* exhibition in Munich (1911/1912), the *Sonderbund* exhibition in Cologne (1912), the *Armory Show* in New York (1913), and the first manifestation of Suprematism at *The Last Futurist Exhibition of Painting 0,10* in St. Petersburg (1915/1916).[1]

In the absence of a broader picture of the rich European exhibition landscape prior to the First World War, it is neither possible to write an accurate history of the art of this period, nor to understand fully the distinctive characteristics of its canonical exhibitions. In order to overcome this limitation, the research project "Exhibitions of Modern European Painting 1905–1915" (led by Raphael Rosenberg) was founded in the Department of Art History of the University of Vienna. The project aimed to outline (1) the geography and networks of modern painting: Where (in which cities, in which institutions), when, and with whom artists exhibited? (2) the chronology and geography of exhibiting new forms and propagating "isms": Which kinds of paintings were exhibited when and where? (3) The exhibition strategies of modern painters: how did artists choose the works to present in which exhibitions? Did they pursue specific practices to make themselves publicly known? (4) The discourses around modern art exhibitions: how did exhibitions and their catalogues relate to contemporary art criticism?

The centerpiece of the research project is the Database of Modern Exhibitions (DoME)[2] that enables detailed research into information extracted from exhibition catalogues. DoME covers as comprehensively as possible the European continent for the years between 1905 and 1915. In this chapter we present the criteria, architecture, challenges, and potential of this database.

## Definitions—Template

DoME aims to store information extracted from catalogues pertaining to exhibitions that took place between 1905 and 1915 and that included modern European painters. The goal was to cover the European continent as completely as possible, as well as to include exhibitions of works by European painters that took place outside Europe. Since resources were limited, we excluded sculpture, prints and applied art, and instead focused only on paintings and drawings. We also ignored traditional and/or academically oriented exhibitions that did not show any modern artists (such as the *Salons de la Société nationale des Beaux-Arts* in Paris or the *Große Berliner Kunstausstellung*). Defining "modern" in an operationalizable manner, without lapsing into established canons was a major challenge. After intensive discussions, we opted to depend largely on Donald E. Gordon's 1974 publication *Modern Art Exhibitions 1900–1916*, which provided a "template at large" for the project.

Gordon's research was a milestone in exhibition history, compiling around 850 exhibitions and including 426 artists over a seventeen-year period. His artist list contains painters "of national or international significance to the origin and early development of modern art"[3] that served as useful starting point, although he does not explain his criteria for "modernity." We implemented Gordon's selection of artists and exhibitions as a starting point. Gordon's two volumes mention locations of catalogue copies and were therefore a crucial aid in locating the original exhibition catalogues in cultural institutions across Europe and North America. However, instead of repeating his highly selective and subjective collection (he only lists artworks exhibited by the 426 artists), we entered *all* paintings and drawings by *all* artists listed in the original exhibition catalogues into DoME. Additionally, as far as our resources allowed, we added exhibitions that were not part of Gordon's volumes, if they (1) included artists already listed in the database; (2) comprised living, non-academic artists; or (3) took place in institutions dedicated to modern art. This method enabled a wide—albeit blurry—treatment of the concept of "modern." As important as Gordon's volumes are, they are not only limited to a restricted canon of artists and sometimes erroneous, but also cumbersome to work with—an issue where digital tools offer a clear advantage.

## Data Entry

Over a two-year period, four broad overarching phases of alternating data entry and quality control structured the manual data entry process. The development and adaptation of the database infrastructure, as well as the design of the database frontend, was continually informed by critical insights from the project team. At the time of writing (August 2019) the database covers more than 1,350 exhibitions, out of which about 1,000 are entered completely, and comprises roughly 12,000 artists and 150,000 catalogue entries of paintings and drawings. Although some original exhibition catalogues have not yet been located, the corresponding exhibitions are still listed in DoME in order for them to be included in the database's statistics and maps. Furthermore, this renders the database transparent about missing data and should encourage users to come forward in case they know of the whereabouts of those missing catalogues.

Copyrights were one of the main challenges for the project and had an extensive impact on the data entry process. Institutions lending digitized versions of catalogues, some exhibiting institutions ("organizing bodies") and some of the artists' estates (still) own a variety of copyrights and rights of use. Hence, we decided not to publish digital reproductions of the original exhibition catalogues and only to provide links where online versions are already freely available. In addition, the option of publishing any historical photographs of the exhibitions or reproductions of exhibited artworks had to be discarded.

Knowing that researchers would likely use the information displayed in DoME in lieu of accessing the original catalogues or reproductions thereof, the information entered needed to be as close as possible to the original. It was, therefore, essential to maintain an accurate view of the catalogue structure in order to ensure that the same insights and correlations from the physical catalogues could be gained when working with the information as data. Beyond basic data—the listings of names of artists and artworks—we also wanted to keep as much "discursive and relational information"[4] as possible, such as introductive and or explanatory texts, artists' addresses, and names of the organizing committees of the exhibition and their honorary members. It was also essential to maintain the order of listings in the catalogues and to render them visible. To stay true to the source, numbering errors, typing errors, handwritten notes or corrections (if decipherable) were included. Artworks realized in media other than painting or drawing were recorded as "other medium," along with their numbering but without title, creator or further information. This way, gaps in the continuously numbered lists of exhibited items were avoided, and the proportions of paintings, drawings and all other media become apparent and can be displayed statistically. This approach also enables us to see in which catalogues these items are listed, which makes it possible to easily add them at a later date, if desired.

To work with the diversity of languages in the catalogues from the entire European continent, the team included members with native language skills in Czech, Dutch, English, French, German, Hungarian, Italian, and Russian. In total, thirteen persons (mainly art history students from the University of Vienna) worked on data entry and quality control under the guidance of the core project staff. To render the database as user-friendly as possible, languages with non-Roman alphabet were transliterated and Russian, Hungarian and Czech information was translated into English. Most importantly, artists' names were linked to "authority files" (see the following section). This presented a time-consuming challenge since it was common to have their names written as a moniker or short-hand in the catalogues, making them difficult or sometimes even impossible to identify today.

While the kind of information provided by the catalogues is relatively consistent, their format is often anything but. Therefore, a customized set of formatting rules for DoME was developed and adopted to make the data entry as coherent and as comprehensive as possible. This extensive manual of format rules for data entry is made available for consultation on the frontend and can be used as a basis for future projects.[5] Since different copies of the same exhibition catalogues can differ from one another—depending on variations in editions, annotations and physical condition—it was important to detail the specific catalogue used, along with the institution that provided the reproduction.

For particularly large exhibition catalogues with several thousand exhibits, such as the *Salon d'Automne* and *Salon de la Société des Artistes Indépendants* in Paris, an alternative to the often-slow manual data entry was sought. Walid Ahmad, data scientist, developed software to automatically extract structured information from such catalogues. This software employed a three-stage pipeline (Figure 30.1).

The first stage used optical character recognition (OCR) to extract text from scanned catalogues. State of the art OCR methods are developed using machine learning and require both large sets of annotated examples and intensive computer power. Rather than training a new OCR model, we used the Google Cloud Vision API[6] to obtain text extracts. For the second stage, we trained a long short-term memory[7] (LSTM) network to predict attributes (see stage 2 in Figure 30.1) for each line in the raw text extract. Lastly, we leveraged the fact that families of catalogues often had consistent formatting to create a rules engine. This engine jointly parsed the text extract and attributes from the first and second stages, respectively, into database entries. After several development cycles, we were able to recognize over 90% of works correctly in an out-of-sample catalogue with this pipeline.

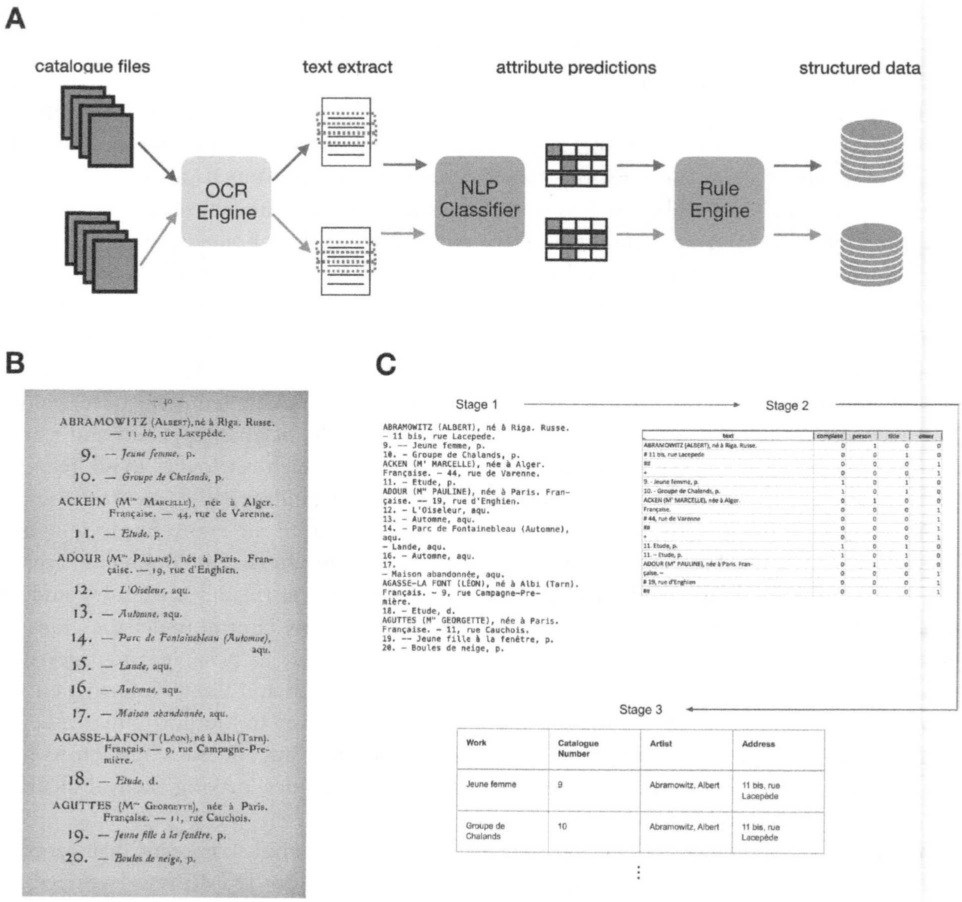


*Figure 30.1* *A*: Schematic depicting the three-stage pipeline employed for automated data entry. *B*: An example of a scanned catalogue page. *C*: (1) Processed scan sent to the Google Cloud Vision API, which returns a text extract; (2) Multiclass text classification model predicts whether or not each line meets the criteria of "complete," "person," "title," and "other"; (3) Multiclass predictions used by a rules engine to extract database-compatible information fields.

However, this automatic data entry system had several limitations. High-quality scans, often unavailable, were needed to ensure coverage (inclusion of works) and accuracy (correct data field attribution). Furthermore, the system's output still required proofreading and the manual linking of artist names to authority files. This was an elaborate task, especially in regard to the very big *Salons*, where many artists appeared only in one single exhibition and were not yet found in any authority file. Therefore, this pipeline was only used for very few catalogues.

## Database Architecture

### *Structure*

When building a database of reusable research data, one can profit from the insights of textual scholarship. There is, however, an essential difference between an analogue and a digital edition or data set: "With new media, the content of the work and the interface become separate. It is therefore possible to create different interfaces to the same material."[8] The ease of building these interfaces and their capabilities crucially depend on the underlying data structures. As with any modeling process, a trade-off between accuracy and simplicity is essential. Models are rarely obviously right or wrong, but rather good enough or not for a set of specific tasks and questions. In addition, a good model provides enough flexibility for incorporating additional requirements which could not be thought of at the beginning of the research process.[9]

The highly relational data model chosen for DoME (see Figure 30.2) is centered around a catalogue entry tied to an exhibition at a specific venue in the order recorded in the exhibition catalogue. Catalogue entries are connected to a single creator (even in very rare cases of collectively created works within our time frame) in order to simplify the queries.

The data model differentiates between "Catalogue entry" and "Work," as a single artwork might have been shown in multiple exhibitions. However, we could not afford the extremely time-consuming and often inconclusive research process of linking catalogue entries across exhibitions. Based on the exhibition catalogues, it is not possible to decide if two catalogue entries refer to the same work (e.g. "8. Cézanne, Paul, Stilleben" in the exhibition *VII. Jahrgang. Frühjahr 1905. VII. Ausstellung. [Collectionen Vincent van Gogh, Félix Vallotton]* (DoME ID: 1004) and "314. Cézanne, Paul, Nature morte" in the catalogue of the *Salon d'Automne. 3e Exposition. 1905* (DoME ID: 30)). Even in the case of Paul Cézanne, an artist with a meticulously researched catalogue raisonné, only a tentative identification of the Paris-entry can be found while the Berlin-entry (with a different catalogue number from our database) is listed as "Unidentified painting."[10] Until authoritative information on cultural works such as the Getty's Cultural Objects Name Authority or GND für Kulturdaten (GND4C) are widely adopted, such an effort must be limited to a few select artists or exhibitions where extensive archival resources or prior research are readily available.

The online database has been implemented on the widespread LAMP[11] Open Source stack which has been in use for more than two decades. This technologically rather conservative approach should not be interpreted as an aversion toward more recent developments. Rather, its use stems from the specific constellation of the research grant which did not provide funding for a dedicated developer role. Accordingly, large parts of the code were adapted from earlier projects that were initiated almost ten years ago.[12] Without such a legacy code-base to build upon, one could start with one of the Open Source solutions used in academic and cultural heritage organizations whose architecture might be flexible enough to implement a similar data model.[13]

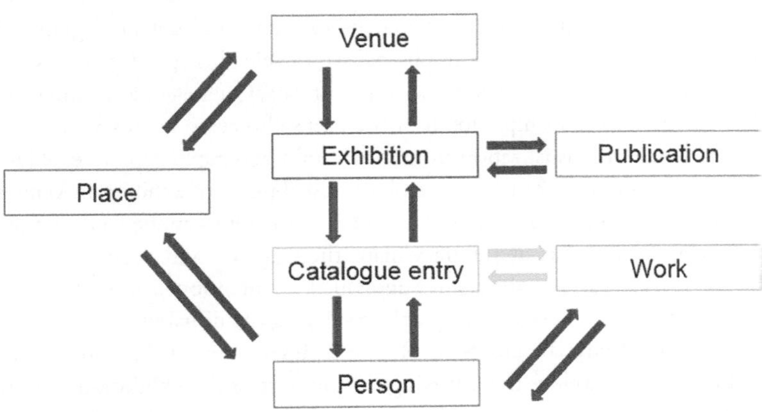


*Figure 30.2* DoME's relational data model.

## *Authority Files*

Wherever possible, database entries were connected to authority files and controlled vocabulary. For persons and organizations, Getty ULAN and/or GND identifiers were used. Though the existing coverage is far from complete, 60% of the slightly less than twelve thousand artists entered could be connected to at least one of these authorities. ULAN and GND are both integrated into the administration interface as machine-readable sources for normative spellings, nationalities, and dates and places of birth and death. The identifiers also build a crucial bridge for the reuse of our data. In addition, they provide the basis for an automated match-up with corresponding Wikidata-identifiers. A third of our person-entries are thus linked not only to corresponding Wikipedia-entries in a variety of languages but also to other human- or machine-readable online resources such as numerous artists' lexica (Benezit, RKD, Art UK, Sikart, Dictionnaire des peintres belges). All places (place of birth, death or activity of an artist and the city of a venue) are drawn from the Getty Thesaurus of Geographic Names (TGN) which provides geographic coordinates and (current day) political divisions (country, state) as linked open data. This information is essential for displaying geographic maps and filters. In addition, art-related vocabulary is drawn from Getty's Art and Architecture Thesaurus (AAT).

## *Functionalities*

The user-interface of DoME is divided into two parts: "Browse" and "Advanced Search." The browse option allows users without a specific research question or goal to peruse lists of exhibitions, artists, catalogue entries, venues, organizing bodies, and exhibiting cities. Furthermore, simple filters can be applied—such as limitations by years, by country or city, as well as by participating artists' nationalities and/or gender. The advanced search option (subdivided along the same basic entities of exhibitions, artists, venues, organizing bodies etc.) enables users to combine the filters from each of those categories with each other. It thus allows one to see, for example, the number and list of exhibitions of works by women artists in shows in the Netherlands between 1908 and 1910 or Van Gogh's presence in exhibitions organized by commercial galleries between 1910 and 1915.

Beyond targeted queries, the advanced search also offers a full text search, permitting the user to track a specific term or name throughout the entire data set: in this case, significant amounts of text in the database are combed through, including references in forewords, jury panels, member lists, organizing committees and the like. The results of both search options—browse and advanced—can be visualized as lists, geographical maps, and statistical graphs. The results, whether already filtered or not, can further be refined by selecting specific items via a checkbox, consequently allowing for a more flexible selection of data. Queries of any kind can be saved in the "My data" section with a simple login of the user's choice, so as to save specific selections the user repeatedly needs. Visualization in the form of a geographical map enables researchers quickly to obtain an overview of the geographical distribution of exhibitions venues, birth and death places of artists, or a combination of factors as per the filters applied. Given the problem of locating historic addresses on contemporary maps, the maps are only accurate to the city level.

The statistical visualizations are again subdivided, as mentioned, into the six categories. "Exhibitions" for example offers various graphs displaying the distribution by gender, by city or by types of organizing body. Bar charts enable the representation of the number of exhibitions by year and by month as well as the artists' age at the start of the exhibitions selected. A more complex matrix shows the artists' nationalities by exhibiting country, thus picturing the stronger or weaker circulation of artists in exhibitions in different countries. The statistics in the "Artists" category provide charts representing the distribution of artists' nationalities, their years of birth and death as well as the extent of their participation in exhibitions.

As a way to quantify differences of artists' popularity—in both their period and today—and to demonstrate the possibilities of linking open data with DoME, the number of Wikipedia page views of an artist (in the past year) and the number of exhibitions in the database they took part in (as an indicator for their success between 1905 and 1915) are presented together (Figure 30.3). This graph shows for instance those artists who were very successful between 1905 and 1915, but who failed to be recognized in 2019. As such, Ulrich Hübner participated in fifty-six exhibitions between 1905 and 1915, but remains largely unknown today, whereas Van Gogh was highly exhibited during this period and remains widely popular now. However, a more meaningful way of measuring the popularity of artists could be to determine how many different organizing bodies they showed with; an artist who exhibited a lot with only very few organizing bodies was in all likelihood less popular than one who exhibited with a larger variety of organizing bodies.

The "Catalogue Entries" category provides a pie chart outlining the distribution of the types of work (by medium), while in "Venues," "Organizing Bodies," and "Exhibiting Cities" the division by types of venue and/or by venues in different countries can be studied. All visualizations (lists, maps, statistics) can be downloaded in different file formats including Microsoft Excel to allow a flexible handling and combination of the data.

In comparison to existing databases such as artist-info.com, DoME is freely accessible online in its entirety. Thanks to its numerous options for combining different filters, it exceeds the carefully constructed Salons 1673–1914 database by the Musée d'Orsay. Thanks to the use of authority files, DoME surpasses large-scale endeavors such as Artl@s in its practicability, although without reaching Artl@s' geographic accuracy.[14]

## Challenges and Limitations

### *Geography—Nationality—Organizers*

Changes in the political geography of the European continent, especially in the aftermath of World War I, but also due to the continuing evolution of cities and changes in street names, were a major challenge for DoME. This influenced both the mapping of old addresses on contemporary maps as well as the allocation of nationalities. As digital mapping is based on the coordinates of indexed inhabited places, problems arise on country and street level, but not however for identifying cities. Exhibitions and locations that took place in Budapest or in Prague are now recorded in the database as having taken place in Hungary and Czech Republic respectively, although they were both part of the Austro-Hungarian Empire at the time of the event. Similarly, the exact address of an exhibition location is documented as given in the catalogue, but only the city is located on the maps, as any further degree of granularity such as the street names and their geographic locations might have changed and/or disappeared in the meantime. As no historic, digital gazetteer—accurate to the pre–World War I street level—exists for Europe in general, the only possible solution within the limits of the project was to combine historic data with contemporary maps and to accept the discrepancy between the two sources. The case of Berlin forms the only exception, where historical maps are available and have been used to assign exact coordinates to the various venues. When historical geocoding services become available in the future, it will be easy to implement them for additional cities.

As for nationalities, how should one classify artists born in Kiev, for example? Should they be listed as Russian (as per pre-WWI borders) or as Ukrainian (as per contemporary borders)? The

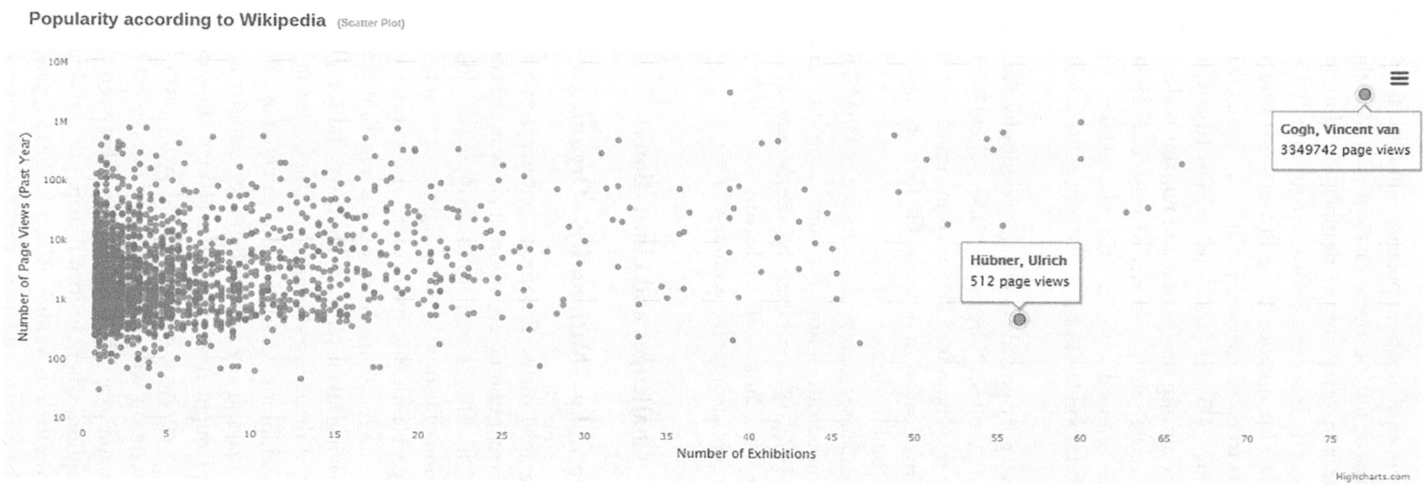


*Figure 30.3* Scatter plot in DoME showing the number of page views in Wikipedia (y-axis) and the number of exhibition participations (x-axis) for all artists registered in DoME. This graph is an attempt to measure the differences in the popularity of artists in the early twentieth century and today. Chart created with highcharts.com.

database allowed the team to choose the nationality manually; therefore, Kiev can be selected as place of birth, but Russian can be selected as nationality—as is the case for Kazimir Malevich. However, as per the use of authority files, the nationality is often set by the link to it, and changes were only made in very rare and obvious cases.

The treatment of information about "Organizing Bodies" posed an additional challenge, as the organizer(s) of an exhibition are rarely explicitly mentioned in catalogues. In such cases, the host institution was selected as the exhibition's organizer. However, this information could generally not be verified and can consequently be erroneous or misleading. It is thus marked as such in the database.

## *Limitations*

When using the database (or any database for that matter), an undeniable amount of bias has to be taken into account. As the data set was constructed with the goal of providing answers to specific research questions, it contains a curated content and by definition can only depict an excerpt of the wide exhibition landscape. However, within its scope, and compared to similar database projects, DoME is very comprehensive; and nevertheless, it is far from exhaustively covering all existing exhibition catalogues. Some catalogues could not be located, others could not be entered, at least not yet. Furthermore, the extension of Gordon's exhibition list could not be realized as systematically as we would have liked. Crucially, even if all catalogues were fully entered, we still have to reflect on the fact that numerous exhibitions of modern European painting took place *without* a catalogue being produced. The database can only aim to mirror the exhibitions *with* catalogues, but not all exhibitions altogether. Last but not least, even for the catalogues that are included in DoME, the nature of the documents has to be remembered: given that exhibition catalogues were generally produced *before* the start of the actual exhibition, the catalogue can merely reflect what was *planned* to be exhibited, not the final facts. When combined with other sources (e.g. archival documents such as photographs, correspondence), it may become evident that specific artworks were in fact not present, replaced, or that additional ones were hung but not listed in the catalogue.

## *Advantages*

Working with DoME makes it possible to grasp the wider context of the landscape of exhibitions in the early twentieth century, and particularly the context into which the so-called Avant-gardes inscribed themselves and their exhibition activity. Some specific topics related to these issues are treated in more depth in the project's online blog that accompanies the database from a qualitative point of view.[15] The open access data set invites users to explore that landscape thanks to the variety of possible combinations of factors, all the while permitting the verification of theories concerning the art-historical canon, encouraging questions of this very canon, and detecting hitherto ignored patterns. By extension, results provided by the database might lead to further and new questions, thus pushing our field further. This has the potential to ultimately break up the canon built on single case studies and to gain a bird's eye view of the art world's exhibition activity of the early twentieth century. DoME was conceived as the core of a collaborative project that would help revising the history of avant-garde painting. To this end, the involvement of students was and still is seminal.[16]

A specific feature of digital tools is that they remain flexible: missing data can be added, errors amended, or even new features implemented. Compared with printed publications, this is a significant advantage, but it raises the question of how to work with and quote an ever-changing data set. While we provide accurate dates of the last change of every database entry in the recommended citation, we currently do not offer reverse time travel to reproduce filtered searches and statistics carried out before certain changes have been made to the database.

## Outlook

What else is desirable? What more could the database provide? The list is long and spans the development of automated data entry, the implementation of digital historic maps, and more advanced visualizations of data through space and time, as well as network dimensions. Plans to offer the option of entering personalized and individual data sets via the availability of the backend structure on the frontend had to be postponed, as well as the option of tagging information contained in the database as per customized needs. The visualization of networks was also deferred in order to allow the development of a more complete and efficient front end.

In order to tackle these issues (particularly more complex visualizations and the perfection of the user-interface), cooperation with specialized projects and institutions should be considered and pursued as a matter of priority. The collaboration and exchange that arises from various international projects focused on basic research, leads to a positive and sustainable aftermath of digital art history endeavors. As such, DoME agreed to provide Getty ULAN with all of the artists names in the database, structured in a way to meet their requirements (c. 6,700 were missing there as of August 2019). In return, for all clearly identifiable artists for whom there is no corresponding authority information, a new entry with a proper identifier will be created. This bolsters the Getty's resource and at the same time creates visibility for artists who have been previously unaccounted. The project has agreed to provide Getty not only with the names of the artists currently not in the ULAN list, but with all of the names in the database; for many artists who already had an entry, additional information can be derived from DoME. Sharing data and capacity across projects and institutions in this way will strengthen both respective databases and simultaneously improve the quality of the data for the wider academic community and beyond.

A critical issue is the long-term storage, maintenance and care of the database; not only from a technical side, but also from a content perspective. Finally, digital information will become outdated unless new information and research is incorporated. We are working on a long-term support plan in order to keep the database useful over time.

## Conclusion

Given its nature, the database gives answers in the form of *data*. The task of interpreting that data continues to lie with the researchers who use it. The project was based on specific research questions, but the database should be useful to tackle even more queries; in any case, however, qualitative research must complete the quantitative results gained through this new tool. Although this is a call for awareness, it also presents an advantage: the data available remains the same, while scholars can research and interpret them in their own ways. In order to guarantee the usability of the data set, it is necessary to communicate clearly and with the utmost transparency its construction and limitations: what the database can and cannot do. DoME and similar databases should be considered as one among many resources in the field of art history. They need to be treated with the same care, questioning, and healthy skepticism as any other resource: specific conditions and reasons led to what is shown and what the user can see as well as to what is *not* shown or *cannot* be seen. Therefore, it is important for researchers to have their own research questions to guide them through the data set.[17] On the other hand, the data itself can yield new and further research questions.

This research project entailed a steep learning curve for its initiators and collaborators. Not only from a content point of view, but also from the point of view of the conception of a database. Although some aspects could have been tackled differently in hindsight, the priority at this point is to share the experiences in order to support similar projects and avoid repeating errors. To that end, the exchange between digitally based research projects is paramount and the discourse they prompt throughout the field of digital art history must be regarded as vital for the digital humanities and for art history in general.

## Acknowledgment

The authors thank Kathryn Brown for the kind invitation to contribute to this publication, as well as the Austrian Science Fund (FWF) for generously funding this project.

## Notes

1. Such as Eberhard Roters, *Stationen der Moderne. Die bedeutenden Kunstausstellungen des 20. Jahrhunderts in Deutschland* (Berlin: Nicolai, 1988); Bruce Altshuler, *The Avant-Garde in Exhibition* (New York: Abrams, 1994); Bernd Klüser, ed., *Die Kunst der Ausstellung. Eine Dokumentation dreißig exemplarischer Kunstausstellungen dieses Jahrhunderts* (Frankfurt am Main: Insel Verlag, 1995); Bruce Altshuler, ed., *Salon to Biennial: Exhibitions that Made Art History,* vol. I, 1863–1959 (London: Phaidon, 2008).
2. Accessed September 3, 2019, https://exhibitions.univie.ac.at/.
3. Donald E. Gordon, *Modern Art Exhibitions 1900–1916*, vol. 1 (Munich: Prestel Verlag, 1974), 12.
4. Béatrice Joyeux-Prunel and Olivier Marcel, "Exhibition Catalogues in the Globalization of Art: A Source for Social and Spatial Art History," *Artl@s Bulletin* no. 2 (2016): Article 8, 84.
5. Accessed September 3, 2019, https://exhibitions.univie.ac.at/pdf/Data_Entry_Guidelines.pdf
6. https://cloud.google.com/vision/. Accessed September 3, 2019.
7. Sepp Hochreiter and Jürgen Schmidhuber, "Long Short-Term Memory," *Neural Computation* 9, no. 8 (1997): 1735–80.
8. Accessed September 3, 2019, www.mfj-online.org/journalPages/MFJ34/Manovich_Database_FrameSet.html.
9. See Jannidis Fotis and Julia Flanders, "A Gentle Introduction to Data Modeling," in *The Shape of Data in Digital Humanities: Modeling Texts and Text-Based Resources*, ed. Jannidis Fotis and Julia Flanders (London: Routledge, 2019).
10. www.cezannecatalogue.com/catalogue/entry.php?id=321; www.cezannecatalogue.com/exhibitions/entry.php?id=1843 (both accessed September 3, 2019).
11. LAMP stands for Linux (operating system), Apache (web server), MySQL (relational database) and PHP (programming language).
12. Daniel Burckhardt and Matthias Speidel, "Verbunddatenbank Bildatlas: 'Kunst in der DDR'," in *Elektronische Medien & Kunst, Kultur, Historie*, ed. Andreas Bienert, Frank Weckend, James Hemsley, and Vito Cappellini (Berlin: EVA Conferences International, 2011).
13. Possible candidates are WissKI (CIDOC-based datamodel, Drupal) which currently lacks a model for catalogue entries as well as nodegoat.net (PHP, MySQL/Postgresql), ConedaKOR (Ruby, MySQL) and Collective Access (PHP, MySQL)—three Web-based DH and cultural heritage platforms flexible enough to implement project-specific relational metadata schemes including normed vocabulary and linked open data. In addition, researchspace.org promotes itself as an open source platform for building user-friendly interfaces to fully graph based data models, but is at the moment still very much in alpha with limited public development activity (https://github.com/researchspace/researchspace).
14. www.artist-info.com/; http://salons.musee-orsay.fr/; and https://artlas.huma-num.fr/fr/ (all accessed September 3, 2019).
15. Accessed September 3, 2019, https://exhibitions.univie.ac.at/blog.
16. Two PhD dissertation are part of this project. Christina Bartosch has written her doctoral thesis on the exhibition of abstract art between 1908 and 1915. Marei Döhring studies the use of picture frames by avant-garde artists. Additionally, so far three research seminars led by Professor Rosenberg invited students to reconsider the canon and to work with the database. So far, they stimulated five Master's theses in which various aspects of exhibitions in the early twentieth century are studied in depth. Vered

Bergmann dedicated her Master's thesis to "Ausstellungsstrategien von fünf Galerien in Deutschland im Vergleich (1905–1914)." Master theses in progress at the time of writing are Filip Blagojevich's (Munch's exhibition strategies in Germany, 1902–1909), Isabel Fischnaller's (Women's internationality in their participations at art exhibitions, 1905–1915), Liisa Hättasch's (Artist networks and strategies among the Bloomsbury Group, 1905–1920), and Irinia Romanova's (Vladimir Izdebsky's International Art Exhibitions).

17. "Data management should be governed by well-considered research questions [. . .], " as Sophie Hatchwell, Fern Insh, and Hana Leaper, "Born Digital: Early Career Researchers Shaping Digital Art History," *Visual Resources: An International Journal on Images and Their Use* (February 2019): 6, https://doi.org/10.1080/01973762.2019.1553448, put it.

## Bibliography


Altshuler, Bruce. *The Avant-Garde in Exhibition.* New York: Abrams, 1994.

———, ed. *Salon to Biennial: Exhibitions that Made Art History*, vol. 1, 1863–1959. London: Phaidon, 2008.

Burckhardt, Daniel, and Matthias Speidel. "Verbunddatenbank Bildatlas: Kunst in der DDR." In *Elektronische Medien & Kunst, Kultur, Historie*, edited by Andreas Bienert, Frank Weckend, James Hemsley, and Vito Cappellini, 75–81. Berlin: EVA Conferences International, 2011.

Fotis, Jannidis, and Julia Flanders. "A Gentle Introduction to Data Modeling." In *The Shape of Data in Digital Humanities. Modeling Texts and Text-Based Resources*, edited by Jannidis Fotis and Julia Flanders, 26–95. London: Routledge, 2019.

Gordon, Donald E. *Modern Art Exhibitions 1900–1916.* Munich: Prestel Verlag, 1974.

Hatchwell, Sophie, Fern Insh, and Hana Leaper. "Born Digital: Early Career Researchers Shaping Digital Art History." In *Visual Resources. An International Journal on Images and Their Uses* (February 2019). https://doi.org/10.1080/01973762.2019.1553448.

Joyeux-Prunel, Béatrice, and Olivier Marcel. "Exhibition Catalogues in the Globalization of Art. A Source for Social and Spatial Art History." *Artl@s Bulletin* 4, no. 2: 81–104. Paris, 2015.

Klüser, Bernd, ed. *Die Kunst der Ausstellung. Eine Dokumentation dreißig exemplarischer Kunstausstellungen dieses Jahrhunderts.* Frankfurt am Main: Insel-Verlag, 1995.

Roters, Eberhard. *Stationen der Moderne. Die bedeutenden Kunstausstellungen des 20. Jahrhunderts in Deutschland.* Berlin: Nicolai, 1988.

# 31

# THE ART-HISTORICAL CATALOGUE IN THE DIGITAL ERA

*Anne Collins Goodyear*

If Walter Benjamin's powerful 1936 essay "The Work of Art in the Age of Mechanical Reproduction" sought to examine the numerous ramifications of reproductive, specifically photographic, technologies upon the political and cultural ramifications of works of art, his observations have proved to be uncannily prescient in describing the relationship of technologies emerging today to the development of new intellectual resources and conventions, particularly those featuring pictorial information. Reflecting upon the anticipation by Dada artists—through their montages of pictorial and literary materials—of efforts later associated with film, Benjamin observed how the technological structure of one set of communicative tools paved the way the way for others that provided even more refined, robust, and efficient delivery of that information. Indeed, in observing the potential for the reproduction to usurp, or perhaps distribute, the impact of the unique original, we might argue that Benjamin was among the first thinkers to develop a theory concerning the flow of metadata—information about a particular cultural form—which took into account how the production of cultural artifacts was, in turn, transformed by the desire to share them: "To an ever greater degree the work of art reproduced becomes the work of art designed for reproducibility," noted Benjamin.[1]

Taking the lead from Benjamin, I seek to provide a historical overview of the appearance of the digital catalogue, looking at the first applications of the computer to cataloguing in the 1960s, exploring the development of an infrastructure to support these efforts, and describing recent achievements and ongoing challenges. For the most part, this chapter concerns developments in American art history, though important achievements in Europe also play a vital role. In examining these themes, this chapter implicitly encourages the reader to consider the very intellectual assumptions and technological structures that have undergirded developments in this field.

The *catalogue raisonné*, aptly defined by Michael Clarke and Deborah Clarke as the "complete published catalogue of an artist's work," has special authority in the history of art.[2] By virtue of its overview of an artist's oeuvre, these publications provide information deemed critical to establishing details of a work's authenticity and provenance, in addition to information about the physical features of the object, such as its physical appearance, subject matter, size and medium. As Matthew Lincoln has noted: "The *catalogue raisonné* can be understood as an object of digital scholarship *avant la lettre*: a volume that structures knowledge by enumerating and categorizing artworks such that the scholar may efficiently locate single objects or gain a synthetic overview of an artist's oeuvre."[3] To date, numerous digital catalogues have appeared or are in preparation in the United States and Europe. A survey of approximately sixty such publications reveals that the majority of these compilations are available free of charge. Organizing institutions include artists' estates, museums, and universities. Artifex Press, established in 2012, provides a commercial model for the publication of digital *catalogues raisonnés*, operating on a subscription basis.[4]

Broadening the accessibility of *catalogues raisonnés* and considering new strategies for developing them may indicate that, in addition to serving experts, such compilations could provide a bridge between specialists and knowledgeable members of the general public—a change that may be characteristic of the digital humanities more broadly. As Elizabeth Honig suggests, such a reconceived approach to the *catalogue raisonné* may help position these publications, not as the site of "outmoded connoisseurship," but rather as an "open-ended, flexible, collaborative enterprise" that may even offer the opportunity for the "crowd-sourcing of catalog data."[5] Indeed, the idea that digital art history might itself more broadly recast "the relationship between the expert and the layman by defining a new and productive role for the latter" has similarly been noted by Max Marmor.[6]

Perhaps not surprisingly, the *catalogue raisonné* has also invited the application of sophisticated new digital technologies, such as the Image Investigation Tool (or ITT), developed by programmers Charles Henderson and Angela Hong for a *catalogue raisonné* of the work of Jan Brueghel at http://janbrueghel.net/. The IIT enables *catalogue raisonné* users to compare and contrast details of the artist's work. Such visual enhancement may enable users to see details not ordinarily accessible to the eye, or to study features such as the facture of a painting. Additionally, Honig argues, such publications improve access, combatting the high cost of purchasing conventionally published volumes. Yet, at the same time, Honig acknowledges the limitations of the model she champions, noting questions about the very nature of sharing scholarly research and inviting public contributions, the question of potential copyright challenges, and access to high-quality reproductions.[7] Perhaps most significant, as she points out, is the larger question of the ongoing sustainability and maintenance of such digital resources. Can these undertakings be supported by individuals, or need they be based in a well-resourced institution capable of ensuring their long-term viability? Other issues that would inevitably require further research and scrutiny include securing the portal and developing editorial strategies for reviewing submissions. In evaluating the longer term promise and possible pitfalls of such projects, from the *catalogue raisonné* to other forms of digital cataloguing, it is worth looking more deeply at the history underlying such efforts. This will afford a better understanding of the historical assumptions and conventions that undergird the integration of digital technologies into the realm of the catalogue—a publication that implies a critical intersection between the academy, the museum, and the market.

The first documented use of the computer for art-historical analysis is Jules Prown's 1963–64 study of John Singleton Copley's American sitters.[8] Focusing on 240 works produced by the artist during the American part of his career, Prown, working with a graduate student assistant, Gerald Warden, used a program originally created for the purposes of studying the medical histories of patients (such as those with heart disease) to process the correlation between education, income, gender, place of residence, and other personal characteristics.[9] As he observed: "The computer, while it had not done our thinking for us, had arranged and clarified the material, pointing us in a fruitful direction and permitting more concrete and comprehensive conclusions to be drawn."[10] Ultimately, Prown and Warden found themselves with concrete indications that the young artist had benefited from the departure from the American colonies of his more experienced competitor, Joseph Blackburn, and that financial pressures, resulting from fewer commissions, may have influenced Copley's decision to leave Boston for London.[11]

But perhaps most significant in Prown's study was the art historian's ability to conceive of a critical element of this study not strictly as a qualitative, but also as a quantitative nature: in other words, the success of Prown's undertaking was premised on his ability to understand a critical dimension of his work as data. Seeking to identify underlying patterns in a body of work by Copley that could not easily be scrutinized through the records of a pre-existing infrastructure of artistic and learned societies, such as those which existed in England, and drawing upon methods from the social sciences, Prown found himself drawn to the "factual data" associated with the artist's American portraits, namely the physical characteristic of the works, as had been recorded approximately twenty-five years earlier in a critical catalogue and the sitters themselves, whose achievements, carefully detailed by their descendants, could be rendered as statistics.[12]

Such an approach to recasting art-historical information, premised upon existing Copley catalogues, such as that published in 1938 by Barbara Neville Parker and Anne Bolling Wheeler, might arguably reflect a broader cultural turn toward "the quantitative" as observed by Martin Heidegger the same year in his "Age of the World Picture." In this essay, Heidegger sketched out trends he observed in the academic world, including the broadening sway of the sciences in the realm of the humanities.[13] As he put it:

> What is taking place in this extending and consolidating of the institutional character of the sciences? Nothing less than the making secure of the precedence of methodology over whatever is (nature and history), which at any given time becomes objective in research. On the foundation of their character as ongoing activity, the sciences are creating for themselves the solidarity and unity appropriate to them.[14]

Indeed, the laying out of discrete descriptive quanta for a catalogue during the 1930s, might, to paraphrase Benjamin, represent "the creation of a demand which could be fully satisfied only later" through the integration of the computer into humanities research. As Professor George W. Pierson noted 1965 in a study exploring the applicability of the computer to humanistic study:

> The humanities are concerned with facts as well as with feelings; they depend upon the accumulation of knowledge and its systematic arrangement; their lifeblood is communication. And if since World War II man has acquired a clinking electronic facility to make possible the recording, storage, comparison, and repossession of information with an accuracy and at speeds undreamed of in human experience, might not the humanities be able to benefit?[15]

The applicability of computational strategies to the study of art history was similarly noted in the mid-1960s by Kenneth C. Lindsay. Recognizing that "sophisticated mechanical instruments can promote both the production of art and a better organization of the data of art history," Lindsay proposed distinguishing "between two kinds of activity: (1) the independent venture which is self-sufficient, and (2) the interdependent venture which makes sense only if organized in long-term cooperative plans."[16] Lindsay's second point is significant for this chapter: the need for coordinated efforts designed to create broadly networked and integrated information. As Lindsay persuasively argued: "Above all, museum planning must be coordinated with the interests, needs, and talents of the art historians' world."[17] To his credit, he also foresaw obstacles that would need to be addressed, particularly that of copyright. "Can the archive remain an open system?" he wondered.[18]

It is noteworthy that at an early moment in the integration of the computer into the discipline of art history as a means of organizing data, pioneers recognized the enduring benefits, needs, and challenges intrinsic to these efforts. The power of the computer to identify meaningful patterns for interpretation by the art historian was evident to Prown, and Lindsay anticipated that large museums, such as the Metropolitan Museum of Art in New York, would see the benefit of developing cooperative efforts to support "the establishment of a comprehensive machine file of visual data and images." He could anticipate art historians retrieving images and related data from a distance. Today the largely wireless network of the internet serves the function he envisioned might be enabled through "coaxial cable."[19]

Lindsay was not alone in foreseeing the important role of computers for organizing information within the context of the museum, and, indeed, in 1967, the Museum Computer Network (MCN) took root, growing out of the work of the New York University Institute for Computer Research in the Humanities (ICRH), established in 1965. Inspired in part by pioneering efforts at the Metropolitan Museum of Art, a cohort of fifteen museums in the New York area established the MCN with the goal of sharing resources and building a joint "data dictionary" to "accommodate the diverse methods used to describe museum collections."[20] The first conference dedicated to museum computing took place in April 1968 with support from IBM, the Metropolitan Museum of Art, and MCN.

But if the promise of the computer and the organization and integration of data related to works of art for registration and basic cataloguing was quickly embraced by museums, the implementation of this capability has encountered a number of technological, organizational, and, to a large degree, cultural hurdles. Even as museum professionals were exploring strategies for the adoption of digital technology into the realm of collections management, the academic art history community evinced reluctance to adopt computational techniques. Indeed, when Prown presented his paper on "The Art Historian and the Computer" at the College Art Association in the mid-1960s, he recalls: "My first slide, which displayed an IBM punch card, was roundly booed. After the conclusion of the session, a senior art historian berated me loudly in the aisle for my apostasy."[21] Later Prown recounted that "The chairman of my department at the time advised me to remove the computer-analysis section from my book manuscript because its publication would jeopardize my chances for tenure."[22] The hostility was noted at the time by Kenneth Lindsay, who likened the "nervous laughter" that followed Prown's presentation to "an example of mass hysteria."[23]

A 2012 report by Diane Zorich, based on research carried out nearly fifty years after the uncomfortable response to Prown's presentation, documented lingering doubts about the merit of the computer. According to Zorich: "These findings reveal disagreements in the art history community about the value of digital research, teaching, and scholarship. [. . .] The community's ambivalence about digital art history also carries into its perception of art history research centers and their role in fostering digital scholarship."[24] In the same year James Cuno similarly pointed to the enduring hesitance of art historians to embrace the digital, noting that:

> The biggest mistake many of us in the arts and humanities academy can make is thinking of that potential only in terms of how we can use the new technology to more quickly and broadly disseminate information. The promise of the digital age is far greater than that. It offers an opportunity to rethink the way we do, as well as to deliver new research in the arts.[25]

Provocatively suggesting that "art history is failing at the Internet," Cuno argued that despite the formation of the information network nearly two decades earlier, the electronic resource had not substantially changed approaches to scholarship in the field of art history, despite the increased ease of access to vital resources, such as journals, databases, and catalogues of museum and library holdings.

In retrospect, the concerns raised by Zorich and Cuno may have signaled a turning point in the field. Indeed, by February 2013, when the CAA offered its first THAT (The Humanities and Technology) Camp, it was possible to point to a number of recent projects and publications reflecting upon the emergence of digital art history, including convenings the previous Summer and Fall at Princeton University and New York University focused on the topic as well as pioneering publications, such as Pamela Fletcher and Anne Helmreich's "Local/Global: Mapping Nineteenth-Century London's Art Market," for *Nineteenth-Century World Wide*.[26] In addition to the rich discussion of pioneering art-historical digital projects that CAA's THAT Camp permitted, the event was equally important in creating a forum for scholars to discuss vital concerns regarding the infrastructure of the field, including shedding light on stumbling blocks to digital scholarship that had little to do with computational strategies themselves. Most significantly, at a 2013 THAT Camp debriefing session chaired by Diane Zorich, at the CAA meeting that immediately followed the session, many scholars were deterred by the lack of credit frequently accorded by tenure and promotion committees to digital scholarship, and emerging professionals were particularly vulnerable. This observation would prove a critical motivation in CAA's partnership with the Society of Architectural Historians on the development of guidelines for the evaluation of digital scholarship for tenure and promotion, thanks to funding from the Andrew W. Mellon Foundation.[27] The spring of 2013 also marked the launch of the CAA's Fair Use Project, a four-year undertaking, supported by the Andrew W. Mellon and Samuel H. Kress Foundations, designed to tackle the chilling effect on scholarship and other forms of creative practice of the pervasive uncertainty about whether fair use applied to the use of copyrighted reproductions by scholars and artists.[28] The educational initiative, which involved input from over 3,200 CAA members, commenced with a detailed report, which, in documenting the myriad concerns about copyright in the field, also marked an important educational initiative. In addition to documenting how a broad range of arts professionals understood what constituted "fair" use of copyrighted images, the project helped to clarify for art historians the distinction between public domain and copyrighted images and introduced a strategy for reasoning about whether a given use of a copyrighted image was likely to be understood as fair. The document has proved an empowering tool.[29]

Half a decade later, the adoption of digital strategies has accelerated. If the CAA Fair Use Guidelines have helped scholars to make reasoned assessments about whether reproductions used online need be licensed, workshops supported by the Getty Foundation and the Samuel H. Kress Foundation in collaboration with institutions such as George Mason University, the University of California, Los Angeles, Harvard University, and Middlebury College have provided training about digital tools enabling new modes of historical documentation and analysis, including OMEKA, Geographic Information System (GIS), Neatline, and Gephi.[30] In addition to benefiting from partnerships with digital humanities programs, the number of art history programs offering digital art history has grown.[31] Numerous colleges and universities now provide centers, departments, and programs dedicated to the digital humanities, another home for scholars of digital art history.[32] Additionally, an increasing number of publications also support the dissemination of digital art-historical scholarship, including the *International Journal for Digital Art History*, the *Journal of the Society of Architectural Historians*, and *Nineteenth-Century Worldwide*. The College Art Association, hosts a born-digital publication, *caa.reviews*, and recently digitized *The Art Bulletin* and *Art Journal*—which also hosts a web page—provides a structure for hosting future digital scholarship. In January 2019, the Digital Art History Society was born, providing a forum for exchange for specialists interested in the digital development and dissemination of scholarship.

These important developments within the field of art history address the significance of training, recognition for intellectual rigor, opportunities for publishing, the reduction of perceived impediments (such as copyright or penalties in promotion and tenure), and the availability of funding in developing an increasingly open stance to pioneering digital projects on the part of art historians. This growing receptivity to computational methods also represents a paradigm shift of critical importance to the development of new digital catalogues that are designed not only to provide access to data, but also new analytical models and insight.

Key to strides in the emergence of digital art history since the late 1960s have been steps taken by museum complexes and research centers to promote the integration of digital data. These leaps forward include the development of the Getty Vocabularies, including the Art and Architectural Thesaurus (AAT) in the late 1970s, ULAN (the Union List of Artist Names) in 1984, the Getty Thesaurus of Geographic Names (TGN) in 1987, the Cultural Objects Name Authority (CONA) in 2004, and the Iconography Authority about 2016 (after originating as a module within CONA).[33] Indeed, the AAT, the first of the Getty Vocabularies resulted specifically from the digital revolution within library and museum cataloguing and the growing need for controlled vocabularies to promote "consistency in cataloging and more efficient retrieval of information." As the Getty history of the AAT notes: "the use of a thesaurus for indexing was not welcomed by art catalogers prior to the advent of computerized cataloging."[34] The Getty Provenance Index, established in the early 1980s by Burton Fredericksson, the Getty Museum's first curator of Paintings, has recently been hailed as an exemplary tool for digital art history by Johanna Drucker, who asserts: "While it may seem counter-intuitive to art historians focused on objects, the strongest benefits of digital and networked technologies for art history are in the use of structured text and data."[35]

In recent years, archivists and librarians, working with information technologists, have built an infrastructure, permitting the integration of data across a range of sources, that has proven critical to success for digital projects. As Matthew Lincoln observes: "Computational research like Fletcher's and Helmreich's is only possible with data prepared in formats amenable to digital analysis. Thus, some of the most crucial, forward-looking work in digital art history involves infrastructural work that might not be recognized as 'art history' per se."[36] These breakthroughs, often happening out-of-sight of traditional departments of art history, have established the channels and interconnections critical to the flow of data that has contributed to the blossoming of computational analysis within the art-historical field. This includes the development of the CIDOC-CRM ontology between 2000 and 2006 to promote the exchange of information within cultural organizations.[37] This organization model has, in turn, proved vital to art institutions utilizing linked open data (released under an open license) to make possible projects such as the American Art Collaborative—a consortium of fourteen museums piloting a shared information project, launched in 2014—and to increase still further the impact of such resources as the Getty Vocabularies.[38] It has also helped to pave the way for the development of a new format for sharing images and metadata data—the International Image Interoperability Framework (IIIF)—originated by the archival community and which greatly eases the ability to share reproductions of works of art and their metadata across institutions. Among other capabilities, the software enables greater facility in studying works in tandem and may even aid in the process of re-associating pictorial elements that have long been separated, such as components of an altarpiece, or manuscript illustrations that have been separated from a page.[39]

The rapid adoption of shared resources promoting collaboration between institutions, such as Linked Open Data and IIIF, in turn reflects a growing culture of openness concerning access to information, particularly that overseen by cultural heritage institutions. In the spring of 2013, led by the Rijksmuseum in Amsterdam, numerous museums around the world began to make available their public domain images free of charge to the public. Since that time many other museum complexes, including the British Museum in London, the National Gallery of Art in

Washington, DC; the Getty Museum in Los Angeles; the Metropolitan Museum, and the Victoria and Albert Museum in London, in addition to smaller institutions, have followed suit. The shift in the policy of numerous museums, which had long protected their reproductions, was prompted to a significant degree by the increasing availability of online reproductions of varying quality and often with little input from the collection housing the original work.[40] Indeed, the growing importance of the internet for the exchange of images was highlighted by the launch of such undertakings as Europeana between 2008 and 2010 and the Google Art Project (now Google Arts & Culture) in 2011.

Fueled by a cultural shift favoring free and open access to cultural data, the digital catalogue, like other digital art-historical publications, represents a critical step in the integration of pioneering work on the part of museum registrars, archivists, and information specialists with the research questions and capabilities of art historians. The digital era points up and increases still further the vital intersection of academic research with the critical work being done by colleagues who focus on the stewardship, development, and dissemination of informational resources, including works of art and documentation about them. Matthew Lincoln notes:

> Museums comprise the largest data stores in our field, acting as repositories of objects, but also of decades and centuries of knowledge about those objects. It is these institutions, along with organizations such as the Rijksbureau voor Kunsthistorisches Documentatie and the Getty Research Institute, that have pioneered vocabularies and ontologies to richly and completely describe the contextual knowledge associated with art objects.[41]

If such organizational efforts were essential to developing an infrastructure to enable the development of digital catalogues, then, so too has the archival field's posture of openness and commitment to sharing cultural information shaped such enterprises in essential ways.

This foundation, then, has not only made possible the enrichment and growth of the *catalogue raisonné*, but also the emergence of new publications that might best be described as hybrid forms of publication that draw on concepts from the world of print publication, but that also integrate the flexibility and interconnectedness of digital technology. The phenomenon invites comparisons to the myriad ways in which "photography," (or drawing with light) diverged from hand-rendered media, and in which "digital photography" has departed from the chemically based medium that formed the operative metaphor for describing electronic-image capturing and production. As Robert S. Nelson observes: "the history of past technological revolutions—whether roll to codex, manuscript to printed book, or manual typewriter to computer keyboard—suggests that prior customs often continue, even as they cease to be understood."[42]

While numerous notable accomplishments have been made to digital publishing by museums, including *Gemini G.E.L.* launched in 2001 by the National Gallery of Art in Washington, DC, arguably the first online *catalogue raisonné*, and the Heilbrunn timeline, launched in 2000 by the Metropolitan Museum of Art, among the most important of these initiatives is the Getty Foundation's Online Scholarly Catalogue initiative.[43] Undertaken between 2009 and 2017 with a cohort of nine leading Anglo-American museums, including the J. Paul Getty Museum, Art Institute of Chicago; Arthur M. Sackler and Freer Gallery of Art, Smithsonian Institution (FSG); Los Angeles County Museum of Art (LACMA); National Gallery of Art, Washington, DC (NGA); San Francisco Museum of Modern Art (SFMOMA); Seattle Art Museum Tate; and the Walker Art Center, the very scope of the undertaking positioned it to stimulate innovative digital cataloguing projects internationally at a range of institutions. The project offered significant financial and technical support, the latter in the form of the OSCI Toolkit. In addition to providing substantial publicity to these undertakings, the Getty also provided close oversight and analysis of the incumbents' accomplishments, ultimately concluding in its final report: "momentum is building for the publication of permanent collection catalogues online."[44]

As I have noted elsewhere, the catalogues, diverse in subject matter, are also diverse in the approaches they have taken to the subject matter they treat.[45] While the format of the catalogues of the Art Institute of Chicago, *Monet Paintings and Drawings at the Art Institute of Chicago* and *Renoir Paintings and Drawings at the Art Institute of Chicago*, resemble a book moved into an electronic environment, many of the others, such as the Tate's *The Camden Town Group in Context*, SFMoMA's *The Rauschenberg Research Project* and the NGA's *Dutch Paintings of the Seventeenth Century*, by Arthur K. Wheelock, Jr., have closer affinities with the traditional design of a website.

The technical accomplishment of each of the websites is remarkable, and the content is impressive. However, with the exception of a visualization of the frequency of publications of illustrated books in Japan from the late seventeenth century to the mid-twentieth century in the FSG Pulverer catalogue, none of the catalogues makes significant use of the tools of digital analysis per se. The audio and visual content of the sites did, however, make remarkable content available for researchers that could not be transmitted through print alone, especially in the case of interviews with the artist Robert Rauschenberg (SFMoMA) and performances by artists included in the Walker Art Center's *On Performativity, Living Collections Catalogue* (three volumes). Nonetheless, in making detailed collections information available online, this project raises the important question of whether the creators of such publications, especially in the context of cultural institutions largely supported by public and charitable contributions, should make the data associated with these publications readily available through open Application Program Interfaces (APIs) to facilitate its use by other scholars who might wish to apply computational strategies to its study.

Contemplating such open access raises the intriguing issue of the relationship between data, its presentation, and interpretation. This, in turn, raises the question of how to address authorship, collaboration, and even the standardization of informational formats, which remains an elusive goal in the field.[46] With the exception of the NGA's catalogue, credited to Arthur Wheelock, none of the OSCI catalogues reflect the perspective of a single individual, but rather reflect input from many scholarly, editorial, and technical experts. Indeed, growing recognition of the multiple specialisms required to build digital catalogues is reflected in the growing range of professional input, including on the part of conservation scientists and computer engineers.[47] But with the proliferating number of experts contributing to digital projects, an important question emerges: Who should be acknowledged, and how should these contributors be recognized? A quick scan of electronic catalogues, such as those developed under the auspices of the Getty Foundation, indicates that no convention has yet emerged for clearly defining the roles of various individuals and technologies in developing the content of digital catalogues.

As we consider the range of partners currently developing electronic projects, an obvious question arises: what is the future of catalogues including content from multiple institutions, and particularly their databases? And what about the aggregation of content from multiple providers? An innovative project along these lines is now underway. The Yale University Press Art and Architectural e-portal provides access to personally authored books and catalogues from a range of participating publishers and integrates records of images between publications and museum holdings. This means that users of the portal can both learn about a given object within the framework provided by a specific scholar, within the context of the institution that owns it, and within the broader universe of multiple voices, as the portal in turn reflects what other books include discussions of a given piece.[48] While the publications included in Yale's portal were not born-digital, the publisher has carefully crafted, in conversation with the authors of the works, a new presentation for the content, befitting their electronic setting. The repository suggests a future promise for the domain of digital publication—an opportunity to compare and contrast scholarship reflecting many voices, to gather detailed information about objects from multiple institutions, and to work with digital reproductions that can be enlarged, rotated, and put into appropriate scale for the purpose of gaining new insight into the relevant objects.

If the technical promise of online art history is tremendous, and matched by a growing body of astute scholars conversant with the capabilities of new software, multiple challenges remain in place as we contemplate the future of the digital *catalogue raisonné* and electronic catalogues more broadly. Many of these challenges have little to do with a burgeoning digital infrastructure, but rather grow out of institutionalized policies and postures rooted in an analogue era.

As noted previously, digital catalogues, like other projects, benefit from the facility with which information can be exchanged. Yet at this time, as noted, too little standardization exists across institutions and across the practices of individual scholars to permit the ready ingestion of data across multiple platforms. And despite the rapidly broadening reach of digital art history, few graduate programs provide training for students in data formats, perpetuating idiosyncratic systems for describing objects.

Furthermore, recognizing that digital projects are susceptible to the threat of technological obsolescence, increased attention to the development of protocols for the preservation of digital publications is needed. In the digital era, one must understand a project to be "launched," with the attendant metaphorical implication that one will tend its safe voyage, as opposed to "published," implying that an effort has come to a close. In the case of the *catalogue raisonné*, which often combines information from many sources, the challenge is particularly acute. Records must be coordinated and a designated institution needs to oversee the life cycle of that resource. To what degree does the ability to refine and preserve the data underlying such online publications significantly narrow the field of sponsors who can participate in the long-term development of such projects? And as the life-span of such publications is considered, further attention deserves to be paid to the question of editioning. How might museums and individual scholars, provide information about how and when entries and other aspects of scholarly interpretation have been altered, particularly if updates to museums' collections management systems are automatically providing such updates? What responsibility exists to document such changes?

Finally, aside from the important challenges related to developing academic standards for the exchange of information, another less visible obstacle must be confronted: that of differing copyright regimes around the world that offer varying degrees of flexibility regarding the unlicensed use of copyrighted works of art and/or their documentation. While "fair use" in the United States has some counterpart in "fair dealing" in the United Kingdom and Canada, substantial differences between nations threaten the efficacy of electronic publications and portals. If access to scholarship can be understood as a human right, how might scholars, institutions, and artists work together to ensure that laws intended to protect intellectual property do not unintentionally undermine the free-flow of data essential to ensuring the potential for creative insight?[49]

Ultimately, realizing the great potential of electronic catalogues, premised on cooperative relationships between scholars, curators, museum professionals, technical developers, and artists will require buttressing the critical partnerships that have made possible past accomplishments. The mindful integration of scholars and the emerging professionals they train with the myriad cooperating professionals, institutions, and systems required for enhanced access to new data, suggests that the future of the digital catalogue may rely not so much on any specific accomplishment, but rather on an ongoing commitment to transforming scholarly methods, practices, and policies. How might we agree to acknowledge the collaborative and experimental nature of the construction of digital catalogues within the academy and beyond? How can we ensure that the potential for digital integration becomes an opportunity to build our collective strength and to expand access to resources further? It is in addressing, and continually reassessing the implications of such questions in the years to come that the greatest promise of the digital catalogue resides.

## Notes

1. Walter Benjamin, "The Work of Art in the Age of Mechanical Reproduction," *Zeitschrift für Sozialforschung* V, no. 1 (1936); republished, in English translation, in *Illuminations: Essays and Reflections*, ed. Hannah Arendt (New York: Schocken Books, 1968), 224.
2. Michael Clarke and Deborah Clarke, "catalogue raisonné," in *The Concise Oxford Dictionary of Art Terms*, 2nd ed. (Oxford: Oxford University Press, 2010), online version, accessed August 12, 2018. On the catalogue raisonné, see also "Catalogues Raisonnés Users' Guide," *International Foundation for Art Research (IFAR)*, www.ifar.org/users_guide.php, accessed August 12, 2018.
3. Johanna Drucker, Anne Helmreich, Matthew Lincoln, and Francesca Rose, "Digital Art History: The American Scene," *Perspective* (Online) 2 (2015), 7, https://journals.openedition.org/perspective/6021.
4. I thank Qianni Zhu for her compilation of a detailed list of these digital publications.
5. Elizabeth Alice Honig, "Art History and Access: The Catalogue Raisonné as Collaborative Research Site," *NANO: New American Notes Online* (published July 2014), https://nanocrit.com/issues/issue5/art-history-and-access-catalogue-raisonne-collaborative-research-site, accessed August 12, 2018.
6. Max Marmor, "Art History and the Digital Humanities," *Zeitschrift für Kunstgeschichte* 79 (2016): 155, accessed July 22, 2019, https://caa.hcommons.org/deposits/item/hc:10121/.
7. Although Honig does not address the question in this publication, the issue of how to vet entries is another important issue for any *catalogue raisonné* to tackle, especially one inviting contributions from donors and others who may not be disinterested scholars.
8. Excellent overviews of the emergence of the field of art history are provided by Pamela Fletcher, "Reflections on Digital Art History," *caa.reviews*, June 18, 2015, www.caareviews.org/reviews/2726#.XTWQjJNKh24, accessed July 22, 2019; Paul B. Jaskot, "Digital Art History as the Social History of Art: Towards the Disciplinary Relevance of Digital Methods," eds. Anne Helmreich and Murtha Baca, *Visual Resources* 35, no. 1–2 (2018): 21–33.
9. Jules Prown, "The Art Historian and the Computer: An Analysis of Copley's Patronage," in *Art as Evidence: Writings on Art and Material Culture* (New Haven and London: Yale University Press, 2001), 40–42.
10. Ibid., 44.
11. Ibid., 44 and 48.
12. Ibid., 38. As Prown explains, his interest in the use of the computer for this project was spurred in part by a course offered while he as at Winterthur by Anthony N.B. Garvan. According to Prown: "A professor in American civilization with a strong interest in anthropology, he introduced his students to a method used by the Human Relations Area Files at Yale that involved the use of punched data cards into which a needle was inserted to pull out cards and effect progressive cross-referencing." (Jules Prown, "Introduction," in *Art as Evidence*, 3). The catalogue in question is Barbara Neville Parker and Anne Bolling Wheeler, *John Singleton Copley: American Portraits* (Boston MFA, 1938); now available electronically through the Hathi Trust: https://babel.hathitrust.org/cgi/pt?id=mdp.39015015669073;view=1up;seq=7, accessed August 20, 2018.
13. Martin Heidegger, "The Age of the World Picture," in *The Question Concerning Technology and Other Essays*, trans. William Lovitt (New York: Harper and Row, 1977), 125, 135. Heidegger first delivered this paper in 1938, as clarified by William's Lovitt's preface to the volume, x.
14. Heidegger, "The Age of the World Picture," 125.
15. George W. Pierson, *Computers for the Humanities* (New Haven, 1965), v. Quoted and cited in Prown, "The Art Historian and the Computer," 51 (note 1).
16. Kenneth C. Lindsay, "Art, Art History, and the Computer," *Computers and the Humanities* 1, no. 2 (November 1966): 28.
17. Ibid., 29.
18. Ibid., 30.
19. Ibid., 28–30.

20. Marla Misunas and Richard Urban, "A Brief History of the Museum Computer Network," Prepared for the Encyclopedia of Library and Information Sciences in 2007; available through the Museum Computer Network website at accessed August 20, 2018, http://mcn.edu/wp-content/uploads/2016/03/HistoryofMCN.pdf

    Misunas and Urban point out that MCN was referenced in the influential 1968 Belmont Report, published in 1968 by American Association of Museums (now American Alliance of Museums) and describing the state of crisis in American museums, which had been overtaxed by their growing popularity.
21. Prown, "Introduction," 4.
22. Bryan J. Wolf, "Jules David Prown: 2010 Distinguished Scholar Session," College Art Association Annual Conference, www.collegeart.org/programs/conference/scholars/julesprown.
23. Lindsay, "Art, Art History, and the Computer," 28.
24. Diane M. Zorich, "Transitioning to a Digital World: Art History, Its Research Centers, and Digital Scholarship," A Report to the Samuel H. Kress Foundation and the Roy Rosenzweig Center for History and New Media George Mason University, May 2012, 6, accessed August 20, 2018, www.kressfoundation.org/uploadedFiles/Sponsored_Research/Research/Zorich_TransitioningDigitalWorld.pdf. (Note that the while the PDF bears the date of May 2012, the web-based version of the report is dated June 2012. It is available at: www.kressfoundation.org/research/transitioning_to_a_digital_world/.)
25. James Cuno, "How Art History Is Failing at the Internet," *The Daily Dot*, November 19, 2012, www.dailydot.com/via/art-history-failing-internet/, accessed August 14, 2018.
26. In my "Introductory Notes for CAA's First THAT Camp," February 12, 2013, offered in my capacity as the current CAA President, I made note of a number of publications and events, which seemed to signal a groundswell, this included the following articles and report: Hasan Niyazi, "The Moment of Digital Art History?" *3 Pipe Problem*, December 7, 2012, accessed August 20, 2018, www.3pp.website/2012/12/digital-art-history.html; Zorich, "Transitioning to a Digital World"; Pamela Fletcher and Anne Helmreich, "Local/Global: Mapping Nineteenth-Century London's Art Market," in a new "Digital Humanities and Art History" section included in *Nineteenth-Century Art Worldwide* 11, no. 3 (Autumn 2012), accessed August 20, 2018, www.19thc-artworldwide.org/autumn12/fletcher-helmreich-mapping-the-london-art-market; and two symposia: "Mellon Research Initiative: Digital Art History," Institute of Fine Arts, New York University, November 30–December 1, 2012 and "The Digital World of Art History," Princeton University, July 12, 2012.
27. College Art Association and the Society of Architectural Historians, "Guidelines for the Evaluation of Digital Scholarship in Art and Architectural History," Funded by the Andrew W. Mellon Foundation; www.collegeart.org/pdf/evaluating-digital-scholarship-in-art-and-architectural-history.pdf, accessed August 20, 2018. The value of the guidelines is noted by Drucker et al., "Digital Art History," 11.
28. An excellent overview of the process, with links to the resulting *Code of Best Practices in Fair Use for the Visual Arts* and the preliminary, preparatory research report, *Copyright, Permissions, and Fair Use Among Visual Artists and the Academic and Museum Visual Arts Communities: An Issues Report* appears in "Code of Best Practices in Fair Use for the Visual Arts," *Art and Education*, February 9, 2015, www.artandeducation.net/announcements/106885/code-of-best-practices-in-fair-usefor-the-visual-arts.
29. CAA's Code of Best Practices in Fair Use for the Visual Arts has been widely endorsed and has inspired a number of shifts in practice, such as a new Fair Use policy by the Robert Rauschenberg Foundation, Yale University Press, and numerous museums. Detailed information is available at: accessed August 20, 2018, www.collegeart.org/programs/caa-fair-use. Its value is noted by Marmor 157. It also helped to inspire the Association of Art Museum Directors to develop new Guidelines for the Use of Copyrighted Materials and Works of Art by Art Museums, available at: file:///Users/anne/Desktop/ACG%20Business/Publications/Digital%20CR/Guidelines%20for%20the%20Use%20of%20Copyrighted%20Materials.pdf, accessed August 20, 2018.
30. See Drucker et al., "Digital Art History," esp. 10–12; Anne Collins Goodyear and Paul B. Jaskot, "Digital Art History Takes Off," *CAA News Today*, October 7, 2014, accessed August 20, 2018, www.collegeart.org/news/2014/10/07/digital-art-history-takes-off/.
31. These now include Duke University, home of the Wired Lab, now offering a Masters of Arts Degree in Art History; the University of Maryland, home of the Michelle Smith Collaboratory for Visual Culture, offering training in Digital Art History; and the University of California, Los Angeles offering "Digital Art History 101." Harvard University's Villa I Tatti, dedicated to the study of the Italian Renaissance, now offers Mellon Fellowships in the Digital Humanities.

32. The literature on this topic is voluminous; see, for example: Chris Alen Sula, S. E. Hackney, and Phillip Cunningham, "A Survey of Digital Humanities Programs," 2017, for the Alliance of Digital Humanities Organizations, accessed August 20, 2018, https://dh2017.adho.org/abstracts/232/232.pdf
33. For more on this history, please see the Getty Vocabularies Frequently Asked Questions, available at: accessed August 14, 2018, www.getty.edu/research/tools/vocabularies/faq.html.
34. The Getty Foundation, "History of the AAT," accessed August 14, 2018, www.getty.edu/research/tools/vocabularies/aat/about.html.
35. Drucker et al., "Digital Art History," 3–4; More information about the Getty Provenance Index and its research potential appear in: Eric Hormell, "New Sales Data Trace the First Hundred Years of the British Auction Market," *The Iris*, March 1, 2017, accessed August 15, 2018, http://blogs.getty.edu/iris/new-sales-data-first-hundred-years-british-auction-market/.
36. Drucker et al., "Digital Art History," 5.
37. According to *Wikipedia*'s entry for the CIDOC Conceptual Reference Model: "The CIDOC CRM emerged from the CIDOC Documentation Standards Group in the International Committee for Documentation of the International Council of Museums. Initially, until 1994, the work focused on developing an entity-relationship model for museum information, however, in 1996, the approach shifted to object-oriented modeling methodologies, resulting in the first '*CIDOC Conceptual Reference Model (CRM)*' in 1999. The process of standardizing the CIDOC CRM began in 2000 and was completed in 2006 with its acceptance as the ISO 21127 standard." Accessed August 15, 2018, https://en.wikipedia.org/wiki/CIDOC_Conceptual_Reference_Model#cite_note-2.
38. A good early definition of linked-open-data is provided by Tim Berners-Lee in "Linked Data," *Design Issues*, added 2010, www.w3.org/DesignIssues/LinkedData.html. An excellent description of its applicability to museums and cultural heritage organizations is provided in "Getty Vocabularies as Linked Open Data," revised October 26, 2017, accessed August 16, 2018, www.getty.edu/research/tools/vocabularies/lod/#definition.
39. Indeed, a IIIF Manuscripts Community Group exists, see: accessed August 20, 2018, https://iiif.io/community/groups/manuscripts/.
40. This shift in perspective is captured in Nina Siegal, "Masterworks for One and All," *The New York Times*, May 28, 2013, www.nytimes.com/2013/05/29/arts/design/museums-mull-public-use-of-online-art-images.html. Museums may also have been responding to research that demonstrated it was not cost effective to charge for reproductions, particularly for public domain works not protected by copyright. See, for example, Kristin Kelly, "Images of Works of Art in Museum Collections: The Experience of Open Access," Prepared for the Andrew W. Mellon Foundation, April 25, 2013, accessed August 21, 2018, http://msc.mellon.org/msc-files/Open%20Access%20Report%2004%2025%2013-Final.pdf
41. Drucker et al., "Digital Art History," 5.
42. Robert S. Nelson, "The Slide Lecture, or the Work of Art History in the Age of Mechanical Reproduction," *Critical Inquiry* 26 (Spring 2000): 415.
43. The National Gallery of Art, *Gemini G.E.L. Online Catalogue Raisonné* can be found at: www.nga.gov/gemini/; Earl A. Powell's "Director's Foreword," indicates that the site was launched around mid-2001. The Metropolitan Museum of Art's *Heilbrunn Timeline of Art History* can be found at www.metmuseum.org/toah/; the copyright, 2000–2018, suggests that the site was launched around 2000. Reports about the Getty Foundation's Online Scholarly Catalogue Initiative and links to each of the publications that resulted can be found at www.getty.edu/foundation/initiatives/current/osci/.
44. The Getty Foundation, "Museum Catalogues in the Digital Age: A Final Report on the Getty Foundation's Online Scholarly Catalogue Initiative (OSCI)," 2017, accessed August 11, 2018, www.getty.edu/publications/osci-report/.
45. Anne Collins Goodyear, "The Getty Online Scholarly Catalogue Initiative (OSCI)," *caa.reviews*, October 6, 2016, accessed August 20, 2018, www.caareviews.org/reviews/2880#.W3vqNZNKjMU.
46. See, for example, Annelisa Stephan, "Conversation with the Getty's New Imaging and Digital Media Architect [Chris Edwards]," *The Iris*, April 27, 2017, accessed August 20, 2018, http://blogs.getty.edu/iris/a-conversation-with-the-gettys-new-imaging-and-digital-media-architect/; Drucker et al., "Digital Art History," 1, 7; Dominic Oldman et al., "Realizing Lessons of the Last 20 Years: A Manifesto for Data Provisioning and Aggregation Services for the Digital Humanities (a Position Paper)," *D-Lib Magazine*, 20/7–8, July–August 2014, accessed August 20, 2018, www.dlib.org/dlib/july14/oldman/07oldman.html.
47. Numerous entries in the Art Institute of Chicago's OSCI catalogue, Monet Paintings and Drawings at the Art Institute of Chicago, for example, include technical studies by conservators (although the

authorship of contributions must be discerned through footnotes), and the Johnson Art Museum at Cornell University, recently received funding from the National Endowment of the Humanities to support the collaborative work of art curator Andy Weislogel, and computer engineer, C. Richard Johnson, on the development of a tool to identify and authenticate watermarks in Rembrandt etchings (see: accessed August 20, 2018, www.engineering.cornell.edu/news/ece-prof-johnson-work-cornells-johnson-art-museum-build-tool-authenticate-watermarks).

48. On Yale University Press's Art and Architecture ePortal see: accessed August 20, 2018, https://yalebooks.yale.edu/art-architecture-eportal.
49. This topic was taken up in a recent panel organized by the College Art Association's Committee on Intellectual Property: "International Copyright Flexibilities and Creative Practice," chaired by Anne Collins Goodyear, with presentations by Riva Symko, Martine Denoyelle, Judith Blijden, and Piotr Adamczyk, and a response by Jeffrey P. Cunard; for more information see: accessed July 22, 2019, https://caa.confex.com/caa/2019/meetingapp.cgi/Session/2115. The question is also implicit in a recent report on the state of copyright in France: Martine Denoyelle, Katie Durand, Johanna Daniel, and Elli Doulkaridou-Ramantani, "Droits des images, histoire de l'art et société (Institut national d'historire de l'art," October 2018, accessed July 22, 2019, https://issuu.com/inha-paris/docs/inha_rapport_images_usages.

## Bibliography


Drucker, Johanna, Anne Helmreich, Matthew Lincoln, and Francesca Rose. "Digital Art History: The American Scene." *Perspective* [Online] 2 (2015). https://journals.openedition.org/perspective/6021.

Fletcher, Pamela. "Reflections on Digital Art History." caa.reviews, June 18, 2015. Accessed July 22, 2019. www.caareviews.org/reviews/2726#.XTWXCJNKh24.

Goodyear, Anne Collins. "The Getty Online Scholarly Catalogue Initiative (OSCI)." *caa.reviews*, October 6, 2016. Accessed August 20, 2018. www.caareviews.org/reviews/2880#.W3vqNZNKjMU.

Goodyear, Anne Collins, and Paul B. Jaskot, Digital Art History Takes Off. *CAA News Today*, October 7, 2014. Accessed August 20, 2018. www.collegeart.org/news/2014/10/07/digital-art-history-takes-off/

Honig, Elizabeth Alice. "Art History and Access: The Catalogue Raisonné as Collaborative Research Site." *NANO: New American Notes Online* (published July 2014). Accessed August 12, 2018. https://nanocrit.com/issues/issue5/art-history-and-access-catalogue-raisonne-collaborative-research-site.

Jaskot, Paul B. "Digital Art History as the Social History of Art: Towards the Disciplinary Relevance of Digital Methods." *Visual Resources* 35 (2018), no. 1–2, edited by Anne Helmreich and Murtha Baca, 21–33.

Lindsay, Kenneth C. "Art, Art History, and the Computer." *Computers and the Humanities* 1, no. 2 (November 1966): 27–30.

Marmor, Max. "Art History and the Digital Humanities." *Zeitschrift für Kunstgeschichte* 79 (2016): 155–58. https://caa.hcommons.org/deposits/item/hc:10121/

Niyazi, Hasan. "The Moment of Digital Art History?" *3 Pipe Problem*, December 7, 2012. www.3pp.website/2012/12/digital-art-history.html

Oldman, Dominic et al. "Realizing Lessons of the Last 20 Years: A Manifesto for Data Provisioning and Aggregation Services for the Digital Humanities (A Position Paper)." *D-Lib Magazine* 20, 7–8, July–August 2014. Accessed August 20, 2018. www.dlib.org/dlib/july14/oldman/07oldman.html

Prown, Jules. "The Art Historian and the Computer: An Analysis of Copley's Patronage." In *Art as Evidence: Writings on Art and Material Culture*, 36–51. New Haven and London: Yale University Press, 2001.

Zorich, Diane M. "Transitioning to a Digital World: Art History, Its Research Centers, and Digital Scholarship." A Report to the Samuel H. Kress Foundation and the Roy Rosenzweig Center for History and New Media George Mason University, May 2012. www.kressfoundation.org/uploadedFiles/Sponsored_Research/Research/Zorich_TransitioningDigitalWorld.pdf

# 32

# DIGITAL PROVENANCE, OPEN ACCESS, AND DATA-DRIVEN ART HISTORY

*Anne Luther*

Researchers concerned with the "social, cultural, and economic mechanisms underlying the circulation of art" conduct studies that are based on data collected about cultural objects and their context.[1] Such data has many forms, formats, and material features. Information about an object's materiality might give information about where it was produced, used and stored; auction records show parties or individuals who sold and bought artifacts; photographs contextualize objects within exhibition histories and document their condition; interviews offer personal recollections of the life of an object in a certain place; archives and museum collections store information about operations such as the cleaning, moving, and exhibiting of objects; and other forms of data are collected in various formats including audio, text, and numeric information. The study of such data introduces the possibility of tracing objects' histories in the context of their institutional provenance.

Depending on the discipline, field of study, and objects, digital provenance research is often interdisciplinary, operating at the interface of computer sciences, design and one of the following theoretical approaches: sociology of art studying the social worlds that construct a discourse of art and aesthetics;[2] the social history of art concerned with the social contribution to the appearance of certain art forms and practices;[3] economics and art business exploring global economic flows and the influence of wealth and management strategies of art;[4] art theoretical discourses on concepts relating to a philosophy of art and therefore closely related to curating and art criticism;[5] and art history with research in provenance, image analysis, and museum studies.[6] Researchers in these disciplines work with manifold data and methodologies such as qualitative and quantitative methods, hermeneutics, iconography, and aesthetics of reception depending on their research focus and discipline.

Approaches that connect the aforementioned disciplines to information technology can be found as early as 1949 in the project *Corpus Thomisticum* by Roberto Busa SJ and associates[7] in cooperation with IBM, a project that developed a concordance of the complete works of St. Thomas Aquinas.[8] More recently, the analysis of cultural data based on computational methods dates back to the "Computers and the History of Art Group" founded in 1985 by international scholars, coining the term 'Digital Art History' with its conference title in 2001.[9] That Group's research, in turn, suggests that The British Museum began its own digitization of records in 1976.[10] In 2015 Lev Manovich used the term "digital art history" and posed the following question:

> Will art history fully adapt quantitative and computational techniques as part of its methodology? While the use of computational analysis in literary studies and history

> has been growing slowly but systematically during 2000s and first part of 2010s, this has not yet happened in the fields that deal with the visual (art history, visual culture, film, and media studies).[11]

Quantitative analysis of "cultural data"[12] such as network analysis[13] and media visualization[14] is mostly based on automated statistical and algorithmical approaches that follow certain hypotheses about relations and patterns in the data sets. Christine Borgman illustrates the current discourse on Big Data/Little Data and the associated methodological approaches in current research communities[15] and argues that "there exists not one method, but many"[16] for digital data analysis in the humanities.

One persistent challenge in this field is the absence of data analysis tools that have been specifically developed for art historical methodologies and provenance research. The majority of tools in digital data analysis were developed for automated, algorithmic analysis in the so-called STEM fields (science, technology, engineering, and mathematics).[17] The tools developed for these fields aim to reveal patterns or information that are not comprehensible without mathematical or statistical approaches. Increasingly, however, art historical research has tested the applicability of such approaches for its own purposes.[18]

One example of a digital provenance project that that uses a network visualization tool developed for biology is the "Network diagram of agents connecting the British, Belgian, Dutch, and French auction markets from 1801–20"[19] developed by Maximilian Schich with Cytoscape in 2011. Although established methods for collecting, analyzing and storing various data sources differ across methodological approaches, it can be said that the need for new computational tools that allow the analysis, storage, sharing and understanding of new digital data sources are needed to understand data sets as a whole, in their full complexity and over various dimensions. Only in recent years have researchers started to develop "standardized, native application programming interfaces (APIs) for providing graphics, animation, multimedia, and other advanced features"[20] necessary for the analysis, visualization and understanding of large data corpi. This standardization allows researchers to develop tools and applications that can be used in multiple browsers and on different devices.[21] While the digitization of object based collections (museum collections, libraries and archives etc.) has an established history, the development of new tools to access, display and analyze these digitized collections based on the development of web standards across browsers and devices is in its infancy. This chapter focuses on the types of data produced by or within galleries, museums, archives and libraries (GLAM), the ways in which such data is made available to audiences and how provenance research relates to open access data. The contextualization of provenance in its entire institutional acquisition, exhibition and loan history can only be comprehended by examining all data collected by an institution. This is only one example that will be shown later that illustrates how complex and large data corpi can reveal new contexts, knowledge, and navigation of cultural object and artifacts.

## Data Publishing and Open Access

After digitization began in large museums in the 1970s and a discourse developed in the 1980s about internal, institutional data structures and standards, institutions began to publish their data in accordance with agreed web standards. It is important to understand that the availability of digitized or born-digital information is accessible on different levels. Data that is viewable online in a website catalogue is, however, not made openly available for computational methods in digital provenance research because it is typically embedded as "view only" information in a website interface. Making GLAM data available as machine readable data means that the data is provided in a structure that can be reshaped, cleaned and edited. This process of altering and reshaping data allows provenance researchers to develop new knowledge that is based on the entirety of a data corpus and its context in a larger semantic web depending on the scale of the research project. Manually and qualitatively created case studies can be embedded in a larger collection context, which can be viewed and visualized in its entirety with different strategies (for example material clusters, semantic topic modeling, time and event context, exhibition networks and other methods).

The digital availability of information has different hierarchies in its quality as open data. The "Five Stars of Open Data"[22] is a hierarchy developed by Tim Berners-Lee that shows different levels of open access data publishing that is currently a standard on the web.[23] The implications of this hierarchy for museums may be summarized as follows:

**One star**: "Make your stuff available on the Web (whatever format) under an open license"
The most common form of data publishing is a digital catalogue on the museum's website. It is often more extensive than the data published as open access data. Provenance data is often published on museum websites, but not as part of open access data.

**Two Star**: "Make it available as structured data (e.g., Excel instead of image scan of a table)"
This form is no longer used in the context of cultural data publishing. Instead institutions now typically publish structured data as CSV files.

**Three star**: "Make it available in a non-proprietary open format (e.g., CSV instead of Excel)"
Data repositories of CSV files and image files are accessible mostly on Github. Museums update their data at different rates (seventy-two hours for the Museum of Modern Art, New York and a one-time data dump in 2014 from Tate for example). The data usually comes from the internal API that museums use to publish their data online. The data is parsed into manageable files and has a clear structure, but is not (graph) relational which makes complex queries harder and slower. However data repositories with open formats often omit information as to provenance, references, exhibition histories, funding bodies, art periods, movements, styles, descriptions or artists' gender although this is often published on museum websites.

**Four star**: "Use URIs to denote things, so that people can point at your stuff (Linked Data)"
A growing trend in the GLAM sector is to release data to wikiData and to the Getty Research Institute as data sources for linked data.[24] Linked Open Data (LOD)—data that is made openly available, identifiable through Uniform Resource Identifier (URI) and linked to other data that is also accessible through HTTP via URI—has however one issue, namely, that it is seldom used by the majority of museum staff, curators or the broader research community. It is hard to grasp how to use, access and share data for the average museum staff working on data.[25]

**Five star**: "Link your data to other data to provide context"
An active LOD community[26] in museums mostly in the US are working on releasing digital collection data under an open license which allows its reuse without cost. The linking of data can be made available in Wikipedia's media repository for entries and images that link directly to the museum's website. The institution provides context internally and externally about the museum's holdings and gives insights about how users might contextualize their data. One exceptional example for this is the donation of "375,000 images of public domain art freely available under Creative Commons Zero on the Wikimedia Blog"[27] by the Metropolitan Museum of Art in 2017. One of the images included in this is *The Adoration of the Christ Child* by the School of Jan Joest (c. 1450–1519).[28] Included in the Wikimedia entry for this work are the terms "Down syndrome" referencing an article in

the *American Journal of Medical Genetics* by Andrew Levitas and Cheryl Reid in which it is suggested that this Early Netherlandish painting is one of the earliest depictions of a person with Down syndrome.[29] The data source of this image that is linked on the media repository of Wikimedia is the online catalogue of The Metropolitan Museum which, in turn, shows full object details, provenance, exhibition history, references and more. The contextualization in the original data source (The Met) that makes information and the object available to the public is here displayed in the context of a history about a genetic disorder. The five star level is therefore used to contextualize the image in a data context that is not restricted to museum collections, curatorial decisions in exhibition making or art historical interpretations of contexts within an art-related narrative, but rather expands into the contexts of diverse disciplines, histories and narratives. The linking of information on the five star level makes a complex network of information and contexts possible and visual museum data becomes part of a larger semantic web outside institutional contexts.

The reason why museums publish their data on different "Star Levels" is related to a social dimension within the institutions themselves. Open access to the data collection of a museum is not yet inscribed in museums' educational missions. Decisions about what data to publish often depend on advice given by legal departments in large institutions and by enthusiastic individuals in smaller institutions. Museums have argued for data entry and publishing standards since the beginning of digitization and although most museums in the United States use the same database management system, institutional structures vary widely across nations. A standardization of data production across international museums is not feasible due to the social dimension of museums, where individual scholars employ terminology from their own discipline and department (time, place, and names differ largely) and use their own style of note taking which can be dependent on the technology that they use to store information. The study of differences, changes and movement in databases is a study of institutional provenance in its own right. As Yanni Loukissas argues, studying information, data collection technology and database structures as an object in itself can lead to a contextual understanding of provenance data.[30] However comprehending provenance in the context of institutional collection patterns is only possible if extensive open data access is made available by institutions.

## Digital Provenance and Software Development

With data about cultural objects openly accessible, digital humanities and digital art history research projects can develop software tools that cater specifically to approaches in digital provenance research. One of the main challenges in software development for cultural data is that information about cultural objects is either undocumented or described by individuals who conceptualize the information as data for computational analysis. This leads to discrepancies of information in databases that are destined for humans, on the one hand, and for machines on the other. One example of such discrepancies concerns artist names. Pablo Picasso has 16 different names in the Union List of Artist Names® (ULAN) (e.g. "Picasso, Pablo Diego José Francisco de Paula Juan Nepomuceno Crispíniano de la Santissima Trinidad Ruiz Blasco" flagged as "vernacular (local) language" as opposed to "p. picasso" flagged as "local use" and "unknown"). For an individual researcher these differences are clearly comprehensible, and it can be assumed that the same person is referenced with a different name tag. For a machine, however, a slight discrepancy in the tag is a *different* tag.

Similarly, time, events, categorization of material and medium, and other descriptive information about an object do not always follow a unified language, but are rather disciplinary terms used by individual specialists, archivists and registrars. Drawing large patterns in collection histories or tracing object movements based on data that reveals large discrepancies, ambiguities and non-unified data entry strategies is a difficult endeavor. Researchers have developed methods to clean and make data points comparable, but every institution, department and individual shapes the diversity of cultural data. Against this background, it is possible to distinguish three open-source software that can help to ameliorate these problems in digital provenance development:

## Standardization of Data Structures and Data Production

A strong argument can be made for a standardization of language when writing provenance data into a museum or archival database. Standardization would enable data from multiple sources (for example multiple museums) to be unified. Linking provenance data from multiple institutions would make it possible to visualize an object's histories without institutional boundaries, to trace trading patterns over time, or to compare and find discrepancies in collection histories on a large scale. Art Tracks, for example, aims to build provenance maps that show the movement of cultural objects through the standardization of provenance data.[31] The CMOA Digital Provenance Standard is a document that provides a "digital model for storing and capturing" provenance data "in a machine readable format" because "there is no machine-readable structure, and it is cumbersome or difficult to automatically analyze the data contained within."[32]

Another example of such a standard approach is the accumulation of data from archives, libraries and museums into one database. Europeana is such a database that currently stores "58,318,521 artworks, artefacts, books, films and music" as digital records.[33] The visualization interface that the platform provides shows the limitations of the project; one can explore the data collection in a catalogue style interface sorted by color, topic, source, people and time period. The rich data diversity and local data context runs the risk of being simplified and flattened due to a normalization of the input data. Both examples share the aim of developing a standard that can be utilized across all museum, archive, and library collections to make information machine-readable across multiple platforms. The social dimension that involves individuals producing and keeping such information up-to-date in ever-changing institutional databases remains a problem in this approach.

## Accumulation of Data From Different Sources

In contrast to the aim of creating a standard for *all* data that describes and documents information about cultural objects is the idea of accumulating pieces of information from different sources and bringing them into a merged data structure that relates to individual case studies. Often art historians or curators employ this approach to accumulate knowledge about a certain topic, event, artist or object in a collection that has been dispersed or that can be found in more than one collection. It is a challenge for the researcher to bring together data from different collections and resources because, as mentioned previously, institutions do not use a unified data description. In consequence, the researcher needs to create a data structure before accumulating information from different sources. Digital Provenance research delivers visualizations that underline a data analysis or tracing of specific patterns. One software example that visualizes historical data is the mapping tool Palladio,[34] developed by Humanities + Design at Stanford. Through a CSV upload, the software allows researchers to map and visualize their provenance data. The accumulation of data from different sources in a singular data structure does not, as described previously, aim to develop a universal standard that can be used across platforms, but is based on a specific data structure that is needed for the use of visualization software.

### *Visually Analyzing Data From One Source or Collection*

The implementation of data visualization and other software for the presentation of historical and provenance data in museum interfaces is being pioneered in institutions. One example is the identification of art works in MoMA's photographed exhibition history since its first exhibition in 1929. The interactive interface displays works that are identified in installation shots of the exhibition archive; by selecting one work, the user receives a full catalogue view of the work, including subsequent exhibitions in which the work has featured at MoMA. Due to the fact that this interface is only developed for works that are still in MoMA's collection, it also reveals the absence of information about their exhibitions in their database. We do not, for example, see information about works that were on loan from other institutions, nor do we have information about the loan history of works from their own collection. The works are identified through machine-learning algorithms, but the manual labor of verification remains an important aspect of human-machine interaction in this branch of digital research.

The Vikus Viewer is another example of the visualization of a museum collection according to "time periods, texture and themes."[35] Recently, institutions such as the Prussian Palaces and Gardens Foundation (Germany), Van Gogh Museum (The Netherlands) and Riksantikvaren (Iceland) have begun using this used tool for the display of their collections. The interface is open-source and can be used by museums to present alternatives to scroll-down or list views of object catalogues. The thematic overview makes it useful for provenance researchers to survey related objects and to create a timeline of collection contexts that relate to specific objects. The interactive design enables the user to switch effortlessly between a broad overview of the relevant collection or to dive into provenance information and high resolution images.

Taken together, these three approaches aim to make large amounts of data machine readable. Nevertheless they differ in their delivery: the implementation of standards for data acquisition and classification across institutional boundaries would enable the development of code for the analysis of data from multiple institutions; data structures for particular software would permit researchers to use existing code or tools that have been developed in a specific collection context; and consistency in data entries in a specific data corpus facilitate the use and development of computer aided data analysis. These examples not only show that data production, storage, and distribution is not only dependent on the digitization of collection records and object documentation, but also reveal that approaches to data histories and changes in databases and data structures are an important part of provenance research.

## Availability of Data Sets and Object Contextualization

Museums, libraries, and archives document large amounts of meta-data about cultural objects that provide provenance researchers with a context for acquisition policies, political, social and historical events, and movements of the objects themselves. This meta-data is however not presented in single "tombstone"[36] paper cards or card file boxes that contain closed information with limited physical connecting systems. Meta-data is linked, related and accessible, and the network of information an institution develops with its data production practice can give information about the technological and ideological interests of the institution itself.

Figure 32.1 shows an example of the influence of historical contexts for acquisitions in museum collection. The visualization was produced in a data sprint that the MediaLab at Sciences Po organized in 2017 with the Centre Pompidou in Paris and an interdisciplinary group of museum staff, researchers, developers and designers.[37] The x-axis shows the year of acquisition in the collection of the Centre Pompidou and the y-axis the percentage of acquisitions from

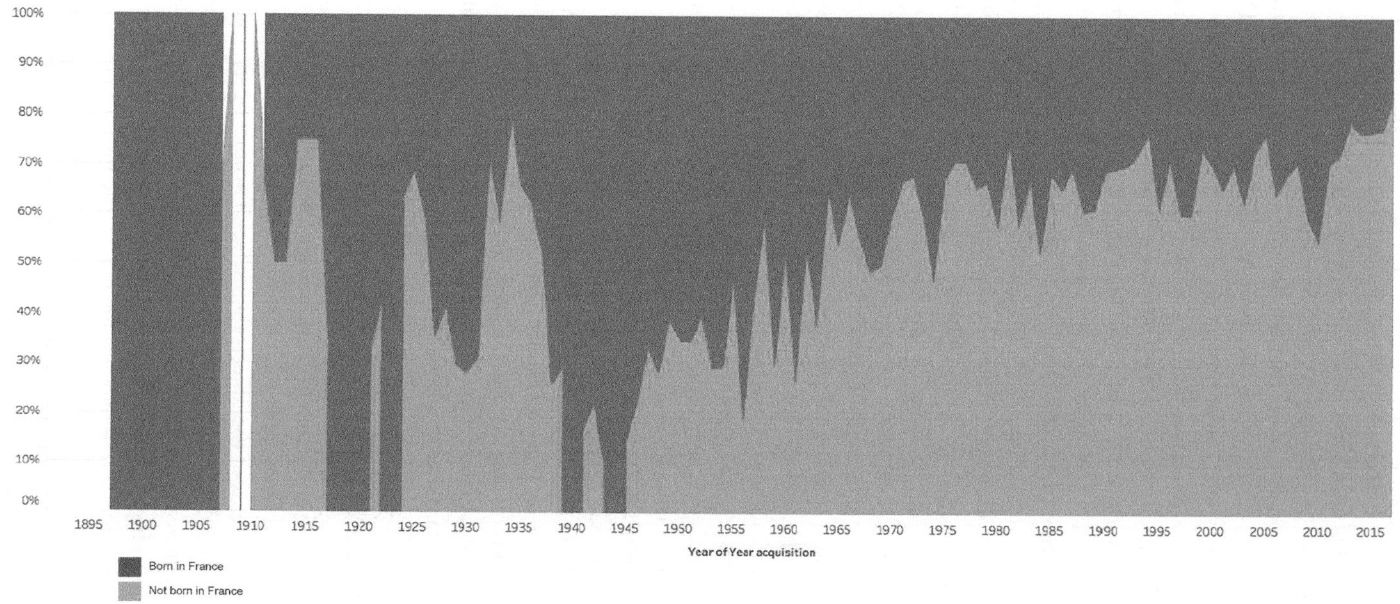


*Figure 32.1* Visualization of the collection of the Centre Pompidou, Paris, according to year of acquisition/nationality.

*Source*: Image courtesy of MediaLab, Sciences Po, Paris.

artists born outside France. With this view of the collection it becomes clear that the museum did not acquire works by any artist who was born outside of France during the First and Second World War. The absence of international artists shows a clear time historical influence on the acquisition practice of the museum during these historic events.

Being able to view the development of collections from such distant views is only possible with the access to the whole.[38] Instead of treating objects as individual items, digital provenance makes it possible to trace objects as part of the evolution of a collection. The embeddedness of individual objects in a collection and the study of the changes within these collections creates a much larger narrative of objects' provenances. Trancing an object's history up to the point at which it becomes part of a collection is one approach that can present itself parallel to the examination of the collection's history. An object does not just appear in a collection independently of external circumstances. Accordingly, it is important to study the patterns, narratives, and factors within the collection that lead to the acquisition of particular objects.

Tracing provenance from the perspective of the whole collection shifts attention to the collecting practices of the institution. Rather than arguing that an object had its own history and appeared in the collection with that history intact, it is important to embed collected items within the logic of the collection itself. This can be understood in terms of actor-network theory as proposed by Bruno Latour: "Using the terminology of actor-network theory (ANT), an actor is defined by its network. This network is not a second level added to that of the individual, but exactly the same level differently deployed."[39] A shift of focus occurs when access to *all* information related to the object and its role in a collection is collated and analyzed. Access to a broader set of digital information significantly influences the approach to provenance research. A more complex set of relationships arises from the digitization and digital documentation of cultural objects because rather than accessing individual paper cards or catalogue pages that describe and document objects as discrete pieces of information, researchers examine objects in wider contexts that can be navigated through digital interfaces. As shown previously with *The Adoration of the Christ Child*, the contextualization of a work of art in different factual environments nevertheless links back to the work's original data source in the museum catalogue.

It is not only published data or open access data that is linked in such a complex network. Rather, museum databases store and develop information about cultural objects in relational ways. Attributes in databases are connected: one work by Picasso can lead to all works by Picasso; and works by Picasso link to time frames in which the artist used specific pigments; the name of this pigment may be linked to all artists that used that pigment. Every object is documented and described with a list of attributes such as provenance, object description, exhibition histories, operations (restoration, storage, cleaning etc.) and others that make up the "biography" of the object. The flexible and fast navigation of attributes in a data set embraces the argument that digital provenance researchers no longer differentiate between the individual object and the collection, but rather seek to contextualize objects in collection histories that comprise a range of changing and related attributes. As much as an object is made up of its meta-data (information about the object) in the data set, its relationship to other objects with associated links can provide information that is equally important about the appearance and role of that object in a particular collection.

Navigation through digital data sets broadens the perspective from object-based, event-driven art history to a distinctively data-driven art history. The diverse ways in which objects can be contextualized, described, and documented configure those objects. An argument can be made in favor of the display of differing provenance meta-data alongside a single object because the latter can be linked to particular data contexts (a collection, an article, a wiki repository etc.) that reveal why such information exists. Rather than using provenance to construct a single, authoritative source of information, more interesting results can be generated by revealing the entire network to which this source is linked. Instead of imposing an institutional hierarchy over certain descriptions and attributes, digital interfaces make it possible to contextualize information in an expanding network of farther reaching information. A data-driven art history links these relationships without removing the information from its context.

## Conclusion

While digital data production in museums, libraries and archives has a long history, the current state of the field of digital provenance is only beginning to develop tools for the analysis of complex data contexts. A data-driven art history depends on open access data (a minimum of three stars) for computational aid in provenance research. Technical and social dimensions in institutions lead to diverse approaches of data production. Standardizations would make a machine-readable approach easier, but also risk diminishing a rich local data history of institutions. Changes, absences, and the formation of new attributes are traceable evidence of institutional decisions to collect, document and deaccession cultural objects. Digital provenance encompasses not only individual objects, but offers the possibility of examining the data contexts of cultural objects in their full complexity.

## Notes

1. See Brill's *Studies in the History of Collecting & Art Markets*, www.brill.com/products/series/studies-history-collecting-art-markets, accessed April 29, 2019.
2. See, for example, Theodor W. Adorno, *Kulturkritik Und Gesellschaft* (Frankfurt Am Main: Suhrkamp, 1977); Howard Saul Becker, *Art Worlds* (Berkeley: University of California Press, 2012); Arnold Hauser, *The Sociology of Art* (London: Routledge, 2013); Pierre Bourdieu, *Die Regeln der Kunst* (Frankfurt am Main: Suhrkamp, 1999); Niklas Luhmann, *Die Kunst Der Gesellschaft* (Frankfurt: Suhrkamp, 1997).
3. Arnold Hauser and M. Harrington, *The Social History of Art* (London: Routledge, 1951).
4. Jos Hackforth-Jones, *Art Business Today* (London: Lund Humphries in Association with Sotheby's Institute of Art, 2016).
5. David Joselit, *After Art* (Princeton: Princeton University Press, 2013); Boris Groys, *Art Power* (Cambridge, MA: MIT Press, 2008).
6. Bénédicte Savoy, *Tempel der Kunst: die Geburt des öffentlichen Museums in Deutschland 1701–1815* (Mainz: von Zabern, 2006).
7. Available online since 2005: www.corpusthomisticum.org/it/, Accessed April 29, 2019.
8. Christine L. Borgman, *Big Data, Little Data, No Data* (Cambridge, MA: MIT Press, 2015), 162; and in Julianne Nyhan and A. Flinn, *Computation and the Humanities* (Ebook: Springer, 2016), 1.
9. William Vaughan, *Digital Art History—A Subject in Transition*, ed. A. Bentkowska-Kafel, T. Cashen and H. Gardiner (Bristol and Portland, OR: Intellect, 2005), 1.
10. Tanya Szrajber, *CDMS: The Computerization of the British Museum Collections* (London: Harwood Academic Publishers, 1989), 9.
11. Lev Manovich, "Data Science and Digital Art History," *DAH-Journal* no. 1 (2015.)
12. Lev Manovich, *The Science of Culture? Social Computing, Digital Humanities, and Cultural Analytics* (2015), http://manovich.net/index.php/projects/cultural-analytics-social-computing, Accessed April 29, 2019.
13. Maximilian Schich, Christian Huemer, Piotr Adamczyk, and Yang-Yu Liu, "Network Dimensions in the Getty Provenance Index," *arXiv:1706.02804* (2017).
14. Lev Manovich, *Media Visualization: Visual Techniques for Exploring Large Media Collections* (2011), http://manovich.net/index.php/projects/media-visualization-visual-techniques-for-exploring-large-media-collections, Accessed April 29, 2019.
15. Borgman, *Big Data, Little Data, No Data.*
16. Ibid., 83.
17. Ibid.

18. See, for example, "Cytoscape," accessed April 29, 2019, www.cytoscape.org/; "The Open Graph Viz Platform," Gephi, Accessed April 29, 2019, https://gephi.org/; and "Stanfordnlp/CoreNLP," GitHub, April 6, 2019, Accessed April 29, 2019, https://github.com/stanfordnlp/CoreNLP.
19. "Auction Market Visualization," Getty Research Institute, accessed April 29, 2019, www.getty.edu/research/tools/provenance/zoomify/index.html.
20. Tim Taylor, J.E. Auerbach, J. Bongard, J. Clune, S. Hickinbotham, C. Ofria, M. Oka, S. Risi, K.O. Stanley, J. Yosinski, "WebAL Comes of Age: A Review of the First 21 Years of Artificial Life on the Web," *Artificial Life* 22, no. 3 (2016): 364–407.
21. Ibid.
22. "5 Star Open Data," accessed April 29, 2019, https://5stardata.info/en/.
23. Anne Luther, Liz Neely, and Chad Weinard, "Cultural Collections as Data: Aiming for Digital Data Literacy and Tool Development—MW19 | Boston," MW19, Accessed April 29, 2019, https://mw19.mwconf.org/paper/cultural-collections-as-data-aiming-for-digital-data-literacy-and-tool-development/.
24. Alexander D. Stinson, Sandra Fauconnier, and Liam Wyatt, "Stepping Beyond Libraries: The Changing Orientation in Global GLAM-Wiki," *JLIS.it* 9, no. 3 (2018): 16–34.
25. "Museums APIs," ProgrammableWeb, Accessed April 29, 2019, www.programmableweb.com/category/museums/api.
26. "Linked Open Data in Libraries, Archives & Museums," LODLAM, Accessed April 29, 2019, http://lodlam.net/.
27. "Met Open Access Artworks Challenge," Commons:Met, Accessed April 29, 2019, https://commons.wikimedia.org/wiki/Commons:Met.
28. "Down Syndrome," Wikipedia, July 12, 2019, Accessed July 16, 2019, https://en.wikipedia.org/wiki/Down_syndrome#/media/File:The_Adoration_of_the_Christ_Child_MET_DT8852.jpg
29. Andrew S. Levitas and Cheryl S. Reid, "An Angel with Down Syndrome in a Sixteenth Century Flemish Nativity Painting," *American Journal of Medical Genetics* 116A, no. 4 (2003): 399–405, doi:10.1002/ajmg.a.10043.
30. Yanni A. Loukissas, *All Data Are Local: Thinking Critically in a Data-Driven Society* (Cambridge, MA: MIT Press, 2019).
31. "Provenance Record," CMOA Provenance Interactive, accessed April 27, 2019, http://arttracks.github.io/provenance-interactive.
32. "The CMOA Digital Provenance Standard," CMOA Digital Provenance Standard, v. 0.2 | Art Tracks, accessed April 27, 2019, www.museumprovenance.org/reference/standard/.
33. Europeana Collections, accessed April 27, 2019, www.europeana.eu/portal/en.
34. "Palladio," Humanities Design Lab, accessed April 28, 2019, http://hdlab.stanford.edu/palladio/.
35. "VIKUS Viewer: Explore Cultural Collections Along Time, Texture and Themes," accessed April 28, 2019, https://vikusviewer.fh-potsdam.de/.
36. "Complete Guide to Adult Audience Interpretive Materials: Gallery Texts and Graphics," *The J. Paul Getty Museum*, 2019, Accessed April 28, 2019, www.getty.edu/education/museum_educators/downloads/aaim_completeguide.pdf
37. Anne Luther, "Activating Museums' Data for Research, Scholarship, and Public Engagement—A New Research Project at the Center for Data Arts," Data Matters, The New School (2018), accessed May 20, 2018, https://data-matters.nyc/?p=18847.
38. Bruno Latour, Pablo Jensen, Tommaso Venturini, Sébastian Grauwin, and Dominique Boullier, "The Whole Is Always Smaller than Its Parts—A Digital Test of Gabriel Tardes Monads," *The British Journal of Sociology* 63, no. 4 (2012).
39. Ibid., 4.

## Bibliography

"5 Star Open Data." 5stardata. Accessed April 29, 2019. https://5stardata.info/en/.

"Auction Market Visualization." Getty Research Institute. Accessed April 29, 2019. www.getty.edu/research/tools/provenance/zoomify/index.html.

Borgman, Christine L. *Big Data, Little Data, No Data: Scholarship in the Networked World*. Cambridge, MA: MIT Press, 2016.

Burdick, Anne. *Digital Humanities*. Cambridge, MA: MIT Press, 2012.

"The CMOA Digital Provenance Standard." CMOA Digital Provenance Standard, v. 0.2 Art Tracks. Accessed April 27, 2019. www.museumprovenance.org/reference/standard/.

"Down Syndrome." Wikipedia. April 15, 2019. Accessed April 29, 2019. https://en.wikipedia.org/wiki/Down_syndrome#cite_note-116.

Europeana Collections. Accessed April 27, 2019. www.europeana.eu/portal/en.

Groys, Boris. *Art Power*. Cambridge, MA: MIT Press, 2013.

Hackforth-Jones, Jos, and Iain Robertson. *Art Business Today*. Lund: Lund Humphries in Association with Sotheby's Institute of Art., 2016.

Hauser, Arnold. *Social History of Art: Naturalism, Impressionism, the Film Age*. Place of New York: Routledge, 2016.

Joselit, David. *After Art*. Princeton: Princeton University Press, 2013.

Latour, Bruno, Pablo Jensen, Tommaso Venturini, Sébastian Grauwin, and Dominique Boullier. "The Whole Is Always Smaller than Its Parts—a Digital Test of Gabriel Tardes Monads." *The British Journal of Sociology* 63, no. 4 (2012): 590–615.

"Linked Open Data in Libraries, Archives & Museums." LODLAM. Accessed April 29, 2019. http://lodlam.net/.

Loukissas, Yanni A. *All Data Are Local: Thinking Critically in a Data-driven Society*. Cambridge, MA: MIT Press, 2019.

Luther, Anne, Liz Neely, and Chad Weinard. "Cultural Collections as Data: Aiming for Digital Data Literacy and Tool Development—MW19 | Boston." MW19. Accessed April 29, 2019. https://mw19.mwconf.org/paper/cultural-collections-as-data-aiming-for-digital-data-literacy-and-tool-development/.

Manovich, Lev. "Data Science and Digital Art History." *DAH-Journal*, no. 1 (2015).

———. "The Science of Culture? Social Computing, Digital Humanities, and Cultural Analytics." Manovich.net. 2015. Accessed April 29, 2019. http://manovich.net/index.php/projects/cultural-analytics-social-computing.

———. "Media Visualization: Visual Techniques for Exploring Large Media Collections." Manovich.net. 2015. Accessed April 29, 2019. http://manovich.net/index.php/projects/media-visualization-visual-techniques-for-exploring-large-media-collections.

"Met Open Access Artworks Challenge." Commons:Met. Accessed April 29, 2019. https://commons.wikimedia.org/wiki/Commons:Met.

"Museums APIs." ProgrammableWeb. Accessed April 29, 2019. www.programmableweb.com/category/museums/api.

Nyhan, Julianne. *Computation and the Humanities*. Ebook: Springer, 2016.

Ono, Keiichiro. "Cytoscape." Accessed April 29, 2019. www.cytoscape.org/.

"The Open Graph Viz Platform." Gephi. Accessed April 29, 2019. https://gephi.org/.

"Palladio." Humanities Design Lab. Accessed April 28, 2019. http://hdlab.stanford.edu/palladio/.

"Provenance Record." CMOA Provenance Interactive. Accessed April 27, 2019. http://arttracks.github.io/provenance-interactive/.

Savoy, Bénédicte. *Tempel Der Kunst: Die Geburt Des Öffentlichen Museums in Deutschland 1701–1815*. Köln: Böhlau Verlag, 2015.

Schich, Maximilian, Christian Huemer, Piotr Adamczyk and Liu Manovich. "Network Dimensions in the Getty Provenance Index." ArXiv.org. June 09, 2017. Accessed April 29, 2019. https://arxiv.org/abs/1706.02804.

Stanfordnlp. "Stanfordnlp/CoreNLP." GitHub. April 06, 2019. Accessed April 29, 2019. https://github.com/stanfordnlp/CoreNLP.

Stinson, Alexander D., Sandra Fauconnier, and Liam Wyatt. "Stepping Beyond Libraries: The Changing Orientation in Global GLAM-Wiki." *JLIS.it*, 9, no. 3 (2018): 16–34.

"Studies in the History of Collecting & Art Markets." Brill book series, History of Collecting & Art Markets. April 26, 2019. Accessed April 29, 2019. www.brill.com/products/series/studies-history-collecting-art-markets.

Szrajber, Tanja. *CDMS: The Computerization of the British Museum Collections*. London: Harwood Academic Publishers, 1989.

Taylor, Tim, Joshua E. Auerbach, Josh Bongard, Jeff Clune, Simon Hickinbotham, Charles Ofria, Mizuki Oka, Sebastian Risi, Kenneth O. Stanley, and Jason Yosinski. "WebAL Comes of Age: A Review of the First 21 Years of Artificial Life on the Web." *Artificial Life* 22, no. 3 (2016): 364–407. doi:10.1162/artl_a_00211.

"VIKUS Viewer: Explore Cultural Collections along Time, Texture and Themes." VIKUS Viewer: Explore Cultural Collections along Time, Texture and Themes. Accessed April 28, 2019. https://vikusviewer.fh-potsdam.de/.

# 33

# RESEARCH, PROCESS, PUBLICATION, AND PEDAGOGY

## Reconstructing the World's Columbian Exposition of 1893

*Lisa M. Snyder*

For six months in 1893, Chicago was the center of the universe. People flocked to the city to experience the grandeur and spectacle of the World's Columbian Exposition. They exhausted themselves exploring enormous exhibition halls filled with the latest technological advances, art from around the world, and every kind of product imaginable. At night, the electrified buildings glowed like jewel boxes, and great searchlights and fireworks displays lit up the sky. Out on the midway, a giant revolving wheel designed by George Washington Ferris induced palpitations in the hearts of many a stalwart fairgoer. And then it was over. The fairgrounds closed, the great buildings were eventually dismantled or destroyed, and the ephemeral city now celebrated as a landmark event was relegated to history.

Large-scale expositions with worldwide participation began in 1851 with the Crystal Palace in London. The first American world's fair, the Centennial International Exhibition of 1876, was held to celebrate the anniversary of the Declaration of Independence. The World's Columbian Exposition (WCE) was similarly focused on a key event in American history—the anniversary of the "discovery" of the New World by Christopher Columbus. For Chicago, the WCE was also a symbol of rebirth following the devastating fire of 1871 that destroyed great swaths of the city. In the United States, the WCE is widely studied. Architectural historians consider it a touchstone for the American Renaissance and City Beautiful movements; in art history, it is revered for the unprecedented number of renowned artists and architects that worked collaboratively to realize the vision of the exposition organizers (Figure 33.1). American historians consider the exposition a landmark event in history both for America at the time and Chicago. In urban planning it is viewed as an exemplar for designed environments; in women's studies as the first fair with a dedicated Board of Lady Managers, and a Woman's Building designed and decorated by women, and dedicated to the work of women. In African-American studies, the fair provides context for the protests of activists Ida B. Wells, Frederick Douglass, and others.[1]

The following describes efforts to create an interactive reconstruction model of the WCE, focusing on four key aspects of three-dimensional (3D) scholarship: research, process, publication, and pedagogy. The intent is to not to provide an overview of 3D scholarship *per se*, but rather to consider key issues for the project across the arc of its development as a guide for other

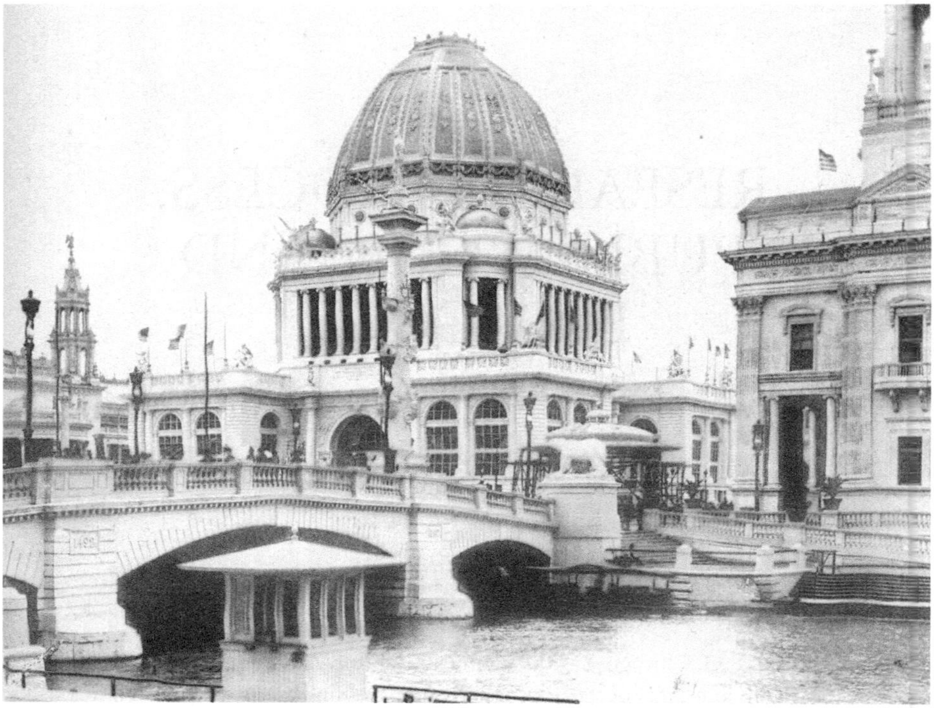

*Figure 33.1* The Administration Building at Chicago's World's Columbian Exposition of 1893.
*Source*: Image from Witteman's *The White City by Lake Michigan*.

scholars interested in engaging with 3D reconstruction work as a form of knowledge production and as a pedagogical tool.

## Research

### *The WCE Reconstruction Project, Technology, and Method*

The WCE project was launched as a testbed for research on the educational applications of interactive computer technologies and explorations of alternative forms of instructional technology for architectural history courses. The first file on the reconstruction was opened in late 1997, and development on the project has continued to the time of this writing, first in conjunction with the Urban Simulation Team at UCLA, then with UCLA's Office of Information Technology and Institute for Digital Research and Education.

While there is a significant amount of published material about the exposition, our modern understanding of the physical infrastructure of the fair is based solely on textual descriptions and static images. As such, it is difficult to appreciate the sheer scale of the enterprise (over 680 acres with well over 400 buildings); consider the relationships of the buildings, one to the next; and build a holistic understanding of the fair. Most critically, because it was held before moving images could effortlessly capture the essence of an ephemeral event, there is no way for modern-day scholars to understand what it may have been like to walk through the fairgrounds and experience the transitions between the different zones of the exposition. Thus, a key requirement of the reconstruction project was that it provide an interactive approximation of the spatial experience of the exposition with as much detail as possible to engender prolonged engagement with the model. The original research questions focused on pedagogy: How would instructors want to use the technology in the classroom? How would students react? What would students learn differently about an environment if they could interact with a computer model rather than read an article or look at a series of images?

It is impossible to gauge the level of completeness of the reconstruction model, because that requires agreement as to what "complete" means for this type of project. If complete means a fully realized virtual simulation of the fair with all buildings—inside and out, including exhibits—and the entire site faithfully reconstructed, then the project will never be finished. If completeness refers to a user's ability to understand the physical elements of the fair, then the reconstruction could be considered around 80% done. The major exhibition halls are all represented—albeit some in greater detail than others—and there is a cohesive route through the model that provides a sense of the different zones of the fair (Figure 33.2). There are, however, still vast areas that have not been addressed (e.g. the stockyards along the southern edge of the fairgrounds). A better metric for an academic project is a comparison against the available evidence. For reconstruction projects, it is critical that the modeling effort be supported by primary textual or visual resource material. In the absence of that incontrovertible evidence, one can only develop strategies to suggest what might have been without compromising the rigor of the project. If judged against this standard—the degree to which the available evidence has been exhausted—then a cautious estimate would put the WCE model at 40% complete, considering the amount of research material that has been collected or identified and not yet incorporated into the reconstruction.

To facilitate the desired interaction, the WCE reconstruction was built in a polygonal surface modeler designed for flight simulation. In the early years of the project, the software was distributed as *MultiGen Pro*, and could only be used on Silicon Graphics systems. Now updated for use on Windows systems, the software is known as *Creator* and distributed by Presagis. *Creator* facilitates spatial organization of the modeled environment with an emphasis on data efficiency, use of nested levels of details, and easy hierarchical file organization for linking individual models

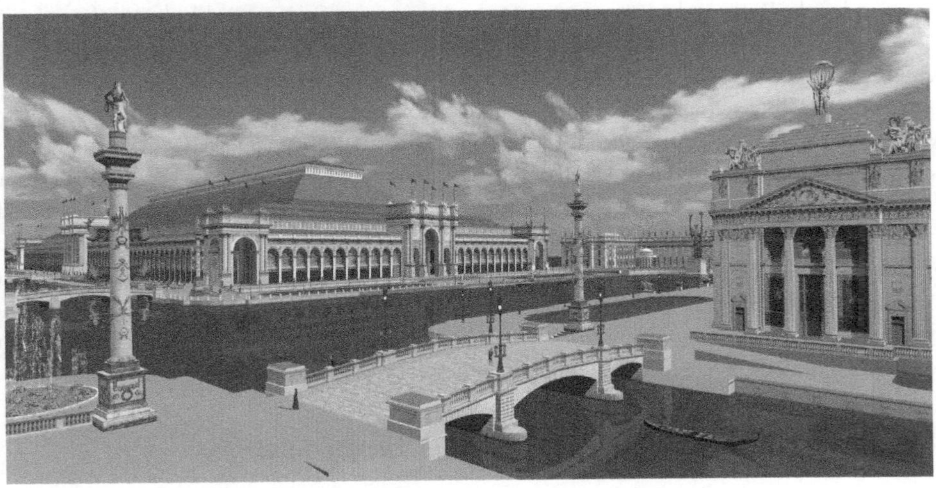

*Figure 33.2* The Court of Honor in the WCE reconstruction model.

*Source*: © 2019 The Regents of the University of California.

into a single, large-scale scene. Interaction with the model would best be described as desktop virtual reality—a virtual environment explored on a desktop computer with a keyboard and mouse, and well suited for projection in classrooms and presentation spaces.

As the project evolved, so did the research questions. As the modeling work progressed and more and more buildings were added, questions of methods emerged. How best to show areas of uncertainty and ambiguity while also preserving visual continuity so as not to break the user's willing suspension of disbelief as they navigate through the environment? How complete does the environment need to be in order to be useful pedagogically (or interesting to a general audience)? As dissemination of the model became viable, questions of publication came to the fore. How might one annotate a model so that it is legible for a secondary user unfamiliar with the exposition? What does the software look like to enable broad distribution and use? What does publishing look like for an interactive 3D model? And finally, as the project stretched into its third decade, sustainability questions became a priority. What mechanisms and workflows need to be in place to preserve 3D material, and ensure long-term access to the scholarship?

## *Sources-Based versus Reality-Based Models*

The WCE reconstruction is an example of a *sources-based* model, the result of the analysis and synthesis of a broad range of primary and secondary textual and visual source materials, with the model as a point of reconciliation for disparate facts.[2] Art and architectural historians, public historians, and others researching long-demolished or significantly altered environments or structures have embraced sources-based modeling. In contrast to this largely manual approach, *reality-based* models are generated with data captured from physical artifacts and sites, whether from photographs, scanners, or sensors.[3] In the case of the WCE, the extant remains are limited, hence the focus on source material rather than reality-based data. The site—Jackson Park—still exists. It would be technically feasible to capture terrestrial information through scans or photographs, and generate a terrain mesh, but the site itself has changed in the 125 years since the exposition, so the information would be of little value for the reconstruction. A few buildings from the exposition still stand, but not enough to seriously consider reality-based scanning options. On site, the Fine Arts Building remains in a fashion. When it was rebuilt in the late 1920s and early 1930s and transformed into the Museum of Science and Industry, the exteriors followed Charles Atwood's original designs but were clad in Indiana limestone instead of staff, while the interiors were completely gutted and remodeled. Other buildings were relocated after the exposition closed. The Maine Building, for example, was moved to Poland Springs, Maine, and the Norway Building was moved multiple times—first to Lake Geneva, then to Blue Mounds Wisconsin, and then to Orkdal, Norway, where it was restored as the Thams Pavilion.[4] The one reality-based modeling test conducted for the project focused on a scale replica of the Statue of the Republic designed by Daniel Chester French, a dominant feature of the Court of Honor. While the test was acceptable, the resultant 3D version of the statue has never been introduced into the WCE model because the density of the geometry generated from this photogrammetric approach is at odds with the overall need for data efficiency, and significant time would be required to "correct" the differences between the replica and original statue.[5]

## *The Scholarship of Reconstruction Modeling*

The reconstruction process privileges minute and specific details about the structures in question over broader historical themes and global phenomena, and knowledge of architectural form over cultural trends and political events. Reconstruction research requires an extremely close reading of the primary source material to pull out elusive references to color, heights, dimensions, and details about how the buildings were constructed and used. While a more traditional architectural historian writing about the WCE might not care about the entasis of the columns used on the entry pavilions of the Manufactures Building, that information is critical for a scholar creating a computer reconstruction model. Considering the eclectic mix of buildings at the fair, the process also requires a broad knowledge of a wide variety of architectural styles, and the ability to research the work of both the principal designers of the fair and the minor architects that contributed to the fabric of the exposition.

For the major buildings of the WCE, the vocabulary of classicism famously dominates, deployed by well-known architects of the day. Charles McKim, for example, from the New York architectural firm of McKim, Mead & White designed the neo-classical Agriculture Building in the Court of Honor. Given the prominence of the architects and the importance of the main exhibition halls for the fair, there is considerable evidence for these structures: Contemporary architecture and engineering magazines published architectural drawings, photos of these buildings are common, and modern scholars have written monographs about the work of these architects and firms. The minor buildings, in contrast, are in an assortment of vernacular and historical styles, many designed by little-known, regional architects. Burnham's 1892 guidelines for the state buildings encouraged a dignified and formal, yet eclectic mix: "The earlier styles that prevailed in this country, such as the architecture of the Old Spanish Missions in Lower California and Mexico, can with propriety furnish the motives for the buildings of the western and southwestern states. For the eastern and southern states, buildings of the old colonial style would be appropriate, and reproductions of historic buildings would prove an interesting feature."[6] Thus, Virginia contributed a replica of George Washington's Mount Vernon, while the Louisiana State Building designed by Herod & Andre was a replica of the Creole plantation house that, in its final use, had been repurposed as the courthouse and police station in Algiers, the city across the Mississippi river from New Orleans.[7] The virtual reconstruction of the latter required research on Louisiana architectural styles, the original plantation house and its history, the two named architects, the city of Algiers, and the wood products of the state to inform the color choices.

The reconstruction process also favors visual materials as the most accurate record of the built environment. The most enduring images of the WCE were taken by the fair's official photographer, C.D. Arnold, who, along with Harlow D. Higinbotham, also held the concession that controlled the sale and distribution of images of the fair. Other photographers and vendors produced significant images of the WCE, all of which have enriched the reconstruction model: the B.W. Kilburn Company held the concession for stereographs; well-known photographer William Henry Jackson produced images that appeared in two major publications (*White City (as it was)* and *Jackson's Famous Pictures of the World's Fair*), and, as Brown documents, there were a host of unofficial vendors that produced views of the fair.[8] The challenge, however, is that the vast majority of these images capture variations of the same "hero" views. The primary facades of the major and minor buildings dominate, leaving the rear and sides of the buildings largely undocumented. The buildings typically fill the frame, providing useful massing information, but little on detail and ornament. And most of the images were taken from ground level, so provide little information about the roofing systems of the buildings. (The notable exceptions to this are the views made from the upper walkways and observation decks of the great exhibition halls, or from the Ferris Wheel on the Midway.) Lacking in these commercial views are images of the lesser buildings of the fair, the elusive backsides and roofs of buildings, and the less-than-photogenic areas of the grounds that will provide the information necessary to complete the reconstruction.

### *The Importance of Both Physical and Digital Collections*

As with more traditional forms of scholarship, the WCE project relies heavily on physical special collections. Significant archival research was necessary for fragile, oversized, and/or unique materials related to the exposition, and low-demand items unlikely to have been digitized. The collections of the Ryerson and Burnham Libraries at the Art Institute of Chicago, for example, include the original leaves for Burnham's eight-volume final official report complete with mounted text panels, drawings, diagrams, and photographs. A two-volume reproduction of the report was released in 1989, but research time with the original documents was critical for the reconstruction process, primarily because the size of the print reproduction compared to the originals (24 × 32 cm versus 55 × 70 cm) and the screening necessary to reproduce the images limited the value of the volumes' dimensioned architectural drawing. In many cases, in-person appointments with collection curators were required to access materials. The Olmsted Archives at the Frederick Law Olmsted National Historic Site in Brookline, Massachusetts, for example, include a significant trove of landscape and hardscape plans unlikely to be digitized in their entirety; to view the plans, an application for an in-person appointment had to be submitted and scheduled at the convenience of archive staff. Similarly, access had to be coordinated with the National Archives and Records Administration to review and request digital copies of their complete large-scale set of working drawings for the U.S. Government Building, and with the Royal Institute of British Architects' Library for an afternoon with a one-of-a-kind report on the design and construction of the exposition prepared by Sir Banister Fletcher following an extended stay in Chicago during which he met with the principles of Burnham's design and construction teams.

Increasingly, however, it is the digitized source materials available online from archives and collections across the world that are making the most transformative contributions to the reconstruction. While it is true that the project itself would not have been technically possible a mere thirty years ago, it is equally true that access to the wealth of information required to produce a reconstruction model with enough detail to foster sustained user interaction is only possible because of the push in the past few decades to digitize text and image archives and collections. Thus, the project has been enabled by two separate, yet equally important advancements in information processing: the technological advancements that make possible the computer model itself (e.g. the developments related to computer modeling, graphics processing, and real-time interaction), and the developments that democratize knowledge and provide online access to critical primary and secondary resources (e.g. ongoing funding initiatives to digitize resources, efforts to archive and link digital collections, and the general explosion of efficient search algorithms that enable discovery).

The WCE project has benefited significantly from ongoing digitization efforts, and the resources made available under three categories of access. The first and most critical are those resources digitized and made freely available from a range of providers. The Ryerson and Burnham Archives at the Art Institute of Chicago have fully digitized and released online their collection of C.D. Arnold photographs of the WCE—"nearly eight hundred large-format photographic prints and twenty-five small-format sepia photographic prints"[9]—as well as WCE material from other sources. The image viewer used on the site facilitates deep engagement with the visuals, revealing minute details that can be incorporated into the reconstruction model. Another freely available resource, the Internet Archive, has become a critical aggregation site for digitized material from across the globe; a recent search on "World's Columbian Exposition" returned 992 results, mostly digitized texts from major academic institutions, and the benefit of having access to digitized versions of these titles *en masse* cannot be overstated. Also immensely valuable and freely available are the unique materials and information posted by minor institutions and private citizens that would be have been functionally inaccessible to an academic project pre-internet (e.g. the Minnesota Historical Society web page on the statue of Hiawatha and Minnehaha from the Minnesota Building at the WCE).[10] A second category of digitized materials are those available behind paywalls, such as Hathi Trust Digital Library's digitized runs of the major architectural periodicals made available courtesy of UCLA's membership, or the architectural drawings for the Philadelphia Building designed by Thomas P. Lonsdale that have been digitized and are available online through a subscription to the A.W. Leh Collection of the Athenaeum of Philadelphia. The final category of digitization includes libraries and collections willing to scan—for a price—images from their archives for research purposes. The cost of "research-only" imagery varies by institution, but is often significantly less than typical rights and reproduction fees and can often be negotiated remotely. The Swedish National Archives (aka Riksarkivet), for example, provided at cost the project scans of Gustaf Wickman's drawings for the Swedish Pavilion.

## Process

### *Model Creation*

The process to build a sources-based reconstruction model is painstaking, requiring skills and an aptitude for both archival research and 3D computer modeling. As with research for more traditional forms of scholarship, the process involves the search for best available evidence, a preponderance of contradictory evidence, and thinking critically about the source material. In the case of the WCE reconstruction, immersion in the subject material was an absolute necessity for developing a fundamental knowledge of key resources, bibliographies, and the physical infrastructure of the fair. The first step of the process was to establish in the modeling software an accurately scaled base model of the exposition grounds. From that foundation, the reconstruction moved forward either building by building, or by geographic zone. For each modeled area, the process followed the same basic steps: research, construction of preliminary geometry, construction of detailed geometry, development of texture maps, and placement of final ornamental elements.

### *Interpretive Decisions as Academic Argument*

As argued by Sullivan, Nieves, and Snyder, sources-based 3D work generates new disciplinary knowledge and should be considered a new form of scholarship: "If modeling is a form of rhetoric, then both the development of the 3-D [sic] reconstruction and the selection and evaluation of source materials constitute interpretive processes."[11] Staley supports that position, referring to virtual environments as visual secondary sources, acknowledging them as the "product of a set of conscious choices by historians."[12] These interpretive processes and conscious choices should rightly be considered academic argument. Inductive logic and reasoning are integral to the reconstructive process, and the resultant digital object—the reconstruction model—can be evaluated in the same fashion as more traditional forms of argument and scholarship. Every reconstruction contains thousands of micro-arguments that draw conclusions about the built form based on the assembled evidence. The strongest arguments are supported by multiple sources; weaker arguments are inferred and potentially extrapolated from the available evidence, with the possibility that the reconstruction will be revised in the face of new information.[13] The preponderance of source material for the WCE reconstruction model means that this process of analysis, inference, and interpretation can be supported and evaluated against visual and textual source material and available photographs.

## *The Sources-Based Reconstruction Workflow: Wooded Island*

The workflow for a sources-based reconstruction model follows a logical and iterative sequence. The creation of the Wooded Island in the heart of the exposition grounds, for example, began with significant archival research. The primary materials included Burnham's atlas of the fair published in his final report; contemporary descriptions, photographs, and paintings of the fair generally and the island specifically; correspondence from the Olmsted archives from the Library of Congress available on microfilm; un-microfilmed correspondence held in the Manuscripts Division of the Library of Congress; plans, letters, and photo albums related to the exposition in the Olmsted archives in Massachusetts; letters and plant lists in the archives of Warren Manning in the Special Collections Department of the Francis Loeb Library in the Harvard Design School; contemporary horticulture accounts (notably the *Annals of Horticulture 1893*); and materials from various sources on the specific firms identified as contributing specimens to the fair or as exhibitors on the island (often both).

Synthesizing the archival research and translating it into a model intended for real-time interaction presented some unique challenges. The first modeling task was to build the digital terrain of the island and surrounding terraces based on Olmsted's plans. Then came the painstaking task of recreating the plant materials and "planting" these specimens on the island and along the shoreline as accurately as possible, but within the constraints imposed by the technology (Figure 33.3). According to Burnham's final report, the landscape department cultivated and planted 7,333 trees, 37,055 shrubs, 100,000 willow cuttings, 156,396 herbaceous plants, and an additional quarter of a million general bedding plants and vines.[14] For the interactive computer, it was critical to give the illusion of those numbers within the context of a fully navigable real-time model. Rather than building, for example, individual specimens of the tule—a type of

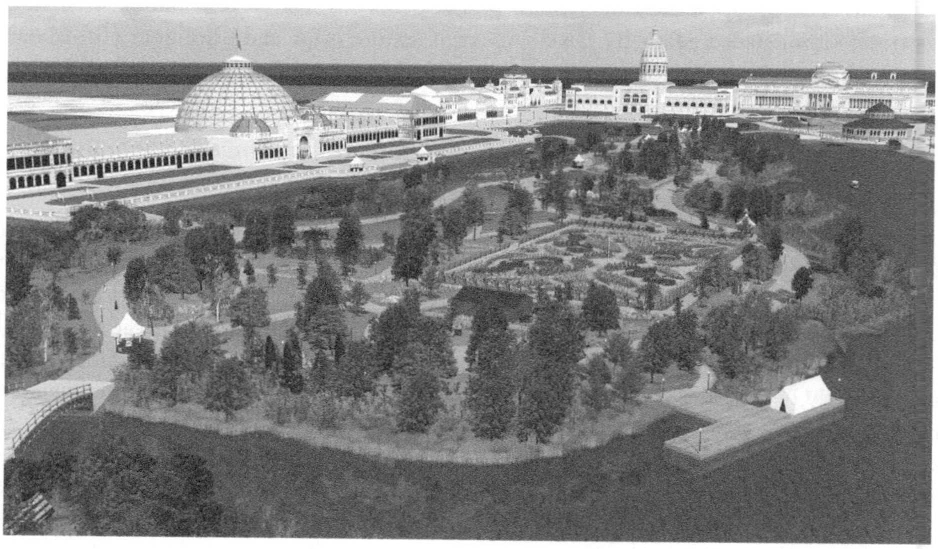

*Figure 33.3* The 2009 reconstruction of Wooded Island.

*Source*: © 2019 The Regents of the University of California.

semi-aquatic sedge—planted around the island's shoreline, a single repeating texture was created and placed on simple polygons placed perpendicularly to the water's edge. A similar technique was used to approximate the one hundred thousand willows.

Approximately 175 specific trees, shrubs, and flowering plants were created for the island. Standard horticultural resources such as Dirr's *Hardy Trees and Shrubs*, the Garden Club of America's *Trees that Merit Attention*, and the American Horticultural Society's *Encyclopedia of Plants & Flowers*; and online sources like the U.S. Department of Agriculture's Plants Database, the plant index of the Chicago Botanic Garden, and sites devoted to heirloom varieties of commonly used plants like roses were used as guides for building recognizable digital surrogates for the specific specimens identified in the WCE planting lists. Finally, reference materials generated for gardeners and landscape architects restoring period landscaping, notably Denise Wiles Adams' *Restoring American Gardens: An Encyclopedia of Heirloom Ornamental Plants 1640–1940*, were used to trace specimen name changes over the years.

The street culture elements—light standards, benches, and buildings—and the horticulture exhibits were the last to be added to the model of the Wooded Island. Contrary to the popular conception of the Wooded Island as a virgin landscape in contrast to the major exhibition halls, the interior of the island was broken into thirty-four plots by the meandering walkways. Of these plots, only one was left as an open greensward; the others contained planting beds and exhibits from nurseries both in the U.S. and abroad. To recreate these exhibits, research on each exhibitor was conducted, and the contemporary accounts of the fair combed for references that connected specific plants to specific exhibitors on specific plots. As these were identified, digital specimens were created and planted within the WCE model.

### *An Architectural Workflow: The Transportation Building*

For the reconstruction of the major exhibition halls, the modeling work followed the same process, but was more focused on architectural documentation and the search for as-built information. For the Transportation Building by Louis Sullivan, for example, a set of construction drawings was assembled from disparate sources. Elevation drawings were digitized from *Inland Architect and News Record*; section and truss detail drawings from *Engineering*; plans from Burnham's final report and *Inland Architect*; detail drawings from Banister Fletcher's report on the WCE at the RIBA, and from the Louis Sullivan Collection of the Avery Library at Columbia University. A reference archive of photographs of the building at various phases of its construction was created using digitized photographs from private collectors; material photographed, photocopied, or downloaded from the Ryerson & Burnham Archives; digitized material from online sources including the Richard Nickel Collection at Southern Illinois University Edwardsville, the Historic American Building Survey, and the Goodyear Archival Collection at the Brooklyn Museum, and the Wisconsin Historical Society; material photographed at the Frederick Law Olmsted National Historic Site, Archives and Museum Collections; and digitized images from books such as *Architectural Details of the Buildings of the Columbian Exposition* held at the New York Public Library, WCE view books, and the four-volume series *A History of the World's Columbian Exposition* edited by Rossiter Johnson. Textual references to the building were also compiled from sources such as the previously mentioned Banister Fletcher report, "The Decoration of the Exposition" by F.D. Millet, "Architecture at the World's Columbian Exposition" by Van Brunt, and, of course, Burnham's final report. Finally, color information was collected that could inform a reconstruction of the building's elaborate polychromatic stenciling. The emphasis was on contemporary sources such as those from *Vistas of the Fair* published by the Poole Brothers, *Art and Architecture of the Fair* by Walton, watercolor drawings in private collections, and tinted lantern slides and drawings in the Ryerson & Burnham Archives.

Construction of the model of the building itself followed the same four basic steps as described earlier for the island. Preliminary geometry was created on the accurately scaled base model of the exposition grounds using dimensions from the digitized construction drawings. This simple massing model was then carved into separate, discrete files for the main building elements, and referenced hierarchically by a single master file. Detailed geometry was constructed as efficiently as possible. A model of a single bay, for example, was constructed using the section printed in *Engineering*, and referenced multiple times into the master file; thus, any changes to the primary bay would update the bays of the entire building. The north and south facades with their elaborate entrances to the building were identical; one file was built and referenced twice into the master file—once at its original location, and once mirrored off the building's center line for the opposite entry. Individual files were created and referenced for the main entrance to the building (the famed Golden Door), the cupola, the building annex, and the elements that connected the repeating bays to the north and south facades. Texture maps for the building were extracted from the assembled photo archive, and digitally colored based on textual descriptions and an element-by-element comparison of the available color references (Figure 33.4). The final step in the process was layering in the ornamental details such as the column capitals, fountains, flagpoles and flags, and interior stairways and trusses.

## Reconstruction Challenges and Ethics

The London Charter for the Computer-based Visualisation of Cultural Heritage provides general guidelines for ensuring the rigor and "intellectual transparency" of 3D scholarship.[15] The most detailed of the charter's principles—and the most relevant for the purposes of this

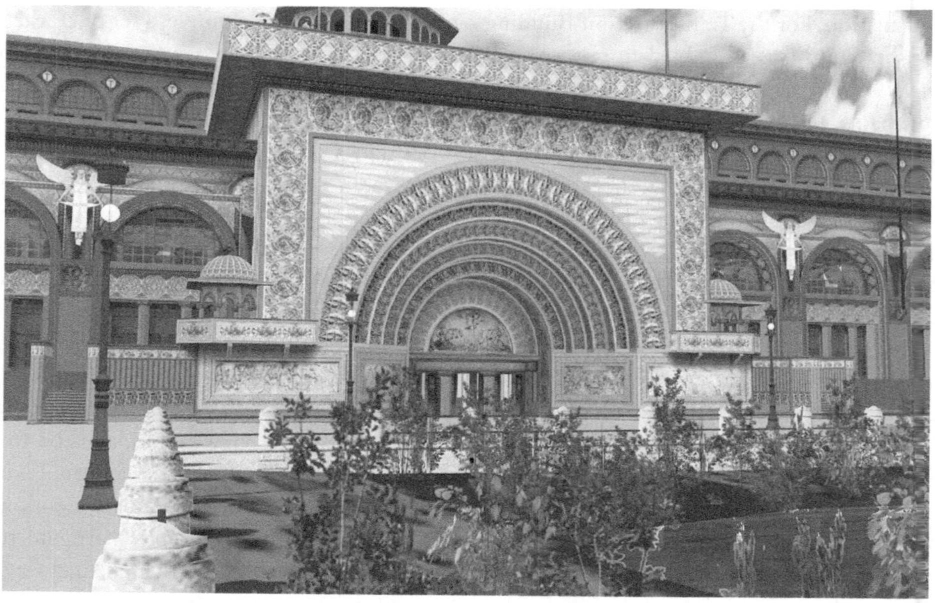

*Figure 33.4* The Transportation Building (reconstructed in 2012).

*Source*: © 2019 The Regents of the University of California.

discussion—focuses on the documentation of source material, knowledge claims, and the reconstruction process, urging that projects make clear the "relationship between research sources, implicit knowledge, explicit reasoning, and visualisation-based outcomes."[16] Early on in the WCE reconstruction project, a decision was made only to include information in the model that could be substantiated with solid evidence. For well-documented buildings and areas of the exposition, this approach yields results that are rich in detail and engender the prolonged user engagement set as a goal of the reconstruction. Structures or areas with limited source material, on the other hand, have been left in a work-in-progress state within the model to signal to users the lack of available evidence. The differences in the amount of available source material can be illustrated with two Midway Plaisance concessions that included crowd-pleasing restaurants, shops, and entertainments: The Street of Cairo and Old Vienna (Figure 33.5).

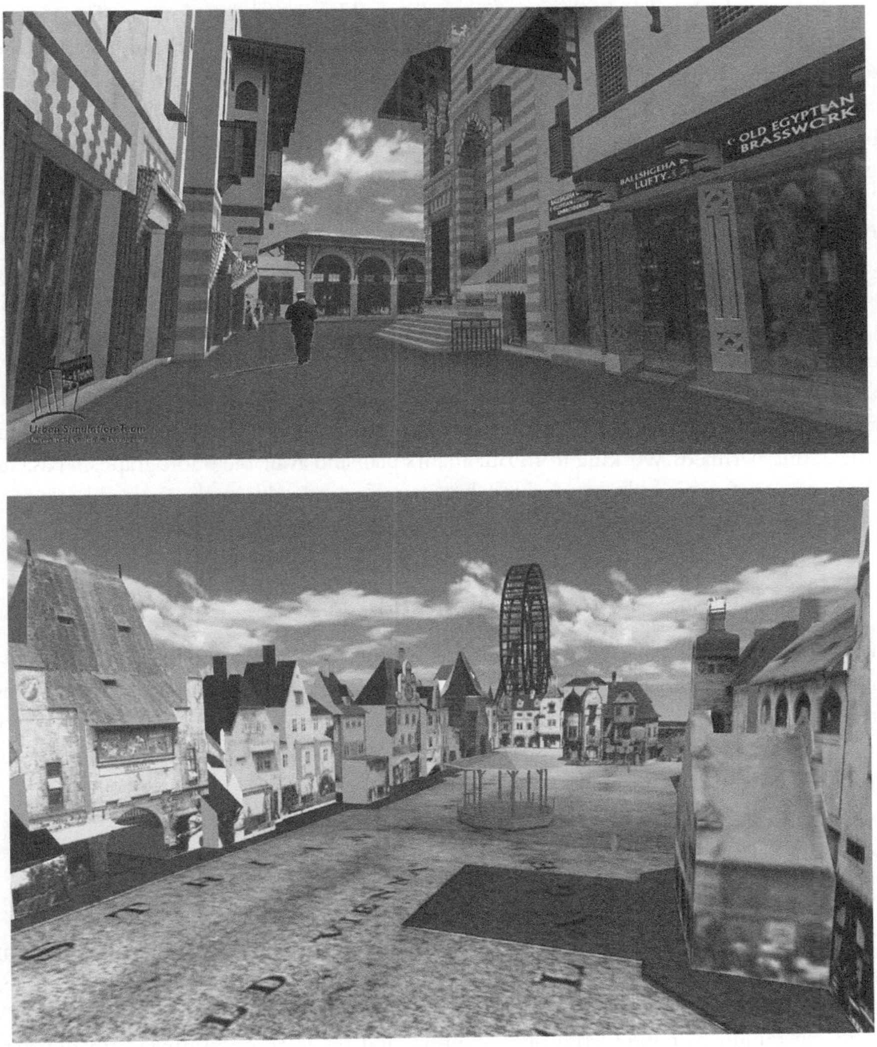


*Figure 33.5* Top: 2011 reconstruction of the Street of Cairo. Bottom: efforts in 2014 to reconstruct Old Vienna.

*Source*: © 2019 The Regents of the University of California.

For the reconstruction of the Street of Cairo installation, there was considerable available evidence. The modeling effort relied on the plan from Burnham's final report; elevation sketches published in the *Chicago Tribune*; historic photos from the fair (which provided easy visual scale references as the faux ablaq-style stonework makes it easy to count courses and calculate heights); modern and historic photos and architectural documentation of the extant Cairene buildings that were replicated in the Street; modern images of Cairo and historic color illustrations distributed at the fair to provide the color palette for the model; concessionaire George Pangalo's written description of the installation; documentation about the architect (Max Herz Bey) and publications about his work and association with the *Comité de Conservation des Monuments de l'Art Arabe* in Cairo; records related to the local Chicago architect that supervised the Street's construction (Henry Ives Cobb); the Street of Cairo guidebook; Gabriel Lekegian and Company's photographs of the Street (on which they had a retail outlet); and the popularity of the installation, which led to its depiction in innumerable textual descriptions. (Even with all of the available evidence, data gaps were inevitable. On the signage throughout, for example, pale grey "Lorem ipsum" text was used for placeholders when the actual text was occluded or illegible in the historic photographs.)

In contrast, a rigorous reconstruction of Old Vienna was impossible. The installation was advertised as "a reproduction of that part of Vienna known as '*die Graben*' as it appeared 200 years ago" or circa 1693.[17] The Graben of modern Vienna is a street in the city center and a major tourist attraction, but the buildings at the WCE bear no resemblance to that district, past or present. Rather, Ingram concludes, Old Vienna is "generically old" and merely evocative of a distant and misleading past.[18] None of the structures were reconstructions of identifiable buildings, and attempts to prove otherwise were futile, including consultations with architectural historians and conservators at the Vienna University of Technology, and research at the Wien Museum and in the City and State Archive of Vienna. Rather than the physical environment, contemporary descriptions of Old Vienna focus on the food establishments, the band concerts, and the young barmaids. Working from Burnham's plan and available photographs, a basic model of Old Vienna was eventually constructed, but the effort was ultimately aborted because of the lack of information.

## Publication

Digital 3D scholarship enables new forms of publication that foreground the interactive environment and support secondary scholarship by providing interactive opportunities for new insights as cross-disciplinary learning objects. One can imagine a spectrum of publication options in terms of the 3D material—from illustrations for text-based arguments at one extreme to fully navigable augmented virtual environments on the other.

### *Digital 3D Edition Fantasy*

The ideal WCE publication centers on the reconstruction model, and encourages user-motivated exploration by providing just-in-time information about the virtual environment in response to their interactions. On approach to the Agriculture Building, for example, spatially aware information about the building would present itself to the user—annotations that describe the building's construction, use, context, and reconstruction; images to illustrate the exhibits and the building across its lifespan; and links to documents to provide users access to primary and secondary resources including contemporary publications and guides, critical appraisals, and websites that feature the building or the fair. Thus, movement through the model would trigger a constantly updating cascade of information about the exposition for the user to explore as befits their own research interests and curiosity. Overlaid on this fabric of model and information, narratives or academic arguments would be available to guide the user through curated discussions about the modeled environment. Variations of this vision have been articulated by a number of scholars in recent years and are evident in commercial online archives like Sketchfab.[19] Indeed, the holy grail of 3D scholarship is a stable technological platform that will enable dissemination of computer models to secondary users, allow content creators to annotate their 3D work, and provide users access to the primary and secondary materials that informed the creation of the reconstruction.

## *VSim: A 3D Interface for Scholarship and Pedagogy*

Concurrent with the WCE project, the author explored, and ultimately designed, software to support academically generated models of historic landmarks and urban environments. The navigation elements for this software (dubbed VSim) built on the functionality of the software (USim) used by the Urban Simulation Team at UCLA written by Scott Friedman. The remaining interface elements were part of a long-term effort to understand and support publishing requirements and pedagogical applications for interactive computer models. Paper designs for a software interface that facilitated teaching and learning with 3D computer models to be developed by a fictitious Virtual Exploration Laboratory were included in the author's doctoral dissertation in 2003. A key figure is a composite image based on a tinted C.D. Arnold view of the WCE's Peristyle that illustrates an early conceptualization of a mechanism to build curated paths through the virtual space that prefigured VSim's Narrative feature. The illustration includes line segments representing both the user's position in the virtual environment and their view, as well as information nodes that provide opportunities to augment the computer model with discussion and analysis.[20] Additional experiments with USim that were partially funded by the Israel Antiquities Authority in 2004 featured the construction of linear paths through the virtual environment with a trigger mechanism that launched supplementary information and images based on the user's position and viewing direction. This work was the precursor to the VSim prototype and VSim 2.0, now in wide release.

With funding from a 2010 Start-Up grant from the National Endowment for the Humanities (NEH) in the United States (HD-50958–10), a prototype was developed and released that included functioning versions of the linear path and resource trigger concepts (now identified as the Narrative and Embedded Resources features), as well as three modes of navigation for free-form exploration. The Narrative feature allowed users to establish keyframes, and augment them with text and imagery, resulting in the equivalent of a PowerPoint or Prezi presentation, but in 3D space. When "played," the software would generate movement between individual keyframes to take users through a guided tour of the modeled environment. The Embedded Resource feature referenced earlier trigger experiments, but was redesigned to allow the user's free-form movement through the virtual space to trigger the display of the supplementary information, rather than requiring that they be constrained to a predetermined linear path.

The current VSim 2.0 software (Figure 33.6), funded by an NEH Digital Humanities Implementation grant (HK-50164–14) refined the functionality of the Narrative and Embedded Resource features, enabled responsive design so that narrative overlays could conform to changes to the simulation window's size and aspect ratio, and expanded the file formats that can be imported into the software. The implementation grant also funded the construction of the VSim Repository and Archive. Hosted by UCLA's Digital Library Program, the repository provides a home for academically generated 3D material, and encourages the use and reuse of

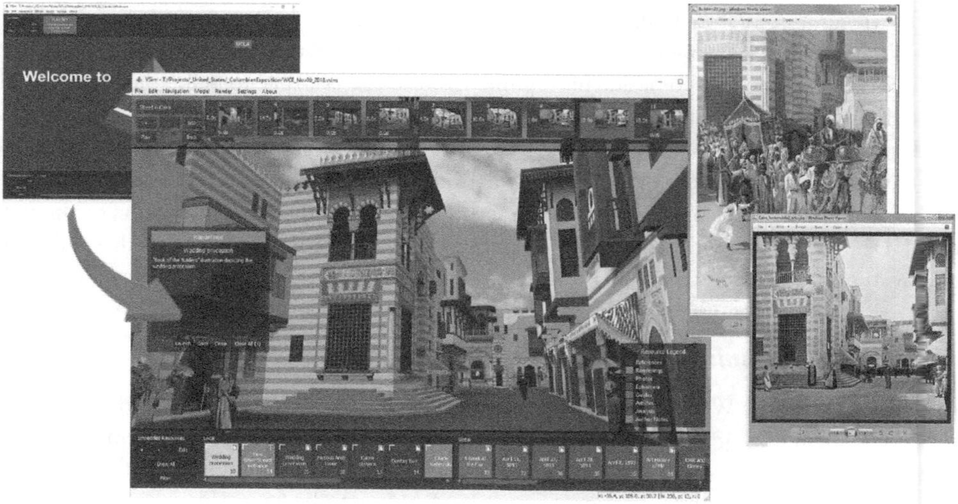


*Figure 33.6* NEH-funded VSim interface supports both the creation of linear arguments in 3D space and annotations that can link to primary and secondary resources.

*Source*: © 2019 The Regents of the University of California.

these models for teaching, learning, and secondary research. The grant resulted in generalizable software that scholars can use to interact with 3D material, build publication packages for distribution that combine a range of computer models, narratives, and embedded resources; and a platform for the distribution and preservation of these materials.[21] The logic for distribution is simple: 3D models can be released by themselves, or in combination with narratives and embedded resources. At the content creator's discretion, these files can also be shared with peer reviewers and/or locked to prevent changes to the material and protect intellectual property.

## Annotations and Access to Primary and Secondary Source Materials

A critical challenge for scholars is the ability to annotate virtual environments for publication and distribution. Building information modeling (BIM), Heritage BIM, and semantic-based solutions and ontologies are targeted toward professional audiences—architects, engineers, and cultural heritage specialists—not researchers, secondary scholars, and the general public.[22] For broad dissemination of academic 3D material, it is imperative that content creators have mechanisms to insert references and annotate their virtual environments to explain the scholarship of the model to peers, and provide enough information to secondary users that they can build knowledge from the reconstruction. In 2014, the author argued that an annotation system for academically generated 3D content needs to accommodate introductory information that provides context for the modeled environment, access to the primary and secondary evidence that informed the reconstruction, paradata that describes any interpretive decisions and areas of uncertainty, academic arguments, and paratextual information that may be introduced into the environment by other scholars.[23]

The challenge to thoroughly annotate a large-scale virtual environment has both technical and organizational components. The "cascade of information" central to the hypothetical WCE publication described previously would require tens of thousands of annotations and links to supplementary images, websites, and digital files. The first test of embedded resources within the Street of Cairo installation—which covered barely half a percent of the total exposition grounds—involved over 313 MB of data across 120 digital files (e.g. PDFs, images, sound, video clips), not counting purely textual annotations. Extrapolating those numbers to the entire exposition suggests that annotating the entire model to that level of density could involve over 62.6 GB of data and 24,000 digital files. Organizing annotations at that scale requires a flexible mechanism for authoring, embedding, managing, and updating the linked resources.

VSim includes mechanisms that address the challenges of embedding and classifying annotations within a virtual environment. Authors have the freedom to define resource categories as best suits their computer models. Anchoring a resource sets its camera position in space as well as the viewing direction (i.e. the XYZ and HPR positions). Resources can be text-only annotations, or include links to locally stored digital resources or online material. These resources can be filtered, sorted, and searched. Settings control their display with auto-launch and auto-reposition options. (With auto-launch, the text description automatically opens in response to the user's movement through the modeled environment; with auto-reposition, clicking on a resource repositions the user to facilitate a match view and accommodate annotations that are view dependent). The interface also allows display filtering, and mechanisms to adjust resource anchors and triggers, all within the context of generalizable software.

## *Range of Academic Publications*

The hypothetical World's Columbian Exposition publication described at the beginning of this section is echoed by the 3D Scholarly Edition (3DSE) envisioned by the scholars (including the author) involved in a 3D Publishing Cooperative planning grant funded by NHPRC/Mellon:

> A 3D Scholarly Edition publishes an interactive digital representation of an (often historic) object or environment following consistent and well-articulated methodologies. Like traditional scholarly editions, 3D Scholarly Editions provide well-researched and sourced explanations of historic material culture and their context through deep annotations, and provide reliable metadata about each document or source used in the presentation of that object or environment.[24]

In this definition, the emphasis of the 3DSE is on the environment itself, as an authoritative and definitive representation of the subject environment. Other forms of publication are also possible, including long-form books, monographs, or journal articles with academic arguments best explicated within the interactive 3D environment. This requirement for spatially organized arguments, however, suggests limits to use of the models for publication. For example, where Potter-Hennessey's dissertation on sculpture at the fair or Karlowicz's examination of the Manufactures Building may be perfectly suited to a spatial approach, Rae's epidemiological study of typhoid in Chicago in the early 1890s may best be included in the model as context for efforts to provide a clean water source for fairgoers.

## Pedagogy

The academic disciplines that have embraced the pedagogical applications of 3D technologies are those traditionally associated with tangible objects of study. Thus, for these disciplines, adoption of 3D models is more a digitalization and expansion of an existing practice (i.e. a shift from analogue to digital). Architects and engineers quickly adopted computer-aided design (CAD) and 3D modeling programs as alternatives for ink, paper, and balsa wood. Hands-on anatomy labs can be supplemented or replaced by *Gale Interactive: Human Anatomy*, "an innovative learning aid that allows students to examine in virtual 3D dissections and immerse themselves in interactive research."[25] Rather than relying solely on physical collections, paleontologists can now turn to the University of Michigan's Online Repository of Fossils (UMORF) to examine photogrammetrically generated 3D representations of specimens. Similarly, the online Protein Data Bank—and its educational portal, PDB-101—augments classic electron microscopy by making available "the 3D shapes of proteins, nucleic acids, and complex assemblies that [help] students and researchers understand all aspects of biomedicine and agriculture, from protein synthesis to health and disease."[26] For art historians, online archives of reality-based 3D models are opening up new opportunities for the study of sculpture, as exemplified by the Uffizi Digitization Project.

## *Digital Art and Architectural History*

In considering the impact of 3D on art and architectural history pedagogy, it is important to draw a distinction between constructivist classroom activities that use 3D models and technologies and the use of academically generated interactive 3D environments as described herein. The two approaches equally involve a transformative re-imagining of teaching and learning, but in very different ways. Mathews[27] and Hoobler[28] both describe exciting classroom activities that involve immersing small groups of students in an art-historical research problem. Mathews' student team worked with digital technologies including photogrammetry to document historical buildings in Coral Gables, Florida, while Hoobler's team focused on Zapotec tombs in Oaxaca, Mexico. Of particular emphasis for both teams was the integration of students into the research process and the experience that they gained as a result of their technological explorations. In contrast, the focus of the WCE project—and the point of the VSim software interface—is to provide a transformative alternative to the static images and texts that are the cornerstones of large-enrollment art and architectural history courses.

## *Pedagogical Applications*

The development of VSim makes pedagogical use possible by supporting both teacher-centered instruction and student-centered learning with an emphasis on prolonged engagement with the 3D content. The software was designed to be as flexible as possible in order to accommodate a broad range of pedagogical uses.

- In a lecture hall, architectural history instructors could interactively navigate through the WCE reconstruction model in the classroom while describing the layout out of the fair and the arrangement of the major exhibition halls around the Court of Honor. This experience with the environment would provide the students a holistic understanding of the fair.
- Rather than reading an article about the fair, students could explore the WCE reconstruction either alone or in small groups, and in doing so, build an understanding of the 3D space, the experience of moving through the exposition, and the relative position and scale of buildings and zones of the fair.
- As a paper-equivalent assignment, students could work alone or in small groups to construct narrative arguments within the interactive model using VSim's Narrative or Embedded Resource features. This type of constructivist exercise would facilitate active engagement with the model and the primary and secondary resources that informed the reconstruction.

- As a term-project-equivalent or course, students could work collaboratively to learn computer modeling, conduct research, and create reconstructions of the structures not currently represented in the WCE model. The students' projects could then be imported into the larger model of the exposition and explored interactively. Like Mathews' and Hoobler's experiments described previously, this use of the reconstruction would immerse students in the research process and allow them to develop significant technical skills.

## Conclusion

Sources-based reconstruction models of historic buildings or environments like the WCE project are potent tools for scholarship and pedagogy, and the construction of these models is a compelling new form of knowledge production. When these models are developed with academic rigor and attention to detail, the process mines primary source material to extract information about the built environment resulting in an impactful interactive experience that transcends disciplinary boundaries. The longevity of this scholarship, and its ultimate contribution to the academy and pedagogy, however, depends on the development of stable, sustainable, and generalizable technology for publication and dissemination that enables the annotation of the virtual environment. The VSim interface is one possible solution to this challenge, and future testing with the fully annotated WCE reconstruction model will establish the software's utility for publishing and sharing 3D scholarship. Another challenge for this form of scholarship and this type of modeling is the time and focus required to generate buildings and/or large-scale environments that can survive academic scrutiny and peer review, and sustain prolonged user interaction. Solutions to these challenges will undoubtedly be found as interest in this type of work continues to grow and new waves of computer-savvy scholars integrate 3D technologies into their research and classrooms. In the meantime, it is critical for working academics to advance the argument that the construction and dissemination of 3D materials is a form of digitally enabled scholarship that provides critical opportunities for research, knowledge production, publication, and pedagogy.

## Acknowledgments

A debt of gratitude is owed to colleagues and friends at UCLA's Urban Simulation Team, Office of Information Technology, and Institute for Digital Research and Education; the Museum of Science and Industry, Chicago; The Brinson Foundation; the National Endowment for the Humanities; the Ryerson and Burnham Archives at the Art Institute of Chicago; the Olmsted Foundation, the Library of Congress, and the National Archives and Records Administration. Thank you also to projects supporters and friends, including Jay Bentz and the entire VSim development team.

## Notes

1. Christopher Robert Reed, *'All the World Is Here!': The Black Presence at White City* (Bloomington and Indianapolis: Indiana University Press, 2000).
2. Fabrizio I Apollonio, "The Production of 3D Digital Archives and the Methodologies for Digitally Supporting Research in Architectural and Urban Cultural Heritage," *Digital Research and Education in Architectural Heritage Communications in Computer and Information Science* 817 (2018): 139–58, https://doi.org/10.1007/978-3-319-76992-9_9. Apollonio discusses the two modeling approaches. The

cultural heritage community has embraced the use of reality-based models and the possibilities they present for conservation, restoration, and analysis. Unlike sources-based models, the generation of reality-based models emphasizes workflows and technologies, with the resultant knowledge production derived from the analysis of the digitized material.

3. Amy Jeffs and Gabriel Byng, "The Digital Pilgrim Project: 3D Modeling and GIS Mapping Medieval Badges at the British Museum," *Peregrinations: Journal of Medieval Art and Architecture* 6, no. 2 (2017): 80–90; Rachel Opitz, Marcello Mogetta, and Nicola Terrenato, eds., *A Mid-Republican House From Gabii* (Ann Arbor, MI: University of Michigan Press, 2016), www.fulcrum.org/concern/monographs/n009w229r. A good example of an art history project that uses reality-based models is the Digital Pilgrim project. An example of a hybrid models that combine elements of both forms is the Gabii archaeological project where users can superimpose manually created models on a reality-based model of the excavations.
4. Colleen Mastony, "Norway Building from 1893 Chicago World's Fair Heads Home," *Chicago Tribune*, September 19, 2015, www.chicagotribune.com/news/ct-little-norway-blue-mounds-met-20150919-story.html.
5. The scale replica is 24 feet tall versus the original that was 65 feet. Minor changes to the statute include adding a laurel wreath topping the staff in place of the Phrygian cap of the original, and the replica is fully gilded, where the 'skin' of the original figure was not.
6. Daniel Hudson Burnham, "World's Fair State Buildings," *The Inland Architect and News Record*, March 1892, 25.
7. "New Orleans," *The American Architect and Building News* 51, no. 1046 (January 11, 1896): 17–18.
8. Julie K. Brown, *Contesting Images: Photography and the World's Columbian Exposition* (Tucson: University of Arizona Press, 1994), 81. Non-commercial images of the exposition are rare, though desirable on the chance that they will provide unique views and information. Brown further explains that amateurs were discouraged from taking images: "The regulations stipulated a payment of two dollars per day for a permit to photograph on the grounds of the Exposition (which was four times the daily admission charge); a prohibition of cameras that used negatives larger than 4" × 5"; and a complete ban on stereo cameras and tripods." Ibid., 94.
9. "World's Columbian Exposition Photographs by C.D. Arnold, 1891–1894: Finding Aids Collection," 1993, http://digital-libraries.saic.edu/cdm/ref/collection/findingaids/id/17574.
10. Molly Huber, "Hiawatha and Minnehaha (Sculpture)," *MNopedia, Minnesota Historical Society*, accessed June 20, 2019, www.mnopedia.org/thing/hiawatha-and-minnehaha-sculpture.
11. Elaine Sullivan, Angel David Nieves, and Lisa M. Snyder, "Making the Model: Scholarship and Rhetoric in 3-D Historical Reconstructions," in *Making Things and Drawing Boundaries: Experiments in the Digital Humanities*, ed. Jentery Sayers (Minneapolis and London: University of Minnesota Press, 2017), 302, www.jstor.org/stable/10.5749/j.ctt1pwt6wq.38?refreqid=excelsior%3Ab0cef490996cf560aec547743dc4f4b5&seq=1#metadata_info_tab_contents.
12. David J. Staley, *Computers, Visualization, and History: How New Technology Will Transform Our Understanding of the Past* (Armonk and London: M.E. Sharpe, 2003), 98.
13. Diane Favro and Bernard Frischer, "Digital Roman Forum," accessed August 13, 2019, http://wayback.archive-it.org/7877/20160919152126/http://dlib.etc.ucla.edu/projects/Forum/. PIs Favro and Frischer noted the level of certainty for the various elements of the reconstructed buildings in the Digital Roman Forum project.
14. Daniel Hudson Burnham, Joan E. Draper, and Thomas S. Hines, *The Final Official Report of the Director of Works of the World's Columbian Exposition*, vol. 2 (New York: Garland Publishing, 1989), 19.
15. Hugh Denard, "A New Introduction to the London Charter," in *Paradata and Transparency in Virtual Heritage Digital Research*, ed. Drew Baker, Anna Bentkowska-Kafel, and Hugh Denard (London and New York: Ashgate Publishing, 2012), 57.
16. Ibid., 66.
17. Harlow N. Higinbotham, *Report of the President to the Board of Directors of the World's Columbian Exposition: Chicago, 1892–1893* (Chicago: Rand, McNally & Co., 1898), 90.
18. Susan Ingram, "Meet Me in Vienna (Alt-Wien), Meet Me at the Fair," in *Placing History: Themed Environments, Urban Consumption and the Public Entertainment Sphere = Orte Und Ihre Geschichte(n)*, ed. Susan Ingram and Markus Reisenleitner (Vienna: Turia & Kant, 2003), 85.
19. Daisy Abbott et al., "Development of Cross-Curricular Key Skills Using a 3D Immersive Learning Environment in Schools," *Communications in Computer and Information Science Immersive Learning Research Network* 725 (2017): 60–74, https://doi.org/10.1007/978-3-319-60633-0_6; David Fredrick

and Greg Herman, "A House of the Ozarks: Fay Jones and the American House," *Tesseract*, accessed August 13, 2019, http://tesseract.uark.edu/mid-century-modern-in-the-ozarks-fay-jones-and-the-american-house/. "The Oplontis Project," accessed June 20, 2019, www.oplontisproject.org/; "Sketchfab," accessed June 20, 2019, https://sketchfab.com/education.

20. Lisa M. Snyder, "The Design and Use of Experiential Instruction Technology for the Teaching of Architectural History in American Undergraduate Architecture Programs" (PhD diss., University of California, Los Angeles, 2003), 229.
21. "VSim Repository and Archive," 2018.
22. Livio De Luca et al., "A Semantic-Based Platform for the Digital Analysis of Architectural Heritage," *Computers & Graphics* 35, no. 2 (2011): 227–41, https://doi.org/10.1016/j.cag.2010.11.009; Jesús Ibáñez and Carlos Delgado-Mata, "Lessons from Research on Interaction with Virtual Environments," *Journal of Network and Computer Applications* 34, no. 1 (2011): 268–81, https://doi.org/10.1016/j.jnca.2010.07.005.
23. Lisa M. Snyder, "VSim: Scholarly Annotations in Real-Time 3D Environments," *Proceedings of the 2nd International Workshop: Collaborative Annotations in Shared Environments: Metadata, Tools, and Techniques in the Digital Humanities DH-CASE II* (DH-CASE '14), Fort Collins, CO, 2014, https://doi.org/10.1145/2657480.2657483.
24. Angel David Nieves et al., "Scholarship in 3D: Digital Publishing Cooperative," Grant Proposal, NHPRC-Mellon Digital Edition Publishing Cooperatives Implementation Grants Program, 2019, 1.
25. Gale, "Gale Interactive: Human Anatomy," accessed August 13, 2019, www.gale.com/c/interactive-human-anatomy.
26. RCSB Protein Data Bank, "RCSB PDB: Homepage," accessed August 13, 2019, www.rcsb.org/.
27. Karen Rose Mathews, Amin Sarafraz, and Chris Mader, "3D Modeling in the Urban Classroom: Using Photogrammetry for the Study of Historic Architecture in Coral Gables, Florida," *Journal of Interactive Technology & Pedagogy* 12, accessed June 20, 2019, https://jitp.commons.gc.cuny.edu/3d-modeling-in-the-urban-classroom-using-photogrammetry-for-the-study-of-historic-architecture-in-coral-gables-florida/.
28. Ellen Hoobler et al., "Of Software and Sepulchers: Modeling Ancient Tombs from Oaxaca, Mexico," *Journal of Interactive Technology & Pedagogy* 12 (2018), https://jitp.commons.gc.cuny.edu/of-software-and-sepulchers-modeling-ancient-tombs-from-oaxaca-mexico/.

## Bibliography

Abbott, Daisy, Stuart Jeffrey, Anastasia Gouseti, Kevin Burden, and Mhairi Maxwell. "Development of Cross-Curricular Key Skills Using a 3D Immersive Learning Environment in Schools." *Communications in Computer and Information Science Immersive Learning Research Network* 725 (2017): 60–74. https://doi.org/10.1007/978-3-319-60633-0_6.

Apollonio, Fabrizio I. "The Production of 3D Digital Archives and the Methodologies for Digitally Supporting Research in Architectural and Urban Cultural Heritage." *Digital Research and Education in Architectural Heritage Communications in Computer and Information Science* 817 (2018): 139–58. https://doi.org/10.1007/978-3-319-76992-9_9.

Brown, Julie K. *Contesting Images: Photography and the World's Columbian Exposition*. Tucson: University of Arizona Press, 1994.

Burnham, Daniel Hudson. "World's Fair State Buildings." In *The Inland Architect and News Record* 19, no. 2 (March 1892): 25.

Burnham, Daniel Hudson, Joan E. Draper, and Thomas S. Hines. *The Final Official Report of the Director of Works of the World's Columbian Exposition*. New York: Garland Publishing, 1989.

Creator. Presagis. Accessed June 20, 2019. www.presagis.com/en/product/creator/.

De Luca, Livio, Chawee Busayarat, Chiara Stefani, Philippe Véron, and Michel Florenzano. "A Semantic-Based Platform for the Digital Analysis of Architectural Heritage." *Computers & Graphics* 35, no. 2 (2011): 227–41. https://doi.org/10.1016/j.cag.2010.11.009.

Denard, Hugh. "A New Introduction to the London Charter." In *Paradata and Transparency in Virtual Heritage Digital Research*, edited by Drew Baker, Anna Bentkowska-Kafel, and Hugh Denard, 57–71. London; New York: Ashgate Publishing, 2012.

Favro, Diane, and Bernard Frischer. "Digital Roman Forum." Accessed August 13, 2019. http://wayback.archive-it.org/7877/20160919152126/http://dlib.etc.ucla.edu/projects/Forum/.

Fredrick, David, and Greg Herman. "A House of the Ozarks: Fay Jones and the American House." *Tesseract*. Accessed August 13, 2019. http://tesseract.uark.edu/mid-century-modern-in-the-ozarks-fay-jones-and-the-american-house/.

Gale. "Gale Interactive: Human Anatomy." Accessed August 13, 2019. www.gale.com/c/interactive-human-anatomy.

Higinbotham, Harlow N. *Report of the President to the Board of Directors of the World's Columbian Exposition: Chicago, 1892–1893*. Chicago: Rand, McNally & Co., 1898.

Hoobler, Ellen, Arturo Hernandez Jr., Ve'Amber Miller, and Catherine Quinn. "Of Software and Sepulchers: Modeling Ancient Tombs from Oaxaca, Mexico." *Journal of Interactive Technology & Pedagogy* 12 (2018). Accessed June 20, 2019. https://jitp.commons.gc.cuny.edu/of-software-and-sepulchers-modeling-ancient-tombs-from-oaxaca-mexico/.

Huber, Molly. "Hiawatha and Minnehaha (sculpture)." *MNopedia, Minnesota Historical Society*. Accessed June 20, 2019. www.mnopedia.org/thing/hiawatha-and-minnehaha-sculpture.

Ibáñez, Jesús, and Carlos Delgado-Mata. "Lessons from Research on Interaction with Virtual Environments." *Journal of Network and Computer Applications* 34, no. 1 (2011): 268–81. https://doi.org/10.1016/j.jnca.2010.07.005.

Ingram, Susan. "Meet Me in Vienna (Alt-Wien), Meet Me at the Fair." In *Placing History: Themed Environments, Urban Consumption and the Public Entertainment Sphere = Orte Und Ihre Geschichte(n)*, edited by Susan Ingram and Markus Reisenleitner, 83–104. Vienna: Turia & Kant, 2003.

Jeffs, Amy, and Gabriel Byng. "The Digital Pilgrim Project: 3D Modeling and GIS Mapping Medieval Badges at the British Museum." *Peregrinations: Journal of Medieval Art and Architecture* 6, no. 2 (2017): 80–90. Accessed June 20, 2019. https://digital.kenyon.edu/perejournal/vol6/iss2/10.

Karlowicz, Titus M. "Notes on the Columbian Exposition's Manufactures and Liberal Arts Building." *Journal of the Society of Architectural Historians* 33, no. 3 (1974): 214–18. https://doi.org/10.2307/988856.

Mastony, Colleen. "Norway Building from 1893 Chicago World's Fair Heads Home." *Chicago Tribune*, September 19, 2015. Accessed June 20, 2019. www.chicagotribune.com/news/ct-little-norway-blue-mounds-met-20150919-story.html.

Mathews, Karen Rose, Amin Sarafraz, and Chris Mader. "3D Modeling in the Urban Classroom: Using Photogrammetry for the Study of Historic Architecture in Coral Gables, Florida." *Journal of Interactive Technology & Pedagogy* 12. Accessed June 20, 2019. https://jitp.commons.gc.cuny.edu/3d-modeling-in-the-urban-classroom-using-photogrammetry-for-the-study-of-historic-architecture-in-coral-gables-florida/.

"New Orleans." *The American Architect and Building News* 51, no. 1046 (January 11, 1896): 17–18.

Nieves, Angel David, Lisa M. Snyder, Mick Gusinde-Duffy, Costas Papadopoulos, and Susan Schreibman. "Scholarship in 3D: Digital Publishing Cooperative." Grant Proposal. NHPRC-Mellon Digital Edition Publishing Cooperatives Implementation Grants Program, 2019.

"The Oplontis Project." Accessed June 20, 2019. www.oplontisproject.org/.

Opitz, Rachel, Marcello Mogetta, and Nicola Terrenato, eds. *A Mid-Republican House From Gabii*. Ann Arbor, MI: University of Michigan Press, 2016. www.fulcrum.org/concern/monographs/n009w229r.

Potter-Hennessey, Pamela. "The Sculpture at the 1893 Chicago World's Columbian Exposition: International Encounters and Jingoistic Spectacles." PhD diss., University of Maryland at College Park, 1995.

Rae, Bronwyn. "Water, Typhoid Rates, and the Columbian Exposition in Chicago." *Northwestern Public Health Review* 2, no. 2 (2015). Accessed June 20, 2019. https://sites.northwestern.edu/nphr/journal-volume-2-issue-2-2015/water-typhoid-rates-and-the-columbian-exposition-in-chicago/.

RCSB Protein Data Bank. "RCSB PDB: Homepage." Accessed August 13, 2019. www.rcsb.org/.

Reed, Christopher Robert. *"All the World Is Here!": The Black Presence at White City*. Bloomington and Indianapolis: Indiana University Press, 2000.

"Sketchfab." Accessed June 20, 2019. https://sketchfab.com/education.

Snyder, Lisa M. "The Design and Use of Experiential Instruction Technology for the Teaching of Architectural History in American Undergraduate Architecture Programs." PhD diss., University of California, Los Angeles, 2003.

———. "VSim: Scholarly Annotations in Real-Time 3D Environments." In *Proceedings of the 2nd International Workshop: Collaborative Annotations in Shared Environments: Metadata, Tools, and Techniques in the Digital Humanities DH-CASE II*. Fort Collins, CO, 2014. https://doi.org/10.1145/2657480.2657483.

Staley, David J. *Computers, Visualization, and History: How New Technology Will Transform Our Understanding of the Past*. Armonk and London: M.E. Sharpe, 2003.

Sullivan, Elaine, Angel David Nieves, and Lisa M. Snyder. "Making the Model: Scholarship and Rhetoric in 3-D Historical Reconstructions." In *Making Things and Drawing Boundaries: Experiments in the Digital Humanities*, edited by Jentery Sayers, 301–16. Minneapolis; London: University of Minnesota Press, 2017. www.jstor.org/stable/10.5749/j.ctt1pwt6wq.38?refreqid=excelsior%3Ab0cef490996cf560aec547743dc4f4b5&seq=1#metadata_info_tab_contents.

"UMORF | University of Michigan Online Repository of Fossils." Accessed June 20, 2019. https://umorf.ummp.lsa.umich.edu/wp/.

"The Uffizi Digitization Project." Accessed June 20, 2019. www.digitalsculpture.org/florence/.

"VSim Repository and Archive." Accessed August 14, 2019. https://vsim.library.ucla.edu/xmlui/.

"World's Columbian Exposition Photographs by C.D. Arnold, 1891–1894: Finding Aids Collection." 1993. http://digital-libraries.saic.edu/cdm/ref/collection/findingaids/id/17574.

# 34
# SOCIAL MEDIA IN THE ART HISTORY CLASSROOM

*Lauren Jimerson and Allison Leigh*

When we were college students, art history courses revolved around a 1960s-era carousel slide projector. Its monotonous humming and clicking in the darkened lecture hall often put our classmates to sleep. For years, the technology used in college art history classrooms was limited. Only in the last two decades have departments transitioned from using the Kodak 35 mm slide projector to computers with PowerPoint presentations.[1] Other digital tools have been more slowly implemented. Though rarely used in art history classes, social media can serve as a highly effective teaching aid.[2] Cost-free and ubiquitous, social media can be leveraged to make lectures more interactive and relatable to a twenty-first-century audience. It can foster scholarly interest in art history while introducing students to current issues and debates in the field. When employed effectively, it increases engagement both inside and outside the classroom and enables students to integrate art history into their daily lives.

Today's college students are immersed in a culture inundated with technology. With smartphones and computers, social media has risen to become a major channel of communication and interaction. The vast majority of college students employ social media on a daily basis. Of the 65% of American adults who use social networking sites and applications, young adults are the most avid users—an estimated 90% aged eighteen to twenty-nine.[3] We aimed to harness digital technologies already employed by most college students and to use them in the art history classroom. Rather than explore the plethora of social media platforms available, this chapter concentrates on the implementation of two of the most popular: Twitter and Instagram. Both are oriented around visual communication. With Twitter, messages are limited by character count and are often accompanied by an image, video, or a link to an article or website. Instagram posts feature an image or short video with a terse caption. Furthermore, each serves as an important source for art and art-historical related news and information. Myriad scholarly and cultural institutions share current events through Twitter and Instagram.

Founded in 2006, Twitter is a social networking site through which users publish short messages, called "tweets," which are visible to other users in real time. Initially, tweets were limited to 140 characters, but this was doubled in 2017 to 280. The open nature of Twitter enables users to communicate not only with friends and colleagues, but with millions of other users globally. As of the time of writing, the number of monthly active users on Twitter is approximately 336 million and it is estimated that the site is used by 23% of all online adults.[4] Twitter has numerous features that make it apposite for teaching. The open nature of the platform and the facility of sharing scholarly and news articles make Twitter an optimal environment for learning about any academic subject. For art history, students can stay abreast of scholarly debates, recent publications, and research discoveries as well as current exhibitions by following museums, galleries, historical sites, professional societies, artists, curators, and art historians from around the world. At the same time, they can learn about major events in the art market. Integrating Twitter or any social media platform into curricula can present challenges though. One disadvantage of Twitter is that it has become a locus of political controversy over the past few years. Fortunately, it is possible to make selective choices about who (and who not) to follow.

Launched in 2010, Instagram is a digital social platform that allows users to upload and share photographs and videos through a mobile application. These posts are visible to the user's followers in their Instagram feeds. When not set on private mode, posts can also be viewed publicly. Like Twitter, Instagram is used by individuals, companies, and organizations alike. Most major art institutions and cultural centers also have accounts and regularly share images from their collections, videos of art performances, or clips of interviews with artists and curators. Instagram is one of the most popular social media platforms, especially among young adults. The total number of monthly active Instagram users has surpassed one billion.[5] In 2018, it was estimated that around 71% of eighteen- to twenty-four-year-olds in the United States use Instagram (45% of that age group are Twitter users).[6] Moreover, Instagram users tend to visit the site multiple times throughout the day. One researcher estimates that teens access Instagram around ten to thirty times daily.[7]

As an application designed specifically for viewing and sharing images, Instagram lends itself to the study of art. Each post must consist of at least one photograph or short video and it is now possible to display a series of up to ten images via a swiping carousel. With more than fifty billion photos shared to date, Instagram is a major conduit of imagery in today's image-saturated environment.[8] By observing, creating, and interacting with images, students learn to communicate effectively through images as they simultaneously develop both visual literacy (VL) and digital visual literacy (DVL) skills.[9] Visual literacy, the ability to construct meaning from images, is fundamental to the field of art history. DVL, the ability to analyze critically digital visual materials, is becoming an increasingly essential skill in academia, the work place and in daily life. VL and DVL are not mutually exclusive; by enhancing them in tandem, students will be better prepared for reading and comprehending images—whether on a screen or in a museum.

Over the past five years, Twitter has been implemented in higher education with increasing regularity. It is often utilized in marketing and management courses, particularly at the graduate level.[10] In fact, in some business classes, Twitter use is a requirement.[11] Less research has been conducted on Instagram's academic applications.[12] Although numerous studies have examined the use of Twitter in pedagogy, most of these have been centered on math and science courses and other non-humanities disciplines.[13] In 2014, when Lauren first implemented Twitter in her curriculum (the first instructor in the Art History department at Rutgers University to do so), there were no published sources on the use of Twitter in an art history course.[14] Overall, there seems to be a degree of cultural resistance to social media use in art history as well as other academic fields.[15] Yet, art and art history are alive and well on social media. And students increasingly rely on these platforms for communication and entertainment. It seemed both constructive and vital to address this cultural phenomenon by engaging with these networks in our own courses. We aimed to steer our students' habitual use of digital technologies toward education in order to make art history a part of their social networks and everyday lives.

Twitter was integrated into an introductory art history survey course at Rutgers The State University of New Jersey, and Instagram was incorporated into a number of art history courses at the University of Louisiana at Lafayette. In neither class was the use of social media mandatory.

While students were incentivized to participate, it was not a graded assignment or obligation. At the end of the Rutgers course, surveys were administered to assess students' response as to whether social media enhanced or detracted from the overall classroom and learning experience. However, we wished to avoid the distraction of formal structured assessments conducted at various times throughout the semester. We pioneered new technologies in our classrooms with the aim of complementing and enhancing pedagogy and academic rigor. In what follows, we will describe how we leveraged social media to enhance art history content learning and reveal the ways in which we found it to be the most useful. In sharing these experiences, we hope to increase understanding of these digital technologies and their utility in higher education settings. However, we remain cognizant of the fact that in the rapidly changing world of technology, these platforms, just like the slide carousel, will someday become obsolete.

## Lauren's Case Study: Twitter

I decided to incorporate Twitter into my curriculum in 2014.[16] I was teaching the Renaissance through Contemporary Art section of the *Introduction to Art History* to a class of sixty-two students. While other academic courses employ social media, I had never personally encountered it in an art history classroom. Therefore, I had to devise an approach that suited the field and the course's pedagogical aims. Participation with Twitter was optional, but I offered an incentive. Students earned two bonus percentage points for the semester if they used the site regularly to interact with lecture, either during or after class. Students were given a very general guideline regarding Twitter usage. Tweets had to be informative and insightful. Students could ask questions, provide links to outside sources, or offer engaged responses to course material and their classmates' posts. All tweets had to include the class hashtag (#arthist106) so that they would be easily searchable. Rather than banning cell phones, I allowed students to use them in class for Twitter in case they did not have access to a laptop computer. To provide a model for students on how to use social media in an academic setting, I frequently shared articles, videos, images and remarks related to course material (Figure 34.1). I responded to their questions on Twitter and liked the most notable tweets. Furthermore, I recognized top tweets each week, displaying them in the PowerPoint presentation. Over the course of the semester, about 50% of the class participated.

I was aware of the fact that most college students already use social media sites, like Twitter, on a daily basis. Thus, it seemed plausible that orienting students' social media use toward academic subjects could produce favorable results. In my art history course, Twitter encouraged active learning. It allowed students to comment on material and ask questions in real time. An average of ten tweets were posted during each class. When a live stream was included in the PowerPoint, this number greatly increased. During a lecture on Van Gogh with a live Twitter feed, a record seventy-two tweets were generated. Twitter also allowed for discussions to continue outside of the classroom. The majority of tweets were posted after class, often in the evenings and on weekends. From the students' activity on Twitter, it was clear that the course material resonated with them and that they continued to reflect on the ideas and concepts during their spare time. Twitter thus served as an extension of the lecture hall, a flexible and open digital forum fostering learning and discussion.

Notably, final grades were on average 8% higher for students who used Twitter consistently. That Twitter use can result in improved learning is corroborated by other studies as well.[17] Research has shown that student engagement is positively linked with increased academic success.[18] Twitter added to the amount of time and effort students devoted to the class, which may have contributed to a favorable outcome. By reorienting their habitual social media use around

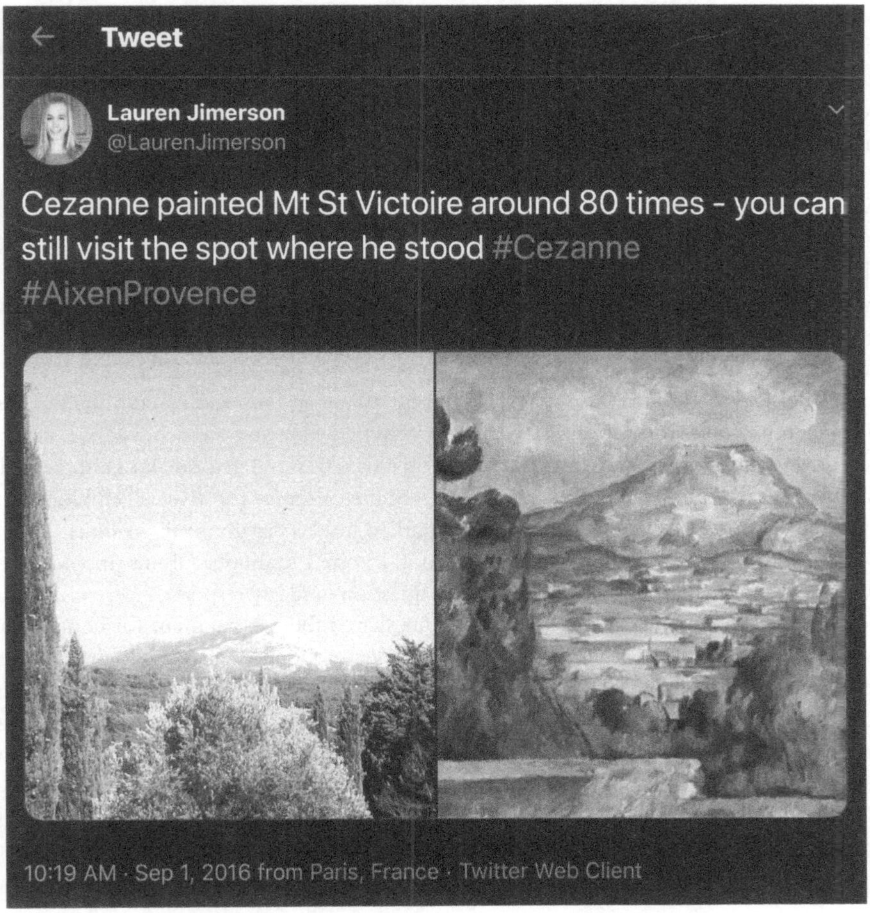


*Figure 34.1* Twitter post from September 1, 2016.

*Source*: Lauren Jimerson via Twitter.

art history, the subject became a major preoccupation for many of the students and fostered content understanding and retention. Many students had no prior exposure to art history and the majority took the class to fulfill a core undergraduate requirement. In the final course survey, most reported that they had only a moderate interest in the subject before taking the course. However, the majority (86%) indicated that they developed a greater interest in art history afterward.

Although multiple factors affected these results, Twitter seemed to play a large role in cultivating an appreciation and enthusiasm for art history. It allowed students to relate the subject to their own academic and leisure pursuits. Students drew connections between art history and science, literature, music, fashion, popular culture and personal experience on Twitter. A biology major shared how J.M.W. Turner's landscapes were used in a scientific study; a music major tweeted about her experience playing Maurice Ravel while gazing at Monet's water lilies; and an art major tweeted about his admiration for Michelangelo and his fascination with the hidden anatomical images in the frescoes on the Sistine Chapel ceiling.

Significant realizations came to fruition when students drew connections between their own academic pursuits and art history. Twitter served as a conduit, a kind of interdisciplinary magnet, through which students could observe and associate art with their own hobbies and passions, making the subject all the more meaningful. Additionally, Twitter served as a powerful resource for expanding students' knowledge of museums and cultural sites. Students could follow a wide range of museums and institutions and learn about ongoing exhibitions and other current events in the art world. This in turn encouraged them to visit new places and to tweet about their experiences.

With a plethora of museums at their doorstep, Rutgers students have a unique advantage. Still, they are not always aware of all of these sites. Through Twitter, students encouraged one another to visit nearby cultural institutions (Figure 34.2). Some students traveled further afield to see art and architecture and zealously shared these experiences with the class. One student tweeted photographs of Cattedrale di Santa Maria del Fiore on her trip to Florence during spring break (Figure 34.3).

Each week, I displayed the "top tweets," the most salient and interesting comments, questions and images, on a PowerPoint slide, and began the class by addressing them and answering important questions. In this manner, I ensured that the material was understood and I also geared each lecture to the needs and interests of my students. Some of these "top tweets" employed humor to reinforce art history concepts, while others sparked heated classroom discussions.

Twitter also proved to be a practical study tool. I posted reminders about upcoming exams and writing assignments. Students tweeted their questions and my responses were visible to everyone prior to exams. On a regular basis, students shared their excitement for course material on Twitter. This was particularly evident during one lecture focused on Van Gogh. As I lectured, students' tweets appeared next to images of Van Gogh's work in real time.[19] This generated a great deal of enthusiasm, and the majority of the students present tweeted responses and questions during class. Afterward, students continued to tweet their reactions, some of which were particularly insightful: one student made a connection between Van Gogh's *Crows Over the Wheatfield* and a Greek myth while another student later shared a link to a psychiatric study examining plausible diagnoses of Van Gogh's illness.

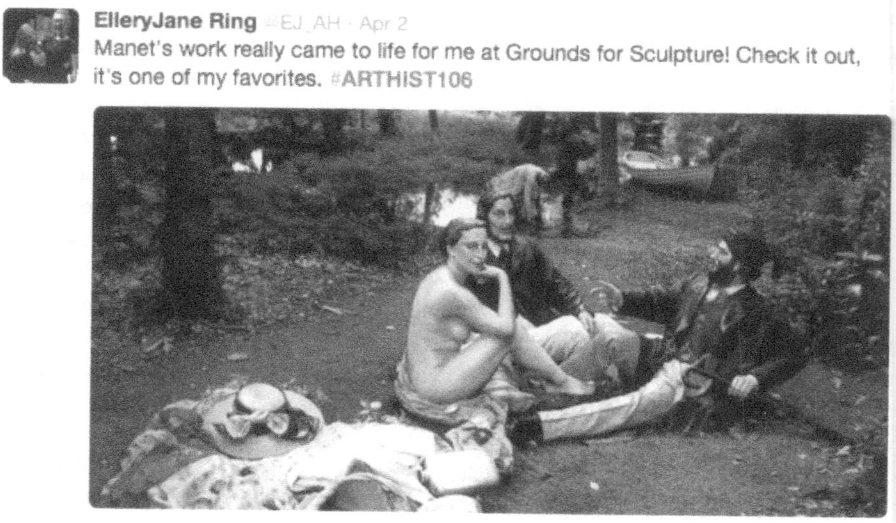


*Figure 34.2* Twitter post from April 2, 2014.

*Source*: Ellery Jane Ring via Twitter.

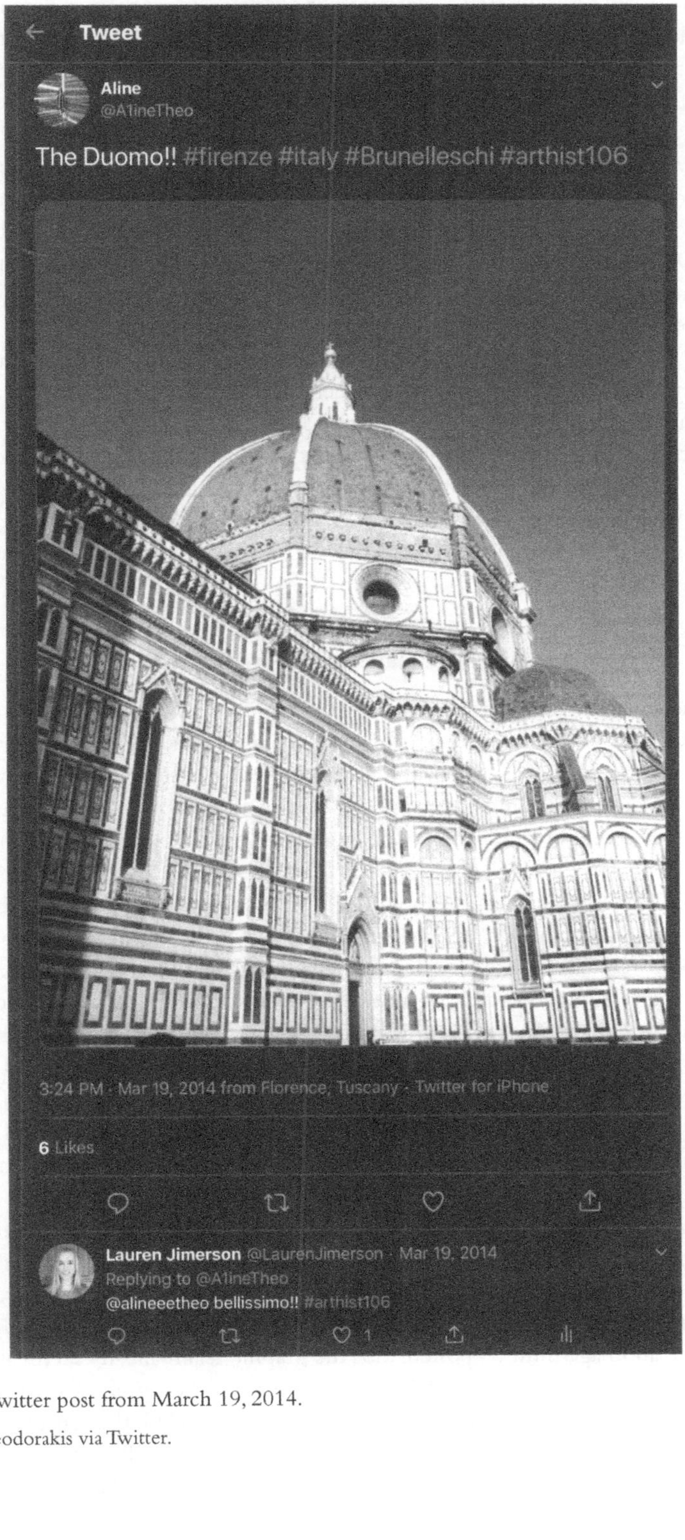


*Figure 34.3* Twitter post from March 19, 2014.

*Source*: Aline Theodorakis via Twitter.

Twitter allowed everyone in the class to express their ideas while simultaneously strengthening the classroom community. I encouraged students to share their viewpoints openly. By allowing students to speak out through Twitter, I acknowledged their opinions as valid and emboldened them to develop their own perspectives on key art historical topics. With an additional outlet for interaction and discussion, individuals felt empowered, and a sense of community amongst students was bolstered as well. Meanwhile, for the shiest students in class, Twitter proved an invaluable asset. In a large lecture hall, it can be intimidating for some students to participate, even in a course that encourages dialogue.[20] One bright student rarely raised her hand during class at the beginning of the semester. Yet, she felt comfortable sharing her insights on Twitter. During one lecture, she tweeted an astute observation that anticipated my own remarks. This must have boosted her confidence, as afterward she increasingly participated in class discussions.

Although Twitter does require some additional effort on the part of the instructor (facilitating discussions, responding to questions, correcting any misinformation), it was worthwhile. The course survey administered at the end of the semester revealed the advantages of implementing Twitter in the classroom. With a free exchange of ideas, Twitter sparked intellectual conversations and helped to establish a cohesive community among students and the professor. When asked what they liked most about the class in the final survey, the majority of students mentioned Twitter as it allowed them to connect art history with their own lives, interests, and experiences.

## Allison's Case Study: Instagram

My use of the social media platform Instagram currently functions more as a supplement to the art history classroom than a core part of my pedagogy. I am interested in further exploring the potential for this platform's use in the classroom, but my current praxis is to tell students that I have an Instagram account that relates to class material and encourage them to follow it beginning in the second or third week of classes. I keep my Instagram account public and have found that students from a range of classes will follow me—from those in basic general education classes like "Art Appreciation" to those in a similar survey to the one described earlier, and even those in my much smaller, upper-level seminars which rotate in terms of art historical topics. Approximately 20–30% of students in my large classes follow me over the course of the semester, and nearly 50% follow my account in upper-level courses designed for more advanced students. I make it clear from the beginning that I will not accept friend requests from students on Facebook so that I am able to maintain a level of privacy, but I tell them that my Instagram account is specifically devoted to posts about art history and the life of an academic. I also often follow my students on Instagram if they do not have private accounts and find this especially helpful in getting to know my students and learn names in those classes where I have more than 120 students.

The Instagram account I maintain contains posts which take a variety of different forms and I do not organize them thematically. Rather, I use the medium most heavily to reflect in real time subjects I am preparing to teach or am researching for my own publications. In both regards, the visual nature of Instagram is well-suited to art history; it is the only social media platform where an image must be posted, thus the graphic realm already serves as the software's driving impetus. Whereas Twitter (and Facebook) posts can be purely textual, Instagram prioritizes imagery, bringing to life what Leo Steinberg once called, though in a very different context, the "sightbite."[21] Along similar lines, Instagram does not allow for the embedding of links within posts like Twitter does, so each post is self-contained in that I cannot link to other material without putting the link in my bio. Consequently, Instagram does not incite students to fall into an internet search rabbit hole, linking from one website to the next in a process of overwhelming data overload.[22]

I reserve links to articles relevant to art history for my Twitter account, which I also mention to students, but find they use it significantly less since I began teaching in Louisiana. My Twitter account is specifically devoted to posting articles about art and the humanities more generally which I glean from a range of academic and journalistic sources. Students who want to keep abreast of developments in the art world can follow my Twitter account for links to articles on everything from recently revised art attributions, upcoming museum exhibitions, and art market trends to scholarly debates about the use of technology in the classroom, the #metoo movement in academia, and the latest developments in 3D printing. After I read the articles, I often choose a salient line or two and use the quote in the tweet to draw students' attention to potentially reading the full article. Of the students who do follow me on Twitter, most are majoring in Visual Art and several have told me they find it an excellent resource for staying "in the know"—a constant challenge for students in less urban areas.

Instagram also allows me to supplement my art history classroom and the material I am covering in lectures in other significant ways. During the semester, I will often post "teasers" about upcoming lectures on the platform. These can include detail photographs I have taken of artworks in museums over the years, screenshots of a PowerPoint I am constructing, or even a photograph of an article I have assigned with my highlighting and notes evident so that students see that I too am reading (and grappling with) the material I have asked them to absorb for class. I find that students especially derive benefit from the close-up photographs of artworks as these can serve to bring the pieces to life (Figure 34.4). Many have never been to a major museum and have never experienced firsthand a single work by a canonical artist, thus the photographs I share on Instagram (and include in subsequent lectures) give them a vital sense of artistic media they may never gain otherwise. In this sense, Instagram is also a vital tool for me as a professor; I often find photographs posted by others that give me a sense of scale—something otherwise missing from standard textbooks. I have taken screenshots of other users' Instagram posts as they visited Giotto's *Arena Chapel* in Padua or the *Woman of Willendorf* in Vienna and I use these in my own lectures. Nothing drives home how big (or small) a work is like a photograph of someone looking at that work of art in person. Outside social media, such photographs can be difficult or even impossible to find. Thus, Instagram is also a resource for me as an educator—one that frequently supports and enhances my pedagogy in the classroom.

Before lectures, students will sometimes reply in the comments section of my post that they are "so pumped" for the upcoming material or ask if they can attend the lecture if it is not a class in which they are currently enrolled. Some former students who go on to become art educators themselves comment that they now teach certain artists I am covering too. This is especially encouraging when the post is about an understudied artist or a non-Western artistic movement. Replying to a post I made of a Rachel Ruysch still-life, a former student mentioned that she had "just introduced her and Jan van Huysum to my fine art survey students at Lafayette High"—thus demonstrating the continuation of work on women artists in pre-modern periods.

I will also sometimes post memes in advance of lectures to get students interested in the upcoming material in ways that engage them at the level of humor or within the pop culture arena (Figure 34.5). Former students often comment that they have never forgotten references like these and that it allowed them to appreciate the works of art in ways that made them newly relevant to their lives. Along similar lines, I will sometimes post new findings about works of art I teach in the survey course or will share when an artist I covered in class attains a new record at auction. In this way, students see that art and its histories develop and change over time. Students,

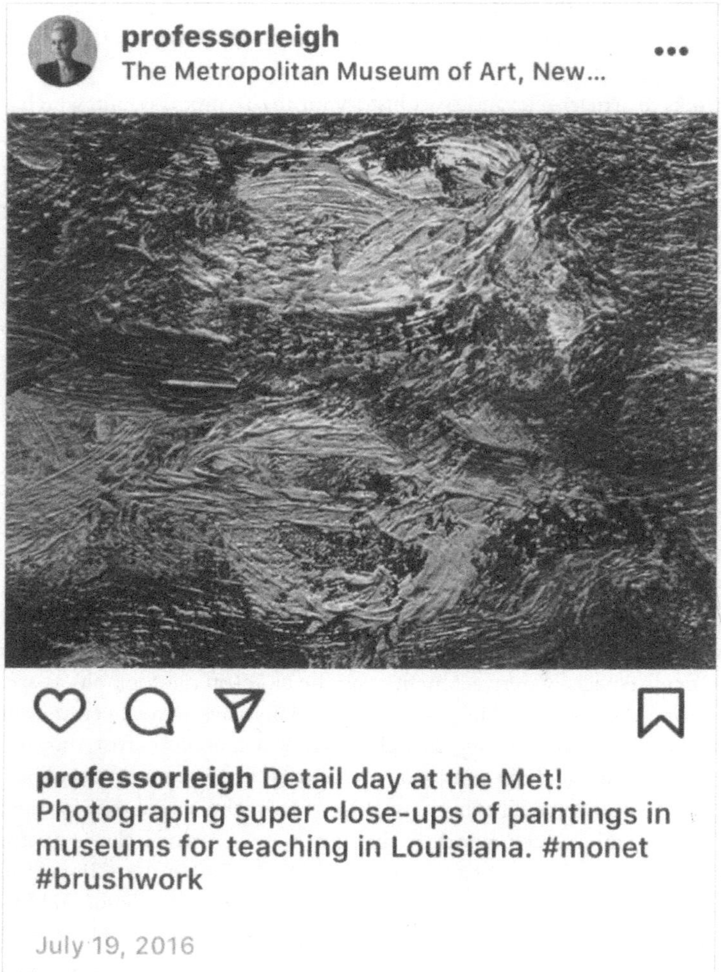


*Figure 34.4* Instagram post from July 19, 2016.
*Source*: Allison Leigh via Instagram.

both current and former, often comment on these posts and express that they see my Instagram account as a resource for staying current on art historical knowledge.

Additionally, I find it useful to post about research I am hearing at conferences and lectures I attend. I will often share illuminating comparisons put forward by other scholars or describe an argument that altered my understanding of a certain work so that students can benefit from the knowledge I gain while traveling. There has been some recent debate as to how properly to attribute social media posts like these so that scholars' intellectual property rights are maintained.[23] I try whenever possible to search for the presenter on Instagram and "tag" them in the post or, if they are not a member of the site, I use their name in a hashtag so that attribution is maintained to some extent. I also frequently post photographs of artworks in exhibitions so that students get a sense of scale and material qualities, but also so that they feel less intimidated about going to museums over the course of their lives. Research shows that museum attendance has

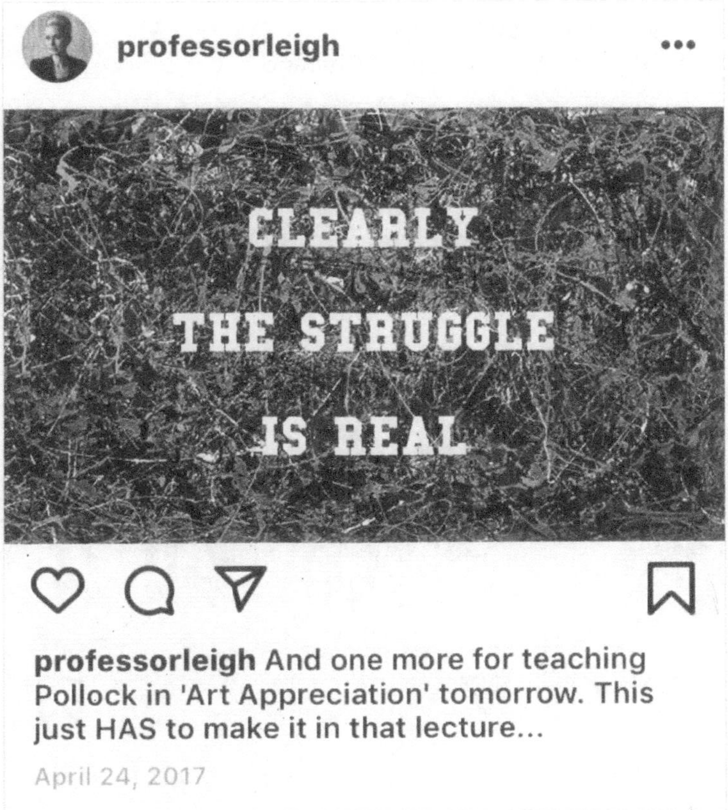


*Figure 34.5* Instagram post from April 24, 2017.

*Source*: Allison Leigh via Instagram.

been declining since the early 2000s and that audiences lack ethnic and socioeconomic diversity.[24] As far back at 1969, Pierre Bourdieu and Alain Darbel investigated the fact that despite the "open to all" stance of museums and art galleries, they are in fact visited only by a small fragment of the population.[25] More recent research has confirmed that this trend has continued; according to one study, only 22.7% of the U.S. adult population visited art museums/galleries in 2008 and of that percentage, 78.9% were non-Hispanic White.[26]

By posting photographs of exhibitions I attend, artworks in gallery settings, wall texts, and even just the museum entrance itself, I seek to help students feel less intimidated by these institutions (Figure 34.6). Positive results have begun to accrue—more and more students every semester tell me in office hours that they went to a museum for the first time because they felt more comfortable seeing that I "go all the time and make it seem fun." Students also email me more frequently since I began maintaining an Instagram account asking for advice on what museums to go to when they are in New York, or Chicago, or Florence. Students also frequently send me pictures via Instagram showing they are finally seeing some of the works we covered in class. As a result, I feel confident that social media platforms like Instagram possess tremendous potential for reaching students in new ways and familiarizing arenas for aesthetic experience.

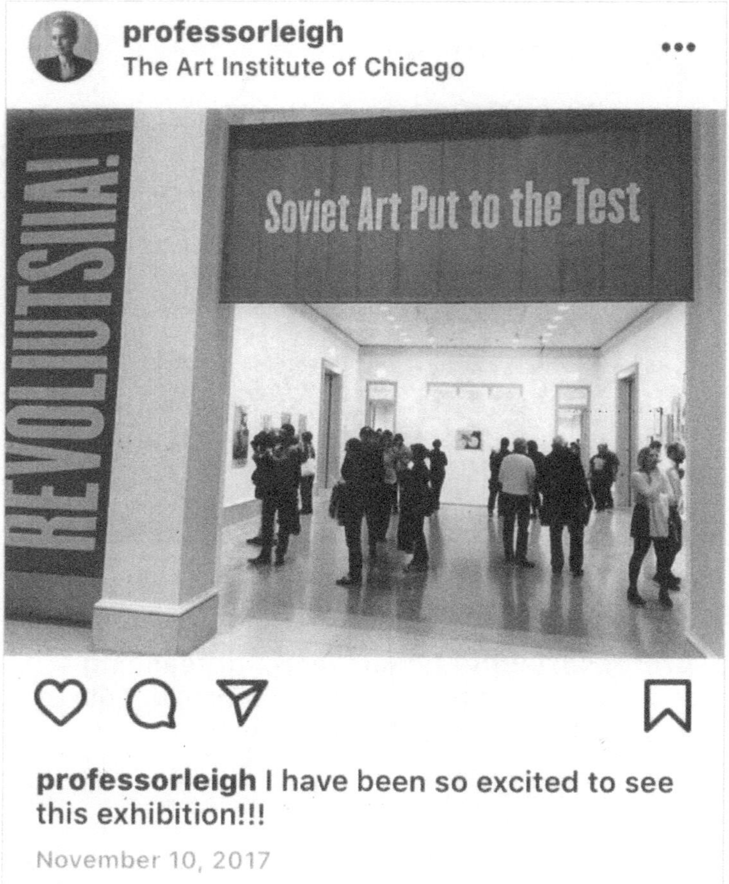


*Figure 34.6* Instagram post from November 10, 2017.

*Source*: Allison Leigh via Instagram.

Along similar lines, I use my Instagram account to show students what the life of a professional scholar consists of from day-to-day. In the interest of growing the profession and attracting students from diverse backgrounds to lead professional lives as artists, designers, historians, and curators, I post frequently about my activities outside the classroom. I share photographs of myself in libraries and archives, while scanning and photocopying books, or in the act of reading and marking up a text. I post photos of the cover of books I am reading with descriptions that might encourage students to try the book themselves; I share shots of my own writing heavily marked up with red pen to show followers how one must always edit and re-edit a text (regardless of their field of study). And I try to show my students through Instagram that the life of a professor frequently means juggling these activities *all* the time—in airports, in waiting rooms, at coffee shops, even at the pool (Figure 34.7).[27] Students frequently come to my office to discuss activities they saw posted on my Instagram account; they want to hear more about a conference I attended, what I saw at a certain museum, or even about why I read the *New York Times* on Sundays. It is my hope that in a broad, and perhaps somewhat ideologically subversive way, these kinds of social media posts expose young men and women to what it means to live

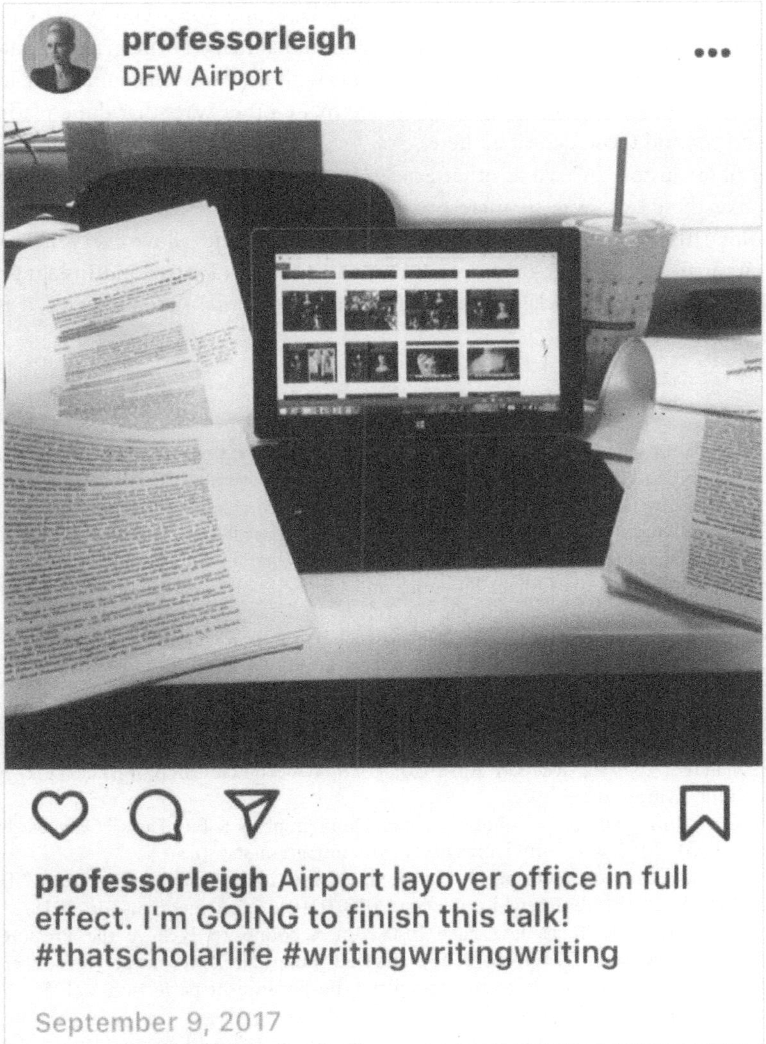


*Figure 34.7* Instagram post from September 9, 2017.

*Source*: Allison Leigh via Instagram.

"the life of the mind" and might inspire them to pursue lives that are similarly thoughtful and intellectually rigorous.

## Conclusions

Implementing Twitter was a small step that made a big impact. With Twitter, art history became more meaningful and exciting to students as they could relate it to their own lives and academic pursuits. Moreover, in a large lecture hall, it permitted all students to participate and to develop their own viewpoints. Similarly, the use of Instagram showed how the art history classroom could be expanded to bring material to students in a way that not only had contemporary relevance but introduced them to ideas well beyond class time (or even beyond when a course had formally ended). Instagram proved to be a medium that helped bring students into museums as well as having the potential to familiarize students with the practical elements of academic life and draw them into careers in the field. There are many other ways that these platforms might be employed beyond those described here.

Faculty of art history as well as other academic subjects should consider using social media platforms like these as a way to increase student engagement, stimulate interest in the subject, embolden the idea of knowledge as ever expanding, and allow everyone to find their voice despite increasingly large class sizes at many institutions. Twitter and Instagram have now become integral parts of our classrooms. As for that old carousel slide projector, it is rusting in the basement.

## Notes

1. In 2004, Kodak stopped manufacturing 35mm slide projectors. Orit Gat, "Projected Projects: Slides, PowerPoints, Nostalgia, and a Sense of Belonging," *Rhizome,* November 28, 2011, accessed June 23, 2018, http://rhizome.org/editorial/2011/nov/28/projected-projects-slides-powerpoints-nostalgia-an/.
2. Constantly evolving, social media is difficult to define. It broadly refers to a "wide range of applications enabling users to create, share, comment and discuss digital contents." Stefania Manca and Maria Ranieri, "Facebook and the Others: Potentials and Obstacles of Social Media for Teaching in Higher Education," *Computers & Education* 95 (2016): 217.
3. Andrew Perrin, "Social Media Usage: 2005–2015," *Pew Research Center,* October 8, 2015, accessed July 3, 2018, www.pewinternet.org/2015/10/08/social-networking-usage-2005-2015/.
4. See "Number of Monthly Active Twitter Users Worldwide from 1st Quarter 2010 to 1st Quarter 2018 (in Millions)," *Statista,* the Statistics Portal, www.statista.com/statistics/282087/number-of-monthly-active-twitter-users/; Drew DeSilver, "5 Facts About Twitter at Age 10," *Pew Research Center,* March 18, 2016, accessed April 20, 2018, www.pewresearch.org/fact-tank/2016/03/18/5-facts-about-twitter-at-age-10/.
5. Salman Aslam, "Instagram by the Numbers: Stats, Demographics & Fun Facts," *Omnicore,* July 18, 2019, accessed July 31, 2019, www.omnicoreagency.com/instagram-statistics/.
6. Aaron Smith and Monica Anderson, "Social Media Use in 2018," *Pew Research Center,* March 1, 2018, accessed May 10, 2018, www.pewinternet.org/2018/03/01/social-media-use-in-2018/.
7. Joanne Orlando, "How Teens Use Fake Instagram Accounts to Relieve the Pressure of Perfection," *The Conversation,* March 6, 2018, accessed June 29, 2018, http://theconversation.com/how-teens-use-fake-instagram-accounts-to-relieve-the-pressure-of-perfection-92105.
8. Aslam, "Instagram by the Numbers."
9. For more on visual literacy, see Danielle Rice, "Museums and Visual Literacy," *Journal of Aesthetic Education* 23, no. 4 (1989): 95–99; Anne Morgan Spalter and Andries Van Dam, "Digital Visual Literacy," *Theory into Practice* 47, no. 2 (2008): 93–101.
10. Abdullah Al-Bahrani, Darshek Patel, and Brandon Sheridan, "Engaging Students Using Social Media: The Student's Perspective," *International Review of Economics Education,* 19 (2015): 36–50.
11. John White, "Don't Have a Twitter Account? It Might Prevent You from Earning an MBA," *Inc.*, October 20, 2016, accessed May 15, 2018, www.inc.com/john-white/dont-have-a-twitter-account-it-might-prevent-you-from-earning-an-mba.html.
12. One of the few studies conducted is Lauren Serpagli's "Social Media in the Science Classroom: Using Instagram with Young Women to Incorporate Visual Literacy and Youth Culture" (PhD diss., Columbia University, 2017).
13. A few examples of studies on the use of Twitter in the classroom include: Stephen J. Jacquemin, Lisa K. Smelser, and Melody J. Bernot, "Twitter in the Higher Education Classroom: A Student and Faculty Assessment of Use and Perception," *Journal of College Science Teaching* 43 (2014): 22–27; Ryan Becker and Penny Bishop, "'Think Bigger About Science': Using Twitter for Learning in the Middle Grades," *Middle School Journal* 47 (April 2016): 4–16.
14. Lauren Jimerson, "How an Art History Class Became More Engaging with Twitter," *The Conversation,* September 22, 2015, accessed March 20, 2018, https://theconversation.com/how-an-art-history-class-became-more-engaging-with-twitter-47133.

15. A nation-wide study on social media in university teaching practices in Italy found that cultural resistance was one main deterrent for academics. Manca and Ranieri, "Facebook and the Others," 216–30.
16. At the time that I employed Twitter, tweets were limited to 140 characters.
17. R. Junco, G. Heiberger, and E. Loken, "The Effect of Twitter on College Student Engagement and Grades," *Journal of Computer Assisted Learning* 27 (2011): 119–32.
18. George D. Kuh, "What Student Affairs Professionals Need to Know About Student Engagement," *Journal of College Student Development* 50, no. 6 (2009): 683–706.
19. To display a live Twitter feed in PowerPoint, create a Tweet wall with a unique url and insert this link into each PowerPoint slide: accessed June 3, 2018, www.tweetwally.com/.
20. Trip Gabriel, "Speaking Up in Class, Silently, Using Social Media," *New York Times,* May 13, 2011, Section A, Page 1.
21. Leo Steinberg, "Who's Who in Michelangelo's Creation of Adam: A Chronology of the Picture's Reluctant Self-Revelation," *The Art Bulletin* 74, no. 4 (December 1992): 556.
22. Two fascinating accounts of the potential liabilities of search jumping and linking between platforms include: Astra Taylor, *The People's Platform: Taking Back Power and Culture in the Digital Age* (New York: Henry Holt and Company, 2014); Michael P. Lynch, *The Internet of Us: Knowing More and Understanding Less in the Age of Big Data* (New York: W. W. Norton & Company, 2016).
23. See especially Steve Kolowich, "The Academic Twitterazzi," *Inside Higher Ed*, October 2, 2012, www.insidehighered.com/news/2012/10/02/scholars-debate-etiquette-live-tweeting-academic-conferences; Roopika Risam, "Conference Live Tweets: Twitter Good or #Twittergate?" *Personal Blog of Roopika Risam*, September 30, 2012, accessed July 5, 2018, http://roopikarisam.com/uncategorized/conference-live-tweets-twitter-good-or-twittergate/.
24. Among numerous examples, see most recently: "Art Museum Attendance," *Humanities Indicators*, November 2017, www.humanitiesindicators.org/content/indicatordoc.aspx?i=102; Peggy Levitt, "Museums Must Attract Diverse Visitors or Risk Irrelevance," *The Atlantic*, November 9, 2015, accessed April 26, 2018, www.theatlantic.com/politics/archive/2015/11/museums-must-attract-diverse-visitors-or-risk-irrelevance/433347/.
25. Pierre Bourdieu, Alain Darbel, and Dominique Schnapper, *L'amour de l'art: les musées d'art européens et leur public* (Paris: Les Éditions de Minuit, 1969).
26. Betty Farrell and Maria Medvedeva, *Demographic Transformation and the Future of Museums* (Washington, DC: The American Association of Museums Press, 2010), 12. Full PDF, accessed May 28, 2018, www.aam-us.org/wp-content/uploads/2017/12/Demographic-Change-and-the-Future-of-Museums.pdf
27. That said, I do try to include posts that show my life as one that is not exclusively about work so that students might gain ideas about what it means to seek work-life balance in their own professional lives. Looking forward, it may prove vital for students to see both male and female professors with families juggle the tasks of professional and personal life. The primary question I hear from female students seeking advice about graduate school in art history and potential careers in the field is how one manages to find time to have children. In this sense, social media sites like Instagram might help students see that it is possible in a way that no other platform can.

## Bibliography


Al-Bahrani, Abdullah, Darshek Patel, and Brandon Sheridan. "Engaging Students Using Social Media: The Student's Perspective." *International Review of Economics Education* 19 (2015): 36–50.

Becker, Ryan, and Penny Bishop. "'Think Bigger About Science': Using Twitter for Learning in the Middle Grades." *Middle School Journal* 47 (April 2016): 4–16.

Jacquemin, Stephen J., Lisa K. Smelser, and Melody J. Bernot. "Twitter in the Higher Education Classroom: A Student and Faculty Assessment of Use and Perception." *Journal of College Science Teaching* 43 (2014): 22–27.

Junco, R., G. Heiberger, and E. Loken. "The Effect of Twitter on College Student Engagement and Grades." *Journal of Computer Assisted Learning* 27 (2011): 119–32.

Kuh, George D. "What Student Affairs Professionals Need to Know About Student Engagement." *Journal of College Student Development* 50, no. 6 (2009): 683–706.

Lynch, Michael P. *The Internet of Us: Knowing More and Understanding Less in the Age of Big Data.* New York: W. W. Norton & Company, 2016.

Manca, Stefania, and Maria Ranieri. "Facebook and the Others. Potentials and Obstacles of Social Media for Teaching in Higher Education." *Computers & Education* 95 (2016): 216–30.
Rice, Danielle. "Museums and Visual Literacy." *Journal of Aesthetic Education* 23, no. 4 (1989): 95–99.
Spalter, Anne Morgan, and Andries Van Dam. "Digital Visual Literacy." *Theory Into Practice* 47, no. 2 (2008): 93–101.
Taylor, Astra. *The People's Platform: Taking Back Power and Culture in the Digital Age*. New York: Henry Holt and Company, 2014.

# INDEX